Exactions and Impact Fees in California

2012

THIRD EDITION

Exactions and Impact Fees in California

A comprehensive guide to policy, practice, and the law

William W. Abbott

Peter M. Detwiler

Thomas Jacobson

Margaret Sohagi

Harriet A. Steiner

Solano Press Books

Exactions and Impact Fees in California

2012 (Third) Edition

Solano Press Books
Post Office Box 773
Point Arena, California 95468
tel: 800 931-9373
fax: 707 884-4109
email: spbooks@solano.com

Cover design by North Star Press
Front cover photos by Jon Handel (top two), RHAA -Royston,
Hanamoto, Alley & Abey www.rhaa.com (bottom photo)
Book design by Solano Press Books
Index by Galen Schroder,
North Dakota Indexing

ISBN 978-0-923956-97-4

Printed by Sentinel Printing
St. Cloud, Minnesota

NOTICE

Before you rely on the information
in this book, be sure you are aware
that some changes in the statutes or
case law may have gone into effect
since the date of publication. The book,
moreover, provides general information
about the law. Readers should consult
their own attorneys before relying
on the representations found herein.

Preface

Land development requirements are a source of recurring debate and controversy in most California cities and counties. Meaningful dialogue is often hampered by the complex and unclear statutes under which project applicants and local governments must operate. This book brings together the myriad of constitutional and statutory schemes that directly affect how a decision-making body determines the appropriate mix of development requirements that can or will be imposed on a particular application.

Essentially, a local government wishing to impose a particular type of development fee or dedication, otherwise known as an "exaction," may do so as long as certain procedures and standards of fairness are followed. The more difficult issues are the ones based on fairness and policy. Proposition 13 enacted in 1978, caused the tax burden reallocation, which, coupled with higher impact fees and special taxes, resulted in the legally justifiable but politically questionable shifting of costs that will doubtless grow over time. The policy issue is of another dimension. Because the housing sector is vital to California's economy, local officials may need to reconsider the tradeoff between public facilities and economic growth. This re-examination is an important component of the decisions by some local governments to reduce, if not eliminate, certain development fees during the recession beginning in 2008.

Chapter 1 examines the combination of federal, state, and local considerations that have combined to calculate demands on developers to contribute to solving the increasing range of community needs. Chapter 2 explains the distinctions between taxes, fees, assessments, land dedication, land reservation, and other development requirements. Chapters 3 and 4 discuss the constitutional and statutory issues governing the imposition of exactions, and chapter 5 is devoted to compliance with the nexus legislation for impact fees, AB 1600. The characteristics particular to school impact fees are addressed in chapter 6, while chapter 7 addresses legal challenges to various exaction requirements. Chapter 8 looks at specific exaction issues of current interest around the state, including child care, inclusionary housing, transit impact fees, and others. Chapter 9 serves as a transition from exactions to operations—in other words, the choices that are available to fund the operation and maintenance of improvements. The appendices contain relevant code sections as well as sample agreements, exaction studies, and a flow chart summarizing key legal considerations. The cases and statutes cited are current to June 2011; in selective circumstances, more current case references are included.

Special recognition must be given to my co-authors, all of whom took time from their very busy schedules to update this book. Peter M. Detwiler, chapter 1; Margaret Sohagi, chapters 2 and 7; Thomas Jacobson, chapters 3 and 4; Cori Badgley, chapter 5; and Harriet A. Steiner and Seth Merewitz, chapter 9.

William W. Abbott

Chapters at a Glance

Contents

Contents

Contents

Contents

Contents

Contents

CHAPTER ONE

Introduction

By Peter M. Detwiler

Whether you call it "infrastructure" or just plain "public works," public capital investment subsidizes private development, and government spending on infrastructure stimulates and sustains the private side of the United States economy. The practice is older than the American republic itself; colonial governments financed the wharves, roads, and waterworks that launched mercantilism, large-scale agriculture, and industry in the New World. Hurdling into the twenty-first century, Californians know that their vibrant economy owes much to long-term public investment. How to pay for these investments is a monumental challenge.

Whether you call it "infrastructure" or just plain "public works," public capital investment subsidizes private development, and government spending on infrastructure stimulates and sustains the private side of the United States economy.

The *fiscalization* of land use is the intersection of three strands of public policies: land use decisions, government structures, and fiscal choices.[1] *Land use decisions* reflect the public institutions that make them, and they result in fiscal consequences. *Government structures*—the organization and political control of counties, cities, redevelopment agencies, special districts—reverberate with the tensions between land use decisions and fiscal choices. *Fiscal choices* propel public agencies and the land use decisions made by public officials.

To trace one of these strands immediately leads to the other two strands. Sometimes a strand is a cause, sometimes an effect, sometimes both. Trace a fiscal decision and you will always discover connections to the strands of government organization and land use. Figure 1 displays these relationships as dirt, dollars, and duties; dirt stands for land use decisions, dollars for public finance, and duties for governance. Builders, planners, public officials, and those who advise them must recognize how government institutions and land use decisions influence public finance.

Figure 1
Dirt, Dollars, and Duties

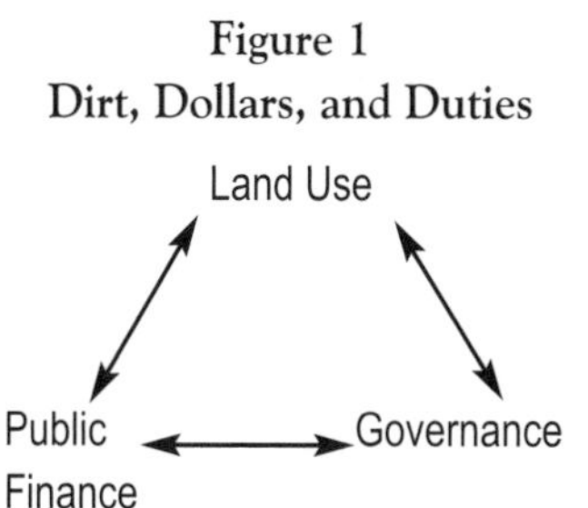

It's Getting Harder to Finance Public Works

California needs to invest $37 billion annually for the next ten years to provide the infrastructure to accommodate future growth. Nearly $200 billion is needed to rehabilitate, maintain, and expand transportation projects in the next twenty years.[2] But public spending has not kept pace with the continuing demand for public works. In the California of the 1950s, about one dollar out of every $100 of personal income went into building public works. By 1997, just seven cents out of the $100 of personal income went to public infrastructure.

After decades of reduced investment, the results include crowded highways, disintegrating schools, run-down parks, cracked sidewalks, and overburdened libraries.

Forces and Results

Four forces have emerged and combined to make it harder for public officials and private investors to accumulate the public capital needed to build infrastructure:

- Persistent population growth and the associated demand for public works
- Cuts in federal and state public works spending
- New constitutional limits on governments
- Ambiguous reactions by voters and their elected officials

One result is that it is much harder for state departments and local agencies to raise public capital for water projects, transportation improvements, sewer systems, parks, recreation facilities, schools, universities, and the other public amenities that make life in the Golden State so attractive. A second result is that it now requires even more managerial skill and political leadership to plan, finance, build, and operate public works.

These themes—the forces and their results—appear throughout this chapter. In hindsight and placed in perspective, these forces and results are the predictable consequences of the public's concerns about land use, governance, and public finance. And yet, no one would have proposed the current arrangement as a desirable outcome.

Government's Roles

One distinctive feature of the American federal system is that no single unit of government ever has enough power to carry out a decision by itself. The separation of federal government's authority into executive, legislative, and judicial branches was a deliberate policy to avoid the concentration of power that could lead to tyranny. The other distinctive feature—the division into national, state, and local governments—further complicates effective governance. The 1950's image of federalism as a "layer cake" gave way in the 1960s to the image of a "marble cake," in which policy was made at all levels all the time. A more current simile is "fruitcake federalism" where policy is "bogged down in government plums and puddings."[3] Understanding the deliberately fragmented nature of American government is not easy, but it is essential. Those who fail to appreciate those complexities will find themselves trapped by them.

Government performs three roles in providing public works: planner, banker, and operator. As a planner, government sets goals and standards for itself and others to follow. Federal officials changed American commerce when they laid out the interstate highway system. The California Transportation Commission's periodic adoption of a State Transportation Improvement Program channels infrastructure dollars into highways and mass transit projects. Cities and counties must follow their own general plans when widening streets and building other public works.[4]

Government performs three roles in providing public works: planner, banker, and operator.

As a banker, all three levels of government spend significant amounts of tax revenue on infrastructure. Recreation and park districts levy special taxes and benefit assessments to buy more parkland. State general obligation bonds allow the state Department of Parks and Recreation to add to the state park system and make grants for local parks. Through the Outdoor Recreation Fund, the U.S. Bureau of Outdoor

Recreation helps state governments and communities acquire more local park and open space land.

As an operator, government runs the public works that make it possible for private firms to stay in business and for many of the public's needs to be served and met. The federal Bureau of Reclamation and the U.S. Army Corps of Engineers operate the dams on California rivers that control floods, generate electricity, and store irrigation water. The state Department of Water Resources has its own dams that feed the State Water Project. Cities and water districts operate reservoirs and canals that carry water great distances from distant sources to urban and suburban consumers.

Many communities have successfully increased their open space holdings as a result of dedications.

Sophisticated observers and participants recognize that all three levels of governments actively engage in the planning, financing, and operation of key public works projects. Public officials must become policy entrepreneurs if they are to succeed in finding funding for their particular projects.[5] Private entrepreneurs must appreciate the complexity of the public sector when they want a government agency to build infrastructure to support private investment.

The Fiscalization of Land Use

Land use decisions have fiscal consequences and fiscal decisions have land use consequences. When the fiscal effects of land use decisions become relatively more important than other factors, public officials approve or deny planning and development proposals based on costs and revenue. One result is that the other factors—air and water quality, transportation mobility, affordable housing—take second place. To understand this fiscalization of land use requires an understanding of the legal and political context of public works funding.

Land use decisions have fiscal consequences and fiscal decisions have land use consequences.

Disengagement of the Federal and State Governments

Competition from other political constituencies and changes in political goals have reduced state and federal spending for public works. By the late twentieth century, spending for health and welfare entitlement programs consumed increasing proportions of state and national budgets. At the federal level, the Reagan Administration's military build-up and deficit spending meant less money for other purposes. Except for transportation, federal infrastructure spending declined substantially in the mid-1980s.[6] In California, state spending on building and operating new prisons consumed funds that state budgets might have otherwise allocated to local public works. The disengagement of the federal and state governments pushed more of these costs to local agencies. In 1984, for example, the California Transportation Commission stopped paying for freeway interchanges and overcrossings intended to serve new growth, shifting the costs to developers and local officials.[7]

Competition from other political constituencies and changes in political goals have reduced state and federal spending for public works.

When faced with declining revenue sources, public managers have just three options:

- **Cut costs.** The traditional managerial response to reduced revenue, cutting spending can be an effective short-term response. Officials delay new projects and defer routine maintenance of existing infrastructure. Over time, however, population growth and deteriorating facilities increase the demand to resume public works spending.

Declining Revenue
- Cut costs
- Shift costs
- Produce new revenue

- **Shift costs.** Often the most politically acceptable response, a cost-shifting strategy involves convincing other governments or the private sector to pay for public facilities. Many medium-sized cities set up community redevelopment agencies in the early 1980s to take advantage of "property tax increment financing." Redevelopment agencies paid for local public works that the cities formerly financed themselves. The use of private toll roads in Southern California is an example of shifting costs from the public sector to the users themselves.
- **Produce new revenue.** Usually the least-popular strategy, some local agencies have tried to raise new revenue to replace the funds that used to come from federal and state public works programs. Voters in 18 counties have approved sales tax increases to pay for highway improvements that in previous decades the state government might have financed.[8]

Limitations on the Actions of Local Government

California voters' enthusiasm for ballot initiatives prompted one political pundit to observe that "we have propositioned ourselves into an economic mess." Indeed, the web of constitutional amendments approved by the voters over the last thirty years has snarled public officials' ability to raise money for their agencies' operating budgets and accumulate the capital needed for public works.

Proposition 13. The passage of Proposition 13 in 1978 fundamentally changed the relationship between the state government and its local agencies.[9] The property tax had been many local governments' primary revenue source and the cornerstone of local political power and fiscal independence. Proposition 13 changed this formerly local revenue source into a state-controlled tax. The constitutional change capped the property tax rate at one percent of the property's assessed value, rolled back the assessed values of real property, limited the growth in property tax assessments, and required two-thirds voter approval for special taxes. With Proposition 13, voters gave the Legislature the constitutional duty to allocate the remaining property tax revenue. When property tax revenue fell by 55 percent, the state government increased its spending for schools and shifted some of the school districts' property tax revenue to cities, counties, and special districts.[10]

Proposition 4. Besides limiting state and local expenditures, the passage of Proposition 4 in 1979 required the state government to reimburse local governments for the costs of state-mandated local programs.[11] The state government must pay for new state-mandated local programs or increased service levels of existing programs. For example, if the state Legislature were to pass a new law requiring cities and counties to amend their general plans to include a new infrastructure element, the state government would have to pay for the local costs of preparing and adopting the new plans. The costs of older mandates—those enacted before 1975—are not reimbursable. The uneven implementation of this constitutional requirement is a source of continuing controversy between local agencies and the state government. Legislators author new laws without appropriating funds, hoping that the cumbersome reimbursement procedures will suffice. County officials particularly chafe under the burden of older state mandates for which they receive no reimbursements. Unreimbursed state-mandated costs limit local officials' discretion over their spending priorities, limiting their ability to spend local revenue on public works projects.

Proposition 218. Reacting to a perceived "end run" around tax-cutting efforts, Proposition 218 in 1996 imposed new requirements on local attempts to raise new revenue. General taxes require majority-voter approval, and special taxes require two-thirds voter approval.[12] Benefit assessments require the approval of the property owners who represent at least fifty percent of the proposed assessments in a weighted ballot election.[13] Local property-related fees require the approval of a majority of the property owners (or two-thirds voter approval), unless they finance water, sewer, or refuse collection.[14]

The Search for a Politically Acceptable Strategy

Confronting truculent voters, those who seek increased funding for their pet projects or favorite programs have crafted political strategies based on statewide propositions or local ballot measures to support popular programs. Voters' skepticism and often outright distrust of elected officials has made it hard to gather political support for tax hikes that put money into governments' general funds. But it is politically feasible to link higher revenues to the expansion of popular programs or specific projects. These targeted tax increases succeed when an aroused electorate embraces the sponsors' causes. Programs that lack political sex appeal languish while voters pass ballot measures that dedicate revenue sources to trendy causes. Those who advocate increased funding for a broad range of public purposes have failed to make their case to the voting public while success has come to those who connect with the public's unease. Voters do not trust their elected officials to spend tax dollars wisely, so they prefer to restrict spending to specific categories. In short, we finance what we can and not what we should.

Earmarking Revenue. A half-dozen statewide ballot measures illustrate the practice of linking popular programs with specific revenue streams. In each case, the sponsors convinced the voters that the problem was worthy of increased spending and reassured them that the state government would spend new tax dollars only for the designated purpose. Proposition 99 (1988) raised tobacco taxes and earmarked the money for anti-smoking programs. Proposition 111 (1988) raised the state tax on gasoline and diesel fuel, dedicating the resulting revenue for state highways and local streets. Proposition 172 (1994) raised the state sales tax and sent the revenue back to counties and cities for law enforcement and other public safety programs. Proposition 10 (1998) hiked tobacco taxes again and restricted the funds to programs for children and public health. Proposition 63 (2004) put an additional 1 percent state tax on personal incomes above one million dollars to pay for expanded mental health services. Proposition 42 (2002) devoted most of the sales tax revenues on gasoline to highways, streets, and transit projects. Cities, counties, special districts, and school districts can adapt the same political strategy by making the case for special taxes that raise and earmark funds for popular purposes.

State Bonds Find Favor. By the late 1990s, voters' attitudes began to shift in favor of statewide bond issues that financed local projects as well as state facilities. Proposition 1A (1998) authorized $9.2 billion in state general obligation bonds for educational facilities, with most of the money ($6.7 billion) going for local schools. The November 2004 elections found voters in favor of nearly $70 billion in state bonds proposed by five ballot measures. Table 1-1 shows the amounts of these bond issues and their politically appealing names.

Table 1-1. Statewide Bond Measures Passed in November 2004

$19.9 billion	Proposition 1B: Highway Safety, Traffic Reduction, Air Quality and Port Security Bonds.
$2.8 billion	Proposition 1C: Housing and Emergency Shelter Trust Fund Bonds.
$10.4 billion	Proposition 1D: Kindergarten-University Public Education Facilities Bonds.
$4.1 billion	Proposition 1E: Disaster Preparedness and Flood Prevention Bonds.
$5.4 billion	Proposition 84: Water Quality, Safety and Supply, Flood Control, Natural Resource Protection, Park Improvements Bonds.

The Results of These Forces

Hemmed in by constitutional limitations on raising new revenue and squeezed by other demands for local revenue, local officials face increasing difficulty in financing public works.

Competition for Revenue. The allocation of most local revenue in California follows the situs method—that is, the revenue goes to the local agency in which the taxable activity occurs.[15] For example, the allocation of local sales taxes depends on the location of the retail sale. When someone buys a car inside the city limits, the local sales tax goes to the city government. If the sale occurs in an unincorporated area, the revenue goes to the county government. The situs method of allocating tax revenue fuels fierce competition for other local revenue, including transient occupancy (hotel/motel) taxes, utility user taxes, and business license taxes; it tempts local officials to compete for development that generates revenue (auto malls, big-box retailers) and to shun land uses that do not (factories, affordable housing, farmland). From this perspective, a large discount store is more desirable to city officials than a factory of the same size. Even though the store offers the community fewer and less-well-paid jobs than the factory, its sales tax revenues are far more attractive to the city treasury. Sales tax sharing between cities and between cities and counties is possible but rare.[16]

City annexations can produce battles for local revenue. Adding territory to a city by annexation can add revenue-generating territory to the municipal tax base and erode the county's tax base. Counties like Napa, Stanislaus, Ventura, and Yolo, whose policies direct new development inside city limits, harm their tax base while implementing the laudable goal of protecting agricultural land in unincorporated areas. While annexations can achieve other desirable goals such as land use control and community representation, boundary changes remain points of contention between cities and counties, and sometimes between cities competing for the same lucrative property and sales revenue.

Redevelopment poses another potential for fiscal competition among and between cities and counties. The diversion of property tax increment revenue[17] can be a reliable revenue stream that finances the bold steps to attract and retain private investors. But diverted revenues have to be diverted from somewhere else. That's why some counties challenge redevelopment projects, alleging that city officials turn to redevelopment not to eradicate blight, but simply to capture property tax increment revenue or attract retailers and their sales tax revenue.[18]

The state government intensified the fiscalization of land use when it created the Educational Revenue Augmentation Fund (ERAF) in 1992. Faced with a serious shortfall in its own budgets in 1992–1993 and 1993–1994, the state government permanently shifted property tax revenue away from counties, cities, and special districts back to school districts and community college districts. In 2004–2005, there was another, temporary ERAF shift. By allocating more property tax revenue to schools, the state reduced its obligation to finance the schools by the same amount, freeing up state general fund dollars for other purposes. This re-allocation of property tax revenue is what economists call a "zero-sum game" in which there must be a loser for every winner. As a new permanent feature on the fiscal landscape, ERAF now automatically diverts about $3.7 billion from counties, cities, and special districts to the schools, benefiting the state budget. The state government eased some of ERAF's fiscal stress on counties with offsetting measures, such as trial court funding, limited relief from state mandates, and new public safety funds from Proposition 172 (1994). Nevertheless, by reducing the amount of property tax revenue available, ERAF sharpens the intergovernmental conflict for other sources of local revenue, especially sales tax revenue.[19] Fed up with what they claimed were repeated fiscal raids, local leaders created the statewide political coalition that resulted in a 2004 constitutional amendment. Proposition 1A (2004) constitutionally protected local property tax and sales tax revenues from diversion to the state, except in extraordinary circumstances.

ERAF = Educational Revenue Augmentation Fund

Continued Demand. Because of persistent population growth and other demographic changes, local officials face continuing demands for more infrastructure. The demand for water supplies, sewer systems, roads, public transit, fire stations, schools, parks, libraries, and other facilities will continue just as the state's population continues to grow. Population growth appeared inevitable when the 1850 federal census counted 92,597 Californians and then nearly 380,000 in 1860. Table 1-2 displays the state's persistent growth. By 2008, there were an estimated thirty-eight million residents, all expecting public facilities and services. Demographers project that there will be fifty million Californians by 2032.[20]

Table 1-2. California's Population Continues to Grow

Year	Population (in millions)
1950	10.6
1960	15.7
1970	19.9
1980	23.7
1990	29.8
2000	33.9
2010	37.3
2020	(projected) 44.1
2030	(projected) 49.2

Source: Department of Finance

While the absolute growth in California residents most certainly boosts the need for more public works, other demographic trends will also accelerate the demand. The decline in the size of households from 2.95 persons per household in 1970 to 2.87 persons per household in 2000 confirms the trend towards smaller families. Conversely, however, it means that the rate of growth in the number of households is higher than population growth. The trend towards smaller but more numerous households signals a comparatively higher demand for housing and associated infrastructure.

New Infrastructure

- Population Growth
- Shifting Demographics
- Neglect

Summary. In short, the demand for infrastructure grows. The political problem of providing infrastructure results from the confluence of three powerful streams: persistent population growth, unavoidable shifts in demographic trends, and the unmet needs that result from nearly three decades of underfunded public works programs. How elected officials, public administrators, landowners, and residents react to these problems will influence state and local politics at the beginning of the twenty-first century.

Local Funding Techniques

Local officials have a wide variety of ways to finance public works projects, despite state constitutional intrusions and statutory limits on their home rule powers.[21] Table 1-3 compares some of the more popular borrowing methods. Successful use of these infrastructure funding techniques requires close attention to legal procedures, as well as a careful matching of the public works project to an appropriate funding source.

General Obligation Bonds

G.O. = General obligation

The most reliable and least expensive way for local agencies to borrow money is also one of the politically most difficult. Since the late nineteenth century, the California Constitution has required most local governments to obtain two-thirds voter approval before issuing general obligation bonds.[22] General obligation bonds rely on ad valorem property tax revenues that are collected outside Proposition 13's one percent limit, making them highly secure investments.[23] Because of this inherent economic security, the municipal bond market usually charges a lower interest rate for general obligation bonds than for other types of public debt. If they can obtain the necessary voter approval, local officials use G.O. bonds to finance projects that cannot be financed with other revenue: parks, jails, city halls, and schools. Successful elections for general obligation bonds share common characteristics. Officials start their efforts more than a year in advance of election day, document the need for specific public works projects, explain why bonds are needed, and connect the proposed spending to specific projects. A sustained public education effort is essential to win an election.

Revenue Bonds

When a local government operates a public enterprise—a sewer system, waterworks, a parking lot—it can borrow money to build or expand the facility by issuing debt secured by the future revenue. Investors in the municipal bond market are willing to lend money for revenue bonds because they are relatively secure, provided that projects generate sufficient revenue to pay off the bonds. Unlike general obligation bonds, revenue bonds require just majority-voter approval. The standard statutory authority is the Revenue Bond Law of 1941.[24]

Assessment Bonds

The concept behind assessment bonds is simple: the more an owner's property benefits from a public works project or a public service, the more that owner should pay. To pay for assessment bonds, local officials collect revenues called benefit assessments—sometimes known as special assessments—because the charges or assessments reflect the special benefit that each property receives. Local officials use a variety of formulas to represent each parcel's benefit. For example, when using assessment bonds to pay for paving a street, local officials might assign each parcel a share of the overall cost in relation to the parcel's front footage on that street. A parcel with 150 feet of front footage on the newly-paved road would pay three times as much as a fifty-foot wide lot, even though the parcels were the same size. When financing a local park, officials might charge assessments based on the parcels' proximity to the new amenity. A parcel across the street from the new park might pay one amount, parcels within an easy three-block

Table 1-3. Public Capital Formation
How Local Officials Use Debt to Accumulate Capital

Type of Debt	Revenue Stream	Required Approval
General Obligation Bonds	Ad valorem property tax revenues outside the standard 1% tax rate	2/3-voter approval: cities, counties. 55% voter approval: schools.
Limited Obligation Bonds	Any existing revenues	2/3-voter approval.
Revenue Bonds	Rates and user charges	Majority voter approval.
Tax Allocation Bonds	Property tax increment revenues	No voter review. Only redevelopment agencies.
Mello-Roos Act Bonds	Special taxes (parcel taxes)	2/3-voter approval. Landowners vote if <12 voters.
Assessment Bonds	Benefit assessments	Weighted ballot approval by property owners.
Certificates of Participation	Payments by borrower	No voter review. COPs are annual contracts to pay, not long-term debts.
Lease-Purchase Contracts	Payments by borrower	No voter review. Borrower contracts to pay lender.
Promissory Notes	Payments by borrower	No voter review. Districts borrow.

walk might pay a lesser amount, and parcels beyond three blocks might pay nothing at all.

State law provides nearly three dozen types of benefit assessments,[25] but the most common are assessment bonds issued under the 1915 Act and the 1911 Act.[26] Counties, cities, and many types of special districts can use assessment bonds to finance public works. Proposition 218 (1996) and its implementing statutes[27] restrict local officials' ability to issue assessment bonds by requiring weighted-ballot approval by the affected property owners. Public officials and their advisors must research and follow these procedures closely to avoid mistakes.

Redevelopment Tax Allocation Bonds

Growing fiscal problems in urban areas have forced cities to develop alternative financing schemes to pay for needed public services and facilities.

Redevelopment has literally changed the way that California looks by clearing slums, financing downtown improvements, building affordable housing, and paying for infrastructure.[28] Redevelopment agencies controlled by city councils and county boards of supervisors issue tax allocation bonds to generate the public capital needed to convert blighted areas into productive land uses.[29] When local officials adopt a redevelopment plan for a redevelopment project area, they freeze the property tax allocations that go to the county government, the city, school districts, and any special districts. In future years, the redevelopment agency's efforts should cause the property values in the project area to rise, resulting in higher assessed values, and consequently more property tax revenue. A ground-breaking study found that redevelopment accounts for about half of the increases in assessed value within redevelopment project areas. The other growth would have occurred anyway without a redevelopment agency's intervention.[30] Redevelopment project areas divert over five billion dollars in annual property tax increment revenue. The redevelopment agency, not the other local governments, captures the property tax increment revenue that it then uses to repay the tax allocation bonds.[31]

Death of Redevelopment Agencies?

The 2011 budget crunch led to the dismantling of Redevelopment Agencies effective February 1, 2012.

Because state law restricts the use of redevelopment to blighted areas[32] and because of the political and social intractability of the problems in these areas, the life of a redevelopment project may extend over many decades. Successfully eradicating blight and producing economic gains for the bond holders often requires considerable patience. Nevertheless, redevelopment is so fiscally attractive that many counties and ninety percent of the cities with populations over 50,000 have redevelopment agencies.

Mello-Roos Act Bonds

When Proposition 13 (1978) restricted property taxes, private builders lacked access to public capital that used to pay for the public works needed to support new development.[33] The Legislature responded by passing the Mello-Roos Community Facilities Act.[34] Mello-Roos Act bonds can finance any type of local public infrastructure, making them a useful and desirable way to pay for the public works that subdividers want.[35] The revenue stream that pays for these bonds comes from special taxes levied on the affected parcels. These so-called parcel taxes are fixed amounts charged to each lot, without regard to the amount of benefit received by any specific parcel. To comply with the constitutional requirement for two-thirds voter approval for new special taxes, the Mello-Roos Act allows landowners to cast ballots if the affected property has less than twelve registered voters. For example, the developer of a large, uninhabited area can approve Mello-Roos Act bonds by casting the sole "yes" vote.

The earliest use of Mello-Roos Act bonds was to build new schools for new subdivisions, avoiding the political entanglements that a school district might face in trying to convince voters in a district-wide election for general obligation bonds. Because builders wanted public capital for new schools, they readily agreed to vote for the bonds. Once the property is subdivided into marketable lots and houses, the new home buyers—not the builder—pay the parcel taxes that retire the bonds. In short, those who pay the parcel taxes weren't there when the bonds passed.

Exactions and Dedications

The police power is the inherent authority of a government to regulate private behavior in the public interest, consistent with constitutional safeguards. Because California's courts regard land development not as a right but a privilege, public officials use their police powers to regulate private projects. Linked to the power to approve or disapprove development proposals is the ability of public officials to impose conditions when approving applications for private development projects.[36] County boards of supervisors and city councils can impose scores of conditions on the builder who seeks local approval of a tentative subdivision map. The builder must satisfy each of those conditions before gaining final subdivision approval. For example, the subdivider may have to annex the property to the local fire protection district and orient the proposed houses to take advantage of passive solar design.

Regarding infrastructure, builders often must pay for the public works that the new development needs. When developer fees run into the tens of thousands of dollars for individual houses, the economic and legal stakes are high. The crucial test is the nexus between the demand triggered by the proposed development and the exactions and dedications that local officials require as the conditions of granting the approval.[37] Among the most common exaction requirements are the construction of streets, curbs, gutters, and sidewalks. Other developer commitments include the water distribution and sewage collection systems for the development, street lights, and traffic signals. Likewise, builders now pay fees to local school districts to fund some or all of the costs of building new schools.[38] Builders readily accept these requirements as a cost of developing property in California. The requirement to dedicate land for local parks or pay fees in lieu of dedicating lands was once controversial, but now it is well accepted.

The Exotics

Invention, adaptation, and variation characterize the attempts to raise public capital for the infrastructure needed to stimulate and sustain private development. Although the voters have imposed constitutional limits on elected officials' ability to charge taxes, levy assessments, and issue bonds, the demand for public capital has not abated. To the contrary, the legacy of disinvestment, the prospect of persistent population growth, together with the accumulated need to upgrade and replace, combine to keep the demand high for infrastructure funding. With the traditional methods limited by constitutional restrictions and political resistance, builders and public officials turn to more exotic techniques.[39]

Certificates of Participation. Financing infrastructure with long-term leases that avoid voter review makes certificates of participation (COPs) attractive to many local governments. With COPs, a local government leases property from another entity, often a nonprofit corporation or a joint powers authority. This lessor raises capital for the project by issuing and selling COPs to private investors. When buying COPs, an investor acquires an interest in the lease payments that the government pays to the lessor. COPs are suitable for nearly any type of property that local governments can lease for public purposes: land, buildings (jails, courthouses, city halls, and other office buildings), vehicles (buses and railcars), and durable equipment (computers and telecommunication systems). Because they are used to financially back COPs, leases are exempt from the constitutional requirement for voter approval of long-term debts.[40]

COP = Certificate of participation

Marks-Roos Act Bonds. The Marks-Roos Local Bond Pooling Act[41] provides the statutory authority for Joint Powers Authorities[42] to issue Marks-Roos Act bonds and loan the proceeds to local agencies as infrastructure capital. These bonds can finance a wide variety of local public works projects, including electrical power, sewers, water projects, recreation facilities, solid waste recovery facilities, and housing. Local agencies use a wide variety of revenue sources to pay for their Marks-Roos Act bonds, including enterprise revenue, income from leases, redevelopment property tax increment revenue, special tax revenue, and benefit assessments.[43] Reviews by legislators and the state treasurer identified perceived abuses and resulted in legislation that reined in the use of Marks-Roos Act bonds by Joint Powers Authorities.[44] Local officials should be wary of unsolicited offers to pay "administrative expenses" in return for issuing these bonds.

Limited Obligation Bonds. Cities, counties, special districts, and school districts can issue limited obligation bonds that are backed by the pledge of specified amount of revenue, including property taxes or local sales taxes. The local agency's general fund, general credit, and taxing powers are not liable for these limited obligation bonds. Investors who buy these bonds can't force a local agency to raise any other taxes to repay the bonds. Limited obligation bonds require two-thirds voter approval.[45]

Integrated Financing Districts. Faced with the prospect of being the first builder in an area that lacks ready access to public capital for infrastructure, a developer can ask local officials to create an integrated financing district. Using the Integrated Financing District Act,[46] the private investor can lend money to the new agency to build the necessary public works, or the developer can build the facilities. The new district issues bonds that will be paid by contingent assessments. The assessments remain dormant until development starts; then the landowner starts to pay. As other developers build in the area that is now supplied with public works projects, they pay their shares of the infrastructure's costs and the original sponsor recoups its investment.[47]

Infrastructure Financing Districts. Another way to use public revenue from future private development to pay for public works before that private development occurs is found in the Infrastructure Financing District Act.[48] Like a redevelopment agency, the infrastructure financing district can issue bonds that are to be repaid from future property tax increment revenue. Unlike redevelopment agencies that are restricted to blighted areas, infrastructure financing districts can finance public works in "greenfields." For several years, local officials were reluctant to form infrastructure financing districts because they worried about the constitutionality of using tax increment revenue from property that was not within a redevelopment project area. When an attorney general's opinion allayed those concerns, the City of Carlsbad became the first community to create an Infrastructure Financing District.[49] Since then, legislators have passed special bills that adapt the Infrastructure Financing District Act to particular communities.[50]

Securitized Limited Obligation Notes. Special districts—but not counties or cities—can issue securitized limited obligation notes (SLONs) to borrow up to two million dollars to be paid back from designated revenues over ten years. Special districts must secure their SLONs by pledging a dedicated stream of revenues. Although SLONs don't require voter approval, they need a four-fifths vote of a special district's governing board.[51]

Some Conclusions

Paying for infrastructure has become a series of political balancing acts—balancing projects with funding sources, balancing demand with supply, and balancing short-term public opinion with long-term needs.

Balancing Projects and Funding Sources

Infrastructure finance is like a three-legged stool in that each leg is essential to achieving balance. The stool's first leg is the set of large-scale public works projects financed by the federal agencies, state departments, and community-wide bond issues. Federal and state dams, aqueducts, freeways, universities, prisons, parks, and public lands are too big to be financed by any individual community. Similarly, K–12 schools are such an important part of public life that Proposition 1A (1998) and Proposition 1D (2004) committed billions in state general obligation bonds to build and rehabilitate local schools. The second leg of the metaphorical stool consists of the community-scale public works projects that benefit nearly everyone. Community-wide general obligation bonds and revenue bonds pay for sewer plants, reservoirs, levees, regional parks, libraries, museums, fire stations, and city halls. School districts' G.O. bonds also invest in local schools. The stool's third leg are the public works that benefit particular neighborhoods and individual properties. A combination of assessment bonds, Mello-Roos Act bonds, and developer exactions pay for this infrastructure (e.g., dedication of land, capital facilities fees, public improvements). Public officials try to match the scale of the infrastructure with an appropriate source of funding, finding a politically acceptable balance.

Balancing Demand and Supply

Another part of the balancing act requires state and local officials to match changing infrastructure demands with the supply of public capital. The sidebar at right lists other sources of information and advice. Population growth and changing demography drive the demand for public works projects, sometimes outstripping public officials' best efforts to build enough capacity before residents show up. The apparent jumble of government institutions makes it hard for builders and residents to navigate this rampant federalism. The state's own revenue and taxation statutes influence the fiscal choices that become obstacles to building the local roads, sewers, water systems, parks, and other public works. Once again, three policy strands intersect–land use decisions, government structure, and fiscal choices. Choosing compact development patterns over suburban sprawl may not reduce the overall demand for public works, but it costs less.

Balancing Public Opinions and Public Needs

In 1887, years before he became President of the United States, Woodrow Wilson wrote the seminal essay that launched the modern study of public administration. "It's getting harder to run a constitution than to frame one," Wilson argued.[52] Indeed, more than 120 years later, it's much easier to rewrite the California Constitution than it is to find ways to invest in future infrastructure.

Taken together, the voters' constitutional initiatives, described on pages 4 and 5 (Limitations on the Actions of Local Government), have placed new constitutional limits on most major infrastructure financing methods. These neo-populist propositions attract support from voters who remain deeply skeptical of elected officials' ability to spend tax revenue wisely. With their favorite funding methods either off limits or sharply restricted, local officials and private builders turn to the devices that remain available to them without voter approval. When Proposition 13 temporarily eliminated the ability of communities to pass general obligation bonds, local officials turned to assessment bonds, Mello-Roos Act bonds, and redevelopment tax allocation bonds. When Proposition 218 changed the rules for issuing assessment bonds, one result was that certificates of participation and redevelopment property tax increment revenue became even more attractive.

Building a Basic Bookshelf

Besides this book, what are the essential publications on public finance that attorneys, planners, and consultants should keep within reach? While individual preferences vary, here's a list of basic books that you should have to start your own reference shelf.

- California Debt Issuance Primer, published by the California Debt and Investment Commission, Sacramento, California (2006).
- A Legal Guide to California Redevelopment (Third Edition), Goldfarb & Lipman LLP, San Francisco, California.
- Mello-Roos Financing in California, published by the California Debt Advisory Commission, Sacramento, California (1991).
- Redevelopment in California (Fourth Edition), published by Solano Press Books, Point Arena, California (2009).

Besides books, other useful sources of public finance information appear on these web sites:

- California Debt and Investment Advisory Commission (reports) www.treasurer.ca.gov/stocda.htm
- Legislative Analyst's Office (reports) www.lao.ca.gov
- Legislative Counsel (full text of the California Constitution and state statutes) www.leginfo.ca.gov
- Public Policy Institute of California (reports) www.ppic.org

Balancing Act:

Projects/Sources
Demand/Supply
Short-term/Long Term

No one will be surprised if the next round of initiatives targets those devices requiring more elections and voter review. This fundamental clash of political cultures—between the values of representative democracy and insistently direct democracy—will demand adroit administrative skills and considerable political leadership. To finance infrastructure in the first quarter of the twenty-first century the challenge will be to win the public's confidence in California's future.

Peter M. Detwiler formerly served as the Staff Director for the California State Senate Committee on Local Government in Sacramento, where he advised legislators about bills affecting public finance, land use, and the powers of local agencies. Mr. Detwiler helped the Legislature write major reform bills on long-term finance, redevelopment, land use planning, LAFCOs, and growth management. This chapter reflects his own views, not necessarily those of the Committee Chair and the other members of the Senate Local Government Committee.

CHAPTER TWO

Defining the Terms

By Margaret M. Sohagi

Introduction

Exactions, taxes, and assessments are three of the most common sources of funding for infrastructure, maintenance, and services in California. Frequently confused, the terms contain important differences that play a crucial role in determining which technique or combination of approaches can be used to solve a financing problem. Sometimes subtle, these distinctions can affect the legality or illegality of the levy. This chapter defines the terms and helps explain why different techniques are used in various situations. Since courts have been wrestling with many of these distinctions for years, a number of the pivotal cases are discussed to clarify the terms and explore the power and limitations of different approaches.

Exactions, taxes, and assessments are three of the most common sources of funding for infrastructure, maintenance, and services in California.

Exactions

The definition of *exaction* is expansive. It includes development fees, interests in and improvements to land, and capital improvements.[1] The following definition is widely used in connection with land development:

> The process by which developers are required, as a condition of development approval, to dedicate sites for public or common facilities; construct and dedicate public or common facilities; purchase and donate vehicles and equipment for public or common use; make payments to defray the cost of land, facilities, vehicles and equipment in connection with public or private off-site facilities or otherwise provide other specifically agreed upon public amenities.[2]

Four major forms of exactions are encountered in land development:

- Dedication of land and fees in lieu of dedication
- Subdivision reservations
- Project design and improvements
- Fees

According to a 2006 California League of Cities report, fees comprise eight percent and service charges 38 percent of annual local government revenues. (League of

Major Exactions

- Dedication of Land/in-Lieu Fees
- Subdivision Reservations
- Project Design and Improvements
- Fees

California Cities, 2006, www.CaliforniaCityFinance.com.) Permit fees, development fees, dedications, in-lieu fees, and exactions are especially important in new and growing suburban municipalities, which commonly have high infrastructure costs but lack an established tax base. Depending on the municipality and type of project, residential development fees in California in 1999 ranged from a low of $4,000 per unit to as high as $60,000 per unit. Single-family homebuilders in California paid an average of $24,325 per unit in residential development fees, based on the results of a sample of 89 cities and counties in 1999. Owners of new infill homes paid an average of $20,327 per unit, and apartment developers paid an average of $15,531 per new apartment unit.

For a detailed study of fees charged by various entities in California, see "Pay to Play: Residential Development Fees in California Cities and Counties 1999," published by the Division of Housing Policy Development, California Department of Housing and Community Development (August 2001).

Given the housing boom of the past decade, development fees have also grown. According to the 2007 National Impact Fee Survey,[3] fees for a $200,000 single-family, three bedroom house on a 10,000 square foot lot at density of four UPA range from $55,863 in Livermore to $6,082 in Rialto. The national average for impact fees was $10,497; the California average was $18,793. As an example of the range of fees, the City of Glendale's 2008 draft Housing Element states that for a single family hillside house on one half acre, the fees would amount to $67,277. If the same single family project were located on flat lands, the fee would be approximately $41,202. The costs per unit for a forty-five-unit, multifamily project on a one acre parcel would be $8,718. Glendale's fees are 10-20 percent lower than its neighboring cities of Los Angeles, Burbank, or Pasadena.[4]

Land Dedication and Fees in Lieu of Dedication

Dedications of land are imposed in one of two ways—an outright dedication of land and/or a mandatory fee in lieu of dedication. Fees are often used in lieu of dedication of land or facilities (in-lieu fees) when the proposed facility is offsite.

Two types of land dedication exist in California: those made under the controlling principles of common law and those made pursuant to statutory provisions of the Subdivision Map Act (Map Act) (Gov. Code §§ 66410– 66499.37).[5] *Subdivision* is defined as "the division, by any subdivider, of any unit or units of improved or unimproved land, or any portion thereof, shown on the latest equalized county assessment role as a unit or contiguous units, for the purpose of sale, lease, or financing, whether immediate or future." § 66424.[6]

San Francisco, facing a continuing decline in federal and state revenues, exacts fees from new development to help finance low-income housing projects and improvements to its public transit system.

A common law dedication occurs when an individual records a map of his or her land with defined areas labeled as public squares or parks. Courts interpret this to be an offer to dedicate that will take effect upon acceptance by the public.[7] Lands may also be dedicated through implied means, such as allowing the public to use one's land over an extended period of time. *Gion v. City of Santa Cruz* (1970) 2 Cal. 3d 29, 43–44. A dedication may occur in conjunction with a zoning or use permit approval. *Scrutton v. County of Sacramento* (3d Dist. 1969) 275 Cal. App. 2d 412, 421–22. Historically, common law dedications played an important role in providing land for public use, but over time the statutory provisions of the Map Act and non-statutory requirements of the zoning law have become more important.

Article 3 of the Map Act, titled "Dedications," expressly permits local agencies (meaning cities or counties) to require dedication of land within the subdivision for streets and drainage (§ 66475), bicycle paths (§ 66475.1), transit facilities (§ 66475.2), solar easements (§ 66475.3), parkland (§ 66477 [the Quimby Act]), access for public resources (§§ 66478.1–66478.14), and school sites (§ 66478). This list is not exclusive, however. Because the definitions of *design* (§ 66418) and *improvement* (§ 66419) both refer to dedications for the purpose of ensuring consistency with the local general plan, the range of allowable dedications most likely extends beyond those items listed in article 3. The expansive effect of the general plan on conditions that can be imposed as part of a subdivision approval is discussed in chapter 4.

Section 66411.1 limits dedications imposed by local ordinance for subdivisions of fewer than five lots to dedications of right-of-way, easements, and the construction of reasonable offsite and onsite improvements for the parcels being created.

Section 66478 of the Map Act directly addresses elementary school site dedications, although it is more akin to a reservation than a dedication because the subdivider is compensated for the original cost of the land plus improvement taxes assessed and maintenance costs. The subdivider is also given the option to repurchase the land not used by the school district as a school site within ten years after being dedicated. (Reservations are described below and in chapter 4, and school facilities are addressed more fully in chapter 6.) Historically, cities and counties used the School Facilities Act (§§ 65970–65981) to require dedication of land and payment of fees for school facilities as a condition for approval of a subdivision map. Although not part of the Map Act, the School Facilities Act applies to residential subdivisions that are governed by the Map Act.

Subdivision Reservations

Chapter 4, article 4, sections 66479–66482, of the Map Act gives local agencies the authority to require a developer to reserve part of a development's real property for public uses such as parks, recreational facilities, fire stations, and libraries. A reservation is analogous to a dedication because it operates as a compulsory requirement for the subdivider to relinquish some portion of his or her property for public purposes. The difference between reservations and dedications pertains to reimbursement. Under the reservation provisions, the subdivider is paid the fair market value of the land plus taxes measured at the time a tentative map is filed, whereas the local agency is not required to pay for a dedication. (See exception above for section 66478.) The agency may impose reservation requirements by local ordinance, subject to the conditions of section 66479.

Project Design and Improvement

The Map Act extends to local government the ability to regulate and control "the design and improvement of subdivisions." § 66411. This legislative grant of power can be used to obtain a dedication of land or the use of land or fees for a variety of public purposes such as streets, bike paths, alleys, local transit facilities, etc., as a condition of approval for a subdivision map. Historically, *design* was limited primarily to such matters as street alignments, grades and widths, drainage and sanitary facilities, utilities, location and size of easements and rights of way, fire roads, lot sizes, traffic access, and grading. Originally, *improvement* only referred to street and traffic work, utilities, drainage facilities, and other similar items necessary for the general use of lot owners in the subdivision.

In the 1970s, the legislature expanded the power of local governments by adding broad passages to the statutory definitions of design and improvement so that the definitions now include such other specific physical requirements or improvements "... necessary to ensure consistency with, or implementation of the general plan or any applicable specific plan." §§ 66418, 66419. This legislation extended the ability of local government to condition development on compliance with goals and policies in either the general plan or a specific plan. See 58 Ops. Cal. Atty. Gen. 41 (1975). See chapter 4 for more information about the Subdivision Map Act and the general plan as additional authority for fees.

Fees

Fees fall into three categories: fees for benefits and services, commonly referred to as *service fees, user fees, or connection fees*; fees for regulatory activities; and development fees.

Fees for Benefits and Services. Local governments can charge fees for a variety of benefits and services. These fees—frequently called service fees, user fees, and connection fees—can be imposed for services such as garbage collection, sewage treatment, and water supply. The basic authority for these fees comes from the police power. As long as they do not exceed the value of the services rendered, courts have held that these fees are not taxes and are thus exempt from the limitations of Proposition 13. Cal. Const. art. XIII A. See also *County of Fresno v. Malmstrom* (5th Dist. 1979) 94 Cal. App. 3d 974, 984; *Mills v. County of Trinity* (3d Dist. 1980) 108 Cal. App. 3d 656, 660. However, if a fee such as a water hook-up fee exceeds the cost of providing the needed facilities, it may be held invalid as a violation of Proposition 13. See *Beaumont Investors v. Beaumont-Cherry Valley Water District* (4th Dist. 1985) 165 Cal. App. 3d 227. A fee that apportions costs based upon the benefits received, such as a water transportation rate that apportions costs based upon the amount of acre-feet of water delivered, and does not exceed the cost of providing the service is reasonable. See *Rincon Del Diablo Municipal Water District v. San Diego Water Authority* (4th Dist. 2004) 121 Cal. App. 4th 813, 824.

Fees fall into three categories: fees for benefits and services, commonly referred to as service fees, user fees, or connection fees; fees for regulatory activities; and development fees.

Fees for many services are codified. For example, section 66483 authorizes storm drainage and sewer connection fees, and Health and Safety Code sections 5470 to 5474 authorize connection fees and charges for water, sanitation, and storm drainage. See *Capistrano Beach Water District v. TAJ Development Corporation* (4th Dist. 1999) 72 Cal. App. 4th 524 (refund of provisions of Mitigation Fee Act (Gov. Code § 66000 *et seq.*) do not apply to capacity charges and connection fees governed by former Gov. Code § 54991 (now § 66013)).

Simply calling a charge a fee does not determine whether it is a fee, a tax, or an assessment. For example, a charge having the earmarks of a service fee, such as a water standby charge, is actually an assessment due to the procedures and mechanisms used to levy the charge. Thus, courts are not bound by the label but will inquire into the method of calculation and imposition to determine the relevant body of law. See *Trumbo v. Crestline-Lake Arrowhead Water Agency* (4th Dist. 1967) 250 Cal. App. 2d 320, 322; *J.W. Jones Companies v. City of San Diego* (4th Dist. 1984) 157 Cal. App. 3d 745. Assessments are discussed more fully on pages 38 to 41 (Assessments).

Sometimes a charge can be defended using more than one legal theory, as in *Kern County Farm Bureau v. County of Kern* (5th Dist. 1993) 19 Cal. App. 4th 1416, 1422. In this case, the court determined that a landfill service charge was valid whether analyzed as a regulatory/service fee or as a special benefit assessment. Instead of charging a gate fee to persons dumping refuse at the county's landfill site, Kern County imposed a charge against property countywide based on the generation of solid waste occurring from the various land use categories. In 1990, the county increased the charge for agricultural land. The Farm Bureau challenged the fee on the basis that it was a special tax because it was calculated on potential use by broad classifications of land uses, rather than actual use by individuals; furthermore the Farm Bureau argued that it was not a valid benefit assessment, because there was no special benefit to the property subjected to the fee.

As long as they do not exceed the value of the services rendered, courts have held that fees for benefits and services are not taxes and are thus exempt from the limitations of Proposition 13.

In rejecting the special tax argument, the court found that the county's studies of the gross percentage of agricultural waste deposited in various landfill sites and other empirical data to support its fees were reasonable, especially in light of the fact that landfill usage "is not susceptible of mathematical calculation." *Kern County*, 19 Cal. App. 4th at 1424. Moreover, because the fees allowed the county to operate the landfill without a gate fee, they had the regulatory effect of reducing illegal dumping by individuals who wanted to avoid the gate fee. This was an additional basis for upholding the fees as a reasonable exercise of the police power for regulatory purposes. *Id.*

Simply calling a charge a fee does not determine whether it is a fee, a tax, or an assessment.

The court also upheld the landfill charges as a "special assessment" authorized by Health and Safety Code section 5471, even though the statute did not use the term "assessments." The general authorization for "other charges" pursuant to Health and Safety Code section 5471 was sufficient under the rationale of *San Marcos Water District v. San Marcos Unified School District* (1986) 42 Cal. 3d 154, 162 (sewer capacity fees upheld pursuant to Health and Safety Code § 5471). *Kern County*, 19 Cal. App. 4th at 1425–26.

The Farm Bureau also unsuccessfully argued that the fee was a special tax because it "exacted from every person or parcel within the county service area regardless of the use of the service and irrespective of the benefit to the land." The court found maintenance of an existing level of service, such as the landfill operations, provided a particular benefit to the assessed properties, citing the California Supreme Court's decision in *Knox v. City of Orland* (1992) 4 Cal. 4th 132, 141. Accordingly, the court in the *Kern County* case found that the direct and indirect benefits to the property justified the landfill assessment. *Kern County*, 19 Cal. App. 4th, at 1426.

Regulatory Fees. Regulatory fees are imposed to cover the cost of regulating some activity, such as a business license fee. The authority for regulatory fees also comes from the police power. In *Sinclair Paint Company v. State Board of Equalization* (1997) 15 Cal. 4th 866, the California Supreme Court held that a regulatory fee was not a tax, and therefore, not subject to the two-thirds vote requirement imposed by the California Constitution, article XIII A, section 3. The fee at issue was imposed on all manufacturers and other persons engaged in the stream of commerce of lead or products containing lead that have significantly contributed, or currently contribute, to environmental lead contamination. Pursuant to the Childhood Lead Poisoning Prevention Act of 1991, the fee would be used for the evaluation, screening, and medically necessary follow-up services for children who were deemed to be at risk for lead poisoning. The Sinclair Paint Company challenged the fee on grounds that it was intended to generate revenue for a non-regulatory program, and therefore constituted an unconstitutional tax.

The court stated that "all regulatory fees are necessarily aimed at raising 'revenue' to defray the cost of the regulatory program in question, but that fact does not automatically render those fees 'taxes.' . . . [I]f regulation is the primary purpose of the fee measure, the mere fact that the measure also generates revenue does not make the imposition of a tax." *Sinclair Paint*, 15 Cal. 4th at 880.

The court further distinguished between taxes subject to a two-thirds vote and fees and assessments. Taxes are generally imposed for revenue generation rather than for a special benefit or privilege. Special taxes are taxes levied for a specific purpose rather than for general governmental purposes.

Special assessments, on the other hand, are charges to a property or business based upon a benefit conferred on the property. They are valid where the assessment reflects the reasonable value of the benefit received by the property. *Id.* at 874. Development fees are exactions made in return for building permits or other governmental privileges. They are valid and not special taxes where the fee bears a reasonable relationship to the probable costs of the development to the community and the benefits conferred to the developer. *Id.* at 875.

Regulatory fees are imposed for a regulatory purpose under the regulatory power, rather than the taxing power. A regulatory fee is valid if it does "...not exceed the reasonable cost of providing services necessary to the activity for which the fee is charged and [is] not levied for unrelated revenue purposes." *Id.* at 876. Determining that the fee did serve a regulatory purpose, the Supreme Court held: "It requires manufacturers and other persons whose products have exposed children to lead contamination to bear a fair share of the cost of mitigating the adverse health effects their products created in the community. Viewed as a 'mitigating effects' measure, it is comparable in character to similar police power measures imposing fees to defray the actual or anticipated adverse effects of various business operations." *Id.* at 877. "In our view, the shifting of costs of providing evaluation, screening, and medically necessary follow-up services for potential child victims of lead poisoning from the public to those persons deemed responsible for that poisoning is likewise a reasonable police power decision." *Id.* at 879. See also *City of Oakland v. Superior Court of Alameda County* (1st Dist. 1996) 45 Cal. App. 4th 740 (upholding regulatory fees charged to alcoholic beverage sale licensees to support a pilot project to address public nuisances associated with those sales); *United Business Commission v. City of San Diego* (4th Dist. 1979) 91 Cal. App. 156 (upholding fees for inspecting and inventorying on-premises advertising signs).

Similarly, in *Mills v. County of Trinity* (3d Dist. 1980), 108 Cal. App. 3d 656, the court found that fees for county services to process subdivision, zoning, and other land use applications are legitimate exercises of regulatory authority, and hence are not special taxes. Thus, regulatory fees are not limited by Proposition 13.[8] The court held:

> . . . "[S]pecial taxes," under article XIII A, §4 . . . do not embrace fees for land-use regulatory activities where the fees charged do not exceed the reasonable cost of the regulatory activities and are not levied for unrelated revenue purposes.
>
> *Mills*, at 663.

The California Attorney General concluded that counties may require applicants for coastal development permits to defend, indemnify, and hold harmless the county in the event a third party sues to void the permit. 85 Ops. Cal. Atty. Gen. 21 (2002).

Under the California Constitution, "[a] county or city may make and enforce within its limits all local, police, sanitary and other ordinances and regulations not in conflict with general laws." Cal. Const., art. XI, § 7. The regulation of land development is a traditional subject for the exercise of the constitutional police power by a county or city. The opinion concluded that county governments have the authority to impose regulatory fees to cover the costs of issuing a development permit. Such costs may include all those incident to the issuance of the license or permit, including investigation, inspection, administration, maintenance of a system of supervision, enforcement, and litigation.

As a matter of public policy, a county may determine whether the litigation costs associated with the granting of a coastal development permit should be borne by the permit holder or by the general taxpayers of the county. No statute precludes a county from making such a determination, and a court will not interfere with a county's decision in this regard. Therefore, a county may enact an ordinance that requires applicants to defend, indemnify, and hold harmless the county in any action by a third party to void the permit.

In *California Association of Professional Scientists v. Department of Fish & Game* (3rd Dist. 2000) 79 Cal. App. 4th 935, the court considered whether the exactions imposed by section 711.4 of the Fish and Game Code constitute a regulatory fee or a tax. The court concluded that as long as the cumulative amount of the fees did not surpass the cost of the regulatory program or service, and the record disclosed a reasonable basis to justify distributing the cost among payors, the fee did not become a tax simply because each payor was required to pay a predetermined fixed amount. *Id.* at 939.

Section 711.4 was enacted in 1990 and imposed a flat fee schedule to defray a portion of the costs incurred by the Department of Fish and Game (DFG) in fulfilling its environmental review obligations under the California Environmental Quality Act (CEQA) and the Z'Berg-Nejedly Forest Practices Act (Forest Practices Act). Pub. Res. Code §§ 4511, 21000 *et seq.*

The DFG presented evidence that $11 million had been collected in fees, but the cost of the reviews was in excess of $20 million. Thus the fees were not revenue raising since they did not generate income beyond the cost of the review services provided. *California Association of Professional Scientists v. Department of Fish & Game* (3rd Dist. 2000) 79 Cal. App. 4th 935. As such, the regulatory fee did not violate the state constitution. *Id.* at 950.

The court further stated that it need not perform an appellate audit of the DFG's accounting systems to determine reasonableness of the fees. *Id.* at 954. Review of the entire record indicated sufficient evidence to support the trial court's finding that the cost of comprehensive environmental review far surpassed the amount of fees generated under section 711.4.

Sometimes a fee is levied for both regulatory and revenue purposes. Also, in some instances, a local agency may not have authority to levy a license fee for regulatory purposes, but it may do so for revenue purposes, and vice versa.

Development Fees

- In Lieu
- Impact/linkage
- Mitigation

Development Fees. Due to the increasing unavailability of federal, state, and local funds for public improvements, especially improvements associated with new development, local governments are constantly looking for new ways to finance construction of such facilities. Two common techniques are to request land for and/or require construction of improvements (discussed previously under dedications), and/or to impose development fees. There are three major types of development fees:

- In-lieu fees
- Impact fees, including a variation called *linkage* fees
- Mitigation fees

Frequently used interchangeably, these terms may refer to the same fee depending on the context.[9]

In-lieu fees. In-lieu fees are used when requiring a developer to dedicate land would not be optimal or feasible. For example, requiring each subdivider to dedicate land for school or recreational purposes might not achieve the goal of providing such facilities for large, developing suburban areas if the sites are either inadequate in size or not in the best locations. Imposing an in-lieu fee can solve this problem by substituting a monetary payment for dedication. Fees collected from numerous subdividers can then be used at a later date to purchase an appropriate site and construct the necessary improvements.[10] In-lieu fees have been upheld by the courts in many cases. *Remmenga v. California Coastal Commission* (2d Dist. 1985) 163 Cal. App. 3d 623.

Impact fees. This category of exactions is one of the most important funding sources for large-scale public facilities and services necessary to serve new developments. Impact fees are designed so that each development pays its proportionate share.

An impact fee is an exaction:

- In the form of a predetermined monetary payment
- Assessed as a condition to the issuance of a building permit, an occupancy permit, or subdivision map approval
- Imposed pursuant to local government powers to regulate new growth and development and provide for adequate public facilities and services
- Levied to fund public facilities and services necessary to serve new development
- Levied in an amount that is proportionate to the need for the public facilities created by the new development[11]

Over time, calculation of impact fees has become more complicated. Impact fees adopted during the 1970s were adopted without enabling legislation, guidelines, or standards, and were based on a straightforward set of factors and calculations. Eventually, however, courts and legislatures around the country scrutinized these fees, which resulted in new requirements. Fees enacted more recently are authorized by specific enabling statutes and are usually designed to reflect the principles of well established case law, such as *Nollan v. California Coastal Commission* (1987) 483 U.S. 825.

Today, many states have laws that set procedural and substantive standards for impact fees. In California, this legislation is commonly referred to as AB 1600 or the Mitigation Fee Act, section 66000 et seq. (See chapter 5 for a more thorough discussion of AB 1600.) Fees adopted in the early 1970s are referred to as *first generation* impact fees, and those adopted after the enactment of AB 1600 are called *second generation.*[12]

In general, second generation impact fees are distinguishable from first generation by the following elements:

Impact Fees

- First Generation—Adopted in early 1970s
- Second Generation—Adopted after AB 1600

Statutory basis. Most communities in the United States now impose impact fees under a state statutory enactment representing clear legal authority for their use. These state statutes reflect the increased political acceptance of impact fees.

Methodology. Second generation impact fees use complex formulas and computer models, incorporating population and employment projections, cost estimates for capital facilities, and/or trip generation data. See Appendices A, B, and C for examples of such studies. First generation impact fees and fees in lieu of dedication frequently were based simply on a fixed cash payment per acre.

Procedures. Second generation impact fees are usually subject to detailed and rigorous notice and hearing requirements, not only to satisfy the ordinance establishing the impact fee, but also to comply with capital improvement plans and land use assumptions that justify the ordinance. These heightened procedural requirements reflect a legislative intent to provide uniform, statewide standards and procedures for impact fees and to limit local abuse of discretion.

Scope of facilities funded. Unlike earlier impact fee ordinances, second generation ordinances are frequently designed to fund a much broader array of capital improvements, i.e., government buildings, libraries, and public services such as police, fire, and emergency medical services.

Exemptions. Early impact fees usually applied to all new development, or to a broad category of new development, such as new residential or office/commercial development. For equitable reasons, some second generation impact fees exempt certain classes of land use in order to avoid the harsh effect development fees have on less profitable, socially beneficial land uses.[13] In California, certain types of housing development may be exempt from some fees. § 65995.1(b) (agricultural migrant worker housing).

In *Ehrlich v. City of Culver City* (1996) 12 Cal. 4th 854, the California Supreme Court held that a city may impose a fee to mitigate impacts resulting from the loss of a land use designation and upheld general legislative fees. The Court examined the scope of the United States Supreme Court's opinions in *Nollan,* 483 U.S. at 825 and *Dolan v. City of Tigard* (1994) 512 U.S. 374. In particular, the court was required to determine the extent to which the unconstitutional dedication test announced in these cases applied to:

- A recreation mitigation fee applied for the first and only time to a developer seeking approval of a specific project
- An "art in public places" ordinance applicable to all new development in the community, and for which no particularized determination is made when a building permit is sought

The recreation mitigation fee was a one-time fee intended to pay for replacement of community recreational facilities that were provided at the proposed development site. The need for community recreational facilities had been evidenced by previous staff reports, consultant reports, and public testimony indicating the use and feasibility of such facilities at the subject site. The amount of the fee was based upon a city study analyzing the replacement costs of each recreational amenity provided on the project site.

The majority of the court determined that *Nollan/Dolan* applied to the city's recreational mitigation fee because it was not levied pursuant to an ordinance but was instead applied ad hoc to a single development application. As the plurality stated: "It is the imposition of land-use conditions in individual cases, authorized by a permit scheme which by its nature allows for both the discretionary deployment of the police power and an enhanced potential for its abuse, that constitutes the sine qua non for application of the intermediate standard of scrutiny formulated by the court in *Nollan* and *Dolan*." *Ehrlich,* 12 Cal. 4th at 859.

The Court recognized the need to allow cities to impose these types of fees. "Such a fee would serve the same purpose as do all development fees: providing the city with a means of escaping the narrow choice between denying plaintiff his project permit altogether or subordinating legitimate public interests to plaintiff's development plans." *Ehrlich,* 12 Cal. 4th at 884. However, the Court ordered the city to recalculate the fee. The Court stated that the city had improperly set the fee by ignoring the fact that new tennis courts at any other private recreational facility would be paid by fees of members and would not have been open to the public at no charge. The Court suggested three methods that the city could use to determine the appropriate fee on remand, including that the city could charge a fee roughly proportional to the cost of inducing a new private recreation facility to locate in the city, or a fee roughly proportional to the impairment that a private recreation facility restriction would impose on another vacant parcel of land. *Ehrlich,* 12 Cal. 4th at 883–85.

The Art in Public Places Ordinance applied citywide and required projects to either provide art work onsite, or to the city, or pay a fee to the city art fund. The amount of art work or fee was to be the equivalent of one percent of the total building valuation. Only new construction projects with building valuations in excess of $500,000 and remodeling projects exceeding $250,000 in building value must comply with the ordinance. There were also certain exclusions for low- and moderate-income housing, earthquake rehabilitation, and small residential projects.

The Court refused to extend the *Nollan/Dolan* analysis to the Art in Public Places Ordinance. The plurality opinion, authored by Justice Arabian, found that: "Such aesthetic conditions have long been held to be valid exercises of the city's traditional police power, and do not amount to a taking merely because they might incidentally restrict a use, diminish the value, or impose a cost in connection with the property." *Ehrlich,* 12 Cal. 4th at 886. The plurality further stated: "we agree with the city that the art in public places fee is not a development exaction of the kind subject to the *Nollan-Dolan* takings analysis." *Id.*

Most significantly, the Court concluded that the Mitigation Fee Act, section 66000 et seq., is the exclusive remedy for developers who contend that fees imposed by the government are excessive: "developers who wish to challenge a development fee on either statutory or constitutional grounds must do so via the statutory framework provided by the Act. (*Cf. Hensler v. City of Glendale,* 8 Cal. 4th at 13–15.)" *Ehrlich,* 12 Cal. 4th at 867.[14]

Earlier examples of impact fees that have been upheld are *Commercial Builders of Northern California v. City of Sacramento* (9th Cir. 1991) 941 F. 2d 872, cert. denied (1992)

504 U.S. 931, 112 S. Ct. 1997, 118 L. E. 2d 593 (linkage fee imposed on commercial development to fund low-income housing); *Blue Jeans Equities West v. City and County of San Francisco* (1st Dist. 1992) 3 Cal. App. 4th 164, cert. denied, 506 U.S. 866, 113 S. Ct. 191, 121 L. E. 2d 135 (impact fee imposed on commercial development to fund mass transit); *Garrick Development Company v. Hayward Unified School District* (1st Dist. 1992) 3 Cal. App. 4th 320 (school fees imposed on development). (See chapter 3 for a more thorough discussion of these cases.) See also *Trent Meredith, Inc. v. City of Oxnard* (2d Dist. 1981) 114 Cal. App. 3d 317, 328 (school facilities fees); *Terminal Plaza Corp. v. City and County of San Francisco* (1st Dist. 1986) 177 Cal. App. 3d 892, 905–907 (fee to replace demolished residential units); *Candid Enterprises, Inc. v. Grossmont Union High School District* (1985) 39 Cal. 3d 878 (fees on new construction to mitigate the impact on school districts); *Russ Bldg. P'ship. v. City and County of San Francisco* (1st Dist. 1987) 199 Cal. App. 3d 1496 (public transit impact fee).

Traffic congestion in urban areas is a growing problem, and development fees offer local government a means to finance, in part, the local share of the cost of new and expanded transit services.

San Marcos legislation. In 1988, the Legislature enacted Government Code sections 54999–54999.6 (the San Marcos legislation) authorizing public agencies providing public utility service on or after July 21, 1996, to continue to charge, or increase, an existing capital facilities fee or to impose a new capital facilities fee on public entities who use their facilities. § 54999.2. The legislation was in direct response to *San Marcos Water District v. San Marcos Unified School District* (*San Marcos I*) (1986) 42 Cal. 3d 154, cert. denied (1987) 479 U.S. 1079, 109 S. Ct. 1291, 94 L. E. 2d 148, in which the California Supreme Court held that public entities could not be made subject to capital facilities fees without statutory authorization. § 54999. The Legislature expressly noted that as a result of *San Marcos I*, "the fiscal stability and service capabilities of the affected public utility service agencies which have in good faith collected and spent these fees for capital improvements are seriously impaired as is the ability to finance essential future facilities." § 54999(a).

The *San Marcos* legislation contains express provisions for the imposition of capital facilities fees on educational entities or state agencies as follows:

- The imposition of capital facilities fees on any educational institution is limited to "[w]here necessary to defray the actual construction costs of that portion of a public utility facility actually serving a public agency." § 54999.3(a)
- A public utility providing service to any of these educational institutions may continue to charge capital facilities fees imposed prior to July 21, 1986, and not protested or challenged, or may increase the capital facilities fees pursuant to the Implicit Price Deflator Index. § 54999.3(a)
- After July 21, 1986, any initial imposition of a capital facilities fee or any increase in an existing fee in excess of the amount permitted in section 54999.3(a) can only occur by agreement between the two agencies. § 54999.3(b)
- Upon request of the affected public agency or upon increase pursuant to subdivision (a), the public agency imposing or increasing the fee shall identify the amount of the capital facilities fee. The public agency imposing or increasing the fee has the burden of producing evidence to establish that "the capital facilities fee is nondiscriminatory and that the amount of the fee does not exceed the amount necessary to provide capital facilities for which the fee is charged." § 54999.3(c)

Impact Fees Compared to Linkage Fees

Used for many forms of development, impact fees are most often used as a funding mechanism for physical improvements that are directly attributable to the development project. Linkage fees, however, describe fees required of commercial/industrial projects to mitigate secondary types of impacts such as child care and affordable housing. The dividing line between the two fees is blurred. Since the same constitutional and statutory limitations apply to both, the label or classification given to these particular fees is not legally significant.

Impact Fees Compared to in-Lieu Fees

Impact fees are functionally and conceptually similar to in-lieu fees in that both are payments for required capital facilities. In some situations the terms can be used interchangeably. However, the uses that can be funded and the methods of assessment distinguish impact fees from fees in lieu of dedication. The true impact fee is a more flexible, cost-shifting tool because in-lieu fees can only fund those facilities for which onsite dedication may be required. For facilities such as libraries, police, and fire stations, for example, which normally provide service to a very wide area, dedications generally do not effectively shift a portion of the capital cost to the development because additional land will do little to extend those services. However, those facilities can be funded with impact fees.

The method for assessing the fees is also different. Dedication of land or in-lieu fees required by local government as a condition for subdivision approval usually depends on the total acreage and projected completion of an entire subdivision or phase of a subdivision. In contrast, the dollar amount of impact fees is usually determined on a per unit basis, depending on the number of units, bedrooms, or square footage of a unit. Thus, because developers are not required to pay large sums prior to development, impact fees are more flexible than mandatory onsite dedications of roads or parkland. Instead, the local government only charges a developer for the proportionate impact new development has on public services and facilities in terms of units actually constructed.

Impact Fees Compared to Connection or User Fees

The main distinction between impact fees and connection or user fees is that impact fees are much more flexible. Connection fees are usually authorized by statute for specific uses, whereas state law does not limit how impact fees may be used. Impact fees can be used to provide almost any public facilities that can reasonably be construed to fall within the enabling legislation and police powers, subject to the limitations imposed by a particular jurisdiction.

Brian W. Blaesser and Christene M. Kentopp, "Impact Fees: The Second Generation," 38 Washington University Journal of Urban and Contemporary Law 55, 64 (Fall 1990), p. 68.

Section 54999.4 provides that "[a]ny capital facilities fees paid prior to [March 24, 1988] and not protested or challenged pursuant to law on or before January 1, 1987, shall not be subject to refund, except for capital facilities fees paid after July 21, 1986, by a public agency subject to Section 54999.3 which are in excess of the maximum amount authorized by Section 54999.3."

In *San Marcos Water District v. San Marcos Unified School District* (*San Marcos II*) (4th Dist. 1987) 190 Cal. App. 3d 1083, the court of appeal applied the 120-day statute of limitations (§ 54995) to bar a school district's action against a water district for a refund of capacity fees sought under section 54999.

In *Rincon Del Diablo Municipal Water District v. San Diego Water Authority* (4th Dist. 2004) 121 Cal. App. 4th 813, the court evaluated an ordinance which set the transportation rate, a component of the water rate. The Water District's transportation rate captured the capital costs as well as the operating and maintenance costs of the Water Authority's aqueduct system. Under the ordinance, revenue generated from the transportation rate were placed in the Water Authority's general fund and were not separated to fund capital costs. The *Rincon* court found that the mere fact that water rates were used to offset capital expenses along with operating expenses did not make water rates a capacity charge pursuant to Government Code section 66013.

In *The Regents of the University of California v. East Bay Municipal Utility District* (*EBMUD*) (1st Dist. 2005) 130 Cal. App. 4th 1361, the court held that the capital component of East Bay Municipal Utility District's water rate constituted a special assessment under the *San Marcos* purpose test and as such, was subject to the *San Marcos* legislation. The court distinguished *Rincon*, noting that the claim in *Rincon* was that the transportation rate was an unreasonable capacity charge under Government Code section 66013 and was totally unrelated to the property tax exemption at issue in the *San Marcos* case.

Linkage fees. The use of linkage fees to fund offsite improvements is of more recent vintage. These fees link the right to construct projects to either the direct provision of new housing or other facilities, the payment of fees to fund construction of housing or other facilities, or payment for providing services such as child care or job training. Linkage is considered the latest stage in a progressive expansion of the police power that began with zoning and subdivision regulations, and has now expanded to exactions for social needs indirectly related to the development projects.[15]

Linkage fees are generally imposed on large-scale, mixed-use, or non-residential projects to promote social programs or policies such as child care and affordable housing. For example, linkage fees have been used in San Francisco, Sacramento, and Boston to fund low- and moderate-income housing. The first major city to adopt a child care linkage ordinance was Concord, California in 1985 (now repealed).[16] Shortly thereafter, San Francisco included child care in its comprehensive Downtown Plan. See chapter 8 for additional discussion of linkage fees.

Mitigation fees. Relying solely on the process outlined in the California Environmental Quality Act (CEQA) (Pub. Resources Code § 21000 *et seq.*), some local agencies levy fees to pay for projects that will offset anticipated harm to the environment from a development. It is important to note, however, that CEQA does not independently authorize fees for these activities. Nonetheless, a public agency may mitigate an adverse effect upon the environment caused by a development project through the levy of an exaction derived from appropriate non-CEQA authority. Pub. Resources Code §§ 21004, 21081. Accord, 68 Ops. Cal. Atty. Gen. 225, 229 (1985). Assuming the public agency has discretionary power or some other source of authority to impose mitigation measures, CEQA can provide appropriate justification, together with a nexus, for requiring conditions. As a result of *Ehrlich* amendments to the CEQA Guidelines that occurred in 1998, special *Dolan* and *Ehrlich* considerations must now be accounted for when applying ad hoc mitigation measures. Guidelines §§ 15041, 15126.4.

CEQA = California Environmental Quality Act

A public agency may mitigate an adverse effect upon the environment caused by a development project through the levy of an exaction derived from appropriate non-CEQA authority.

Assuming the public agency has discretionary power or some other source of authority to impose mitigation measures, CEQA can provide appropriate justification, together with a nexus, for requiring conditions.

Local agencies may also rely on authorities other than CEQA to impose environmental conditions. For a case upholding a non-CEQA environmental condition (scenic open space easement dedication), see *Paoli v. California Coastal Commission* (1st Dist. 1986) 178 Cal. App. 3d 544. Accord, *Leroy Land Development v. Tahoe Regional Planning Agency* (9th Cir. 1991) 939 F.2d 696 in which the court applied the nexus test from *Nollan*, 483 U.S. 825, and upheld the agency's requirement that the developer acquire adjacent or nonadjacent land for open space as mitigation for the environmental impacts of building a condominium project near Lake Tahoe.[17]

Taxes

The California Supreme Court discussed the definition of a tax and its inherent characteristics in *Sinclair Paint Company v. State Board of Equalization* (1997) 15 Cal. 4th 866, 874 as follows:

> In general, taxes are imposed for revenue purposes, rather than in return for a specific benefit conferred or privilege granted. (*Shapell Industries, Inc. v. Governing Board* [1991] 1 Cal. App. 4th 218, 240; *County of Fresno v. Malmstrom, supra*, 94 Cal. App. 3d at 983 ("Taxes are raised for the general revenue of the governmental entity to pay for a variety of public services").) Most taxes are compulsory rather than imposed in response to a voluntary decision to develop or to seek other government benefits or privileges. (*Shapell Industries, Inc. v. Governing Board, supra*, 1 Cal. App. 4th at 240; *Russ Building Partnership v. City and County of San Francisco, supra*, 199 Cal. App. 3d at 1505–1506; see *Terminal Plaza Corporation v. City and County of San Francisco, supra*, 177 Cal. App. 3d at 907.)

A tax may be levied to raise revenue for a general or specific purpose and can cover a wide or narrow range of persons, property, or activities. 62 Ops. Cal. Atty. Gen. 254, 256 (1979). See also *Westfield-Palos Verdes Co. v. City of Rancho Palos Verdes* (2d Dist. 1977) 73 Cal. App. 3d 486, 497.

If the analysis of the incidence[18] of the charge leads to the conclusion that its primary purpose is to raise revenue generally, as opposed to regulating some specific activity or providing a service, the charge is a tax. *Weisblat v. City of San Diego* (4th Dist. 2009) 176 Cal. App. 4th 1022. In *Weisblat*, the court determined that the levy imposed on rental property owners for the purpose of raising revenue to cover the cost of administering the business tax program was a general tax, not a fee. There was no evidence of a benefit conferred on the payor and the proceeds went into the City's general fund. *Id.* at 1042-1045. However, just because a levy places money in the public treasury, does not mean the levy is a tax. 62 Ops. Cal. Atty. Gen. 254, 256 (1979). Many governmental charges are not taxes. For example, a water charge is not a tax. *Arcade County Water Dist. v. Arcade Fire Dist.* (3d Dist. 1970) 6 Cal. App. 3d 232, 240; *Trumbo v. Crestline-Lake Arrowhead Water Agency, supra*, 250 Cal. App. 2d 320, 322. Also, certain regulatory license charges have been determined not to be taxes. *Pennell v. City of San Jose* (1986) 42 Cal. 3d 365. Where the charge exceeds the cost of the benefit or service provided, the payment will most likely be called a tax and will therefore be governed by the strict rules on taxes dictated by Proposition 13. These stringent rules are described below.

Development Taxes

- Property
- Parcel
- Excise/Business License
- Special

Four major types of taxes relate to land development:

- Property taxes
- Parcel taxes
- Excise taxes (including business license taxes)
- Special taxes

Property Taxes

Until Proposition 13 passed in 1978, the ad valorem property tax—a tax based on some percentage of value of the property—was the main source of local revenue for local governments in California. Proposition 13 froze property taxes for homeowners at their 1976 value and limited the ability of local government to increase the property tax each year by no more than two percent. As properties sell, the new property tax can be no more than one percent of the acquisition value, and thereafter the tax assessment cannot increase by more than two percent annually. This feature was upheld by the U.S. Supreme Court in *Nordlinger v. Hahn* (1992) 505 U.S. 1. Additionally, section 4 of article XIII A of the California Constitution prohibits any additional "ad valorem taxes on real property or a transaction or sales tax on the sale of real property. . . . "

Parcel Taxes

Parcel taxes are typically levied as a flat rate on each parcel or classification of parcel, regardless of property value. Under Proposition 13 parcel taxes are considered to be special taxes requiring approval by two-thirds of the voters for passage. Sometimes a parcel tax cannot be approved without also approving an increase in a local agency's Gann spending limit to allow the expenditure of the revenue generated by the new tax. Such measures are sometimes called "parcel tax/Gann measures."

Excise Taxes and Business License Taxes

Excise taxes or *privilege taxes* are collected from developers for exercising their right or privilege to develop or use property and municipal services. The tax is imposed on the *occupants* of property rather than on actual property owners. An excise or privilege tax is not a property tax within the meaning of Proposition 13; therefore, cases applying or construing either Proposition 13 or Proposition 62 (which requires a two-thirds vote for special taxes) are not relevant. These taxes, considered to be general purpose, only require a majority vote for approval.

The primary purpose of an excise tax must be to raise revenue, not to regulate. *Westfield-Palos Verdes County v. City of Rancho Palos Verdes*, 73 Cal. App. 3d at 495. The best known excise tax in California is the sales tax, imposed "for the privilege of selling tangible personal property at retail" (Rev. and Tax. Code § 6051) and the use tax imposed "on the storage, use, or other consumption in this state of tangible personal property." Rev. and Tax. Code § 6201. Counties are authorized to levy sales and use taxes (Rev. and Tax. Code § 7201), and the State Board of Equalization is authorized to administer the sales and use taxes of cities and counties (Rev. and Tax. Code § 7203.5 *et seq.*). Other examples of excise taxes are business license taxes, hotel or bedroom taxes, and payroll taxes.[19]

Excise taxes can be imposed on new development to alleviate the burdens they create. For example, a license tax–a type of excise tax–imposed on a company engaged in the business of acquiring, subdividing, improving, selling, and otherwise disposing of real property was upheld in *City of Los Angeles v. Rancho Homes, Inc.* (1953) 40 Cal. 2d 764. A bedroom tax ordinance was upheld in *Associated Home Builders of the Greater East Bay, Inc. v. City of Newark* (1st Dist. 1971) 18 Cal. App. 3d 107. The ordinance required the payment of a tax computed according to the number of bedrooms in the proposed structure, payable at the time a building permit is issued. Monies were to be used for parks and other capital improvements. An environmental excise tax that levied $500 per bedroom with a maximum of $1,000 per dwelling unit was approved in *Westfield-Palos Verdes Co. v. City of Rancho Palos Verdes*, 73 Cal. App. 3d at 495.[20]

The primary impediment to the use of excise taxes is the potential for litigation that claims the tax is either a special tax or a disguised development fee. Local agencies wishing to impose an excise tax must determine whether the proposed tax is a *special tax* within the meaning of the California Constitution, article XIII A, section 4. In November 1990, voters in the City of Novato passed an excise tax measure to purchase open space for public use. The tax was later struck down in a court decision that found the tax to be a special tax requiring a two-thirds rather than a majority vote for passage.[21]

How the tax is collected and disbursed must also be considered. By definition, an excise tax must be levied on each occupant rather than on each property owner. Thus, the measure must be carefully drafted or a court may find that the tax in question is a *parcel tax* rather than a true excise tax. This issue also arose in the Novato case where the court found that the tax in question was a *parcel tax* rather than a true excise tax because the tax was collected on a *per parcel basis* rather than upon each occupant of the city.[22]

A number of communities increase their business license taxes to raise revenue. Because these taxes are exempt from Proposition 13, the vast majority of increases throughout the state have been adopted through the

The Reluctant Electorate

Despite the equity of spreading public facility costs across a wider base, Californians are hesitant to vote to increase their own taxes. In the 1998 Primary and General Elections, 39 of 109 special tax measures were approved by the required two-thirds majority. This amounts to approximately 36 percent of the special tax measures being approved in 1998. In the Primary Election, special tax measures for multiple capital improvements and public works were relatively successful with three of four passing. In contrast, in this election only three of eight special tax measures for fire protection and suppression were successful. Other measures included: five library service measures with two passing; five public safety measures with two passing; three street improvement measures with only one being approved; and of nine communication system measures only three gained approval.

In the General Election, special tax measures for emergency medical services ended up with the best relative success rate, with ten out of twelve being approved. Only three of thirteen fire protection measures were approved, two of three library services and facilities, and one of eight special tax measures for mosquito abatement. Both public safety and parks and open space had only two of seven measures pass in each category.

Results from more recent election data show that while Californians support more general taxes, special municipal service (parcel) taxes and bonds continue to be rejected by the public. In the 2005 Special Election, only 13 percent of these taxes for libraries, street, sidewalks, and other improvements passed. See "Lessons of the November 2005 Special Election," Western City Magazine, January 2006 for more data.

ordinance process. However, a number of communities have decided to submit business license tax proposals to voter approval. Sometimes the proposed tax increase includes all business within the community, but more often the measures are proposals to increase the taxes or surcharges levied on certain activities or industries such as a percentage surcharge on the receipts of a waste disposal facility. In *The Pines v. City of Santa Monica* (1981) 29 Cal. 3d 656, the court upheld imposition of a thousand dollar business license tax per saleable unit for new or converted condominiums.

In October 1993, the First District Court of Appeal upheld the City of Vallejo's property development excise tax. *Centex Real Estate Corp. v. City of Vallejo* (1st Dist. 1993) 19 Cal. App. 4th 1358. The City of Vallejo's ordinance imposed an excise tax on the "privilege of developing property and benefiting from city services...." *Id.* at 1361. The tax was in the amount of $3,000 per residential unit and $.30 per square foot for nonresidential development, collected at the time of building permit issuance.

The developers argued that the tax was actually a development fee, and had been adopted without following the procedures of AB 1600. The court disagreed, relying upon the authority in the city's charter (providing generally for any taxes permitted by the charter itself or state law), and the fact that the excise tax was not preempted by state law. The court was persuaded that the city had followed the procedures of AB 1600 in rescinding and re-adopting other charges for specific capital improvements, while at the same time enacting the excise tax for general revenue purposes. Because the excise tax was deposited in the general fund, and was not earmarked "for the limited purpose of funding public facilities or services related to a new development," it was not considered a development impact fee subject to AB 1600. *Id.* at 1364.

Although not discussed by the court, the excise tax did not require a two-thirds vote of the public because it was neither a property tax nor a "special tax." For further explanation, see the discussion of Propositions 13 and 62 beginning on page 31.

The authors note that the particular tax upheld in this case depended upon the city charter provision authorizing taxes generally. Section 707 of the city charter provides that "[t]he [city council of the City of Vallejo] may, by ordinance, provide for any tax... permitted by this Charter or by the constitution or general laws of the State." *Centex,* 19 Cal. App. 4th at 1362 fn 4. The court relied upon a long line of cases that accord charter cities a special status with regard to the power to tax for local purposes, citing *Weekes v. City of Oakland* (1978) 21 Cal. 3d 386, 392.

The Fourth District Court of Appeal found that the City of Riverside did not have the right to require a telecommunications company to pay a $1.50 for each foot of conduit it laid in the city's streets while installing fiber optic cable. *Williams Communications, LLC v. City of Riverside* (4th Dist. 2003) 114 Cal. App. 4th 642. The city argued that this charge, like the one in *Centex*, was not a development fee and was valid because it did not conflict with a state statute.

The court disagreed with the city and distinguished this case from *Centex*, in which the exaction was a tax, finding that the charge here was instead "compensation" charged for the use of the city's streets. *Id.* at 659. As such, the charges could not exceed the reasonable cost of providing the service. The court explained, "[T]he City of Vallejo in Centex had the right to impose an excise tax on the privilege of developing property. But Riverside did not have the right to require Williams to pay $750,103 to use the City's streets for its conduits." *Id.*

The city also argued that the Mitigation Fee Act did not apply to this payment because it was not a fee. The court found, however, that it was an "other exaction," and thus subject to the Act. The court also rejected the city's argument that the Mitigation Fee Act was inapplicable because the city did not "impose" the charge on Williams but that it was part of a negotiated agreement between the parties. The court found that "[s]ince the payment was required as a condition of the license agreement, and the license agreement was required before the necessary permits would issue, we must conclude that the payment was imposed on Williams." *Id.* at 660.

Another city's attempt to impose an excise tax on the use of city services, when levied simply on property ownership, was unsuccessful. In *Thomas v. City of East Palo Alto* (1st Dist. 1997) 53 Cal. App. 4th 1084, the appellate court affirmed the trial court invalidation of an "excise" tax imposed by the City of East Palo Alto. This tax was originally enacted in 1989, and was approved by a simple majority of the voters. By its own terms, the tax expired in 1993– 1994, but a similar tax was put before the voters where again it received a simple majority vote. *Id.* at 1087.

The tax was structured on a flat fee basis: $175 for single-family homes, $60 for multi-family units, $1000 for commercial properties, and $100 for vacant parcels. Several taxpayers filed for administrative refunds and, when denied, filed the ensuing litigation. As part of the litigation, the plaintiffs sought certification as a class action. *Id.*

Both the trial court and the appellate court ruled in favor of the taxpayers. Citing the earlier decision of *City of Oakland v. Digre* (1st Dist. 1988) 205 Cal. App. 3d 99, the appellate court concluded that the East Palo Alto tax was indistinguishable from the tax held invalid in *Digre*. "The City parcel tax is imposed upon every owner of real property in the City, without regard to the use of the property or the use of any city services. It is imposed upon real property that is vacant and unused, and upon owners who reside elsewhere but own land in the city. It is collected by the county tax assessor annually as part of the regular property tax collection, and nonpayment of the tax results in imposition of a tax lien on real property, just as would nonpayment of other real property taxes." *Id.* at 1089. The fact that the tax was labeled an "excise" tax was entitled to some legal weight, but was not dispositive; rather, a reviewing court is required to look at the true incidence of the tax in order to determine whether or not it is a true excise tax or a property tax.

Finally, the appellate court approved the use of a class action. However, the class was limited to those who filed administrative claims for refunds, thereby distinguishing this class from *Neecke v. City of Mill Valley* (1st Dist. 1995) 39 Cal. App. 4th 946 and *Woosley v. State of California* (1992) 3 Cal. 4th 758, in which certification was held improper.

Special Taxes and Special Districts

The Debate Created by Propositions 13 and 62. Article XIII A, section 4 of the California Constitution states:

> Cities, counties and special districts, by a two-thirds vote of the qualified electors of each district, may impose *special taxes* on such district, except ad valorem taxes on real property within such City, County or *special district.*

One of the first problems that emerged after enactment of article XIII A, section 4, was that no one was clear about the definition of a *special tax* or a *special district*. To clear up the confusion, the California Legislature in 1979 defined the terms, adding section 50075 *et seq.*, to authorize "all cities, counties and districts" to impose "special taxes" pursuant to the provisions of article XIII A. Section 50076, as amended by chapter 672 of the 1980 Statutes, defined special tax:

> ..."special tax" shall not include any fee which does not exceed the reasonable cost of providing the service or regulatory activity for which the fee is charged and which is not levied for general revenue purposes.

In another 1980 amendment, the Legislature defined *district* to mean "...an agency of the state, formed pursuant to general law or special act, for the local performance of governmental or proprietary functions within limited boundaries." § 50077(d).

Two important court cases followed that addressed the meanings of *special tax* and *special district*. In *Los Angeles County Transportation Commission v. Richmond* (1982) 31 Cal. 3d 197 the California Supreme Court held that a "special district," as used in section 4 of article XIII A, means only a district that has the power to levy a property tax. In that case, the L.A. County Transportation Commission levied a one-half cent sales tax with only the approval of the *majority* of those voting on the issue. Because the Transportation Commission did not have the authority to levy a property tax, the Supreme Court ruled it was not a special district and thus a two-thirds voter approval was not required. *Id.* at 205.

In *City and County of San Francisco v. Farrell* (1982) 32 Cal. 3d 47, 57, the California Supreme Court held that "special tax" as used in article XIII A, section 4, applied only to a tax whose proceeds were to be deposited or dedicated to a *specific fund or purpose, and not to funds deposited in the agency's general fund for general governmental purposes.*

Proponents of Proposition 13 retaliated against the *Farrell* decision with Proposition 62, which the voters passed overwhelmingly in 1986. Proposition 62 did not amend the California Constitution, but instead added article 3.7 (§ 53720 et seq.) to the Government Code, which included the following six major provisions:

- It adopted the section 50077(d) definition of *district* (this became section 53720(b)).
- General and special taxes were defined. General taxes are taxes imposed for general governmental purposes. Special taxes are taxes imposed for specific purposes. § 53721
- It attempted to overrule *Los Angeles County Transportation Commission v. Richmond*, by imposing a two-thirds voter approval of *any* "special tax," the same as required by section 4 or article XIII A, but applied it to all districts as defined. § 53722
- It attempted to partially overrule *Farrell* by imposing a majority vote requirement on the imposition of any "general tax." § 53723
- It mandated that a "general tax" can be enacted only if approved by two-thirds vote of all the members of a city's legislative body and then ratified by a majority vote of the electorate. §§ 53723 and 53724(b)
- It required a majority vote validation requirement for any tax imposed by local government between August 1, 1985, and November 5, 1986, the effective date of Proposition 62. § 53727

Proposition 62 was significantly weakened by subsequent court decisions. In *City of Westminster v. County of Orange* (4th Dist. 1988) 204 Cal. App. 3d 623, the court of appeal declared that the retroactive validation provision of section 53727 (also called the window period provision) was unconstitutional. Although the precise holding of *City of Westminster* invalidated only the window period provisions of Proposition 62, some thought its reasoning called into serious question the requirement for voter approval of any local tax for general revenue purposes.[23]

In *City of Woodlake v. Logan* (5th Dist. 1991) 230 Cal. App. 3d 1058 (overruled, *Santa Clara County Local Transportation Authority v. Guardino* (1995) 11 Cal. 4th 220, 246), the city imposed a utility tax without voter approval. The appellate court ruled in favor of the city and declared that Proposition 62's voter approval requirements for general taxes were unconstitutional. The court also held that Proposition 62's enforcement provisions, which reduce a local government's share of property taxes on a dollar-for-dollar basis for general taxes collected without voter approval, are also unconstitutional insofar as they are used to enforce the voter approval requirement for general taxes. The California Supreme Court subsequently disapproved of the *Woodlake* decision, holding that Proposition 62 was constitutional. *Guardino,* 11 Cal. 4th at 226.

The California Supreme Court subsequently expanded the definition of special district and greatly set back the ability of a special district to impose taxes without a two-thirds vote in *Rider v. County of San Diego* (1991) 1 Cal. 4th 1. In *Rider*, the County of San Diego established a special agency to raise and use supplemental sales tax for jails and courts. A sales tax to fund the agency was adopted by a majority, rather than by two-thirds, of the voters. A taxpayers' group challenged the validity of the sales tax under Propositions 13 and 62. The trial court declared the tax invalid and ruled that the tax was a deliberate attempt to circumvent the requirement of Proposition 13 for a two-thirds voter approval of special taxes. The appellate court, relying on *Los Angeles County Transportation Commission v. Richmond,* 31 Cal. 3d 197, concluded that Proposition 13 did not apply to special districts that had no power to levy property taxes. Because the special criminal justice agency did not have power to levy property taxes, the appellate court found that the sales tax, passed with only a majority approval of the vote, did not violate Proposition 13.

The California Supreme Court rejected the appellate court's narrow definition of *special district* and expanded it to conclude that special district should be interpreted to "include any local taxing agency created to raise funds for city or county purposes to replace revenues lost by reason of the restrictions of Proposition 13." *Rider*, 1 Cal. 4th at 11. Thus, the Supreme Court deemed San Diego's criminal justice agency to be a special district under article XIII A, section 4. The Supreme Court also held that the half-cent sales tax levied by the agency qualified as a special tax subject to a two-thirds vote because tax revenues were "being collected for the special and limited governmental purposes of constructing and operating the County's justice facilities." *Id.* at 13. Because only a majority vote had been obtained, the Supreme Court struck down the tax.

The Supreme Court also found that the county's retention of substantial municipal control over the criminal justice agency's operations created the inference that the agency was established to circumvent Proposition 13. Because the required two-thirds voter approval had not been obtained, the tax ordinance was invalid under article XIII A, section 4.

In summary, the Supreme Court ruled:

- The tax levied by the agency was unconstitutional. *Id.* at 5
- The *Farrell* doctrine ("general taxes" are immune to Proposition 13's two-thirds vote requirement) applies only to general taxes levied by more or less general purpose governments (such as cities and counties). *Id.* at 10–12
- The *Los Angeles County Transportation Commission v. Richmond* doctrine (special districts not authorized to levy property taxes are immune to the two-thirds vote requirement) applies only to (a) pre-1978 districts or (b) districts that lack property tax power and are not "essentially controlled" by cities and counties.[24] *Id.* at 13–14

Some experts believe that the *Rider* decision may invite a new round of *experimentation* with finding permissible ways to fund infrastructure and other particular purposes, subject merely to majority voter approval. For example, *Rider* strongly suggests that there is (or might be in the future) a set of special districts not "essentially controlled" by cities and counties, which are not special districts subject to the two-thirds vote requirement for special taxes. *Rider,* 1 Cal. 4th at 11–13. Old districts might fit in the same way the transit district fit in *Los Angeles County Transportation Commission v. Richmond,* but the court declined to establish the rules for old districts. *Rider* at 13. A newly created district might fit if it meets the court's tests for independence, which includes:

- Cities and counties should not have substantial control over the district's operations, revenue, or spending
- Cities and counties should not own or control district property
- The district should not have the same boundaries as a city or county
- The district should not be governed by boards that are common or overlapping with cities or counties
- Cities and counties should not be overly involved in creation of the district
- The district should not perform functions "customarily or historically performed by municipalities and financed through levies of property taxes"[25]

One particularly interesting aspect of the *Rider* decision is that it creates the possibility for financing functions not *customarily* or *historically performed* by cities or counties that are not financed with property taxes. Eventually, some of the following functions may possibly be financed through *special districts*:

- Transportation facilities, if they were not historically financed with the property tax and not by local government (i.e., through gas tax revenue or sales tax revenue, and by state or federal government)
- Wildlife habitat or bio-diversity preservation areas (traditionally not financed by local government)
- Regional detention and rehabilitation centers (if different from traditional county facilities, and involving new multi-county cooperation)
- City and county high technology extensions of libraries
- Child care facilities, if neither cities or counties have historically provided them in the area

Many had hoped that the Supreme Court's decision in *Rider* would settle Proposition 62 issues raised in *City of Woodlake* and *City of Westminster*. However, because a majority of the Supreme Court did not address the Proposition 62 issues raised in

Rider, City of Woodlake is still considered the definitive case on Proposition 62 issues. (*Woodlake* overruled by California Supreme Court in *Guardino*, 11 Cal. 4th 220, 246).

It is important to remember that Propositions 13 and 62 do not limit the authority of local governments to impose fees and exactions under their police power in connection with the development of real property. *Trent Meredith, Inc. v. City of Oxnard*, 114 Cal. App. 3d 317. For example, local agencies can still impose school impact fees, parkland dedication fees, and similar fees and exactions, or levy special assessments to finance public improvements that benefit specific property. *J.W. Jones Companies v. City of San Diego*, 157 Cal. App. 3d 745, 751.

One court case found that a "major facilities charge" imposed on a developer was a permissible use fee rather than a *special tax* subject to the two-thirds vote requirement of Proposition 13. *Carlsbad Muni. Water Dist. v. QLC Corp.* (4th Dist. 1992) 2 Cal. App. 4th 479. In that case, the QLC Corporation applied for and received building permits to construct a 300-unit condominium project, and Carlsbad Municipal Water District imposed a $95,400 fee on the developer for water service. QLC refused to pay the fee, arguing that the resolution that established the fee imposed development fees nominally necessitated by new development but explicitly permitting the water district to expend those fees for wholly unrelated general revenue purposes in violation of Proposition 13's two-thirds vote requirement. *Id.* at 481–82.

QLC relied on a prior decision, *Bixel Associates v. City of Los Angeles* (2d Dist. 1989) 216 Cal. App. 3d 1208. In *Bixel*, the court found that an ordinance authorizing a fire hydrant fee did not limit the use of the fee solely to installations and repairs associated with new development, and thus imposing the fee without a two-thirds vote violated Proposition 13. In *QLC*, the court found the water district's ordinance bore no resemblance to the ordinance and fee in *Bixel* for two reasons. First, the water district's resolution did not conflict with the "reasonable cost" and "fair and reasonable relationship" limitations set forth in statutes and case law. Second, the ordinance targeted the use of the fees for acquiring or constructing water facilities necessitated by the increased demand created by new or revised development. Thus, because the ordinance did not include language that permitted the fees to be used for unrelated or arbitrary revenue purposes, the charge was categorized as a fee and not as a tax subject to a two-thirds vote. *Id.* at 491.

The case of *Brydon v. East Bay Municipal Utility District* (1st Dist. 1994) 24 Cal. App. 4th 178 builds upon the *Richmond* and *Rider* cases in further defining one exception to Proposition 13's coverage of "special districts." In *Brydon*, the East Bay Municipal Utility District adopted an inclining block rate structure as part of a water conservation program to conserve its limited supply of water. The rate structure imposed higher charges per unit of water as the level of consumption increased. Water customers in single-family residences challenged the rate structure on the grounds that it was a "special tax" prohibited by Proposition 13.

The court of appeal held that because the district was formed prior to the passage of Proposition 13, and was not authorized to levy real property taxes, it was not a "special district" for purposes of Proposition 13. ". . . *Rider* unmistakably carves out an exception for those local agencies that were in existence before 1978 and which lack the power to levy property taxes as a means of replacing the loss of tax revenues pursuant to article XIII A." *Brydon*, at 189. This is consistent with prior cases that considered "the probable intent" of the framers of California Constitution, article XIII A, in interpreting "special district" to include "any local taxing agency created to raise funds for city or county purposes to replace revenues lost by reason of the restrictions of Proposition 13." *Id.* at 189, citing *Rider*.

In addition, the court upheld the rate structure as a regulatory tool that did not need to meet the strict statutory standard of section 50076 for capital improvement fees. Section 50076 defines a limited exception from the special tax provisions of article XIII A for those fees that do not exceed the reasonable cost of the service provided. In *Brydon*, the court held that the inclining block rate structure was a reasonable vehicle with which the District could carry out its constitutional and statutory mandate for water conservation. The court analogized the District's water conservation program with the air pollution control and water conservation programs upheld in prior cases. "Just as the regulatory scheme set forth by the APCD (in *San Diego Gas & Electric Company v. San Diego County Air Pollution Control District* (4th Dist. 1988) 203 Cal. App. 3d 1132) was designed to achieve a legislatively mandated ecological objective, so is the inclined block rate structure of the District a response to state-mandated water-resource conservation requirements." *Brydon, supra* at 192.

Following *Rider*, the California Supreme Court again addressed local government financing, focusing for the second time on Proposition 62. In *Santa Clara County Local Transportation Authority v. Guardino* (1995) 11 Cal. 4th 220, Santa Clara County created an interjurisdictional (county/cities in the county) governmental entity for transportation planning and construction. The newly created entity was given authority to impose a sales tax subject to a simple majority vote of the people pursuant to a 1987 state law (the Local Transportation Authority and Improvement Act, Pub.Utilities Code §§ 180000–180264). A local ballot measure was submitted to the voters where it was approved, but by only 54.1 percent of the voters. Several plaintiffs filed suit, seeking a judicial determination that the measure was invalid under Propositions 13 and 62. The newly formed Transportation Authority sought to issue tax anticipation bonds, but Guardino, the auditor-controller, refused to sign the bonds. The Authority filed its own legal action directly in the appellate court, seeking a determination that the bonds were validly issued. The appellate court ruled against the Authority, finding the tax invalid under Proposition 13. The California Supreme Court granted review.

The Supreme Court also ruled against the Authority, but in so doing relied upon Proposition 62 (§§ 53720–53730), following the judicial preference to dispose of a case on statutory, rather than constitutional grounds, where feasible. The Court rejected all of the legal distinctions offered up by the Authority as it sought to exempt itself from the supermajority vote requirement of section 53722. In so doing, the Court determined that Proposition 62 was intended to apply to any district, not just those with the authority to impose a property tax. The Court also stated its belief that the voters intended that Proposition 62 be applied broadly. The Authority's next argument was that the voter approval requirement was in effect a referendum on a tax, and that there was a long line of cases invalidating such measures. Relying in part on another Supreme Court decision involving a repeal of a utility tax by initiative (*Rossi v. Brown* (1995) 9 Cal. 4th 688), the Court rejected this argument, in effect finding that voter approval was a condition precedent to a valid enactment, and not a referendum taking place after a valid enactment by the public entity.[26] Although the Court acknowledged that Proposition 62 may not apply to charter cities, this limitation would not be a basis to set aside the entire measure. As a result of voter approval of Proposition 218 on the November 1996 ballot, charter cities are now subject to the two-thirds voter approval requirement.

Four other cases have added to the Proposition 13 debate. In *Howard Jarvis Taxpayers' Association v. State Board of Equalization* (3d Dist. 1993) 20 Cal. App. 4th 1598, the ubiquitous Howard Jarvis Taxpayers' Association challenged two statutes that authorized certain counties to establish county regional justice facilities financing agencies. Under these two acts, the newly created agencies were authorized to adopt a countywide sales tax of one-half of one percent if approved by a majority of the voters in the county. Applying the *Rider* test for a "special district," i.e., whether the "local taxing agency [was] created to raise funds for city or county purposes to replace revenues lost by reason of the restrictions of Proposition 13," the court of appeal found that because the new tax agency was "essentially controlled" by the counties, it fell within the definition. In support of its conclusion that such control existed, the court cited the fact that the activities being funded—construction and operation of jails and courthouses—were "squarely within the core functions customarily and historically performed by municipalities and financed through levies of property taxes." *Id.* at 1604.

Rider was further construed in *Hoogasian Flowers, Inc. v. State Board of Equalization* (*San Francisco Educational Financing Authority, RPI*) (3d Dist. 1994) 23 Cal. App. 4th 1264, where the court of appeal found that school districts are "special districts" for purposes of Proposition 13. The taxing agency in *Hoogasian Flowers*, the San Francisco Educational Financing Authority (EFA), was controlled by the San Francisco Unified School District and the San Francisco Community College District. EFA argued that because it was not "essentially controlled" by a city or county, it did not come within the *Rider* test for a special district. However, the *Hoogasian Flowers* court understood the *Rider* decision to mean that "special district" includes taxing agencies controlled by a city or county, but is not limited solely to such agencies. "The lesson of *Rider* is that entities subject to article XIII A, section 4, cannot circumvent the constitutional restrictions through the device of creating new entities to do what the creating entity cannot do....The material questions are whether EFA was created and is controlled by an entity that is subject to Proposition 13's supermajority requirement." *Id.* at 1273. The court concluded that school districts are subject to the supermajority voting requirement; therefore, the EFA being created and controlled by the school district must also comply with the supermajority voting requirement. *Id.* at 1279.

EFA = San Francisco Educational Financing Authority

In addition, the *Hoogasian Flowers* decision illustrates another holding of the *Rider* court, which is that a limited purpose district cannot avoid the limitations on special taxes merely by designating its new tax as one for "general purposes." Where the taxing agency does not possess general governmental powers, all of its funds would come within the scope of "special taxes" because of the very nature of a special purpose district. Citing *Rider*, the court held that "a 'special tax' is one levied to fund a specific governmental project or program...," such as the construction and financing of the county's justice facilities, regardless of whether it is placed in a general or special fund. *Id.* at 1283.

In 1985, a bare majority of voters in Mill Valley approved a municipal services tax levied on the occupancy of real property (generally, $145 per year). *Neecke v. City of Mill*

Valley (1st Dist. 1995), 39 Cal. App. 4th 946. The tax was to be collected with property taxes, and all proceeds were to be deposited into the city's General Fund, without limitation on the purpose for which the funds could be used. After the passage of Proposition 62, the city readopted the ordinance, and again submitted it to the voters where it again received a bare minimum of approval. A taxpayer challenged the tax, arguing that the tax was in fact a special tax. This argument was based upon the prior history of the first tax measure in which the city's voters failed to pass a special tax for road improvements. Subsequently, the voters approved the special tax, and most if not all of the proceeds were then used for road improvements. Thus, the taxpayer argued that the general tax was simply a disguised special tax for road improvements. Distinguishing *Rider*, the appellate court affirmed the city's ability to collect the tax. Unlike *Rider*, in which the funds were collected for a special purpose agency, the City of Mill Valley was a general purpose government. Therefore, in the absence of specific earmarking of the funds for particular purposes, this tax remained a general tax and was not subject to Proposition 13. *Id.* at 959.

Assessments

A special assessment is a ". . . charge imposed on a particular real property for local public improvement of direct benefit to that property.... The rationale of a special assessment is that the assessed property has received a special benefit over and above that received by the general public." *J.W. Jones Companies v. City of San Diego,* 157 Cal. App. 3d 745, 751, quoting from *Solvang Municipal Improvement District v. Board of Supervisors* (2d Dist. 1980) 112 Cal. App. 3d 545, 552–554. Exactions that amount to assessments are often called fees, charges, special taxes, or special property taxes. However, an imposition that operates as an assessment will be classified as such by the court, regardless of its label. See also *Sinclair Paint Com. v. State Bd. of Equalization* (1997) 15 Cal. 4th 866, 874.

The passage of Proposition 13 threatened the future of special assessments in two ways. First, special assessments could arguably be viewed as ad valorem taxes subject to the one percent *ad valorem* real property tax limit. Second, if they were not to be treated as *ad valorem* taxes, special assessments could be characterized as special taxes that could not be imposed without a two-thirds vote of the qualified electors according to section 4 of Proposition 13.[27]

The holdings in *County of Fresno v. Malmstrom* (5th Dist. 1979), 94 Cal. App. 3d 974 and *Solvang,* 112 Cal. App. 3d 545, helped clarify whether special assessments are *ad valorem* taxes. In *Malmstrom,* the Fresno County tax collector refused to collect routine street improvement assessments in order to test whether Proposition 13 applied to assessments. The *Malmstrom* court found that to include special assessments within the one percent tax limit of Proposition 13 would be illogical. The court determined that the practical effect of inclusion would have been to eliminate special assessments entirely, because the maximum one percent *ad valorem* property tax was already being levied. *Malmstrom* at 981–982.

The *Malmstrom* court noted that in most states constitutional tax limitations like Proposition 13 have been held inapplicable to special assessments. *Malmstrom* at 981–982. In fact, special assessments usually are not even considered taxes. Instead, a special assessment is a charge imposed on property for a local improvement of special benefit to the property assessed. *Id.* at 980 fn 2 (citing Sts & Hwys Code §§ 6400–6441). Thus, the *Malmstrom* court reasoned that, unlike a tax, a special assessment resembles an improvement loan to an individual property owner secured by a lien against the property that benefits.

The *Malmstrom* court also interpreted the purpose of Proposition 13 as not simply to limit *ad valorem* taxes, but rather to control government spending and taxes generally. The court reasoned that, because special assessments have no direct impact on the overriding concerns of Proposition 13, general governmental spending and taxes, it could not justify a broad and liberal construction of the term special taxes to include special assessments. *Malmstrom* at 984.

A few months after the *Malmstrom* decision, special assessments withstood another Proposition 13 attack in *Solvang Municipal Improvement District v. Board of Supervisors,* 112 Cal. 3d at 545. In that case, an appellate court upheld the validity of special assessments for public parking improvements measured by the assessed value of the parcels benefiting. The assessments at issue in Solvang even varied annually with the assessed value of the benefiting property. Despite this fact, the court held that the charges were true special assessments because they were levied only against real property that benefited directly from the public parking improvements. *Id.* at 557. Following the reasoning of the *Malmstrom* case, the *Solvang* court concluded that Proposition 13 did not apply. *Id.* at 556–557. The *Solvang* court ruled that special assessments, including those assessed on a fixed, variable, *ad valorem*, or other basis, are excluded from the one percent limitation of section 1 of article XIIIA. However, the court cautioned that, in its opinion, this exclusion applied only to true special assessments designed to directly benefit the real property assessed to make it more valuable. The court reasoned that levies to meet general expenses of the taxing entity and to construct facilities to serve the general public, such as fire stations, police stations, and schools, could not be transformed from general ad valorem taxes to special assessments by a "mere change in the name of the levy." *Id.* at 557.

Despite the court's warning in *Solvang* that local governments could not switch to special assessments for projects commonly financed with general revenue—such as police stations, fire stations, and schools—later cases ruled that these uses of special assessments can be legal. For example, in *Trent Meredith, Inc. v. City of Oxnard,* 114 Cal. App. 3d 317, the court upheld the use of special assessments for school facilities. In *J.W. Jones Companies v. City of San Diego,* 157 Cal. App. 3d 745, the City of San Diego, under the authority of its charter, adopted a system of "facility benefit assessments" that were imposed when a developer applied for a building permit. *Id.* at 749, 756. Proceeds were deposited into a special fund to build a broad spectrum of public works such as parks, transit and transportation, libraries, fire stations, school buildings, and police stations. The court upheld the use of special assessments for these facilities. A companion case (*City of San Diego v. Holodnak* (4th Dist. 1984) 157 Cal. App. 3d 759) upheld assessments for community and neighborhood parks, a branch library, and a fire station, as well as for other facilities.

Proposition 218 (articles XIIIC and XIIID of the California Constitution) added new requirements for using assessments to finance public services. These changes include the requirements that the agency segregate general from special benefits with assessments limited to special benefits only, that government property must be assessed, and that there be both disclosure of the procedures for completion and return of ballots and weighted voting. The notice must be sent at least forty-five days prior to a public hearing on the proposed assessment, and the local agency must tabulate the ballots at the hearing. At the conclusion of the hearing, if the agency determines that a majority protest has occurred (comparing weighted votes in favor and opposition), then the agency cannot proceed with the assessment. In any subsequent litigation challenging the assessment, the burden is on the agency to show that the property receives special benefits, and that the amount of the assessment is proper. Article XIII D, section 4. Proposition 218 also adds to the Constitution the authority of voters to reduce assessments by initiative in the future. Article XIII C, section 3.

Implementing Proposition 218

The League of California Cities has published an in-depth analysis of implementation strategies for Proposition 218, entitled Proposition 218 Implementation Guide. This publication is available from the League at 1400 K Street, 4th Floor, Sacramento, California 95814. The price of the publication can be confirmed by calling (916) 658-8200.

The approval of Proposition 218, the Right to Vote on Taxes Act, in the November 1996 general election, dramatically increased existing voter approval requirements for general taxes, property-related fees, and assessments. It also imposed restrictions and new procedural requirements for the passage of local fees and assessments. In addition, Proposition 218 allows voters to repeal, by initiative, previously approved taxes.

In anticipation of Proposition 218, a select few local agencies placed eleven measures representing ongoing assessments on the November ballot for voter approval. If they received voter approval, this strategy would allow them to take advantage of Proposition 218's grandfathering provisions for previously voter-approved taxes and assessments.

In the November election, voters approved all eleven of the local measures motivated by Proposition 218. Of the eleven, five measures were for parks and open space; four were for multiple capital improvements and public works; and the remaining two measures were for a K–12 school facility and library services. (*Source*: California Debt and Investment Advisory Commission, State and Local Bond and Tax Ballot Measures, Results of the November 1996 General Election.)

Section 4 of article XIII D, as well as the remainder of Proposition 218, has generated a significant number of questions regarding interpretation and application. In early 2004, the California Supreme Court, in *Richmond v. Shasta Community Services District* (2004) 32 Cal. 4th 409, declared that a capacity charge imposed as a condition for making a new connection to a water system, the proceeds of which were used to finance capital improvements, was not an assessment within the meaning of article XIII D. The Court made this distinction by looking at article XIII D's requirement that an agency imposing an assessment identify "all parcels which will have a special benefit conferred upon them and upon which an assessment will be imposed." Art. XIII D, § 4, subd. (a). The Court observed that the capacity charge at issue in *Richmond* would be imposed on property owners who apply for a new service connection. Because the District could only estimate the number of new connection applications and could not identify the specific parcels for which new connection applications would be made, it would be impossible for the District to comply with the identification requirements of XIII D. Furthermore, because many undeveloped parcels would likely be subdivided into an indeterminable number of smaller parcels, for which a connection might be requested, it would be impossible for the District to determine the "proportional financial obligation of the affected property" as required by XIII D. The *Richmond* Court concluded that an assessment within the meaning of XIII D must not only confer a special benefit on real property, but must also be imposed on identifiable parcels of real property. *Id.* at 419.

The Court in *Richmond* explained that its construction of XIII D is consistent with the article's definition of an assessment as a "levy or charge upon real property" since the capacity charge at issue was not imposed upon real property as such, but on individuals who applied for new service connections. Further, the construction is consistent with Proposition 218's aim of enhancing taxpayer consent because the charge was only imposed on users applying for new connections. In other words, whereas any new impositions of costs on existing customers would be subject to article XIII D's voter approval requirements, users who apply for new connections give their consent by the act of applying. *Id.* at 419–420.

Comparing Impact Fees, Taxes, and Assessments

In 1993, the Legislature adopted section 54954.6, which required an additional "public meeting" prior to adoption of a new or increased tax or assessment. The public meeting must be in addition to any noticed public hearing at which the public agency proposes to enact or increase the tax or assessment. This new requirement does not, however, apply to impact fees, service charges, standby charges, or previously enacted assessments.

Impact Fees Compared to Taxes

A common legal attack against impact fees is that they constitute taxes. In California, opponents of impact fees frequently claim that the fees are *special taxes* under Proposition 13, and thus require a two-thirds vote of the people. However, impact fees are distinguishable from taxes in several ways. For example, each is authorized under different delegated powers of local government, and is subject to different constitutional requirements. Generally, a local government's authority to impose fees derives from the state's police power to regulate businesses or activities for the health, safety, or general welfare of the public. The more restricted taxing power is exercised only to raise general revenue.

One of the more significant California cases distinguishing impact fees from taxes was *Russ Building Partnership v. City and County of San Francisco* (1st Dist. 1987) 199 Cal. App. 3d 1496. In *Russ Building*, the appellate court upheld the imposition of a $5.00 per square foot transit impact fee on new office space to benefit the San Francisco Municipal Railway System. (The *Russ Building* case is discussed in more detail in chapter 3.)

Another noteworthy case was *California Building Industry Association v. Governing Board of the Newhall School District of Los Angeles County* (2d Dist. 1988) 206 Cal. App. 3d 212. The court distinguished fees from taxes in the following way:

> Whereas taxes are compulsory in nature, development fees are imposed only if a developer elects to develop. (*Russ Building Partnership v. City and County of San Francisco, supra*, 199 Cal. App. 3d at 1505; *Terminal Plaza Corporation v. City and County of San Francisco, supra*, 177 Cal. App. 3d at 907.) Furthermore, a special tax levies a fee to replace revenue for services which were affected by the reduction [in taxes] caused by article XIII D. . . . In contrast, [a development fee] is not intended to replace revenues lost as a result of article XIII A. It is triggered by the voluntary decision of the developer to [proceed with his development] and is directly tied to the increase in [residents, students, riders, etc.] that this construction would possibly generate. (*Russ, supra*, at 1505.)

California Building Industry Association, supra, 206 Cal. App. 3d at 235. See also *Sinclair Paint Company v. State Board of Equalization*, 15 Cal. 4th 866–874.

In distinguishing between fees and special taxes, courts also focus on whether the amount of the fees received is proportional to the costs of the service for which the fee is charged. In *Collier v. City and County of San Francisco* (1st Dist. 2007) 151 Cal. App. 4th 1326, San Francisco's Department of Building Inspection defrayed its building permit, inspection, and enforcement costs by charging regulatory fees, the surplus of which went into a Building Inspection Fund. San Francisco officials transferred part of the surplus to the city's Planning Department and to the Fire Department. The court held that the transfer of the funds did not render the fee a 'special tax' as alleged by the plaintiffs. The court held that Planning Department and Fire Department activities—land use planning and building inspection—were sufficiently related to the function of the Department of Building Inspection, and the amount of the charged fees was proportional to the costs of conducting those activities.

Impact Fees Compared to Assessments

Fees are also frequently confused with special assessments. The primary difference is that special assessments represent a measure of the benefit public improvements give to new or existing development. In contrast, impact fees typically measure only the cost of the demand or need for public facilities resulting from new development.[28]

Taxes Compared to Assessments

Despite the similarities between special assessments and taxes, a number of differences should be noted. First, special assessments must be based on a unique benefit to the assessed land. *County of Fresno v. Malmstrom* 94 Cal. App. 3d at 974, 981. A general property tax, on the other hand, can be imposed without showing any benefit to the taxed land. Local governments must limit the use of special assessments to situations in which special benefit to assessed parcels can be shown and in which rational formulas for calculating and assessing benefits can be applied. General taxes are not subject to these same tests. Unlike general property taxes, each specially assessed property owner is constitutionally entitled to notice and a hearing before the special assessment is imposed. *City Council of the City of San Jose v. Kent South* (1st Dist. 1983) 146 Cal. App. 3d 320, 332. Finally, in contrast to a property tax, a majority of the property owners have the statutory opportunity to vote down a special assessment. The key to understanding an assessment is the requirement that it be levied on property in proportion to the benefits received from the improvements. *Anaheim Sugar Company v. County of Orange* (1919) 181 Cal. 212, 216. If the levy is designed to ". . . benefit the members of the taxing district in common with the public, and not merely as individual property owners . . ." or if the assessment exceeds the actual cost of the improvements, it is a tax and not an assessment. *Id.* at 217; *City of Los Angeles v. Offner* (1961) 55 Cal. 2d 103, 108.

In *Evans v. City of San Jose* (6th Dist. 1992) 3 Cal. App. 4th 728, an appellate court reiterated that special assessments are not special taxes even if the assessments are not traditional or true special assessments. In that case, the City of San Jose imposed an assessment pursuant to the Parking and Business Improvement Area Law of 1989 (Sts. & Hwys. Code § 36500 et seq.). That law authorizes cities to form parking and business improvement areas to fund various kinds of activities and facilities that benefit the local businesses. San Jose imposed the assessment to fund general downtown promotion, music, and other non-capital projects.

In *Evans*, a downtown apartment owner challenged the assessment, claiming that it was a special tax that could only be imposed by a two-thirds vote. Relying on a long list of prior cases, the appellate court disagreed, explaining that Proposition 13 does not apply to revenue-generating procedures such as regulatory and service fees employed by local governments. Specifically, the court emphasized that section 4 does not apply to special assessments. *Id.* at 737.[29]

The court explained that special assessments are charges imposed by a local district ". . . upon real property within a pre-determined district, made under express legislative authority for defraying in whole or in part the expense of a permanent public improvement therein. . . ." *Id.* at 737 (relying on *San Marcos Water District v. San Marcos Unified School District* (1986) 42 Cal. 3d 154, 161, cert. denied (1987) 479 U.S. 1079 (emphasis added, inside quotes deleted).)

Because it was neither a charge on real property nor intended to pay for permanent public improvements that specifically benefit the assessed real property, the *Evans* court found that San Jose's assessment was not a *true* special assessment. Nonetheless, the court determined that simply because an assessment is not a *true* special assessment does not necessarily mean that it is a *special tax* within the meaning of section 4 of article XIIIA of the California Constitution. This was because the assessment benefited a discrete group, and that group bore the burden of paying for the assessment. The court stated:

> The reasons the regulatory and development fee cases and the special assessment cases are exempt from the reach of Proposition 13 are the same reasons the Act and ordinance should also be exempt from its reach. With each of these cases, a discrete group receives a benefit (for example, a permit to build or inspection of produce) or a service (for example, providing and administering a rental dispute mediation and arbitration hearing process) or a permanent public improvement (such as a local park or landscaped median islands on a local road) which inures to the benefit of that discrete group. The public as a whole may be incidentally benefitted, but the discrete group is specially benefitted by the expenditure of these funds. . . . The public should not be required to finance an expenditure through taxation which benefits only a small segment of the population. (Cf. *Rider v. County of San Diego, supra*, 1 Cal. 4th 1). . . . If it is asked to do so, it must agree by a two-thirds vote. *On the other hand, where the burden for these expenditures is borne by the group specifically benefitted by them, Proposition 13 is not implicated. Evans* at 738 (emphasis added).

The California Supreme Court also recently rejected allegations that a special assessment was a special tax in *Knox v. City of Orland* (1992) 4 Cal. 4th 132. In this case, the Orland City Council formed an assessment district under the Landscaping and Lighting Act of 1972 (Sts. & Hwys. Code § 22500 et seq.) for maintenance and servicing of lights, playground equipment, landscaping, irrigation systems, public restrooms, bleachers, and other improvements at several existing city parks. Alleging that the assessment was instead a *special tax* that required a two-thirds vote under section 4 of Proposition 13, Knox and several other homeowners challenged the assessment. Additionally, they charged that the Landscaping and Lighting Act of 1972 could only be used for parks constructed pursuant to the Act, not for pre-existing parks.

The Supreme Court ruled in favor of the city for two reasons: It found that the levy was a special assessment, not a special tax, and it ruled that the Landscaping and Lighting Act of 1972 permits maintenance of existing parks. Regarding the distinction between special assessments and special taxes, the court found that a special assessment differs from a tax, noting that a special assessment is "levied against real property particularly and directly benefited by a local improvement in order to pay the cost of that improvement." *Knox* 4 Cal. 4th at 142, quoting *Solvang Municipal Improvement District v. Board of Supervisors* 112 Cal. App. 3d 545, 554. A tax, on the other hand, is very different:

> "Unlike a special assessment, a tax can be levied 'without reference to peculiar benefits to particular individuals or property'" (*Fenton v. City of Delano* (5th Dist. 1984) 162 Cal. App. 3d 400, 405, citing Black's Law Dictionary (5th ed. 1979) at 1307, cols. 1–2). . . . The same holds true even for a special tax which, for purposes of section 4, is a tax levied to fund a specific governmental project or program (*Rider v. County of San Diego* (1991) 1 Cal. 4th 1, 15 [2 Cal. Rptr. 2d 490, 820 P. 2d 1000]). *Malmstrom, supra*, 94 Cal. App. 3d at 984 [a special tax "need not . . . specifically benefit the taxed property" in the same manner as a special assessment].) *Knox* 3 Cal. App. 4th at 142.

The Supreme Court then drew the following critical distinction between a special tax and a special assessment:

> Therefore, while a special assessment may, like a special tax, be viewed in a sense as having been levied for a specific purpose, a critical distinction between the two public financing mechanisms is that a special assessment must confer a special benefit upon the property assessed beyond that conferred generally. Accordingly, if an assessment for park maintenance improvements provides a special benefit to the assessed properties, then the assessed property owners should pay for the benefit they receive. If it does not, the assessment effectively amounts to a special tax upon the assessed property owners for the benefit of the general public. (See *Spring Street Company v. City of Los Angeles* (1915) 170 Cal. 24, 30) *Knox, supra*, at 142–143.

The plaintiffs argued that parks do not provide benefit to specific properties, and therefore, the Landscaping and Lighting Act was an end run around Proposition 13. The Supreme Court found that parks have long been considered public amenities that benefit specific properties, and a lengthy history of legislative and judicial recognition that parks constitute a proper subject for special assessments exists. The Supreme Court also found that the propriety of a special assessment for maintenance has also been recognized for decades by both the Legislature and the courts. *Knox* at 144, 145.

Property Related Fees and Charges

Proposition 218 introduced a new legal phrase, "property related fees and charges." Section 6 of article XIII D of the California Constitution now requires that local agencies follow certain procedures when imposing or increasing certain fees and charges. The fees and charges are defined as "any levy other than an *ad valorem* tax, a special tax, or an assessment, imposed by an agency upon a parcel or upon a person as an incident of property ownership, including user fees or charges for a property related service." Cal. Const. art. XIII D, section 2(e). The additional steps that must be followed include identification of the parcels affected and written notice to the owner of record including the amount of the fee or charge to be imposed on each parcel, the basis upon which the fee was calculated, the reason for the fee or charge, together with the date, time, and location of the public hearing. The agency must conduct a public hearing no less than forty-five days from the mailing of the notice. At the hearing the agency must consider protests and, if a majority of the owners file written objections, then the agency may not impose the fee. Cal. Const. art. XIII D, § 6.

This new measure includes additional restrictions on revenues as they relate to the cost of service, as well as the requirement that the service is actually used by, or immediately available to, the owner of the property in question. Fees or charges based upon potential or future use are not permitted. Standby charges are to be considered as assessments and levied in accordance with section 4 of the same proposition. *Ibid.*

In *Howard Jarvis Taxpayers Association v. City of Fresno* (5th Dist. 2005) 127 Cal. App. 4th 914, the court confirmed that requirements for property-related fees and charges in Proposition 218 apply to a city's existing in-lieu fee for utilities, even though the city had taken no formal action to extend the fee after the enactment of Proposition 218.

The *Howard Jarvis Taxpayers Association v. City of Fresno* court also determined that the city's assessment of a fee in lieu of property taxes upon its own utility departments, which was passed through to rate payers, was not a "utilities consumption tax," as the city argued, but was a fee imposed directly on ownership of property. As such, it was subject to Proposition 218's restrictions on property-related fees and charges. Therefore, the city could not collect this fee in absence of its establishing the cost of actual city services to utility departments. *Id.* at 923–27.

Two later cases addressed the question of when fees for water services fall under Proposition 218's restrictions on property related fees and charges. In *Bighorn-Desert View Water Agency v. Verjil* (2006) 39 Cal. 4th 205, the Court concluded that a public water agency's charges for ongoing water delivery were property related charges, and were thus subject to reduction by voter initiative under Section 3 of Article XIII C. The *Bighorn* Court relied on the reasoning in *Richmond v. Shasta Community Services District* (2004) 32 Cal. 4th 409 (discussed above under Assessments):

> A fee for ongoing water service through an existing connection is imposed "as an incident of property ownership" because it requires nothing other than normal ownership and use of property. But a fee for making a new connection to the system is not imposed "as an incident of property ownership" because it results from the owner's voluntary decision to apply for the connection.

Richmond, 32 Cal. 4th at 427.

In *Pajaro Valley Water Management Agency v. Amrhein* (6th Dist. 2007) 150 Cal. App. 4th 1364, the court relied on the same *Richmond* reasoning to address whether charges on extraction of groundwater were subject to Article XIII D. The court held that they were, finding no distinction between groundwater extraction and the water delivery at issue in *Bighorn-Desert View* that would justify a different result. The *Pajaro* court bolstered its finding that groundwater extraction was "an incident of property ownership" by reasoning that groundwater extraction is more intimately related with property ownership than is the mere receipt of delivered water. *Id.* at 1391.

In 2009, for the first time, the court of appeals addressed the meaning of the term "immediately available," as used in Article XIII D section 6, subd. (b) (4). *Paland v. Brooktrails Township Community Services District Board of Directors* (1st Dist. 2009) 179 Cal. App. 4th 1358. The issue before the court was whether the imposition of a monthly base charge for water and sewer services, regardless of whether those services were turned on, was a stand-by charge subject to the owner ballot approval requirements of section 4, or a fee for a property-related charge exempted from those requirements under section 6. The court held that services are immediately available "as long as the agency has provided the necessary service connections at the charged parcel and it is only the unilateral act of the property owner . . . that causes the service not to be actually used." *Id.* at 1370. In *Paland*, the charge was held to be a fee because it was applied to parcels equipped with water and sewer connections which were either active or inactive at the direction of the parcel owner.

Margaret M. Sohagi is owner and Principal of the Sohagi Law Group, a Los Angeles environmental and land use firm, where she represents only public agencies, both from a legal and planning perspective. Ms. Sohagi is also an Adjunct Professor of Land Use Law at USC Law School, where she teaches Land Use Law, and an Instructor for the Judicial Council of California, teaching CEQA courses to Superior, Appellate, and Supreme Court Judges and court attorneys.

CHAPTER THREE

Constitutional Authority for and Limitations on Exactions

By Thomas Jacobson

This chapter begins by identifying and describing the constitutional authority to impose exactions, and then goes on to describe the various constitutional limitations on the exercise of that authority. This is an area of constant evolution, particularly as cities and counties continue to expand the range and degree to which they require new development to "pay for itself," as described in chapter 1.

The chapter discusses constitutional provisions in two contexts. The first is the California Constitution's grant of authority to cities and counties to exercise the "police power." The second is the set of limitations on the exercise of the police power established by the United States Constitution. Authority and limitations that derive from state statutes (i.e., "statutory" provisions) are discussed in chapter 4.

Constitutional Authority for Exactions

California cities and counties rely on two sources of authority for imposing exactions. One, discussed in detail in chapter 4, relies on statutes, that is, specific provisions of state law. The other is the more general authority, held by certain agencies of government, known as the "police power," which is described here.

The police power authorizes government to act to protect the public's health, safety, and welfare. *Euclid v. Ambler Realty Company* (1926) 272 U.S. 365; *Miller v. Board of Public Works* (1925) 195 Cal. 477, 490. The federal government does not hold the police power. Rather, it is an inherent power of the states, reserved to them through the Tenth Amendment to the United States Constitution.[1] Local governments have no inherent police power, but it may be delegated to them.[2] As is described below, this delegation is accomplished by the California Constitution.

The police power authorizes government to act to protect the public's health, safety, and welfare.

The police power has been treated by the courts as being broad and elastic, and over time has gone well beyond more limited health and safety concerns. For instance, speaking for the U.S. Supreme Court in 1954, Justice William O. Douglas characterized the "public welfare," one of the central components of the police power, as representing a wide range of public concerns. (See the sidebar on page 49.)

Under this broad grant of authority, local governments have enacted a wide variety of regulatory controls, including land use regulations. In fact, many of the early court cases addressing exercises of the police power were concerned with various types of land use regulations. See, e.g., *Welch v. Swasey* (1909) 214 U.S. 91 (upholding building height limitations), *Eubank v. City of Richmond* (1912) 226 U.S. 137 (upholding setback requirements), *Euclid v. Ambler Realty Company* (1926) 272 U.S. 365 (upholding a zoning ordinance creating an exclusive single-family district).

The California Constitution Delegates the Police Power to Cities and Counties

Article XI, section 7 of the California Constitution provides:

> A county or city may make and enforce within its limits all local, police, sanitary, and other ordinances and regulations not in conflict with general laws.

This provision delegates the police power to California cities and counties. The courts have determined that the police power of a city or county is as broad as that of the state, subject to certain limitations. *Candid Enterprises, Inc. v. Grossmont Union High School District* (1985) 39 Cal. 3d 878, 885. These limitations are described below under Constitutional Limitations on Exactions.

The police power is not held by special districts (e.g., water and sewer districts) or school districts. *Grupe Development Company v. Superior Court of San Bernardino County* (1993) 4 Cal. 4th 911, fn 3. These agencies must rely on specific authorizations in order to impose regulations, including exactions. See, e.g., *California Building Industry Association v. Governing Board of the Newhall School District* (2d Dist. 1988) 206 Cal. App. 3d 212.

The Police Power and Land Use Regulation

Early attempts at regulating the use of private property were, predictably, often challenged, requiring the courts to determine the applicability of the police power in this context. As early as 1925, the California Supreme Court upheld as a proper exercise of the police power a local zoning ordinance that excluded commercial and apartment uses from residential zones, because the restrictions had "a real or substantial relation to the public health, safety, morals, or general welfare." *Miller v. Board of Public Works* (1925) 195 Cal. 477, 490. A year later, the U.S. Supreme Court upheld the constitutionality of a zoning ordinance restricting land use to single-family dwellings. The Court articulated a deferential standard applicable in such cases, determining that before a zoning ordinance will be held unconstitutional, it must be shown "that [its] provisions are clearly arbitrary and unreasonable, having no substantial relation to the public health, safety, morals, or general welfare." *Euclid v. Ambler Realty Company* (1926) 272 U.S. 365.

Later cases looked at the widening range of regulation that California cities and counties have engaged in to deal with land use and related matters. Thus, for instance, in *Birkenfeld v. City of Berkeley* (1976) 17 Cal. 3d 129, the City's rent control ordinance was upheld. So was the City of Petaluma's growth management plan, which limited new residential development to 500 units per year. *Construction Industry Association v. City of Petaluma* (9th Cir. 1975) 522 F.2d 897, 908; cert. denied, (1976) 424 U.S. 934. Likewise, Carmel's restriction on short-term rentals in areas zoned for single-family dwellings was upheld (*Ewing v. City of Carmel-by-the-Sea* (6th

Dist. 1991) 234 Cal. App. 3d 1579), as was Livermore's growth management ordinance tying new development to the availability of infrastructure and public services (*Associated Home Builders, Inc. v. City of Livermore* (1976) 18 Cal. 3d 582).

The police power can be used to regulate for aesthetic reasons, such as limiting offsite, commercial billboards (*Metromedia, Inc. v. City of San Diego* (1981) 453 U.S. 490), or prohibiting "monotonous" development (*Novi v. City of Pacifica* (1st Dist. 1985) 169 Cal. App. 3d 678), or to protect "community character" (*Village of Belle Terre v. Boraas* (1974) 416 U.S. 1). As noted in *Village of Belle Terre*, "a quiet place where yards are wide, people few, and motor vehicles restricted are legitimate guidelines in a land-use project addressed to family needs." *Id.* at 9. Recent court decisions have upheld land use regulations affecting the location of types of economic activity (*Wal-Mart Stores, Inc. v. City of Turlock* (5th Dist. 2006) 138 Cal. App. 4th 273; *Hernandez v. City of Hanford* (2007) 41 Cal. 4th 279).

The Police Power and Exactions

Although specific statutory provisions authorize imposing certain exactions (discussed in chapter 4), the police power provides a general authority to impose exactions. In other words, cities and counties do not need an express authorization to impose specific types of exactions. Rather, they can do so based on their police power, subject to the limitations described below. See, e.g., *Candid Enterprises, Inc. v. Grossmont Union High School District* (1985) 39 Cal. 3d 878.

Local exercises of the police power for the purposes of imposing exactions can take two basic forms: (1) local ordinances, resolutions, etc., of general applicability throughout the jurisdiction; and (2) "ad hoc" conditions, determined for and imposed on a specific project.

An example of a measure of general applicability is a city-wide enactment (or enactment applicable throughout the

The Police Power: Broad, Elastic Source of Land Use Authority

Exactions and other types of land use regulation are exercises of the "police power"—the authority to regulate private activity in order to protect the public's health, safety, and welfare. The state and California counties and cities hold this authority.

In interpreting the police power, the courts have recognized its breadth. It includes not just the health and safety concerns that many early land use regulations addressed, but also the broad array of "quality of life" considerations that fall within the public "welfare."

For instance, in 1954, Justice Douglas, speaking for the U.S. Supreme Court, characterized the "public welfare," one of the central components of the police power, in this way:

> The concept of the public welfare is broad and inclusive . . . The values it represents are spiritual as well as physical, aesthetic as well as monetary. It is within the power of the legislature to determine that the community should be beautiful as well as healthy, spacious as well as clean, well-balanced as well as carefully patrolled.
>
> *Berman v. Parker* (1954) 348 U.S. 26, 33

Furthermore, the courts have recognized that the range of topics that are appropriately subject to regulation under the police power can change over time.

The elasticity of the police power was reflected in one of the seminal land use cases, *Euclid v. Ambler Realty Company* (1926) 272 U.S. 365, a 1920s U.S. Supreme Court case that upheld zoning as a legitimate exercise of the police power. In *Euclid*, Justice Sutherland described the need for an evolving sense of the police power's scope:

> Regulations, the wisdom, necessity and validity of which, as applied to existing conditions, are so apparent that they are now uniformly sustained, a century ago, or even half a century ago, probably would have been rejected as arbitrary and oppressive. Such regulations are sustained, under the complex conditions of our day, for reasons analogous to those that justify traffic regulations, which, before the advent of automobiles and rapid transit street railways, would have been condemned as fatally arbitrary and unreasonable. And in this there is no inconsistency, for while the meaning of constitutional guaranties never varies, the scope of their application must expand or contract to meet the new and different conditions that are constantly coming within the field of their operation. In a changing world, it is impossible that it should be otherwise.
>
> *Euclid, supra*, at 387

Applying these principles, in *Metromedia Inc. v. City of San Diego* (1980) 26 Cal. 3d. 848, the California Supreme Court overturned seventy-year old legal precedent in assessing a ban on offsite commercial billboards, finding that aesthetic reasons alone could justify this regulation under the police power. In so doing, the Court overruled *Varney and Green v. Williams* (1909) 155 Cal. 318, which had held that aesthetics alone cannot justify assertion of the police power to ban billboards. The *Metromedia* Court found the older rule to be "unworkable and discordant with modern thought as to the scope of the police power." *Metromedia* at 861.

unincorporated portion of a county) establishing a traffic impact mitigation fee or capital facilities fee.[3] Exactions of this type have been described as "legislatively-enacted" (*Ehrlich v. City of Culver City* (1996) 12 Cal. 4th 854), a distinction of some significance, as described in the discussion of the *Ehrlich* case on page 57.

In contrast, an "ad hoc" condition is one established and imposed on a project-by-project basis. Examples include the dedication requirements addressed in *Dolan v. City of Tigard* (1994) 512 U.S. 374, and *Nollan v. California Coastal Commission* (1987) 483 U.S. 825, and the "recreational mitigation fee" addressed in *Ehrlich v. City of Culver City, supra*, discussed on pages 55, 54, and 57, respectively.

Constitutional Limitations on Exactions

Exercise of the police power is generally subject to the standard that it must be "reasonably related" to the public welfare. Other applicable standards are that an enactment under the police power may not conflict with state law and must be confined to the territorial limits of the jurisdiction. Nor may police power actions conflict with the U.S. Constitution or federal statute. Each of these standards takes on special meaning when applied to the imposition of exactions, described below.

In addition, specific limitations are imposed by California's "Mitigation Fee Act," which is discussed in detail in chapter 5.

Limitation: Police Power Actions Must Be Reasonably Related to the Public Welfare

An action taken under the authority of the police power must bear a "real and substantial relation to the public welfare." *Associated Home Builders, Inc. v. City of Livermore* (1976) 18 Cal. 3d 582, 609. This fairly modest limitation is further limited by the breadth of the term "public welfare," as defined by the courts and described on page 49, to include a wide array of public purposes.

Furthermore, the courts (i.e., the judicial branch) have typically shown deference to the police power actions of the legislative branch. See, e.g., *Ewing v. City of Carmel-by-the-Sea* (6th Dist. 1991) 234 Cal. App. 3d 1579. This recognition of the separation of powers between the various branches of government is not without limits, however. For example, as the discussion beginning on page 52 indicates, the courts have rejected exactions that conflict with the U.S. Constitution.

Limitation: Preemption by State Law

While special districts—such as fire districts—lack police power authority to levy fees, cities and counties are empowered to exact development fees to support public services (e.g., fire, police, and library).

A local ordinance is preempted when it conflicts with a state law on the same subject matter (recall that the California Constitution's delegation of the police power, described above, excludes enactments "in conflict with general laws"). Such a conflict is present when a local regulation "duplicates, contradicts, or enters an area fully occupied by general law, either expressly or by legislative implication." *People ex rel. Deukmejian v. County of Mendocino* (1984) 36 Cal. 3d 476, 484 (citations omitted).

Where a state law preempts local regulation, the local enactment would be invalid. The question of preemption is relevant to imposing exactions through the local police power, as state law may preclude or limit an exaction based on local exercise of the police power.

Express preemption precludes local regulation in the same field by explicit statutory language. For example, in adopting a statutory scheme for school districts to impose impact fees for school facilities, the Legislature determined that financing school facilities and mitigating impacts of land use approvals on the need for school facilities are matters of statewide concern, and that it has "occupied" that subject matter to the exclusion of locally-adopted approaches. Gov. Code § 65995(e). See also, *RRLH, Inc. v. Saddleback Valley Unified School District* (4th Dist. 1990) 222 Cal. App. 3d 1602.

For a thorough discussion of school fees and the provision of school facilities through exactions, see chapter 6.

Implied preemption can be more difficult to identify. The courts have described the governing principles in this way:

> In determining whether the Legislature has preempted by implication to the exclusion of local regulation we must look to the whole purpose and scope of the legislative scheme. There are three tests: "(1) the subject matter has been so fully and completely covered by general law as to clearly indicate that it has become exclusively a matter of state concern; (2) the subject matter has been partially covered by general law couched in such terms as to indicate clearly that a paramount state concern will not tolerate further or additional local action; or (3) the subject matter has been partially covered by general law, and the subject is of such a nature that the adverse effect of a local ordinance on the transient citizens of the state outweighs the possible benefit to the municipality."
>
> *People ex rel. Deukmejian v. County of Mendocino* (1984) 36 Cal. 3d 476, 485 (citation omitted) (initiative ordinance prohibiting aerial application of herbicides preempted by state law). See also *Candid Enterprises, Inc. v. Grossmont Union High School District* (1985) 39 Cal. 3d 878, 885 (no preemption when the subject matter of the state law does not cover the same subject matter as the local ordinance).

An historic example of implied preemption is provided by the Subdivision Map Act's authorization to require provision of bicycle paths in subdivisions of 200 parcels or more. § 66475.1.[4] It would appear, by implication, that this provision would have precluded a bike path requirement as a condition to approval of a smaller subdivision. Note, however, that effective January 1, 2002, the Legislature removed from this statutory authorization the limitation that it only applies to subdivisions of 200 parcels or more.

At times the Legislature recognizes local regulation in an area that is also addressed by state law. In such cases, no implied preemption will be found. *IT Corporation v. Solano County Board of Supervisors* (1992) 1 Cal. 4th 81, 94 (hazardous waste storage and disposal statute does not preempt local regulation where state scheme includes delayed effectiveness of state permit until local land use permit application is granted). See also *Casmalia Resources, Ltd. v. County of Santa Barbara* (2d Dist. 1987) 195 Cal. App. 3d 827.

The principles of preemption described here also apply to federal statutes.

Limitation: Territorial Limits

A city or county only has authority to exercise its police power within its own territory. ("A county or city may make and enforce *within its limits* all local, police, sanitary, and other ordinances and regulations not in conflict with general laws." Cal. Const. art. XI, § 7, emphasis added.)

An unresolved question is whether a county can impose fees on new development within a city in order to pay for infrastructure provided by the county. Several California counties have experimented with this approach; there are no published court decisions to date addressing the practice. As an alternative and possibly more defensible strategy, a number of cities and counties now work in a collaborative manner in which the cities adopt fees to address impacts to county facilities. These fees, once collected, are typically passed to the county, based upon a memorandum of understanding or similar agreement.

Limitation: Conflicts with the U.S. Constitution

While the reach of the police power is broad and deep, it does not authorize violating a right protected by the U.S. Constitution. Thus, even an action that is reasonably related to the public welfare may be found to be an invalid exercise of the police power if it violates constitutionally-recognized rights. Two constitutional provisions are most commonly raised in challenges to exactions. They are: (1) the Fifth Amendment's prohibitions against the "taking" of private property for a public use without just compensation; and (2) the Fourteenth Amendment's assurance of equal protection of the law. Each of these is discussed below.

Challenges Based on the "Takings Clause"

The Takings Clause. The Fifth Amendment to the United States Constitution[5] provides "... nor shall private property be taken for a public use without just compensation." Effectively, this is a reverse statement of the power of eminent domain—government's ability to take private property for public use, as long as government pays fair market value for it.

However, along with the emergence of land use regulation in this country a legal theory developed to challenge government's ability to regulate land use. This concept is called "regulatory taking." Under this theory, land use regulation affecting private property could have essentially the same effect on the property owner as government seizing the property. Thus, the theory goes, in the absence of "just compensation," these regulations violate the Fifth Amendment.

While the reach of the police power is broad and deep, it does not authorize violating a right protected by the U.S. Constitution.

An early statement by the United States Supreme Court attempted to delineate when a land use regulation amounts to a compensable taking. In *Pennsylvania Coal v. Mahon* (1922) 260 U.S. 393, the Court addressed a regulation limiting the ability to extract subsurface coal. Justice Oliver Wendell Holmes, Jr., in this opinion, said: "The general rule... is, that while property may be regulated to a certain extent, *if regulation goes too far* it will be recognized as a taking." *Pennsylvania Coal* at 415 (emphasis added). For the better part of a century, the courts have struggled with determining when a regulation "goes too far."

In so doing, two types of regulations have been challenged as "regulatory takings": (1) those that restrict the use of private property (e.g., "downzonings," as in the *Agins* case, discussed below); and (2) those that impose conditions on the development of private property (i.e., exactions).[6]

Tests for When a Taking Has Occurred. The process of determining when a regulatory taking has occurred has produced a number of rules, if not standards that will apply in every instance. While the courts have spoken of the fact-based, case-by-case nature of an inquiry into when a regulatory taking has occurred (*Penn Central Transportation Company v. City of New York* (1978) 438 U.S. 104, 124), certain principles have emerged.

For instance, *Agins v. City of Tiburon* (1980) 447 U.S. 255, established a "two-prong" test for determining when a regulatory taking has occurred. This test was applied, unchanged, for many years by both federal and California courts. Agins' five-acre parcel was rezoned from allowing five units to a designation permitting as few as one unit. Agins alleged that the regulations amounted to a taking for which compensation was due. The U.S. Supreme Court held that a regulation results in a taking if one of the following is true: (1) the regulation does not substantially advance legitimate state interests; or (2) the regulation denies an owner economically viable use of his land.[7] *Id.* at 260. (Subsequent cases have made clear that this second part of the test requires that all economic benefit be lost as a result of the regulation. *Lucas v. South Carolina Coastal Council* (1992) 505 U.S. 1003.) Here, the Court found that Tiburon's regulations substantially advanced legitimate state interests (protecting against air, noise, and water pollution, traffic congestion, destruction of scenic beauty, etc.). *Id.* at 261. Furthermore, it had not been shown that the regulations left Agins without economically viable use of the property. *Id.* at 262. Thus, the regulation of Agins' property was not shown to be a taking.

In 2005, however, the U.S. Supreme Court corrected its "regrettable imprecision" in articulating the *Agins* rule. In *Lingle v. Chevron USA, Inc.* (2005) 544 U.S. 528, the Court eliminated the first part of the test. While not a case challenging a land use regulation, this case altered the legal standards by which such regulations will be reviewed. Chevron challenged Hawaii's law regulating the rents that oil companies could charge dealers who lease service stations owned by the company. Chevron alleged that the regulation failed to substantially advance a legitimate state interest in that, in fact, Hawaii's rent cap did not promote the state's claimed interest in controlling retail gas prices. The Court determined that the "substantially advances" portion of the *Agins* test is not appropriately part of deciding when a taking has occurred and rejected the first prong of *Agins* as a takings test. Rather, the Court said, it is a standard for determining whether there has been a denial of due process under the Fourteenth Amendment of the U.S. Constitution (which provides "nor shall any State deprive any person of life, liberty, or property, without due process of law"). Thus, *Agins* now provides a basis for finding a regulatory taking only when the regulation denies the property owner all economically viable use of the property. (The *Lingle* Court also clarified the legal basis under which exactions can be challenged as takings, discussed on page 58.)

In addition to the standard that a land use regulation will be a taking if it denies the owner all economically viable use, the courts have recognized circumstances when a less-than-total deprivation can still result in a taking. In *Penn Central Transportation Company v. City of New York, supra*, the Court based its takings analysis on three considerations: (1) the economic impact of the regulation on the claimant; (2) the extent to which the regulation has interfered with distinct investment-backed expectations; and (3) the character of the governmental action. In *Kavanau v. Santa Monica Rent Control Board* (1997) 16 Cal. 4th 761, the California Supreme Court, relying on *Penn Central*, held that a regulation that leaves some economically beneficial use of the affected property may still amount to a regulatory taking. The *Agins* test, the Court said, establishes categorical bases for finding a regulatory taking. But it may be possible to show, on a case-by-case basis, that a regulation that does not remove all economically viable use has still gone too far and amounts to a taking. The Court identified thirteen possible considerations, derived from earlier cases, and indicated that there might be other valid factors, as well.

The Takings Clause and Exactions. The courts have articulated several tests for determining when an exaction violates the takings clause. The applicable test is a function of the type of exaction imposed. While the tests vary to some degree, their common thread is that they address the relationship between the impacts of a project and the conditions that may be imposed on them. The following describes the most important exactions-related takings cases, grouped by the rule each illustrates.

The "Essential Nexus" Requirement. *Nollan v. California Coastal Commission.* This case added the term "nexus" to the vocabulary regarding the legitimacy of exactions. In *Nollan v. California Coastal Commission* (1987) 483 U.S. 825, the U.S. Supreme Court found that the Coastal Commission's condition to a coastal development permit requiring dedication of access along the beach across Nollan's property was a taking. The Court addressed the required relationship between conditions imposed on development and the impacts of that development.

The Nollans sought approval to replace the existing house on their property with a larger one. The Coastal Commission had characterized one impact of the new house as blocking the view of the ocean, thereby contributing to the development of "a 'wall' of residential structures" that would prevent the public "psychologically . . . from realizing a stretch of coastline exists nearby, that they have every right to visit." *Nollan* at 828. In addition, the new house was expected to increase private use of the beach. *Id.*

As a development condition, the Coastal Commission required dedication of an easement across Nollan's property and parallel to the beach, above the mean high tide line. While the Court recognized the value to the public of enhanced access along the beach, it found an inadequate connection or "nexus" between the project's identified impacts, described above, and this condition imposed upon its approval. The easement, the Court said, did not further the same governmental purpose (addressing blocked views) advanced as justification for the condition. The Court found that the absence of the required nexus turned an otherwise valid system of land use regulation into "an out-and-out plan of extortion." *Nollan* at 837.

The Court did indicate that other conditions furthering the public's ability to see the beach notwithstanding the impact of building a new house–such as a height limitation, a width restriction, a ban on fences, or even a dedicated "viewing spot" on the Nollans' property–might have been upheld. *Id.* at 836.

Thus, from *Nollan*, the term "nexus" entered the vocabulary of the courts with regard to development conditions and became part of discussions and debates in planning departments, planning commission meetings, and city council chambers around the country.

Associated Home Builders, Inc. v. City of Walnut Creek. The decision in *Nollan* was consistent with earlier California law on the question of the required relationship between an exaction and the development approval on which it was imposed. In *Associated Home Builders, Inc. v. City of Walnut Creek* (1971) 4 Cal. 3d 633, the California Supreme Court upheld the City's requirement that a subdivider contribute to the cost of new parks in the general vicinity of the subdivision, even though use of the park would not be limited to the residents of the subdivision. The City's rationale was that construction of the new homes reduced the amount of open space generally available throughout the region, while at the same time increasing the need for park and recreational land. The Court upheld the local ordinance and its state law authorization, the Quimby Act (section 66477, discussed in chapter 4), without requiring a direct relationship between a particular subdivision and the new park facilities provided.

Ayres v. City Council of the City of Los Angeles. The California Supreme Court's decision in *Associated Home Builders, Inc. v. City of Walnut Creek, supra*, cited its prior holding in *Ayres v. City Council of the City of Los Angeles* (1949) 34 Cal. 2d 31. In *Ayres*, the court upheld a dedication requirement imposed as a condition of a subdivision approval, even though its benefits would extend beyond the residents of the subdivision. Los Angeles's required dedication of a street right-of-way abutting a proposed subdivision was not an unconstitutional taking, the *Ayres* Court held, even though the condition would "incidentally benefit" the city as a whole.

The "Rough Proportionality" Requirement. *Dolan v. City of Tigard*. In *Dolan v. City of Tigard* (1994) 512 U.S. 374, dubbed the sequel to *Nollan* by the U.S. Supreme Court, the Court addressed the required degree of connection under *Nollan*'s nexus requirement. The Court held that two conditions imposed on a building permit approval, dedications of Dolan's land for a portion of the City's "greenway" system, met *Nollan*'s "essential nexus" requirement. However, the Court said that the conditions did not meet the applicable "rough proportionality" standard with regard to their relationship to the impacts of the project.

The City had required, as conditions to approving a building permit to enlarge a plumbing supply store and pave the accompanying parking lot, that Dolan dedicate to the City all of her land within the 100-year floodplain of a creek bordering her property, and an additional fifteen-foot wide strip of land for a bicycle path. In all, the dedication requirements amounted to approximately ten percent of the site. These dedication requirements reflected policies in the City's master plans for drainage and bicycle pathways. *Dolan* at 378, 391. Dolan charged that the conditions violated the principles established in the *Nollan* case.

In assessing this claim, the Court characterized as an unanswered question from *Nollan* the required degree of connection between the development conditions imposed by the City and the projected impacts of the proposed development. The Court determined that development conditions, at least of the type imposed in *Dolan*, must bear a "rough proportionality" to project impacts.

The Court arrived at its term "rough proportionality" after reviewing standards applied by various state courts. The Court rejected both the relaxed "very generalized statement" requirement of some states and the demanding "specific and uniquely attributable" standard applied by others. Instead, the Court selected the "reasonable relationship" standard used by California and a number of other states, although the Court opted for the term "rough proportionality" to describe that standard.

In characterizing "rough proportionality," the Court spoke of the need for an "individualized determination," involving "some quantification," although a "precise mathematical calculation" is not required. *Id.* at 391.

Significantly, the Court also held that the City had the burden of showing that it had met the rough proportionality standard, contrary to the traditional rule applied to municipalities' exercise of the police power. The Court justified shifting the burden of proof by characterizing the dedication requirements as "an adjudicative decision to condition petitioner's application for a building permit on an individual parcel."[8] This distinguished *Dolan* from the earlier land use cases decided by the Court, which considered "legislative" approvals—those establishing rules of general applicability, such as zoning ordinance revisions. With regard to non-legislative approvals, according to the Court, it was appropriate to shift the burden of proof. *Dolan* at 391, fn 8.

Here, although the Court did not question the City's analysis that the proposed expansion would both increase run-off due to additional impervious surface and add to traffic congestion (and that addressing these effects were "legitimate state interests"), it found that the City had not met its burden of showing rough proportionality between these impacts and the conditions imposed. With regard to the floodplain dedication, the Court found that the City had failed to justify a dedication requirement, rather than simply a setback requirement that limited development in the floodplain. "The City has never said why a public greenway, as opposed to a private one, was required in the interest of flood control." *Dolan* at 393.

Regarding the bicycle pathway, the Court found that the City had failed to complete the calculation on which to base a finding that the bike path would offset the increased traffic congestion resulting from Dolan's expanded store. The City had calculated that the impact of the proposed expansion would be 435 additional trips per day. However, the City did not determine the effect of the bike path dedication in offsetting that impact. In other words, the City had failed to establish the "rough proportionality" between impact and condition that the Court required.

Various components of the *Dolan* case had been addressed by the California courts in ways that foreshadowed the U.S. Supreme Court's opinion in *Dolan*. One case, *Surfside Colony, Ltd. v. California Coastal Commission, infra*, looked at the issue of "individualized determination," though not using that expression. Another, *Rohn v. City of Visalia, infra*, addressed "misplaced reliance" on planning documents, taking an approach similar to that later adopted by the Court in *Dolan*. Both of these cases are discussed below.

Individualized Determination: Surfside Colony, Ltd. v. California Coastal Commission. In *Surfside Colony, Ltd. v. California Coastal Commission* (4th Dist. 1991) 226 Cal. App. 3d 1260, the Court of Appeal invalidated the requirement for a dedication of a public easement along a private beach as a condition to a Coastal Commission permit. The permit was needed to maintain a protective rock barricade, or "revetment," in front of beachfront homes. In support of its dedication requirement, the Coastal Commission relied on studies indicating that revetments generally result in beach erosion. The Commission reasoned that since the revetment was likely to reduce the amount of beach available to the public, requiring additional public beach access was a reasonable condition to offset this impact. However, no studies demonstrated that this particular revetment would cause erosion.

The *Surfside* court rejected reliance on "general studies," instead looking for evidence specific to the subject property and the exaction being imposed.

While general studies may be sufficient to establish a mere rational relationship between revetment and erosion, *Nollan* requires a "close connection" between the burden and the condition. At the very least, a "close connection" entails evidence more "substantial" than general studies which, because of unique or unusual wave conditions, may not even apply to the case at hand. Substantial evidence must be reasonable in nature, credible, and of solid value. (*People v. Johnson* (1980) 26 Cal. 3d 557, 576.) Evidence which may not necessarily even apply to the case at hand hardly meets such a definition. *Surfside* at 270.

Misplaced Reliance on the General Plan: *Rohn v. City of Visalia*. In *Dolan*, the Court rejected the idea that simply because the flood plain dedication and bike path dedication requirements reflected the City's master plans for drainage and pedestrian/bicycle paths, they were valid exactions. For instance, regarding the bike path dedication requirement, the Court said:

In rejecting petitioner's request for a variance from the pathway dedication condition, the city stated that omitting the planned section of the pathway across petitioner's property would conflict with its adopted policy of providing a continuous pathway system. But the Takings Clause requires the city to implement its policy by condemnation unless the required relationship between the petitioner's development and added traffic is shown. *Dolan* at 395, fn 10.

An earlier California case had made much the same point. In *Rohn v. City of Visalia* (5th Dist. 1989) 214 Cal. App. 3d 1463, the court found that a dedication requirement to facilitate a road widening, imposed as a condition to a use permit, was invalid because the identified adverse traffic impacts of the project (none, according to the administrative record) did not justify the condition. The fact that the City's planning efforts identified the need for a road widening did not alter the limitations on the City's ability to impose conditions on development.

***Nollan/Dolan* "Heightened Scrutiny"—When Does It Apply?** Taken together, *Nollan*'s "essential nexus" and *Dolan*'s "rough proportionality" requirements make up a "heightened scrutiny," one that demands more of government than is true for most exercises of the police power. Because of these greater demands and the corresponding greater protections afforded developers, developers have sought to have heightened scrutiny apply in a variety of contexts. Questions have arisen with regard to which kinds of exactions are subject to a less demanding standard of review, and as to whether land use regulations not involving exactions should also be subject to heightened scrutiny. These questions are discussed below.

Does *Nollan/Dolan* Heightened Scrutiny Apply to Development Fees? Both *Nollan* and *Dolan* involved exactions requiring a dedication of land as a condition of development approval. Later cases have addressed when *Nollan/Dolan* heightened scrutiny applies to development fees. And, as described in the discussion of *San Remo* on page 59, the California Supreme Court has articulated the standard, less demanding of government, which will apply when heightened scrutiny does not.

Ehrlich v. City of Culver City. The leading case with regard to when heightened scrutiny applies to development fees is *Ehrlich v. City of Culver City* (1996) 12 Cal. 4th 854. In *Ehrlich*, the California Supreme Court addressed whether the *Nol-*

U.S. Supreme Court Clarifies Basis for Takings-Based Challenges to Exactions

Rulings from the U.S. Supreme Court have clarified that takings clause-based challenges to exactions rely on the doctrine of "unconstitutional conditions." It had been commonly stated (including in earlier editions of this book) that the basis for such challenges derived from the "substantially advances a legitimate state interest" component of the *Agins* two-part test for regulatory takings. Did, then, the U.S. Supreme Court's *Lingle* decision (*Lingle v. Chevron USA, Inc.* (2005) 544 U.S. 528), which discredited this component of the *Agins* test, disturb the Court's position on when an exaction can amount to a taking? No, said the Court. While the Court seemed to accept some responsibility for any misconception in this regard ("It might be argued that this formula [the "substantially advances" prong of the test] played a role in our decisions in *Nollan* . . . and *Dolan*") (see, e.g., *Nollan* at 835), the Court explained the actual legal basis for evaluating whether an exaction amounts to a regulatory taking is a "special application of the doctrine of 'unconstitutional conditions'" *Lingle* at 547.

Both *Nollan* and *Dolan* involved a takings challenge to a development condition requiring an easement dedication for public access across the subject properties. Both cases recognized that, had government simply appropriated the easement absent an application for a development approval, this would have been a per se physical taking. The issue in both cases was whether the easements could be required as conditions for granting a development permit the government was entitled to deny. The Court had concluded in *Nollan* that the easement exaction could be required, provided it would substantially advance the same government interest that would provide a basis for denying the permit application. *Lingle* at 547. The Court had gone on, in *Dolan*, holding that the easement exaction must also be "'roughly proportional' . . . both in nature and extent to the impact of the proposed development." *Lingle* at 547.

The *Lingle* Court explained that the question in *Nollan* and *Dolan* was not whether some legitimate state interest was advanced by the exactions at issue in those cases. Rather, it was whether the exactions substantially advanced the same interests as would have allowed government to deny the land use approvals being sought. The Court had described the doctrine of "unconstitutional conditions" and its application in *Dolan* in this way: "... the government may not require a person to give up a constitutional right—here the right to receive just compensation when property is taken for public use—in exchange for a discretionary benefit conferred by the government where the benefit has little or no relationship to the property." *Lingle* at 547, quoting *Dolan* at 385.

lan/Dolan standards of "essential nexus" and "rough proportionality" apply to development fees. Since both *Nollan* and *Dolan* involved exactions requiring easement dedications, it was not clear whether the standards established in those cases would apply to development fees as well.

In *Ehrlich*, the challenge involved two development fees imposed by the City as conditions to the rezoning of property to allow a change of use from a private tennis club to residences. One, a $280,000 "recreational mitigation fee," was intended to offset the loss of recreational facilities in the City resulting from the rezoning. The second fee was in lieu of providing public art under the City's "art in public places" ordinance. The fee, $33,000, represented one percent of the building's valuation.

With regard to the recreational mitigation fee, which was created by the City specifically to address *Ehrlich*'s rezoning proposal, the Court determined that the "heightened scrutiny" established by *Nollan*'s and *Dolan*'s "essential nexus" and "rough proportionality" requirements did apply, reserving this standard for development fees imposed "neither generally nor ministerially, but on an individual and discretionary basis." *Id.* at 876, 899. The "ad hoc" recreational mitigation fee, said the Court, met the latter description.

Applying the *Nollan* standard, the Court determined that the essential nexus requirement had been met. *Id.* at 879, 901, 912. "Unlike *Nollan*, where the high court found no logical connection between the commission's demand for a lateral easement across the owner's property and the purported governmental purpose of enhancing visual access, the 'essential nexus' in this case is plain." *Ibid.*

With regard to meeting *Dolan*'s "rough proportionality" standard, however, the Court rejected the City's method of calculating the fee. The fee, the Court said, should not be based on the cost of providing replacement facilities. The Court, instead, suggested other approaches that might pass muster. For instance, the City might show the "additional administrative expenses incurred in redesignating other property within Culver City for recreational use," or the cost of attracting a developer of private recreational facilities because Ehrlich's property would no longer be providing this use. Fees determined in this way, the Court suggested, might be roughly proportional to the "land use incentive it [the City] relinquished when it removed the recreational use restriction from plaintiff's property." *Id.* at 884. Ultimately, the Court remanded the case to allow the City to recalculate the fee.

In addressing the public art fee, the Court determined that the heightened scrutiny established in *Nollan* and *Dolan* did not apply. The Court based this on its characterization of the public art requirement on which the in lieu fee was based as being in the nature of a development standard, such as a building setback, landscaping requirement, or other design condition. As such, it was subject to less strict review as a traditional exercise of the City's police power. *Id.* at 886.

San Remo Hotel v. City and County of San Francisco. In *San Remo Hotel v. City and County of San Francisco* (2002) 27 Cal. 4th 643 (*San Remo I*), the California Supreme Court upheld San Francisco's "Hotel Conversion Ordinance," pursuant to which the plaintiff had paid a $567,000 "housing replacement" in lieu fee. In reaching its decision, the Court rejected application of the "heightened scrutiny" standard articulated by the U.S. Supreme Court in *Nollan v. California Coastal Commission* and *Dolan v. City of Tigard*. Rather, because the fee in question was legislatively-enacted and for general application, the Court applied a more deferential standard.

San Francisco's Hotel Conversion Ordinance (HCO) was first enacted in 1981 to "benefit the general public by minimizing adverse impact on the housing supply and on displaced low income, elderly, and disabled persons resulting from the loss of residential hotel units through their conversion and demolition." *San Remo* at 650. The HCO makes it unlawful to eliminate a residential hotel without a "one-for-one" replacement of converted units. An applicant may satisfy this requirement by either constructing or rehabilitating other types of housing for low income, disabled, or elderly persons, or by paying an in lieu fee equal to the replacement site acquisition costs plus a portion (established by the HCO) of the replacement construction costs. San Remo paid an in lieu fee under protest and challenged it as an unconstitutional taking. San Remo did not seek relief for violation of the takings clause of the Fifth Amendment to the U.S. Constitution, explicitly reserving its claims under federal law. (See Access to Federal Courts for Takings Challenges to Exactions, below, regarding the outcome of this strategy.) Rather, San Remo brought its claim based on the California Constitution's counterpart provision to the U.S. Constitution's takings clause. Article 1, Section 19(a) of the California Constitution provides: "Private property may be taken or damaged for public use only when just compensation . . . has first been paid." Noting the similarity between the federal and California provisions, the Court analyzed San Remo's taking claim under the relevant decisions of both the California and United States Supreme Courts.

As a threshold question, the Court considered the applicable standard of review. San Remo urged applying the "heightened scrutiny" standard, requiring an "essential nexus" and "rough proportionality," for reviewing exactions articulated by the U.S. Supreme Court in *Nollan v. California Coastal Commission* and *Dolan v. City of Tigard*, discussed above.

Both *Nollan* and *Dolan* were concerned with exactions requiring dedication of a portion of the applicant's real property. In *San Remo*, the Court noted, the exaction was monetary. Thus, it looked to its earlier decision in *Ehrlich v. City of Culver City* (1996) 12 Cal. 4th 854, for guidance. There, the Court had addressed whether the heightened scrutiny required in *Nollan* and *Dolan* applies to development conditions requiring the payment of a fee (see page 57). The *Ehrlich* Court held that development fees are subject to heightened scrutiny when imposed on an ad hoc basis (i.e., when the developer is singled out for a development fee not imposed on others). But when a development fee is "legislatively enacted" for general application it is not subject to heightened scrutiny.

In *San Remo*, the Court of Appeal had held that housing replacement fees assessed under the HCO were subject to heightened scrutiny because they were only applied to a small number of property owners, and were exacted in a discretionary manner. The California Supreme Court rejected this characterization, holding that the HCO does not provide the city with any discretion as to the imposition or size of a housing replacement fee. The applicant, the Court pointed out, must meet the housing replacement requirement by selecting one of the available options. The amount of the in lieu fee, if that approach is selected by the applicant, is determined by a set formula. "Thus, no meaningful government discretion enters into either the imposition or the calculation of the in lieu fee." *San Remo* at 669.

Furthermore, the Court said, the city did not single San Remo out for payment of the housing replacement fee—it applied to every residential hotel in the city. A condition of general application need not apply to every other property in the city, but only to all property in the class logically subject to it (e.g., all residential hotels). Here, the HCO applied to more than 500 properties with more than 18,000 guest rooms. "The HCO is generally and non-discriminatorily applicable within a class of properties reasonably defined according to the purpose of the ordinance." *Id.* at 669, n.12. The Court distinguished the Recreational Mitigation Fee found to be subject to heightened scrutiny in *Ehrlich*. That fee was not based on a specific legislative mandate to impose the fee, or on a legislatively set formula to calculate its amount.

In justifying limiting heightened scrutiny to ad hoc fees, the Court pointed to the "ordinary restraints of the democratic political process" that apply to legislatively-enacted fees. "A city council that charged extortionate fees for all property development, unjustifiable by mitigation needs, would likely face widespread and well-financed opposition at the next election." *Id.* at 671. Ad hoc development fees, which, the Court said, affect fewer citizens and evade systematic assessment, are more likely to escape such political controls. Thus, they are more likely to be subject to arbitrary treatment for "extortionate motives."

The Court went on to describe the more deferential standard applicable to legislatively-enacted fees, established by constitutional limitations and by California's Mitigation Fee Act (Gov. Code § 66000), discussed in detail in chapter 5. The relationship between such a fee and the impact it is intended to address need not be as close or thoroughly established as is required by heightened scrutiny. However, the more deferential standard of review that does apply still requires a "reasonable relationship," in both intended use and amount, between the fee and the impacts that the fee was intended to mitigate. "[T]he arbitrary and extortionate use of purported mitigation fees, even where legislatively mandated, will not pass constitutional muster." *Id.* at 671.

The Court then applied this deferential standard to San Remo's allegations, which challenged the HCO's housing replacement provisions both on their face and as applied to the San Remo Hotel. With regard to the facial challenge, the Court found that the HCO's methodology for determining the amount of the housing replacement fee is reasonably related to the loss of housing resulting from hotel conversions. "Plaintiffs fail to demonstrate from the face of the ordinance that fees assessed under the HCO bear no reasonable relationship to housing loss in the *generality* or *great majority* of cases, the minimum showing we have required for a facial challenge to the constitutionality of a statute." *Id.* at 673 (emphasis in original).

Likewise, the Court rejected San Remo's as-applied challenge, which was based on the claim that the $567,000 fee imposed bears no connection to tourist use of the San Remo Hotel. The Court noted that, under the HCO, the fee was based on the number of units reported as being in residential use on September 23, 1979, and then proposed for conversion to tourist use. San Remo had made no allegations specifically relating to the San Remo Hotel's use as of that date. "Nowhere do plaintiffs allege that the San Remo Hotel was, in 1979 or at any time, entirely in tourist use, as would be required to support their claim that the housing replacement fee has 'no connection at all' to the hotel's historical use." *Id.* at 678.

Loyola Marymount University v. Los Angeles Unified School District. In *Loyola Marymount University v. Los Angeles Unified School District* (2d Dist. 1996) 45 Cal. App. 4th 1256, a California Court of Appeal rejected the argument that *Dolan*'s standard of "rough proportionality" should apply in this challenge to a development fee. Loyola Marymount University had challenged the requirement that it pay school development fees pursuant to Government Code section 65995 and former Education Code section 53080 (recodified as section 17620) as a condition to a permit to develop a portion of its property. In denying applicability of the rough proportionality standard to the fee in question, the court followed the reasoning in *Ehrlich, supra*, recognizing that the U.S. Constitution is "specially protective of property against physical occupation or invasion" (*Ehrlich* at 875), which was not present here. The court also recognized that *Ehrlich* draws a distinction between legislatively-enacted fees of broad application and adjudicatively-adopted, individually-determined fees. As one of the former, the fee challenged in *Loyola Marymount* was determined not to be subject to *Dolan*'s rough proportionality standard. (See chapter 6 for a detailed discussion of exactions for school facilities.)

Tahoe Keys Property Owners' Association v. State Water Resources Control Board. In *Tahoe Keys Property Owners' Association v. State Water Resources Control Board, et al.*, (3d Dist. 1994) 23 Cal. App. 4th 1459, a California Court of Appeal decision published shortly before *Dolan*, the court held that a challenge to a water quality mitigation fee was not governed by any heightened scrutiny for exactions established by the *Nollan* case. Affected property owners had sought a preliminary injunction against imposition of the fee, payment of which was a condition to obtaining a building permit, and against spending fees already collected. The $4,000 mitigation fee was to fund projects to offset nutrients entering Lake Tahoe as a result of the applied-for new development. *Id.* at 1469.

Challenges to Inclusionary Housing Requirements

"Inclusionary housing" requirements have become a widespread practice in California. They require that new residential development provide some measure of affordable housing or pay a fee for that purpose. And, they have generated a number of published court decisions. The following cases illustrate various ways in which such requirements have been challenged and the outcome in the courts.

Home Builders Association of Northern California v. City of Napa. In *Home Builders Association of Northern California v. City of Napa* (1st Dist. 2001) 90 Cal. App. 4th 188, the California Court of Appeal upheld dismissal of a facial takings challenge to the City's inclusionary housing ordinance. ("Facial" challenges are based solely on the text of the regulation and not its application in a particular circumstance.) The City had adopted an "inclusionary" ordinance requiring residential developers to set aside ten percent of new units for lower income housing or, alternatively, to dedicate land or construct affordable units off-site or pay an "in-lieu" fee. The court analyzed the ordinance under the "*Agins* two part test," the first prong of which plaintiffs alleged was violated—the ordinance failed to substantially advance legitimate state interests. (See the discussion of *Lingle v. Chevron U.S.A.* on p.62 regarding the now-discredited "first prong" of *Agins* in takings analysis and the effect on analyzing exactions as takings.) The court rejected this argument, noting first that creating affordable housing is a legitimate state interest and, second, that the ordinance would substantially advance it. In making the latter determination, the court denied application of the *Nollan/Dolan* "heightened scrutiny" standard, which requires "essential nexus" and "rough proportionality" between the impacts of a project and the conditions imposed on it. The court relied on *Ehrlich v. City of Culver City* in rejecting application of that standard to development fees that are generally applicable through legislative action (here, the City's inclusionary ordinance).

Action Apartment Association v. City of Santa Monica. In *Action Apartment Association v. City of Santa Monica* (2nd Dist. 2008) 166 Cal. App. 4th 456, plaintiff Action Apartment Association challenged provisions of the City of Santa Monica's inclusionary housing program, alleging that the regulation, on its face, was a taking. Plaintiffs argued that the heightened scrutiny established by the *Nollan* and *Dolan* cases applies to facial challenges (again, challenges based not on the application of a regulation in a particular instance, but on the provisions of the regulation itself) and is not limited to adjudicative decisions. Plaintiffs had alleged that the City's requirement that developers include affordable housing within their multifamily residential projects bore no "nexus" and was

Avoiding Common Errors in Imposing Exactions

Misplaced Reliance on the General Plan

Dolan v. City of Tigard (1994) 512 U.S. 374. In addition to the Court's articulation of the "rough proportionality" standard, this case includes a reminder that putting a policy in a city's planning documents does not insulate its implementation from constitutional attack. In other words, a city must still abide by the limitations of the "taking" clause of the Fifth Amendment to the U.S. Constitution ("...nor shall private property be taken for public use without just compensation"), and all other provisions of the Constitution, when implementing its general plan.

Rohn v. City of Visalia (5th Dist. 1989) 214 Cal. App. 3d 1463. In this case the court found that a dedication requirement to allow a road widening, imposed as a condition to a use permit, was invalid because the identified traffic impacts of the project (none, according to the administrative record) did not justify the condition. The fact that the City's planning efforts identified the need for a road widening did not alter the limitations on the City's ability to impose conditions on development.

Requiring New Development to Pay for Existing Infrastructure Deficiencies

Bixel Associates v. City of Los Angeles (2nd Dist. 1989) 216 Cal. App. 3d 1208. The California Court of Appeal found invalid a development fee intended to upgrade a portion of the City's water delivery system for fire protection. The fee represented the amount needed to remedy deficiencies in the aged system, as well as meeting the needs created by the new development on which the fee was being imposed. The court determined that new development could not be required to pay for fixing existing deficiencies.

Relying on "Everyone Else Does It"

Russ Building Partnership v. City and County of San Francisco (1st Dist. 1987) 199 Cal. App. 3d 839. The California Court of Appeal upheld imposition of a transit impact fee on office development in San Francisco against a variety of challenges. Of particular interest to cities is the court's deference to the "impact studies" prepared by San Francisco and relied on in establishing the fee. In other words, it was San Francisco's "homework" regarding the impacts of development in the City on its transit system, and the costs of addressing those impacts, that carried the day.

(Continuation of **Challenges to Inclusionary Housing Requirements**)

not "roughly proportional" (standards articulated in the *Nollan* and *Dolan* cases) to the impact of their projects. Plaintiffs maintained that in the *Lingle* case the U.S. Supreme Court had broadened application of heightened scrutiny to include facial challenges to exactions. The court disagreed, holding that "*Lingle* does not abrogate the rule that the *Nollan/Dolan* nexus and rough proportionality test applies only in the context of judicial review of individual adjudicative land use decisions."

Building Industry Association of Central California v. City of Patterson. While *Building Industry Association of Central California v. City of Patterson* (5th Dist. 2009) 171 Cal. App. 4th 886, involves a development agreement (development agreements are discussed on pages 91 and 94), its primary importance is its interpretation of the law generally applicable to inclusionary housing requirements. Here, the City had adopted a fee ($20,946 per market rate residential unit) based on a fee justification study. The fee was essentially based on the estimated cost of providing for the City's projected need for affordable housing spread among the estimated number of new residential units that would be developed in the City. In evaluating the validity of the fee, the court rejected that methodology. The "legislatively-enacted" fee adopted by the City here (see *San Remo Hotel v. City and County of San Francisco* (2002) 27 Cal. 4th 643, regarding the distinction between such fees and "ad hoc" fees) is subject to this standard: there must be a reasonable relationship between the amount of the fee and "the deleterious public impact of the development." Here, while the City stated that its fee study "clearly shows the need for affordable housing generated by the new construction," the study failed to actually show that the fee was reasonably related to the need for affordable housing *associated with the project*.

Palmer/Sixth Street Properties, L.P. v. City of Los Angeles. *Palmer/Sixth Street Properties, L.P. v. City of Los Angeles* (2nd Dist. 2009) 175 Cal. App. 4th 1396, while not based on a takings challenge, illustrates a limitation on imposing an inclusionary requirement as a condition to new residential development. In *Palmer*, the City of Los Angeles approved a specific plan with an inclusionary housing requirement. Under this condition, residential and mixed use projects were required to either construct rental units, subject to long-term rent restrictions at regulated, affordable levels, or pay an in-lieu fee that the city would use to build affordable housing off-site. The city imposed this inclusionary requirement on a mixed-use project in the specific plan area, requiring developers to either construct sixty affordable rental units or pay approximately $100,000 for each of these affordable units as an in-lieu fee. The court found this requirement invalid, determining that it was preempted by California's Costa-Hawkins Act (see the general discussion of "preemption" as a limitation on local exercise of the police power on p.50). The Costa-Hawkins Act allows landlords to set rents as they see fit when a tenancy begins (i.e., initial rents are not subject to otherwise applicable rent control restrictions). The court found LA's requirement (including the in-lieu requirement) in conflict with, and thus preempted by, Costa-Hawkins.

In denying the preliminary injunction, the *Tahoe Keys* court held that the *Nollan* decision was not controlling because the challenged exaction did not involve a physical invasion of the subject property, as had the exaction in *Nollan*. Characterizing the *Nollan* decision, the *Tahoe Keys* court said, ". . . the Court held that where the government accomplishes a permanent physical invasion through its land-use regulations the courts must be 'particularly careful' to ensure that the regulations substantially advance a legitimate state interest. . . ." *Tahoe Keys* at 1477, citations omitted. The

Tahoe Keys court instead analyzed the takings challenge to the water quality mitigation fee in a more deferential manner, assuming "the propriety of the land use regulation . . ." where "it falls upon the plaintiff to establish its invalidity." *Id.* at 1478. Applying the first prong of the *Agins* test in this fashion, the court held that the state's justification for imposing the mitigation fee, *i.e.*, to ameliorate the effects of pollution from the Tahoe Keys development, was a legitimate state interest. And, since the mitigation fund was "specifically dedicated to partial mitigation of the effects of that source of pollution through projects to abate or at least offset the polluting effects of the Tahoe Keys" development, the court found an adequate connection between "the effect of the regulation and the objectives it was supposed to advance to support the regulatory scheme." *Id.* at 1480.

Blue Jeans Equities West v. City and County of San Francisco. In *Blue Jeans Equities West v. City and County of San Francisco* (1st Dist. 1992) 3 Cal. App. 4th 164, another case decided after *Nollan* but before *Dolan* and *Ehrlich*, a California court of appeal held that any heightened scrutiny established by *Nollan* did not apply to a development fee–San Francisco's Transit Impact Development Fee (TIDF). The plaintiff challenged the condition imposed on the construction of its five office buildings that required "a good-faith effort to participate in future funding mechanisms to assure adequate transit service to the area in the City in which the project is located." After the project was approved, San Francisco enacted the TIDF ordinance, which imposed a $5.00 per square foot fee on new downtown buildings to offset the cost of resulting increased peak period ridership. (See *Russ Building, infra,* for a discussion of the TIDF ordinance and the method for calculating the fee.)

The *Blue Jeans Equities* court upheld the TIDF ordinance and determined that the heightened scrutiny required by *Nollan* is limited to exactions that require conveying an interest in property (e.g., the easement in *Nollan*). The court quoted language from *Nollan* pointing out that "[w]e are inclined to be particularly careful about the objectives where the actual conveyance of property is made a condition to the lifting of a land use restriction, since in that context there is heightened risk that the purpose is avoidance of the compensation requirement, rather than the stated police-power objectives." *Blue Jeans Equities* at 169.

Commercial Builders of Northern California v. City of Sacramento. In *Commercial Builders of Northern California v. City of Sacramento* (9th Cir. 1991) 941 F. 2d 872; cert. denied, 112 S. Ct. 1997 (1992), a case also decided after *Nollan* but before *Dolan* and *Ehrlich*, the U.S. Court of Appeal for the Ninth Circuit upheld a fee imposed by the City of Sacramento on commercial development for the purpose of providing low-income housing. In doing so, the court rejected the notion that the *Nollan* standard applied to the fee. The fee was intended to address the effects of low-income workers moving to the area to fill jobs related to the development being approved. The City had enacted its Housing Trust Fund Ordinance based on a detailed study showing that new commercial development "is related to an increase in the need for low-income housing." (See Appendix D for an updated version of this study.) Developers

Selecting the Wrong Condition for a Project's Impact: the "Failure of Fit"

Nollan v. California Coastal Commission (1987) 483 U.S. 825. The U.S. Supreme Court found that the Coastal Commission's condition to a coastal development permit requiring dedication of access along the beach across Nollan's property was a taking. The Court addressed the required relationship between conditions imposed on development and the impacts of that development, and held that there must be a connection or "nexus" between the condition and the impact. Here, the Court said that there was no such nexus between the lateral beach access condition and the identified impact of the project: blocked views of the ocean from areas inland of Nollan's property.

Dolan v. City of Tigard (1994) 512 U.S. 374. This case addressed the required degree of connection under *Nollan*'s nexus requirement. The Court held that two conditions imposed on a building permit approval, dedications of land within the 100-year flood plain and for a bicycle path, met *Nollan*'s "essential nexus" requirement. However, the Court said that the conditions did not meet the required standard of "rough proportionality" with regard to their relationship to the impacts of the project. In order to establish rough proportionality, a city must make an "individualized determination" based on some quantification.

Inappropriate Reliance on CEQA

Public Resources Code section 21004 provides, "In mitigating or avoiding a significant effect of a project on the environment, a public agency may exercise only those express or implied powers *provided by law other than this division* [Division 13, the California Environmental Quality Act (emphasis added)]."

Thus, CEQA does not provide independent legal authority for imposing exactions. For that, public agencies must look to the authority described in this chapter and in chapter 4. However, impact analysis under CEQA may provide the factual basis on which exercises of that authority rely.

Thomas Jacobson, J.D., MCP, AICP
Department of Environmental Studies and Planning
Sonoma State University

challenged the fee, arguing that the ordinance did not demonstrate that their commercial development was directly responsible for the social problems that the fee was designed to alleviate—the shortage of low-income housing. In upholding the ordinance, the Ninth Circuit held that the heightened scrutiny required by *Nollan* was inapplicable to regulations not involving a physical encroachment upon land. The court found a "reasonable relationship" between the fee and the development on which the fee would be imposed, and stated that for a "purely financial exaction" this was the applicable standard.

Does *Nollan/Dolan* Heightened Scrutiny Apply to Development Conditions Requiring Improvements? In *McClung v. City of Sumner* (9th Cir. 2008) 545 F. 3d 803, the Federal Ninth Circuit Court of Appeals considered a different type of development conditon—an improvement—than had been the subject matter of the leading cases in the field. Other cases have focused on dedication requirements and impact fees; here, a city ordinance required new developments to include storm drainage pipes with a minimum twelve-inch diameter. Plaintiffs sought to develop their property and were required to replace the existing six-inch storm pipes with twelve-inch pipe. Plaintiffs alleged that this "six- to twelve-inch" upgrade requirement was a taking. At issue was the standard for making this determination. Plaintiffs maintained that the requirement should be judged under the "heightened scrutiny" articulated in the *Nollan* and *Dolan* cases. The court disagreed, instead determining that the *Penn Central* test (discussed above) was the appropriate standard. Rather than employing a "set formula," *Penn Central* identifies three factors relevant to when, in a specific situation, a regulation amounts to a taking. These factors are: the economic impact of the regulation on the claimant; the extent to which the regulation has interfered with distinct investment-backed expectations; and the character of the governmental action.

Does *Nollan/Dolan* Heightened Scrutiny Apply to Regulations That Restrict Development? The courts have been unwilling to apply the rough proportionality standard outside the exactions context, declining to do so with challenges to other types of land use regulations.

Breneric Associates v. City of Del Mar. In *Breneric Associates v. City of Del Mar* (4th Dist. 1998) 69 Cal. App. 4th 166, the court rejected the notion that the "heightened scrutiny" standard articulated by the U.S. Supreme Court in *Nollan v. California Coastal Commission* (1987) 483 U.S. 825 and *Dolan v. City of Tigard* (1994) 512 U.S. 374 applies to a design review decision. This more demanding standard, the court said, applies only to development exactions (e.g., dedications of land and fees required as conditions to development approvals). Here, the land use decision at issue was an application of the City's ordinance requiring a design review permit as a condition to obtaining a building permit for certain types of remodeling projects. The court determined that the applicable standard of review for design review cases is the deferential "substantial evidence" test. That is, in reviewing a challenge to a city's design review decision, the court must uphold the city's decision if there is substantial evidence to support the city's findings and if those findings support the city's decision. The burden is on the challenger of that decision to show that the evidence on which the city relied is insufficient.

Furthermore, the court must resolve all reasonable doubts in favor of the city and only reverse the city's decision if, based on the evidence before the city, a reasonable person could not have reached the city's conclusion.

City of Monterey v. Del Monte Dunes at Monterey, Ltd. Subsequent to its *Dolan* decision, the U.S. Supreme Court held that the "rough proportionality" standard does not apply to land use regulations other than exactions. In *City of Monterey v. Del Monte Dunes at Monterey, Ltd.* (1999) 119 S. Ct. 1624, the Court stated that:

> [W]e have not extended the rough-proportionality test of *Dolan* beyond the special context of exactions—land-use decisions conditioning approval of development on the dedication of property to public use. [Citations omitted]. The rule applied in *Dolan* considers whether dedications demanded as conditions of development are proportional to the development's anticipated impacts. It was not designed to address, and is not readily applicable to, the much different questions arising where, as here, the landowner's challenge is based not on excessive exactions but on denial of development. *Id.* at 1635.

Which Standard of Review for "Legislatively-Enacted" Dedication Requirements?

While the courts have described the standards to apply in evaluating the constitutional validity of ad hoc dedication requirements (*Nollan, Dolan*), ad hoc development fees (*Ehrlich*), and legislatively-enacted developments fees (*San Remo*), to date there has been no clear statement as to the standard to apply to legislatively-enacted dedication requirements. Some commentators have argued that it is more appropriate to use the less demanding standard applicable to legislatively-enacted development fees, while others maintain the stronger legal support is for applying heightened scrutiny.

Does *Nollan/Dolan* Heightened Scrutiny Apply to Facial, Non-Adjudicative Decisions? In *Action Apartment Association v. City of Santa Monica* (2d Dist. 2008) 166 Cal. App. 4th 456, plaintiff Action Apartment Association challenged provisions of the City's inclusionary housing program, alleging that the regulation, on its face, was a taking. The plaintiff argued that the heightened scrutiny established by the *Nollan* and *Dolan* cases applies to facial challenges and is not limited to adjudicative land decisions (i.e., quasi-judicial decisions applying land use regulations to a specific project proposal). Plaintiffs had alleged that the City's requirement that developers include affordable housing within their multifamily residential projects bore no "nexus" and was not "roughly proportional" (standards articulated in the *Nollan* and *Dolan* cases) to the impact of their projects. Plaintiffs also maintained that in the *Lingle* case, the U.S. Supreme Court had broadened application of heightened scrutiny to include "facial" challenges to exactions (that is, challenges based solely on the text of the regulation and not its application in a particular circumstance). The court disagreed, holding that "*Lingle* does not abrogate the rule that the *Nollan/Dolan* nexus and rough proportionality test applies only in the context of judicial review of individual adjudicative land use decisions."

An increase in commuter traffic resulting from San Francisco's downtown development led to the city's enactment of a TIDF for the purpose of adding new commute service on the city's transit lines.

The Importance of Adequate Fee Studies and Other Justification *Russ Building Partnership v. City and County of San Francisco.* In *Russ Building Partnership v. City and County of San Francisco* (1st Dist. 1987) 199 Cal. App. 3d 1496, the court upheld imposition of a $5.00 per square foot "Transit Impact Development Fee" on new office development in San Francisco against a variety of challenges. The fee, intended to fund transit facilities, was based on two impact studies by the City estimating the costs of improvements necessary to accommodate new riders during peak commute hours resulting from construction of additional downtown office space. The studies arrived at two figures: one $6.57 per square foot of new development and the other $8.36 per square foot. These figures represented the actual costs of the improvements disaggregated by the anticipated amount of new development. The City adopted a $5.00 per square foot fee. Of particular interest to cities and counties is the court's deference to the studies prepared by San Francisco and relied on in establishing the fee.

Shapell Industries, Inc. v. Governing Board of the Milpitas Unified School District. In *Shapell Industries, Inc. v. Governing Board of the Milpitas Unified School District* (6th Dist. 1991) 1 Cal. App. 4th 218, the Milpitas School District adopted fees for new residential and commercial development pursuant to Government Code section 65995 and Education Code section 53080 (since recodified as section 17620) (discussed further in chapter 6). The court described the basic criteria for a defensible study to support school fees imposed on new residential development within the district. The district must: (1) project the total amount of new housing expected to be built; (2) determine approximately how many students will result from the new housing; and (3) estimate what it will cost to provide the necessary school facilities for that number of students. The second element was missing from the Milpitas School District's report. However, using data found in the administrative record, the court determined how much enrollment would increase, calculated a fee based on this data, and ordered a refund of that portion of the fee charged that exceeded the amount calculated by the court ($1.35 per square foot).

Balch Enterprises, Inc. v. New Haven Unified School District. In *Balch Enterprises, Inc. v. New Haven Unified School District* (1st Dist. 1990) 219 Cal. App. 3d 783, a developer successfully challenged imposition of a school facilities fee on new commercial and industrial construction. The court found that the school district had failed to make adequate findings justifying the amount of the fee, as required under section 65995(b)(2). The court noted that section 65995(b)(2) requires establishing a "reasonable relationship" between the fee and the needs for schools caused by the new development. In finding that this requirement had not been met, the court stated:

> We are obliged to affirm the order invalidating the fee only because we can find nothing in the record that can be reasonably construed to support the findings required by the statute. While the staff study did address the question, it offered little substance apart from observing the difficulty of estimating the impact of commercial and industrial development on school enrollment. However well-founded, this court cannot accept such a plea of difficulty as compliance with the statutory requirements. *Balch* at 795.

The general topic of preparing adequate fee studies is discussed at length in chapter 5.

Limitations on Requiring New Development to Remedy Existing Infrastructure Deficiencies: *Bixel Associates v. City of Los Angeles.* In *Bixel Associates v. City of Los Angeles* (2d Dist. 1989) 216 Cal. App. 3d 1208, a California Court of Appeal found invalid a development fee intended to upgrade a portion of the City's water delivery system for fire protection. The fee represented the amount needed to remedy deficiencies in the aged system, as well as meeting the needs created by the new development on which the fee was being imposed. The court determined that new development could not be required to pay for fixing existing deficiencies.

In *Bixel*, a developer was required to pay $135,520 as a fire hydrant fee for a 32-story office building. In calculating the fee, the City included the costs of long-delayed maintenance and replacement costs. In other words, the fee was not limited to the cost of capital projects made necessary by the new development. For example, the cost of replacing a nearly 100-year-old water main was included in fee imposed on Bixel, even though, according to the administrative record, the main should have been replaced almost fifty years earlier. Therefore, the court held that the resulting fee did not bear, as required, a fair and reasonable relationship to the burden on public services created by the development. *Bixel* at 1220.

In 2006, the Legislature added section 66001(g), which provides that a fee may not include costs attributable to existing deficiencies in public facilities. The fee may, however, include costs attributable to the increased demand for public facilities reasonably related to the development project either in order to refurbish existing facilites to maintain the existing level of service, or to achieve an adopted level of service that is consistent with the general plan. This provision must be read in light of the constitutional principles discussed in this chapter.

Access to Federal Courts for Takings Challenges to Exactions: *San Remo Hotel v. City and County of San Francisco.* In *San Remo Hotel v. City and County of San Francisco*, 545 U.S. 323 (2005) ("*San Remo II*"), the U.S. Supreme Court addressed whether a plaintiff was entitled to a review of its exactions-related takings claim in the federal courts. This case is part of the long-running saga of the San Remo Hotel's objection to having to pay San Francisco's Hotel Conversion Ordinance fee. The fee was enacted in order to offset the effect that converting residential hotels to tourist use would have on the city's affordable housing stock. San Remo challenged the ordinance and its application, which required San Remo to pay a $567,000 housing replacement in lieu fee, under the California Constitution's prohibition against taking or damaging private property without just compensation. In its challenge, San Remo expressly reserved its claims under the Takings Clause of the Fifth Amendment of the U.S. Constitution. In 2002, the California Supreme Court upheld the HCO ordinance and its application to San Remo (see the discussion of *San Remo I* on page 59).

San Remo then sought review of its federal takings claim in the federal courts. In doing so, however, *San Remo* ran afoul of the federal "full faith and credit" statute. That statute (28 U.S.C. § 1738) provides generally that judicial proceedings in any state shall be recognized in every other court within the United States. The effect of the statute is to prevent re-litigating issues and claims already decided. San Remo's attempt to preserve a federal takings claim distinct from its California takings claim was thwarted by the fact that the California Supreme Court's decision was based on federal takings jurisprudence. The California Supreme Court had noted its practice of construing the federal and California takings clauses "congruently," and utilized "the relevant decisions of both this court and the United States Supreme Court." *San Remo*, 27 Cal 4th at 656.

San Remo argued that takings claims present a unique circumstance, justifying an exception to the full faith and credit statute. San Remo pointed out that a claim that state or local government has violated the Fifth Amendment's Takings Clause cannot be heard in federal court until the property owner has been denied just compensation through available state compensation procedures. See *Williamson County Regional Planning Commission v. Hamilton Bank* (1985) 473 U.S. 172. Thus, San Remo maintained that since bringing a federal takings claim first in state court is required, plaintiffs should also be able to bring that claim in federal court despite the strictures of the full faith and credit statute. This, San Remo asserted, would ensure the opportunity to have federal takings claims considered on their merits in federal court. San Remo argued that when, as here, plaintiffs in a state court action reserve a federal court claim, federal courts should review such reserved claim, regardless of what issues the state court may have decided or how it may have decided them.

The Court declined the invitation to create an exception to the full faith and credit statute. Thus, the Court noted that while San Remo could certainly reserve some of its federal claims, such reservation would be effective only if the state courts did not decide those claims. The reservation would be of no effect when, as here, the state courts decide plaintiff's federal law claims; in that circumstance, the attempted reservation would not keep the state court judgment from precluding re-litigation of the same claim in federal court. The issues San Remo wanted heard in federal court, subsequent to the California Supreme Court's ruling in 2002, had been decided in valid state court judgments. This, the Court held, deprived San Remo of the ability to have the same claims heard in federal court.

Challenges Based on the "Equal Protection" Clause

In addition to challenges to exactions based on the takings clause of the Fifth Amendment of the U.S. Constitution, some Constitutionally-based challenges have relied on the Fourteenth Amendment's "equal protection" clause. The Fourteenth Amendment provides that no state may "deny to any person within its jurisdiction the equal protection of the laws." This provision does not guarantee that a law have the same effect on all persons. Rather, it recognizes reasonable classification and only requires that all members of each classification be treated the same. When strictly economic regulations are involved, as is the case with most exactions, legislative determinations of classification will be upheld as long as they have a "rational basis." *Russ Building Partnership v. City and County of San Francisco* (1st Dist. 1987) 199 Cal. App. 3d 1496. (A stricter level of scrutiny will apply when a "suspect classification" (e.g., race) or a "fundamental right" (e.g., voting) is involved. However, the courts have held that developers are not a "suspect class," nor is development a "fundamental right." *Id.* at 1507.)

In *Russ Building Partnership v. San Francisco, supra,* San Francisco's Transit Impact Development Fee, applicable only to new development, was found not to violate the equal protection rights of the developers of new office buildings, despite the fact that existing office space received a benefit from the improvements that new office development was funding:

> Consistent with the purpose of the Ordinance, the owners of new office space are required to pay for additional public facilities, the need for which is generated by their development. That the existing buildings will indirectly benefit from improved services does not result in such inequity as to offend equal protection principles. [Citations omitted] *Russ Building* at 1508.

The court also rejected the argument that retail development, which also generated increased ridership, received an unacceptable windfall:

> The Ordinance imposes the fee on the projected ridership directly and reasonably arising from the new office space. The city may rationally conclude that office workers increase the need for transit services during peak hours. The conclusion that it is office space, and not retail stores, which is primarily responsible for the need for improved transit services, is properly left to the sound discretion of the local governing body. Since the trial court found this determination to be reasonably arrived at, this Ordinance must be upheld as being directly and additionally related to legitimate governmental goals. *Russ Building* at 1508.

In *Village of Willowbrook v. Olech* (2000), 528 U.S. 562, the U.S. Supreme Court held that, for the purposes of the equal protection clause, a challenge can be brought on behalf of a "class of one." At issue in *Olech* was an easement required as a condition of connecting to a municipal water supply. Faced with an easement condition wider than that required of others connecting to the water supply, plaintiffs alleged a violation of equal protection. Although the plaintiff was not part of a class or group, the Court concluded that the number of individuals in a class is immaterial for equal protection analysis.

Thomas Jacobson is a Professor and Director of the Institute for Community Planning Assistance in the Department of Environmental Studies and Planning at Sonoma State University. He was formerly an attorney with McCutchen, Doyle, Brown & Enersen's Land Use and Local Government Group, where he represented both public agencies and project applicants, and adjunct professor at University of San Francisco School of Law, where he taught land use law. He is a member of the American Institute of Certified Planners and the California Planning Roundtable, serves as a consultant to public agencies on land use law and planning matters, and is Of Counsel to the Sohagi Law Group.

CHAPTER FOUR

Exactions—Statutory Authority and Limitations

By Thomas Jacobson

City and county authority to regulate land use is expressed in both statutory grants of specific authority and the more general delegation of authority under the "police power," to act to promote the public's health, safety, and welfare. The police power was discussed at length in chapter 3. This chapter will focus on statutory sources of authority to impose exactions. These sources include state laws governing general plans, zoning, subdivision, and building codes. Following each of these discussions of statutory authority are descriptions of corresponding limitations established by statute. In addition, this chapter discusses the authority to negotiate development conditions under both the California Community Redevelopment Law and state law authorizing "development agreements."[1] It also addresses "vesting" as a limitation on imposing exactions, other limitations on the ability to impose exactions, and the relationship of the exactions process to the California Environmental Quality Act. (Note that certain specific types of exactions, such as school impact fees, child care facilities, etc., are addressed in chapters 6 and 8.)

The General Plan

Each city and county in California must adopt a "general plan" consisting of seven mandatory elements addressing land use, circulation, housing, conservation, open space, noise, and safety. Gov. Code § 65302.[2] The general plan also may include one or more other elements that, in the judgment of the city or county, relate to its physical development. § 65303. Among the wide array of such optional elements are growth management, economic development, urban design, and recreation elements.[3]

Authority

California's general plan "consistency requirement" provides the authority for imposing exactions based on the general plan. The consistency requirement places the general plan "atop the hierarchy of local government law regulating land use." *Neighborhood Action Group v. County of Calaveras* (3d Dist. 1984) 156 Cal. App. 3d 1176, 1183. In California, virtually all land use decisions (zoning, subdivision, etc.), must be consistent with the general plan. (Note that there is an exception to this consistency requirement with regard to zoning in charter cities other than Los Angeles, although many charter cities have "self-imposed" such a requirement. § 65860(d).) Because of the consistency requirement, the general plan has been referred to as the "constitution for future development." *Lesher Communications, Inc. v. City of Walnut Creek* (1990) 52 Cal. 3d 531, 540.

One of the implications of the consistency requirement is that since virtually all land use approvals must be consistent with the general plan, conditions can be imposed to achieve the general plan's goals. See 58 Ops. Cal. Atty. Gen. 41 (1975). For instance, in *Soderling v. City of Santa Monica* (2d Dist. 1983) 142 Cal. App. 3d 501, the court upheld Santa Monica's condition to a condominium conversion requiring a developer to install smoke detectors, despite the absence of a specific city ordinance or regulation establishing this requirement. To justify this exaction, Santa Monica relied on its general plan policies to "promote safe housing for all" and "to protect the health and safety of the resident."

Similarly, in *J.W. Jones Companies v. City of San Diego* (4th Dist. 1984) 157 Cal. App. 3d 745, the court upheld San Diego's "Facilities Benefit Assessment," imposed to implement the growth management program established by the City's general plan. The court recognized the critical role the Facilities Benefit Assessment program would play in implementing the provisions of the general plan.

In some instances, state law requires that the general plan include specified contents before certain exactions can be imposed. These requirements relate to parkland dedication, section 66477(d), and fees for bridges and major thoroughfares, section 66484(a)(1). Both of these exactions are discussed in the section on conditions imposed through the subdivision process, below.

Limitations

The authority to impose exactions based on the consistency requirement is not without limitations. For example, as is generally true regarding the police power (discussed in chapter 3), the consistency doctrine does not outweigh constitutional guarantees. It will not, for instance, justify a taking of private property for public use without just compensation, in violation of the Fifth Amendment of the U.S. Constitution. *Dolan v. City of Tigard* (1994) 512 U.S. 374; *Rohn v. City of Visalia* (5th Dist. 1989) 214 Cal. App. 3d 1463.

Likewise, the consistency requirement will not authorize exactions that are preempted by state law (see chapter 3 for a more in-depth discussion of the principle of "preemption"). Thus, for example, in *Corona-Norco Unified School District v. City of Corona* (4th Dist. 1993) 13 Cal. App. 4th 1577, the court held that the general requirement that subdivision map approvals be consistent with the general plan, coupled with general plan policies that require adequate school facilities as a precondition to new development, do not supersede the specific provisions of state law (§ 65996) that establish an exclusive method of addressing impacts on school facilities. (See chapter 6 for a detailed discussion of school fees. See also 60 Ops. Cal. Atty. Gen. 44 (1977) (city has no authority to require a developer to pursue an affirmative marketing program to prevent housing discrimination, even though the program may be part of the city's general plan, because the proposed regulation would have added to a field already fully occupied by state law (Health and Safety Code §§ 35700–35739).)

Working with developers, local government can provide trail access to open space adjacent to new development.

Zoning

Zoning is authorized by section 65800 et seq. This authorization includes the ability to establish zoning districts (§ 65851) and to regulate uses and establish development standards (§ 65850).

Authority

There are two types of authority to impose exactions through the zoning process. One relates to the legislative act of adopting and amending the zoning ordinance itself. The other is based on "quasi-judicial"[4] processes that implement the zoning ordinance—use permits (or "conditional use permits") (§§ 65901(a), 65902), variances (§ 65906), and similar site-specific development approvals.

"Contract" or "conditional" zoning. No express provision of state law authorizes imposing conditions on rezoning, a practice often referred to as "contract" or "conditional" zoning. Rather, it is a local exercise of the police power under the general statutory grant of authority to zone (§ 65800 et seq.). Conditional zoning is not widely employed, but its use has been upheld. *Scrutton v. County of Sacramento* (3d Dist. 1969) 275 Cal. App. 2d 412. In *Scrutton*, however, the court found that failure to comply with a condition could not result in an *automatic* reversion to the previous zoning, as this would amount to a rezoning without following the procedures required by state law for amendments to the zoning ordinance. *Scrutton* at 417; *J-Marion Company v. County of Sacramento* (3d Dist. 1978) 76 Cal. App. 3d 517.

The Sacramento County zoning ordinance includes specific provisions that authorize imposing conditions on rezonings. Such conditions may be imposed where the Board of Supervisors finds that they are necessary "so as not to create problems inimical to the public health, safety and general welfare of the County of Sacramento." Conditions must be agreed to by the property owner and the County, and the agreement recorded. Typical conditions address street improvements, drainage facilities, lighting and landscaping, transit improvements, etc. Sacramento County's ordinance and sample form agreement are included as Appendices E and F.

Another example of exactions imposed through zoning is provided by *Ehrlich v. City of Culver City* (1996) 12 Cal. 4th 854. In *Ehrlich*, the California Supreme Court considered the validity of two conditions imposed on a rezoning. The case is discussed in detail in chapter 3.

Imposing conditions on use permits and variances. Although state law does not specifically authorize imposing exactions on the approval of use permits and variances, such exactions are recognized in statutory provisions placing limits on their imposition. These limitations are discussed below.

Limitations

Zoning, and exactions imposed through the zoning process, are subject to the limitation, discussed in chapter 3, that such actions may not violate a provision of the U.S. Constitution (e.g., the "Takings Clause" of the Fifth Amendment). Furthermore, state law, through preemption, creates some limitations on exercises of the zoning power, both in its legislative and quasi-judicial forms. These limitations include:

General limitations on use permits and variances. Local governments may not impose conditions on use permits or variances that result in: (1) a dedication of land for any purpose not reasonably related to the use of the property for which the use permit or variance is requested; or (2) the posting of a bond to guarantee installation of public improvements not reasonably related to the use of that property. § 65909. (Note, however, that it is unlikely that § 65909 adds anything to the standards established in *Nollan*, *Dolan*, *Ehrlich*, and other cases discussed in chapter 3.)

Second units. In order to promote the development of "second units" as a form of housing, state law establishes both parameters for local regulation and standards for the consideration of second units in the absence of local standards.[5] §§ 65852.150, 65852.2. A city or county may adopt, by ordinance, a full range of development requirements governing the construction of second units in single-family and multifamily residential zones, however, applications for second units must be considered "ministerially," that is, without discretionary review. § 65852.2. Where no local ordinance governing second units is adopted, state law limits the authority of local governments to impose conditions by mandating issuance of a conditional use permit for a second unit where specified circumstances are met. § 65852.2(b). Fees charged for the construction of second units are to be determined in accordance with the Mitigation Fee Act (§ 66000 et seq., discussed in depth in chapter 5). § 65852.2(f).

Care facilities. A variety of provisions of state law limit the exercise of the local zoning power, including the ability to require use permits and to impose exactions, with regard to a range of care facilities. Each has its unique characteristics and should be consulted for its specific applications. They include provisions governing intermediate care and congregate living health facilities (see, e.g., Health and Safety Code § 1267.8), residential care facilities (see, e.g., Health and Safety Code § 1566.3), residential care facilities for persons with chronic life-threatening illness (see, e.g., Health and Safety Code § 1568.0831), and alcoholism or drug abuse recovery or treatment facilities (see, e.g., Health and Safety Code § 11834.23). Likewise, there are provisions relating to family day care homes (see, e.g., Health and Safety Code § 1597.40), and facilities housing six or fewer mentally disordered, or otherwise handicapped persons or dependent and neglected children (see, e.g., Welfare and Institutions Code § 5116). For a more thorough discussion of these restrictions, see *Longtin's California Land Use* (1987 edition with 2011 Update).

Subdivision

Since the provision of affordable housing is a statewide policy, state law creates certain limitations on the ability to impose exactions on residential development if the exactions will affect affordability.

The subdivision process in California is the product of both state law (most notably, the Subdivision Map Act, § 66410 et seq.), and city and county subdivision ordinances.

The Subdivision Map Act (the "Map Act") governs divisions of land for the purposes of sale, lease, or financing. § 66424. The Map Act is distinct from the Subdivided Lands Act (Business and Professions Code §§ 11000–11030), which governs the sale of parcels created by subdivision. The Map Act and associated statutory provisions provide authority for imposing exactions, as well as some limitations on this authority. In addition, as described below, the Map Act requires that exactions be imposed in certain instances.

In addition to the Map Act, each city and county must adopt an ordinance regulating subdivisions requiring tentative and final maps or a parcel map. § 66411. As with all local exercises of the police power, city and county subdivision ordinances are subject to limitations based on preemption by state law. Thus, a local ordinance may not conflict with a provision of the Map Act.

The Map Act's authorization for imposing exactions takes a variety of forms. This chapter discusses them in the following categories:

- Specific authorization for certain types of exactions
- More general authorization under the concept of ensuring consistency of the subdivision's "design and improvement" with the general plan
- A general authority to impose exactions in order to address environmental impacts
- Specific provisions for requiring "oversized" infrastructure and reimbursement
- Provisions relating to imposing exactions on parcel maps (as opposed to "tentative" and "final" maps)
- Provisions for imposing exactions on "lot line adjustments"
- Provisions for judicial partitions of lands under Williamson Act contract
- Conditions imposed on certificates of compliance

In addition, this section discusses a type of exaction—involving access to public waterways—that is required, and not merely authorized as are the other exactions discussed here.

It also addresses limitations that apply to imposing exactions as part of the subdivision process.

Subdivision Exactions Based on Specific Authorization

The Map Act expressly authorizes a range of exactions that may be imposed on subdivision map approvals. These can be grouped according to the type of exaction authorized: dedications, dedications/in lieu fees, reservations, and "impact" fees. Each type of exaction is discussed below.

Dedications. A dedication exaction requires that a property owner relinquish an interest in property either in the form of an easement or the "fee" interest, as a condition to obtaining development approval. (The fee interest is what is usually thought of when we say that we "own" land. Property ownership is often described as a "bundle of sticks," with each stick representing a type of interest. The fee interest is the entire bundle, rather than a more limited interest, such as an easement.)

The following are dedication requirements expressly authorized by the Subdivision Map Act. Note that failure to complete a dedication under the provisions of the Map Act does not necessarily negate the possibility of a common law dedication. See, e.g., *Hanshaw v. Long Valley Road Association* (3d Dist. 2004) 116 Cal. App. 4th 471. This section also describes various rules that govern dedications imposed under the Map Act's authority.

Dedications for streets, drainage, and utilities. A local ordinance may require a dedication of real property within a subdivision for streets and alleys, including access rights and abutters' rights, drainage, public utility easements, and other public easements. § 66475.

In addition, a local ordinance may prescribe conditions and procedures allowing dedication of real property needed by the city or county for local transportation, or by the state for transportation projects that will not receive any federal funds, or as satisfaction or partial satisfaction of a required assessment, fee, or charge, for transportation purposes (but not a tax). § 66006.5.

According to the Attorney General, an offer of dedication of roads for public use may be accepted by a county without sanctioning the roadway's entry into the county maintained road system. Then, as a condition for subdivision approval, the county may require that the owners of parcels within the subdivision maintain the roads dedicated for public use. In this way, the county is relieved of the burden of maintenance until the roads are accepted into the county highway system. *See* 61 Ops. Cal. Atty. Gen. 466 (1978).

A local ordinance may require a dedication of real property within a subdivision for streets and alleys, including access rights and abutters' rights, drainage, public utility easements, and other public easements.

An offer to dedicate real property for streets or public utility easement purposes does not include any public utility facilities located on or under the real property unless, and only to the extent that, an intent to dedicate those facilities is expressly declared by the use of a written statement on the final map. § 66439.

Pursuant to section 66476, local ordinance may require that street dedications include a waiver of direct access rights for property shown on the final or parcel map as abutting that street.

Dedications for bicycle paths. The Map Act authorizes requiring dedications of land as may be necessary and feasible to provide bicycle paths for the use and safety of subdivision residents, if the subdivider is also required to dedicate roadways pursuant to section 66475. § 66475.1. Until 2002, this provision was limited to subdivisions that contained 200 or more parcels. This limitation no longer applies.

Dedications for transit facilities. Local ordinance may require that land within a subdivision be dedicated for local transit facilities. Such facilities may include bus turnouts, benches, shelters, landing pads, and similar items that directly benefit the residents of the subdivision. This provision at one time included an exception for condominium projects and stock cooperatives consisting of the subdivision of airspace in an existing apartment building more than five years old when no new dwelling units were added. This limitation has been deleted. The statute now provides that subdivision of airspace in existing buildings into condominium projects, stock cooperatives, or community apartment projects, as those terms are defined in section 1351 of the Civil Code, are covered by this section. However, only the payment of in lieu fees may be required for these subdivisions. § 66475.2.

Dedications for solar access easements. Section 66475.3 authorizes local ordinances requiring the dedication of "solar access easements" as a condition of the approval of a tentative map. The purpose of these easements is to assure that each parcel or unit in the subdivision has the right to receive sunlight for a solar energy system across adjacent parcels in the subdivision. The ordinance must specify:

San Francisco, facing a continuing decline in federal and state revenues, exacts fees from new development to help finance low-income housing projects and improvements to its public transit system.

- Standards for determining the exact dimensions and locations of such easements
- Restrictions on vegetation, buildings, or other objects that would obstruct the passage of sunlight through the easement
- Any terms or conditions under which an easement may be revised or terminated
- That in establishing such easements, consideration will be given to the feasibility, contour, and configuration of the parcel to be divided, as well as costs, and that such easements will not reduce allowable densities or the percentage of a lot that

may be occupied by a building or structure under the planning and zoning in effect at the time the tentative map was filed

- That the ordinance does not apply to condominium projects consisting of the subdivision of airspace in existing buildings, where no new structures are to be added

The following specific provisions of state law govern dedications required as conditions to subdivision approval.

Procedures for dedications and offers to dedicate. Dedications and offers to dedicate interests in real property required as part of a tentative/final map process must be made by a statement appearing on the final map, signed and acknowledged by those parties having any record title interest in the real property. § 66439(a). Procedures for parcel maps are similar, although local ordinance may require that the dedication or offer of dedication be made by separate instrument, rather than by statement on the parcel map. If a separate instrument is used, it must be recorded concurrently with, or prior to, the parcel map. § 66447.

In 2009, the Map Act was amended to provide that if a subdivider is required under the Map Act or any other provision of law to make a dedication for specified public purposes on a final map, the local agency must state whether the dedication is to be in fee or an easement. Goverment Code § 66439(d). Section 66439(d) specifies language to be used by the subdivider in the dedication clause on the final map or any separate instrument. A counterpart provision was also added for parcel maps. § 66447(c).

If any street shown on the final map is not offered for dedication, the certificate may contain a statement to that effect. If the final map is approved, the use of any such street by the public is permissive only. § 66439(b).

Local government can promote the use of solar energy by exacting solar easements from new development.

Accepting or rejecting offers to dedicate. The legislative body, or the official designated pursuant to section 66458, must either accept, accept subject to improvement, or reject any offer of dedication at the time it approves a final or parcel map. §§ 66477.1(a), 66463. The clerk of the legislative body shall certify or state on the map the action the legislative body or designated official has taken. Pursuant to Streets and Highways Code section 941, the legislative body of a county, or a designated county officer, may accept into the county road system any road for which an offer of dedication has been accepted or accepted subject to improvements. § 66477.1(b).

In *Mikels v. Rager* (4th Dist. 1991) 232 Cal. App. 3d 334, the court held that a public easement was not created by an offer of dedication that had been accepted on the condition that it be improved in accordance with county standards. San Bernardino County had qualified its acceptance of the dedication, stating on the parcel map that the easement was "subject to . . . improvement, in accordance with county standards." *Id.* at 351. In fact, after the offer of dedication, no improvements were ever made to the roadway. Thus, the court held, no public easement was created.

In *Hanshaw v. Long Valley Road Association, supra*, 116 Cal. App. 4th 471, the court held that a county's accepting a portion of a road offered for dedication pursuant to section 66477.1 was not an acceptance of all portions of the road offered for dedication and, thus, did not create maintenance or liability burdens on the county.

Rejected dedication offers remain open; later termination. An offer of dedication for streets, paths, alleys, public utility easements, rights-of-way for local transit facilities such as bus turnouts and similar items that directly benefit the residents of a subdivision, or storm drainage easements, shall remain open despite the fact that, at the time the final map or parcel map is approved, they were rejected. §§ 66477.2(a), 66463. The legislative body may, by resolution at a later date and without further action by the subdivider, rescind its action and accept and open these streets, paths, alleys, rights-of-way for local transit facilities, and storm drainage easements for public use. This acceptance must be recorded with the county recorder. Offers of dedication covered by this provision may be terminated and abandoned in the same manner as prescribed in Streets and Highways Code section 8300 et seq. § 66477.2(c).

For subdivisions fronting on the ocean coastline or a bay shoreline, offers of dedication for public access routes must be accepted within three years after approval of a final or parcel map for any subdivision. The same three-year limit applies to public access routes for any subdivision fronting on a public waterway, river, or stream (as well as public easements along the banks of such waterways, rivers, or streams). An offer of dedication of public access routes must be accepted within five years after approval of a final or parcel map for a subdivision fronting on any lake or reservoir owned in part or entirely by any public agency. All other offers of dedication may be accepted at any time. §§ 66477.2(b), 66463.

Offers of dedication that are not accepted within the above-described time limits are deemed abandoned. § 66477.2(d). Subject to certain restrictions, a rejected offer of dedication will be terminated if a resubdivision of the property or a reversion to acreage is approved. § 66477.2(e). (For a further explanation of reversions to acreage, see below.)

Effective date of acceptance. Acceptance of offers of dedication on a final or parcel map is not effective until the final map or a resolution of acceptance by the legislative body is filed in the office of the county recorder. §§ 66477.3, 66463.

Effect on dedications of reversion to acreage and resubdivision of lands. Subdivided real property may "revert to acreage" (i.e., effectively be "unsubdivided") at the initiation of the city's or county's legislative body or all of the owners of the subject property, subject to a series of requirements. § 66499.11 et seq. One is that the legislative body must find that dedications or offers of dedication that would be vacated or abandoned by the reversion are unnecessary for present or prospective public purposes. § 66499.16. Reversion is effective when the final map is recorded, at which time all previous dedications and offers of dedication not shown on the map are terminated. § 66499.18.

In addition, as a condition to reversion, the local agency must require dedications or offers of dedication necessary to satisfy the purposes specified by local ordinance following reversion. § 66499.17.

A local ordinance may also provide for the filing of a parcel map that constitutes legal reversion to acreage and abandonment of all streets and easements not shown on the map. § 66499.20 ¼.

An alternative to reverting to acreage and then submitting a new subdivision map allows a subdivider to file a new subdivision map on the property covered by the old map, effectively merging the parcels and resubdividing them without first reverting to acreage. § 66499.20½. Filing the new final map constitutes legal abandonment of all streets and easements not shown on the new map.

Reconveyance of dedicated land to the subdivider if purpose no longer exists. For property dedicated "in fee" (i.e., as opposed to an easement) for public purposes, making public improvements, or constructing public facilities (excluding property dedicated for open space, parks, or schools), the local agency to which the property is dedicated must record a certificate in the county where the property is located. The certificate is to be attached to the subdivision map and must contain: (1) the subdivider's name and address; (2) a legal description of the property dedicated; and (3) a statement that the property will be reconveyed to the subdivider if the same public purpose for which the property was dedicated no longer exists or if the property or any portion of it is not needed for public utilities. § 66477.5(a). If the local agency does determine that the property or any portion of it is not needed for the same public purpose for which the dedication was required, it must reconvey the property to the subdivider or the successor in interest, except for all or any portion of the property that is required for that purpose. § 66477.5(c).

The subdivider may request that the local agency determine that the same public purpose for which the dedication was required still exists, but must pay the reasonable costs of making such a determination. § 66477.5(b).

If a local agency decides to vacate, lease, sell, or otherwise dispose of the dedicated property, the subdivider whose name appears on the certificate shall receive at least 60 days notice. This notice is not required if the property will be used for the same public purpose for which it was dedicated. § 66477.5(d).

These provisions for reconveyance only apply to property required to be dedicated on or after January 1, 1990. § 66477.5(e).

Dedications/In lieu fees. In addition to the Map Act's authorization to impose dedication requirements, it also provides for imposing fees in lieu of such dedications. Both the Map Act's provisions regarding parkland dedication exactions and provisions found elsewhere in the Government Code regarding school facilities allow the city or county to require payment of a fee in place of complying with a dedication requirement. Furthermore, since there is no statutory limitation on imposing in lieu fees for other purposes for which dedications of land might be required, it is arguable that in lieu fees would be valid in these circumstances, as well.

Parkland dedication and in lieu fee requirements (the "Quimby Act"). The Quimby Act, section 66477, gives a city or county the authority to impose as a condition to subdivision map approval the dedication of land, the payment of fees, or a combination of both for park and recreational purposes.

The city or county must adopt an ordinance authorizing such conditions, and must comply with a series of requirements established by section 66477. The Quimby Act requires that, in order to apply to a given subdivision, the ordinance have been in effect for a period of 30 days prior to the filing of the tentative or parcel map. The city or county must also have adopted a general or specific plan containing policies and standards for parks and recreation facilities that are in accordance with definite principles and standards. § 66477(a)(4). Further, the ordinance must include definite standards for determining the proportion of the subdivision to be dedicated and the amount of any in lieu fee. This amount is based on residential density, which is determined by the average number of persons per household estimated on the approved or conditionally approved map. Under the Quimby Act, the dedication of land, or payment of fees, or both, cannot exceed the proportionate amount necessary to provide three acres of park area per 1,000 persons residing within the subdivision, unless the amount of existing neighborhood and community park area exceeds that limit. If existing park areas exceed three acres per 1,000 persons, the legislative body may adopt the calculated amount as a higher standard not to exceed five acres per 1,000 persons residing within a subdivision. § 66477(a)(2).

The land and/or fees can be used only to develop new or rehabilitate existing neighborhood or community park or recreational facilities to serve the subdivision. § 66477(a)(3). This may include "recreational community gardens." § 66477(f). The California Attorney General has interpreted this provision of the statute broadly, opining that fees collected under the Quimby Act may be spent to buy an existing theater, to build a theater, or to buy land on which to place a theater. 81 Ops. Cal. Atty. Gen. 293 (1998).

The amount and location of land to be dedicated or fees to be paid must bear a reasonable relationship to the use of the park and recreational facilities by future residents of the subdivision. Note that the facilities do not have to be physically located within the subdivision. In *Associated Home Builders, Inc. v. City of Walnut Creek* (1971) 4 Cal. 3d 633, the court held that the fees would be justified if used for park and recreational facilities generally available to subdivision residents, but the facilities did not have to be located within the subdivision or reserved exclusively for use by the subdivision's residents. *Associated Home Builders* remains one of the leading California cases on the constitutionality of exactions. (See chapter 3 for additional discussion of this case.)

The city, county, or other local public agency to which the land or fees are conveyed or paid must develop a schedule specifying how, when, and where it will use the land or fees to develop park or recreational facilities to serve residents of the subdivision. Any fees collected under the ordinance must be committed within five years after the payment of the fees or the issuance of building permits on one-half of the lots created by the subdivision, whichever occurs later. If not committed, the fees shall be distributed and paid to the record owners of the subdivision in the same proportion that the size of their lot bears to the total area of lots within the subdivision. § 66477(a)(6).

In subdivisions containing fewer than fifty parcels, only the payment of fees, rather than dedications of land, may be required. However, when a condominium project, stock cooperative, or community apartment project, as those terms are defined in Civil Code section 1351, exceeds fifty dwelling units, a dedication of land may be required, even though the number of parcels may be less than fifty. § 66477(a)(7).

The Quimby Act does not apply to subdivisions containing fewer than five parcels if they are not used for residential purposes. However, if within four years a building permit is requested for construction of a residential structure or structures on one or more of the parcels, the fee may be required from the owner of each parcel as a condition to the issuance of the permit. § 66477(a)(8).

The authority to impose Quimby Act fees or dedications does not apply to commercial or industrial subdivisions, or to condominium and stock cooperative conversions of existing apartment buildings that are more than five years old when no new dwelling units are added. § 66477(d).

If the subdivider provides park and recreational improvements to the dedicated land, the value of those improvements, together with any equipment located on the land, must be credited against the payment of fees or dedication of land required by the ordinance. The California Attorney General has addressed the requirement that the subdivider be given a credit for the value of recreational improvements. 73 Ops. Cal. Atty. Gen. 152 (1990). The subject of the opinion was a proposed ordinance that would have required the subdivider to make specified recreational improvements "without credit." The Attorney General opined that this would violate the express provision of section 66477(i) (since recodified as § 66477(a)(9)), which states that "the value of the improvements . . . shall be a credit. . . ." The opinion stated that a city or county may not lawfully require the dedication of land improved for park and recreational purposes without credit being given to the subdivider for the value of the recreational improvements. See also 66 Ops. Cal. Atty. Gen. 120 (1983).

Alta Bates Medical Center, through mutual agreement with its surrounding neighborhoods and the City of Berkeley, provides playgrounds for use by the community.

"Common interest developments," as defined in Civil Code section 1351, are eligible to receive a credit, as determined by the city or county legislative body, against the amount of land required to be dedicated or the amount of the fee imposed, for the value of "private open space" within the development usable for active recreational uses. § 66477(e). In *Branciforte v. City of Santa Cruz* (6th Dist 2006) 138 Cal. App. 4th 914, a developer sought credit for such private open space within a development under section 66477(e). The developer sought credit for an amount equal to the value of the usable open space included as common area in the development and the improvements to that land. The City refused this request, as its land use regulations had no provision for granting credit for private open space. In determining whether a subdivider is entitled to a credit for private open space under section 66477(e), the court noted the ambiguity of that section. Considering whether it mandates a credit, or merely authorizes it, the court compared section 66477(e) with section 66477(a)(9), which clearly requires credit for the value of park and recreational improvements to land dedicated under the requirements of the Quimby Act. Relying on the legislative history of the two provisions, enacted in the same year, the court concluded that, "As subdivision (e) of Section 66477 now reads, local legislatures retain the flexibility to implement a private open space credit as they determine reasonable under local conditions." As the City had not adopted legislation providing a credit for private open space under section 66477, the court held the City had no duty to provide Branciforte with a specific amount of credit for private open space. However, the court did note that it did not need to reach the question of whether the City could be compelled to enact an ordinance providing some credit for private open space consistent with section 66477(e), as the developer did not seek such relief.

Interim school facilities. When specified conditions are met, a local agency may require as a condition to subdivision map approval the dedication of land and/or payment of in lieu fees for interim school facilities to address overcrowding. §§ 65970–65981. Although not part of the Subdivision Map Act and not limited to subdivisions, these provisions apply to residential development, including residential subdivisions governed by the Map Act. (Exactions for school facilities, in general, are discussed in detail in chapter 6.)

Reservations. In addition to dedication requirements, which require an uncompensated transfer of an interest in land from the property owner to a public agency as a condition to development approval, "reservation" requirements involve setting aside a portion of the subject property for a specific period of time, during which time a public agency may buy the property at a price determined by statute.

Reservations for school facilities. Although the Map Act refers to this as a "dedication" requirement, these provisions are more accurately characterized as authorizing a reservation requirement. Section 66478 authorizes local ordinances to require land be set aside for one or more elementary schools, as a condition of tentative map approval. A school district may purchase the property at the subdivider's purchase price plus specified costs incurred by the subdivider in holding title to the land. § 66478. The school district must offer to enter into a binding commitment to accept the dedication within thirty days of approval of the tentative map, or the opportunity automatically terminates. If once purchased, the land is not used by the school district as a school site within ten years after "dedication," the subdivider has the option of repurchasing the property.

An ordinance adopted under section 66478 does not apply to a subdivider who has owned the land for more than ten years prior to the filing of a tentative map.

Reservations for other public facilities. Section 66479 gives local agencies the authority to require that real property within a subdivision be reserved for public use including parks, recreational facilities, fire stations, libraries, and other public purposes.

A city or county may impose reservation requirements by local ordinance, subject to the following conditions:

- The agency's requirement must be based on an adopted general or specific plan containing policies and standards for the proposed use or uses, and the required reservation must in accordance with those policies and standards. § 66479(a)
- The ordinance requiring the reservation must have been in effect for at least 30 days prior to the tentative map being filed. § 66479(b)
- The size and shape of the reserved area must permit the balance of the property within which the reservation is located to develop in an orderly and efficient manner. § 66479(c)
- The required reservation must not make development of the subdivider's remaining land economically unfeasible. § 66479(d)

The reserved area must be in such multiples of streets and parcels as to permit an efficient division of the reserved area if the area is not acquired within the prescribed period. If it is not acquired, the subdivider shall make "those changes as are necessary to permit the reserved area to be developed for the intended purpose consistent with good subdividing practices." § 66479.

At the time the final or parcel map is approved, the local agency must enter into a binding agreement to acquire the reserved area within two years after the completion and acceptance of all improvements. The two-year period may be extended by mutual agreement. The purchase price of the reserved land is set at fair market value at the time of filing the tentative map, plus taxes from the date of reservation, and any other costs, including loan interest, incurred by the subdivider relating to the reserved area. § 66480.

If the public agency fails to enter into the binding agreement required by section 66480, then the reservation automatically terminates. § 66481.

This authority to require reservations is in addition to any other authority the local agency has relating to subdivisions, and is not to be construed as limiting or diminishing that other authority. § 66482.

Impact Fees. In addition to the dedication, in lieu fee, and reservation requirements described above, the Map Act authorizes imposing fees for a variety of purposes as conditions to development approvals. These are classic "impact fees," intended to provide public facilities made necessary by the proposed new development. The primary purpose of such a fee is to provide service to the proposed development and/or to "mitigate" the impacts of the new development on the surrounding community. This statutory scheme applies to ordinances regulating the division of land, but not other police power ordinances. 66 Ops. Cal. Atty. Gen. 120 (1983).

Storm Drainage and Sanitary Sewer Off-site Improvements. By ordinance, cities and counties may impose fees for storm drainage and offsite sanitary sewer improvements. § 66483. The ordinance will only apply if in effect at least thirty days prior to the filing of a tentative or parcel map, and must refer to a drainage or sanitary sewer plan adopted for a particular drainage or sanitary sewer area. The plan must contain an estimate of the total costs of constructing the facilities required by the plan, and a map showing the location of the facilities.

Fees imposed under this provision must be paid to the local agency and deposited into a planned local drainage facility or sewer fund. The fees must be fairly apportioned within the planned drainage or sewer area either on the basis of benefits conferred on the property proposed for subdivision, or on the need for the facility created by the proposed subdivision and development of other property within the project.

The fees collected can be spent to: (1) construct, or reimburse those who construct, local drainage or sanitary sewer facilities in the designated area; or (2) reimburse the local agency for the costs of engineering and administrative services to form the district and design and construct facilities.

Any local agency within a local drainage or sanitary sewer area may adopt the drainage plan and map designated in section 66483 and impose a reasonable charge on property within the area that benefits from the facilities. § 66488.

After completion of the facilities, any surplus funds remaining can be: (1) transferred to the general fund of the county or city, subject to certain limitations; (2) used for the construction of additional or modified facilities within that particular area; or (3) refunded to the current owners of the property for which a fee was previously collected. § 66483.1. Section 66483.2 provides specific procedures for refunding surplus funds.

These provisions governing the transfer and disposition of surplus funds should be considered in light of the Mitigation Fee Act (§ 66000 et seq., discussed in detail in chapter 5), enacted after sections 66483.1 and 66483.2. The Mitigation Fee Act requires local agencies to place development fees in separate accounts to be used only for the purpose for which the fees were collected, and to provide information to the public about each separate account. The Mitigation Fee Act also addresses the disposition of surplus funds.

Fees for Constructing Bridges and Major Thoroughfares. The Map Act authorizes local ordinances requiring a fee to defray the actual or estimated costs of constructing bridges over waterways, railways, freeways, and canyons, or to defray the cost of building major thoroughfares, as a condition of approval of a final map or as a condition of issuing a building permit. § 66484. The ordinance must:

- Refer to the circulation element of the general plan
- Provide for a public hearing to determine a fair method of allocating costs to the area of benefit, as well as how fees will be apportioned
- Provide timelines within which written protest may be filed by the owners of more than one-half of the area of the property benefiting by the improvement § 66484(a)

Fees collected under the ordinance must be deposited in a planned bridge facility or major thoroughfare fund. A fund must be established for each planned bridge facility project or for each planned major thoroughfare project, although if the benefit area is one in which more than one bridge is required to be constructed, a fund may be established covering all of the bridge projects in the benefit area. The funds may be expended only to construct the identified improvements or to reimburse the local agency for constructing such improvements. § 66484(e).

Section 66489 provides for reimbursement to either a subdivider or local agency that constructs a bridge or major thoroughfare by imposing a reasonable charge on property within the area of benefit established pursuant to section 66484.

Fees for Constructing Bridges and Major Thoroughfares—Special Provisions for Orange County. Legislation applicable only to Orange County grants authority to city councils in Orange County and the County's Board of Supervisors to impose development fees for the construction of bridges and major thoroughfares, and includes specific provisions regarding toll roads. § 66484.3. In *Committee of Seven Thousand (COST) v. Superior Court* (City of Irvine) (1988) 45 Cal. 3d 491, the California Supreme Court held that this statute, which expressly grants authority to the legislative bodies of those jurisdictions, precludes the use of an initiative to enact ordinances limiting the power of those legislative bodies to impose such fees.

Fees for Ground Water Recharge Facilities. A local agency may adopt an ordinance requiring the payment of a fee for the purpose of constructing ground water recharge facilities, in order to encourage the replenishment of underground aquifers, as a condition of approval of a final or parcel map, or as a condition of issuing a building permit. § 66484.5. A ground water recharge facility plan for the area to be benefited must first be adopted, which includes planned facilities and a fair method of allocating costs and apportioning fees within the area of benefit. §§ 66484.5(a)(1), (a)(3). Fees paid must be kept in a planned recharge facility fund and can be expended only for construction within the area of benefit. § 66484.5(f). Section 66484.5 provides for public hearings and majority protests.

Subdivision Exactions Based on Consistency of Subdivision "Design and Improvement" with General Plan

Since 1971, state law in California has required that subdivision map approvals be consistent with the general plan. Among the manifestations of this requirement are the Map Act's definitions of "design" and "improvement." The Map Act requires that cities and counties regulate and control the "design and improvement" of subdivisions. § 66411. The definition of "design" includes: street alignments, grades, and widths; drainage and sanitary facilities and utilities, including alignments and grades thereof; location and size of all required easements and rights-of-way; fire roads and firebreaks; lot size and configuration; traffic access; grading; land to be dedicated for park or recreational purposes; *and other specific physical requirements in the plan and configuration of the entire subdivision that are necessary to ensure consistency with, or implementation of, the general plan or any applicable specific plan.*" § 66418. "Improvement" is defined as street work and utilities to be installed by the subdivider for public or private streets, highways, ways, and easements, needed for the general use of the lot owners of the subdivision and local neighborhood traffic and drainage needs, as well as improvements *necessary to ensure consistency with, or implementation of, the general plan or any applicable specific plan.* § 66419. See also 58 Ops. Cal. Atty. Gen. 41 (1975).

This requirement has broadened the scope of exactions that may be imposed under the authority of the Map Act. For instance, in *Soderling v. City of Santa Monica* (2d Dist. 1983) 142 Cal. App. 3d 501, the court upheld Santa Monica's condition to a condominium conversion (condominium conversions are covered by the Map Act) requiring a developer to install smoke detectors, despite the absence of a specific city ordinance or regulation establishing this requirement. To justify this exaction, Santa Monica relied on its general plan policies to "promote safe housing for all" and "to protect the health and safety of the resident" by enforcing housing regulations. The court found this to be an adequate basis for imposing the condition.

Under this concept, the general plan can provide the basis for a wide array of exactions, including dedications for trails, riparian corridors, and wildlife habitat, as well as fees for libraries, senior and community centers, affordable housing, etc.

Subdivision Exactions Based on Environmental Impact Analysis

Section 66474(e) requires that a city or county deny a subdivision if it finds that the design of the subdivision or its proposed improvements are likely to cause substantial environmental damage or substantially injure fish or wildlife or their habitats. This power to deny a subdivision has been interpreted to create a corresponding power to impose development conditions to address what would otherwise be the basis for denial. *City of Buena Park v. Boyar* (4th Dist. 1960) 186 Cal. App. 2d 61; see also *Nollan v. California Coastal Commission* (1987) 483 U.S. 825. This can be contrasted with CEQA, which by its own terms states that CEQA does not establish the authority to impose "mitigation measures" as conditions. Pub. Resources Code § 21004 (see the discussion later in this chapter regarding the "Relationship of the Exactions Process to the California Environmental Quality Act"). Furthermore, the courts have determined that section 66474(e) provides authority for environmental review that is independent from the requirements of CEQA. *Topanga Association for a Scenic Community v. County of Los Angeles* (2d Dist. 1989) 214 Cal. App. 3d 1348.

Subdivision Exactions Requiring Oversizing Infrastructure; Reimbursement Agreements

Local governments may by ordinance impose a requirement that a subdivider "oversize" the project's infrastructure for the benefit of property outside the subdivision, and that those improvements be dedicated to the public. §§ 66485–66487. The local agency is required to enter into an agreement to reimburse the subdivider for the cost of such improvements, including an amount attributable to interest, in excess of the construction required for the subdivision. § 66486. To pay the costs required by the reimbursement agreement, the local agency may:

- Collect a reasonable charge for the improvement from others not within the subdivision
- Contribute to the subdivider that part of the cost of improvements deriving from the benefit outside the subdivision, by levying a charge on the real property benefited together with interest; or
- Establish and maintain local benefit districts for the collection of such charges or costs from the property benefited

The Legislature has exempted fees imposed pursuant to a reimbursement agreement from sections 66001 and 66002 of the Mitigation Fee Act (the Mitigation Fee Act is discussed in chapter 5). § 66003.

The Attorney General has opined that a school district, having benefited by the increased capacity in a supplemental storm drainage system, could be required to pay reimbursement costs to the subdivider. 71 Ops. Cal. Atty. Gen. 163 (1988).

Exactions Imposed on Parcel Maps

Generally, the Map Act requires a parcel map, rather than a tentative map and final map, for divisions of land creating four or fewer parcels. For such subdivisions, the approving agency may only require dedications of rights-of-way, easements, and the construction of reasonable offsite and onsite improvements for the parcels being created. Except where necessary for public health and safety or for orderly development of the area, performance of conditions is not required until a permit or other grant of approval for development of the parcel is issued, or as otherwise agreed to by the subdivider and the local agency. § 66411.1.

Exactions Imposed on Lot Line Adjustments

The Map Act was amended in 2001 with regard to lot line adjustments. The amendments limit the circumstances in which a lot line adjustment may be employed and potentially expand the degree to which a lot line adjustment may be a basis for imposing conditions. A lot line adjustment is now limited to four or fewer existing adjoining parcels, where land taken from one parcel is added to an adjoining parcel and does not result in a greater number of parcels than originally existed. § 66412(d). Bases for review and approval and, thus, for imposing conditions, were expanded beyond conformity with local zoning and building ordinances, requiring the prepayment of real property taxes prior to the approval of the lot line adjustment, or facilitating relocation of utilities, infrastructure, or easements. They now also include conformity with the local general plan, any applicable specific plan, and any applicable coastal plan. § 66412(d)

Provisions for Judicial Partitions of Williamson Act Lands

The Williamson Act (§ 51200 et seq.) provides preferential property tax treatment for lands committed, by contract, to agricultural use for a specified period of time. Special statutes govern exactions for Williamson Act lands. §§ 51200–51295. Whenever a parcel or final map is required to effectuate a judicial partition of land that will remain subject to a Williamson Act contract after map approval, the local agency approving the map may establish the amount of any exaction, dedication, or improvement requirement as a condition for approval, but may not require payment of the exaction, the undertaking of the improvement or the posting of security for future performance, or accept any required offer of dedication, until the Williamson Act contract on the land terminates or is canceled. However, this deferral is not required as to fees and assessments that are due and payable for governmental services provided to the parcel prior to termination or cancellation of the contract. § 66411.5(b). In the opinion of the California Attorney General, the authority of a city or county to impose conditions when approving a division of contracted land includes requiring the owner to rescind a previous notice of non-renewal. 75 Ops. Cal. Atty. Gen. 278 (1992).

Conditions Imposed on Certificates of Compliance

In circumstances where the legal status of a parcel is in question, an owner or a purchaser who has entered into a contract of sale for the parcel may apply to the local agency for a certificate of compliance. § 66499.35. If the parcel was lawfully created, the local agency must issue a certificate of compliance. § 66499(a); *Findleton v. Board of Supervisors of El Dorado County* (3d Dist. 1993) 12 Cal. App. 4th 709. No conditions may be imposed on the certificate. However, if the parcel was created in violation of the Map Act or the local subdivision ordinance, and the applicant for the certificate of compliance was the owner at the time of the unlawful division, the approving body may impose conditions applicable to a current division of land. § 66499.35(b). If the applicant for the certificate of compliance acquired his or her interest in the parcel after the unlawful division, the local agency may impose those conditions that would have been applicable to the division of property at the time the applicant acquired an interest. § 66499.35(b).

Subdivision Exactions Requiring Access to Public Resources

Section 66478.1 et seq., "Public Access to Public Resources," was enacted to implement Article X, Section 4 of the California Constitution, which prohibits private landowners from impeding the right-of-way to any navigable water whenever the right-of-way is required for a public purpose. Unlike many of the Map Act provisions regarding exactions, these establish a requirement applicable to local governments, rather than an authorization.

Pursuant to these provisions, no tentative or final map for property fronting on a "public waterway" river or stream, ocean coastline or bay shoreline, or lake or reservoir, may be approved unless the subdivider dedicates, by fee or easement, reasonable public access from a public highway to those resources. "Reasonable public access" is to be determined considering a set of criteria established by statute. §§ 66478.4, 66478.11, 66478.12.

Likewise, local agencies cannot approve a tentative or final map for a subdivision fronting on a public waterway, river, or stream that does not dedicate a public easement along a portion of the bank of the river or stream bordering or lying within the proposed subdivision. § 66478.5.

Notwithstanding the public access requirements described above, the local agency need not require access through or across the subdivision if it finds that reasonable access is otherwise available within a reasonable distance of the subdivision and identifies the location of this access. § 66478.8. However, this exception has been held not to apply to the easements along the banks of rivers and streams contemplated by section 66478.5. *Kern River Public Access Committee v. City of Bakersfield* (5th Dist. 1985) 170 Cal. App. 3d 1205.

The various access requirements described here refer to tentative or final maps, but not parcel maps. However, in light of the constitutional purpose to be served, and the apparent lack of preemption, it appears that a city or county could require similar exactions in conjunction with parcel maps through its subdivision ordinance.

Limitations Related to Development Standards

In regulating subdivisions, cities and counties cannot impose standards or criteria for public improvements including, but not limited to, streets, sewers, fire stations, schools, and parks, that exceed the standards and criteria being applied at that time to its publicly financed improvements located in similarly zoned districts within that jurisdiction. § 65913.2(c). There is some uncertainty as to whether section 65913.2(c) applies to nonresidential development. Since it is found in Chapter 4.2 of the Planning and Zoning Law ("Housing Development Approvals"), it could be interpreted as only applying to requirements for residential developments. However, while subsections (a) and (b) of section 65913.2 specifically refer to housing projects, subsection (c) does not, leaving open the argument that this limitation applies to other forms of development involving subdivision maps, as well.

Limitations Related to Housing and Housing Affordability

In exercising its authority to regulate subdivisions, cities and counties must refrain from imposing criteria for design or improvements for the purpose of rendering infeasible the development of housing for any and all economic segments of the community. § 65913.2(a).

Further, in regulating subdivisions, local agencies are required to consider the effect of ordinances adopted and actions taken by it with respect to the housing needs of the region. § 65913.2(b). Likewise, section 66412.3 requires that a local agency consider the effect of ordinances and actions adopted in implementing the Map Act on the housing needs of the region, and balance those needs against the public service needs of its residents and available fiscal and environmental resources.

Building Permits

Authority

Historically, cities and counties have treated the issuance of building permits as "ministerial," based strictly on compliance with the applicable zoning ordinance and building codes. This precluded the city or county from imposing additional conditions on building permit issuance. *See, e.g., Sunset View Cemetery Association v. Kraintz* (lst Dist. 1961) 196 Cal. App. 2d 115. (Note that this limitation does not prevent imposing conditions on tentative subdivision maps or other approvals, to be complied with at the time of building permit issuance.)

More recently, however, some local governments have begun to characterize their building permit approval processes as "discretionary"—involving an exercise of judgment—rather than ministerial, thus opening the door to imposing conditions on the issuance of building permits. For example, the approval sought in *Dolan v. City of Tigard* (1994) 512 U.S. 374, discussed in detail in chapter 3, was a building permit. In *Russ Building Partnership v. City and County of San Francisco* (1st Dist. 1987) 199 Cal. App. 3d 1496, also discussed in chapter 3, the court upheld a development fee imposed as a condition to a building permit in San Francisco. Furthermore, section 65961 limits conditions imposed on residential building permits that could have been imposed as conditions to tentative maps, impliedly recognizing the ability to impose conditions on building permits absent these restrictions. Likewise, section 65909 places limitations on dedication and bonding requirements imposed as conditions to building permit approval, an additional indication that conditions to building permits are not necessarily prohibited. (For a discussion of circumstances under which a building permit may be a discretionary approval, see *Friends of Westwood, Inc. v. City of Los Angeles* (2d Dist. 1987) 191 Cal. App. 3d 259 or when design review may be ministerial, see *Health First v. March Joint Powers Authority* (4th Dist. 2009) 174 Cal. App 4th 1135.)

With regard to open space issues, the general plan can provide a basis for requiring conditions to building permit approval. Pursuant to section 65567, no local agency may issue a building permit that is inconsistent with the open space element in the general plan. *See also* § 65560. Since the power to deny has been recognized as authority to approve with conditions (*Nollan v. California Coastal Commission* (1987) 483 U.S. 825, 837), a local agency should be able to impose conditions on building permits as necessary to ensure consistency with the open space element. (Note that this ability would still be subject to constitutional limitations, as discussed in chapter 3.)

However, other than with regard to the open space element, the courts have rejected a consistency requirement between building permits and the general plan. *Elysian Heights Residents Association, Inc. v. City of Los Angeles* (2d Dist. 1986) 182 Cal. App. 3d 21, 28; review denied. Thus, general plan consistency does not provide a more general authority to impose exactions on building permits. Instead, cities and counties wishing to impose conditions through a discretionary building permit process should expressly provide so by local ordinance (including, perhaps, the requirement that building permits be consistent with all elements of the general plan, and not just the open space element).

Limitations

Several provisions of state law limit the ability to impose conditions on the approval of a building permit.

Local agencies may not require as a condition to a building permit either: (1) the dedication of land for any purpose not reasonably related to the use of the property for which the building permit is sought; or (2) the posting of a bond to guarantee installation of public improvements not reasonably related to the use of that property. § 65909.

Generally, for five years after recording a final map or parcel map for a subdivision of single- or multiple-family residential units, a city or county cannot require, as a condition to the issuance of any building or equivalent permit, conformance with or performance of any conditions that could have been lawfully imposed as a condition to the tentative or parcel map for the subdivision. § 65961. However, this limitation does not apply if failure to impose a condition or conditions would place the residents of the subdivision and/or the immediate community in a condition per-

Addressing affordable housing goals can be realized through fees and dedications imposed on new commercial and residential development.

ilous to their health or safety. *See Beck Development Company, Inc. v. Southern Pacific Transportation Company* (3d Dist. 1996) 44 Cal. App. 4th 1160. Likewise, a condition may be imposed if it is required in order to comply with state or federal law.

The provisions of 65961 were modified with regard to certain tentative maps and parcel maps extended by the Legislature in 2009 (*see* Gov. Code §66452.22). For purposes only of a tentative subdivision map or parcel map that is extended pursuant to Section 66452.22, the five-year period described in section 65961 is reduced to three years. § 65961(e). Furthermore, for purposes only of a tentative subdivision map or parcel map that is extended pursuant to Section 66452.22, Section 65961 does not prohibit a city or county from levying a fee or imposing a condition that requires the payment of a fee, including an adopted fee that is not included within an applicable zoning ordinance, upon the issuance of a building permit, including, but not limited to, a fee defined in Section 66000. §65961(f).

The effect of section 65961 was addressed in *Golden State Homebuilding Association v. City of Modesto* (5th Dist. 1994) 26 Cal. App. 4th 601. The City of Modesto approved a vesting tentative subdivision map, at which time the City had not yet adopted a capital facilities fee. Therefore, the City did not impose a condition that the subdivider pay such a fee. Subsequently, the City adopted a capital facilities fee, as well as entering into an agreement to collect comparable facilities fees on behalf of Stanislaus County, where Modesto is located.

Final subdivision maps were recorded and, nearly three years later, the developers sought residential building permits to develop specific parcels. At that time, the City imposed the two capital facilities fees that had been adopted after the vesting tentative map had been approved (by this time the "vesting" protections afforded by the vesting tentative map had expired). The developer challenged the fees on the basis that section 65961 precluded imposing the fees because the City could have lawfully imposed the fees as conditions to the tentative map. By failing to do so, the City had lost the opportunity to do so now, as a condition to a building permit.

The Court of Appeal disagreed. Although acknowledging that its ruling regarding the effect of section 65961 favors local governments that are slow to establish exactions, the court sided with the City. The court found that, because the fees were not in effect at the time of the tentative map approval, the City could not have "lawfully imposed" them at that time. As a result, the City could require the fees as conditions to the issuance of building permits. *Id.* at 612. See also *Laguna Village, Inc. v. County of Orange* (4th Dist. 1985) 166 Cal. App. 3d 125; *Beck Development Company, Inc. v. Southern Pacific Transportation Company* (3d Dist. 1996) 44 Cal. App. 4th 1160, 1199.

"Bargained for" Exactions

Cities and counties have the ability to reach agreements with property owners that will, among other things, establish the development conditions that will apply to the subject property. This ability is established through state law provisions governing redevelopment (Health and Safety Code § 33100 et seq.) and development agreements (Gov. Code § 65864 et seq.). In each case, agreements must be consistent with the general plan. Health and Safety Code § 33367(d)(4); Gov. Code § 65867.5. Subject to this requirement and applicable procedural requirements, the conditions established are limited only to those to which the parties can agree.

Redevelopment

Under California's Community Redevelopment Law, Health and Safety Code section 33100 et seq., redevelopment agencies enter into agreements in order to implement their redevelopment plans. One type, the disposition and development agreement (DDA), is an agreement between the redevelopment agency and a developer for the sale and development of property within a "redevelopment area," and provides the conditions under which the subject property will be developed. For example, pursuant to a DDA, the redevelopment agency will agree to acquire the subject property and sell it to the developer. The developer will agree to develop the property subject to certain limitations on use and design. The redevelopment agency may agree to construct certain public improvements and/or provide public financing.

Following the dismantling of redevelopment agencies by the legislature during the 2011 legislative cycle, the future for redevelopment remains uncertain at best.

Another type of redevelopment agreement is the owner participation agreement (OPA). These agreements are similar in content to DDAs, except that they are utilized with a developer who already owns property within the redevelopment area.

A sample disposition and development agreement and a sample owner participation agreement are provided as Appendices G and H. They offer examples of the kinds of issues that may be addressed in these agreements. For an in-depth discussion of redevelopment under the Community Redevelopment Law, see *Redevelopment in California*, Solano Press Books (2009).

Development Agreements

State law authorizes a city or county to enter into a development agreement with a property owner. § 65865. While the potential scope of these agreements is quite broad, typically the development agreement provides the property owner with a level of certainty by "freezing" the ordinances, resolutions, standards, etc., that will apply to developing the project, as of the date the agreement is entered into. For its part, the city or county may bargain for development conditions (*e.g.*, traffic fees, parks, community centers) beyond what could be required legally pursuant to the rules described in this chapter and chapter 3. Furthermore, the Mitigation Fee Act does not apply to development fees established through a development agreement. § 66000(b). (Note that obtaining a vested right through a development agreement can also limit the ability of a city or county to impose additional or increased exactions by freezing these provisions. These limitations are discussed below.) Development agreements are interpreted in a manner similar to contracts. *Building Industry Association of Central California v. City of Patterson* (5th Dist. 2009) 171 Cal. App. 4th 886. Sample development agreements are provided in Appendices I and J. Regarding the permissible scope of development agreements, *see, e.g., Santa Margarita Area Residents Together v. San Luis Obispo County* (2nd Dist. 2000) 8 Cal. App. 4th 221.

Vested Rights as Limitations on Exactions

A city's or county's ability to impose exactions can be limited through the principle of "vested rights." Under this principle, a developer who has obtained a vested right to develop a particular piece of property is entitled to move forward with development in accordance with the scope of that right. The developer may also have obtained a right to be free of additional exactions, subject to certain limitations.

A vested right may be obtained through application of California's "common law" (court-recognized) vested rights rule. In addition, there are several statutory provisions that can create vested rights of some magnitude. Each of these is described below.

Common Law Vesting as a Limitation on Imposing Exactions

Once a developer has obtained a vested right to develop land, the local agency has limited authority to impose additional exactions. However, under the rule established by California courts (i.e., the "common law rule") a vested right is established quite late in the development process, limiting its ability to prevent additional exactions from being imposed. Under the common law vested rights rule in California, a property owner does not obtain a vested right to complete a particular project, regardless of subsequent changes in the law, until:

"Common Law" Vested Right Requires:

- Building Permit Issued
- Substantial Work Performed
- Substantial Liability Incurred

- A building permit has been issued for the project
- The property owner has performed substantial work in good faith reliance on that permit, and
- The property owner has incurred substantial liability, also in good faith reliance on the permit issued

Avco Community Developers, Inc. v. South Coast Regional Commission (1976) 17 Cal. 3d 785, 791.

The common law rule was clearly demonstrated in *Avco, supra*, a 1976 case involving the newly enacted California Coastal Act. In that case, the developer had received local government approval for a planned development, a final subdivision map, and a grading permit, and had installed street and drainage improvements worth two million dollars to serve the project. Subsequently, the Coastal Act was adopted, which required an additional permit from the Coastal Commission. The developer applied to the Coastal Commission for an exemption from the Coastal Act's permit requirements on the basis that it had already acquired a vested right to complete the project. The California Supreme Court rejected this argument, holding that, because no building permit had been issued, no vested right to develop had been acquired.

The "*Avco* Rule" is made even more stringent by the requirement that a landowner cannot rely on an invalid permit or on a permit that has expired or been revoked. In addition, the scope of the vested right is defined by the terms of the permit itself. Thus, the vested right does not protect subsequent phases of the project if these phases are not approved as part of the permit. *Oceanic California, Inc. v. North Central Regional Commission* (lst Dist. 1976) 63 Cal. App. 3d 57.

The potentially harsh result of *Avco*'s "late vesting" rule and associated limitations may be avoided by one or more statutory mechanisms that provide at least a degree of vesting at an earlier time. Descriptions of these strategies follow.

Statutory Vesting as a Limitation on Imposing Exactions

The California Legislature has provided several mechanisms that offer at least some relief from the late vesting established by the common law vesting rule. Each of these statutory mechanisms can limit the imposition of exactions.

The "Map Filing Freeze." The Map Act generally provides that a local agency, when considering a tentative map, may only rely on those ordinances, policies, and standards in effect at the time the application for that map was determined to be complete. § 66474.2. However, section 66474.2(b), provides that, as long as the local agency initiates proceedings before the tentative map application is complete and follows certain public notice requirements, ordinances, policies, and standards adopted after an application is complete may apply. Furthermore, whatever vesting benefits this provision may provide to a subdivider apply only to the subdivision process, and not to all of the steps in the development process. Following the enactment of a moratorium, a developer cannot file a pre-emptive declaratory relief action under 66474.2 where the developer's map application is incomplete and follow-up rezonings have not yet occurred. *Stonehouse Homes LLC v. City of Sierra Madre* (2d Dist. 2008) 167 Cal. App. 4th 531.

Vesting Tentative Subdivision Maps. A more powerful form of vesting is triggered when an applicant elects to use a "vesting tentative subdivision map." (Note that this tool is also available to applicants for parcel maps in those jurisdictions that utilize "tentative parcel maps.") § 66463.5(g). The approval of a vesting tentative map confers a right to proceed with development in substantial compliance with ordinances, policies, and standards in place at the time the map application was complete. § 66498.1. As such, it "freezes" the applicable regulations for the purposes of development, and not just subdivision. The effect may be dramatic, keeping at bay a subsequently enacted growth moratorium or a subsequently enacted or increased development fee or other exaction.

Exceptions to the above-described rule include those circumstances where failure to deny the project or to impose a new condition would place the residents of the subdivision or the immediate community in a condition dangerous to their health and safety, or where a condition or denial is required to comply with state or federal law. § 66498.1(c). Note, also, that filing an application for a vesting tentative map does not guarantee approval of the map. The application may still be denied, although not because of the vesting nature of the map. § 66452.

In *Bright Development Company v. City of Tracy* (3d Dist. 1993) 20 Cal. App. 4th 783, the court considered the legal effect of a vesting tentative map approval on a city's ability to impose exactions. In particular, this case illustrates the importance of formally authorizing development conditions prior to an application for a vesting tentative map. Bright Development's application for a vesting tentative map was approved with a condition requiring the undergrounding of offsite utilities. The City had not, up to that point, adopted an ordinance or other provision authorizing the imposition of this type of condition. Subsequently, the City formally adopted such a measure.

The court upheld Bright Development's challenge to the utility undergrounding condition imposed on its map approval, on the basis that it was not authorized by the City's "ordinances, policies and standards" in place at the time the vesting tentative map application was complete. The court characterized the vesting map statute as requiring reasonable notice to the applicant of the rules governing development.

> If developers had no knowledge nor reasonable means of acquiring knowledge before "expending resources and incurring liabilities" of the ordinances, policies, and standards to which they were subject, this legislative objective would be frustrated. We thus conclude the statute requires prior notice, either actual or constructive, as a condition to imposing ordinances, policies and standards upon an applicant who is entitled to rely on a complete vesting tentative map. An ordinance, policy or standard of a public agency which is written and accessible is reasonably calculated to apprise interested parties of their responsibility and would suffice to supply constructive notice. *Id.* at 799

The degree to which an approved vesting tentative map will limit a city's ability to impose new fees was addressed in *Kaufman and Broad Central Valley, Inc. v. City of Modesto* (5th Dist. 1994) 25 Cal. App. 4th 1577. (See the article, "Do Vesting Tentative Maps 'Freeze' Development Fees," on the following page.)

The "One Bite of the Apple Rule." Section 65961 precludes local agencies from imposing conditions on building permits that could have been lawfully imposed at the time of the tentative map or parcel map approval. A provision of the Permit Streamlining Act (§§ 65920–65963.1), section 65961 specifies that, notwithstanding any other provision of law, a city or county cannot impose a condition on a building permit or its equivalent for single-or multifamily dwelling units if that condition could have been imposed on a tentative or parcel map for the subject property. This restriction runs for five years from when a final map or parcel map is recorded. However, a local agency may impose additional conditions during this five-year period if a failure to do so would place the residents of the subdivision and/or the immediate community in a condition perilous to their health or safety, or if required in order to comply with state or federal law. § 65961(a). Section 65961 is addressed in detail in the discussion of building permits as a source of exactions, above, and is modified for maps extended as a result of legislation enacted in 2009. Government Code Section 66452.22.

Development Agreements. As discussed above, state law authorizes a city or county and a property owner to enter into a "development agreement." §§ 65864–65869.5. A primary benefit of a development agreement, from the standpoint of the property owner, is to preclude application of subsequently-enacted ordinances, resolutions, policies, standards, etc. As a result, fees enacted or increased after the date established by the development agreement (typically, but not necessarily, the date the development agreement goes into effect) do not apply to the subject property for the term of the agreement.

A development agreement may exempt specified exactions or types of exactions from the local rules, regulations, and policies otherwise "frozen" by the agreement (or, alternatively, "freeze" only those exactions spelled out in the agreement). Thus, for instance, the development agreement may provide that development of the subject property will be subject to the traffic fee in place at the time building permits are issued. Whether any fees or other exactions will not be subject to the freeze of regulations is a matter to be negotiated as part of the development agreement process. Various approaches to using a development agreement to establish applicable impact fees are illustrated in the article, "Addressing Impact Fees through a Development Agreement–To Freeze or Not to Freeze?" (*see* page 97). Sample development agreements are provided in Appendices I and J.

General Limitations on Imposing Exactions

Limitations on Exactions Based on State Housing Policy

State law creates certain limitations on exactions that would be contrary to state policies regarding housing. These policies recognize a housing shortage in California and the high cost of housing in this state, and are generally intended to support providing housing affordable to all income groups.

Exactions and Housing Affordability: Housing Element Requirements. As part of the housing element required to be in every general plan (§§ 65580–65589.8), each city and county must include:

> [A]n analysis of potential and actual governmental constraints upon the maintenance, improvement or development of housing for all income levels, including land use controls, building codes and their enforcement, site improvements, *fees and other exactions required of developers*, and local processing and permit procedures. § 65583(a)(5) (emphasis added).

The basis for this requirement is a concern that fees and exactions, along with the other "governmental constraints" identified, can substantially affect housing affordability.

The housing element must also include a program setting forth a five-year schedule of actions to implement the policies and achieve the goals and objectives of the housing element. Among the required components of this action program is that the city or county "[a]ddress and, where appropriate and legally possible, remove governmental constraints to the maintenance, improvement, and development of housing." § 65583(c)(3). Read together with the description of such constraints that includes "fees and other exactions," this creates a requirement that the housing element at least address the degree to which exactions create an obstacle to housing affordability.

Cities and counties also must address their efforts to remove governmental constraints to the provision of housing in the planning agency's annual report to the legislative body regarding the status of the general plan and progress toward its implementation. § 65400(b).

Very Low-, Low-, and Moderate-Income Housing Projects, Emergency Shelters. Section 65589.5(d) prohibits a local agency from denying a housing development project or (more relevant to this discussion) imposing conditions rendering it infeasible for the use of very low-, low-, and moderate-income households or as an emergency shelter, unless it makes one of a number of findings, based on substantial evidence. Among these findings are, generally:

Do Vesting Tentative Maps "Freeze" Development Fees?

The effect of a vesting tentative subdivision map on a city's ability to impose exactions was illustrated in *Kaufman & Broad Central Valley, Inc. v. City of Modesto* (5th Dist. 1994) 25 Cal. App. 4th 1577. In *Kaufman & Broad*, at issue was the City's "Capital Facilities Fee." The following outlines the critical events and corresponding dates. After reviewing these facts, decide what the fees owed by the subdivider should have been. Then check your answer against the court's decision on the following page.

June 1987	City adopts "Capital Facilities Fee" ($1,417)
October 1987	City adds provision to Capital Facilities Fee, requiring annual adjustment to reflect increases in the Building Cost Index
April 1988	City staff, concerned that the City's capital improvement projects were "woefully underfunded," recommends recalculating the Capital Facilities Fee
June 1988	Applicant's vesting tentative map application (for its "River Terrace" subdivision) is complete. Capital Facilities Fee now equals $1,434 per residential unit (the original $1,417 per unit, plus the annual adjustment based upon the Building Cost Index)
August 1988	City issues a request for proposals to develop a revised Capital Facilities Fee
August 1988	City Council adopts a standard condition for vesting maps requiring subdividers to pay the Capital Facilities Fee in effect at the time of the issuance of building permits
October 1988	River Terrace vesting tentative map approved, including the condition requiring paying the Capital Facilities Fee in place at the time of building permit issuance
February 1989	City adopts an interim revised Capital Facilities Fee—$2,653—the increase based on a "comprehensive reevaluation" of the fee, and not the "relatively modest and predictable" increase in the Building Cost Index by which the fee would be increased per the City's October 1987 provision
June 1989	Application complete for a second vesting tentative map on an adjacent piece of property ("River Terrace II")
July 1989	River Terrace II vesting tentative map approved, including the condition requiring payment of the Capital Facilities Fee in place at the time of building permit issuance
November 1989	City increases the Capital Facilities Fee to $4,890 per unit, based on the completed "fundamental recalculation" of the fee and not simply an increase in the Building Cost Index
October 1991	Kaufman and Broad applies for building permits; City charges Capital Facilities Fee of $4,890 per unit

Question: What Capital Facilities Fee should Kaufman and Broad pay for its River Terrace subdivision? For its River Terrace II subdivision?

Answer

(to question on previous page)

The California Court of Appeal found that the appropriate fees, under the vesting tentative map statutes, were:

For the River Terrace subdivision: $1,434 (the fee in place when the application for this subdivision was complete), plus changes subsequently approved to reflect increases in the Building Cost Index.

For the River Terrace II subdivision: $2,653 (the fee in effect at the time its application was complete, plus changes subsequently approved to reflect increases in the Building Cost Index)

The California Court of Appeal rejected the City's "open-ended" approach to determining the applicable Capital Facilities Fee, holding that a fundamental recalculation of the fee (unlike the annual adjustments for increases in the Building Cost Index) conflicted with the purposes of the vesting tentative map statute.

- The jurisdiction has adopted a housing element and met or exceeded its share of the regional housing need allocation.
- The project as proposed would have a specific, adverse impact on public health or safety [but not the broader "welfare"] and there is no feasible method to mitigate or avoid that impact without rendering the development unaffordable to low- and moderate-income households or rendering the development of the emergency shelter infeasible.
- Denying the project or imposing the conditions of approval is required in order to comply with state or federal law, and there is no feasible method to comply without rendering the development unaffordable to low- and moderate-income households or rendering the development of the emergency shelter infeasible.
- The project is proposed for land: (1) zoned for agriculture or resource preservation and is surrounded on at least two sides by land being used for those purposes; or (2) which does not have adequate water or wastewater facilities.
- The project is inconsistent with the general plan's land use designation for the project site, and the city or county has adopted a housing element.

See section 65589.5(d) for the specifics of this provision.

Nothing in the foregoing relieves a local agency from the obligation to comply with the state law requirements governing either Congestion Management Programs (§ 65088 et seq.) or the California Coastal Act (Public Resources Code § 30000 et seq.). § 65589.5(f).

Furthermore, nothing in section 65589.5 is to be construed as prohibiting a local agency from requiring development projects to comply with development standards, conditions, and policies appropriate to, and consistent with, meeting the jurisdiction's share of the regional housing needs. § 65589.5(f).

Finally, fees and other exactions that are otherwise authorized by law and that are essential to providing necessary public services and facilities to a project are not prohibited by the general limitations of section 65589.5. § 65589.5(f).

In addition to the foregoing, special requirements apply to low- and moderate-income housing within the "coastal zone," as that term is defined in the California Coastal Act, Public Resources Code section 30000 et seq. § 65590(d). These include the requirement that new housing developments constructed within the coastal zone provide, where feasible, housing units for persons and families of low- or moderate-income. Where it is not feasible to provide these units within the proposed new development itself, the local government must require that the developer provide such housing, if feasible, at another location within the same city or county, either within the coastal zone or within three miles of it. Thus, unlike section 65589.5(d), which generally limits the ability to impose exactions in order to promote housing affordability, this provision requires certain conditions to promote the same goal. (Note that under section 65590, local governments are required to offer density bonuses or other incentives in order to assist in providing new housing units.)

When Development Fee Payment Can Be Required

Subject to certain exceptions, payment of fees imposed on a residential development for the construction of public improvements or facilities may not be required until the date of final inspection of the project or the date the certificate of occupancy is issued, whichever occurs first. § 66007(a), (e). If the residential development contains more than one dwelling, the local agency may determine whether the fees or charges shall be paid on a pro rata basis for each dwelling when it receives its final inspection or certificate of occupancy (whichever occurs first); on a pro rata basis when a certain percentage of the dwellings have received their final inspection or certificate of occupancy (whichever occurs first); or on a lump-sum basis when the first dwelling in the development receives its final inspection or certificate of occupancy (whichever occurs first). § 66007(a).

Beginning in 2009, a local agency may defer collection of one or more fees up to the close of escrow. This provision does not apply to fees and charges levied pursuant to section 17620 et seq. of the Education Code. § 66007(g). (See chapter 5 for an in depth discussion of these and related provisions.)

Limitations on Fees for Operation and Maintenance of Public Facilities

Generally, development fees may not be required for the maintenance or operation of public facilities. § 65913.8. However, such fees may be required if the improvement is designed and installed to serve only the specific development project on which the fee is imposed, and the improvement serves nineteen or fewer lots or units, provided that the city or county finds, based on substantial evidence, that it is infeasible or impractical to form a public entity for maintenance of the improvement or annex to one. § 65913.8(a).

Likewise, a fee may be required for maintenance and/or operation for a limited amount of time, if for an improvement within a water, sewer maintenance, street lighting, or drainage

Addressing Impact Fees through a Development Agreement—To Freeze or Not to Freeze?

One of the benefits that a property owner can derive from a development agreement is to establish and "freeze" impact fees applicable to the subject property during the term of the agreement. Particularly for a project with a long build-out period, this type of certainty can be very valuable to a developer. In order to secure this benefit, a property owner may want to negotiate language into a development agreement that prevents applying to the subject property any future enactment that would:

> Establish, enact, or increase in any manner applicable to the Project, or impose against the Project, any fees other than those specifically permitted by this agreement [these might include, for instance, traffic impact fees, park fees, other capital facilities fees, etc.]

Conversely, a city or county entering into a development agreement may want to ensure that some or all new development fees adopted within the jurisdiction will apply to the property subject to a development agreement. For example, a development agreement might provide that a city may impose fees that:

> (a) Are adopted after the effective date [of the development agreement] and applied citywide including, but not limited to, fees related to regional traffic, capital facilities, schools, and parks; or
>
> (b) Exist as of the effective date but are increased thereafter to provide additional facilities or services necessary to accomplish the purposes of the fee or to reflect the costs associated with providing the facilities or services to be financed by the fee

A middle ground might be reflected in the following language, which calls out certain impact fees that will not be subject to a general freeze of applicable regulations:

> (a) Except as provided in (b), the City may not apply to the Project any future enactment that would establish, enact, or increase in any manner applicable to the Project, or impose against the Project, any fees other than those specifically permitted by this Agreement;
>
> (b) City may apply to the Project any increases to its [Traffic Impact Mitigation Fee, Capital Facilities Fee, etc.] subsequently enacted for general application within the City

As an alternative approach, a development agreement might provide that fees are not frozen, allowing newly enacted fees and fee increases to apply, except in those instances called out in the development agreement:

> City may impose fees that are adopted after the effective date [of the development agreement] and applied citywide including, but not limited to, fees related to regional traffic, capital facilities, schools, and parks, provided, however, that the City shall impose no fees or dedication requirements for the acquisition of trails and open space other than those specified in this agreement.

Note: The examples provided here are for illustration purposes only. As such, they look at some of the issues relating to vesting and fees in isolation from the wide range of other issues that typically are addressed in the negotiation of a development agreement.

district, subject to certain restrictions. § 65913.8(b). Funding approaches for operation and maintenance of public facilities are discussed in detail in chapter 9.

Relationship of the Exactions Process to the California Environmental Quality Act

By its own terms, CEQA does not provide the authority to impose exactions as mitigation measures. "In mitigating or avoiding a significant effect of a project on the environment, a public agency may exercise only those express or implied powers provided by law other than this division [Division 13—Environmental Quality]." Pub. Resources Code § 21004. Although the environmental review processes required by CEQA may provide precisely the type of information needed to justify an exaction, a public agency must rely on its ability to impose exactions provided by other legal authority. Fortunately for public agencies, there is no shortage of such authority, as illustrated in this and the preceding chapter.

In *Woodward Park Homeowners Association, Inc. v. City of Fresno* (5th Dist. 2007) 150 Cal. App. 4th 683, the court found invalid an EIR's treatment of mitigation for traffic impacts. The EIR identified certain freeway-related traffic impacts associated with the project, but did not require mitigation for them. The city took the position (apparently its long-standing practice) that it need not require any form of mitigation for project impacts on freeway traffic—not because there were no impacts or that identified impacts were not significant, or that mitigation was infeasible, but because the city was not satisfied with Caltrans' performance in providing information related to those impacts. Thus, the city left out a substantial component of the needed improvements identified by Caltrans. Caltrans, the city alleged, had failed to provide a "nexus study" for the cost per trip by improvement or segment identified in the EIR (see the discussion of such studies in chapters 3 and 5). The court rejected this as a basis for not requiring mitigation. "The city's practice is illegal. There is no foundation for the idea that the city can refuse to require mitigation of an impact solely because another agency did not provide information [here, proposed mitigation from Caltrans and Caltrans's analysis showing that requiring the mitigation would be legal]. This is not how CEQA works." Caltrans' behavior, the court said, did not change the city's obligations under CEQA. *Woodward Park* at 728–729.

Alternatively, the city said it did not need to impose any mitigation requirements for these impacts because the EIR determined the project would generate less traffic than buildout under existing zoning. The court rejected this argument, as well. The baseline against with project impacts are to be measured is existing conditions on the project site, and not buildout under existing plans and regulations. *Woodward Park* at 730.

Thomas Jacobson is a Professor and Director of the Institute for Community Planning Assistance in the Department of Environmental Studies and Planning at Sonoma State University. He was formerly an attorney with McCutchen, Doyle, Brown & Enersen's Land Use and Local Government Group, where he represented both public agencies and project applicants, and adjunct professor at University of San Francisco School of Law, where he taught land use law. He is a member of the American Institute of Certified Planners and the California Planning Roundtable, serves as a consultant to public agencies on land use law and planning matters, and is Of Counsel to the Sohagi Law Group.

CHAPTER FIVE

Overview of the Fee Adoption Process—AB 1600 Nexus Legislation

By William W. Abbott and Cori Badgley

In 1987, the California Legislature enacted Assembly Bill 1600 in part to codify the United States Supreme Court's holding in *Nollan v. California Coastal Commission* (1987) 483 U.S. 825, that a reasonable relationship or nexus must exist between a governmental exaction and the purpose for which the condition was imposed. (Chapter 927, Stats. 1987, California Government Code § 66000 et seq.[1]) In addition to formalizing some of the restrictions found in the *Nollan* decision, AB 1600 established a uniform process for formulating, adopting, imposing, collecting, accounting for, and protesting certain fees. AB 1600 is now known as the Mitigation Fee Act, following the California Supreme Court's utilization of the name in the *Ehrlich* decision. *Ehrlich v. City of Culver City* (1996) 12 Cal. 4th 854. Sample studies used as the basis for imposing development fees for inclusionary housing and major public improvements may be found in Appendices A–D.

The Mitigation Fee Act established a uniform process for formulating, adopting, imposing, collecting, accounting for, and protesting certain fees.

This chapter provides an overview of the fee adoption process required by AB 1600. It is important to remember that the Subdivision Map Act and the School Facilities Act also require special procedures when adopting certain fees. (See chapters 4 and 6 for a review of those procedures.) In general, AB 1600 sets forth a series of specific steps implementing two basic rules: First, the record must clearly demonstrate how the facility relates to the project subject to the fee; second, the fee must not exceed the estimated, reasonable cost of the project's proportionate share of the proposed facility.

Fees for Development Projects

Definitions

Local Agencies Affected by AB 1600—Section 66000(c). AB 1600 is all encompassing and applies to all local agencies in the state, including cities, counties, and special districts. As defined in the statute, "local agency" means a county, city, whether general law or chartered, city and county, school district, special district, authority, agency, any other municipal public corporation or district, or other political subdivision of the state. This includes fire districts, water districts, and joint powers authorities composed of local agencies and redevelopment agencies, although certain redevelopment fees are excluded from the statute. See below.

AB 1600 is all encompassing and applies to all local agencies in the state, including cities, counties, and special districts.

Five Rules for Local Governments to Follow When Setting Development Standards and Fees

Be fair. Don't try to make new development pay for problems it did not create. Separate out existing deficiencies, and don't charge new development for the cost to remedy deficiencies.

Plan ahead. Use the facilities plan in your capital improvement program (CIP) or general plan to forecast your community's projected needs for a realistic period of time. If you don't know the type, amount, and general location of your community's future capital facility needs, there may not be a way to pay for them when they are needed.

Avoid over-generalizing. Connect the impacts of the project with the benefits of each facility or class of facility. Think about what each type of development has to do with each proposed capital facility. For example, how does a self-storage warehouse place a demand on the need for a new library? If you can't explain the connection, rethink the fee. Areas already served by adequate levels of facilities may be exempt from fees charged elsewhere in the same community, *Homebuilders Association of Tulare/Kings Counties, Inc. v. City of Lemoore* (5th Dist. 2010) 185 Cal. App. 4th 554.

Don't be greedy. The fee imposed should reflect a reasonable cost estimate to build the facility, and a fair allocation of the new project's demand for the facility.

Consider alternatives to exactions. New development is unable to carry unlimited levels of new exactions. Demanding too much of development may be counter-productive to the local economy. Investigate reducing development standards or using alternative sources of funding, such as the general fund, taxes, Mello-Roos and assessment districts, and general obligation bonds.

CIP = Capital improvement program
EDU = Equivalent dwelling unit
LOS = Level of service
MPFP = Major Projects Financing Plan

Development Project and Public Facilities—Section 66000(a). AB 1600, which applies to a wide range of projects that provide funding for a variety of public facilities, defines "development project" as any project "undertaken for the purpose of development." This includes a project involving the issuance of a permit for construction or reconstruction, but not a permit to operate. (See chapter 6 for a full discussion of development projects.) "Public facilities" that can be funded pursuant to AB 1600 include "public improvements, public services, and community amenities," but otherwise the phrase is not limited by statute or case law as of yet.

However, section 65913.8 narrows the permissible range of uses that can be funded by fees. Fees imposed as a condition of approval for a public capital facility improvement cannot be used for maintenance or services. A limited exception exists where an improvement serves 19 or fewer lots, or where the payment is used as a temporary measure by certain special districts. Together, these provisions (§§ 66000(d) and 65913.8) limit the use of most fees to public capital improvements.

Fees—Section 66000(b). "Fee" is now defined as "a monetary exaction, other than a tax or special assessment, whether established for a broad class of projects by legislation of general applicability or imposed on a specific project on an ad hoc basis." § 66000(b). Thus, AB 1600 applies to individually negotiated fees as well as fees applicable to a large class, such as school impact fees. However, for purposes of this statute, "fee," by definition, does not include the following:

- Park fees specified in the Subdivision Map Act (imposed pursuant to the Quimby Act, § 66477)
- Fees for processing applications for governmental regulatory actions or approvals
- Fees collected under development agreements adopted pursuant to section 65864
- Fees collected pursuant to agreements with redevelopment agencies
- Reimbursement agreements between a developer and an agency for the cost of a public facility which exceeds the developers proportionate share of the cost (§ 66003)
- Penalties assessed against developers who received a density bonus pursuant to section 65917.5, but failed to use the space for child care facilities (§ 65917.5(f))
- The Fourth Appellate District concluded that water hook up and capacity charges governed by § 66013 are not "development fees" subject to § 66000. *Capistrano Beach Water District v. Taj Development* (4th Dist. 1999) 72 Cal. App. 4th 524. See also § 66013(h).

Even though AB 1600's procedural and substantive requirements do not apply to the above categories of exactions, the implication of the California Supreme Court's decision in *Ehrlich* is that the heightened scrutiny standards enunciated in the *Nollan* decision must still be met for individually determined impact fees. Caution would suggest documenting at least a rough connection between the fee and the need for the facility resulting from these kinds of projects unless the statutory scheme clearly contemplates that no relationship is necessary (e.g., development agreements).

Nexus Requirements Sections 66001(a) and (b)

The heart of AB 1600 is the requirement for findings that connect any impacts stemming from a development project to the type and amount of the fee imposed. Section 66001(a) provides that on or after January 1989, in any action "establishing, increasing, or imposing a fee as a condition of approval of a development project," the local agency shall do all of the following:

- Identify the *purpose* of the fee
- Identify how the fee is to be used. If the use is for financing public facilities, *the facilities must be identified.*[2] That identification may be made in applicable general or specific plans, in other public documents that identify the public facilities for which the fee is charged, or by reference to a capital improvement program or CIP (as specified in § 65403) or a capital improvement plan (§ 66002).
- Determine how a *reasonable relationship exists between the fees use and the type of development project on which the fee* is imposed
- Determine how a *reasonable relationship exists between the need for the public facility and the type of development project* on which the fee is imposed

Included as Appendix K is a sample ordinance adopting a revised comprehensive fee program.

In addition to these four steps, AB 1600 also requires that the local agency demonstrate a reasonable relationship between the amount of the fee and the cost of the public facility or portion of the public facility attributable to the development on which the fee is imposed. § 66001(b).

The distinction between section 66001(a), the first four findings, and section 66001(b), the fifth finding, was discussed in *Garrick Development Company et al. v. Hayward Unified School District* (1st Dist. 1992) 3 Cal. App. 4th 320, 336. The *Garrick* court found that subsection (a) applies to an initial quasi-legislative adoption of development fees, while subsection (b) applies to adjudicatory case-by-case actions. The court held that the data to support the first four findings of section 66001(a) does not require a *site-specific* study because it refers to the "type" of development. Only at the later stage, the *Garrick* court reasoned, when the agency is evaluating the particular project, can it be known what share of the public facility's cost that project should bear. Consequently, for subsection (a), a

To satisfy the requirements of AB 1600, an agency must determine the benefit from the public facility, the impact the project will have on the public facility, and the proportionate share of the cost attributable to a particular development project. The following excerpt, from a study of impact fees conducted for the City of Dana Point, describes these elements more fully.

Reasonable Relationship Requirement

Assembly Bill 1600 requires that a reasonable relationship be demonstrated between: (1) the use of the fee and the type of development on which it is imposed (referred to herein as "benefit"); (2) the need for a facility and the type of development on which the fee for that facility is imposed (referred to herein as "impact"); and (3) the amount of the fee and the facility cost attributable to the project on which the fee is imposed (referred to herein as "proportionality").

Impact Relationship. All new development in a community affects some or all public facilities and services provided by local government by increasing the demand for those facilities or services. If the supply of services is not increased to meet that new demand, the quality of service for the existing community declines. The improvements necessary to mitigate the impacts of new development and to maintain an adequate level of service are quantified in the sections of this report which address types of individual facilities.

Benefit Relationship. A reasonable benefit relationship is present as long as the fees are expended to construct the facilities for which they are collected, and those facilities are available to satisfy the needs of new development for that type of facility. In some cases, the location of a facility relative to the development paying the fees has brought the benefit relationship into question. For example, collecting fees for road improvements located across town may be too tenuous of a relationship.

Proportionality Relationship. A reasonable proportionality relationship must be established through the procedures used in calculating impact fees for various types of development. The first step is to identify the facility costs attributable to future development. The second step is to establish fee rates that allocate those costs in proportion to the demands created by each type of development project.

In this study, a capacity-based approach will be used. The distribution of costs between existing and future users is based on capacity utilization. The capacity of facilities is analyzed to determine how much is needed by existing users, and how much is available for new users. Fee rates are defined in terms of cost per unit of capacity. That definition ensures that costs are allocated in proportion to demand because the fee applied to a project depends on the particular capacity utilization characteristics of that project.

From: City of Dana Point Impact Fee Study

Measuring a Level of Service

When designing a legally-defensible impact fee program for any particular public facility, the measurement standard is important. Some facilities can be easily quantified. For example, capacity-driven facilities—such as water or wastewater treatment—can be measured by average daily or average annual consumption. Roadways are typically measured in six standard "levels of service" labeled A through F (LOS A–LOS F). This standard, which gauges the amount of traffic congestion on a particular roadway, measures increased traffic volume and delay when moving from Level A through F. See the chart below for a description of LOS A through F for traffic.

A different measurement tool is necessary when apportioning the cost of the new roadway facilities required to maintain the current level of service on a project-by-project basis. To project demand on roadway capacity, it is common to use the number of peak trips caused by the land use of a particular project, as measured by the Institute of Transportation Engineers' industry standards.

For other facilities, such as libraries and parks, measurements of levels of service are less direct and more difficult to quantify. Some studies use a population-based measurement—for example, five acres of parkland per 1000 residents. Another method would be to quantify the number of square feet of library floor space per resident or per employee working in the jurisdiction.

Level of Service Definitions for Intersections and Highways with Signals

LEVEL OF SERVICE	SIGNALIZATION INTERSECTION	HIGHWAY
A	Uncongested operations, all queues clear in a single-signal cycle	Free flow of vehicles unaffected in traffic stream
B	Uncongested operations, all queues clear in a single cycle	Higher speed range of stable flow; volume 50% of capacity or less
C	Light congestion, occasional backups on critical approaches	Stable flow with volumes not exceeding 75% of capacity
D	Significant congestion of critical approaches but intersection functional; cars required to wait through more than one cycle during short peaks; no long queues formed	Upper end of stable flow conditions; volumes do not exceed 90% of capacity
E	Severe congestion with some long-standing queues on critical approaches; blockage of intersection may occur if traffic signal does not provide for protected turning movements; traffic queue may block nearby intersection(s) upstream of critical approach(es)	Unstable flow at roadway capacity; operating speeds 30 to 25 mph or less
F	Total breakdown, stop-and-go operation	Stop-and-go traffic with operating speeds less than 30 mph

relationship between each class of development project will suffice. *Garrick, supra*, at 335.

In order to document improvements needed to accommodate new growth, cities typically will prepare a capital improvement plan establishing a schedule for each facility needed based on its existing capacity or level of service and projections of population growth. These statistics may be available in a jurisdiction's general plan, or from the regional council of governments or State Department of Finance projections. It is important to distinguish between the baseline—existing residential dwelling units and businesses—versus projected growth for the relevant jurisdiction. The difference between the two should reflect the pool of new development over which to spread the cost of the new facilities.

Generally the process for establishing fees involves four basic steps:

- First, project the future population to be served, both residential and non-residential, by each category of facility for the relevant service area. The service area may be citywide, or may only cover the area benefiting from the project, as would be the case with a wastewater trunkline serving only a portion of a city. Often, the projection is for a ten- or fifteen-year period, or is related to the jurisdiction's general plan projections. A twenty-year period was upheld in *Garrick, supra*, at 333, as not too speculative or long-term. See also *Russ Building Partnership v. City and County of San Francisco* (1st Dist. 1987) 199 Cal. App. 3d 1496 (upholding fee based on a forty-five-year projection).
- Second, identify existing and appropriate future service levels for each needed public facility. In some cases, these may not be the same. For example, where it expects significant new development, a small town, instead of adding six-lane roads to maintain the current level of traffic flow, may prefer some increase in traffic congestion. Fees imposed on new development cannot be used to substantially improve service levels to existing residents. If a community wishes to improve the ability to provide certain services, funding must come from another source, such as the general fund or a voter-approved tax increase.
- Third, determine the additional facilities needed in each category to serve the pro-

jected future population at the appropriate level. (These first three steps may already have been completed as part of an existing capital improvement plan.) Then identify the cost of these projects.[3]

- Fourth, apportion these costs between the existing population and new residents and businesses in a manner proportional to their contribution of the need for the facility. Since fees cannot be used to upgrade existing deficiencies or to improve the level of service for existing homes or businesses, those costs should be subtracted from the total cost of future facilities.

As illustrated in *Homebuilders Association of Tulare/Kings Counties, Inc. v. City of Lemoore* (5th Dist. 2010) 185 Cal. App. 4th 554, a carefully drafted study goes a long way towards successful defense of a fee.

In addition to the four steps outlined above, a local agency has a new obligation that must be discharged either at the time a project is approved or at the time fees are imposed. Section 66020(d) now states that "each local agency shall provide to the project applicant a notice in writing at the time of the approval of the project or at the time of the imposition of the fees . . . a statement of the amount of the fees . . . and notification that the ninety-day approval period in which the applicant may protest has begun." It is the experience of the authors that this provision is routinely overlooked by local agencies leaving open the opportunity for a much later legal challenge. Sample language used by one California city to address this requirement can be found in the sidebar to the right. Moreover, once the fees have been collected, there is an ongoing duty to make periodic findings regarding the fees.

Where existing residents receive some incidental benefit as a consequence of constructing new facilities, the methodology is not necessarily invalid. For example, *Shapell Industries, Inc. v. Governing Board of the Milpitas Unified School District* (6th Dist. 1991) 1 Cal. App. 4th 218, supported the principle of requiring new development to pay for new science laboratories, libraries, gymnasiums, and administrative offices needed to support additional classrooms if these supporting facilities were necessary to maintain the existing level of service. As a result, all students, including those who live in older neighborhoods, will benefit from more modern structures.

This last step, when the fee is actually imposed on a specific project, requires the local agency to apportion the cost of the facility among different categories of uses on the basis of the contribution of each use to the need for the facility. Sometimes this is measured in appropriate service units for which average usage factors are readily available, such as gallons per day of treated water needed per household. The calculations are fairly straightforward where indus-

Transportation Impact Fee Breaks for Mixed-Use Projects

For certain qualifying residential mixed-use projects, the Legislature directs that a lower trip generation rate be used unless the local agency adopts special findings. § 66005.1.

Putting the Applicant on Notice

The following is the notice routinely given by the City of Rocklin in conjunction with various approvals. This notice is intended to trigger the statute of limitations to any legal challenge.

Notice to Applicant of Fees and Exaction Appeal Period

The conditions of project approval set forth herein include certain fees, dedication requirements, reservation requirements, and other exactions. Pursuant to section 66020(d), these conditions constitute written notice of the amount of such fees, and a description of the dedications, reservations, and other exactions.

The applicant is hereby notified that the 90-day protest period, commencing from the date of approval of the project, has begun. If the applicant fails to file a protest regarding any of the fees, dedication requirements, reservation requirements or other exaction contained in this notice, complying with all the requirements of section 66020, the applicant will be legally barred from later challenging such exactions.

The Use of Existing Facilities as the Benchmark

An alternative approach to using level of service standards is to measure the cost of existing facilities and to determine the pro rata value per capita. This approach was upheld in *Homebuilders Association of Tulare/Kings Counties, Inc. v. City of Lemoore* (5th Dist. 2010) 185 Cal. App. 4th 554. This value is then used as the standard for setting fees designed for similar facilities to serve new growth. Whether or not this value should be reduced by an amount equal to state and federal funding is often debated. No court case has addressed this particular issue, although the source of funding should not affect the calculation since external funding could be used to reduce the financial burden of facilities required to serve new growth.

Appendix C contains the introduction and road impact fee analysis the City of Davis approved as part of a 1998 update to its development impact fees. The report compares existing and projected population growth and discusses how and why the City relied upon the current replacement value of existing facilities as well as the allocation of those costs to existing service populations. The example also illustrates how credits for existing special funding sources like community facilities districts are accounted for in a road fee program.

Existing vs. Future Facilities

Most often, capital facilities fees are used to recover the estimated costs of future facilities. However, AB 1600 only requires the facilities be identified, NOT that the facilities in question be "future" facilities. Thus, where local governments have previously oversized facilities in anticipation of growth, the cost of that portion required to serve new development may be recoverable through fees. In many jurisdictions, this logically includes the cost of debt financing.

In applying fees for such projects as a new wastewater treatment plant, the concept of equivalent dwelling units (EDUs) is used to ensure that all users pay a fair and reasonable share of the total cost.

try standards are available; these include facilities for wastewater treatment capacity, water capacity, and, in certain cases, flood drainage. Other fees, such as those for roadway construction or police protection facilities, involve additional projections to equitably apportion the cost of the facilities to different kinds of projects.

Although spreading the cost of facilities among residential and commercial users may seem like adding apples and oranges, many fee studies have used the concept of an equivalent dwelling unit (EDU) to even out the differences. For example, assume the average wastewater treatment capacity needed for a single-family unit is 350 gallons per day. A condominium or apartment that may have fewer occupants per unit will have a lower average usage. If a typical commercial business consumes 150 gallons per day for every 1,000 square feet of building space, an appropriate EDU formula would be used to calculate the equivalent demand for commercial uses. When the total units of capacity (gallons per day) needed over the life of the study are known, the facility is designed to meet that capacity, and the total cost is then allocated to the projected new growth according to each project's share of total EDUs for that facility, or its proportionate demand.

At a minimum, the categories of users typically include commercial, industrial, and residential. Within each of these broad categories, a subcategory may be appropriate, depending on the facility being built. If the proposed fee is for road improvements and widening, for example, the portion of the cost attributable to a particular project would be measured by the amount of traffic it caused. Thus, separate subcategories for office commercial, restaurants and fast-food restaurants, and warehouse industrial may be necessary, because each one generates a different amount of traffic. This calculation needs to be tailored to the type of facility, kind of development, and the unique geographical and infrastructure circumstances of each jurisdiction.

Similarly, a subarea or zone that benefits from certain improvements in a proportion substantially different from citywide or agency-wide projects should have its own subcategory for that particular facility. A good example would be where one discrete undeveloped area of a city subject to major flooding requires extensive drainage improvements before construction can be authorized. In that case, the drainage design and fee structure should be unique to that area, similar to the benefit analysis used for assessment districts.

Findings Section 66001(d)

The local agency must make findings with respect to any portion of a fee remaining unexpended, whether committed or uncommitted in its account, beginning the fifth fiscal year following the first deposit and every five years thereafter. Those findings must address or identify:

- The purpose for which the fee is to be put
- The reasonable relationship between the fee and the purpose for which it is charged
- All sources and amounts of funding anticipated to complete financing in incomplete improvements
- The approximate dates on which the funding referred to above is expected to be deposited into the appropriate account or fund (§ 66001(d))

The above findings need only be made with respect to moneys in possession of the local agency, and need not be made with respect to letters of credit, bonds, or other instruments taken to secure payment of the fee at a future date. If the findings are not made, the agency is required to follow the steps for refunds. § 66001(d)(4).

Looking Back

A potential tool to evaluate the reasonableness of impact fees is the audit. Secion 66023. It serves as a non-litigation option to test the validity of existing fees. The cost of the audit is paid for by the person requesting it.

Refunds Sections 66001(e) and (f)

Unless the administrative costs exceed the amount of the refund, a local agency must refund, on a pro-rated basis, the unexpended or uncommitted revenue portion for which a need could not be demonstrated in the findings required by section 66001(d). Once the required funds have been collected to complete the financing of the improvements, the agency is required, within 180 days of determining that sufficient funds exist, to finance the improvements, to identify the approximate date by which construction will commence, or to refund the funds. The unexpended portion of the fees are to be refunded, including any accrued interest, to the current record owners. The duty to give a refund may be satisfied by direct payment, by providing a temporary suspension of fees, or any other reasonable means. § 66001(e).

If the administrative costs of refunding unexpended or uncommitted revenues exceed the amount to be refunded, the local agency—after a public hearing, notice of which has been published and posted in three prominent places within the area of the development project—may determine that the revenues shall be allocated to some other purpose for which fees are collected that serves the project on which the fee was originally imposed. § 66001(f).

Water and sewer fees and related capacity charges are not subject to the refund provisions. § 66013; *Capistrano Beach Water District v. Taj Development* (4th Dist. 1999) 72 Cal. App. 4th 524 (discussing legislative amendments in 1998 extending the right to a refund).

When Are Fees Established and Imposed for the Purposes of Section 66001?

Although the term "established" was not defined in section 66001, by general agreement a local government "establishes" a fee when a general obligation to pay that fee is created. Thus, a local agency "establishes" a fee when it adopts an ordinance or resolution requiring the fee. Section 66001 also does not define the word "imposed." However, the provisions regarding protesting and challenging of fees addresses the term. For the purposes of section 66020—the "pay under protest" statute—the "imposition" of fees or other exactions occurs "when they are imposed or levied on a specific development." § 66020(h). In addition, the Legislative Counsel issued an

Which Agency Is Responsible for Accounting?

The annual and five-year obligations appear to be the responsibility of the local agency maintaining the fund, not necessarily the local agency collecting the fee. Section 66006 states that the "local agency receiving the fee shall deposit it with the other fees," and the requirements under section 66001 apply to "moneys in possession of the local agency." This language suggests that the local agency maintaining the fund and building the capital facilities must carry out the necessary accounting under sections 66001 and 66006. This means that when two or more local agencies cooperate on imposing multijurisdictional fees, it is the agency building the improvements and maintaining the fund that will satisfy the accounting requirements.

opinion interpreting "imposed" to mean the actual application of the fee to a particular development in the course of the approval process. (Legislative Counsel of California Opinion No. 18851, July 20, 1988.)

The term "imposition of fees" as used in the "pay under protest" statute, section 66001, was interpreted by the appellate court to mean that it occurs at the time the local agency requires the fees, not at the time the fees must be paid. *Ponderosa Homes, Inc. v. City of San Ramon* (1st Dist. 1994) 23 Cal. App. 4th 1761.

As applied here, "imposition" refers to the creation of a condition or fee by authority of local government; it is not synonymous with the act of complying with that condition or fee. Just as creation is different from compliance, so is "imposition" of a fee different from payment thereof. *Id.* at 1770. See also the discussion of the *Ponderosa* case starting on page 138.

The court in *Garrick Development Company v. Hayward Unified School District* (1st Dist. 1992) 3 Cal. App. 4th 320, 335, addressed these two terms in the context of school fees. *Garrick* concluded that in section 66001(a) "establishing, increasing, or imposing" fees applies to an initial quasi-legislative adoption of development fees in relation to a "type" of development project, as opposed to the process of "imposing" the fees as part of an adjudicatory case-by-case action. As a consequence, no second stage findings under section 66001(b) are required for school fees authorized under Education Code section 17620 et seq.

Capital Improvement Plans Section 66002

Section 66002(a) permits, but does not require, any local agency that levies fees pursuant to section 66001 to adopt a capital improvement plan. If adopted pursuant to this statutory authority, the plan must indicate the approximate location, size, time of availability, and estimates of costs for all improvements or facilities to be financed with the fees. Moreover, section 66002(b) requires that the capital improvement plan be updated annually and adopted at a noticed public hearing pursuant to section 65090.[4] The notice that must be given to any cities or counties significantly affected by the capital improvement plan is described in section 66002(b).

Reimbursement Agreements Section 66003

When a local agency and a property owner or developer enter into a reimbursement agreement authorizing the property owner or developer to fund that portion of the cost of a public facility that exceeds the need for the facility attributable to and reasonably related to the project, sections 66001 and 66002 do not apply.

Accounting Section 66006

Section 66006 requires that the local agency responsible for collecting the fee deposit it with other fees for the specific improvement in a separate capital facilities fund. Except for temporary investments, the fees in this fund may not be commingled with other local agency revenues and must be expended solely for the purpose for which they were collected. Interest earned must be deposited into the appropriate accounts and *must be expended only for the purpose for which the fee was originally collected.* § 66006.

Within 180 days of the close of each fiscal year, the local agency is required to make available to the public, for each separate account or fund established pursuant to section 66006(a), specific information.

This information consists of:

- A brief description of the type of fee
- The amount of the fee
- The beginning and ending balance of the account or fund
- The amount of fees collected and interest earned
- An identification of the improvements for which fees were expended
- The amount of the expenditures for each improvement
- The total percentage of the cost of the public improvement that was funded with fees
- Approximate date by which construction of the improvements will commence
- The amount of refunds paid pursuant to section 66001 (§ 66006(b)(1))

If the fund is authorized to engage in interfund transfers, then the local agency must also describe the loan, the interest rate to be paid, and the date upon which the loan will be repaid. § 66006. The local agency is also required to review the information made available to the public at the next regularly scheduled public meeting no earlier than fifteen days after the information is made available to the public. Further, mailed notice is required at least fifteen days prior to the public meeting to all parties who have requested notice in writing. § 66006(b)(2).

Good accounting practices can track money from different funds and accounts and thereby avoid commingling. However, a potentially greater restriction on the use of funds comes from the requirement that the money only be spent "for the purpose for which the fee was collected." This restriction makes the range of facilities included in the category for each separate fee a critical factor. For example, a fee for "citywide roadways, bridges, and signalization improvements" is more flexible than discrete accounts for each class of facility. When the category is for only one road or intersection, fewer development projects will place a demand on the facility and thus contribute to the fee. Consequently, accumulating sufficient funds to pay the full cost of constructing the proposed infrastructure will also take longer.

How narrowly a fee category is described could limit interfund borrowing. This is when money from one fund is temporarily used to pay for facilities in another category that may be needed earlier, with repayment to the first fund made from subsequently collected fees. When describing the purpose of a fee, to clarify that it is authorized, some cities include interfund borrowing as an additional stated purpose. Although no judicial interpretation of AB 1600 specifically permits interfund borrowing, it has been indirectly recognized by the Legislature. In the authors' opinion, allowing such temporary borrowing is a reasonable interpretation, as long as the money is available when needed to build the targeted facilities and the findings on uncommitted fees required by section 66001(d) can be made (see discussion on page 105). While development agreements are generally exempt from the Mitigation Fee Act (66000(b)), the accounting and reporting requirements still apply to agreements entered into after January 1, 2004. See Government Code section 65865(e).

Interfund Borrowing

While not expressly recognized as a stated purpose in AB 1600, interfund borrowing is referenced as part of the required analysis for the annual review. § 66006. This practice, along with the use of credits, can substantially reduce the financial impact of a capital facilities program on new development. For example, a capital facilities for a new growth area may set forth a fee for facilities that may not be needed or constructed for 15 years. Without interfund borrowing, the initial developer is faced with not only paying the AB 1600 fee for all facilities, but may also be required to construct the backbone infrastructure as well as the first stage of sewer, water, parks, and drainage systems. With interfund borrowing and/or credits, the initial developer is still required to build the same infrastructure as before, but will be permitted to take a credit against those future facilities to be constructed in later phases for which the fee is currently collected.

This practice requires the local agency to develop accurate cost forecasting methodology and establish accounting practices and procedures that will work over the life of the fee program.

Timing Section 66007

Section 66007 specifies when fees can be collected; however it only applies to fees collected by a local agency for the construction of public improvements or facilities.

It does not apply to fees for code enforcement, inspection services, or to other fees for enforcement of local ordinances or state law. § 66007(d).

Section 66007(a) governs when local agencies may require payment of fees for residential development, and section 66007(b) covers the exceptions. Section 66007(a) states that, except as otherwise provided in subsection (b), any local agency that imposes any fees or charges on a residential development for the construction of public improvements or facilities shall not require the payment of those fees or charges until the date of final inspection, or the date the *certificate of occupancy* is issued, *whichever occurs first*. However, utility service fees may be collected at the time an application for service is received. "Final inspection" or "Certificate of Occupancy," as used in section 66007, has the same meaning as described in sections 305 and 307 of the Uniform Building Code, International Conference of Building Officials, 1985 edition. § 66007(e). If the residential development contains more than one dwelling, section 66007(a) gives the local agency several options to determine whether fees shall be paid on a prorated or lump-sum basis. (As a result of the economic downturn starting in 2007, local agencies can now defer collection of fees until the close of escrow. § 66007(g).)

It's All About Cash Flow
Local agencies are authorized to delay collection of the fee until close of escrow. Section 66007(g)

Section 66007(b) recognizes important exceptions, stating that the local agency may require payment of fees or charges at an earlier time than provided in subsection (a) if:

- The local agency determines that the fees or charges will be collected for public improvements or facilities for which an account has been established and funds appropriated and for which the local agency has adopted a proposed construction schedule or plan prior to final inspection or issuance of the Certificate of Occupancy; or
- Fees or charges are to reimburse the local agency for expenditures previously made.

Qualified Affordable Housing Projects are not subject to the early collection option. Section 66007(b)(2).

There are no words of limitation on how far back an agency can look for previous expenditures. The section says, "the fees or charges are to reimburse the local agency for expenditures previously made." With this in mind, there may be an opportunity to look back to previous expenditures when making the findings required for new fees. Practitioners should review, however, the holding in *Homebuilders Association of Tulare/Kings Counties, Inc. v. City of Lemoore* (5th Dist. 2010) 185 Cal. App. 4th 554 as a possible limitation on this effort.

Additionally, section 66007(b) defines "appropriated" as authorization by the governing body of the local agency for which the fee is collected to make expenditures and incur obligations for specific purposes. Methods for complying with the requirement that a proposed construction schedule or plan be adopted include, but are not limited to, (1) the adoption of the capital improvement plan described in section 66002, or (2) the submittal of a five-year plan for construction and rehabilitation of school facilities pursuant to section 17717.5(c) of the Education Code. § 66007(f).

If any fee or charge specified in section 66007(a) has not been fully paid prior to the issuance of a building permit to construct any portion of a residential development encumbered by the fee or charge, section 66007(c)(1) permits the issuing agency to require the property owner (or lessee in certain circumstances), as a condition of issuance, to execute a contract to pay the fee or charge, or applicable portion, prior to the date of final inspection or the date the occupancy permit is issued. If the fee or charge is prorated, the obligation under the contract shall be similarly prorated. Sections 66007(c)(2) and 66007(c)(3) establish a method by which the contract is recorded at the time escrow is opened for the sale of property for which the building permit was issued.

One court has held that section 66007 does not apply to school impact fees. In *RRLH, Inc. v. Saddleback Valley Unified School District* (4th Dist. 1990) 222 Cal. App. 3d 1602, the court ruled that school impact fees imposed through section 53080 (now Education Code § 17620), the Stirling legislation, take precedence over the general provisions in section 66007. Thus, the school fees had to be paid *before* the building permit was obtained.

Some analysts also think that the *RRLH, Inc.* ruling applies to the timing of fees for bridges and major thoroughfares specified in the Subdivision Map Act. § 66484. Under this interpretation, these fees could be collected earlier than section 66007 would otherwise allow.

Expenditure of Fees Solely for Purpose for Which the Exaction Was Imposed Section 66008

Fees may only be expended for the purpose for which the fee was collected. Fees may not be levied, collected, or imposed for general revenue purposes. Gov. Code, § 66008; see also § 66006.

Procedures for Adopting Various Fees

Sections 66016, 66017, 66018, 66018.5, and 66019 of the Government Code govern the procedures for adopting various fees pursuant to AB 1600. Local agencies must follow these procedures strictly, and developers and other entities subject to the fees should scrutinize the process closely to ensure that the proper procedures are followed. A sample time line is included in Appendix L.

Special Rules for Development Projects Section 66017

Public Hearing and Effective Date—Section 66017(a). Any development project fee which applies to filing, accepting, reviewing, approving, or issuing an application, permit, or entitlement to use, must comply with the notice and public hearing procedure specified in section 54986 (fees imposed by counties) or section 66016 (see page 16). The fee or charge, or increase in the fee or charge, shall be effective sixty days following final adoption.

Urgency Measure as Interim Authorization—Section 66017(b). The legislative body of a local agency, to protect the public health, welfare, and safety, may adopt an urgency measure as interim authorization for a fee or charge, or increase in a fee or charge, without following the procedures otherwise required. The interim authorization requires a four-fifths vote of the legislative body for adoption. In addition, findings must be made describing the current and immediate threat to the public health, welfare, and safety. The authorization has no force or effect 30 days after its adoption unless the legislative body, after notice of public hearing (pursuant to §§ 54986 or 66016), extends the interim authority for an additional thirty days. No more than two extensions may be granted, and any extension also requires a four-fifths vote of the legislative body. § 66017(b).

Declaration of Urgency

While the courts normally will not investigate the truth of the facts cited by a city council to support its declaration of urgency, "the mere declaration of the council…that the ordinance has passed for the immediate preservation of the public health is neither conclusive nor yet sufficient." *Crown Motors v. City of Redding* (3d Dist. 1991) 232 Cal. App. 3d 173. Courts have generally supported a broad definition of public health, safety, and welfare as being a legitimate exercise of a local government's police powers. However, it is important to include a statement of the facts supporting the mandatory findings that immediate adoption of the fee is necessary to protect the public. "Where the facts constituting the emergency or urgency are recited in the ordinance and are such that they may reasonably be held to constitute an emergency, the courts will not interfere, and they will not undertake to determine the truth of the recited facts." 45 Cal. Jur. 3d, Municipalities, § 199 at 315.

Public Hearings Section 66018

Applicability—Sections 66018–66018(c). Section 66018 contains public hearing requirements which apply only to adopting or increasing fees to which no specific requirement for statutory notice—other than section 54954.2 notice requirements for regular meetings of a local agency—applies. § 66018(c).

Public Hearing—Section 66018(a). Before an ordinance, resolution, or legislative action can be adopted, and before approving a new fee or an increase in an existing fee to which section 66018 applies, a local agency must hold a public hearing at which oral or written presentations can be made, as part of a regularly scheduled meeting. Notice of the time and place of the meeting, including a general explanation of the matter to be considered, shall be published in accordance with section 6062(a) requiring publication of notice twice—at least five days apart—ten days prior to the hearing. Note: this section does not permit adoption of the fees at a special meeting of the legislative body, but fees could be adopted at a continued regular meeting that is scheduled at the same time as a special meeting.

Costs—Section 66018(b). Any costs a local agency incurs to conduct a hearing required by section 66018(a) may be recovered as part of the fees which were the subject of the hearing. Education Code section 17620(a)(5) also allows school facilities fees to be spent for the cost of conducting a study to satisfy AB 1600.

General Procedures for New Fees and Increases in Existing Fees

Applicability—Section 66016, 66019. Section 66016 provides procedures for establishing new fees or increasing existing fees, which apply only to the following:

- Section 57004 (fees imposed by conducting authorities pursuant to the Cortese-Knox Act)
- Section 65104 (fees imposed by local legislative bodies to support the work of planning agencies)
- Section 65456 (fees imposed by local agencies for specific plans)
- Section 65863.7 (fees incurred by local agencies in association with mobile home park conversions)
- Section 65909.5 (fees imposed by local agencies for use permits, zone variances, and zone changes)
- Section 66013 (fees imposed by local agencies for water and sewer connection fees)
- Section 66014 (fees imposed by local agencies for zoning and permit fees, fees associated with implementing the Cortese-Knox Act, and fees associated with implementing the Subdivision Map Act)
- Section 66451.2 (fees imposed by local agencies to process parcel maps, tentative subdivision maps, and final subdivision maps)
- Health and Safety Code section 17951 (fees imposed by local agencies for permits, certificates, and other forms of documents associated with the building codes)
- Health and Safety Code section 19132.3 (fees for keeping copies of building plans)
- Health and Safety Code section 19852 (fees for building permits)
- Public Resources Code section 41901 (fees for preparing and implementing a countywide integrated waste management plan)

- Public Utilities Code section 21671.5 (fees imposed by airport land use commissions)

  § 66016(d)

Section 66019 (discussed below) governs impact fees not covered by Section 66016.

Public Meeting and Notice—Section 66016(a), 66019. Prior to levying a new fee or service charge, or prior to approving an increase in an existing fee or service charge, a local agency shall hold *at least one public meeting* at which oral or written presentations can be made as part of a regularly scheduled meeting.

Any interested party who files a written request with the local agency for a mailed notice of the meeting on new or increased fees or service charges, shall be sent a notice of the time and place of the meeting, including a general explanation of the matter to be considered and a statement that the data required by section 66016 or 66019 is available at least fourteen days prior to the meeting. Unless a renewal request is filed, a written request for a mailed notice is valid for one year from the date filed. Note: regularly scheduled meetings are also subject to the notice requirements in section 54954.2 (the Brown Act).

Public Report—Section 66016(a). The public agency must make available to the public the cost, or estimated cost, required to provide the service for which the fee or service charge is levied, and the revenue sources anticipated to provide this service, including general fund revenues, at least ten days prior to the regularly scheduled meeting.

Cannot Exceed Estimated Amount Required to Provide Service—Section 66016(a). Unless voters have approved new fees as prescribed in section 66013 (water and sewer connection fees) or section 66014 (zoning and permit fees), no local agency shall levy a new fee or service charge, or increase an existing fee or service charge, in an amount which exceeds the estimated amount required to provide the service. (See discussion below.) Any excess revenue resulting from the fees or service charges shall be used to reduce the fee or charge creating the excess. In *County of Orange v. Barratt American, Inc.* (4th Dist. 2007) 150 Cal. App. 4th 420, the court held that "[u]sing the surplus fee revenue to cover the reasonable and necessary costs of the services rather than merely lowering the fees until the surplus is dissipated has the effect of 'reducing' the future fees." In other words, as long as the costs are reasonable and necessary, a local agency may apply the surplus to pay for costs that the fee would normally pay for, instead of simply reducing the amount of the fee charged to the developer or applicant.

Ordinance or Resolution Necessary—Section 66016(b). A local agency may only levy a new fee or service charge, or approve an increase in an existing fee or service charge, by ordinance or resolution. Ordinarily, if local government takes action by ordinance, any amendment to that action must also be by ordinance, following the equal dignities doctrine. For example, rezoning of use districts or changes of uses and restrictions within a district can be accomplished only through an amendment of a zoning ordinance, and the amendment must be made in the same mode as its original enactment. *City of Sausalito v. County of Marin* (1st Dist. 1970) 12 Cal. App. 3d 550. With respect to fee amendments, the agency may use a resolution to amend the fee sched-

Because the statutory language speaks in terms of new fees or increased existing fees, fee reduction would apparently not require any findings or determinations.

ule previously set by ordinance. *Richmond v. Shasta Community Services District* (2004) 32 Cal. 4th 409 ("*SCSD*").

In *SCSD*, the issue was whether a water district's increase of its two component water connection fee violated Proposition 218's voter approval requirement. The district adopted an ordinance that established a capacity fee and a fire suppression fee for new water service connections. Later, the district adopted a resolution that amended the ordinance. Several owners within the district challenged the resolution, alleging that: (1) the resolution imposed an assessment with the meaning of Article XIIID, but the district failed to satisfy the constitutional requirements (*i.e.*, voter approval) for imposing an assessment; (2) the fire suppression fee was a fee or charge within the meaning of Article XIIID, and it violated the prohibition against fees or charges for general governmental services; and (3) the original ordinance could only be amended by another ordinance, not a mere resolution.

The California Supreme Court reversed, holding that both the capacity and fire suppression fees imposed as a condition of making a new connection to a water system are not "property assessments" or "property-related fees" subject to the voter approval requirements of Article XIIID. With respect to the use of a resolution to amend the ordinance, the court held:

> Government Code section 66016, part of the Mitigation Fee Act (Gov. Code, § 66000 et seq.), provides in subdivision (b): "Any action by a local agency to levy a new fee or service charge or to approve an increase in an existing fee or service charge shall be taken only by ordinance or resolution." We agree with the Court of Appeal that this provision authorizes the District to use a resolution to increase existing connection fees, and that this authorization applies even when the fees were initially imposed by ordinance.

CEQA Review. The adoption or increase of a fee is a "project" as defined by the California Environmental Quality Act, Public Resources Code sections 21000 et seq. (CEQA). The local agency must either rely upon an existing environmental document or prepare new CEQA documentation. In some circumstances, a fee not tied to a specific improvement may be viewed as not a "project." See *Kaufman and Broad-South Bay, Inc. v. Morgan Hill Unified School District* (6th Dist. 1992) 9 Cal. App. 4th 464. However, if the local agency elects to not conduct CEQA review, then the effectiveness of the fee as a form of CEQA mitigation can be more readily challenged in the context of individual project approvals. *California Native Plant Society v. County of El Dorado* (3d Dist. 2009) 170 Cal. App. 4th 1026.

Recovery of Costs—Section 66016(c). Any costs a local agency incurs to conduct a meeting required by section 66016(a) may be recovered from the fees charged for services which were the subject of the meeting.

Remedy for Fees with Both Valid and Invalid Purposes. The court held in *County Sanitation District No. 2 of Los Angeles County v. County of Kern* (4th Dist. 2005) 127 Cal. App. 4th 1544 that the appropriate relief when a fee is imposed for both valid and invalid purposes is to uphold the fee to the extent that the funds generated are otherwise severable from invalid ones.

Recovering the Cost of Planning and Fee Studies

Although the use of development fees is generally limited to capital facilities (see section 65913.8), a number of specific statutory provisions authorize fees to recover the cost of various planning and fee studies:

- Fees for conducting a public hearing on fee adoption may be recovered as part of the fee. § 66018(b).
- Fees for preparing an AB 1600 study for school fees may be charged. Education Code § 17620(a)(5). Three percent of the fees collected may also be used for reimbursement of administrative costs incurred in collecting school fees.
- Fees for preparing, adopting, and administering a specific plan can be required of any applicant who requests an approval which is required to be consistent with the specific plan. If the plan is prepared at the request of an applicant, the local agency can require an initial deposit for any costs incurred. § 65456(a).
- Fees for preparing a negative declaration or environmental impact report as required by the California Environmental Quality Act may be charged. Public Resources Code § 21089(a).

Fees for Specific Purposes

Fees for Projects Damaged by Declared Natural Disaster Section 66011

Section 66011 prohibits the application of fees to the reconstruction of any residential, commercial, or industrial development project damaged or destroyed as a result of a natural disaster, as declared by the governor. However, complete or partial reconstruction of real property, *which is not substantially equivalent to the damaged or destroyed property*, will be considered new construction, and only that portion that exceeds substantially equivalent construction may be assessed a fee. The term "substantially equivalent," as used in section 66011, has the same meaning as the term in section 70(c) of the Revenue and Taxation Code.

Water or Sewer Connection Fees Section 66013

Section 66013 applies specifically to water and sewer connection fees. Its three important provisions are described below.

Reasonable Cost or Two-Thirds Vote Required—Section 66013(a). When a local agency imposes fees for water or sewer connections, or imposes capacity charges, the fees or charges shall not exceed the estimated reasonable cost of providing the service, unless the fee is approved by a two-thirds vote of those electors voting on the issue.

Definitions—Section 66013(b)

- "Sewer connection" is the connection of a building to a public sewer system.
- "Water connection" is the connection of a building to a public water system, as defined in section 116275 of the Health and Safety Code.
- "Capacity charges" are charges for existing public facilities or charges for new public facilities to be constructed in the future which benefit the person or property being charged. See *N.T. Hill Inc. v. City of Fresno* (5th Dist. 1999) 72 Cal. App. 4th 977, 983 (Water fees constitute "capacity charges" because they were to be used to pay "for facilities in existence" or "for new facilities to be constructed in the future that are of benefit to the person or property being charged"). In 2007, the definition of capacity charge was expanded to include supply or capacity contracts for rights, entitlements, or property interests involving capital expenses of local public facilities. (See SB 699 (Stats. 2007, Ch. 94).)
- "Local agency" refers to a local agency as defined in section 66000 (see page 99).
- "Fee" means a fee for the physical facilities necessary to make a water or sewer connection not exceeding estimated reasonable cost of labor and materials for installation of these facilities.

Payments of Charges—Section 66013(c). Local agencies must deposit charges in a separate capital facilities fund along with other charges received. The local agency must also account for the funds in a manner that avoids commingling of the fund with other moneys, except for investments. The charges also must only be expended for the pur-

Impact Fees as CEQA Mitigation: A Primer

Properly administered impact fee programs can operate to streamline CEQA review of later development projects. At the same time, impact fee programs that are not implemented in accordance with the original expectations or that are founded upon unrealistic assumptions may offer the lead agency and affected applicant little or no real legal relief, and may be a trap for the unwary.

Impact fees are controlled by Government Code sections 66000–66022. Fees may be imposed based upon a comprehensive impact fee program (*Blue Jeans Equities West v. City and County of San Francisco* (1st Dist. 1992) 3 Cal. App. 4th 164) or as calculated on an ad hoc basis (*Erlich v. City of Culver City* (1996) 12 Cal. 4th 854). The methodology (broad-based vs. ad hoc) determines which findings must be adopted by the imposing agency. *Loyola Marymount University v. Los Angeles Unified School District* (2nd Dist. 1996) 45 Cal.App.4th 1256. Generally, impact fees of broad application receive less judicial scrutiny. *Ehrlich v. City of Culver City, supra* at p. 875.

CEQA requires lead agencies to mitigate the impacts associated with project approvals. For a developer, it is far simpler to pay an impact fee than it is to design, engineer, and construct an offsite improvement. From this perspective, impact fees are a cost-effective means by which project impacts can be properly mitigated. Moreover, impacts are considered mitigated, even when the fee funded facility is constructed after the project that contributes to the need for the facility. *Save Our Peninsula Committee v. Monterey County Board of Supervisors* (6th Dist. 2001) 87 Cal. App. 4th 99. In this context, paying impact fees could well be the lesser of two evils. However, recent cases illustrate that simply paying the local impact fee does not constitute full absolution of CEQA responsibilities in every instance.

In *Napa Citizens for Honest Government v. Board of Supervisors* (1st Dist. 2001) 91 Cal. App. 4th 342, the court of appeal found that a pre-existing fee program failed to provide the "mitigation cover" to avoid a determination that a project impact may be cumulatively significant. The county previously adopted a Napa Airport traffic fee, and collected over $2 million pursuant to this fee. However, the improvements necessary to maintain an adequate circulation totaled over $70 million, and although the current project was obligated to pay its fair share of fees, the evidence showed that the necessary improvements would never be funded. As a result, there could be no assumption that cumulative impacts would be mitigated simply by paying the adopted fee.

A different result was reached in *Save Our Peninsula Committee v. Monterey County Board of Supervisors, supra*. In this case, the petitioners challenged a development project approval located in scenic Carmel Valley. One of the legal challenges was to the payment of traffic impact fees as a form of mitigation. The project approval followed the 1995 enactment of a Carmel Valley road impact fee, which called for funding of improvements consistent with the Carmel Valley Master Plan. The fee was set at $16,000 per unit, with annual increases tied to the construction cost index. The mitigation program called for regular monitoring of traffic conditions to determine if specified thresholds were met, which in turn would call for construction of specified improvements. The appellate court characterized the fee program as a "pay-as-you-go" program. The project also contributed to Highway 1 congestion improvements, based upon a mitigation measure that called for developer pro-rata contribution to these improvements. The appellate court found sufficient evidence upon which it could conclude that a reasonable commitment to mitigation was demonstrated. In these circumstances, the use of previously adopted fees, as well as ad-hoc fees imposed as part of the project approval, constituted effective mitigation.

Two later cases have delineated the outer limits of the ability to use fee programs as mitigation for traffic impacts. In *Anderson First Coalition v. City of Anderson* (3d Dist. 2005) 130 Cal. App. 4th 1173, the appellate court held that paying a "fair-share fee" is permissible as effective mitigation if the fees are "part of a reasonable plan of actual mitigation that the relevant agency commits itself to implementing." Project opponents challenged the use of an impact fee to mitigate cumulative traffic effects in the EIR for a proposed Wal-Mart Supercenter. The court held that a fee program would be permissible as long the mitigation measure specified the amount of the fee and the percentage of future improvements for which this developer would be responsible. The court also emphasized that the fees must be a reasonable, enforceable part of an improvement plan that will actually mitigate the cumulative effects. But *Endangered Habitats League, Inc. v. County of Orange* (4th Dist. 2005) 131 Cal. App. 4th 777 demonstrates how an incomplete fee program fails to serve as CEQA mitigation. Opponents challenged a fee program to fund road improvements needed due to a proposed residential development. The appellate court held that there was no evidence of a firm and certain plan for improvements because the record showed only the existence of a fee program as well as a planned study to identify needed improvements. The court said, "Since there is no evidence here of what improvements will be funded by the fee programs . . . we cannot find the mitigated project is consistent with the general plan," and held that the fee program was not adequate mitigation under CEQA.

What's the key? In order to count on a previously adopted fee program, or project imposed "fair share" fees, the lead agency must have reasonable evidence in the record to find that the program is sufficiently

pose that the charges were collected. Moreover, all interest income earned from the investment of moneys in the capital facilities fund shall be deposited in that fund.

Accounting for Capital Facility Funds—Section 66013(d). For funds established pursuant to section 66013(c), local agencies must make the following information, for the fiscal year, available to the public within 180 days after the last day of each fiscal year.

- A description of charges deposited
- The beginning and end balance, including interest earned from investment
- The amount of charges collected in that fiscal year
- An identification of the following:
  - Each improvement on which charges were expended and the amount of the expenditure for each improvement funded with those charges if more than one source of funding was used
  - Each public improvement on which charges were expended that was completed during the fiscal year
  - Each public improvement that is anticipated to be undertaken in the following fiscal year

The local agency must also provide a description of each interfund transfer or loan made from the capital facility fund. When there has been an interfund transfer the agency must identify the public improvements which the transferred moneys are, or will be, expended on, the date on which the loan will be repaid, and the rate of interest that the fund will receive on the loan. Accounting requirements apply to capacity charges. *N.T. Hill Inc. v. City of Fresno* (5th Dist. 1999) 72 Cal. App. 4th 977, 984.

Annual Report—Section 66013(e). This section allows for all the accounting information required by section 66013(d) to be included in the local agency's annual report.

Exceptions to Sections 66013(c) and (d) Requirements. Monies received to construct public facilities pursuant to a contract between a local agency and a person or entity, including but not limited to a reimbursement agreement pursuant to section 66006, are not required to comply with sections 66013(c) and (d).

Charges used to pay existing debt service, or that are subject to a contract with a trustee for bondholders, that requires a different accounting of the charges, or charges that are used to reimburse the local agency or to reimburse a person or entity who advanced funds under a reimbursement agreement or contract for facilities in existence at the time the charges are collected, need not comply with sections 66013(c) and (d).

Additionally, any charges collected on or before December 31, 1998 are not required to comply with sections 66013(c) and (d).

Finally, it is also important to note that sections 66013(c) and (d) only apply to capacity charges levied pursuant to this section. § 66013(i).

In *Richmond v. Shasta CSD* (2004) 32 Cal. 4th 409, landowners challenged the actions of the Shasta CSD in establishing fees for new connections. The district operates a water system for its users as well as a volunteer fire department, and in 1994 it adopted an ordinance which established a fee for new water connections. The connection fee consisted of a capacity charge for future water improvements and a fire suppression charge. The money from these fees was used for capital improvements and purchasing water and fire equipment. In 1997, after Proposition 218 was passed, the district passed a resolution amending the ordinance and increasing the capacity charge. Landowners within the district challenged the resolution on three grounds: (1) the resolution was an assessment under Article XIIID and the district had not satisfied the applicable constitutional requirements; (2) the fire suppression fee was a fee and violated Article XIIID's prohibition against fees or charge for general governmental services; and (3) the original ordinance could only be amended by an ordinance.

The court held that because the capacity charge was not imposed on identifiable parcels, but instead on individuals who request a new water connection, the charge is not an assessment within the meaning of Article XIIID and is not subject to the notice and vote requirements. The court also held that the fire suppression charge was not imposed as an incident of property ownership, but instead was done at the request of the property owner as part of a new connection. Since it is not a property-related fee or charge under Article XIIID, it is not subject to Proposition 218's requirements. Finally, the court held that Government Code section 66016 gave the district the authority to amend an ordinance by resolution.

Judicial Challenges—Section 66013(e). Any judicial action or proceeding to attack, review, set aside, void, or annul the ordinance, resolution, or motion imposing a fee or capacity charge subject to this section shall be brought pursuant to section 66022, the "pay-under-protest" statute (see chapter 7). Fees paid on or before December 31, 1998 are not required to comply with § 66013(c) and (d) (§ 66013(f)(3)) and are not subject to the refund provisions that would otherwise apply to development fees.

Special Rules—Section 66013(h). Section 66013(h) provides that fees and charges subject to this section are not subject to the provisions of Chapter 5 (commencing with section 66000), but are subject to sections 66016, 66022, and 66023.

certain and can be implemented in its entirety over time. "We do not believe, however, that CEQA requires that the EIR set forth a time-specific schedule for the County to complete specified road improvements. All that is required by CEQA is that there be a reasonable plan for mitigation." *Save Our Peninsula Committee v. Monterey County Board of Supervisors, supra* at p. 139. Where improvements call for significant state or federal funding and that funding is in doubt, then assumed mitigation of cumulative impacts is doubtful and reversal is likely.

In 2006, the discussion of impact fees and CEQA mitigation was visited by the California Supreme Court in *City of Marina v. Board of Trustees of California State University* (2006) 39 Cal. 4th 341. There, the court addressed the refusal of a state university campus to pay funds toward the construction of offsite improvements. The campus claimed that it lacked the legal authority to pay those fees. The California Supreme Court disagreed, and introduced into the fee lexicon the phrase "voluntary mitigation," inviting significant speculation as to where the duty to mitigate (and in appropriate circumstances, pay impact fees) ends.

In 2009, the appellate court cast doubt over the effectiveness of impact fees as a mitigation measure if the fees were adopted without accompanying CEQA review. *California Native Plant Society v. County of El Dorado* (3d Dist. 2009) 170 Cal. App. 4th 1026.

Road Usage Fees. A road usage fee, imposed upon permittees receiving biosolids, was banned by Vehicle Code section 9400.8 which provides in part:

> No local agency may impose a tax, permit fee, or other charge for the privilege of using its streets or highways, other than a permit fee for extra legal loads after December 31, 1990, unless the local agency has imposed the fee prior to June 1, 1989.

This limitation was not trumped by the Mitigation Fee Act, as Kern County's fee was largely based upon road usage. To the extent that the fee was imposed for valid purposes, imposition of a portion of the fee may be valid. *County Sanitation District No. 2 of Los Angeles County v. County of Kern* (5th Dist. 2005) 127 Cal. App. 4th 1544.

Local Agency Zoning and Permit Fees Section 66014

Section 66014 governs fees for the cost of processing land use decisions and permits. Its important provisions are summarized below:

Applicable Processing Fees—Section 66014(a). Section 66014 applies when a local agency charges fees for any of the following:

Section 66014—

- Zoning Variances and Changes/Use Permits
- Building Permits and Inspections
- LAFCO Petitions/Cortese-Knox
- Map Processing
- Planning Services

- Zoning variances, zoning changes, and use permits
- Building inspections
- Building permits
- Filing and processing applications in petitions filed with local agency formation commissions, or when conducting preliminary proceedings or proceedings under the Cortese-Knox Local Government Reorganization Act of 1985, Division 3 (commencing with § 56000) of Title 5
- Processing of maps under provisions of the Subdivision Map Act, Division 2 (commencing with § 66410) of Title 7
- Planning services under the authority of Chapter 3 (commencing with § 65100) of Division 1 of Title 7, or under any other authority

Reasonable Fee or Two-Thirds Vote Required—Section 66014(a). Any fees charged for the services listed above (zoning and permit fees) must not exceed the estimated reasonable cost of providing the service for which the fee is charged, unless the issue has been submitted to the electors and approved by two-thirds of those voting on the issue.

California's Attorney General has expressed doubt as to the use of the Uniform Building Code Valuation Tables for calculating fees. In 76 Ops. Cal. Atty. Gen. 4 (1993), the attorney general rendered the following opinion:

- A local agency is prohibited from charging building permit and similar fees which exceed the estimated reasonable costs of providing the services rendered unless the amounts of the fees are approved by the electorate.
- A local agency may not charge building permit and similar fees based upon the Uniform Building Code Valuation Tables which are in excess of the estimated reasonable costs of providing the services rendered unless the amounts of the fees are approved by the electorate.
- If a local agency charges building permit and similar fees based upon the Uniform Building Code Valuation Tables without supporting evidence regarding the relationship between the fees and the services rendered, these fees are invalid to the extent they exceed the reasonable costs of providing the services rendered.

Relying upon section 66014, the attorney general opined that this statute exclusively established the rules applicable to calculating the fee. The opinion notes that there is no indication that the actual costs of providing the service are factors upon which the chart's publisher bases the fee calculations and, as a private publication, the task does not carry with it a presumption of reasonableness. Finally, the opinion concludes that the Department of Housing and Community Development (HCD) had not adopted the tables in conjunction with the adoption of the uniform codes as provided for in Health and Safety Code sections 17910–17995.5. As a consequence, there is no conflict between the building standards in the uniform codes and the procedural requirements of section 66016.

Costs of Preparation and Revision of Plans. Cities and counties may now include within processing fees an amount reflecting the reasonable costs necessary to prepare and revise plans and policies the city or county is required to adopt before it can make necessary findings. Gov. Code, § 66014(b). This should embrace the full range of amendments to land use documents triggered by an application.

Judicial Challenge—Section 66014(c). Any judicial action or proceeding to attack, review, set aside, void, or annul the ordinance, resolution, or motion authorizing the local agency zoning and permit fees (§ 66014) must be brought pursuant to section 66022. (See chapter 7.) A court held that building permit fees are not "development fees" under the Mitigation Fee Act (Gov. Code, §§ 66000–66025), and thus the remedy for excessive permit fees is limited to a reduction of future fees through a challenge to the enacting resolution. Gov. Code, § 66022. Section 66014(a) permits local agencies to impose building inspection and permit fees not in excess of the estimated reasonable cost of providing the service for which the fee is charged. *Barratt American, Inc. v. City of Rancho Cucamonga* (2005) 37 Cal. 4th 685.

Fees for Aerial Tramways Section 66012

Cities and counties may levy any fee or charge in connection with the operation of an aerial tramway within its jurisdiction. § 66012(a). If anyone disputes whether the fee or charge levied is reasonable, the auditor or the fiscal officer of the local entity, upon request by the legislative body of the local agency, must conduct a study to determine whether the fee or charge is reasonable. § 66012(b).

William A. Abbott is a partner in the Sacramento, California law firm, Abbott & Kindermann, LLP, where he practices land use, environmental, municipal, and real estate law, representing both public and private clients. He was assisted by Cori Badgley, an associate in the firm.

CHAPTER SIX

School Facilities

By William W. Abbott

The methods by which developers are required to participate in the financing and development of school facilities is as controversial a subject as any in the field of land development. While historically the State of California was responsible financially for the construction of public schools, various budgetary limitations have triggered a transfer of a significant share of the financing obligation to local government—which, in turn, has passed on that responsibility to developers and new home buyers. The state's failure to act effectively in the matter of school funding has received longstanding judicial recognition. *Serrano v. Priest* (1971) 5 Cal. 3d 584; *Candid Enterprises, Inc. v. Grossmont Union High School District* (1985) 39 Cal. 3d 878. Coupled with the recession of the early 1990s, the state's non-responsiveness created an increasing burden on local governments, developers, and home buyers.

The methods by which developers are required to participate in the financing and development of school facilities is as controversial a subject as any in the field of land development.

To remedy this situation, in 1998 the California Legislature passed SB 50, Stats. 1998, Ch. 407, which included Proposition 1A, the largest school construction bond measure in California history. The voters approved Proposition 1A on November 3, 1998, thereby putting into motion $9.2 billion for local and state school construction. Additionally, SB 50, in conjunction with the approval of Proposition 1A, made significant revisions to developer fees and mitigation procedures. The net effect is to remove cities and counties from the school mitigation fee business.

This chapter addresses three fundamental sources of legal authority historically relied on by municipalities and school districts to mitigate the impact of development on public schools. The first of these is the police power, used in conjunction with legislative enactments (California Constitution art. XI, § 7). This option was in use extensively, but has now been curtailed by SB 50 and the approval of Proposition 1A. The second source of legal authority, which has moved into the forefront with the passage of SB 50 and Proposition 1A,[1] is Stirling fees[2] (§ 65995 and Education Code § 17620). The third legal option is the School Facilities Act (§§ 65970–65981).[3] Reservations of school sites permitted by the Subdivision Map Act (§ 66410 et seq.) are discussed in chapter 4. Neither Mello-Roos district financing (another important source of school funding) nor state funding are addressed in this book except to the extent either method directly affects exactions required of developers.

The three fundamental sources of legal authority historically relied on by municipalities and school districts to mitigate the impact of development on public schools are the police power, Stirling fees, and the School Facilities Act.

The Police Power Exactions in Conjunction with Legislative Approvals

Detailed information on School Facility Planning can be found in *California School Facility Planning*, published by Solano Press.

Until the passage of SB 50 and Proposition 1A, the most significant of the three listed powers had been the police power. Local governments and school districts shifted attention to the police power in response to several appellate court decisions. These cases concluded that monetary caps and other limitations created by the Stirling fees and School Facilities Act simply did not apply to exactions imposed in conjunction with legislative approvals. *Murrieta Valley Unified School District v. County of Riverside* (4th Dist. 1991) 228 Cal. App. 3d 1212 review denied (1991); *William S. Hart Union High School District v. Regional Planning Commission of the County of Los Angeles* (2d Dist. 1991) 226 Cal. App. 3d 1612; *Mira Development Corporation v. City of San Diego* (4th Dist. 1989) 205 Cal. App. 3d 1201 review denied (1989). In other words, the police power operated unfettered by the statutory scheme when local legislative action was involved.

In 1992, Assembly Constitutional Amendment 6 (ACA 6) attempted to amend the State Constitution. Had it passed, it would have overruled *Murrieta, Hart,* and *Mira*, however, its failure at the state ballot box left the holdings of the trilogy intact. Nevertheless, six years later in November 1998, SB 50 was passed, and Proposition 1A was approved by the voters, effectively overturning the holdings of *Murrieta, Hart, and Mira*, bringing an end to the trilogy's exception for legislative acts.

With the passage of SB 50 and Proposition 1A, changes were enacted that revised both developer fees and mitigation measures for school facilities. Proposition 1A amended section 65995[4] to not allow any fees for school facilities other than those allowed under the Stirling fee legislation (as amended by SB 50) for both adjudicative as well as legislative approvals. § 65995(a). This amendment effectively abrogated the holdings of *Murrieta, Hart, and Mira* (discussed, *infra*), thereby making the Stirling fee legislation the controlling law for both legislative and adjudicatory decisions.

Stirling Fees

The Stirling fee revisions (SB 50) do not apply the same requirements to all contracts or conditions of approval entered into or applied to projects prior to the operative date of Proposition 1A (November 4, 1998). Therefore, this chapter will initially discuss what law applies to contracts and conditions of approval in place prior to the effective date of Proposition 1A, and then will look at both the post-SB 50 analysis and the pre-SB 50 analysis, each being applicable in certain circumstances under the new law. Additionally, this chapter will examine the Stirling fee legislation as a whole.

The Continuing but Limited Role for *Murrieta, Hart,* and *Mira*

The threshold question raised by SB 50 and Proposition 1A is, in what circumstances does the new law apply to contracts or conditions of approval concerning school facilities for projects approved prior to November 4, 1998? The legislature addressed this question in section 65995(c).

SB 50 initially divides contracts into two categories. The first includes contracts entered into on or before January 1, 1987, between *subdividers or contractors* and either a school district, city, county, or city and county concerning *residential construction* (unless otherwise indicated contracts and conditions relate to fees, charges, or dedications for the construction of school facilities). A contract meeting these criteria is not subject to section 65995 or Education Code section 17620 and is controlled by the terms of the contract. § 65995(c)(1). Therefore, the issue of school fees would be controlled by the terms of the contract and any other applicable law.

The second category of contracts are those entered into after January 1, 1987 and before November 4, 1998. The contract must be between a person and either a school district, city, county, or city and county concerning construction (no reference to residential). Contracts meeting these criteria are not affected by SB 50 and are controlled by the law as it existed prior to the passage of SB 50 and Proposition 1A (discussed starting on pages 127). § 65995(c)(2). Accordingly, a pre-SB 50 analysis would control contracts meeting these criteria.

SB 50 also affects construction not subject to a contract. If the construction does not meet the requirements of section 65995(c)(2), and the conditions were imposed concerning school facilities in conjunction with a legislative act after January 1, 1987 and before November 4, 1998, the conditions must be complied with until January 1, 2000. After January 1, 2000, the construction, regardless of what the original condition was, cannot be subjected to any fees, charges, or dedication in excess of those allowed under the Stirling fees legislation as amended by SB 50 in sections 65995(b)(1), 65995(b)(2), 65995.5, or 65995.7. § 65995(c)(3).

All construction not subject to a contract described in section 65995(c)(2) or section 65995(c)(3) may never be subject to any fees, charges, dedications, or other requirements concerning school facilities in excess of those amounts specified in sections 65995(b)(1) and 65995(b)(2), if two requirements are satisfied. The two requirements are: (1) the construction must have had a tentative map, development permit, or conditional use permit approved prior to November 4, 1998; and (2) a building permit must have been issued before January 1, 2000. § 65995(c)(4).

Section 65995(c)

Although section 65995(c) discusses the application of SB 50 to both contracts and conditions of approval, it focuses on those contracts either entered into prior to November 4, 1998 (the effective date of SB 50), or related to approvals prior to that date. §§ 65995(c)(1), 65995(c)(2), and 65995(c)(4). This leaves open the question of whether a development agreement, providing for school fees and entered into subsequent to November 4, 1998 is allowed under SB 50. While this question has not yet been answered, an agreement freely entered into by the developer does not seem to violate the restriction found in section 65995(a) which states that "a fee, charge, dedication, or other requirement... may not be levied or imposed...." Further, it seems to follow that a developer would be free to waive any protection granted SB 50; however, the question would remain as to the ability of a third party, such as a successor in interest, to challenge the enforceability of such an agreement.

Stirling Analysis/Post-SB 50

With the passage of SB 50 and the approval of Proposition 1A in November 1998, *Murrieta, Hart, and Mira* no longer control approvals of legislative acts. The 1998 amendments require public agencies to observe the limits of the Stirling legislation regardless of whether they are acting in a legislative or adjudicative capacity. The result is that the post SB 50 Stirling fee analysis is dictated by section 65995 et seq. and Education Code section 17620 et seq. as amended by SB 50. The Stirling fee legislation limits the amount of fees, charges, dedications, or other requirements that can be imposed for school impacts, regardless if made in connection with a legislative act.

Section 65995 limits the fees for residential construction to $1.93 per square foot of assessable space and $0.31 per square foot of chargeable covered and enclosed space for commercial or industrial construction[5] (discussed in detail, infra). However, exceptions do exist allowing school districts to charge fees exceeding these amounts.

Under sections 65995.5 and 65995.7, school districts may impose fees in excess of the limits set forth in section 65995(b). School districts can increase developer fees to fund the fifty percent matching requirement for new school construction if they meet certain conditions regarding capacity problems and local bonding efforts. Districts may also increase the fees to cover 100 percent of a school project if there are no state funds available for new school construction. If a district subsequently receives funding from the state, the district may reimburse the parties that originally paid the fee. These exceptions are discussed in greater detail later in this chapter.

Proposition 1D

The passage of Proposition 1D by the voters in November 2006 had the effect of extending the preemptive quality of the *Stirling* fee provisions. Thus the *Murrieta, Hart*, and *Mira* case holdings remain in legislative limbo.

Between November 4, 1998, and the primary election of 2012, cities and counties may not require any fees for school construction in excess of those allowed under the Stirling fee legislation section 65995 as a condition of project approval. However, if in the year 2012 or thereafter, a statewide school bond measure is rejected, cities and counties can assess an increased fee up until such time as a statewide bond measure for school facilities is passed by the voters. § 65997. However, the amount of the increased fee is limited by sections 65995.5 and 65995.7. The original time limitation was increased when Proposition 1D was approved by the voters in November 2006.

The new law also prohibits cities and counties from denying approvals of legislative or adjudicative acts that involve the use, planning, or development of real property on the basis of inadequate school facilities. § 65996(b). The existing law prior to SB 50 and Proposition 1A only prohibited the denial of projects based on inadequacy of school facilities under CEQA or the Subdivision Map Act. Under current law, a project cannot be rejected for inadequacy of school facilities until the year 2012 or thereafter unless a land measure fails. If the land measure fails, legislative approvals may be denied for inadequacy of school fees. However, it is important to note that no fee beyond those imposed pursuant to section 65995 may be required. § 65997(d). This is also discussed in more detail later in this chapter.

Triggering Events for Increasing Fee Level

According to the Attorney General, the triggering event authorizing an increase from Level II to Level III fees is as set forth in the statute, Ed. Code, §§ 17072.20–17072.35. but not as provided for by regulation of the State Allocation Board. 85 Op. Atty. Gen. Cal. 25. By statute, this trigger is pulled when the State Allocation Board (SAB) is "no longer approving apportionments." The SAB adopted a regulation providing that as soon as requests for funds exceeded remaining funds, that for purposes of increasing fees, the statutory trigger was satisfied. Not so, according to the Attorney General. As long as state funds were available for apportionment, then the threshold event leading to Level III fees could not occur.

Pre-SB 50 Analysis

In 1985, the legislature passed what was then intended to be a uniform scheme for assessing and imposing school impact fees. Commonly referred to as the Stirling fee legislation, this authority established a basic upper limit for development fees at $1.50 per foot for residential space and $0.25 per square foot for commercial and industrial construction. However, this legislation only covered exactions imposed in conjunction with the approval of *development projects*, as defined in section 65928 of the Permit Streamlining Act. Ed. Code § 17620. Appellate courts had previously held that the Permit Streamlining Act did not include legislative decisions, such as amendments to general plans and rezoning actions (*Landi v. County of Monterey* (1st Dist. 1983) 139 Cal. App. 3d 934), or adjudicatory decisions undertaken in conjunction with legislative decisions. *Land Waste Management, Inc. v. Contra Costa County Board of Supervisors* (1st Dist. 1990) 222 Cal. App. 3d 950).

In construing the authority to impose Stirling fees, the appellate courts, following the precedent of *Landi* and related cases, concluded that, when acting in a legislative capacity, local governments may impose additional exactions beyond those permitted by the Stirling legislation. This broader authority encompasses both the adoption or amendment of a general or specific plan (*Murrieta, supra*) and rezoning actions (*Mira, Hart, supra*). In *Murrieta*, the County of Riverside previously had included policies in its general plan which required that developers must arrange to help school districts provide for adequate school facilities when land use proposals have a negative impact on schools. The county later approved a major comprehensive general plan amendment which, from the perspective of the Murrieta Valley Unified School District, failed to make adequate provision for schools. The District subsequently challenged the comprehensive plan amendment on multiple grounds, with the perceived gap in school funding common to all.

A portion of the county's defense was the argument that its authority was limited by both the Stirling legislation and the School Facilities Act. Ruling against Riverside County, the court relied on the well established rule that an amendment to a general plan is a legislative act, which is not subject to the Permit Streamlining Act. Accordingly, the court found that the county, in considering additional measures apparently contemplated by the existing text of the general plan, was not completely bound by Stirling fee legislation.[6] Faced with the same argument from Los Angeles County, that its ability to mitigate impacts was restricted when acting on a rezoning application, the Second District Court of Appeal reached the same conclusion in *William S. Hart, supra*.

The above cases were significant because, intentional or otherwise, it is common practice for local general plans to include a goal or policy that ties new development to the adequacy of public facilities. Where the city or county specifically identified schools as a facility to be protected by the policy, or perhaps where the list is non-specific, school districts or other affected individuals relied on the Murrieta trilogy either to demand higher fees or otherwise argue against a proposed project. As noted in *Murrieta*, a district could demand higher fees even though it had not exhausted mitigation options under the Stirling legislation or the School Facilities Act.

In addition to the *Mira*, *Hart*, and *Murrieta* trilogy, the decisions of *Grupe Development Co. v. Superior Court of San Bernardino County* (*Chino Unified School District*) (1993) 4 Cal. 4th 911 (invalidating a "special tax" (not a Mello-Roos tax) on new residential development for new school construction on grounds that Stirling legislation preempted the field); *Corona-Norco Unified School District v. City of Corona* (4th Dist. 1993) 17 Cal. App. 4th 985 (holding annexation consistent with the general plan and school district failed to exhaust administrative remedies under CEQA); and *Western/California Limited v. Dry Creek Joint Elementary School District* (3d Dist. 1996) 50 Cal. App. 4th 1461 defined the law as it applied to pre-SB 50 Stirling fee analysis.

The Stirling Legislation Examined

In 1986, the legislature enabled school districts to adopt and impose exactions on developers for school construction and reconstruction. This enactment (§ 65995 et seq. and Education Code § 17620 et seq.) as amended by SB 50 and Proposition 1A in

Adjudicative
- Tentative Map
- Parcel Map
- Conditional Use Permit
- Special Permit
- Variance

Vs.

Legislative
- Amendments to Zoning
- Ordinances or General Plan

What's in a Name?

"School impact fees" is a generic term often used to describe exactions imposed by school districts or municipalities to pay for school facilities, the need for which is caused by new growth. In this chapter, the relevant legal authorities are divided into three categories: legislative fees ("*Mira*"); Stirling fees (§ 65995 and Education Code § 17620); and the School Facilities Act (§ 65970). The label "Stirling" is used to describe the fee legislation authored by Assemblyman Stirling in 1986 which was amended by the Leroy F. Greene School Facilities Act of 1998. The School Facilities Act describes the legislation passed in 1977 authorizing fees for interim facilities. Technically, while simply codified as "School Facilities," it is often referred to as the School Facilities Act. *Candid Enterprises, Inc. v. Grossmont Union High School District* (1985) 39 Cal. 3d 878, 881. Regardless of the label, the Stirling legislation limits School Facilities Act exactions, and as a result, although these laws were separately enacted, they work in conjunction with one another. Accordingly, courts often have failed to distinguish the two enactments when discussing fee disputes. For example, in *Shapell Industries, Inc. v. Governing Board of the Milpitas Unified School District* (6th Dist. 1991) 1 Cal. App. 4th 218, the court indirectly described Stirling fees as fees imposed pursuant to the School Facilities Act; and in *William S. Hart, supra*, 226 Cal. App. 3d 1612, the Second District Court of Appeal coined the term "School Facilities Legislation" to describe the Stirling legislation.

November 4, 1998 and Proposition 1D in November 2006, authorizes the governing body of any school district to impose fees, charges, dedications, or other requirements on new construction within prescribed limits.

Purpose. The purpose of the Stirling legislation is to provide funding for the construction or reconstruction of school facilities. However, the terms "construction" and "reconstruction" are only defined by exclusion. Because these terms are only defined by exclusion, Stirling fees arguably can be collected to fund the construction and reconstruction of a broad range of facilities. Ed. Code § 17620(a)(3). The specific purposes for which fees *may not* be collected are:

- Regular maintenance or routine repair
- Asbestos inspection and removal
- Deferred maintenance as described in section 17582 of the Education Code

Scope of the Act

Applicable to Legislative and Adjudicative Acts. Prior to the passage of SB 50 and Proposition 1A, the Stirling legislation was interpreted by the courts to apply only to adjudicatory decisions. Tentative maps, parcel maps, conditional use permits, special permits, and variances, all are administrative acts. Therefore, when making these types of decisions, local governments were bound by the monetary limits and funding authorities of the Stirling legislation. However, they were not bound by these constraints when making legislative decisions such as amendments to zoning ordinances or to a general plan.

This distinction was done away with by SB 50 and Proposition 1A. Under SB 50 and Proposition 1A, any legislative or adjudicative decision must abide by the Stirling fee monetary limits. § 65995(a). (The effect of SB 50 and Proposition 1A on existing projects is discussed on page 118.)

CEQA and Mitigation in General. The law prior to SB 50 and Proposition 1A set forth the exclusive mitigation methods for environmental effects concerning school facilities related to the approval or conditions of approval of projects under CEQA. However, SB 50 and Proposition 1A, with section 65996, extends this by establishing the exclusive methods of considering and mitigating impacts on school facilities occurring as a result of any legislative or adjudicative act by state or local agencies involving, but not limited to, the planning, use, or development of real property. This does not limit local agencies from utilizing alternative methods of providing school facilities as long as the method is not imposed in connection with a legislative or adjudicative act. § 65996(d). The exclusive methods for considering and mitigating impacts on school facilities under section 65996 are:

The limitations on CEQA do not apply to the offsite impacts of school construction. *Chawanakee Unified School District v. County of Madera* (5th Dist. 2011) 196 Cal. App. 4th 1016.

- Section 17620 of the Education Code
- Chapter 4.7 (commencing with § 65970) of Division 1 of Title 7

Section 65996 provides that the above statutory schemes amount to full and complete school facilities mitigation, notwithstanding section 65858, or Division 13 (commencing with section 21000) of the Public Resources Code (CEQA), or any other provision of state or local law. Accordingly, a state or local agency may not deny or refuse to approve a legislative or adjudicative act, or both, involving, but not limited to, the planning, use, or development of real property or any change in governmental organization or reorganization, as defined in section 56021 or section 56073, on the basis that school facilities are inadequate.

However, section 65996 is only operative as long as section 65997 is inoperative. § 65996(f). Section 65997 becomes operative on or after the year 2012, if a statewide general obligation bond measure, including bond issuance authority to fund construction of kindergarten and grades 1 thru 12 inclusive, is submitted to the voters in 2012 or thereafter, and fails to be approved. § 65997(c)(1). If an appropriate bond measure is submitted in 2012 or thereafter and is approved, section 65996 remains or becomes operative, accordingly, making section 65997 inoperative. Section 65997 makes the following provisions the exclusive methods of mitigating environmental effects related to the adequacy of school facilities when considering the approval or the establishment of conditions for the approval of a development project, as defined in Education Code section 17620, pursuant to CEQA:

- Chapter 12 (commencing with section 17000) of Part 10 of the Education Code or Chapter 12.5 (commencing with section 17070.10)
- Chapter 14 (commencing with section 17085) of Part 10 of the Education Code
- Chapter 18 (commencing with section 17170) of Part 10 of the Education Code
- Article 2.5 (commencing with section 17430) of Chapter 4 of Part 10.5 of the Education Code
- Section 17620 of the Education Code
- Chapter 2.5 (commencing with section 53311) of Division 2 of Title 5 of the Government Code
- Chapter 4.7 (commencing with section 65970) of Division 1 of Title 7 of the Government Code.

Moreover, section 65997 states that "[n]otwithstanding any other provision of law, a public agency may deny or refuse to approve a legislative act involving, but not limited to, the planning, use, or development of real property, on the basis that school facilities are inadequate, except that a public agency may not require the payment or satisfaction of a fee charge, dedication, or other financial requirement in excess of that levied or imposed pursuant to section 65995 and, if applicable any amounts specified in sections 65995.5 or 65995.7." § 65997(d).

In addition, under section 65997 a public agency may not deny the approval of a project on the basis of the adequacy of school facilities, pursuant to CEQA or Division 2 (commencing with § 66410) of this code. § 65997.

In other words, if on or after 2012 a bond measure, described above, is either presented and not approved or not presented, section 65997 increases the number of statutory schemes that can be used to mitigate the environmental effects related to the adequacy of school facilities. These increased mitigation options are the only options that may be considered in the approval or establishment of conditions for the approval of a development project (defined above) under CEQA. These options are the only choices for CEQA mitigation and are deemed sufficient to mitigate environmental effects under CEQA; therefore, a public agency cannot deny the approval of a project based on inadequate school facilities under CEQA. § 65997(a).[7]

CEQA Charity and Voluntary Mitigation

In *City of Marina v. Board of Trustees of the California State University* (2006) 39 Cal. 4th 341, the California Supreme Court decided in part the duty to consider extraterritorial impacts. The state university (CSU) assumed the legal position that it was not authorized to mitigate for offsite impacts, and on that basis, the trustees rejected the feasibility of mitigation measures sought by a local city (Marina) and a base reuse authority (Fort Ord Reuse Authority or FORA).

FORA, responsible for the redevelopment of Fort Ord, had statutory authority very similar to a city or county, including the authority to impose fees and assessments. FORA previously prepared a plan for the eventual development of the base, including the required infrastructure. FORA's plan assumed that the CSU campus would be responsible for financing some of the required infrastructure, to the tune of about $20.5 million. In conjunction with the adoption of a master plan for CSU Monterey Bay, the trustees certified an EIR. The master plan acknowledged that the eventual growth of the Monterey campus would lead to a population of approximately 25,000 students. The EIR identified five significant impacts which could not be mitigated to a less than significant level: water supply, drainage, wastewater management, traffic, and fire protection.

With respect to roads and fire protection, no agreement had been reached between FORA and CSU, and CSU had not committed any funds directly. CSU ultimately concluded that the mitigation responsibility was that of another responsible agency (FORA), and that it lacked legal authorization to expend money for these purposes. With regards to drainage, water supply, and wastewater management, CSU took the position that these matters were the responsibility of FORA, and that the improvements proposed by FORA would provide the necessary mitigation, assuming that the parties completed the statutory negotiations pursuant to Government Code section 54999 et seq. To justify the certification of the EIR and the adoption of the master plan, the CSU Trustees adopted a statement of overriding considerations, and FORA petitioned for review. Eight years later, the Supreme Court finally weighed in on the issues.

First, the court considered the trustees' finding that they could not feasibly mitigate the environmental effects of the master plan campus expansion. The trustees claimed that they were prohibited from contributing funds to FORA as mitigation and relied on *San Marcos Water District v. San Marcos Unified School District* (1986) 42 Cal. 3d 154 in support of their assertion. The court disagreed, and held that while San Marcos addressed compulsory assessments imposed on public entities, voluntary payments were not discussed in that case. The court said, "An assessment connotes, at the very least, a compulsory charge imposed by the government on real property... FORA has imposed no charge on the Trustees, let alone a compulsory one." CEQA requires avoidance or mitigation, if feasible, of significant environmental effects, and voluntary payments to FORA may be a feasible way to mitigate those effects. A payment made for purposes of mitigation is not compulsory or an assessment merely because it is a feasible method of mitigation under CEQA. The court reiterated the duty to mitigate and said,

> ...if campus expansion requires that roads or sewers be improved, the Trustees may do the work themselves on campus, but they have no authority to build roads or sewers off campus on land that belongs to others. Yet the Trustees are not thereby excused from the duty to mitigate or avoid CSUMB's off campus effects on traffic or wastewater management, because CEQA requires a public agency to mitigate or avoid its projects' significant effects not just on the agency's own property but on the environment.

The court also held that there was no prohibition against CSU making voluntary payments to FORA, notwithstanding the lack of specific legal authorization by the Legislature. After *San Marcos*, the Legislature enacted Government Code section 54999 et seq., which authorizes public utilities to charge public-entity customers a fair share of capital costs. Though this statute did not literally apply because FORA had not imposed an assessment or capital facilities fee, the court held that a negotiated agreement between the trustees and FORA for mitigation of significant effects resulting from the campus expansion would likely satisfy CEQA requirements. Also, the fact that the legislature had spoken to three of the five issues in section 54999 (drainage, water supply and wastewater), did not operate as a prohibition against voluntary payments for the remaining matters (roads and fire protection). The court said,

> We discern...no evidence of intent to bar the Trustees from voluntarily contributing, as a way of meeting their CEQA

CEQA Charity and Voluntary Mitigation

> obligations, their fair share of the cost of improvements to roads and fire protection necessitated by CSUMB's expansion.

CSU also argued that mitigation would not be feasible, as there was no assurance that the fees would be used to provide the required mitigation. Acknowledging that there might be some uncertainty as to the success of long term mitigation, the court found that this was not a basis to reject its own ability to make a voluntary payment. The Supreme Court then favorably cited *First Anderson* and *Save our Peninsula* for the position that payment of fair share impact fees can constitute adequate CEQA mitigation for cumulative impacts. Though the court emphasized that that the payment of fees without a showing that mitigation would actually occur is inadequate for CEQA purposes, it found that here there was no reason to believe that FORA would not meet its obligation. *Save our Peninsula* was used to illustrate the notion that there need only be a "reasonable plan" for mitigation, and FORA's plan met that requirement.

Undaunted, the trustees also argued that mitigation was the sole responsibility of FORA and that the CSU did not have the responsibility to mitigate environmental effects under Public Resources Code section 21081(a)(2). However, the court drew a careful distinction. While true that FORA had the legal authority to construct the offsite improvements, this did not mean that CSU lacked the authority to make a supporting financial contribution. In other words, the impact areas of offsite mitigation were not exclusively the responsibility of FORA. It is true that the trustees cannot enter the land of another to make improvements, and the court pointed to Public Resources Code section 21004, which says that "in mitigating or avoiding a significant effect of a project on the environment, a public agency may exercise only those express or implied powers provided by law . . ." But the court also highlighted the fact that CEQA does not limit that agency's obligation to mitigate those significant effects. Payment to FORA to mitigate would be a feasible alternative.

A similar line of reasoning, as it applies to community colleges, is found in *County of San Diego v. Grossmont-Cuyamaca Community College District* (4th Dist. 2006) 141 Cal. App. 4th 86. Feasibility, and its counterpart infeasibility, is an integral part of CEQA analysis. Feasibility is defined by the Guidelines as follows: "... capable of being accomplished in a successful manner within a reasonable period of time, taking into account economic, environmental, legal, social, and technological factors." Guidelines, § 15364. A mitigation measure may be determined by the lead agency to be infeasible, and on that basis would not be required as a condition of project approval. Unlike other areas of CEQA practice, there has been less frequent and less critical analysis of what constitutes a valid finding of infeasibility. A recent court decision begins to shed light on what is likely to be a new chapter of CEQA challenges.

The Grossmont-Cuyamaca Community College District prepared a master plan, approving twenty remodeling and new construction projects. The EIR forecasted substantial increases in student population, triggering a significant increase in offsite traffic impacts. With respect to those impacts, the district found that it was legally and economically infeasible for the district to pay for offsite improvements. The County of San Diego disagreed with the infeasibility determination, and filed suit to set aside the EIR and master plan approval.

With respect to offsite mitigation of traffic impacts, the appellate court reviewed the relevant statutes governing community college construction. First, as a general proposition, the court confirmed that CEQA by itself does not create the legal basis for mitigation. Rather, the authority to mitigate must be based upon separate legal authority. Next, the court found no words of limitation which would support the district's position that it lacked the legal authority to expend funds offsite on improvements in the control of the county. The court then reviewed the district's claim of economic infeasibility. As local governments are already aware (but apparently not the district), a claim of economic infeasibility must be based upon substantial evidence in the record. In this case, there was none.

> The administrative record contains no estimate of the District's proportional share of off-campus traffic mitigation measures identified in the final EIR. Without evidence of the amount of any such cost, we must conclude there is no substantial evidence to support the District's claim that mitigation of the adverse project-related off-campus traffic impacts is economically infeasible.

However, section 65997, unlike section 65996, allows a public agency to deny or refuse a legislative act on the basis of inadequacy of school facilities as long as it does not require payment in excess of fees, charges, dedications, or other financial requirements allowed under sections 65995, 65995.5, and 65995.7.[8]

Exceptions. Property within a Mello-Roos District established to finance school facilities is exempt from any fee, increase in fee other than a cost of living increase, or other requirement first levied, increased, or imposed subsequent to the resolution of formation. This exemption applies to exactions imposed pursuant to Education Code section 17620 (Stirling fees) or sections 65970 et seq. This exemption lasts for ten years, and is measured from the latest issuance of bonds or, if no bonds are issued, then ten years following formation of the district, or until the school district applies for state funding as provided for in subdivision (d) of section 17705.6 of the Education Code. § 53313.4. (§ 17705.6 has been repealed, so it is unclear how a current application would affect the exemption.). In addition, a developer should receive credit against his or her Stirling fees for Mello-Roos special taxes. The procedure that must be followed requires that the special tax be calculated as an amount per square foot of assessable space. This amount of tax per square foot is then credited against the applicable fee as required under the Stirling legislation (§ 17620 of Education Code and § 65995 et seq.). Residential projects located within redevelopment areas are not exempt from SB 50 impact fees. *Warmington Old Town Associates, L.P. v. Tustin Unified School District* (4th Dist. 2002) 101 Cal. App. 4th 840.

Commercial, Industrial, and Residential Construction. Section 17620 of the Education Code is comprehensive in scope. A district may impose school fees on new residential, commercial, and industrial construction, except in circumstances of reconstruction after a disaster. Ed. Code § 17620(a)(1). To the extent that additional space is built, the fees paid must relate to the net increase. Where the proposed development involves new commercial and industrial space, the chargeable area must be covered and enclosed, and may not include the square footage of any existing structure. Ed. Code § 17620(a)(1)(A)(B). Residential additions may also be assessed, but only to the extent that at least 500 square feet (net) of assessable space is added. Any decrease in space that occurs as a result of the expansion must be granted a credit. Ed. Code § 17620(a)(1)(C).

The court has also interpreted Education Code section 17620 to apply to construction undertaken by private colleges. A private college had constructed a new business graduate school and parking structure. According to the college, its existing business school would relocate to the new facility, resulting in no increase in students or faculty. The court held that the Los Angeles Unified School District could impose the Stirling fee applicable to commercial and industrial development. The fact that the applicant/builder was a nonprofit, educational entity was not a basis to exempt the college from the fee. *Loyola Marymount University v. Los Angeles Unified School District* (2d Dist. 1996) 45 Cal. App. 4th 1256.

General Procedure

Collecting the Fee. Once a school district imposes a fee schedule, no city or county may issue a building permit for any construction without the district having certified compliance. This limitation applies equally to general law and charter cities. Ed. Code § 17620(b). However, a local government is not subject to this limitation unless it has first received notification of the new fee, or of an increase in the existing fee. Ed. Code § 17620(d). In contrast to the omnibus fee provisions of section 66007 that ordinarily delay fee collection until the date of final inspection or certificate of occupancy, the school board may elect to collect the impact fee prior to issuing a building permit. Ed. Code § 17620(c). (See chapter 5 for further discussion of § 66007.)

The Resolution. Any resolution adopting or increasing a fee, or otherwise imposing a development requirement, has to follow the general provisions of AB 1600 (§ 66000 et seq.), or section 65995.6 procedural and notice requirements where applicable, for the adoption of new or increased fees. Ed. Code § 17621(a). In a rare departure from prior legislative enactments, the new fee, increased fee, or development requirement is not subject to the CEQA. Ed. Code § 17621(a).

Notification to Cities and Counties. When the fee is adopted, the district is required to forward to each city and county affected a copy of the resolution and all supporting documentation, and a map depicting the development area. Ed. Code § 17621(c). At that time, the district must inform the city or county whether the fee is subject to the limitation of section 66007(a), which generally limits collection to when a final inspection is made or a permit to occupy is granted.

Effective Date. As in the omnibus fee statute, unless an interim authorization is adopted on an urgency basis with a four-fifths vote, resolutions that impose or increase a fee or exaction do not take effect for sixty days. Ed. Code § 17621. An interim authorization must be reapproved within thirty days after a noticed hearing. *Ibid.*

The Nexus

AB 1600. The enacting agency must establish the nexus for the proposed fee pursuant to the general fee statute provisions of AB 1600, which are discussed in greater detail in chapter 5. Therefore, fees or exactions must be supported by sufficient analysis to meet the requirements of AB 1600, or they will be invalidated by a reviewing court. See *Shapell Industries, Inc. v. Governing Board of the Milpitas Unified School District* (6th Dist. 1991) 1 Cal. App. 4th 218; *Balch Enterprises, Inc. v. New Haven Unified School District* (1st Dist. 1990) 219 Cal. App. 3d 783.

In *Shapell Industries, supra*, the school district passed two resolutions imposing fees on residential and non-residential development. The district estimated the amount of new facilities to be constructed, and then assigned 100 percent of this cost to students brought in by the new development, even though only 54.9 percent of the students attending the school would come from new residential development. Relying heavily on the fact that the fee generated from residential construction would be insufficient, the district also imposed the fee on commercial and industrial development without the benefit of a particular study. In granting partial relief to the developer, the court of appeal found that school districts, when imposing fees on residential development, must: (1) project the total amount of new housing expected to be built within the district; (2) determine approximately how many students the new housing will attract; and (3) estimate the cost necessary to provide school facilities to accommodate those new students. *Shapell Industries, supra*, at 235.

The developers, even though they demonstrated that the district had assigned the total cost of new facilities specifically to residents of new development, were not entitled to a complete refund. Rather, the district was allowed to keep the portion of the fees on new residential development it had shown could be reasonably justified. *Id.* at 244.

The court did strike down the fees the district attempted to impose on non-residential development. The court concluded that since no rationale for the fee was offered other than a perceived insufficiency of revenue from residential development, the nexus test could not be met. *Shapell Industries, supra*, at 245.

The court also reviewed a later fee imposed on commercial and industrial development which was based on a study that assumed that commercial and industrial development would attract new employees with families, and would therefore generate new students. The study showed the average number of employees per square foot for each of seven sub-categories of commercial and industrial property. It also estimated the average number of school age children per employee household in each of these categories. Next, the study calculated the number of students expected per square foot for each category of industrial and commercial development. The study then went on to estimate the approximate cost per student for new facilities (using only the students resulting from new commercial and industrial development), and adjusted the cost per student by subtracting the amount the district expected to collect from residential development. Since the amount remaining was less than the estimated cost of providing the necessary new facilities, the court found the imposition of fees on commercial and industrial development was warranted. *Id.* at 247. Shapell was applied in *Warmington Old Town Associates, L.P. v. Tustin Unified School District* (4th Dist. 2002) 101 Cal. App. 4th 840 to invalidate the application of a fee study to a project involving the demolition of existing units (fifty-six multi-family) and replacement with thirty-eight new single family homes, as the school study, as most do, focus on the impacts of new students joining the district in new homes. Thus, the agency failed to meet the requirements that there be a reasonable relationship between the fee's use and type of project and the need for the public facility and the type of project on which the fee is imposed. Gov. Code, §§ 66001(a)(3) and (4). The court also stated that impact fee studies do not have to analyze the effect of individual development projects, and rather must analyze the class of development projects generally.

In *Balch Enterprises, supra*, the school district imposed a fee on commercial and industrial development, and Balch brought an action to set aside the fee. The district, relying in part on a staff study demonstrating a need for new revenues, found that the fee on residential development alone would fall short of community requirements. However, the court found nothing in the record to support the statutorily required findings that the fee was reasonably related to the needs of the community and the need for schools caused by new development. *Balch Enterprises, supra*, at 795.

The quality of the underlying data supporting the fee was examined in *Garrick Development, Inc. v. Hayward Unified School District* (1st Dist. 1992) 3 Cal. App. 4th 320. Prior to this decision, school districts were left to speculate about the level of detail necessary to adopt impact fees. The *Garrick* decision is important because it recognizes that school districts (and inferentially other public agencies) are entitled to leeway when determining the need and type of facilities for which fees may be collected.

Plaintiff's first argument against the fee was that the supporting studies did not include specific plans for new school facilities. The court noted that, while it may be common for such plans to be the basis for the fee, the statute was silent as to a mandatory duty to have plans for specific facilities. Accordingly, the court determined that since the law requires only that a reasonable relationship exist between the fees charged and estimated costs of services, specific development plans were not essential to that determination.

The plaintiff also challenged the twenty-year planning horizon for the fees, arguing that this length of time was too extensive to reasonably estimate facility needs. The appellate court disagreed, noting that the time frames corresponded with the demographic projections of the regional government, and that, in fact, a 45-year time frame used for estimating fees for transit impacts had been upheld by another court. *Garrick, supra*, at 333.

Finally, the appellate court rejected the builder's argument that fees should be collected only for temporary, not permanent facilities, in light of the school district's recent decision to use temporary facilities. Recognizing the deferential role of the courts when reviewing legislative actions, the court noted, "[t]he choice between permanent and movable facilities, we think, is a legislative one whose wisdom we cannot second guess." *Ibid.*

From *Garrick* it is clear that local agencies are not required to produce very specific studies to meet the requirements of the Stirling fee limits and AB 1600. Coupled with the fact that a court will not substitute its own reasoning regarding the type of facility, its useful life, or the methodology used to calculate the fee, this case suggests that logical and reasonable fee programs should withstand judicial review.

It is also important to note that in determining whether a sufficient nexus exists, a reviewing court will not apply the heightened scrutiny of *Ehrlich* to broadly applied Stirling impact fees. *Loyola Marymount, supra.*

Section 65995.6. Under sections 65995.5 and 65995.7, specific statutory notice and procedural requirements have been established for conducting school facilities needs analysis. § 65995.6. These particular statutory requirements apply when a school district wishes to increase the Stirling fees beyond the amounts allowed under sections 65995(b)(1) and 65995(b)(2). Otherwise, the general requirements of AB 1600 apply to the calculation of the fee.

Commercial and Industrial Development. The required findings for proposed commercial or industrial development may be made either by treating a project individually or by considering it to be part of a category of commercial or industrial projects. To estimate the number of employees expected to result from new development, and the effect on existing facilities, the district must conduct a study based on commercial and industrial factors within the district, or in whole or in part on an employee generation study published in January 1990 by the San Diego Association of Governments. Ed. Code § 17621(e)(1).

Administrative Appeals. Where exactions for commercial or industrial projects are levied not on the basis of individual projects but on categories, the governing board of the school district must allow for an administrative appeal. Ed. Code § 17621(e)(2). The party appealing the levy has the burden to demonstrate that the fee is unreasonable.

Special Findings for Agricultural Uses. Where fees or other exactions are imposed on greenhouses or other covered or enclosed agricultural spaces, the school district must make the following findings based on substantial evidence (Education Code § 17622):

- Proposed fees, other requirements, and/or land to be dedicated bear a reasonable relationship, and are limited to, the needs of the community for elementary or high school facilities caused by the development
- The fees or other requirements do not exceed the reasonable cost of school facilities necessitated by the project

In imposing the fee or other requirement, the governing board must consider the proposed increase, if any, in the number of employees, the size and use of the structure, and the costs of construction. The board must also consult with the agricultural commissioner or the county director of the cooperative extension service. In those cases where no increase in the number of employees will result, or where the employer provides the additional housing for which the Ed. Code section 17620 fees have been paid, no fees can be imposed. Ed. Code § 17622.

Statutory School Facilities Needs Analysis. When dealing with Stirling fee increases allowed under sections 65995.5 and 65995.7, a school district is required to conduct a school facilities needs analysis in compliance with section 65995.6. § 65995(b)(2). This section provides for identifying growth, surplus property, and fund sources other than fees, and for the adoption of the school facility needs analysis by resolution at a public hearing. §§ 65995.6(a)–(f). The California Environmental Quality Act does not apply to the adoption, preparation, or update of the school facility needs analysis. § 65995.6(g).

School districts empowered with the authority to exact fees for new facilities must adhere to the provisions of AB 1600, mandating that districts establish a reasonable relationship between fees charged and the need for facilities caused by new development.

Fee Calculations. The ability of school districts to impose fees is not without limitation. The basic authority of a local agency to impose a fee or dedication under the Stirling legislation or the School Facilities Act (discussed elsewhere in this chapter) is limited to $1.93 per square foot for residential construction, or $0.31 per square foot for commercial or industrial construction. § 65995 (b)(1)(2). The effect of the new fee limits was essentially to codify the existing level of fees as they stood due to adjustments for inflation at the time Proposition 1A went to the voters. Therefore, effectively no increase in level of fees was made by this amendment. While these figures are subject to readjustment by the State Allocation Board (discussed below), local agencies must still prepare all the analysis otherwise required for new fees. Thus, these numbers represent maximum levels and cannot be construed as legislatively preapproved fee levels. (See AB 1600 Nexus Requirements in Chapter 5.)

The State Allocation Board may increase the base fee every two years beginning in 2000, and the changes take effect immediately. § 65995(b)(3).

Residential. For residential projects, the maximum school fee is based on assessable space. This is defined to be all of the square footage within the perimeter of a residential structure, not including any carport, walkway, garage, overhang, patio, enclosed patio, detached accessory structure, or similar area. The amount of assessable space is to be calculated by the building department of the city or county issuing the building permit. § 65995(b)(1). As noted below, limited types of residential projects are subject to the lower fee rate for commercial and industrial projects.

Commercial, Industrial, and Senior Citizen Housing. For commercial and industrial projects, the fee is based on the amount of "chargeable covered and enclosed space," which is determined by the building department. Excluded from this calculation are storage areas incidental to the principal use of the construction, garages, parking structures, unenclosed walkways, or utility or disposal areas. § 65995(b)(2).

This same maximum rate also applies to senior citizen facilities.[9] §§ 65995.1, 65995.2. However, if these facilities are later converted to a land use not subject to age restriction, or where residency of a non-senior is permitted in one of the mobile homes, then current school impact fees must be paid, and the district must give credit for previously imposed fees. §§ 65995.1, 65995.2.

A developer (CRH) of an age-restricted residential project for residents 55 years or older mistakenly paid the regular school impact fee of $1.56 per square foot rather than the reduced rate of $.26 per square foot for senior housing. Upon learning of the reduced rate applicable to senior housing projects, CRH filed suit seeking a refund of the excess payment. The appellate court concluded that CRH's failure to file the written protest mandated by section 66020 and failure to file the lawsuit within 180 days from the date the fee was imposed barred any recovery. *California Ranch Homes Development Company of Hemet v. San Jacinto Unified School District* (4th Dist. 1993) 17 Cal. App. 4th 573.

Assessable

- All Square Footage within Perimeter of Residential Structure

Vs.

Non-Assessable

- Carport
- Walkway
- Garage Overhang
- Patio/Enclosed Patio
- Detached Accessary Structure

Exceptions to Fee Limitations. The fee limits imposed by subdivisions (b)(1) and (b)(2) of section 65995 are not absolute; sections 65995.5 and 65995.7 both allow fee increases above the fee limits of section 65995(b).

Eligibility—Section 65995.5. Section 65995.5 offers an alternative for school boards when imposing fees for residential construction. § 65995.5(a). To be eligible to impose the fee, charge, dedication, or other increases allowed under this section, the following requirements must be complied with:

- Timely application is made to the State Allocation Board for new construction funding for which it is determined to be eligible by the State Allocation Board, and the Board fails to notify the school district of the district's eligibility within 120 days of receipt of the application. § 65995.5(b)(1)
- The school district conducts and adopts a school facility needs analysis pursuant to section 65995.6. § 65995.5(b)(2)
- Until January 1, 2000, one or more of the following requirements must be complied with; and on or after January 1, 2000, two or more of the following requirements must be satisfied. § 65995.5(b)(3)
  * The district is a unified or elementary school district having substantial enrollment of its elementary school pupils on a multitrack year-round schedule. "Substantial enrollment" for the purposes of this paragraph means at least thirty percent of district pupils in kindergarten and grades 1 to 6, inclusive, in the high school attendance area in which all or some of the new residential units identified in the needs analysis are planned for construction. A high school district shall be deemed to have met the requirements of this paragraph if either of the following apply:
  * At least thirty percent of the high school district's pupils are on a multitrack year-round schedule.
  * At least forty percent of the pupils enrolled in public schools in kindergarten and grades one to twelve, inclusive, within the boundaries of the high school attendance area for which the school district is applying for new facilities are enrolled in multitrack year-round schools. § 65995.5(b)(3)(A).

- The district has placed on the ballot in the previous four years a local general obligation bond to finance school facilities and the measure received at least fifty percent plus one of the votes cast. § 65995.5(b)(3)(B)
- The district meets one of the following:
  - * The district has issued debt or incurred obligations for capital outlay in an amount equivalent to fifteen percent of the district's local bonding capacity, including indebtedness that is repaid from property taxes, parcel taxes, the district's general fund, special taxes levied pursuant to Section 4 of article XIIIA of the California Constitution, special taxes levied pursuant to Chapter 2.5 (commencing with section 52211) of Division 2 of Title 5 that are approved by a vote of registered voters, special taxes levied pursuant to Chapter 2.5 (commencing with section 52211) of Division 2 of Title 5 that are approved by a vote of landowners prior to November 4, 1998, and revenues received pursuant to the Community Redevelopment Law (Part 1 (commencing with section 33000) of Division 24 of the Health and Safety Code). Indebtedness or other obligation to finance school facilities to be owned, leased, or used by the district, that is incurred by another public agency, shall be counted for the purpose of calculating whether the district has met the debt percentage requirement contained herein.
  - * The district has issued debt or incurred obligations for capital outlay in an amount equivalent to thirty percent of the district's local bonding capacity, including indebtedness that is repaid from property taxes, parcel taxes, the district's general fund, special taxes levied pursuant to Section 4 of article XIIIA of the California Constitution, special taxes levied pursuant to Chapter 2.5 (commencing with section 52211) of Division 2 of Title 5 that are approved by a vote of registered voters, special taxes levied pursuant to Chapter 2.5 (commencing with section 52211) of Division 2 of Title 5 that are approved by a vote of landowners after November 4, 1998, and revenues received pursuant to the Community Redevelopment Law (Part 1 (commencing with section 33000) of Division 24 of the Health and Safety Code). Indebtedness or other obligation to finance school facilities to be owned, leased or used by the district, that is incurred by another public agency, shall be counted for the purpose of calculating whether the district has met the debt percentage requirement contained herein. § 65995.5(b)(3)(C)
- At least twenty percent of the teaching stations within the district are relocatable classrooms. § 65995.5(b)(3)(D)

Increased Fee Calculation—Section 65995.5. The maximum fee, charge, dedication, or other requirement authorized by section 65995.5, must be calculated as follows:

- The number of unhoused pupils identified in the school facilities need analysis shall be multiplied by the appropriate amounts provided in subdivision (a) of section 17072.10. This sum shall be added to the site acquisition and development cost determined pursuant to subdivision (h) of section 65995.5. § 65995.5(c)(1)
- The full amount of local funds the governing board has dedicated to facilities necessitated by new construction shall be subtracted from the amount determined pursuant to paragraph (1). Local funds include fees, charges, dedica-

tions, or other requirements imposed on commercial or industrial construction. § 65995.5(c)(2)

- The resulting amount determined pursuant to paragraph (2) shall be divided by the projected total square footage of assessable space of residential units anticipated to be constructed during the next five-year period in the school district or the city and county in which the school district is located. The estimate of the projected total square footage shall be based on information available from the city or county within which the residential units are anticipated to be constructed or a market report prepared by an independent third party. § 65995.5(c)(3)

While the 1986 Stirling legislation gave school districts similar powers to those of cities and counties to exact fees and dedications from new development, the amount districts may charge is strictly prescribed.

Limitation on Fee Increases—Section 65995.5. An important limit of this section is that the site acquisition costs shall not exceed half the amount determined by multiplying the land acreage determined under State Department of Education guidelines by the estimated cost determined pursuant to section 17072.12 of the Education Code. Site development costs also may not exceed twice the amount funded by the State Allocation Board. § 65995.5(h).

Eligibility—Section 65995.7. Section 65995.7 applies only when state funds for new school facility construction are not available and the school district has complied with the requirements of section 65995.5. § 65995.7(a).

Fee Calculation—Section 65995.7. This section allows the calculation of fees by multiplying the number of unhoused pupils identified in the school facilities needs analysis by the appropriate amounts provided in section 17072.10(a). The resulting number shall then be added to the site acquisition and development cost determined pursuant to section 65995.5(h). Section 65995.7 also allows for reimbursement if state funds are later received and provides for alternative reimbursement agreements. §§ 65995.7(b) and 65995.5(c).

Exemptions. The following facilities are exempt from fees under the Stirling legislation (§§ 65995, 65995.1):

- Religious facilities used exclusively for religious purposes that are also exempt from property taxes
- Private, full-time day schools, as described in Education Code section 48222, which are used exclusively for that purpose
- Buildings owned and occupied by federal, state, or local government
- Residential hotels as described in Health and Safety Code section 50519 (b)(1)
- Agricultural migrant worker housing owned by the State of California and financed in whole or part pursuant to Chapter 8.5 of Part 2, Division 31 of the Health and Safety Code (commencing with § 50710).

Construction and installation of utilities, as compared to construction of actual structures, is insufficient to qualify for the exemption. *Canyon North Company v. Conejo Valley Unified School District* (2d Dist. 1993) 19 Cal. App. 4th 243. (For projects begun prior to November 4, 1998, see page 118.)

Manufactured and Mobile Homes

Fees or other exactions may only be imposed on the initial installation of a manufactured or mobile home, and then only when no other similar structure existed on the same site or space.

Initial Installation on New Pads. Fees or other exactions may only be imposed on the initial installation of a manufactured or mobile home, and then only when no other similar structure existed on the same site or space. Additionally, the levy may only be imposed where construction of the foundation or pad was begun after September 1, 1986. § 65995.2.

Exemptions. The following exemptions from school fees also apply to manufactured or mobile homes (Education Code § 17625):

- Units for which building permits were issued on or before September 1, 1986
- Any replacement or addition to an existing unit on or in the same space
- Replacement as a result of any form of natural disaster
- Accessory structures as defined in section 18008.5 or section 18213 of the Health and Safety Code
- Conversion of a park to resident ownership
- Pursuant to legislation adopted in 1994, a school district has the discretion to waive school facilities fees for persons aged 55 or older who are members of a lower income household, as defined in Health and Safety Code section 50079.5, who have moved a mobile home from a mobile home park space in one school district to another school district. Otherwise, the school district must permit the homeowner to pay the fee in installments over a 36-month period. Ed. Code § 17625(g)

Credit for Previously Paid Fees. Where Education Code section 17620 fees are paid for a manufactured or mobile home, and subsequently a permanent structure is built for which new Education Code section 17620 fees are to be paid, credit must be given for the previously paid fees. Ed. Code § 17625.

Levies by Non-Unified Districts. Where two non-unified districts overlap in their imposition of Education Code section 17620 fees, and the total of those fees exceed the maximum amount authorized by section 65995, the districts must either enter into an agreement dividing the amount within the statutory limit collected, or, if they cannot agree, enter into binding arbitration. Ed. Code § 17623. Allocations set through arbitration are effective for three years.

Refunds. Individuals possessing building permits which expire on or after January 1, 1990, without having begun construction, are entitled to a refund of fees or other exactions, less administrative costs. Ed. Code § 17624.

Legal Protests. Legal challenges to fees are subject to the rules and procedures of the Uniform Protest Act, section 66020 et seq. Ed. Code § 17621(d).

Local procedures must include administrative appeals for fees imposed on commercial and industrial development when relying on development categories rather than the specifics of a particular project. Ed. Code § 17621. However, most school boards provide appeals for all types of projects. Thus, a party seeking to challenge a fee should determine whether an administrative appeal is available. A developer who successfully challenges the nexus underpinnings of a school impact fee is entitled to a refund plus interest at eight percent, not ten percent. *Warmington Old Town Associates, L.P. v. Tustin Unified School District* (2002) 101 Cal. App. 4th 840, 868.

School Facilities Act

In contrast to the Stirling legislation, which empowers school districts to adopt fees, the School Facilities Act grants exaction authority only to cities or counties to require exactions for temporary school facilities. This statute is complementary to the Stirling legislation. However, in light of the fact that districts may impose fees directly on their own behalf, most cities and counties rely upon the districts to levy the exaction and do not exercise the powers permitted by the School Facilities Act.

The legislative origins of the act can be traced back to the temporary school facilities legislation (SB 201) enacted in 1977. *Trent Meredith, Inc. v. City of Oxnard* (2d Dist. 1981) 114 Cal. App. 3d 317. The focus of the School Facilities Act was and continues to be temporary facilities, and the inadequacy of the statute was the basis for rewriting the school fee legislation in 1986.

Findings

For School Facilities Act fees or land dedications to be adopted, the governing body of the local school district providing elementary or high school facilities must first make two findings. Those findings are that: (1) conditions of overcrowding exist in one or more attendance areas which impair educational functions; and (2) all reasonable methods of mitigating conditions of overcrowding have been evaluated, and no feasible method for reducing those conditions exist. § 65971(a). "Conditions of overcrowding" occur when planned enrollment exceeds the capacity of the school. § 65973(a). Reasonable methods of mitigation include agreements with developers to lease temporary facilities, or agreements with other districts to lease or purchase excess facilities.

Notice of Findings

When notifying the appropriate city council or board of supervisors that the required findings have been made, the school board must specify all mitigation measures considered by the school district. The notice of findings must also include a completed application to the Office of Local Assistance for preliminary determination of eligibility under the School Building Lease-Purchase Law of 1976. § 65971(b).

Schedule of Fees

Either as part of the notice sent to the city or county, or prior to the decision to require a dedication of land or the payment of fees, the school district is required to submit a schedule specifying how the fees or land will be used to relieve overcrowding. § 65976. The schedule must list the sites where the fees will be used, the facilities to be made available, and the schedule of availability. The district must notify the city or county of any later modifications to the schedule. *Ibid.*

Concurrence of Local Government

A city or county cannot take any action until the findings have been made available to the public for sixty days. § 65971(b). After 60 days from the date of receipt, but not longer than 150 days, the local government is required to either concur or not concur. Although the local government may extend this period for thirty days, failure to act may not be deemed concurrence. *Ibid.*

Agreements Between Districts with Same Attendance Area

Where two districts are subject to overcrowding in the same attendance area, the city or county and affected districts are required to enter into an agreement regarding distribution of School Facilities Act funds or dedications. § 65977.

Authorized Facilities

With one exception, collected fees are limited to interim facilities. Interim facilities are defined as (1) temporary classroom and bathroom structures constructed without a permanent foundation; (2) reasonable site preparation and facility installation; and (3) the land necessary for the structures. § 65980.[10] However, a district that receives funds pursuant to the Act, under an ordinance in effect on September 1, 1986, may expend those funds for any of the construction or reconstruction purposes authorized by Education Code section 17620. § 65974.5.

Residential Project Approvals by Local Agencies

Once overcrowding is demonstrated pursuant to the School Facilities Act, the local legislative body must adopt a fee ordinance or make specified findings when approving residential developments. Approvals affected include rezonings for residential uses, issuing discretionary permits for residential uses, and approval of tentative subdivision maps for residential purposes. § 65972. The term "residential projects" includes mobile homes. § 65973(c).

To exempt a project from compliance with the ordinance, findings must be made which demonstrate specific overriding fiscal, economic, social, or environmental factors which warrant project approval. § 65972.

Ordinance Provisions

In order for a city or county to require payment of fees, dedication of land, or both, the legislative body must adopt an ordinance. The ordinance may only be adopted when the following conditions can be met (§ 65974(a.)):

- The general plan must provide for the location of public schools
- Exactions transferred to the district are used solely for interim purposes
- A reasonable relationship must exist between the need for schools caused by the development and the amount of the exaction
- A finding must demonstrate that the facilities to be constructed are consistent with the general plan

The ordinance must be in effect no less than 30 days prior to imposing the fee or condition. Note, however, the 60-day minimum period requirement found in section 66017 may supersede the specific time period enumerated in the School Facilities Act.

Additional Limitations

The total amount of the land to be dedicated, or fees paid, or both, shall not exceed the amount of five annual lease payments for the interim facilities. If fees are required, the payment shall be made at the time the building permit is issued, or later if specified by the ordinance. If the residential project involves the subdivision of fifty or fewer parcels, only fees may be required. §§ 65974(b), (d).

The overall financial limitations established by the Stirling legislation apply to the School Facilities Act, as do the special limitations regarding mobile homes occupied by older adults. § 65995.2.

Property within a Mello-Roos District established to finance school facilities is exempt from any fee, increase in fee other than a cost of living increase, or other requirement first levied, increased, or imposed subsequent to the resolution of formation. This exemption applies to exactions imposed pursuant to Education Code section 17620 (Stirling fees) or the School Facilities Act section 65970 et seq. This exemption lasts for ten years, and the exemption is measured from the latest issuance of bonds or, if no bonds are issued, then ten years following formation of the district or until the school district applies for state funding as provided for in subdivision (d) of section 17705.6 of the Education Code. (This latter section has been repealed, so it is unclear how a current application would affect the exemption.) § 53313.4.

Relationship to Other School Funding Statutes

Collection and expenditure of School Facilities Act funds is modified by various state school funding requirements. The Act is impacted as follows:

- Where a joint powers authority agrees to and implements a school facility master plan, the monetary limitations of section 65995(b) do not apply. § 65974(e)
- Where a district has received approval for a project under the Building Lease-Purchase Law of 1976 for which fees have already been collected, interim facility fees may be used as the local district's matching funds. § 65975(a). Where land has been dedicated for interim facilities, the fair market value of the land may be used as the district's contribution. § 65975(b)
- One year after receiving an apportionment of funds under the Lease-Purchase Law, the city or county may not impose a new levy unless the legislative body finds additional overcrowding which the additional fee can be used to relieve. § 65979. If an excess of fees or land results from apportionment of Lease-Purchase funds, the excess exaction must be returned to the source. § 65979

Legal Challenges

The School Facilities Act does not have specific provisions governing legal challenges. Thus, judicial review should follow the requirements of the Uniform Protest Act found in sections 66020 and 66021 et seq. These requirements are discussed at length in chapter 7.

William W. Abbott is a partner in the Sacramento, California law firm, Abbott & Kindermann, LLP, where he practices land use, environmental, municipal, and real estate law, representing both public and private clients.

CHAPTER SEVEN

Challenging Exactions—Protests, Legal Actions, and Audits

By Margaret M. Sohagi

Challenges to development exactions commonly claim that an exaction is one or more of the following: (1) a special tax instead of a fee; (2) a "taking" under the Fifth and Fourteenth Amendments to the U.S. Constitution; (3) unreasonable as it relates to the proposed development; (4) not supported by adequate evidence in the record.

Regardless of the relied upon theory, the challenger must follow strict protest procedures prior to filing a lawsuit. Furthermore, the nature of the legal proceedings depends upon the type of exaction imposed and the statutory scheme governing the specific exaction.

This chapter begins with a discussion of the two principal forms of judicial review: traditional mandamus and administrative mandamus. The level of scrutiny the court will apply to analyze an agency's decision is dependent upon the form of mandamus proceeding that is required. The discussion of mandamus is followed by a explanation of the uniform protest provisions contained in Chapter 9 of the Planning and Zoning Law, Government Code sections 66020–66025,[1] which govern protests, legal challenges, and audits for numerous exactions.[2] The next section explains new procedures relating to mediation (§§ 66030–66037), followed by an explanation and discussion of the special provisions applicable only to protests of fees and other exactions imposed under the Subdivision Map Act and a description of the special provisions applicable only to sewer, water, and land use permit processing fees. Finally, the chapter addresses statutes of limitations and attorney fee awards. See Appendix M for a sample complaint alleging excessive development fees.

Judicial Review

Legislative Acts

Many decisions creating or imposing exactions are considered "legislative" or "quasi-legislative" acts. Legislative acts generally predetermine the rules for future cases. In the land use context, adoption or amendment of zoning ordinances, general and

The Role of Administrative Findings

Courts have held that local officials, especially when acting in an administrative capacity, must show how they arrived at their land use decisions. This written explanation is called the "findings." When land use decisions are challenged, the courts usually demand that the record reflect how the agency processed raw evidence to reach its final decision to approve or deny a certain project. The findings should expose the way the agency analyzes facts and applies regulations and policies. Findings help to:

- Provide a framework for making principal decisions that enhance the integrity of the administrative process
- Make analysis orderly, reducing the likelihood that an agency will leap randomly from evidence to conclusions
- Serve a public relations function by persuading the parties that the administrative decision making is careful, reasoned, and equitable
- Enable the parties to determine whether and on what basis the parties should seek judicial review and remedy
- Apprise the reviewing court of the basis for the agency's decisions, *Topanga Association for a Scenic Community v. County of Los Angeles* (2d Dist. 1974) 11 Cal. 3d 506, 514–517
- For additional information, see Daniel J. Curtin, Jr., *Curtin's California Land Use and Planning Law*, Solano Press Books (2011, thirty-first edition); Michael H. Remy et al., *Guide to the California Environmental Quality Act (CEQA)*, Solano Press Books (2007, eleventh edition).

specific plans,[3] and development agreements are the most commonly recognized forms of legislative acts. In effect, the adoption or amendment of a plan or ordinance draws upon the legislative powers of a city council or board of supervisors, and reflects the codification of new policy to be applied to all future cases. *Strumsky v. San Diego County Employees Ret. Assoc.* (1974) 11 Cal. 3d 28, 34; *Horn v. County of Ventura* (1979) 24 Cal. 3d 605.

As an example, a city council may determine that future commercial development within the community will increase the demand for low-income housing, which may be already lacking in the jurisdiction. The council may then decide that all commercial development projects will be assessed a fee to be paid into a fund to finance low-income housing. In this case, the agency has determined the course of action to take for all future commercial developments to fill a specific need created by that class of development. This constitutes a legislative or quasi-legislative act.[4] When the city council imposes the fee on a specific project, however, it is acting in its adjudicatory capacity, which is discussed below.

Legislative acts are reviewable only in a traditional mandamus proceeding, pursuant to Code of Civil Procedure section 1085. Confined to an examination of the agency proceedings, this review determines whether the action taken was arbitrary, capricious, or entirely lacking in evidentiary support, or whether the agency failed to conform to procedures required by law. *Balch Enterprises. v. New Haven Unified Sch. Dist.* (1st Dist. 1990) 219 Cal. App. 3d 783. "The limited scope of review of quasi-legislative administrative action is grounded upon the doctrine of separation of powers which: (1) sanctions legislative delegation of authority to an appropriate administrative agency; and (2) acknowledges the presumed expertise of the agency." *Stauffer Chemical Com. v. Air Resources Bd.* (1st Dist. 1982) 128 Cal. App. 3d 789, 795.

No inquiry into an agency's reasons for its legislative actions is tolerated. As long as a reasonable basis for the action exists, the motives of the decision makers, or how the decision was reached, is generally immaterial. *City of Fairfield v. Superior Court of Solano County* (1975) 14 Cal. 3d 768, 722; *Mike Moore's 24-Hour Towing v. City of San Diego* (4th Dist. 1996) 45 Cal. App. 4th 1294.

Traditionally, in its review of evidence, the reviewing court is not limited only to those matters in the administrative record. Where the legal issue is limited to whether or not the agency proceeded in a manner required by law, however, review of post administrative hearing evidence may be inappropriate. *Shapell Industries, Inc. v. Governing Bd. of the Milpitas Unified Sch. Dist.* (6th Dist. 1991) 1 Cal. App. 4th 218.

A developer's challenge to a city-imposed obligation to provide underground utilities is reviewable pursuant to Code of Civil Procedure section 1085. In response to the City of Tracy's requirement that the developer provide underground utilities, the developer appealed the requirement to the planning commission and city council. Unsuccessful, the developer filed a petition for writ of mandate. At trial, the judge permitted additional evidence to be admitted. Counsel for the applicant objected to the new evidence on the grounds that the trial was one in administrative mandamus (Code of Civ. Proc. § 1094.5), effectively precluding the introduction of new evidence except under narrow circumstances. The appellate court held that the admission of additional evidence was not in error, because the administrative proceeding involving the city and plaintiff was not an adjudicatory-type hearing involving the presentation of evidence and adoption of findings as required by Code of Civil Procedure section 1094.5. The subsequent legal proceeding was, therefore, in traditional mandamus, with judicial review conducted pursuant to Code of Civil Procedure section 1085. *Bright Devel. Com. v. City of Tracy* (3d Dist. 1993) 20 Cal. App. 4th 783.

In a traditional mandamus action to determine whether the Air Resources Board abused its discretion in adopting regulations under the California Environmental Quality Act (CEQA), the California Supreme Court affirmed that in CEQA and non-CEQA actions, extra-record evidence is generally not admissible in traditional mandamus actions challenging quasi-legislative administrative decisions on the ground that the agency "has not proceeded in a manner required by law." *Western States Petroleum Assoc. v. Superior Court* (1995) 9 Cal. 4th 559. The Court also held, however, that extra-record evidence may be admitted in such actions challenging ministerial or informal administrative actions if the facts are in dispute, as was the case in *Bright*.

Adjudicatory Acts

An "adjudicatory" act involves the application of an existing rule to a specific set of facts, and a determination of rights or obligations concerning matters or transactions which already exist. In other words, an adjudicatory act implements a plan, policy, or rule already adopted by the legislative body. Actions by agencies other than courts are generally called "quasi-adjudicatory," although the term is used interchangeably with "adjudicatory" or "administrative." Approval of conditional use permits, special permits, tentative subdivision maps, and actions imposing conditions or exactions under the Subdivision Map Act are considered quasi-adjudicatory.

Review of adjudicatory decisions that do not affect expressive conduct protected by the First Amendment is by administrative mandamus pursuant to Code of Civil Procedure section 1094.5. Adjudicatory decisions that do implicate the First Amendment are reviewable pursuant to Code of Civil Procedure section 1094.8. Review pursuant to Code of Civil Procedure section 1094.5 requires a more rigorous standard than that imposed by traditional mandate under Code of Civil Procedure section 1085 and focuses on: (1) whether the agency proceeded without, or in excess of, its jurisdiction; (2) whether a fair hearing was held; and (3) whether there was a prejudicial abuse of discretion. An additional and sometimes critical distinction is that when operating under Code of Civil Procedure section 1094.5, the court's review is generally limited to the information actually presented to the city council or board of supervisors during the administrative proceedings. This can only be supplemented in unusual circumstances. Code Civ. Proc. § 1094.5(e).

Alleging abuse of discretion is the most common method to challenge an adjudicatory act. An abuse of discretion is established if the agency has not proceeded in the manner required by law, the decision is not supported by the findings, or the findings are not supported by the evidence. The crux of this determination is whether substantial evidence existed in support of the agency's findings and decision, and whether the agency's findings are legally sufficient to uphold its decision. *Topanga Assoc. for a Scenic Cmty. v. County of Los Angeles* (2d Dist. 1974) 11 Cal. 3d 506. The findings must be supported by substantial evidence in light of the whole record, and any reasonable doubts will be resolved in favor of the agency. *McMillan v. American General Financial Corp.* (1st Dist. 1976) 60 Cal. App. 3d 175, 182.

An agency's findings are adequate if they enable a proponent to determine whether, and on what grounds, to seek review of the decision, and if they make clear to the reviewing entity the basis for the agency's decision. However, boilerplate findings made without deliberation or reference to supporting facts have been found to be inadequate because they fail to "bridge the analytic gap between the raw evidence and the ultimate decision." *Topanga* at 515; *Honey Springs Homeowners Assoc. v. Bd. of Supervisors of San Diego* (4th Dist. 1984) 157 Cal. App. 3d 1122, 1152. Findings are liberally construed to support rather than defeat the decision being reviewed. The court must resolve reasonable doubts in favor of the administrative findings and decision. *Topanga* at 514; *City of Carmel-by-the-Sea v. Monterey County* (1st Dist. 1977) 71 Cal. App. 3d 84, 92.

Application of Code of Civil Procedure section 1094.5 is restricted to those agency decisions made in proceedings which involved a hearing required by law, presentation of evidence, and findings of fact. By itself, a statutory requirement of findings does not render the action adjudicatory. *Langsam v. City of Sausalito* (1st Dist. 1987) 190 Cal. App. 3d 871. A statutory scheme such as the uniform rules for adopting or imposing fees, for example, may oblige the agency to make a finding in conjunction with a legislative or quasi-legislative act. However, "[a]lthough the statutory obligation to make a 'finding' is a characteristic shared with adjudicatory proceedings, it does not stamp the function with an adjudicative character." *Joint Council of Interns and Residents v. Board of Supervisors* (2d Dist. 1989) 210 Cal. App. 3d 1202, 1212. As a result, judicial review of an ordinance adopting fees is conducted according to Code of Civil Procedure section 1085, a less demanding standard.

In *Balch Enterprises* 219 Cal. App. 3d 783, a school board adopted fees applicable to commercial and industrial development. From the appellate court's perspective, the school board prescribed a new rule or plan applicable to all future development in that class. Thus, even though the school board had been required to make certain determinations, the local agency's decision was deemed legislative and reviewable under the less vigorous standard of Code of Civil Procedure section 1085.

Multi-Entitlement Approvals

When acting on a single project, a local agency makes many separate decisions—for example, rezoning, use permit, and tentative map approval may all be part of one project—and the distinctions between adjudicatory and legislative acts are easily blurred. In *Mountain Defense League v. Board of Supervisors* (4th Dist. 1977) 65 Cal.

App. 3d 723, the appellate court held that the stricter requirements of Code of Civil Procedure section 1094.5 apply where a project approval involves both legislative and adjudicatory approvals—e.g., general plan amendment and private development plan. *Id.* at 729. More recent appellate court decisions outside the land use field have held that, where the action of an agency involves both legislative and adjudicatory approvals, each element is subject to the appropriate standard of review. *Dominey v. Dep't. of Personnel Admin.* (3d Dist. 1988) 205 Cal. App. 3d 729.

Finally, each local ordinance must be scrutinized for its own vagaries. The fact that a local ordinance requires a hearing and findings—normally the benchmark of an adjudicatory decision—does not automatically make the decision reviewable under Code of Civil Procedure section 1094.5 where discretion is not contemplated. *Langsam v. City of Sausalito* (1st Dist. 1987) 190 Cal. App. 3d 871.

The Blurring of Distinctions—Do They Matter Anymore?

As noted below, the former bright line test applicable to legislative and adjudicatory decisions has been muddled by both the courts and the Legislature. Recently, the courts have focused on the nature of the exaction, rather than on the nature of the underlying approval to which the exaction is attached. For example, exactions involving dedication of interests in land are subject to the higher level of review set forth by the United States Supreme Court in *Dolan v. City of Tigard* (1994) 512 U.S. 374. The California Supreme Court matched this volley by applying a similarly vigorous review pursuant to the Mitigation Fee Act (AB 1600, discussed further in chapter 5) in *Ehrlich v. City of Culver City* (1996) 12 Cal. 4th 854. The unusual circumstances of the latter case involved a one-time fee incorporated into a legislative approval. In contrast, a broadly applied fee is not subject to the scrutiny of *Dolan* and *Ehrlich*. *Loyola Marymount Univ. v. Los Angeles Unified Sch. Dist.* (2d Dist. 1996) 45 Cal. App. 4th 1256. Similarly, a more deferential standard of judicial review applies to land use requirements affecting height, bulk, and setback. *Breneric Assoc. v. City of Del Mar* (4th Dist. 1998) 69 Cal. App. 4th 166; *Ehrlich* 12 Cal. 4th 854.

The Mitigation Fee Act itself muddies the water. The Act applies to "development projects," a term historically interpreted as not encompassing legislative acts. *Landi v. County of Monterey* (1st Dist. 1983) 139 Cal. App. 3d 934. Yet it was this statute which was embraced by the California Supreme Court in its application of the Mitigation Fee Act to a fee attached to a legislative act. *Ehrlich* 12 Cal. 4th 854. In *City of Monterey v. Del Monte Dunes at Monterey, Ltd.* (1999) 526 U.S. 687, the United States Supreme Court held that *Dolan's* "rough proportionality" test for analyzing regulatory taking claims is not applicable where a landowner's challenge is based solely on denial of development approval, rather than on excessive exactions.

Finally, without distinction as to either legislative or adjudicatory acts, the CEQA guidelines attach the higher scrutiny of *Dolan* and *Ehrlich* to all ad hoc mitigation measures. Guidelines § 15126.4.

Judicial Review—Burden of Proof

In *Dolan v. City of Tigard* (1994) 512 U.S. 374, the U.S. Supreme Court held that the City had the burden to show that the impacts of the project justified the extent of the condition. This is contrary to the presumption of constitutionality that courts have traditionally applied to municipalities' exercise of the police power. See *Euclid v. Ambler Realty Company* (1926) 272 U.S. 365 (a zoning ordinance is upheld unless its "provisions are clearly arbitrary and unreasonable, having no substantial relation to the public health, safety, morals, or general welfare."). The majority in *Dolan* distinguished this line of cases as only applicable to legislative decisions, as opposed to adjudicatory decisions such as the one at issue in the *Dolan* case. In addition, *Dolan* was a case involving dedication of land, and not "simply a limitation on the use petitioner might make of her own parcel. . . ." *Dolan v. City of Tigard* (1994) 512 U.S. 374. Therefore, according to the court, it was appropriate to shift the burden of proof. A similar burden now applies in the case of one-time fees (*Ehrlich*), as well as all ad hoc mitigation measures. Guidelines § 15126.4.[1] In contrast, a land use limitation affecting land use height, bulk, or setback, or involving application of a generalized fee, is reviewed under a more deferential standard of review. *Breneric Associates v. City of Del Mar* 69 Cal App 4th 166; *Ehrlich* 12 Cal 4th 854.

The burden of proof may often depend upon how the charge is characterized. For example, in *Knox v. City of Orland* (1992) 4 Cal. 4th 132, the California Supreme Court upheld the use of a deferential standard of review accorded to a municipality's in making a benefit determination for a benefit assessment district, relying upon *Dawson v. Town of Los Altos Hills* (1976) 16 Cal. 3d 676. Where "[t]he record contains no evidence contradicting the city's benefit determination, and no facts that otherwise tend to show nonproportionality or absence of benefit to the assessed properties . . ." the city's determination of benefit must be "deemed conclusive in the absence of any contradictory evidence in the record." *Knox* at 149, 150.

More recently, the California Supreme Court applied a less deferential standard of review to determine the validity of an assessment. Rather than using the abuse of discretion standard, the Court exercised its independent judgment and instructed other courts to do the same. *Silicon Valley Taxpayers Assoc., Inc. v. Santa Clara County Open Space Auth.* (2008) 44 Cal. 4th 431, 450.

This change is a result of the adoption of Proposition 218 in 1996, which shifted the burden of proof in actions challenging the validity of any assessment from the challenging party to the agency. Proposition 218 provides: "In any legal action contesting the validity of any assessment, the burden shall be on the agency to demonstrate that the property or properties in question receive a special benefit over and above the benefits conferred on the public at large and that the amount of any contested assessment is proportional to, and no greater than, the benefits conferred on the property or properties in question." Cal. Const., art. XIIID, §4, subd. (f). See Chapter 9 of this book, "Finding Neighborhood-Specific Infrastructure and Amenities," for an in-depth discussion of special assessments under Proposition 218.

Notice to Applicant of Fees and Exaction Appeal Period

The conditions of project approval set forth herein include certain fees, dedication requirements, reservation requirements, and other exactions. Pursuant to section 66020(d)(a), these conditions constitute a written notice of the amount of such fees, and a description of the dedications, reservations, and other exactions.

The applicant is hereby notified that the 90-day protest period, commencing from the date of approval of the project, has begun. If the applicant fails to file a protest regarding any of the fees, dedication requirements, reservation requirements, or other exactions contained in this notice, complying with all the requirements of section 66020, the applicant will be legally barred from later challenging such exactions.

Source: City of Rocklin

Uniform Protest Provisions for Fees, Taxes, Assessments, Dedications, Reservations, or Other Exactions

Chapter 9 of the Planning and Zoning Law (Government Code §§ 66020–66025) sets forth the procedures for protests and legal actions challenging fees imposed by local agencies.[2] "Local agency" is defined in section 66000 as a county, city, whether general law or charter, city and county, school district, special district, authority, agency, and any other municipal corporation or district, or other political subdivision of the state. Gov. Code § 66025. See Appendix N for the complete text of these sections.

There are different procedures for challenging different types of fees. Sections 66020 and 66021 govern protests and legal challenges of development fees. Section 66022 governs legal challenges to fees charged for water and sewer connections, zoning changes, building permits and other fees.

Applicability

Before determining how to comply with these protest provisions in mounting a challenge to fees levied by a local agency, it is necessary to first determine which provisions apply to the fee in question. This section examines which fees come under which provisions.

As an initial matter, Chapter 9's protest and legal challenge provisions apply only to the imposition of fees, dedications, reservations and other exactions. Chapter 9 does not apply to land use decisions by local government, such as zoning changes, that may be intended to mitigate impacts of development. See *Fogarty v. City of Chico* (3rd Dist. 2007) 148 Cal. App. 4th 537. It also must be noted that section 66020's provisions constitute the exclusive method for challenging development fees. In *California Ranch Homes Development Company v. San Jacinto Unified School District* (4th Dist. 1993) 17 Cal. App. 4th 573, the court held that an agency's mistaken collection of excess impact fees for development of a senior housing project was challengeable only under section 66020. In *California Ranch Homes*, the developer asserted that section 66020 applies only to suits to challenge a fee in total or to challenge a fee's constitutionality as applied to a particular project. The court rejected this argument, holding that section 66020 also applies to erroneously calculated fees, and thus the developer's suit was barred by section 66020's 120-day statute of limitations.

A common question is whether a fee must be challenged pursuant to section 66020 or section 66022. This determination is important because, as explained below, these different sections have different statutes of limitations and provide for different remedies. As noted above, section 66020, and thus section 66021, apply to challenges to fees imposed on individual development projects, whereas section 66022 applies to challenges to "an ordinance, resolution, or motion adopting a new fee or service charge." Furthermore, section 66022 governs challenges to fees imposed under sections 66013 and 66014, which guides the imposition of charges for water and sewer service, building permits and inspection, charges for zoning administration, and other similar charges.

The courts have articulated the distinction between sections 66020 and 66022 on several occasions. In *Western/California Limited v. Dry Creek Joint Elementary School District* (3rd Dist. 1996) 50 Cal. App. 4th 1461, the Court rejected the defendant School District's contention that a lawsuit was governed by Section 66022 (and its shorter limitations period) because the suit challenged the resolution imposing the disputed fee, rather than the fee itself. The Court noted that Section 66020 also contemplated a challenge to a resolution imposing a fee, and held that the fact that the fees were imposed on specific development projects brought the challenge under section 66020.

The California Supreme Court further clarified the distinction in the applicability of these two provisions in *Barratt American, Inc. v. City of Rancho Cucamonga* (3rd Dist. 2005) 37 Cal. 4th 685. Here, a developer challenged building permit and plan review fees, alleging that the fees were "development fees" imposed on a particular development project, and were subject to the refund provisions of section 66022. The Court rejected this argument. Quoting Government Code section 66000, the Court noted that development fees are fees charged "in connection with approval of a development project for the purposes of defraying all or a portion of the cost of public facilities related to the development project, but [do] not include . . . fees for processing applications for governmental regulatory actions or approvals." *Id.* at 696. The Court concluded that the fees charged by the City were imposed to cover the costs of regulating construction quality and ensuring public safety, and thus were subject to remedies provided by section 66022.

In *N.T. Hill, Inc. v. City of Fresno* (5th Dist. 1999) 72 Cal. App. 4th 977, the Court of Appeal held that lawsuits challenging a local agency's legislative decision to promulgate or change a water or sewer capacity charge were subject to section 66022 and the provisions therein relating to validation actions and the 120-day statute of limitations, while lawsuits challenging a local agency's adjudicatory decision imposing such a charge on a specific development were subject to section 66020.

In *Utility Cost Management v. East Bay Municipal Utility District* (1st Dist. 2000) 79 Cal. App. 4th 1242, Utility Cost Management (UCM) filed a complaint against the East Bay Municipal Utility District (EBMUD) seeking a refund of sums paid by the Berkeley Unified School District (BUSD) for water and wastewater fees. The complaint was based on Government Code section 54999.3, which limits the amount a municipal utility can charge a school district for capital improvements the utility has constructed or will construct. The trial court granted EBMUD's motion for summary judgment based on the argument that UCM's claim was barred, as a matter of law, by the 120-day statute of limitations contained in Government Code section 66022 and by the 120-day statute of limitations in Public Utilities Code section 14402.

The appellate court affirmed the trial court decision holding that the 120-day statute of limitations set forth in Government Code section 66022 applies to an action under Government Code section 54999.4. Government Code section 66022 applies only to fees, capacity charges, and services charges described in and subject to sections 66013 and 66014. The court focused on Government Code section 66013, which sets forth rules that apply when a local agency imposes fees for water connections or capacity fees. The court found that UCM was seeking reimbursement for fees that were synonymous with the term "capacity charges" as defined in section 66013(b)(3) and thus the statute of limitations in section 66022 was applicable.

The Supreme Court of California later decided a sister case, *Utility Cost Management v. Indian Wells Valley Water District* (2001) 26 Cal. 4th 1185, in which it reversed an appellate court's ruling expressly rejecting the reasoning in *Utility Cost Management v. East Bay Municipal Utility District*. The Supreme Court decision solidifies that the 120-day statute of limitations set forth in Government Code section 66022 applies to an action by a public agency to recover amounts paid to a public utility for capital improvements. The fees for which UCM sought reimbursement fell directly within the definition of "capacity charges" as defined in

Government Code section 66013 and were thus subject to Government Code section 66022's 120-day statute of limitation.

The Fifth District Court of Appeal refined the distinctions set forth in *N.T. Hill* in 2003 in a case in which a developer challenged a 1997 ordinance establishing connection charges for users of the County's water and sewer services. *California Psychiatric Transitions, Inc. v. Delhi County Water Dist.* (5th Dist. 2003) 111 Cal. App. 4th 1156. The court specified that where there is an "adjudicatory" determination of a fee, "that determination . . . is itself a 'resolution or motion' establishing the fee." Therefore, the statute of limitations is 120 days under section 66022 and begins to run with the adoption of the resolution or motion. *Id.* at 1162-63.

In *Capistrano Beach Water District v. Taj Development Corporation* (1999) 72 Cal. App. 4th 524, a developer unsuccessfully argued that it was entitled to a refund of sewer connection fees paid to a sanitary district pursuant to section 66001(e) of the Mitigation Fee Act. The Court of Appeal held that the sewer connection fee was not a development fee under the Mitigation Fee Act, but rather, was a connection fee or capacity charge governed by former section 54991 (now section 66013), which did not authorize such a refund.

In *Branciforte v. City of Santa Cruz* (6th Dist. 2006) 138 Cal. App. 4th 914, the court held that the statute of limitations applicable to a claim related to the Subdivision Map Act's provisions regarding credit for "private open space" was that established by section 66020. The court rejected the City's argument that the applicable statute of limitations was the 90-day statutory period, running from the time of the challenged decision, generally applicable to Map Act challenges. Based on its review of legislative history, the court concluded that where a party properly avails itself of the fee protest provisions of Mitigation Fee Act's Section 66020, the limitations period is the one established by that section. If a party does not comply with Section 66020's fee protest procedures to challenge conditions based on the Quimby Act, an action must be brought within the ninety-day statute of limitations generally applicable to subdivision decisions under the Map Act's section 66499.37.

Challenging Development Fees under Government Code Sections 66020 and 66021

Section 66020 lays out the rules for challenging development fees. This section explicitly applies to fees imposed on "a development project," as defined in section 66000. Section 66021 states that section 66020's procedures also apply to challenges to fees, taxes, and assessments required for approval of "a development," as described in Government Code section 65927.[3]

In order to challenge development fees in court, an applicant must first pay the charged fees and file a protest stating the reasons why the fee is invalid. Gov. Code § 66020(a). A statement of protest may be filed at the time a development is approved or conditionally approved, or within ninety days after the fees are imposed. For residential projects, the development is approved when a tentative map, tentative parcel map, or parcel map is approved or conditionally approved or, if a tentative map is not required, when the parcel map is recorded. Gov. Code § 66020(g).[8] For projects not involving a subdivision map, it is unclear when approval occurs.[9] Section 66020(d) requires the local agency to provide the project applicant with written notice when the project is approved or fees are imposed. The notice can be given either at the time of project approval or the imposition of the fees or other exactions, and must include the amount of fees, describe the exactions, and state the ninety-day period in which the applicant has to protest. See the sidebar for a typical notice. A legal challenge pursuant to section 66020 must be brought within 180 days from delivery of the notice required by section 66020(d).

Relationship of Parties after Initiation of Litigation

The fact that a developer has filed a challenge under section 66020 is not sufficient grounds for a local agency to withhold later approvals—such as a building permit necessary for a residential development. Gov. Code § 66020(b). This section does not limit the ability of a local agency to ensure compliance with all applicable provisions of law when determining whether or not to approve a development project in the first instance.

Where a reviewing local agency makes proper and valid findings that certain public improvements or facilities—the need for which is directly attributable to a proposed residential housing development—are necessary for reasons related to public health, safety, and welfare, and elects to require construction of those improvements or facilities as a condition for the approval of the development, then, in the event a protest is lodged pursuant to section 66020(c), that approval shall be suspended pending any of the following:

- Withdrawal of the protest
- The expiration of the 120-day limitation period for filing a lawsuit pursuant to § 66020(d) without an action being filed
- Resolution of any action filed

Section 66020 confers no new or independent authority for imposing fees, dedications, reservations, or other exactions not presently governed by other law.

Refund or Return of Payment

When ruling in favor of the plaintiff in any action or proceeding brought pursuant to section 66020(d), the court shall direct the local agency to refund the unlawful portion of the payment, with interest at the rate of eight percent per annum, or return the unlawful portion of the exaction imposed. Gov. Code § 66020(e). If an action invalidates an ordinance or resolution which had permitted an invalid exaction, the rate of interest on the unlawful portion of the paid sum is based upon the Pooled Money Investment Account. Gov. Code § 66020(f)(1).

In *Shapell Industries, Inc. v. Governing Board of Milpitas Unified School District* (6th Dist. 1991) 1 Cal. App. 4th 218 a developer was entitled to a refund of a portion of school fees, paid under protest, which exceeded the actual cost incurred by new development. The governing board of the school district had adopted resolutions requiring developers to pay development fees of $1.50 per square foot for residential development and $0.25 per square foot for commercial or industrial development. To obtain building permits, Shapell Industries was required to pay the fees. Paying the fees under protest, Shapell then sued the board for declaratory relief and petitioned for a writ of mandate to invalidate the resolutions adopting the school fees. *Id.*

The Interplay Between CEQA and Challenges Under the Mitigation Fee Act

The amendments to CEQA incorporate the rules of *Dolan* and *Ehrlich* to ad hoc mitigation measures (Guidelines § 15126.4). These new regulations raise an interesting dilemma for developers. To the extent that a developer feels that a mitigation measure is an improper exaction, a successful challenge may result in striking down a mitigation measure which was required to support a determination that an impact was mitigated to a level of less than significant. In those circumstances, does it make sense for the developer to be able to proceed with the project "under protest"? Equally tortured considerations go into the identification of the appropriate statute of limitations. Ordinarily in CEQA, the most relied-upon statute of limitations expires thirty days following the posting of the notice of determination. Public Resources Code § 21167. Subsection (e) applies to "any action or proceeding alleging that any other act or omission of a public agency does not comply with this division shall be commenced within thirty days of the filing of the notice. . . ." This raises the issue of whether a developer's challenge to a mitigation measure on the grounds of lack of means is governed by CEQA or the Mitigation Fee Act. There is no way to harmonize these two statutory schemes.

The appellate court held that, although the board had the authority to adopt the fees, a reasonable relationship had to exist between the fees and the need for the school facilities created by the commercial, industrial, and residential development. While sufficient evidence existed for imposition of the fees on commercial and industrial development, the fees imposed on residential development were held to be excessive. Evidence showed that estimates for the exaction were flawed because the calculations reflected costs to accommodate the entire potential increased enrollment without having apportioned those costs only to students associated with new development. Thus, under section 66020(e), the district was required to refund the portion of the fees which did not reasonably reflect the cost of services provided. The court found that this was the precise situation for which section 66020(e) was intended: the authority for the exaction is lawful, but the amount is excessive. To determine the excessive amount of the fee, the court referred to evidence which contained simple arithmetical means for correcting the proportional costs of projects associated solely with new development. This evidence had been before the school board at the time it enacted the resolution. The evidence showed that the fee should have been set at $1.35 per square foot, and that the developer was entitled to a refund of ten percent, plus interest. *Id.*

The effect of 1992 legislative amendments was to expand the obligation of an agency to pay refunds to include those who protested but did not file a lawsuit. If the legal action is filed within 120 days from the effective date of an ordinance or resolution establishing or modifying an exaction on residential housing, and the court determines the exaction to be invalid, then the agency must grant similar relief to others who performed or paid the exaction under protest during the ninety-day period before the action was filed. § 66020(f)(2).

Refunds of sewer service charges that fall under Health and Safety Code Division 5, Chapter 6, Article 4, also requires payment under protest. See the discussion below under Challenges to Exactions Under Other State Law Provisions.

Challenges to Fees Under Section 66022

Any judicial action to attack, review, set aside, void, or annul an ordinance, resolution, or motion adopting a new water and sewer fee (Section 66013), zoning permit fee (Section 66014), or service charge adopted by a local agency must be initiated within 120 days of the effective date of the ordinance, resolution, or motion. The same rule applies to actions that modify or amend an existing fee or service charge. Where the ordinance, resolution, or motion provides for an automatic fee or service charge adjustment, and the adjustment results in an increase in the amount of a fee or service charge, a judicial challenge to the increase must also be initiated within 120 days of the effective date of the increase. Gov. Code § 66022(a). The protest provisions of Sections 66020 and 66021 do not apply here.

Any action by either a local agency or an interested person shall be brought pursuant to the validation procedures contained in Chapter 9 (beginning at section 860) of Title 10 of Part 2 of the Code of Civil Procedure. These are the validation procedures which may be used by "interested parties" to challenge certain actions by local agencies. This body of law has very strict notice, summons, and publication procedures which the plaintiff must follow carefully. *Cmty. Redevelopment Agency of Los Angeles v. Superior Court of Los Angeles County* (2nd Dist. 1967) 248 Cal.App.2d 164, 170.

These timelines do not apply to ordinances or resolutions which establish exactions. To gain relief from these ordinances the legislative act must be challenged at the time the exaction is imposed on a specific development. Gov. Code §§ 66020, 66021. See also *Balch Enterprises v. New Haven Unified Sch. Dist.* (1st Dist. 1990) 219 Cal. App. 3d 783, where the action challenging a school district resolution imposing school facility fees on new commercial and industrial construction was governed by the four-year catch-all period of limitations set forth in Code of Civil Procedure section 343. In that case, the court concluded that neither the 180-day period of limitation set forth in former section 66008 (now Section 66020), nor the 120-day statute of limitations set forth in section 54995 (now Section 66022) applied. However, this gap was closed by amendments in 1991 to section 53080.1 (since repealed and replaced with Education Code § 17621) which applied the "pay under protest" statutes (Sections 66020 and 66021) to commercial and industrial development.

In *Branciforte v. City of Santa Cruz* (6th Dist. 2006) 138 Cal. App. 4th 914, the court rejected the City's allegation that a developer should be barred from challenging the City's failure to grant a credit for "private open space" against its parkland dedication requirements because the developer had failed to exhaust administrative remedies. The City had no provisions for such credit in its land use regulations. The City maintained that the developer should have requested a credit using the administrative procedure available under the City's subdivision ordinance for requesting modifications to the provisions of that ordinance. By not doing so, the City argued that Branciforte had failed to exhaust its administrative remedies. The court disagreed, holding that the City's procedure did not provide a mechanism for obtaining administrative review of the City's decision not to grant credit for private open space. The procedure allows a subdivider to seek minor adjustments to the requirements of the subdivision ordinance under certain limited circumstances. Here, by contrast, the subdivider sought creation of an entirely new provision, granting private open space credit, which was not provided for in the subdivision ordinance.

Challenges to Exactions Under Other State Law Provisions

In *Howard Jarvis Taxpayers Association v. City of La Habra* (2001) 25 Cal. 4th 809, plaintiffs sued the City of La Habra for imposing and collecting a utility users tax. The City contended that the suit was barred by the three-year statute of limitations applicable to a liability created by statute. Code Civ. Proc. § 338(a). The taxpayers argued that the statute began to run when the Supreme Court of California declared Proposition 62 to be constitutional, or in the alternative that the limitations period starts to run anew with each collection of taxes.

Approved by the voters in November 1986, Proposition 62 provided that local governments may not impose any general tax without approval of the proposed tax by a majority of voters. A few years after the passage of Proposition 62, an appellate court declared its voter approval requirements to be unconstitutional. In December of 1992, the city established a utility users tax by ordinance to raise revenue for general governmental purposes. The city did not submit the ordinance to the voters for approval. In September of 1995, the California Supreme Court decided in *Santa Clara County Local Transportation Authority v. Guardino* (1995) 11 Cal. 4th 220, that the voter approval requirements of Proposition 62 were constitutional. In March 1996, the taxpayers filed their lawsuit.

The Court rejected the taxpayers' first argument that the statute of limitations began to run when *Guardino* was decided. "Plaintiffs were free to challenge the tax when it was first imposed, and might, as in *Guardino*, have obtained a favorable result in the Court of Appeal despite the adverse *City of Woodlake v. Logan* (5th Dist. 1991) 230 Cal. App. 3d. 1058, decision." However, the Court agreed with the plaintiffs' alternative argument that the limitations period starts to run anew with each collection of taxes. The Court held that "plaintiffs have alleged an ongoing violation of Proposition 62's commands, for which they seek relief in mandamus (Code Civ. Proc. § 1085(a)), and a presently existing actual controversy between themselves and the city over the validity of the utility tax, which they seek to resolve by declaratory judgment (Code Civ. Proc. § 1060); those causes of action are not barred merely because similar claims could have been made at earlier times as to earlier violations, or because plaintiffs do not at this time also seek a refund of taxes paid." *Howard Jarvis Taxpayers Association* at 821–822. Thus, where the three-year limitations period for action on a liability created by statute applies, and no other statute or constitutional rule provides differently, the validity of a tax measure may be challenged within the statutory period after any collection of the tax, regardless of whether more than three years has passed since the tax was enacted. *Id.* at 825.

The theory of continuous accrual applied in *Howard Jarvis* is not applicable where a statute expressly provides a statute of limitations. For example, in *Barratt American, Inc. v. City of San Diego* (1st Dist. 2004) 117 Cal. App. 4th 809, a residential developer challenged a City resolution authorizing a facilities benefit assessment for a certain property. The developer claimed its lawsuit was timely under the theory of continuous accrual applied in *Howard Jarvis*. The Court rejected this argument and refused to adopt a different date of accrual where California Code of Civil Procedure section 329.5 expressly states that the statute runs from the date the assessment is levied. *Id.* at 820.

In rejecting the theory of continuous accrual, the *Barratt* court likened the case to *Utility Cost Management v. Indian Wells Valley Water District* (2001) 26 Cal. 4th 1185, in which the California Supreme Court found that an action seeking a refund of allegedly excessive capital facilities fees was barred by the limitations period given in section 66022 of the Government Code. *Id.* at 820. See also *Travis v. County of Santa Cruz* (2004) 33 Cal. 4th 757, 774 (rejecting theory of continuous accrual and holding challenges based on later-enacted state statutes must be brought within the limitations period of the first time the challenge could be brought).

As with refund actions under section 66020, a cause of action challenging sewer fees under the Health and Safety Code is not perfected unless the fees have been paid under protest. In *Los Altos Golf and Country Club v. County of Santa Clara* (6th Dist. 2008) 165 Cal. App. 4th 198, taxpayers brought an action against the City of Los Altos ("City") and County of Santa Clara ("County") alleging an excessive overcharge of sewer fees. The City and County demurred on the grounds that taxpayers had no claim because they did not pay the fees "under protest" pursuant to Health and Safety Code section 5472. *Id.* at 202.

Taxpayers argued "payment under protest" was not a prerequisite to filing a legal challenge, relying upon Health and Safety Code section 5473.8, which makes all laws pertaining to general taxes applicable to fees. Section 5473.8 authorizes a procedure found in the Internal Revenue Code, which allows the taxpayer to directly bring an action in superior court. The court disagreed with plaintiffs, holding the more specific claim provision prevails over procedures for general taxes. "The plain language of section 5472 thus contemplates payment under protest, followed by an action if the payer is unable to secure a refund." *Id.* at 205.

Mediation

In an effort to expedite the resolution of lawsuits involving land use matters, including CEQA, the California Legislature enacted new legislation in the 1993–94 session: SB 517. (Bergeson, Chapter 300, Stats. 1994.) This enactment added Chapter 9.3 to the Planning and Zoning Law, beginning with section 66030. The law authorizes mediation of lawsuits relating to the following land development concerns: approval or denial of a project; the scope of environmental review; compliance with the Permit Streamlining Act; development fees, including school impact mitigation; legality of a general plan or redevelopment plan; and actions taken pursuant to the Cortese-Knox Local Government Reorganization Act. While imposition of exactions by a city or county, including dedications, are not formally listed, such actions would reasonably be included within a lawsuit concerning a project approval.

Within five days after the deadline for the defendant or respondent to file its reply in a lawsuit, the court is authorized to invite the parties to pursue mediation. Thus, the parties to the lawsuit themselves are not at liberty to initiate mediation, although presumably a party could simply request that the court initiate the statutory process. The parties are free, without prejudice, to decline the mediation option. If the parties do not reject mediation, but have not selected the mediator within a thirty-day period, then the action must proceed in court. Once a mediator has been selected, then the litigation time lines are tolled. Gov. Code § 66032(a). This suggests that the litigation timelines during the thirty-day decision period, established to allow the parties to consider acceptance of a mediator, are not automatically tolled.

The law also provides that mediation meetings conducted with less than a quorum of local government officials are not subject to the Brown Act or the Bagley-Keene Open Meeting Act. All other current requirements of law governing actions of public agencies would apply. Gov. Code § 66032(c). By statute, the litigation timelines are reinstated after ninety days (and every 90 days thereafter if initially continued), unless the parties reach a settlement, or agree by written stipulation to extend the mediation period for another ninety days. Gov. Code § 66032(d).

Unless stipulated to by the parties, the mediator is not to file a statement with the court, nor can the court consider, any statement of the mediator other than a statement of agreement or nonagreement by the parties. Gov. Code § 66032(e).

Upon completion of the mediation, the mediator must file a report with the Office of Permit Assistance. This report is to include the title, the names of the parties, and an estimate of costs avoided, if any, resulting from the parties using mediation rather than litigation to resolve their dispute. Gov. Code § 66033. It is ambiguous as to whether a mediator, after an unsuccessful mediation, must file the report. Since the particular code section speaks of costs avoided as a result of mediation in conjunction with resolving the dispute, the better reading is that the report is only required after successful mediation.

If the mediation is unsuccessful, the court has the option to set the matter for a settlement conference before a superior court judge other than the judge who will later hear the merits of the lawsuit. Gov. Code § 66034. The Judicial Council is authorized to adopt necessary procedures and forms.

The above procedures are somewhat at odds with the rules governing CEQA lawsuits. Public Resources Code section 21167.8 envisions that a CEQA settlement conference be conducted within a specified time period, with potential sanctions for noncompliance. Public Resources Code § 21167.8(e). No sanctions are included within the new mediation statute. More importantly, the litigation timelines under the CEQA statute are designed to run concurrently with the settlement discussions, the opposite result of the mediation statute. However, since the new mediation statute states that its sections apply "notwithstanding any other provision of law," the new provisions govern, at least to the extent that the parties agree to engage in mediation. If mediation is summarily rejected, then the CEQA provisions still apply.

Audits

Any person may request an audit to determine whether any fee or charge levied by a local agency exceeds the amount reasonably necessary to cover the cost of any product or service provided. If a person makes that request, the legislative body of the local agency may retain an independent auditor to determine whether the fee or charge is reasonable. Gov. Code § 66023(a). Any costs incurred by a local agency in having the audit conducted pursuant to section 66023(a) may be recovered from the person who requested the audit. Gov. Code § 66023(b). Any audit conducted by an independent auditor pursuant to section 66023(a) shall conform to generally accepted auditing standards. Gov. Code § 66023(c). As an alternative procedure, audits of county-approved fees may also be required pursuant to section 54985.

The interplay between section 66023 and the review statutes of sections 66020 and 66021 is unclear. An audit under section 66023 may be requested only after the fee or charge is levied. However, neither sections 66020 nor 66021 provide for tolling the statute of limitations during the audit period. ("Tolling" means postponing or suspending the statute of limitations until a dispute is resolved.) Consequently, even if a party requesting the audit receives a favorable report, the limitations period may have begun. A person in that position should either obtain an agreement from the local agency to toll the statute of limitations or, if necessary, file an action to prevent the limitations period from beginning.

Special Subdivision Map Act Procedures

Bridges and Major Thoroughfares Fees

A landowner may protest the imposition of a fee for construction of bridges and major thoroughfares under section 66484 in a manner similar to the Majority Protest Act of 1931 (Sts. & Hwys. Code § 2900 *et seq.*). Those procedures typically apply to assessment districts. If a written protest is filed by the owners of more than one-half the property area benefiting from the improvement, the legislative body is banned for one year from carrying on proceedings for improvement or acquisition. Under sections 66484(a) and (b), any protest may be withdrawn by the owner in writing at any time prior to the conclusion of a public hearing. These majority protests may be directed against all or only a portion of the improvements. In either case, if successfully protested, proceedings are halted for a year on all or a part of the improvement under protest. Notwithstanding this limitation, the legislative body may still continue with proceedings for the uncontested portion. In addition, proceedings involving the protested facilities may begin where the owners of more than one-half of the property benefited support district formation and the legislative body approves the action by a four-fifths vote.

Groundwater Recharge Facilities Fees

Under section 66484.5, a local ordinance may impose a fee for groundwater recharge facilities to replenish the underground water supply within a benefiting area. As with fees for bridges and major thoroughfares, protests by majority landowners can be filed under the provisions of the ordinance. If a protest is filed and not withdrawn by owners of more than one-half of the area of the property to be benefitted, the proposed proceedings shall be abandoned and the legislative body shall not commence or carry out any proceedings for the same acquisition or improvement for one year from the filing of the protest.

Statute of Limitations

Judicial review of a challenge based on a violation of the Subdivision Map Act must be instituted within ninety days after the date of the decision being challenged. Gov. Code § 66499.37. This limitation requires the action to be initiated and a summons served within ninety days.

In *Hensler v. City of Glendale* (1994) 8 Cal. 4th 1, the California Supreme Court held that an action seeking compensation for inverse condemnation as the result of application of the city's subdivision ordinance was governed by the ninety-day statute of limitations prescribed in the Subdivision Map Act, Government Code section 66499.37. See also *Maginni v. City of Glendale* (2d Dist. 1999) 72 Cal. App. 4th 1102, 1104.

Hensler, a developer in the City of Glendale, submitted a proposed map for 588 residential units. The map was approved, but with a limitation that prohibited any development along the ridge tops in compliance with the City's subdivision ordinance. Hensler later filed an action in inverse condemnation, arguing that the ordinance effectuated a taking of forty percent of his property as a result of the ridge top limitations. In an effort to avoid the statute of limitations, the plaintiff sought only damages for the taking. The Supreme Court held, however, that for all practical purposes the plaintiff was seeking to invalidate the subdivision ordinance on its face or as applied to his property. In other words, Hensler could not leave the land use decision unchallenged and then separately seek damages. Accordingly, the court held that the broad language of section

66499.37 governed.[10] As a result, Hensler's complaint was barred by the ninety-day statute of limitations. *Id.*

The court's ruling disposes of an often argued position that a property owner, when pursuing a claim based upon the United States Constitution, need not exhaust administrative remedies or follow state statutes for filing his or her claim in court. Thus, property owners will, at least for regulatory takings claims, have to challenge the underlying approval, both administratively and judicially, prior to making an inverse condemnation claim. Similarly, the United States Supreme Court in *San Remo Hotel v. City and County of San Francisco* (2005) 545 U.S. 323, held that the full faith and credit clause barred petitioner from having its federal takings claim heard in federal court after dismissal of its takings claim in state court. See Chapter 4, for a more in depth discussion of the *San Remo* case and its consequences.

Integrating Exaction Challenges with Other Legal Theories—Statutes of Limitations

In most circumstances, a party challenging an excessive exaction based upon sections 66020 or 66021 will incorporate additional legal theories. The field of municipal law is replete with varying statutes of limitation, depending on the particular theory. The more commonly encountered statutes of limitation are as follows:

Fees and Exactions

- Zoning permits, water and sewer fees–120 days from the effective date of the enactment. Gov. Code § 66022(a)
- Exactions, administrative protest–ninety days. Gov. Code § 66020(d)
- Exactions, other than those pursuant to the Map Act–120 days. Gov. Code § 66020(d)
- Map Act exactions challenged pursuant to section 66475.4–ninety days. Gov. Code § 66499.37
- Conditional use permit or other permits and variances–ninety days. Gov. Code § 65009(c)
- General/specific plans and zoning actions must commence and service completed within 120 days. Gov. Code § 65009

CEQA

In cases where agencies are proceeding without complying with CEQA, aggrieved parties have 180 days to file a legal challenge. The time within which to bring this action begins with the agency's formal decision to approve or carry out the project or, where no such decision is made, when the project begins. Pub. Res. Code §§ 21167(a), (d). However, when an agency substantially changes a project after preparing and certifying an Environmental Impact Report, but fails to prepare a subsequent EIR or to notify the public, a legal challenge may be filed within 180 days of the time the complaining party either knew, or reasonably should have known, of the changes. *Concerned Citizens of Costa Mesa, Inc. v. 32nd Dist. Agri. Assoc.* (4th Dist. 1986) 42 Cal. 3d 929, 937–939.

All other limitation periods under CEQA are much shorter, either thirty or thirty-five days. For the following agency actions the period is thirty days:

- Filing a notice of determination (NOD) after approving a project for which an EIR or negative declaration was prepared. Pub. Res. Code §§ 21167(b), (c), and (e); CEQA Guidelines § 15112(c)(1)
- Filing a Notice of Decision by a certified state regulatory agency program. Pub. Res. Code § 21080.5(g); CEQA Guidelines § 15112(c)(3)
- Decision by the Secretary of Resources to certify a state agency's regulatory program. Pub. Res. Code § 21080.5(h); CEQA Guidelines § 15112(c)(4)

The limitations period to challenge the filing of a notice of exemption (NOE) is thirty-five days. Pub. Res. Code § 21167(d); CEQA Guidelines § 15112(c)(2). Where a local agency's notice of exemption is filed with the county clerk but not posted properly, the period is 180 days. *Lewis v. Seventeenth Dist. Agri. Assoc.* (3d Dist. 1985) 165 Cal. App. 3d 823, 835.

Takings Claims: The Need for Ripeness

As a general jurisdictional requirement, a case must be "ripe" before the plaintiff is entitled to review in federal court. The U.S. Supreme Court addressed the ripeness issue in the context of a regulatory takings claim involving transferable development rights (TDRs). In *Suitum v. Tahoe Regional Planning Agency* (1997) 520 U.S. 725, the petitioner, Suitum, owned an undeveloped lot near Lake Tahoe. The respondent, Tahoe Regional Planning Agency, determined that the lot was ineligible for development under agency regulations, but that Suitum was entitled to receive certain allegedly valuable TDRs that she could sell to other landowners with the agency's approval. Suitum did not seek those rights, but instead filed a 42 U.S. Code section 1983 action alleging that the regional planning agency committed an unconstitutional regulatory taking when it determined that her residential lot was ineligible for development, even though she had not attempted to sell the TDRs to which she was entitled as owner.

The district court held that Suitum's claim was not ripe for adjudication because she had not attempted to sell her TDRs and, therefore, there was no final decision as to how she would be allowed to use her property. The court of appeals for the Ninth Circuit agreed that Suitum's claim was not ripe in the absence of an application for transfer of her development rights, reasoning that an action on a TDR transfer application would be the requisite "final decision" by the agency regarding the application of its regulations to Suitum's lot. The U.S. Supreme Court granted certiorari for the sole purpose of determining whether Suitum's claim of a regulatory taking of her land in violation of the Fifth and Fourteenth Amendments was ready for judicial review under prudential ripeness principles.

The Supreme Court noted that there are two independent prudential hurdles to a regulatory taking claim brought against a state entity in federal court. *Id.* at 1664. First, the plaintiff must demonstrate that she has received a final decision regarding the application of the challenged regulations to the property at issue from the government entity charged with implementing the regulations and, second, has sought compensation through the procedures the State has provided for doing so. *Williamson County Reg'l. Planning Comm'n. v. Hamilton Bank of Johnson City* (1985) 473 U.S. 172.

The first requirement follows from the principle that only a regulation that "goes too far" results in a taking under the Fifth Amendment. "A court cannot determine whether a regulation has gone 'too' far unless it knows how far the regulation goes," hence the requirement for a "final agency decision." *MacDonald, Sommer & Frates v. County of Yolo* (1986) 477 U.S. 340. The second hurdle stems from the Fifth Amendment's proviso that only takings without "just compensation" infringe that amendment. "[I]f a State provides an adequate procedure for seeking just compensation, the property owner cannot claim a violation of the Just Compensation Clause until it has used the procedure and been denied just compensation." *Williamson County* at 195.

Because the district court only addressed the "final decision" prong of *Williamson County*, the Supreme Court confined its discussion to that issue without deciding the question of how definitive a local zoning decision must be to satisfy Williamson County's demand for finality. The court did state, however, that two points about the requirement are clear: (1) it applies to decisions about how a taking plaintiff's own land may be used, and (2) it responds to the high degree of discretion characteristically possessed by land use boards in softening the strictures of the general regulations they administer.

The Supreme Court found that the demand for finality was satisfied by Suitum's claim as there was no question about how the regulations at issue applied to the particular land in question. The agency had finally determined that Suitum's land lay entirely within a Stream Environment Zone and, consequently, no additional land coverage or other permanent land disturbance on the parcel was permitted. Therefore, because the agency had no discretion to exercise over Suitum's right to use her land, no occasion existed for applying the *Williamson County's* requirement that a landowner take steps to obtain a final decision about the use that would be permitted on a particular parcel. In its opinion, the Supreme Court indicated that, upon remand, the district court should consider the second prong of the two-part test from *Williamson County*. The Supreme Court held that Suitum's claim was ripe for review since the agency had no discretion to exercise over the landowner's right to use her land because it had conclusively determined that the land was in an area that rendered it ineligible for development.

In *Ehrlich* 12 Cal. 4th 854, a developer complied with the requirements of section 66020 by filing a protest with the city which enumerated all of the bases of his challenge to recreational and art fees imposed on a proposed condominium project, including his constitutional takings claim. The California Supreme Court affirmed that all protests to a development fee that challenge the sufficiency of its relationship to the effects attributable to a development project, regardless of the legal theory for the challenge, must be brought in accordance with the administrative procedures set forth in section 66020.

Under the futility exception to the ripeness doctrine, a developer is relieved from submitting multiple development applications when the manner in which the first application was rejected makes it clear that no project will be approved. *Milagra Ridge Partners, Ltd. v. City of Pacifica* (1st Dist. 1998) 62 Cal. App. 4th 108 (holding that when the regulatory authority has drawn the line, clearly and emphatically as to the permissible use of the property, the developer is not required to submit additional development applications).

In *Home Builders Association of Northern California v. City of Napa* (1st Dist. 2001) 90 Cal. App. 4th 188, the city enacted an inclusionary zoning ordinance that required a residential developer to set aside ten percent of new units for low or moderate income housing. Developers had two options: (1) satisfy the requirement through an alternative equivalent proposal such as a dedication of land, or the construction of affordable unites on another site; or (2) pay an in-lieu fee to satisfy the requirements. The court held that the ordinance did not constitute a taking on its face, because the City had the ability to reduce or completely waive the requirements imposed by the ordinance. Nor did the ordinance fail to substantially advance a legitimate government interest. The Mitigation Fee Act portion of the opinion was not certified for publication.

Attorney Fee Awards

In the field of land use law, courts operating under the authority of Code of Civil Procedure section 1021.5 have frequently awarded attorney's fees to successful plaintiffs based on factors such as benefit to the public, time spent, preclusion of other employment, etc. *San Bernardino Audubon Soc'ty., Inc. v. County of San Bernardino* (4th Dist. 1984) 155 Cal. App. 3d 738, 755. If a successful court challenge to an exaction is based simply on procedural issues, an award of fees is unlikely. *Balch Enter. v. New Haven Unified Sch. Dist.* (1st Dist. 1990) 219 Cal. App. 3d 783, 796. Project applicants who successfully overturn an excessive exaction normally will not bring themselves within the scope of the fee statute, since typically a sufficient private economic basis exists for them to undertake the litigation. *Beach Colony II v. California Coastal Comm'n.* (4th Dist. 1985) 166 Cal. App. 3d 106, 109. In *Beach Colony II*, for example, the developer paid $50,500 in litigation costs, but, as a result of the litigation, saved $300,000 in development costs. In these circumstances, the economic incentive that would be generated by an award of fees pursuant to section 1021.5 was unnecessary.

A nonpecuniary interest in the outcome of litigation may also justify a refusal to award fees under section 1021.5. In *Williams v. Board of Permit Appeals* (1st Dist. 1999) 74 Cal. App. 4th 961, the appellate court held that the trial court did not abuse its discretion in refusing to award attorney fees under the private attorney general statute to a homeowner for a successful effort to prevent construction of a four-story building adjacent to his residence on a block of Victorian homes. The court held that the homeowner's interest in maintaining the aesthetic integrity of his immediate neighborhood and protecting both his property's privacy and its access to light, air, and views, constituted an "individual stake" as important as any pecuniary interest that, when weighed against the lesser public interest, did not justify a fee award.

A court may, however, grant attorneys fees where it can be shown that plaintiffs have incurred fees out of proportion to their personal, non-pecuniary interests in the due process rights at stake. In *Bowman v. City of Berkeley* (1st Dist. 2005) 131 Cal. App. 4th 173, the Court awarded attorneys fees to a group of seven neighbors, two of whom lived directly adjacent to a proposed housing project for senior citizens which the group successfully opposed on due process grounds. The *Bowman* Court distinguished the plaintiffs from the homeowner in *Williams v. Board of Permit Appeals*, finding that their personal nonpecuniary interests, although similar to those of the Williams homeowner, were "far more attenuated" since they filed their petition on behalf of 250 other residents and received financial support from approximately forty other citizens. *Id.* at 182.

Margaret M. Sohagi is owner and Principal of the Sohagi Law Group, a Los Angeles environmental and land use firm, where she represents only public agencies, both from a legal and planning perspective. Ms. Sohagi is also an Adjunct Professor of Land Use Law at USC Law School, where she teaches Land Use Law and an Instructor for the Judicial Council of California, teaching CEQA courses to Superior, Appellate, and Supreme Court Judges and court attorneys.

CHAPTER EIGHT

Meeting Local Needs Through Exactions and Other Techniques

By William W. Abbott

This chapter focuses on innovations in local strategies for affordable low-income housing, school facilities, art in public places, open space, habitat conservation, equestrian trails, county facilities funded by projects in cities, and transportation systems. Although each community has its own particular needs and goals, all face similar economic conditions. The reality is that available funding for government services is scarce, and when development slows very little revenue is generated by fees.

The reality is that available funding for government services is scarce, and when development slows very little revenue is generated by fees.

Fees and other exactions frequently lag far behind service needs, and for large capital improvements, often only a fee that has been implemented through several business cycles will generate enough revenue to fund the desired capital facility. If a public improvement is critically needed and substantial short-term funding is required, the creation of a new linkage or impact fee may not be a viable option. Bonds in conjunction with taxes and/or fees may be a more efficient strategy to collect needed revenue.

Housing Trust Funds

City of Sacramento

In 1989, the City of Sacramento established the Sacramento Housing Trust Fund. The fund actually consisted of two separate funds: the North Natomas Fund and the City-Wide Low Income Fund. The funds were supported by linkage fees imposed on commercial development.

The city amended its zoning ordinances to require that developers of all commercial projects, whether new construction, major additions, or remodels, pay fees into these funds. At its inception, fees ranged from $0.18 per square foot for warehouse space to $0.95 per square foot for offices. After a slight adjustment in 1992, the City Council adopted a resolution to increase the fees by forty-four percent in December 2004 and 81.3 percent in July 2005.

Already in existence when the city created the Low Income Fund, the North Natomas Fund was the result of a 1987 development agreement and the settlement of several lawsuits over development in North Natomas between the developers, the city

BMR = Below-market rate
SRO = Single-room occupancy

council, and citizen groups. Its revenue is used to increase the supply of housing units located within the adjacent North Sacramento Community Plan.

The purpose of the City-Wide Low Income Fund, made up of fees on all commercial development throughout the City of Sacramento except for North Natomas, is to finance low-income housing throughout the city. Twenty-five percent of these revenues are for new construction or rehabilitation of single-room occupancy (SRO) residential hotels, which provide housing for low-income single persons typically working at minimum wage. The remaining seventy-five percent is used as local leverage to obtain state and federal tax credits for family housing in new construction projects, or for other programs that require matching grants. The ordinance allows for those desiring to build their own affordable housing units to pay an in lieu fee that amounts to twenty percent of the original fee amount, in addition to building the units.

California Housing Trust Funds

In addition to Sacramento, a number of other cities in California have housing trust funds in place and operating. Those communities include: Berkeley, Cupertino, Los Angeles, Menlo Park, Morgan Hill, Palo Alto, San Diego, San Francisco, Santa Monica, and West Hollywood. n

In 2005, the Sacramento Housing and Redevelopment Agency, which runs the Housing Trust Fund program, commissioned Keyser Marston Associates, Inc. to update the prior nexus analysis drafted in 1989. The Housing Trust Fund Nexus Analysis: City of Sacramento was finalized in March 2006.

SRO = Single Room Occupancy

This study updates the information in the original fee study and provides for different fee options. Although the study was finished in 2006, the fees have not yet been implemented by the city. (See Appendix D for excerpts from the March 2006 study.)

In 1989, a building association, claiming that the City of Sacramento had failed to establish a sufficient nexus between commercial development and the increased demand for low-income housing, challenged the ordinance in court. Both the District Court and the Ninth Circuit Court of Appeals ruled in favor of the city. In 1992, the Supreme Court declined to hear the case. *Commercial Builders of Northern California v. City of Sacramento* (9th Cir. 1991) 941 F.2d 872, cert. denied 112 S. Ct. 1997 (1992). See chapter 3 for a discussion of the case.

For more information, contact City of Sacramento, (916) 808-8931.

Local Funding for Schools Beyond Fees

In Roseville, both the Roseville City Elementary School District and the Roseville Joint Union High School District have successfully presented bond measures to local voters to fund modernizations and renovations, new additions, and technology improvements needed due to an overcrowding problem within the city's school districts. This alternative to relying exclusively on school impact fees has made it possible for the city to support the demand for construction of new school facilities and improvements as the city's housing development has continued to increase.

In 2002, Roseville Elementary School District passed Measure H, which issued $29,117,071 in bond funds to build a new elementary school, construct several new multipurpose rooms, and complete school office modifications and a number of general improvements including installation of energy efficient heating and cooling systems, plumbing repairs, asbestos removal, and so on.

Following the successful passage of Measure H, Roseville High School District, with overwhelming support from district officials, community members, and a well-organized campaign that focused on the overcrowded high school system, was able to pass the seventy-nine-million-dollar bond Measure J in 2004. Monies from this particular bond have been authorized for use in construction, reconstruction, rehabilitation, or replacement of school facilities, including the furnishing and equipping of school facilities. An average homeowner pays approximately $175 per month in special taxes, which is calculated based on a tax formula merging both capital and services taxes. By combining the bond monies with state matching funds and developer fees, the Roseville High School District has received a top grade in meeting the school facility demands in its rapidly growing community.

Equestrian Trails

Beginning with its 1981 General Plan, the City of Rancho Cucamonga has enforced the basic maintenance, construction, and rehabilitation of equestrian trials throughout the city via their Master Plan of Trails. In late 1991, the city approved the Trail Implementation Plan, which is designed to provide detailed development standards, trail alignments, and funding mechanisms necessary to make the trail system a reality.

As outlined in the City's Development Code, all new residential developments within the Equestrian/Rural area are required to include local feeder trail easements for equestrian purposes in their plans prior to approval of any subdivision maps and other development approvals. The Planning Commission decides which non-residential projects within the Equestrian/Rural area must also be required to include these easements in their plans in order to link residential areas with the trail system. In addition, community trails and regional trails are provided where required by the adopted Master Plan of Trails. Developers construct the new trails within their communities, and payment for the development of the trail is included in the price of the home (typically equivalent to or less than the costs of community landscaping).

In October 2007, the city, acting as the lead agency, joined together with the San Bernardino Associated Governments and surrounding cities and opened The Pacific Electric Trail corridor. This twenty-one-mile-long trail runs along the discontinued Southern Pacific Railway from Claremont to Rialto. The purpose of the trail is to provide recreational opportunities for cyclists, pedestrians, runners, and equestrians. Many sources of federal and state funds are available for these types of trails. The State Transportation Fund was the main funding source for this particular project, with additional monies gathered from grants and corporate and private donations, for an estimated total of $8.2 million. For additional information contact: Larry Henderson, Principal Planner, City of Rancho Cucamonga, 10500 Civic Center Drive, Rancho Cucamonga, California 91730, (909) 477-2750.

Art in Public Places

The City and County of Sacramento have worked together since 1977 to integrate artwork from local and regional artists into the landscape of the city and county. In order to facilitate the art in public places program, the city and county jointly established the Sacramento Metropolitan Arts Commission (SMAC). SMAC allocates the funds given to the program and decides which artworks will be displayed at which locations.

The funding for the program comes from the budgets for various capital improvement projects within the city and the county. Both jurisdictions passed ordinances providing that for each eligible public construction project, not less than two percent of the

Developers of new projects in the City of Brea are required to obtain, conserve, and maintain art for public display as part of the city's Art in Public Places program.

cost of the project must be spent on procuring artworks. Sacramento City Code, § 2.84.120; Sacramento County Code, § 2.96.150. In the city, an "eligible construction project" means "any capital project paid for wholly or in part by the city or the parking authority of the city to construct or remodel any [public] building." Sacramento City Code, § 2.84.110. The county uses a narrower definition, namely any capital building project or remodeling project "in excess of one hundred thousand dollars." For these projects, two percent of the budgeted cost will be used by SMAC to place artworks outside or inside the building being constructed or remodeled.

The types of artworks placed in, on, or about the buildings include permanent as well as temporary art. As of 2008, SMAC had placed 400 permanent artworks within the city and county. SMAC has also expanded since its small beginnings in 1977 to include exhibit spaces, such as City Hall, Sacramento Municipal Utility District, the Sacramento International Airport, and educational programs. These new programs have required new sources of funding, and along with receiving funds from the city and county for public projects, SMAC's 2008–2013 business plan looks to expand the sources of funding to other public sector sources as well as sources from the private sector. Overall, the Sacramento program has been very successful and continues to grow.

For more information, see http://www.sacmetroarts.org/index.html.

Innovations

Supercharging the Repayment Schedule

Reimbursement agreements often result in a large delay between the developer building the public facility and the developer getting reimbursed for the excess costs. In order to ensure that the developer gets reimbursed in a timely manner, some localities are entering into agreements with subsequent developers in which the subsequent developers agree to pay a surcharge to connect to the public facility. This surcharge reimburses the first developer, and that initial reimbursement agreement is then fulfilled. The locality then enters into reimbursement agreements with the subsequent developers whereby the subsequent developers will get reimbursed for the surcharges by the impact fees charged on new development. This surcharge will only apply to a certain percentage of subsequent developers, such as the first one-third. After the first one-third has paid the surcharge and the first developer is reimbursed, new developments will no longer have to pay the surcharge. These types of reimbursement plans provide incentives for developers to build the public facility and spread the cost among many developers, instead of one. (See Appendix B for a sample Nexus Study.)

City of Oxnard's Financing Plan for Street Repairs

The City of Oxnard, with the assistance of a legal team and bankers, developed a pioneering $27.7 million Certificate of Participation (COP) program, the first long-term gas-tax financial improvement in California that requires no general fund pledge. The goal of this pioneering financing program is to allocate the funds directly toward major capital improvements, avoiding the typical "patch-work" that the city streets have suffered from over the years as a result of limited funds provided via the state gas tax. These long-term improvements along with ongoing maintenance of the street improvements should help the city save more money in the long run. The city achieves this goal by securitizing the future gas tax revenues.

The legal structure of the city's transaction involves the city selling certain unimproved streets to a joint powers authority. The joint powers authority then has the responsibility to make the improvements to the streets, and the city agrees to repurchase the streets back through an installment purchase agreement. The installment payments consist of gas tax revenue only, allowing the city to steer clear from borrowing from the general fund. The right to receive installments under the purchase agreement is assigned by the joint powers authority to a trustee, which then issues the COP, backed by the future gas tax funds. The COP is used to generate significant capital, upfront, for major improvements. Each time the city makes an installment payment, the investors in the COP receive tax-exempt interest from that installment. Historically, using the gas tax revenue effectively for major improvements has been difficult because of the legislative caps in bonding gas tax revenues. Cities such as Santa Ana, Coachella, Indio, La Puente, and Long Beach are interested in joining Oxnard in similar programs.

County Fees within Cities

Stanislaus County

Growth in the cities also increases demands on services provided by counties, which typically include the coroner's office, county roads between cities and towns, the district attorney's office, the courts, crime lab, jail, and other criminal justice activities. Counties are searching for additional sources of revenue to maintain these services.

At the end of 1989, the Stanislaus County Board of Supervisors established a public facilities fee for development within the county, which was allocated to nine categories countywide and eleven categories for incorporated areas. As of May 2008, the program divides the fees among eleven categories countywide and twelve categories for the incorporated areas. Paid when a building permit is issued, or at the earliest time permitted by law, the fee depends on usage and relies on various units of measure. Residential use is by unit, hotel by room, commercial by square footage, and recreational use by acre or court. The general units used to determine the fee are residential and non-residential. Residential is divided into three types: single family, multi-family, and senior housing. Non-residential is divided into five different use categories: office, industrial, commercial-retail, restaurants, financial, and miscellaneous. The miscellaneous category encompasses uses such as day care centers, manual car washes, and nursing homes. The following are a few examples of countywide fees charged by the type of use after the 2005 annual adjustment:

- A gas station is $3,028.81 per pump
- A convenience market is $40,700.66
- A golf course at $2,320.92 per acre
- A single family residential use has a total fee of $8,037.73

The controversial element is that the fee is exacted countywide and not just applied to the unincorporated areas. The fees vary depending on whether the area in which it is imposed is unincorporated, within a city's sphere of influence, or within a city. The amount of the fee imposed within a city's sphere or within a city is determined by an agreement entered into between the particular city and the county, and the county has agreements with all nine incorporated cities within the its boundaries. The cities collect fees that cover both the city's services and the county's, and then the city transfers the agreed upon portion to the county.

From the beginnings of the program through June 30, 1998, the nine incorporated communities and the unincorporated area of Stanislaus County raised more than $20,496,000 in the original thirteen funds. In 2003, the county implemented its first update, in which the number of categories was increased and the fees were adjusted. As of May 2008, the county was in the process of overhauling the fee program for the first time since 1989 and identifying new capital improvements for the program.

Yolo County

Yolo County also has an ordinance establishing fees for county facilities, and several other counties have either adopted or are in the process of completing studies to adopt similar ordinances. The Yolo County ordinance may be unique because it makes noncompliance a misdemeanor (Yolo County Ordinance No. 1119). Fees in Yolo County are based on both location and use. The county facility fee must be paid directly to the county before a city will issue the other permits necessary, with the exception of West Sacramento, which now collects the county facilities fees for development within that city.

For more information, contact the County of Yolo, 625 Court Street, Room 202, Woodland, California 95695, (530) 666-8150.

City of Ripon

Following the adoption of the San Joaquin County Facilities Fee Program by the County Board of Supervisors in 2005, the City of Ripon immediately responded with the enactment of the Capital Facility Fee Program in order to implement the county's plan. This detailed program was passed via city ordinance and is outlined in the city's Municipal Code (see Chapter 17.20 of the City of Ripon Municipal Code for the full ordinance). The ordinance clearly lists the steps the city and county shall follow to successfully collect and manage capital facilities fees as allowed by Government Code section 66000 et seq. Fee revenues collected by the city are held in a separate County Facilities Fee account for remittance to the county on a quarterly basis. The county then allocates the fees as required for mitigating impact to the county's facilities affected by new development in the City of Ripon.

Open Space

Placer County

With Placer County being one of the fastest growing counties in the state, the need for a long-term program to protect, improve, and maintain the county's variety of natural and open space resources prompted the county's board of supervisors to implement the Placer Legacy Program. The Placer Legacy Program was designed to execute polices contained within the county's 1994 General Plan, while remaining consistent with evolving local, state, and federal regulations.

The Placer Legacy Program, initiated in April 1998, achieved support from environmental, development, and agricultural interests in Placer County. This support stemmed from varying concerns including the need to comply with state and federal environmental regulations threatened by the rapid suburbanization, and developer's needs for a wide range of well-funded mitigation options. The program involves a voluntary working relationship between the county and property owners/buyers in which the parties enter into purchase and sale agreements for lands having value for conservation purposes. Acquisition funding has been secured through state and federal grants, voluntary donations, and public/private sector funding partners. For more information, contact Loren Clark, Assistant Planning Director, at (530) 745-3016.

San Francisco

In the past few decades, San Francisco has seen dramatic changes in the land use and demographics of the city. These changes, along with the lack of an aggressive policy implementation program, have prompted city staff, with support from the Neighborhood Parks Council, to develop open space policies that engage the general public in the decision-making process of land acquisition, maintenance, and funding.

In February 2008, San Franciscans passed Proposition A, approving the $185 million Clean and Safe Neighborhood Parks General Obligation Bond. A portion of the bond funds will be allocated toward improvement programs focused on a series of open space areas known as the Blue Greenway. The Blue Greenway project will provide San Francisco with much-needed open space that includes a 13-mile greenway/waterway/public art trail network.

Additionally the city launched Open Space 2100. This long-term plan is focused on uniting various branches of local government with members of the community to develop a strong framework for securing the vision, maintenance, and acquisition of open spaces. The project is seeking additional donations to match the $175,000 already obtained in contributions from the city, funding partners, and private donors. For more information on these programs, visit the San Francisco website at http://sfgov.org/.

Open Space Districts

Other alternatives to exactions for open space include the creation of assessment districts, state bonds (Proposition 70), user fees, and sales taxes. However, the use of assessment districts is expected to decrease in response to the California Supreme Court's decision in *Silicon Valley Taxpayers Association v. Santa Clara County Open Space Authority* (2008) 44 Cal. 4th 431 (see chapter 9 for more information). Often open space is protected by trusts and easements. Sonoma County has an agricultural preservation and open space district created by voters in 1990 and funded by a 0.25 percent sales tax through the year 2010. In 2006, voters again showed their commitment to the conservation program by passing Measure F, which secured the funding to the Sonoma County District through 2031. In order to avoid continuous, corridor-style urbanization, Sonoma County has identified "community separators," scenic landscape units, scenic corridors/roadside landscapes, critical habitat areas, riparian corridors, and biking, hiking, and other outdoor recreation areas. Since its first acquisition in 1992, the District has protected 142 properties, totaling almost 70,000 acres, through conservation easement and fee purchases.

The preservation and acquisition of open space can be accomplished through special tax districts as an alternative to exactions.

Local governments have utilized assessment districts, state bonds, user fees, and sales taxes for the purpose of acquiring and maintaining open space as an alternative to exactions.

Transportation

Coachella Valley

The Transportation Uniform Mitigation Fee (TUMF) was first established by the Coachella Valley Association of Governments (CVAG) in 1989 in order to prevent the severe traffic congestion likely to occur due to future growth. The program has grown to become the nation's largest multijurisdictional transportation fee program. The real change took place in February of 1999 when the County of Riverside Supervisor requested that the Western Riverside Council of Governments (WRCOG) evaluate the feasibility of a uniform mitigation fee program for jurisdictions in southwestern Riverside County. Eventually TUMF grew to encompass all of western Riverside County. Studies have shown that eight of the 14 cities in Riverside's western region will more than double their current populations within the next twenty-five years. The most extreme example is the City of Beaumont, which is projected to grow more than 800 percent by the year 2030.

WRCOG has administered TUMF for Riverside's western region since 2003, and in that time, a detailed process has been established to effectively allocate revenues and prioritize transportation project improvements. Since TUMF must comply with the MFA, the TUMF Program Nexus Study was created in order to ensure that the fees maintained a reasonable relationship to the impacts of any given development. Between 2003 and 2006, TUMF generated $374 million in revenues.

The creation of a single fee and ordinance for the entire valley required the coordination and cooperation of all political jurisdictions involved. For more information, contact the Coachella Valley Association of Governments, 73710 Fred Waring Drive, Suite 200, Palm Desert, California 92260, (760) 346-1127.

Habitat Conservation Plan Mitigation Fees

Fees imposed on developers to mitigate the loss of habitat for endangered and threatened species listed under the Federal Endangered Species Act and the California Endangered Species Act continue to become more common.

Tracy

In 1991, the City of Tracy adopted by resolution a fee of $125 per acre developed in the Interstate 205 project area. The fee was to partially mitigate the loss of forage for the Swainson's hawk due to the approval of the I-205 Corridor Specific Plan. The California Department of Fish and Game (DFG) felt that this fee was not adequate mitigation for the impact of the project and threatened legal action unless the conditions of the project were modified by the city. The city and developers entered into an agreement that was approved by the DFG for the acquisition of 350 acres of land to be preserved for the hawk.

This situation illustrates the importance of conducting sufficient studies and consultations with the appropriate agencies prior to the adoption of the fee so that the goal of the fee is realized. In this case, the amount of the fee should have been sufficient to mitigate the harm caused by the use the fee was being imposed on. The $125 per acre fee was not sufficient to mitigate for the loss of forage for the hawk, and as a result, the city inherited a different legal problem.

Additionally, the city realized that the mitigation measures outlined in the I-205 Corridor Specific Plan EIR did not include any defined land purchase or location programs to provide for ongoing habitat conservation. The city was relieved of its duty to implement its own detailed plan when, in 2001, the County of San Joaquin developed a uniform Habitat Conservation Plan. This comprehensive plan had all of the elements of a successful conservation program, and the city already had the funding mechanism established via their I-205 Fund to contribute toward the county's HCP.

Transportaton System Improvement Programs can be used to charge new development impact fees to pay for a variety of projects, such as through-lanes, overpasses, and widening of existing arteries.

Natomas Basin

The Natomas Basin Habitat Conservation Plan was adopted for the purpose of preserving, enhancing, and managing the wildlife habitat values in the Natomas Basin, in addition to allowing economic development and the continuation of agriculture in the Basin. The Natomas Basin Conservancy continues to implement the plan, which covers portions of the City of Sacramento, Sacramento County, and Sutter County. The main emphasis of the plan is the protection of the giant garter snake and the Swainson's hawk. Although similar in nature to an impact fee, this plan is voluntary, and therefore no AB 1600 study was conducted, although a study was conducted to decide on the amount of the fee. Accordingly, developers are required to either pay a fee (calculated to be $38,133 per acre of development in 2008, subject to adjustments), or show that they have complied with an alternative mitigation or an exemption from mitigation approved by the U.S. Fish and Wildlife Service and the California Department of Fish and Game.

Placer County

While not yet adopted, Placer County has made substantial progress toward a Natural Community Conservation Plan (NCCP) and Habitat Conservation Plan (HCP) for Western Placer County addressing approximately 221,150 acres of unincorporated land, primarily located in the City of Lincoln. The Placer County Conservation Plan (PCCP) is designed to address the uncertainties associated with continued rapid urbanization and the effect this may have on the threatened and endangered species within the area. If approved, this will be one of the largest and most comprehensive habitat conservation plans in the state.

Funding will come from a variety of resources, including grants and locally funded acquisitions and funds from local, state, and federal sources. While having an approved conservation program in place enhances the likelihood of financial support from governmental funding programs and private conservation organizations, these sources alone will be inadequate to successfully develop and maintain the PCCP. Mitigation fees, land dedications, acquisition of conservation easements, and conservation banking are just some of the optional sources for acquiring reserve land and funding the maintenance of the ongoing habitat protection and monitoring system.

For more information on the status of the PCCP, visit the Placer County website at www.placer.ca.gov.

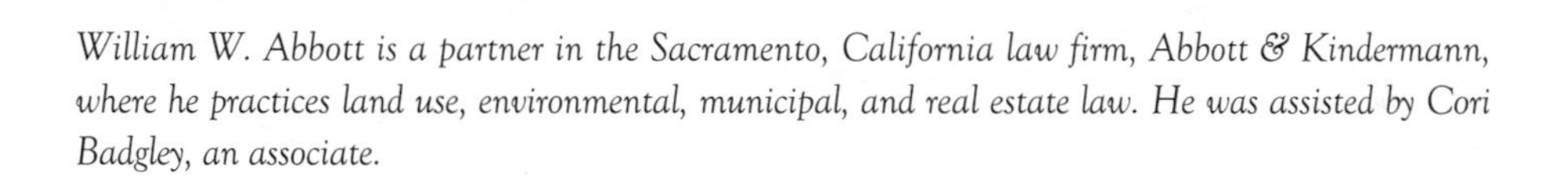

William W. Abbott is a partner in the Sacramento, California law firm, Abbott & Kindermann, where he practices land use, environmental, municipal, and real estate law. He was assisted by Cori Badgley, an associate.

CHAPTER NINE

Funding Neighborhood-Specific Infrastructure and Amenities

By Harriet A. Steiner and Seth Merewitz

In this chapter, the focus shifts from exactions based on land use approvals to funding for the ongoing operation and maintenance (O&M) costs of public improvements and services. While exactions partially address the capital financing of public improvements, the long-term O&M costs are often not provided with a stable funding source. This chapter moves beyond the *Nollan, Dolan,* and AB 1600 debate and looks at the implementation phase and the required maintenance of community infrastructure and amenities.

Public amenities that are well maintained are a gift to future generations.

During the past thirty years, California has experienced significant shifts in the funding of local government services, and in the O&M costs of public improvements. Historically, local government could look to general fund sources, including the property tax, sales tax, transient occupancy tax, or business license tax, to fund O&M costs of public improvements and the costs of public services. However, the authority for local governments to increase general fund revenues has been severely limited by statewide initiative measures, beginning with Proposition 13 (Cal. Const., art. XIII A) and continuing through Proposition 218 (Cal. Const., arts. XIII C, XIII D), which changed the voter approval requirements for special assessments and certain types of property-related fees for services. Moreover, acts of the Legislature, including the imposition of the Educational Revenue Augmentation Fund and the state budget actions related to local government revenues, have further limited the ability of local governments to identify and rely on stable funding sources.[1]

Other chapters have focused on methods by which public improvements are funded. However, the O&M costs of these improvements are often left out of the financing equation. This chapter focuses on the mechanisms available to fund O&M costs of public improvements, including parks and open space, drainage and flood control, street lighting, landscaping, roads, and even public services such as police, fire, and libraries.

In response to these developments, many local governments are reexamining the funding sources for the O&M costs of public improvements and facilities and other public services. To serve existing communities, and to accommodate new development that requires increased operations and services, many local governments are trying to identify and establish stable revenue sources, not only to provide services and build needed facilities, but also to operate and maintain them as well.

This chapter provides an overview of mechanisms used in California to provide stable funding for services and O&M costs of public improvements. In addition to traditional general fund revenue sources, the Legislature has provided local governments in California with numerous mechanisms to fund O&M costs of public improvements and services. Available property-based[2] funding mechanisms can be broadly categorized as either of the following:

Support for public amenities requires ongoing funding for operation and maintenance.

- Special taxes, including Mello-Roos Community Facilities Districts
- Special benefit assessments and districts

In addition, private mechanisms, such as homeowners' associations, are used to fund or insure funding of the O&M costs of some improvements in common-interest developments.

Examples of Special Taxes

Mello-Roos Special Taxes

The Mello-Roos Community Facilities Act of 1982 (the "Mello-Roos Act," Government Code § 53311 et seq.[3]) is generally used to finance capital projects and other infrastructure for new development. However, the Mello-Roos Act may also be used to finance public services, including both maintenance and operations. In appropriate circumstances, special taxes imposed and collected under the Mello-Roos Act can assist in providing the level of public services and maintenance desired by a new development or an existing community.

The Mello-Roos Act authorizes the establishment of community facilities districts, commonly called "Mello-Roos districts" or "community facilities districts," and the imposition of special taxes within these districts. A Mello-Roos district may include a specific area within a jurisdiction or may encompass an entire city or special district. The Mello-Roos district may also include either contiguous or non-contiguous areas of a jurisdiction. § 53325.5.

Following the procedures set forth in the Mello-Roos Act, an area is first proposed to be subject to the special tax. After notice and hearing, the special tax is set for election. As with all special taxes, approval of the special tax requires an affirmative vote of two-thirds of those voting. For Mello-Roos special taxes, the special tax election may be a landowner election or a registered voter election, generally depending on whether there are twelve or more registered voters within the proposed Mello-Roos district. § 53326(b).

Mello-Roos special taxes may be imposed for the public services enumerated in the Act. Examples of these services include:

- Police protection services, including certain criminal justice services
- Fire protection and suppression services
- Ambulance and paramedic services
- Park, parkway, and open space maintenance and lighting
- Street and road maintenance and lighting
- Storm drainage systems operation and maintenance
- Plowing and snow removal services
- Services related to removal or remediation of hazardous materials
- Recreation program services, library services, the maintenance costs of elementary and secondary school sites and structures, and the O&M of museums and cultural facilities § 53313

Mello-Roos special taxes for authorized services can provide an attractive alternative mechanism for financing necessary O&M costs, and particular services, with the consent of the voters.

The tax may be used to finance these services regardless of whether the services are performed within the Mello-Roos district or outside of the district. See §§ 53313.5, 53316.2. This allows the district to participate in funding the costs for maintenance for regional facilities and services as well as those services performed within the district. For example, a Mello-Roos special tax may be used to maintain parks and open space located outside of the boundaries of the Mello-Roos district, as well as regional drainage or flood control facilities.

The Mello-Roos special tax authorization creates an alternative to the traditional landscaping and lighting districts for park maintenance. It also provides a method of financing higher levels of police or fire protection.

The Mello-Roos Act imposes certain restrictions on the use of special taxes for services. If the special tax is approved by landowner vote, the tax may only finance services "to the extent that they are in addition to those provided in the territory of the district before the district was created." § 53313. The additional services may not supplant services that were already available within the Mello-Roos district when the district was created. *Id.*

In addition, bonds may not be issued to fund the services noted above, although bonds may be issued to fund capital facilities to be used in providing those services. § 53313.

Another restriction imposed on Mello-Roos districts is that districts formed after January 1, 1992, if requested by a resident or property owner located in the district, have to prepare an "annual report" containing certain information. § 53343.1. The district may recover the costs of preparing the report by charging a fee. *Id.*

Mello-Roos special taxes are not a panacea for all government financing. The amount of the special tax must be reasonable to meet market and consumer concerns. Many cities have adopted policies that, as a general rule, provide that the total of property taxes and Mello-Roos special taxes should not exceed two percent of the value of a residential parcel. Even if the Mello-Roos special tax is reflected by a discount in the purchase price of a home, there may be buyer resistance to the additional taxes. In all cases, full disclosure of the special tax, its amount, and the facilities and services the tax funds is critical to avoid misunderstandings and taxpayer dissatisfaction.

A Mello-Roos special tax for authorized services or for the maintenance of parks and open space has the potential for greater use in this post-Proposition 218 era. This is because a Mello-Roos special tax can be designed to meet the needs and desires of a particular area, both as to the amount of the tax and the structure or allocation of the tax burdens. Further, this special tax does not need to meet the "special benefit"standards for special assessments required by California law.

See also League of California Cities, Proposition 218 Implementation Guide (2007), avaiable, along with other resources from the League of California Cities, at www.cacities.org.

The Mello-Roos Act provides for setting a maximum tax rate. Below the maximum allowable tax, the tax can be adjusted year to year. The Act also provides for a mechanism for the change or alteration of a special tax, including the dissolution or repeal of the special tax. § 53330 et seq. For Mello-Roos districts financing infrastructure and capital improvements, the issuance of bonds generally will preclude the repeal of the special tax until the bonds are fully paid. § 53332(a). However, if the special tax is used to finance maintenance or services, then, through the procedures in the Mello-Roos Act, the registered voters or landowners of the district may petition for an election to alter or change the special tax, up to and including a repeal of the tax. *Id.* In addition, as discussed below, Proposition 218 may also provide the basis for an initiative to repeal a Mello-Roos special tax.

Police/Fire Special Taxes

Section 53978 authorizes any local agency[4] that provides fire protection, fire prevention services, and/or police protection to levy a special tax for those services. Specifically, the statute provides for maintenance by authorizing "obtaining, furnishing, operating, and maintaining fire suppression and police protection equipment or apparatus or either such service." § 53978(b). The special tax may also be used to pay salaries and benefits for firefighting or police protection personnel and for related expenses. *Id.*

This special tax does not have to be imposed as a jurisdiction-wide special tax—rather, particular areas or zones may be assessed taxes to pay for services in those areas. The graduated application of this tax based on zoning classifications, where a flat tax rate was applied on all parcels within each zone regardless of size or other characteristics, was upheld in a 1986 California Supreme Court case. *Heckendorn v. City of San Marino* (1986) 42 Cal. 3d 481.

Many cities and fire protection districts have been successful in passing police and/or fire special taxes within their jurisdictions. Thus, in the appropriate circumstances, this authorization can provide a viable tool for maintaining or upgrading public safety services. In addition, the adoption of a special tax for fire protection services has been coupled with the formation of a fire protection special district or the reorganization of existing fire protection districts to provide the funding necessary to operate and maintain equipment and pay personnel expenses.

Green Initiatives

State and local policymakers have begun a more concerted effort to address global warming, energy use, and other environmental issues. The League of California Cities, for example, has developed a set of Climate Change Principles to guide its activities. Many communities have adopted green building ordinances to encourage environmentally-efficient building design and construction.

A local government may develop and administer a program to encourage the construction of buildings that use solar thermal and photovoltaic systems that meet applicable standards and requirements imposed by the state or the local government for certain eligible solar energy systems. See Pub. Res. Code § 25406.

Public Library Special Tax

Section 53717 et seq. authorizes a city, county, or library district to impose a special tax within its jurisdiction for the purpose of "providing public library facilities and services." This special tax may be applied on a uniform basis to real property on the basis of benefit, cost of providing service, or other reasonable basis. § 53717.2.

In addition, the Attorney General has opined that certain counties have the authority to impose a transactions and use tax, at a rate of 0.5 percent, for the support of libraries, as well as education, parks, and recreation. 81 Ops. Cal. Atty. Gen. 147 (1998). The basic authority is found in Revenue & Taxation Code section 7285.5; however, prior approval by two-thirds of the electorate is necessary. A county may impose a tax for the construction, acquisition, programs, and operations of a public library within the county. Rev. & Tax. Code § 7286.59. These revenues shall be used only to supplement existing expenditures for public libraries and shall not be used to supplant existing funding. Rev. & Tax. Code § 7286.59(4).

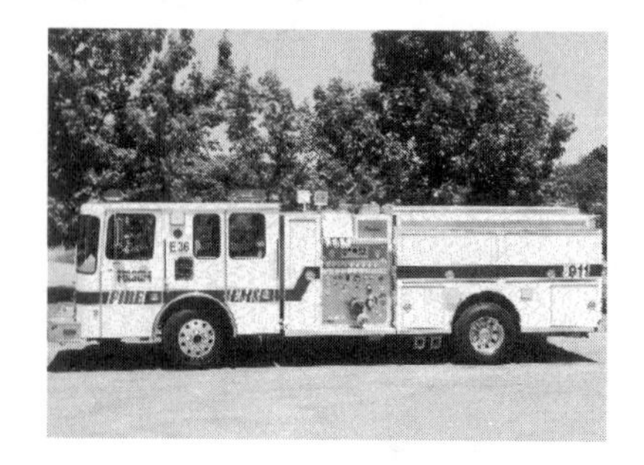

As with all special taxes, a police/fire protection tax is dedicated to the use for which it was levied and is subject to approval by two-thirds of the registered voters within the jurisdiction or zone proposed for the tax.

Retail Transactions and Use Tax

The Local Transportation Authority and Improvement Act (Public Utilities Code §§ 180000–180264) authorizes counties to create local transportation authorities empowered to impose a retail transactions and use tax of up to one percent to fund transportation improvements and services in the county. Pub. Util. Code § 180202. The revenues may be used for the construction and improvement of state highways, the construction, maintenance, improvement, and operation of local streets, roads, and highways, and the construction, improvement, and operation of public transit systems. Pub. Util. Code § 180205. The board of supervisors may designate an existing agency or create a new one. Pub. Util. Code § 180050. The board determines the membership of a new authority with the concurrence of a majority of the cities having a majority of the population in the incorporated area of the county. Pub. Util. Code § 180051. Each member of a new authority must be an elected official of a local government entity within or partly within the county. Pub. Util. Code §180051.

In order to adopt a retail transaction and use tax ordinance, the following must occur, according to statute: (1) the ordinance must be adopted by a two-thirds vote of the authority; (2) it must be approved by the electorate in a special election; and (3) the authority must adopt a transportation expenditure plan. Pub. Util. Code § 180201. The transportation expenditure plan must set forth the expenditure of the revenues expected to be derived from the tax and must be adopted prior to the special election. In addition, the Attorney General has opined that an authority may not reimpose a retail transactions and use tax for an additional period of time without first adopting a new county transportation expenditure plan. 87 Ops. Cal. Atty Gen. 5 (2004).

General Authorization for Special Taxes

While this chapter has identified a few of the specific special taxes available to local governments, section 37100.5 authorizes general law cities to levy any special tax that may be levied by a charter city, subject to voter approval pursuant to Article XIII A of the California Constitution. In addition, sections 50075 through 50077, generally, authorize cities and counties to impose special taxes, also subject to voter approval. This broad authority provides another option for a local government exploring alternatives for funding of O&M costs.

Special Benefit Assessments

Over twenty statutes provide mechanisms for municipalities to levy special assessments to finance O&M costs of public improvements such as streets, storm drains, sewers, curbs, gutters, street lights, and landscaping. See sidebar. Unlike special districts, special assessment districts are not separate legal entities. *Dawson v. Town of Los Altos Hills* (1976) 16 Cal. 3d 676. Rather, special assessment districts are defined and administered by the legislative body of the local municipality.[5]

Proposition 218 Considerations

With the approval of Proposition 218 by the voters in the November 5, 1996, election, the procedures for establishment of assessment districts and the substantive requirements for assessment districts have changed significantly. Proposition 218 affects special assessments in three primary ways:

- Proposition 218 establishes more rigorous procedural requirements for adoption of special assessments, including a mailed ballot process.
- Proposition 218 changes or modifies many of the standards used to determine the scope of the assessment and its propriety, including changing the burden of proof on the legality of the assessment from the challenger to the public agency imposing the assessment.

Various Assessment Laws Providing for Maintenance

Improvement Act of 1911
Streets and Highways Code §§ 5000 et seq.
Maintenance of transportation and navigational facilities

Municipal Improvement Act of 1913
Streets and Highways Code §§ 10100.8 et seq.
Maintenance and repair of works installed under 1911 Act proceedings

Municipal Lighting Maintenance District Act of 1927
Streets and Highways Code §§ 18600 et seq.
Operation and maintenance, but not installation (§ 18606)

Street Lighting Act of 1931
Streets and Highways Code §§ 18300 et seq.
Operation and maintenance, but not installation (§ 18306), limited to 5 years (§ 18321)

Tree Planting Act of 1931
Streets and Highways Code §§ 22000 et seq.
Planting, maintenance or removal of trees (§ 22012), assessment for maintenance limited to 5 years (§ 22087)

Vehicle Parking District Law of 1943
Streets and Highways Code §§ 31500 et seq.
Construction and operation and maintenance of parking facilities, including garages (§ 31506 (d)–(f))

Parking District Law of 1951
Streets and Highways Code §§ 35100 et seq.
Maintenance and operation of parking places acquired (§ 35108)

Pedestrian Mall Law of 1960
Streets and Highways Code §§ 11000 et seq.
Maintenance, operation, repair, or improvement (§ 11806)

Landscape and Lighting Act of 1972
Streets and Highways Code §§ 22500 et seq.
Operation and maintenance of street lights and many other park and landscape improvements

Parking and Business Improvement Area Law of 1989
Streets and Highways Code §§ 36500 et seq.
Improvement includes maintenance of tangible property with a useful life of 5 years or more (§ 36510)

Property and Business Improvement District Law of 1994
Streets and Highways Code §§ 36600 et seq.
Improvement includes maintenance of tangible property with a useful life of 5 years or more (§ 36610)

Geologic Hazard Abatement District
Public Resources Code §§ 26500 et seq.
Maintenance, repair, or operation of any improvements (§ 26505(c))

Habitat Maintenance Assessment District
Government Code §§ 50060 et seq.
Maintenance and servicing of landscaping, irrigation systems, sidewalks, and drainage (§ 50060(b)(3)(B))

Fire Suppression Assessment
Government Code §§ 50078 et seq.
Obtain, furnish, operate, or maintain fire suppression equipment (§ 50078)

Open Space Maintenance Act
Government Code §§ 50575 et seq.
Maintenance and improvement of open areas and the doing of those acts set forth in § 50583 (§ 50579)

Ongoing maintenance of public amenities contributes to neighborhood stability.

- Proposition 218 provides that assessments are subject to repeal or reduction by initiative.

Procedures for Adoption of Special Assessments Under Proposition 218

Prior to the passage of Proposition 218, the general procedure for creation of special assessment districts and the imposition of special assessments involved the following: preparation of an engineer's report delineating the area subject to the assessment, the amount of the assessment, and the method of spreading the assessment; setting a noticed protest hearing on the assessment and mailing notice of the proposed assessment hearing to all affected property owners; holding the hearing on the assessment for the purpose of determining whether there was a majority protest of the property owners (namely, have fifty percent of the property owners protested the assessment, affirmatively and in writing); and then imposing the assessment. In many circumstances, even with a majority protest, the legislative body could still impose the assessment with a four-fifths vote of its members.

Proposition 218 significantly changes this procedure. To impose a special assessment now, the public agency must take the following steps:

- **Identify the property subject to the assessment.** All the property, including property owned by federal, state, or local public agencies, that will receive a special benefit from the assessment must be included in the proposed assessment district. Special benefit is defined as "particular and distinct benefit" over and above the benefit received by the public at large. "General enhancement of property value" is not a "special benefit." Cal. Const., art. XIII D, §§ 2(i),4(a)
- **Apportion or "spread" the benefit.** Determine the proportionate benefit derived by each parcel in the assessment district. The proportionate benefit is an individual parcel's share of the cost of the improvement or maintenance to be financed by the assessment. Cal. Const., art. XIII D, § 4(a)
- **Segregate out any "general benefit."** Special assessments may only be imposed for special benefit. In the past, parcels receiving special benefit could also be assessed for the general benefit that resulted from the improvement so long as the general benefit was incidental to the special benefit. Proposition 218 requires that general benefits be segregated out and, presumably, paid from a different source of funds. Cal. Const., art. XIII D, § 4(a)
- **Prepare an engineer's report.** A registered professional engineer certified by the State of California must prepare this report. Cal. Const., art. XIII D, § 4(b)
- **Mail notice of the proposed assessment.** Notice must be sent to the record owners of each identified parcel 45 days prior to the assessment hearing. The Proposition specifies the content of the notice in detail. It must include: the amount of the assessment for the particular parcel, the total assessment, the duration of the assessment, the basis for the calculation of the assessment, and the reason for the assessment. The notice must also include the date, time, and place of the public hearing on the assessment. Most significantly, the notice must explain the procedures for the mailed ballot and the effect of a majority protest. Cal. Const, art. XIII D, §§ 4(c), (d), and (e)
- **Mailed ballot protest.** This is probably the single most significant procedural change made by Proposition 218. Under the prior law, property owners had the right to protest, but they each had to affirmatively file a protest. Silence was presumed to be acquiescence in the assessment. Under Proposition 218, the notice must include a ballot on which the property owner can indicate support

or opposition to the assessment. Such ballots may be weighted according to the proportional financial obligation of the affected party. Cali. Const., art. XIII D, § 4(e); *Not About Water Committee v. Solano County Board of Supervisors* (2002) 95 Cal. App. 4th 982, 1001

- **Determine majority protest.** Only those ballots that are returned prior to the close of the hearing are counted. Of those ballots returned, if a majority of the ballots opposes the assessment, a majority protest exists and the assessment may not be imposed. In determining whether there is a majority protest, ballots are tabulated according to the proportionate financial obligation of the properties, i.e., one "protest" for each one dollar of assessment. Cal. Const., art. XIII D, § 4(e)
- **Conduct the public hearing.** Under Proposition 218, there is still a public hearing before the legislative body; the ballot does not supplant or take the place of the public hearing. At the conclusion of the public hearing, the agency must tabulate ballots to determine whether or not a majority protest exists and, if appropriate, take any further action required to establish the assessment. Cal. Const., art. XIII D, § 4(e)

The Legislature, through the enactment of the Proposition 218 Omnibus Implementation Act, sections 53750 et seq., clarified some of the procedural requirements for assessments. Among the sections added was section 53753, which explicitly supersedes any statutory provisions applicable to the notice, protest, and hearing requirements for the levy of any new or increased assessment.

Substantive Requirements for Special Assessments Under Proposition 218

Proposition 218 added several new, different, or expanded substantive requirements for special assessments. With the exception of certain assessments in existence on November 6, 1996 (the date of the passage of Proposition 218), beginning July 1, 1997, "all existing, new, or increased assessments shall comply with [Proposition 218]."[6]

First, as mentioned above, the Proposition defined special benefit and general benefit. The Proposition states that "only special benefits are assessable, and an agency shall separate the general benefits from the special benefits conferred on a parcel." Cal. Art. XIII D, § 4(a). After the adoption of Proposition 218, there was some question as to whether the definitions and requirements of "special benefit"under Proposition 218 significantly changed the traditional standards. Under prior law, after all, the power to assess was based on the existence of special benefit to the assessed property. *Harrison v. Board of Supervisors* (1975) 44 Cal. App. 3d 852, 856–857. And the law historically has been that the general public should not pay for that which benefits only a few and the few should not pay for that which benefits the public generally. *Roberts v. City of Los Angeles* (1936) 7 Cal. 2d 477, 491; *Solvang Municipal Improvement District v. Board of Supervisors* (1980) 112 Cal. App. 3d 545, 552–553.

However in a 2008 decision, *Silicon Valley Taxpayers Association v. Santa Clara County Open Space Authority* (2008) 44 Cal. 4th 431, the California

Special Assessment District Formation: The Engineer's Report

The engineer's report has always played an important role the assessment process. But in light of the California Supreme Court's decision in *Silicon Valley Taxpayers Association v. Santa Clara County Open Space Authority* (see text), its importance cannot be overstated. Not only did the Court determine in *Silicon Valley* that Proposition 218 altered the substantive requirements for assessments, but the Court also determined that "courts should exercise their independent judgment in reviewing local agency decisions that have determined whether benefits are special and whether assessments are proportional to special benefits within the meaning of Proposition 218." 44 Cal. 4th 431, 448. This standard of review is in sharp contrast to the more deferential position taken by courts in pre-Proposition 218 decisions.

This heightened standard of review means that the engineer's report—the primary exhibit in any litigation challenging an assessment as violating Proposition 218—will be subject to more exacting scrutiny by the courts. The result of this is illustrated in the *Silicon Valley* decision, where the Court, upon closely analyzing the engineer's report, held that the broad, uniform assessment in that case did not satisfy the "special benefit" or "proportionality" requirements under Proposition 218 (see text).

In light of *Silicon Valley*, an agency should make sure that its engineer's report specifies the special benefits accorded properties in the assessment district as distinguished from general benefits, and that the assessment is proportionately connected to such special benefits. To assist in this, among other things, as is the case with most professionals, the use of an engineer already familiar with assessment district practice is preferable.

Supreme Court put this question to rest by holding that Proposition 218 "made several changes to the definition of special benefits" that ultimately "tightened the definition of special benefits." *Id.* at 451. Therefore, reasoned the Court, "pre-Proposition 218 cases... are not instructive in determining whether a benefit is special under Proposition 218." *Id.* at 452. Instead, "under the plain language of article XIII D, a special benefit must affect the assessed property in a way that is particular and distinct from its effect on other parcels and that real property in general and the public at large do not share." *Id.*

Under this tightened standard, the Court rejected the assessment imposed by the Santa Clara County Open Space Authority (OSA) for the acquisition and maintenance of open space lands (importantly, the specific activities were not specified). In that case, the engineer's report determined that all properties in the assessment district—encompassing approximately 314,000 parcels over 800 square miles—would benefit equally and thus set the assessment at twenty dollars per single-family household (adjusted for condominiums and commercial properties). Although the OSA engineer's report enumerated several "special benefits" that would be accorded properties in the district, according to the Court (which was applying a more exacting standard of review—see the sidebar) the report did not show any "distinct benefits to particular properties above those which the general public using and enjoying the open space receives." *Id.* at 455. Factors that might give rise to such distinct benefits, the Court held, such as proximity to, expanded or improved access to, or views of, the open space, were not indentified in the engineer's report. *Id.* As a result, OSA "failed to demonstrate that the properties in the assessment district receive a particular and distinct special benefit not shared by the district's property in general or by the public at large within the meaning of Proposition 218." *Id.* at 456. Moreover, the Court held that OSA violated the "proportionality" requirement under Proposition 218 since this aspect of the engineer's report, as with its analysis of special benefits, was not exacting enough. Namely, it failed to identify with sufficient specificity the open space activity to be financed, identify the cost of such activity, and to "directly connect any proportionate costs of and benefits received from" the open space activity to the specific assessed properties. *Id.* at 457.

Prior to embarking on a special assessment district formation, the provisions of Proposition 218 and the implementing legislation should be carefully reviewed with the assistance of legal counsel.

Second, Proposition 218 made another fundamental and basic change to traditional assessment law—it changed the burden of proof on the determination of special benefit. Under traditional assessment district law, there was a near conclusive presumption in favor of the public agency's determination of benefit. *Knox v. City of Orland* (1992) 4 Cal. 4th 132; *Dawson v. Town of Los Altos Hills* (1976) 16 Cal. 3d 676. Proposition 218 expressly and specifically states that the burden is on the public agency to "demonstrate that the property . . . received special benefit over and above the benefits conferred on the public at large. . . ." Cal. Const., art. XIII D, § 4(f). Under the procedures established by Proposition 218, since the public agency establishes special benefit, it must be able to defend its determination.

For new development that truly wishes to provide protection amenities for its residents, the 1911 Act specifically provides for the maintenance of bomb shelters.

Third, Proposition 218 requires that property owned by public agencies be assessed. Cal. Const., art. XIII D, § 4(a). In the past, there was a legislatively created exemption for public property from special assessments. Proposition 218 provides that property owned or used by any agency, the state, or the federal government, is not exempt and must be included in the assessment unless "the agency can demonstrate by clear and convincing evidence that those publicly owned parcels in fact receive no special benefit." *Id.* This is an extremely high standard and will require either assessing most public property or contributing public funds to pay those shares of the cost.

The assessing of public property raises many legal issues including what happens if the public agency does not pay and where will the funds come from if some public agencies are found to be exempt from payment obligations.[7] Legislative clarification will be helpful in implementing this provision.

Proposition 218 also requires that a public agency prove that "the amount of any contested assessment is proportional to, and no greater than, the benefits conferred on the property . . ." Cal. Const., Art. XIII D, § 4(f). The California court has construed this burden to mean that a public agency "must prove that the assessment imposed on a parcel does not 'exceed . . . the reasonable costs of the proportional special benefit conferred on the parcel.'" *Dahms v. Downtown Pomona Property & Bus. Improvement Dist.* (2nd Dist. 2009) 174 Cal. App. 4th 708.

Repeal of Assessment by Initiative

Proposition 218 may subject assessments to amendment, reduction, or repeal by initiative. Cal. Const., art. XIII C, § 3. Under traditional law, special assessments could not be challenged by voter initiative. *Chase v. Kalber* (3d Dist. 1915) 28 Cal. App. 561. Proposition 218 seeks to expand the power and scope of the initiative to include reduction or repeal of special assessments, as well as taxes, fees, and charges.

There is debate over the scope of this change and its validity and applicability to municipal securities issued after November 5, 1996; the potential ramifications of this provision of Proposition 218 are beyond the scope of this chapter.[8]

Impact of Proposition 218 on Maintenance Assessments

Pre-Proposition 218 assessment districts, such as landscaping and lighting maintenance districts, were used to obtain funding for park, open space, and other maintenance activities needed for new development. At times, assessment through a maintenance district was expanded to include large areas or entire jurisdictions to provide the funding for needed maintenance activities. This ability to impose special assessments for maintenance of public improvements was upheld by the California Supreme Court in *Knox v. City of Orland* (1992) 4 Cal. 4th 132.

An example of park improvements without adequate ongoing maintenance.

One of the areas Proposition 218 attempted to constrict was this growing use of maintenance assessments.

Proposition 218, in exempting certain assessments that existed at the time it was adopted, did not exempt assessments for park and open space maintenance. Thus, while a case-by-case-analysis is required to determine whether a pre-Proposition 218 assessment is exempt, assessments for the maintenance of park landscaping or open space would probably require new approvals under Proposition 218. If new maintenance assessments are established, care should be taken to assure that all the requirements of Proposition 218 are met.

Utility Rates After Proposition 218

Besides assessment districts, Proposition 218 also had an impact on certain fees and charges. Proposition 218 defines a "fee" or "charge" subject to its provisions as any levy other than an *ad valorem* tax, a special tax, or an assessment, imposed as an incident of property ownership, including a user fee or charge for a property related service. Cal. Const., art. XIIID, § 2. Such property-related fees and charges are subject to certain procedural requirements under Proposition 218, including notice, a hearing, and voter approval of certain new or increased fees and charges.

Arguably the biggest question related to this was whether consumption-based utility rates were subject to the provisions of Proposition 218. Under previous law, it appeared they were not, as metered water rates were held as not subject to Proposition 218. See *Howard Jarvis Taxpayers Association v. City of Los Angeles* (2000) 85 Cal. App. 4th 79.

Proposition 218 also imposes limitations on the manner in which a public agency may impose fees and charges. Cal. Const., Art. XIIID, § 6. One limitation is that a fee or charge may not be imposed for a service unless that service is actually used by, or immediately available to, the owner of the resepctive property. "immediately available" pertains to the conduct of the public agency, not the property owner's *Paland v. Brooktrails Township Comty. Servs. Dist.* (1st Dist. 2009) 176 Cal. App. 4th 158 (review granted).

In the wake of Proposition 218, the 1972 Act will be more difficult to utilize. Proposition 218 has defined "special benefit" to exclude a "general enhancement of property values." This limitation of the definition of "special benefit" will force local agencies to provide specific justification for linking the improvement with the particular benefit to the property.

However, this changed with the decision in *Bighorn-Desert View Water Agency v. Verjil* (2006) 39 Cal. 4th 205. Reinforcing dicta in *Richmond v. Shasta Community Services District* (2004) 32 Cal. 4th 409, the Supreme Court ruled that consumption-based water rates are subject to Proposition 218. See also *Pajaro Valley Water Mgmt. Agency v. Amrhein* (6th Dist. 2007) 150 Cal. App. 4th 1364 (holding, in light of *Bighorn*, that a groundwater augmentation charge for operators of wells is a fee or charge subject to Proposition 218).

Other Service or User Fees under Propositions 13 and 218

In addition to property related fees, Propositions 13 and 218 also impact other fees and charges. In general terms, a user charge is a charge to the person using a service and the amount is related to the cost of providing the goods or service. *Isaac v. City of Los Angeles* (2nd Dist. 1998) 66 Cal. App. 4th 586, 596–597. Typical user charges include park and recreation fees, equipment rental fees, and the like. As with development impact fees, user charges that are new, different, or are significantly increased are often challenged as invalid special taxes. For example, some cities attempted to adopt a user fee applicable to all telephone and wireless phone lines to fund a portion of their 911 Emergency Dispatch. The theory was that this flat fee is a user charge for the use of the 911 system. 911 fees were challenged in several separate actions. In *Bay Area Cellular Telephone Company v. City of Union City* (1st Dist. 2008) 162 Cal. App. 4th 686, the California Court of Appeal invalidated the fee holding that the fee was a tax because it was imposed on virtually everyone in the city and not only on the people who actually used the 911 system. Since the Union City 911 charge was not adopted as a special tax and was not approved by the voters, it was invalid. The Court's analysis is instructive on the legal bases for special taxes and fees. (The appeal of this case to the California Supreme Court was denied.) In addition there are other formulations of a 911 charge, or other similar charges, that may be adopted using different legal theories, and may, in the future either be upheld or invalidated by the courts. However, as public agencies look for operation funds, one area that continues to be explored is user charges for services provided.

Proposition 26

On November 2, 2010, the voters adopted Proposition 26 (Cal. Const. arts. XIIIA and XIIIC). This proposition defines the term "tax" to mean all levies and charges imposed by the state and local governments except for seven identified exceptions, which are:

"(1) A charge imposed for a specific benefit conferred or privilege granted directly to the payor that is not provided to those not charged, and which does not exceed the reasonable costs to the local government of conferring the benefit or granting the privilege." Charges that may be included in this category are government permits, franchises, and parking permits.

"(2) A charge imposed for a specific government service or product provided directly to the payor that is not provided to those not charged, and which does not exceed the reasonable costs to the local government of providing the service or product." Charges that may be included in this category are fees for classes and other program participation, such as park and recreation program charges, utility fees that are not subject to Proposition 218, and some emergency response fees.

"(3) A charge imposed for the reasonable regulatory costs to a local government for issuing licenses and permits, performing investigations, inspections, and audits, enforcing agricultural marketing orders, and the administrative enforcement and adjudication thereof." These charges may include buidling permit fees, and other inspection program fees.

As the maintenance obligation of public improvements grows, public agencies will be forced to explore existing mechanisms, as well as innovative techniques, to identify stable funding for public amenities.

"(4) A charge imposed for entrance to or use of local government property, or the purchase, rental, or lease of local government property." These charges may include leases, day rentals, admission charges and fees for use of city property or equipment.

"(5) A fine, penalty, or other monetary charge imposed by the judicial branch of government or a local government, as a result of a violation of law.

"(6) A charge imposed as a condition of property development." Impact fees, conditions of approval on development and construction permits would liekly fall within this category.

"(7) Assessments and property-related fees imposed in accordance with the provisions of Article XIII D [Proposition 218]." User fees for government provided water, sewer or trash service are imposed purusant to Propstiion 218. Most special assessments are also property based and imposed under Proposition 218. However, certain business improvement district ("BID") assessments on businesses may need to be re-evaluated under Proposition 26 since the BID assessment is not real property based and is not subject to Proposition 218. A BID assessment may, or may not, meet the requirements of Proposition 26 that the charge be "imposed for a specific benefit conferred. . . ." (See, Art. XIIIC, §1(e)(1).)

Fees and charges that do not fall within one of the identified seven exceptions are not defined as "taxes" and would require voter approval. In addition, under Proposition 26 the governmental agency has the burden to prove by a preponderance of the evidence that the fee or charge is not more than the reasonable cost of the governmental activity and that the manner of allocating the costs bear a fair or reasonable relationship to the person paying the charge's burden on the activity or benefit from the activity. Proposition 26 raises many issues regarding the structure and amount of fees currently in use in California. As with many initiatives, its scope and impact may not be known for some time.

Proposition 26 applies to fees imposed by the state as of January 1, 2010. For local agencies, Proposition 26 only applies to those fees and charges newly imposed or increased after November 2, 2010.

Description of Selected Assessment Laws

Improvement Act of 1911

The Improvement Act of 1911 (the "1911 Act") was established primarily for the construction of capital improvements. Streets and Highways Code § 5000 et seq. The 1911 Act authorizes the establishment of a district, the levying of assessments, and the issuance of bonds.[9] The 1911 Act may be used to provide maintenance for limited purposes, such as transportation and navigational facilities. Sts. & Hwy. Code

1913 Act—A Separate Fund for Maintenance

In 1984, the Legislature added a provision to the 1913 Act to allow the creation of a separate fund for the maintenance, repair, or improvement of works, systems, or facilities constructed or substantially reconstructed after January 1, 1985. Sts. & Hwy. Code §§ 10100.8(a), (c).

For the purposes of this provision, "maintenance, repair, or improvement" includes only expenses that are ordinarily incurred no more frequently than every five years, unless the legislative body finds that expenses have to be incurred to maintain the level of benefit to the assessed parcels, and the level of benefit would otherwise decline more rapidly than usual for public works of the type involved. Sts. & Hwy. Code § 10100.8(d). This "five year" restriction results in this provision only being used to a limited extent. ■

§§ 5101, 5101.5. In addition, a city or county may use the 1911 Act to create a maintenance district to fund the O&M of sewer facilities and lighting systems. Sts. & Hwy. Code §§ 5820, 5835.2, 5835.3.

Municipal Improvement Act of 1913

Similar to the 1911 Act, the Municipal Improvement Act of 1913 (the "1913 Act") provides mainly for the construction of capital improvements. The 1913 Act specifically authorizes the maintenance of improvements in its definition of "install." Sts. & Hwy. Code § 10006. Some of the improvements specifically authorized under the 1913 Act are listed in section 10100 and include the following:

- Water services
- Electrical power
- Gas services
- Lighting purposes
- Any "works, utilities or appliances necessary or convenient for providing any other public service"

Once the improvement has been completed, any surplus remaining in the improvement fund from the original assessment or any supplemental assessment may be used for the maintenance of the improvement. Sts. and Hwy. Code § 10427(c).

The 1913 Act authorizes the establishment of a district and the levy of an assessment, but does not provide for the issuance of bonds to finance any improvements. Sts. and Hwy. Code §§ 10000 et seq. Most commonly, a 1913 Act assessment district will be used to issue bonds pursuant to the Improvement Bond Act of 1915 ("1915 Act"). The 1915 Act is a statute that provides only for the issuance of bonds. However, a 1913 Act assessment district may also issue bonds pursuant to the 1911 Act. Sts. & Hwy. Code §§ 10600 et seq.

County Service Areas

In 1953, the Legislature responded to the intensive residential, commercial, and industrial development in the unincorporated areas of many counties with the passage of the County Service Area Law. § 25210 et seq. A County Service Area (CSA) is not a special district, but rather provides counties with an alternative method to furnish extended services to landowners and to levy taxes in an amount sufficient to pay for the extended services provided. Section 25210.4 enumerates the various types of extended services that may be provided, including extended police protection, structural fire protection, local parks, recreation, or parkway services. The county is authorized to levy charges to pay the costs and expenses of maintaining, operating, extending, and repairing waterworks or sewers of a CSA. § 25210.77(c). Moreover, the board of supervisors is explicitly authorized to maintain libraries within a CSA. § 25210.78.

Services provided through a CSA can be funded through user fees or special assessments. There is no statutory limit on the amount of a special assessment levied or fees charged by a CSA. However, any new or increased fee or assessment is subject to the requirements of Proposition 218.

The county board of supervisors acts as the governing body of the CSA. The preliminary proceedings to establish a CSA are discussed in sections 25210.10 through 25210.20. Section 25210.11 provides three methods for the institution of proceedings for the establishment of a CSA: (1) a written request by two members of the board of supervisors filed with the board; (2) a resolution adopted by a majority vote of the governing body of any city in the county and filed with the board of supervisors; or (3) a petition signed by the requisite number of registered voters within the proposed area filed with the board.

Landscape and Lighting Act of 1972

A popular mechanism to fund public improvements for the past twenty-five years has been the Landscape and Lighting Act of 1972 (the "1972 Act"). Sts. & Hwy. Code § 22500 et seq. Section 22525(f) of the 1972 Act authorizes assessments for maintenance and servicing of the following:

- Landscaping
- Statuary, fountains, and other ornamental structures and facilities
- Public lighting facilities, including traffic signals
- Park or recreational improvements

Under the 1972 Act, maintenance includes the furnishing of services and materials for the ordinary and usual operation of any improvement or landscaping, as well as the removal of graffiti. Sts. & Hwy. Code § 22531. Maintenance can apply to existing public parks even if the park itself was not installed pursuant to the 1972 Act. *Knox v. City of Orland* (1992) 4 Cal. 4th 132. Servicing includes furnishing electric current or energy, gas, or other illuminating agent for public lighting, or water for irrigation of landscaping or fountain operation. Sts. & Hwy. Code § 22538.

The 1972 Act may be used by any local agency whose annual taxes are carried on the county assessment roll and are collected by the county, including a city, county, or special district. Sts. and Hwy. Code § 22501. School districts are treated as "special districts" within the meaning of the 1972 Act and are authorized to furnish the maintenance and servicing provided for in the 1972 Act. See *Howard Jarvis Taxpayers Association v. Whittier Union High School District* (2nd Dist. 1993) 15 Cal. App. 4th 730. While bonds may be issued to finance the cost of improvements under the 1972 Act, the cost of maintenance and services may not be financed through bond proceeds. See Sts. & Hwy. Code § 22662.5(a). However, the maintenance and servicing of improvements may be funded pursuant to provisions in the Public Contract Code section 20890 et seq., relating to the Tree Planting Act of 1931. Sts. & Hwy. Code § 22679.

Geologic Hazard Abatement District

One of the methods of maintaining public improvements that remediate a geologic hazard is through the creation of a Geologic Hazard Abatement District (GHAD). Pub. Res. Code § 26500 et seq. A GHAD may levy and collect assessments to pay for the maintenance and operation of improvements "necessary or incidental to the prevention, mitigation, abatement, or control of a geologic hazard." Pub. Res. Code §§ 26505, 26650. A "geologic hazard" is defined as an actual or threatened landslide, land subsidence, soil erosion, earthquake, fault movement, or any other natural or unnatural movement of land or earth. Pub. Res. Code § 26507.

Benefit Assessment Act of 1982

The Benefit Assessment Act of 1982 (the "1982 Act") (§ 54703 et seq.) can be used to finance maintenance and operation of drainage, flood control, and street lighting services. § 54710(a). In 1989, the 1982 Act was amended to include the maintenance of streets, roads, and highways. § 54710(b). The 1982 Act authorizes assessments to be levied on parcels, classes of improvements to property, use of

Assessments for Flood Protection

The devastation wrought by Hurricane Katrina has been termed a "wake-up call" to the residents of flood-prone areas of the state about their own vulnerability to catastrophic flooding. Of all the states in the country, California is particularly vulnerable to flooding, especially its Central Valley.

A major factor contributing to such vulnerability is the lack of sufficient levee protection. Many of the levees protecting communities today were built decades ago without adequate materials or design standards. Moreover, many were intended primarily to protect farmland, as opposed to the urban centers they now protect due to subsequent development.

In response to such vulnerability, affected communities have sought to strengthen their levees and to operate and maintain such levees at an adequate level of protection. In addition, by ensuring that certain design and operation and maintenance systems are in place, such levees will be "recognized" by the Federal Emergency Management Agency (FEMA) under the National Flood Insurance Program (NFIP). See 44 C.F.R. § 65.10. A lack of such recognition could pose problems for the community under the NFIP.

To pay for this, many communities are planning to use special benefit assessments adopted in accordance with the provisions of Proposition 218. Other possible funding sources include development fees, as well as funds from the statewide bond measures adopted in the November 2006 election, Propositions 1E and 84.

Landscape funded by a Landscape and Lighting Act assessment, pictured above.

property basis, or a combination thereof. § 54715(c). The 1982 Act requires voter approval. Assessments for flood control services may be levied on the basis of proportionate storm water runoff from each parcel, only if and to the extent that a parcel will benefit from the service. *Id.* at (e).

The approval of new or increased assessments under the 1982 Act, as amended, is governed by Government Code section 53753, which is the procedure employed under Proposition 218, as outlined above.

Other Mechanisms

Proposition 218's requirements for voter approvals, and risk of voter repeals of traditional funding mechanisms,[10] are reasons for local governments to consider other funding options. A number of alternatives are open to local governments to protect funding for new public improvements and the required maintenance.

Homeowners' Association

As an alternative or supplement to traditional funding mechanisms, a homeowners' association (HOA) may be required of new developments to ensure the financing of public improvement maintenance and operation. The HOA is a common feature of planned developments and condominiums authorized under California law, and provides a mechanism that allows for the assessment of private property to pay for maintenance of common areas such as private streets, open space, landscaping, and recreational facilities. Civ. Code §§ 1350 et seq. Property owner associations are often used in nonresidential projects such as a business park; the legal concept is the same.

The creation of a HOA may bring a residential project under the jurisdiction of the Department of Real Estate. Bus. and Prof. Code § 11000 et seq. To ensure funding for maintenance, the HOA should include the requisite assessment mechanism in the declaration of covenants, conditions, and restrictions (CC&Rs) recorded against the property. Moreover, in order to protect against the repeal of a traditional funding mechanism under Proposition 218, the CC&Rs should include a requirement that the HOA pay the assessment, and that the particular CC&Rs provision regarding maintenance may only be amended with approval of the local legislative body. With this structure, private liens may be used to enforce the assessment and insure the funding for maintenance and operation of the public improvements.

Community Services Districts

Another device to fund maintenance is the creation of a community services district (CSD).[11] § 61000 et seq. A CSD may fund the operation and maintenance of numerous services and facilities, including water, sewer, libraries, police services, streets, public airports, and flood protection works and facilities. § 61100.

A CSD can be formed in two ways: (1) by petition signed by twenty-five percent of the registered voters residing within the district; or (2) by "resolution of application"adopted by the legislative body of the county or city that contains territory proposed to be included in the district. §§ 61011, 61013. The petition for formation or the resolution of application must contain, among other things, a

LAFCO Requirements for a General Tax for Incorporation of a New City

Although this chapter focuses on special taxes and assessments, we wanted to note a 2006 Attorney General opinion regarding the authority of a local agency formation commission (LAFCO) to require voter approval of a general tax as part of an incorporation of a new city. In Opinion Number 06-210, the Attorney General confronted the issue of a LAFCO conditioning its approval of the incorporation of a city upon voters within the proposed city approving a general tax by majority vote.

The first of two questions analyzed by the Attorney General is if Proposition 218 requires voter approval of a general tax, can a LAFCO condition an incorporation upon the approval of such a tax? The Attorney General answered in the affirmative, reasoning that since LAFCOs have the authority to impose conditions when approving a city's incorporation, including general taxes Gov. (§ 56886(s)), and then must hold a vote on that incorporation and associated conditions, the LAFCO approval vote serves as the mandated vote under Proposition 218. In other words, in the words of the Opinion, the LAFCO approval vote "complements" Proposition 218.

The second question analyzed by the Attorney General in the Opinion is whether providing for a majority vote in such a manner violates Proposition 62, which requires a supermajority of the taxing authority (in this case LAFCO) for imposing general taxes. See Gov. Code § 53724(b). To this, the Attorney General responded that the LAFCO is not ultimately imposing a tax here—rather the voters. Therefore, in this case, the requirement that the local entity legislative body approve submitting the tax to the voters by a supermajority vote of that body did not apply.

Based on this opinion, a LAFCO, at least for an incorporation or formation of a special district, would have authority to require voter approval of taxes as a condition of approval of the new local entity.

description of the boundaries, methods by which the district will be financed, the proposed name of the district, and reason(s) for formation. *Id.*

Once complete, the petition or resolution must be filed with the LAFCO. § 61014. LAFCO then decides whether to approve the formation and, if so, may establish a set of terms and conditions that will govern the formation of the district. See § 56825 et seq. If LAFCO approves the formation, an election is conducted, unless a majority protest its creation under the LAFCO *Id.* The formation of the district may be conditioned on the approval of a special tax or assessment. § 61014(c). Once the requisite votes are cast, the LAFCO commission will certify that the CSD is duly organized. § 57176 et seq.

Once formed, a CSD may be further authorized to provide additional services through the passage of special legislation. See § 61105.

Development Agreements

As mentioned in chapter 4, development agreements can provide flexibility and certainty for both the developer and the legislative body approving the new development. Since development agreements are contracts based on mutual consent, they provide the ability to tailor requirements and benefits for the particular development. Most often, development agreements establish a term during which the developer has a vested right to proceed with his or her development. In exchange for this vested right and the certainty it gives to the developer, the developer agrees to provide infrastructure or amenities in excess of what the city or county could otherwise require as exactions.

For example, often a developer would like parks and other amenities built in the time frame that best suits the developer's schedule. The city or county, however, may not want to build the park or other amenity until significantly later in the development, in part because the development will not generate sufficient funds for O&M until that later time. However, with a development agreement the developer may decide to build the park earlier and agree to maintain the park for the time between the date the developer completes the park and the time the city or county would have completed the park under the city or county's own time frame.

Natural Resource Mitigation and Preservation

The preservation of natural resources is an important aspect of land use practice today. Developments and public projects are sometimes required to mitigate for natural resource impacts through, for example, the California Environmental Quality Act (CEQA) or other state or federal natural resources laws, such as the Endangered Species Act and the Clean Water Act. Under Section 404 of the Clean Water Act, for example, the Army Corps of Engineers (ACOE) may require compensatory mitigation for unavoidable impacts to wetlands, rivers, and other aquatic resources in the form of mitigation banks, in-lieu fees, or permittee-responsible mitigation. Other entities have a purely charitable motive for conserving resources such as wetlands, habitat, and agricultural land.

Whatever the reason, various methods are being used to preserve and maintain these resources. The most common methods used include conservation easements, habitat programs, or outright fee ownership. Although these strategies are relatively diverse, they are similar in that they generally require on-going expenditures. Besides the initial purchase, there are, notably, the costs of monitoring and maintenance, documentation, insurance, and legal enforcement/ defense. Funding sources for such costs include, among others, endowments, mitigation funds from developers, or Mello-Roos districts.

Such costs, besides being substantial, can also be challenging to predict over time. Entities may fail to create a sufficient endowment for proper stewardship through lack of experience, inadequate funding sources or mismanagement. This can sometimes lead to entities providing insufficient funds for proper stewardship. In response to this, the Center for Natural Lands Management (CNLM) has developed materials to assist in estimating costs over time through the property analysis report. See http://www.cnlm.org. Furthermore, ACOE and the Environmental Protection Agency have promulgated new regulations intended to improve the standards, including financial planning, of compensatory mitigation measures. See 33 C.F.R. § 325 et seq.

More information on these issues may be obtained from the Land Trust Alliance at http://www.landtrustalliance.org

The Development Agreement

In the past, the focus of most cities and counties has been to assure that the developer provides all-necessary infrastructure and capital improvements. Today, however, many developers, as well as cities and counties, are looking to development agreements to establish a total package of financing requirements for the development, including funding or financing for the maintenance responsibilities.

Another example of use of a development agreement may be to establish the parameters of a landscaping and lighting maintenance district and to agree to include the maintenance costs of certain facilities within the maintenance district. This use of development agreements would provide additional certainty that the maintenance costs of a facility would be fully funded within the district and reduce the chance of future disagreements on the scope and spread of any assessments.

By focusing on the O&M costs of public improvements at the time the development is being reviewed and the development agreement negotiated, cities, counties, and developers can address funding shortfalls for operations and maintenance, as well as the capital needs of the development.

Although there is no established case law on the subject, a development agreement could provide a roadmap for the financing of O&M obligations. For example, the developer could agree, through a development agreement, to fund certain maintenance; to consent to the establishment of certain maintenance districts and assessments; or to create a homeowners' association or other entity to assure that the public improvements within the development will be adequately maintained. Since development agreements are recorded contracts that run with the land, the obligations of the development agreement are binding on the successors and assignees of the developer.

Maintenance Endowment Funds

With a Maintenance Endowment Fund (MEF), the developer would create an endowment fund by depositing money into a trust account for the benefit of the public agency responsible for the facility. The principal should be prudently invested and sufficient in amount to meet the maintenance and operational needs of the particular service or improvement. One example of an MEF occurs with the requirements for dedication of conservation and habitat easements to offset the impacts of new development. Often, habitat mitigation or other types of mitigation with on-going obligations include a component for implementation and monitoring. The implementation or monitoring fee may be used by a land manager of a nonprofit land trust to assure that the conserved lands are properly managed.

Public/Private Partnerships

The variety of creative approaches presently being employed by cities, counties, special districts, and developers or property owners is one of the most dynamic aspects of the quest for stable or additional funding sources.[12]

Today, we routinely see public agencies seeking out corporations, local businesses, and individuals to become involved in supporting public facilities. For example, the naming of a public stadium for a corporate sponsor in exchange for the corporation's support, either by significantly assisting in the construction of the stadium or its maintenance, has become commonplace. Cities often actively solicit individuals and corporations to assist with the maintenance of parks and other recreational facilities. Urban revitalization projects have also been an area of beneficial public/private partnerships.

When Public/Private Cooperation Projects May Be Subject to Prevailing Wages

Public-private innovation may take many forms, including but not limited to, land write-downs, investment of public funds, fee waivers, or reinvestment of project-generated tax proceeds into infrastructure cost, debt, or O&M. However, there should be careful review of the rules applicable to the projects. For example, a result of legislation enacted in 2001 (and amended in 2002), an innovative, cooperative agreement between a public agency and a developer may trigger "prevailing wages," significantly raising development costs.

Labor Code section 1720(b) provides that the phrase "paid for in whole or in part out of public funds," which may evince a public work requiring a prevailing wage, includes:

(1) The payment of money or the equivalent of money by the state or political subdivision directly to or on behalf of the public works contractor, subcontractor, or developer

(2) Performance of construction work by the state or political subdivision in execution of the project

(3) Transfer by the state or political subdivision of an asset of value for less than fair market price

(4) Fees, costs, rents, insurance or bond premiums, loans, interest rates, or other obligations that would normally be required in the execution of the contract, that are paid, reduced, charged at less than fair market value, waived, or forgiven by the state or political subdivision

(5) Money loaned by the state or political subdivision that is to be repaid on a contingent basis

(6) Credits that are applied by the state or political subdivision against repayment obligations to the state or political subdivision

This definition significantly broadens the prevailing wage requirement and is likely to render infeasible many projects that historically had been financed through public/private partnerships.

Such efforts have commanded the attention of policy makers. California Governor Arnold Schwarzenegger, for example, has proposed a set of policies to encourage public/private partnerships in the area of public infrastructure. These include establishing "PBI California," a center devoted to assisting in implementing Performance Based Infrastructure (PBI)—or, public/private partnerships—in state and local projects. The proposals also include broad authorization for state and local governments to use PBI in the construction and O&M of state and local projects.

Privatization of Utilities

Local governments also look to privatizing certain public utilities in an effort to become more efficient. The state is looking at this as well (see the section on Public/Private Partnerships). Municipalities considering privatization of utilities should undertake an economic analysis of the costs and benefits of such an arrangement. Municipalities should also explore requiring the private contractor to provide maintenance at specified levels during the life of the contract so as not to discover a substantial maintenance cost at the end of the operating period.[13]

Harriet A. Steiner is a partner in the Sacramento office of Best Best & Krieger LLP. She practices land use, environmental, municipal, and telecommunications law, and has served as City Attorney for the City of Davis for more than twenty-five years.

Seth Merewitz is a partner with Best Best & Krieger LLP. He provides advisory and transactional services to land owner groups, public agencies, and private entities, with a focus on residential master-planned communities, land use, infrastructure financing, affordable housing, redevelopment, public-private partnerships and general municipal law.

The authors wish to thank Ann Schwing, of counsel with Best Best & Krieger LLP, for her substantive review, advice, and creativity.

The Importance of Planning Ahead

While there are many ways to fund the maintenance of public improvements, the options are generally more effective and understandable when addressed in the early stages of a project. Often public agencies review the cost of a capital improvement without considering the cost of long-term maintenance. When these costs are not part of the equation, the agency is implicitly accepting an unfunded obligation to its general fund.

Public improvements are amenities that citizens appreciate initially, but may not feel compelled to fund after the fact. When considering the placement of public improvements, public agencies and developers should try to locate them in areas with which residents can easily identify. Fostering identification with an improvement creates an opportunity to increase civic pride and secure funding. Often by the time a public agency identifies the unfunded maintenance costs for an existing public improvement, it is generally too late to locate a viable source of funding. By examining the funding for O&M early, one can reduce a portion of the strain on the public agency's general fund in the future.

Appendices

Appendix A prepared for:
City of Sacramento
Prepared by:
Economic & Planning Systems, Inc.
May 24, 2009
EPS #17625

APPENDIX A

North Natomas Nexus Study and Financing Plan 2008 Update

Source: EPS, July 2011

1.Executive Summary of Development Impact Fee Program

Development Impact Fee Adoption and Administration

On October 31, 1995, the City adopted Ordinance 95-058, which added Title 84, Chapter 84.01 and 84.02 to the Sacramento City Code. Chapter 84.02 authorizes certain development impact fees to be assessed upon owners of residential and nonresidential property located in the Finance Plan Area. Map 1 shows the area included in the Finance Plan Area. The development impact fees are assessed to pay for the design, construction, installation, or acquisition of public facilities as required for the development of North Natomas. As development impact fees are collected at the time of building permit issuance, the City will administer the development impact fee programs (Fee Programs) through the Building Department.

The development impact fees are subject to an automatic annual adjustment to account for the inflation of public facilities costs. In addition to the automatic annual adjustment, the City will also conduct both annual and periodic reviews (every three years) of the Fee Programs. The annual and periodic review process is summarized later in this chapter and discussed in more detail in Chapter 7.

Existing Fee Programs

Several existing City and County fees will continue to be collected in addition to the fees discussed in this report. Existing City and County fees applicable to new development in North Natomas include these:

- School fees collected for the School Districts serving North Natomas.
- Sewer fees collected by Sacramento County Regional Sanitation District (SCRSD) and Sacramento Area Sewer District No. 1 (SASD–No. 1).
- Habitat fees for the North Natomas Habitat Conservation Program collected by the City.
- Water connection fees, the Major Street Construction Tax, and the Housing Trust Fund fees collected by the City.
- Quimby Act park land in-lieu fees.
- Building permit, plan checking, and other processing and entitlement fees.
- Citywide Park Development Impact Fees.

Development Impact Fee Summary

Of the 6,439 acres in the Finance Plan Area, approximately 4,244 acres are planned for urban development. For development to occur on these 4,244 acres, a series of public infrastructure improvements must be constructed. References to acres in the text and tables of this report are net of major and minor roads unless otherwise indicated. Development impact fees fund a total of $281.1 million of general public facilities infrastructure and $53.3 million transit facilities (both in 2008 dollars), before adjustments and excluding drainage improvements. Drainage improvements are primarily funded through bond proceeds. Tables 2-1, 2-2, and 2-3 show the list of facilities and facilities costs for each improvement category to be funded through three development impact fees in the City: the North Natomas Public Facilities Fee (PFF), the North Natomas Transit Fee (Transit Fee), and the North Natomas Drainage Fee.

In addition, approximately $135.0 million will be funded through the North Natomas Land Acquisition Program (NNLAP). The NNLAP includes the North Natomas Public

Facilities Land Acquisition Fee (PFLAF), and the North Natomas Regional Park Land Acquisition Fee (RPLAF), both of which will be discussed further in Chapter 6 of this report. The NNLAP program is updated annually and is not updated as part of this 2008 Nexus Study Update.

The remaining infrastructure and public facilities will be funded by other fee programs established by or for other jurisdictions, other existing City and countywide fees, an areawide Mello-Roos Community Facilities District (CFD 97-01), private funding to build facilities required as conditions of map approval, and other Citywide, State, and Federal sources.

Table 2-4 shows the PFF and the Transit Fee for each land use. No changes were made to the Transit Plan for 2008; therefore, the North Natomas Transit Fee was only adjusted to 2008 dollars. As the costs for drainage improvements were not revised for the 2008 Nexus Study Update, Table 2-5 shows the North Natomas Drainage Fee for each basin inflated to 2008 dollars. Table 2-6 shows the PFLAF and the RPLAF. NNLAP fees shown reflect the current fees adopted in November 2008. The nexus findings and calculations of each of these fees are presented in the following chapters. The fees shown on all of these figures include a 3.0-percent allowance for the cost of administering the programs. These tables also reflect the adjustment of fees by lot size for single-family, by density for multifamily, and by percentage of office use for light industrial land uses as discussed in Chapter 3.

North Natomas Public Facilities Fee

Collected as one fee, the Public Facilities Fee (PFF) funds the following public facilities:

- Roadway, Signals, Bridges, and Freeway.
- Freeway and Roadway Landscaping.
- Fire Facilities.
- Library Facilities.
- Police Facilities.
- Community Center Facilities.
- Bikeways and Shuttles.
- Planning Studies.

Although the PFF will be collected as one fee, this report makes separate findings concerning the nexus between each component of the fee and the new development in North Natomas on which the fee is imposed. The cost of each facility is allocated to the entire project area and fees vary only by land use.

Table 2-2	Summary of Transit Fee Facilities Costs
Table 2-3	Summary of Drainage Facility Costs
Table 2-4	Total Public Facilities and Transit Fee
Table 2-5	Total Drainage Fee by Drainage Basin
Table 2-6	Land Acquisition Fees

The PFF includes the costs of improvements that have been or will be funded up-front by landowners such as a portion of the

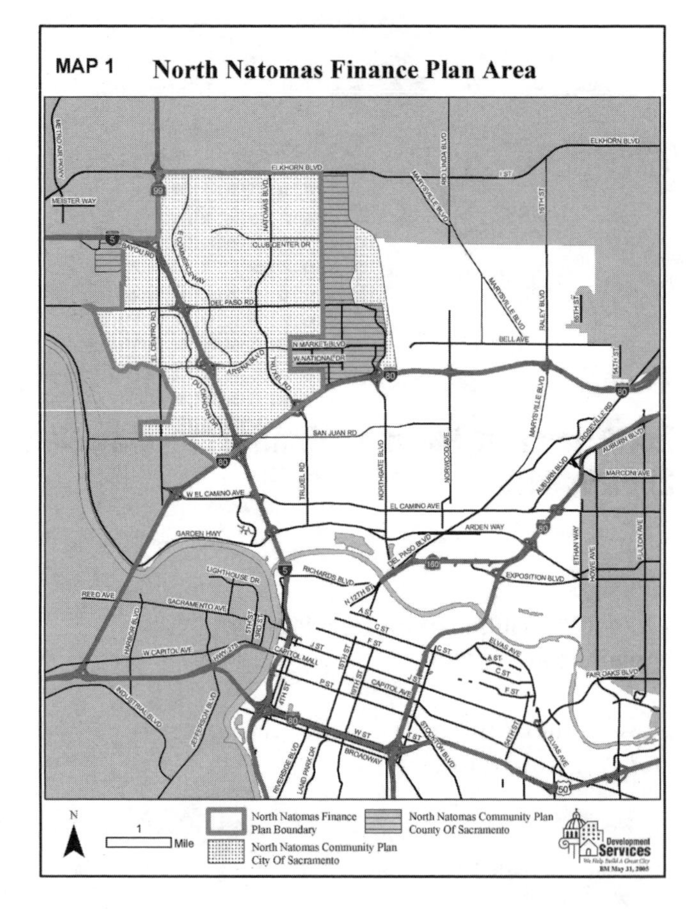

costs funded in AD 88-03, NNLAP planning costs and the Truxel interchange construction costs. The landowners that provided advanced funding for any of these items will be reimbursed by the fee program according to the procedures described in Appendix C.

The PFF fee is allocated to all residential and nonresidential parcels based on net acreage. Residential fees are collected on a per-unit basis; while nonresidential fees are collected on a net acreage-basis. See the following section entitled "PFF and Transit Fee Calculation Changes" and Chapter 7 for more detailed information.

North Natomas Transit Fee

The North Natomas Transit Fee (Transit Fee) funds construction and acquisition of light rail transit (LRT) facilities. The transit facilities funded by the Transit Fee were changed in the 2002 Update. In the 1995 Nexus Study and 1999 Nexus Study Update the transit facilities listed included track, rolling stock, stations, and electronic equipment as well as other transit facilities including buses, shelters, bus turnouts or other transit equipment. The fee also could be used to fund soft costs such as formation of the North Natomas Transportation Management Association (TMA), and planning/studies related to expansion of Regional Transit (RT) in North Natomas.

Table 2-1
North Natomas Nexus Study Update 2008
Summary of PFF Facility Costs (2008$)

Facility	Total Costs (2008$)	Total PFF Funded Costs	Other Funding	Other Funding Sources	Note
Road and Freeway Facilities [1]					
Roadways (includes utilities) [2]	$133,678,362	$108,849,246	$24,829,116	MSCT / Private Funding [3]	See Note [4]
Freeways	$158,573,760	$57,469,215	$101,104,545	State, Federal, & Other Areas	See Note [4]
Signals (4x4 intersection and larger)	$5,791,846	$5,791,846	$0	NA	Provided by Harris & Associates
Signals (2x4, 2x6, and 2x8)	$6,602,494	$654,452	$5,948,042	Developers	Provided by Harris & Associates
Bridges	$10,086,145	$10,086,145	$0	NA	Provided by Harris & Associates
Subtotal Road and Freeway Facilities	**$314,732,607**	**$182,850,904**	**$131,881,703**		
Other Non-Road Facilities					
Freeway and Roadway Landscaping	$31,044,130	$31,044,130	$0	NA	Provided by Harris & Associates
Fire Stations and Equipment	$17,287,049	$17,287,049	$0	NA	See Note [4]
Library	$17,139,271	$10,126,271	$7,013,000	Grant	See Note [4]
Police Substation	$15,142,800	$5,290,705	$9,852,095	General Fund	See Note [4]
Community Center Facilities	$32,545,312	$8,136,328	$24,408,984	General Fund & Other Funding	See Note [4]
Bikeways and Shuttles	$20,495,044	$9,130,923	$11,364,122	Regional & Grants	Provided by Harris & Associates
Planning/Studies	$17,231,226	$17,231,226	$0	NA	Provided by Harris & Associates
Subtotal Other Facilities	**$150,884,832**	**$98,246,631**	**$52,638,201**		
TOTAL PFF FACILITY COSTS	**$465,617,439**	**$281,097,535**	**$184,519,904**		

"PFF cost sum"

Source: Harris and Associates, City of Sacramento, and EPS.

[1] Total roadway cost does not include overwidth reimbursement costs for completed roadway segments. This does not impact total PFF-funded costs. Some facilities, such as designated traffic signals, will receive funding from Panhandle development and were included in this analysis.
[2] Roadway segment costs added in 2002 that are not funded by the PFF will be funded through private sources.
[3] MSCT = Major Streets Construction Tax. Private funding includes exactions from development in North Natomas and other Plan Areas.
[4] Information provided by Harris & Associates and City of Sacramento.

Prepared by EPS 8/11/2009

P:\17000\17625 North Natomas Public Facility Fee Update\Model\1. Final Draft - August 2009\17625 NN2008.8.xls

Table 2-2
North Natomas Nexus Study 2008 Update
Summary of Transit Fee Facilities Costs (2008$) [1]

Facility	Total Costs	Remaining Costs	Other Funding/ Completed Facility Costs	Other Funding Sources
Light Rail Stations	$46,106,800	$15,405,232	$30,701,568	Federal, State, and Other
Light Rail Right-of-Way	$7,239,861	$0	$7,239,861	Land Acquisition Program
TOTAL	**$53,346,661**	**$15,405,232**	**$37,941,429**	

"transit cost sum"

Source: City of Sacramento, Harris & Associates, and EPS.

[1] Transit costs increased by the change in ENR-CCI since the 2005 Nexus Update.

Table 2-3
North Natomas Nexus Study 2008 Update
Summary of Drainage Facility Costs (2008$)

Facility	Total Costs	Costs Funded by Fees	Other Funding	Other Funding Sources	Source Table
DRAINAGE FEE FACILITIES					
Basin 1	$41,408,382	$0	$41,408,382	CFD No. 4	Table 5-2
Basin 2	$8,878,111	$0	$8,878,111	CFD No. 4	Table 5-2
Basin 3	$17,819,336	$0	$17,819,336	CFD No. 2001-3	Table 5-2
Basin 4	$13,006,928	$0	$13,006,928	CFD No. 4	Table 5-2
Basin 5	$9,084,846	$0	$9,084,846	CFD No. 2	Table 5-2
Basin 6	$17,513,874	$0	$17,513,874	CFD No. 2	Table 5-2
Basin 7A	$0	$0	$0	privately financed	Table 5-2
Basin 7B	$0	$0	$0	privately financed	Table 5-2
Basin 8A	$12,433,193	$0	$12,433,193	CFD No. 2000-01	Table 5-2
Basin 8B	$10,603,494	$0	$10,603,494	[1]	Table 5-2
Basin 8C	$9,107,667	$0	$9,107,667	CFD No. 99-04	Table 5-2
Basin-Wide Improvements	**$139,855,831**	**$0**	**$139,855,831**		
Area-Wide Improvements [2]	$38,600,451	$0	$38,600,451	CFD 97-01	Table B-67
Subtotal Drainage	**$178,456,282**	**$0**	**$178,456,282**		

"drainage_cost_sum"

Source: City of Sacramento, Harris & Associates, and EPS.

[1] Costs are estimated and source of funding had not yet been determined.
[2] Estimate is from the North Natomas Drainage CFD No. 97-01 Formation Hearing Report and Financing Plan Report dated March 4, 1997. Costs shown have been inflated to 2008 dollars.

Prepared by EPS 8/11/2009

2-7

Such expenditures would be deducted from the funds for Regional Transit. The fees will be used as part of the local match for State and Federal transit funding. The Transit Fee will not acquire land in North Natomas because stations and right-of-way acquisition are funded through the NNLAP.

In 2002, the City and RT agreed to change the basis for calculating the North Natomas local share of the transit facilities funding for light rail station construction costs, which is unchanged for 2008 as described in Chapter 4. The cost of transit facilities for the Transit Fee is not being updated in the 2008 Nexus Study Update. Thus, Transit Fees will increase in 2008 based on the annual inflation adjustment.

The Transit Fee is allocated to all residential and nonresidential parcels in Finance Plan Area based on net acreage. Residential fees are collected on a per-unit basis; while nonresidential fees are collected on a net acreage-basis. See the following section entitled "PFF and Transit Fee Calculation Changes" and Chapter 7 for more detailed information.

North Natomas Drainage Fee

The North Natomas Drainage Fee (Drainage Fee) funds drainage improvements and land acquisition for each drainage basin that does not have an alternative funding mechanism in place, or the fee can be used as an alternative to a planned funding mechanism. The drainage improvements in each basin include construction of detention basins, detention basin land acquisition, trunk facilities, channels, and certain pump stations.

While a Drainage Fee is calculated for each drainage basin, many of the basins have other funding mechanisms that entirely fund the necessary drainage improvements. In basins with other funding sources, the Drainage Fee will be collected

Table 2-4
North Natomas Nexus Study Update 2008
Total Public Facilities and Transit Fee (2008$) [1]

Land Use	2008 Public Facilities Fee (PFF) [1]	2008 Transit Fee [1]
RESIDENTIAL [2]	*Fee per Unit*	
Single-Family Detached/Attached		
Rural Estates [3]	*See Note [3]*	
Lot Size > 5,000 Sq. Ft.	$8,466	$423
Lot Size 3,250 - 5,000 Sq. Ft. [4]	$7,155	$387
Lot Size < 3,250 Sq. Ft.	$5,845	$351
Age-Restricted	$6,744	$277
Multifamily (>2 attached units)		
8-12 units per acre	$5,845	$351
12 - 18 units per acre [5]	$5,087	$315
> 18 units per acre	$4,330	$277
Age-Restrict. Apartments	$2,822	$136
Age-Restrict. Congregate Care	$1,379	$76
NONRESIDENTIAL	*Fee per Net Acre*	
Convenience Commercial	$238,272	$29,026
Community Commercial	$140,361	$14,952
Village Commercial	$192,376	$22,430
Transit Commercial	$194,636	$22,430
Highway Commercial	$141,161	$15,393
Regional Commercial	$127,541	$13,194
EC Commercial	$140,361	$14,952
EC 30 - Office	$75,669	$5,718
EC 40 - Office	$95,765	$7,917
EC 50 - Office/Hospital	$110,918	$9,675
EC 65 - Office	$136,519	$12,754
EC 80 - Office	$160,944	$15,393
Lt. Industrial w/ < 20% Office	$49,752	$2,639
Lt. Ind. w/ 20% - 50% Office [6]	$57,527	$3,562
Age-Restricted Convalescent Care/Skilled Nursing	$49,563	$3,063
Arena [7]	*See Note [7]*	
Stadium	$129,458	$13,341

"adj fee"

[1] Includes 3.0% administrative allowance.
[2] Residential fees are charged on a per unit basis. However, North Natomas Public Facilities Fees are allocated on a net acre basis assuming target densities.
[3] Currently, no land is designated as Rural Estates in the Finance Plan Area. In the event that such a land use is approved for development, the fee program will be updated to include a fee for Rural Estates.
[4] SFR - 3,250-5,000 sq. ft = 50% Low-Density and 50% Medium-Density.
[5] MFR 12-18 dwelling units/acre = 50% Medium-Density and 50% High-Density.
[6] Modified Light industrial PFF equals 1.35 times Road portion of PFF for Light Industrial plus 70% of the non-Road PFF for Light industrial and 30% of the non-Road PFF for EC-30.
[7] Arena site is already developed. The City of Sacramento and Arco Arena owners have an agreement regarding PFF and Transit Fees and deferred payments.

Table 2-5
North Natomas Nexus Study 2008 Update
Total Drainage Fee by Drainage Basin (2008$)

Land Use	Basin 1	Basin 2	Basin 3	Basin 4	Basin 5	Basin 6	Basin 7A Basin 7B	Basin 8A	Basin 8B	Basin 8C
					Includes 3.0% Administrative Allowance					
RESIDENTIAL [1]					*Fee per Gross Developable Acre*					
Rural Estates	$0	$0	$0	$0	$0	$0		$0	$0	$0
Low Density Residential	$25,729	$31,482	$42,032	$30,577	$0	$23,828		$39,191	$22,402	$25,095
Medium Density Residential	$33,447	$40,926	$54,642	$39,750	$0	$30,976		$50,949	$29,123	$32,624
High Density Residential	$38,593	$47,222	$63,048	$45,865	$19,982	$35,742	NOT	$58,787	$33,603	$37,643
NONRESIDENTIAL										
Convenience Commercial	$41,166	$0	$0	$0	$0	$38,125		$0	$35,843	$0
Community Commercial	$0	$50,371	$67,251	$48,923	$0	$0	AVAILABLE	$62,706	$0	$0
Village Commercial	$41,166	$0	$0	$48,923	$21,314	$0		$0	$0	$0
Transit Commercial	$41,166	$0	$0	$0	$0	$38,125		$0	$0	$0
Highway Commercial	$0	$0	$0	$0	$22,646	$0		$0	$0	$42,662
Regional Commercial	$0	$0	$0	$0	$0	$0	PRIVATELY	$0	$0	$0
Employment Commercial (EC)	$38,593	$0	$0	$0	$19,982	$35,742		$58,787	$33,603	$37,643
Light Industrial	$0	$0	$0	$0	$0	$0		$54,868	$0	$0
Arena	$0	$0	$0	$0	$22,646	$0	FUNDED	$0	$0	$0
Stadium	$0	$0	$0	$0	$22,646	$0		$0	$0	$0
Institutional	$0	$0	$63,048	$45,865	$0	$35,742		$58,787	$33,603	$0
Civic	$38,593	$0	$63,048	$45,865	$0	$35,742		$58,787	$33,603	$0
School	$20,583	$25,185	$33,626	$24,462	$0	$19,062		$31,353	$17,922	$0

"basins"

[1] Drainage fees are based on land use designation for residential gross developable acres, rather than lot size, as for PFF and Transit fees.

only from those land uses not participating in the existing funding program (e.g., schools and parks). In basins with no alternative funding program, the full Drainage Fee could be collected to fund necessary facilities unless or until an alternative funding program is established.

The cost of drainage facilities for the Drainage Fee is not being updated as part of this 2008 Nexus Study Update. Drainage Fees will increase in 2008 based on the annual inflation adjustment. Table 2-5 shows the current Drainage Fee for each basin as of November 23, 2008.

The Drainage Fee does not include the areawide components of the Comprehensive Drainage Plan that will be funded in CFD 97-01. These areawide facilities include the widening and deepening of the RD 1000 canals and the expansion or addition of pumping facilities, detention basins, and major trunk lines. Additional costs include Canal C-1 reimbursement, freeway drainage, and a portion of drainage flows north of Elkhorn Boulevard.

North Natomas Land Acquisition Program

The North Natomas Land Acquisition Program (NNLAP) includes the North Natomas Public Facilities Land Acquisition Fee (PFLAF), and the North Natomas Regional Park Land Acquisition Fee (RPLAF)

The NNLAP funds the acquisition of land for public facilities and the regional park. The PFLAF funds the acquisition of land for uses such as freeway and agricultural buffers, civic lands, light rail right-of-way, drainage easements, street oversizing right-of-way, and AD 88-03 land. The RPLAF funds the acquisition of land required for the regional park. Because no change is being made to the NNLAP at this time, the current PFLAF and the RPLAF (effective November 23, 2008) are shown in Table 2-6.

Changes Included in the 2008 Update

The 2008 Nexus Study Update takes into account current development conditions in the North Natomas Community and Finance Plan Area, as well as changes that occurred during its development between 2002 and 2008. Infrastructure and public facilities costs and requirements have been defined in greater detail since the implementation of the North Natomas Financing Plan and previous updates. Land use estimates of total acres and residential units are current as of March 2008. This section describes other changes.

The changes include extensively updated cost estimates of facilities, revised list of facilities funded by the PFF, and identification of additional revenue sources. In addition, specific procedural and policy changes are proposed and are described in Chapter 7 including revised inflation adjustment procedures and revised fee collection policy regarding changes in land use.

Table 2-6
North Natomas Nexus Study Update 2008
Land Acquisition Fees (2008$) [1]

Land Use	2008 Public Facilities Land Acquisition Fee	2008 Regional Park Land Acquisition Fee
	[2]	[2]
Fee Effective	*11/23/2008*	*11/23/2008*
RESIDENTIAL	*Fee per Unit*	
Single-Family Attached/Detached		
Rural Estates	$0	$0
Lot Size > 5,000 sq. ft.	$6,301	$1,766
Lot Size 3,250 - 5,000 sq. ft.	$5,185	$1,445
Lot Size < 3,250 sq. ft.	$4,070	$1,124
Age-Restricted Single-Family	$7,487	$2,109
Multifamily (>2 attached units)		
8-12 units per net acre	$3,310	$1,128
12-18 units per net acre	$2,412	$832
> 18 units per net acre	$1,514	$536
Age-Restricted Apartments	$1,520	$528
Age-Restricted Congregate Care	$803	$277
NONRESIDENTIAL	*Fee per Net Acre*	
Convenience Commercial	$34,360	$11,899
Community Commercial	$34,360	$11,899
Village Commercial	$34,360	$11,899
Transit Commercial	$34,360	$11,899
Highway Commercial	$34,360	$11,899
Regional Commercial	$34,360	$11,899
EC Commercial	$34,360	$11,899
EC 30 - Office	$34,360	$11,899
EC 40 - Office	$34,360	$11,899
EC 50 - Office/Hospital	$34,360	$11,899
EC 65 - Office	$34,360	$11,899
EC 80 - Office	$34,360	$11,899
Light Industrial with <20% Office	$34,360	$11,899
Light Industrial with 20%-50% Office	$34,360	$11,899
Arena	$25,062	$11,899
Stadium	$21,000	$11,899

"land_fees08"

[1] Fees provided by City of Sacramento. Land Acquisition Fees are before credits for land dedicated.

[2] Based on the Appraisal Report for North Natomas (2008) prepared by Clark-Wolcott, Inc.

PFF and Transit Fee Calculation Changes

Significant development has occurred in North Natomas since the North Natomas Financing Plan was prepared in 1995. Development to date has achieved densities somewhat lower than the planned densities included in the North Natomas Community Plan. For each major update (2002, 2005, and 2008), the decreased densities have been incorporated by updating expected buildout densities thereby reducing the remaining development.

This 2008 Nexus Study Update incorporates additional fee calculation procedures to ensure the City collects the appropriate fee allocation for each parcel based on the Community Plan designation in the Community Plan. Each parcel has a total fee allocation, defined as its Target Revenue.

For nonresidential parcels, the Target Revenue is calculated by multiplying the number of net acres by the appropriate fee from the current fee schedule. This is done for each parcel or portion of parcel included in a proposed Planned Unit Development Schematic Plan (PUD Schematic Plan). The total of all included parcel or portion thereof equals the PUD Schematic Plan's Target Revenue.

For residential parcels, the total allocation of required costs is converted from a per-unit cost to a per-net acre allocation by calculating number of net acres multiplied by the appropriate target density shown in the Community Plan land use assumptions. For each parcel in the PUD Schematic Plan, the resulting number of units is multiplied by the appropriate fee from the current fee schedule to determine the PUD Schematic Plan's Target Revenue.

When the City approves a PUD Schematic Plan, the PFF and Transit Fees will be calculated as proposed, using the current fee schedules, for all parcels and development projects proposed. The PFF and Transit Fee revenues for the entire or undeveloped portion of a PUD Schematic Plan will be compared against the Target Revenues (separately for each fee) for the PUD Schematic Plan.

PFF and Transit fee revenues from a PUD Schematic Plan must equal 100 percent of the Target Revenues for the PUD Schematic Plan. An adjustment as described in Chapter 7 is warranted if the proposed PUD Schematic Plan results in lesser or greater revenue than the Target Revenue. For instance, if the proposed PUD Schematic Plan results in lower total revenue than the Target Revenue, a fee surcharge is added to ensure that adequate fee revenue is collected to fund all required PFF-funded improvements. See Chapter 7 for detailed fee calculation procedures for nonresidential and residential projects.

Updated Cost Estimates

Harris & Associates reviewed all cost estimates and revised all facilities to reflect 2008 dollars. Where updated cost information is available, an actual unit cost estimate was used in the 2008 Nexus Study Update. Improvements based on recent bids or costs provided by the City include: roadways (except underground utilities), landscaping, signals, freeways and overcrossings, bridges, bike paths, fire station and library costs.

If specific unit costs were unavailable, costs were adjusted by either the percentage increase of the Engineering News Record Construction Cost Index (ENR-CCI1) for San Francisco on March 1, 2008, which is currently 11.22 percent; or the three-year moving average of the California Department of Transportation Highway Construction Cost Index (CalTrans Index 2), which is currently 16.91-percent. A detailed summary of adjustments made to the 2008 Nexus Study Update is shown below.

Roadway and Utility Unit Costs

- Roadway costs increased based on recent bids.
- Underground costs increased by change in ENR-CCI.

Signal Costs

- Costs shown in 2005 PFF retained for completed signals: Includes Signal Numbers: 11, 15, 16, 48, 50, 53, 54, and 55.
- Costs Increased per City direction for these:
  - Signal No. 2—cost increased to $814,000.
  - Signal No. 7—cost increased to $400,000.
  - Signal No. 8—cost increased to $400,000.
  - Signal No. 9—cost reduced to $438,000.
  - Signal No. 17—cost increased to $342,000.
  - Signal No. 44—cost increased to $342,000.
- Signals No. 3 and No. 4 were removed from this category and are now included with corresponding interchange cost.
- Remaining signals increased based on recent bids.

Freeway Costs

- Interchange located at West El Camino and Interstate-80 increased to $22.5 million per project study report (PSR).
- Auxiliary lane located at Del Paso Interchange cost increased to $1.6 million per PSR and City. Note that the cost of Signals No. 3 and No. 4 now included with this cost item.
- Elkhorn/ State Route 99 costs increased to $12.9 million per change in ENR-CCI.
- Overcrossing at State Route 99/Meister Way costs increased to $8.1 million per cost estimate shown in Greenbriar Public Facilities Financing Plan.

- Cost of overcrossings at Natomas Crossing Blvd and El Centro Road increased based on recent bid provided by City. They also reflect a reduction of width to fifty-two feet.
- Remaining projects increased by CalTrans Index three-year average.

Bridge Costs

- Bridge No. 4—Terracina Drive over East Drain Canal—Costs increased to $1.2 million per current estimate from City.
- Bridge No. 5—Costs were adjusted based on square footage costs from the Fong Road bridge estimate.
- Bridge No. 6—Costs were adjusted based on square footage costs from the Fong Road bridge estimate.
- Bridge No. 7—Gateway Park Boulevard over C-1 Canal—Cost increased to $2.0 million per current estimate from City.
- Bridge No. 8—Costs were adjusted based on square footage costs from the Fong Road bridge estimate.

Landscaping Unit Costs

- Costs increased based on recent bids.

Fire Station

- Cost for initial fire station increased to $8.5 million to reflect actual cost of construction.
- Cost of second fire station increased to $9.6 million per City direction.

Library

- Costs increased to $15.8 million per actual costs from City.

Police Substation

- Costs increased by ENR-CCI Index.

Community Center

- Total costs increased to $32.5 million for four community centers with fee-funding of $8.1 million for the first community center.

Bikeway Costs

- Projects increased by recent costs and ENR-CCI index.

Shuttle Bus

- Costs increased by ENR-CCI Index.

Light Rail Costs

- Costs increased by ENR-CCI Index.

Other Adjustments

- Cost estimates include a contingency (including management) where appropriate that was reduced from twenty-nine percent to twenty-six percent for all projects adjusted with the ENR-CCI Index. Similar facilities such as bridges, overcrossings, etc. have been constructed throughout the City since the Nexus Study 2005 Update. This experience results in greater understanding of anticipated costs for these facilities planned within the Plan Area and an ability to reduce the cost contingency where appropriate.

Revised Facilities Funded by PFF

In preparation of this 2008 Nexus Study Update, the City undertook a thorough review of facilities funded by the PFF. The City, with the participation of the North Natomas Working Group (comprising community residents, City staff, developers, and representatives for the City), reviewed all facilities for scope, cost, need, and the relationship to actual development in North Natomas. As a result, adjustments can be made that both significantly reduce fee support for some facilities and increase support for under-funded but high priority projects. Using traffic analysis and nexus criteria as governing tools, some facilities permitted reduction in fee-funding because volumes from the Financing Plan area did not support the share of fee support currently in the plan.

In addition, cost of three of the four overcrossings of Interstate 5 and State Route 99, were increased to reflect true costs with funding provided entirely by fees. Additional fee-funding for high-priority projects include a total of $8.1 million in funding for fee-funded community centers and $9.6 million in funding for the second fire station. This section describes each improvement and the source and reason for change in fee-funding status.

Roadway and Utility Unit Costs

- **Segment 1A—Snowy Egret Way from El Centro Road to Duckhorn Drive.** Removed from the Fee Program, but still included in the North Natomas Finance Plan. The City's Department of Transportation (City DOT) conducted a traffic analysis and determined that the segment was designed to accommodate traffic created by the initially planned baseball stadium. Should future development with similar intensity require the improvement to be constructed, the City will require the roadway constructed as a condition of entitlement approval.
- **Segment 17—Natomas Crossing Way from El Centro Road to Duckhorn Drive.** Removed from the Fee Program, but still included in the North Natomas Finance Plan. The City DOT conducted a traffic analysis and determined that the segment will primarily serve the

County area to the west and is not justified for development within the Fee area.

Freeway Costs

- **Snowy Egret Way Overcrossing**—Similar to Road Segment 1A above, the facility was removed from the Fee Program, but is still included in the North Natomas Finance Plan. City DOT conducted a traffic analysis and determined that the segment was designed to accommodate traffic created by the initially planned baseball stadium. Should future development with similar intensity require the improvement to be constructed, the City will require the overcrossing constructed as a condition of entitlement approval.
- **El Centro Overcrossing**—Community Plan calls for two-lane roads, which is justified by traffic analysis by City DOT. Therefore, cost estimates for this facility assume a two-lane overcrossing.
- **Natomas Crossing Overcrossing**—Community Plan calls for two-lane roads, which is justified by traffic analysis by City DOT. Therefore, cost estimates for this facility assume a two-lane overcrossing.
- **Meister Way Overcrossing**—Analysis from City Planning indicates the overcrossing will primarily serve the Greenbriar and Metro Air Park plan areas and should primarily be funded as part of their Finance Plans. The North Natomas contribution was reduced as a correction reflecting this analysis.
- **West El Camino/I-80 Interchange**—Existing and planned patterns of growth were analyzed by City DOT resulting in a revised fair share contribution of North Natomas land uses. These analyses indicate a 9.0-percent fair-share contribution from North Natomas and the PFF.

Signal Costs

- Signal No. 10—El Centro Road and Natomas Crossing Way—Removed from fee support per City direction.

Bridge Costs

- Bridge No. 9—San Juan Road Over West Drain Canal—Cost of this facility removed from fee support. It is considered primarily a drainage improvement and should be funded by CFD 97-01.
- Bridge No. 10—Natomas Crossing Drive Over West Drain Canal—Removed from fee support based on City's direction. Facility is not likely to be built.

Fire Station

- Second Fire Station—Add second fire station at cost of $9.6 million per City direction. The original PFF indicates the second fire station was to be funded from other non-PFF funding sources.

Inclusion of Additional Revenue Sources

In preparing the 2008 Nexus Study Update, the City identified additional sources of revenue that would appropriately offset the cost of funding of PFF-funded infrastructure. Sources not included in the Nexus Study 2005 Update but included herein include these:

- Deferred Arco Arena PFF funding.
- Interest Earned on PFF Fees held in Reserve.
- Bond Arbitrage Funds Earned.

Adjustments to the Fee Program

The fees presented in this report are based on the best available cost estimates and land use information at this time. If costs or land uses change significantly in either direction, or if other funding becomes available, the fees will need to be updated accordingly. Updates to the development impact fees, other than the automatic annual adjustments described below, must be adopted by City Council resolution as explained in Section 84.02.212 of the Sacramento City Code.

The Financing Plan automatically adjusts fees and costs in accordance with the annual change in the ENR-CCI. The ENR-CCI is a commonly-accepted cost index; however, it has proven to be unreliable in California over at least the last three years. It measures material costs but not gross margins in construction contracts. Over the past few years, actual contract cost changes far exceeded material cost changes. This has been true for governments and developers alike.

In recognition that the period since 2005 may have been a historic aberration, the adjustment procedure allows fees to decrease if declines in actual construction costs deem it appropriate. The following procedures improve the method by which the PFF program is annually adjusted as well as ensure that adequate PFF revenues are produced to fund the capital improvement programs.

The automatic annual adjustments take into account the potential for inflation of public facility design, construction, installation, and acquisition costs. As detailed in Chapter 7, the revised automatic adjustment proposed in this 2008 Nexus Study Update is tied to the annual percentage change of the ENR-CCI or the CalTrans Index. This index-approach will be checked for appropriateness with a cost evaluation prepared by a professional third-party engineering consultant. The automatic annual adjustment shall be effective on July 1 of each Fiscal Year. See the next section and Chapter 7 for more information regarding the automatic cost adjustment procedure.

In addition to automatic annual adjustments, the City will perform annual reviews of the PFF to ensure adequate revenues are collected to fund required public facilities. The annual reviews will be supplemented by periodic updates to the Nexus Study and Fee Programs approximately every three years. The 2008 Nexus Study Update identifies several items the City will consider during annual and periodic updates of the Fee Programs (included in Chapter 7).

The comprehensive review includes the two cost-adjustment procedures found in Chapter 7 Procedure A and Procedure B) to reallocate costs to remaining undeveloped land uses in accordance with "nexus" principles.

The following summarizes the adjustment procedure.

Annual PFF Adjustment for PFF Eligible Facilities

Each July 1, the City shall adjust the PFF in accordance with the difference between these:

- The Funding Requirement 3 for the current year.
- The funding that would be available, after deducting revenue on hand and adding outstanding PFF credits, if the then-existing PFF were applied to remaining development.

In other words, the City shall adjust the PFF in accordance with the difference between the then-current year's cost estimate and an amount calculated by applying the then-existing PFF to remaining development. See Chapter 7 for additional information.

Procedure A: Adjusting Costs of Uncompleted Transportation Facilities[4]

The City shall use the following procedure to adjust the funding amount being provided by the PFF for all uncompleted Transportation Facilities (see Chapter 7 for more information and sample calculations):

a. **Method of Adjustment.** Each year, the City shall determine the cost adjustment for uncompleted Transportation Facilities using either the Benchmark Change determined below (section titled, "Determination of Benchmark Change") or the percentage change in the index selected under section titled, "Selection of Index." If, for the year in question, the difference between the Benchmark Change and the percentage change in the selected index is five or more percentage points, then the City will use the Benchmark Change to adjust costs for uncompleted Transportation Facilities. Otherwise, the City will adjust costs for those facilities using the percentage change in the selected index.

b. **Determination of Benchmark Change.** The City shall follow the following steps to determine the "Benchmark Change" for each year:

- **Step 1.** Before April 1, have a third-party professional engineering consultant who is under contract to the City estimate the cost to construct all uncompleted Transportation Facilities. The cost estimate will anticipate cost changes to the next July 1.
- **Step 2.** Determine the "Benchmark Estimate" of the cost to construct all uncompleted Transportation Facilities by adding an estimated contingency to the cost estimate from Step 1. The estimated contingency may not exceed twenty-six percent of the cost estimate.
- **Step 3.** Divide the Benchmark Estimate from Step 2 by previous year's adjusted cost estimate for uncompleted Transportation Facilities (which was determined in accordance with this section) and express the resulting quotient as a decimal.

Illustration: If, for example, the Benchmark Estimate from Step 2 is $206,514,000 and the previous year's cost estimate for uncompleted Transportation Facilities is $188,275,000, then the resulting quotient (to nine decimal places) is 1.094258842 (i.e., $206,514,000 ÷ $188,725,000 = 1.094258842).

- **Step 4.** Subtract 1.0 from the resulting quotient in Step 3.

Illustration: If, for example, the quotient from Step 3 is 1.094258842, then subtracting 1.0 from that quotient yields a difference of 0.094258842 (i.e., 1.094258842 – 1.0 = .094258842).

- **Step 5.** Express the difference from Step 4 as a percentage by multiplying it by 100 and adding a percentage sign, and then round the percentage to the nearest thousandth. This rounded percentage is the Benchmark Change for the year.

Illustration: If, for example, the difference from Step 4 is 0.094258842, then multiplying that difference by 100 and rounding the product to the nearest thousandth yields a Benchmark Change of 9.426 percent.

c. **Selection of Index.** Each year, the City shall adjust the cost of the Transportation Facilities remaining to be completed by using either the percentage change in the ENR-CCI or the percentage change in the CalTrans Index, according to the following criteria:

- If both indexes are positive on March 1 of the year in question, then the City shall adjust the cost of the remaining Transportation Facilities using the index with the greater percentage change.
- If the change in one index is positive and the change in the other is negative on March 1 of the year in question, then the City shall adjust the cost of the remaining Transportation Facilities using the index with the positive change.

- If the change for both indexes is negative on March 1 of the year in question, then the City shall adjust the cost of the remaining Transportation Facilities using the index with the negative change that is closer to zero.

d. **Precision.** The City shall carry out all calculations to three decimal places.

Procedure B: Cost Adjustment for Police Substation, Second Fire Station, Library, Freeway Landscaping, and Community Center

For the police substation, second fire station, library, freeway landscaping, and community center, the PFF Share for each facility will not exceed the amount established in the 2008 Nexus Study Update, except as follows: the City shall adjust the PFF Shares for the police substation, second fire station, library, freeway landscaping, and community center by using only the positive change in the ENR-CCI from March to March, effective each July 1. If, however, there are two consecutive years of decreases in the ENR-CCI, then, beginning with the second year of the decrease, the City shall decrease the PFF Shares for the police substation, second fire station, library, freeway landscaping, and community center by an amount equal to the decrease in the ENR-CCI for that second year.

Refined Facility Descriptions

This 2008 Nexus Study Update includes refined facility descriptions for each bridge, overcrossing, interchange and public building (fire, police substation, library, and community centers) funded by the PFF. The descriptions provide greater design details for planned facilities and place limits on the physical design, appearance, enhancements, and landscaping for each facility.

Changes in Community Plan Land Use Designation

Changes in Community Plan land use designations present unique problems for the Fee Program when a change would result in reduced revenue or increased infrastructure requirements. Reduced revenue causes difficulties because the Financing Plan depends on Target Revenues from each Community Plan land use type. As stated above, the cost allocation, and thus Target Revenue, required from each acre varies by land use as a result of the differing cost burdens of each land use. Changes in land use designations that would reduce revenues below target amounts cannot be practically managed because (1) much of the backbone infrastructure is complete, (2) remaining facility requirements will not be reduced by a designation change, and (3) costs would need to be reallocated to all land uses on a case-by-case basis as changes occur, which is impractical. Similarly, costs cannot be reallocated to all fee payers in the event of increased infrastructure requirements, as many land uses have already paid fees.

Any future change in land use designation cannot result in increased costs or reduced revenues to the fee program. To implement this policy, each proposed change will be evaluated as a whole for its impact on the Fee Programs. As appropriate, conditions of approval will be placed on the project in question stating that the applicant is subject to the North Natomas fee rates applicable under the original Community Plan land use designation or to certain infrastructure improvements.

APPENDIX B

Plumas Lake Specific Plan/North Arboga Study Area Road Fee Nexus Study

2005 Update Prepared for: Yuba County
Prepared by: Economic & Planning Systems, Inc.
December 20, 2004
EPS #14488
Hearing Report

I. Executive Summary

The 2005 Update to the Plumas Lake Specific Plan/North Arboga Study Area (PSLP/NASA) Road Fee Nexus Study (the "PLSP/NASA Road Fee Program") revises the Plumas Lake Specific Plan Road Fee Nexus Study prepared in September of 2003. The 2005 update takes into account current development conditions in the PLSP and adds land uses located within the NASA. The Update uses revised land use information as well as revised and updated costs to calculate the PLSP/NASA Road Fee. The cash flow for the PLSP/NASA Road Fee program is also updated to reflect the changes made in land use and roadway costs.

The purpose and methodology of this report is similar to the 2003 Road Fee program. The reader may wish to refer to the 2003 PLSP Road Fee Nexus Study to compare contents of the hearing report to this 2005 Update.

Background

Economic & Planning Systems, Inc., (EPS) has prepared this 2005 Update to the Plumas Lake Specific Plan Road Fee/North Arboga Study Area Nexus Study. Yuba County retained EPS to establish the nexus between the Plumas Lake Specific Plan (PLSP), the North Arboga Study Area (NASA), and the portion of the public roadway facilities that will be funded by the PLSP/NASA road development impact fee program proposed for adoption by the Yuba County Board of Supervisors.

Yuba County adopted the PLSP with the Plumas Lake Financing Plan as a companion document on September 21, 1993. The NASA was established in 1993. Map 1 shows the boundaries of the PLSP and NASA. The Yuba County Board of Supervisors adopted an updated Financing Plan in June 2000. Construction of housing in the southern portion of the PLSP began in late 2003 and throughout 2004.

The updated 2000 Financing Plan describes the financing strategy for infrastructure in the Plumas Lake Specific Plan and North Arboga areas. While the cost estimates and land use plan have been updated for this Nexus Study, the financing strategy for transportation infrastructure has not changed from the updated Financing Plan. That strategy is to adopt a fee program for the PLSP and NASA to ensure the roadway system to serve the area is fully funded from a variety of available financing sources.

In September of 2003, EPS provided a Hearing Report for the Plumas Lake Specific Plan Road Fee Nexus Study. The 2003 study provided the basis to establish the PLSP Road Fee, which was adopted by Yuba County. This report serves as an update to the Hearing Report, and takes into account changes in land use, improvement costs, absorption, and assumptions for the PLSP/NASA Road Fee cash flow. The updates and changes are summarized in this report.

Purpose of the Study

The purpose of this study is to establish the nexus between new development that occurs in the PLSP/NASA and the need for additional roadway facilities, for which Yuba County is the service provider. After establishing the nexus, this study calculates the roadway development impact fees (the PLSP/NASA Road Fee) to be levied for each land use in the PLSP/NASA based upon the proportionate share of the total road facility use.

Authority

This Nexus Study has been prepared to establish a development impact fee program pursuant to the Yuba County police power in accordance with the procedural guidelines as codified in California Government Section 66000 et seq. This code section sets forth the procedural requirements for establishing and collecting development impact fees. These procedures require that "a reasonable relationship," or nexus, "must exist between a governmental exaction and the purpose of the condition." Specifically, each local agency imposing a fee must:

- Identify the purpose of the fee;
- Identify how the fee is to be used;
- Determine how a reasonable relationship exists between the fee's use and the type of development project on which the fee is imposed;
- Determine how a reasonable relationship exists between the need for the public facility and the type of development project on which the fee is imposed; and
- Demonstrate a reasonable relationship between the amount of the fee and the cost of public facility or portion of the public facility attributable to the development on which the fee is imposed.

The development impact fees to be collected for each land use are calculated based upon the proportionate share of the total facility use that each land use represents.

Summary of Updates and Updated Road Fee

A series of roadway infrastructure is needed which will benefit development in the PLSP, NASA, and surrounding area. The required roadway system is shown in Map 2. The total cost of the off-site and on-site roadway improvements in the area is estimated at $186.6 million (2005$) as outlined in Table 1.

Approximately $34.3 million or eighteen percent of the total roadway projects is anticipated to provide a benefit to both the PLSP/NASA development and the neighboring areas. The funding sources for the $34.3 million include the roadway portion of the Yuba County Capital Facilities Fee, Yuba County gas taxes and State Transportation Improvement Program (STIP) funds, the California Department of Transportation (Caltrans), and developers outside of the PLSP/NASA.

Nearly all of the $34.3 million is required for the construction of the interchange at State Route 70 (Highway 70) and Plumas Lake Parkway/Arboga Road. Approximately $1.9 million will construct portions of Feather River Boulevard and portions of McGowan Parkway.

The remaining $152.3 million or eighty-two percent of the total roadway projects are anticipated to directly benefit the PLSP/NASA. Approximately $71.1 million will be funded by PLSP and NASA developers, and the remaining $81.2 million is proposed to be funded through the new PLSP/NASA Road Fee. Nearly one-third of the roadway system costs included in the PLSP/NASA Road Fee is for construction of the interchange at Highway 70 and Feather River Boulevard.

Under the 2003 Nexus Study, the PLSP Road Fee was established to fund road improvements for the PLSP. The purpose of this study is to update the Road Fee to include the NASA, and establish an updated PLSP/NASA Road Fee to fund improvements in both the PLSP and the NASA. This report incorporates the following changes:

Addition of the NASA to the Road Fee Program: The North Arboga Study Area is adjacent to the northeast boundary of the Plumas Lake Specific Plan, and includes approximately 426 acres. At projected buildout, NASA will include approximately 2,060 Single-family units. NASA has been included in the Road Fee Program because it receives benefit from the PLSP roadway infrastructure identified in the roadway capital improvement program (CIP) included in the report. In March of 2004, a Combined Traffic Study Update was conducted by K.D. Anderson Transportation Engineers.

Update to the land uses included in the PLSP/NASA Road Fee: Several land use adjustment factors have been revised as projections for future development in the PLSP have changed since the 2003 Road Fee was established. Land uses in the PLSP and NASA are updated, as approximately 1,400 units will pay their share of the PLSP/NASA Road Fee before the implementation of this Road Fee Update. Chapter II summarizes changes made to the PLSP/NASA land uses.

Update the Capital Improvement Program (CIP): Improvements to the Highway 70 Interchanges have increased by approximately forty-three percent since the 2003 Road Fee Nexus Study. Several cost estimates for improvements to roads, bridges, streetlights, and other road-related improvements have been added or changed.

To reflect changes in construction costs, the December Engineering News and Report 2005 Cost Index has been applied to previous current construction cost estimates. Appendix B shows the updated Roadway CIP.

For 2005, updated improvement costs for the PLSP/NASA road infrastructure will require approximately $81.2 million in funding from the Road Fee program.

The 2005 update to the Road Fee Cash Flow and Fee Calculation: To accurately calculate the 2005 Road Fee, adjustments for improvements constructed and Road Fee collections must be taken into account. Approximately $1.7 million of improvements have been made to River Oaks Boulevard in the PLSP, leaving approximately $79.5 million of roadway improvements to be constructed.

As of March of 2005, approximately 1,400 units will have contributed approximately $7.0 million in base Road Fees. The 2005 Road Fee Update accounts for the constructed improvements and collected road fees, leaving approximately $74.4 in improvements to be allocated to the remaining 14,620 dwelling unit equivalents (DUEs). Updated costs and changes to the improvement schedule are outlined in Chapter IV.

The PLSP/NASA Road Fee will comprise a Base Road Fee and an Advance Funding Charge (AFC): As documented in the 2003 Road Fee Nexus Study, the Base Road Fee, which will be applicable to all developing PLSP/NASA land uses, will be based on the cost allocations contained in this Nexus Study. Because approximately sixty-five percent of the PLSP/NASA Road Fee-funded facilities (approximately $53.1 million) have to be completed in the first six years of the PLSP/NASA Fee Program, an Advance Funding Charge (AFC) also is required.

The AFC, which is outlined in Chapter V, will only apply to residential development and will only be in effect for a specified period of time. The AFC is required to ensure adequate funding will be available primarily to construct initial PLSP/NASA roadways and to fund or construct both Highway 70 interchanges by 2009.

The necessary findings and calculations for the PLSP/NASA Road Fee are presented in the following chapters.

The proposed PLSP/NASA Road Fees are summarized in Table 2. The cost estimates presented in this report are in constant 2005 dollars. The proposed PLSP/NASA Road Fee Program presented in this Nexus Study is based on the best available cost estimates and land use information at this time. If costs change significantly in either direction, if assumptions significantly change, or if other funding to construct the facilities becomes available, the fees would be adjusted accordingly. The county periodically will conduct a review of road improvement costs and will make necessary adjustments to the fee program.

Applicability of PLSP/NASA Road Fee Program

Once the new fee program is in effect, the PLSP/NASA Road Fee will be collected from new development in the PLSP/NASA at the time of final building inspection. The fee is applied on a per unit basis for residential development, and on a per-building-square-foot basis for nonresidential development.

Public and recreational land uses that will be developed in the PLSP and NASA are incidental/supportive uses to the residential and nonresidential land uses and will not be subject to the PLSP/NASA Road Fee.

Existing development located in the PLSP or NASA will not be subject to the PLSP/NASA Road Fee. Existing development does not meet the procedural requirements for establishing and collecting development impact fees as codified in California Governmental Section 66000 et seq.

Expansions, modifications of, or change of use at existing facilities may be subject to the new PLSP/NASA Road Fee as determined by the Yuba County Public Works Director. With written approval from the Yuba County Public Works Director, or his/her designee, any or all of the PLSP/NASA Road Fee may be waived if the director determines that a proposed expansion, modification, or change in use will not impact the roadway facilities for which the fee is being collected.

Organization of Report

The report is divided into seven chapters including this Executive Summary. Chapter II describes land use in the PLSP/NASA Road Fee program. Chapter III discusses the updated Roadway CIP. Chapter IV provides the cost allocations and the PLSP/NASA Road Fee calculation. Chapter V outlines the Cash Flow Analysis and AFC. Chapter VI describes how the PLSP/NASA Road Fee will be implemented. Chapter VII provides the nexus findings for the PLSP/NASA Road Fee.

This report includes five appendices. Appendix A provides the detail on the land use projections. Appendix B shows the roadway CIP and Appendix C provides the construction cost allocations and fee calculations for the PLSP/NASA Road Fee. Appendix D contains the PLSP/NASA Road Fee Program cash flow and cash flow assumptions. Appendix E contains an example of PLSP/NASA Road Fee Program reimbursements and fee credits.

APPENDIX C

City of Davis Development Impact Fee Study

City of Davis
Development Impact Fee Study
Adopted in 1997
Fee Schedule updated February 24, 2008

Introduction/Overview

History of MPFP and Review Process

The Major Projects Financing Plan (MPFP) was first adopted by the Davis City Council in 1989. The plan, some two years in development, was devised as a tool for implementing the public facilities in eight functional categories called for in the 1987 general plan. At the time, the MPFP was arguably one of the most comprehensive and complex capital improvement plans in Northern California, if not the entire state. Whereas most capital facility plans aim for a five to ten year planning horizon, the MPFP attempts to identify all of the infrastructure projects necessary within the General Plan horizon of 2010. At the time, this represented a twenty-three-year planning horizon.

The MPFP attempts to catalog the physical infrastructure needs of the City in terms of facility descriptions, timing, and funding sources. The document provides detailed information relating to the expected cost of facilities and the allocation of such costs among various service populations, including new and existing development areas, and various land use classifications. It also provides projections of when revenues will be available for facility construction based on estimates of future development.

In addition to listing the description, timing, and funding of major capital projects, the MPFP serves as the legal documentation to support imposition of development impact fees. State law limits the extent to which local governments can place the burden for new facilities on new development (Cal. Gov. Code Sec. 66001 et seq., also known as AB 1600). While not precisely defined, the basic requirement is that such fees must demonstrate a "reasonable" relationship, or nexus, between the type of development on which the fee is imposed and the public facilities being financed by the fee revenue.

In the first few years following its adoption, the MPFP went through several major revisions in addition to annual updates. Subsequent implementation of the MPFP, however, has raised a number of difficult issues. The City Council directed formation of an ad hoc Committee charged to conduct a detailed analysis of the MPFP, including the theory of the plan, underlying assumptions, and legal constraints. Among several recommendations, the Committee suggested several modifications to the method by which the City calculates and imposes development impact fees.

Another recommendation of the MPFP Review Committee was the establishment of the City's Finance and Economics Commission (FEC), which was initially charged with overseeing the MPFP Review Committee's recommendations. Since February of 1997, the FEC has overseen the development of data and techniques to implement the recommended changes to the City's impact fee methodology. This report is the first product of these two important efforts.

Role of the Study

This study is intended to establish the legal and policy basis for the calculation and imposition of impact fees on new development activity in the City of Davis. Impact fees are imposed on new development activity as one means to mitigate the public facility demand created by such activity. Pursuant to State law as found in Government Code 66001 et seq., this study intends to:

- Identify the purpose of the fee.
- Identify the use to which the fee is to be put.
- Determine how there is a reasonable relationship between the fee's use and the type of development project on which the fee is imposed.
- Determine how there is a reasonable relationship between the need for the public facility and the type of development project on which the fee is imposed.

Fee revenues thus attained will be combined with a variety of other revenue sources and used to fund capital facilities as articulated in the City's various capital planning documents. Examples include the General Plan, the Recreation and Parks Master Plan, the Public Facilities Master Plan, and other facility master plans.

This study, if adopted by the City Council, will supersede the existing Major Projects Financing Plan. It will establish new development impact fees, project descriptions and cost estimates, and project priorities for certain types of projects. The next step in this process will be development of a "Financial Master Plan," which will incorporate the information in this study, and attempt to reconcile the needs articulated in facility master plans with available resources.

Description and Organization of the Study

Section I of the plan is this brief introduction and overview.

Section II of the plan provides detailed estimates of current and future development within the City. Such estimates serve to establish existing standards and provide the basis for estimating future facility demand.

Section III explains the methodology by which the City calculates its development impact fees. Many of the recommendations of the MPFP Review Committee are incorporated here.

Sections IV–X provide the detailed impact fee calculations for seven functional categories of facilities. Each category includes a description of the City's performance standards and a description of development impact fee calculations. In some categories, a preliminary listing of prioritized projects is included.

Section XI provides a summary of impact fee calculations and estimated fee revenue cashflow for next five years.

Sections XII–XIV are technical appendices which contain detailed descriptions and cost estimates for roadways, water, and drainage projects.

Existing and Potential Development

This section presents information relating to the amount of existing and anticipated development which forms the basis for both determining the need for capital facilities and the basis for spreading costs via development impact fees. These data are also integral to establishing the legal basis—the so-called "rational nexus"—which links the need for various capital facilities to the development responsible for creating such needs.

Residential Development and Population

The California Department of Finance (DOF) estimates that there were 53,423 residents in the City as of January 1, 1997. Of that total, 2,009 resided in so-called "group quarters," or housing designed to accommodate groups typically larger than families such as college sororities and fraternities. The remaining 51,414 residents reside in 20,762 housing units which, after accounting for an assumed vacancy rate of about 1.95 percent, suggests an average of 2.476 persons per household. This number is essentially the same as the 1990 census average of 2.46. This information is summarized in Table 1.

Table 1. Residential Unit and Population Summary

Type of Unit	No. of Units	Type of Population	No. of Persons
SF Detached	9,268	Household	51,414
SF Attached	2,224	Group Quarter	2,009
Multi Family	9,281	Household Population per Occupied Unit	2.476
Mobile Homes	402		
Total Res'l Units	21,175	Total Population	53,423
Occupied Units	20,762		
Vacant	413		
Vacancy Rate	1.95%		

Source: California Department of Finance, Report E-5. May 1997

Non-Residential Development and Employment

The City Finance Division maintains building square footage data for non-industrial employers for use in levying its municipal services and public safety taxes. As of January 1997, total commercial development was estimated to be about 2.8 million square feet (not including educational or industrial uses).

The Sacramento Area Council of Governments (SACOG) maintains land use data for regional transportation modeling purposes. SACOG aggregates such data by "minor analysis zones." By extracting data for the minor analysis zones which closely correspond to the City limits, one derives an employment estimate for the City. Table 2 summarizes this information.

Subtracting education and industrial employment from the total shown above five leaves about 8,640 employees occupying the estimated 2.8 million square feet of commercial development. This suggests an average employment density of about 325 square feet of building per employee.

Table 3 summarizes the current development within Davis which is categorized as industrial.

Note that the total industrial employment estimate of about 807 is less than the SACOG estimate shown above. This appears to be the result of SACOG's use of peak employment, which in the case of Hunt-Wesson is substantially different from their average employment. The average employment density is 1,250 square feet per employee.

Table 2. City of Davis Employment Estimate

Plan Area (1)	Retail	Office	Medical	Education	Industrial	Other	Total
West Davis	160	32	230	80	0	67	569
Central Davis	665	401	362	280	0	338	2,046
Core Area	1,103	687	27	18	26	721	2,582
East Davis	450	517	70	128	2	535	1,702
North Central	0	83	0	0	1,000	59	1,142
South Davis	567	901	200	44	13	460	2,185
Mace Ranch	0	2	0	0	0	2	4
Totals/Average	2,945	2,623	889	550	1,041	2,182	10,230

NOTES

(1) Based on aggregations of SACOG Minor Analysis Zones (MAZs) which correspond closely to City boundaries.

Source: SACOG 1996 estimate

Table 3. Industrial Employment

Use	Parcel SF	Building SF	Employees	FAR (1)	Employees/SF
Hunt-Wesson	2,178,000	550,000	390	25.3%	1,410
PGE	1,197,465	156,000	131	13.0%	1,191
TCI	44,867	6,250	16	13.9%	391
Calgene	91,090	86,430	118	94.9%	732
Post Office	103,673	19,481	59	18.8%	330
Cort Galvanizing	81,196	62,740	16	77.3%	3,921
DWR	304,920	50,037	45	16.4%	1,112
Moller	189,922	27,316	9	14.4%	3,035
South Davis Storage	128,225	48,430	1	37.8%	48,430 (2)
Misc. Other	NA	48,348	22	NA	2,198
Totals/Average	4,319,358	1,055,032	807	24.4%	1,250

NOTES

(1) FAR is floor area ratio, which is the ratio of building area to lot area.

(2) This number skews the average significantly; thus, it is not included in the derivation of the overall average.

Source: City of Davis Building and Finance Divisions

Existing Development Summary

Table 4 summarizes existing development estimates.

Future Development—General Plan Buildout Estimates

The current City of Davis General Plan was adopted in 1987, and had been subsequently amended several times. Not long after its adoption, questions arose about the capacity of the General Plan to accommodate new development, particularly in light of the traffic analysis and resulting recommendations relating to roadway improvements. This led to a detailed review and reassessment of the General Plan's buildout capacity. The revised development estimates became the basis for the MPFP.

The City has been in the process of updating its General Plan since 1993. Information developed for that effort revealed that in many cases, residential development has been occurring at densities less than anticipated. In addition, because of the time lag between adoption of the General Plan in late 1987 and the MPFP in mid-1989, some development had occurred which was exempt from paying impact fees.

Non-residential development potential has changed as well. In some cases, the estimates shown in the traffic analysis database assumed denser development than now seems likely. In addition, there have been several General Plan amendments, including the proposed annexation of the Nishi property, which have change the potential for future non-residential development. Table 5 shows the original MPFP development assumptions and Table 6 shows the latest estimate of buildout development potential. Finally, Table 7 shows the estimated remaining unbuilt development potential as of June 30, 1997.

Pending Land Use Changes

It is important to note that several pending Council decisions may substantially affect the development estimates shown above. The so-called Covell Center development proposes a substantially different mix of land uses than that assumed above, as shown in Table 8.

In addition, the City is in the process of updating its General Plan. Once the land use map has been updated and adopted, the development potential described above will be amended to be consistent.

DUE Conversion Factors

The City uses the concept of "dwelling unit equivalents" (DUEs) as a measure of public service demand. A DUE is the amount of a particular land use which, on average, is occupied by the average number of persons residing in a single family residential unit. In this regard, a DUE creates a base measurement by which quantities of various land uses can be readily compared. For example, assume the average household contains 2.5 persons and the average commercial development has 500 square feet of building for each employee. If we set a DUE equal the average household size, 2.5 persons, we can therefore say:

1 DUE = 2.5 persons/unit = (500 square feet/person *
2.5 persons per DUE) = 1,250 sq.ft. per DUE).

Residential Development

During review of the plan, it was suggested that the City reevaluate the DUE conversion factors. Among other reasons, anecdotal evidence suggested that household sizes in new development areas may on average be larger than DOF estimates. In addition, it was felt that larger physical units such as single family units generally have larger average household sizes than smaller units such as apartments.

Review of the 1990 census data revealed different average household sizes by type of units, as summarized in Table 9.

It is recommended that for purposes of deriving development impact fees the DUE be set equal to the persons per household in a single family detached unit, namely 2.83.

Table 4. Existing Development Summary

Type of Development	Units	Amount
Single Family Detached	dwellings	9,268
Single Family Attached	dwellings	2,224
Multi-Family	dwellings	9,281
Mobile Homes	dwellings	402
Total Residential	dwellings	21,175
Commercial	square feet	2,800,000
	employees	8,640
Industrial	square feet	1,050,000
	employees	807
Total Non-residential	square feet	3,850,000
Total Non-residential	employees	9,447

Non-Residential Development

The information presented in the preceding section relating to non-residential development and employment is summarized in Table 10.

DUE Conversion Factors Summary

Based on the data presented above, the DUE conversion factors to be used in calculating capital facility demand and corresponding development impact fees are shown in Table 11.

Development Impact Fee Calculation Methodology

Legal Requirements

California law provides the statutory authority for the imposition of fees on new development activity. Government Code section 66001 requires local agencies to satisfy four general requirements to impose such fees:

- Identify the purpose of the fee.
- Identify the use to which the fee is to be put.
- Determine how there is a reasonable relationship between the fee's use and the type of development project on which the fee is imposed.
- Determine how there is a reasonable relationship between the need for the public facility and the type of development project on which the fee is imposed.

This section of the plan describes the methodology by which the City calculates its impact fees, and how this technique not only satisfies state law, but also addresses a variety of policy concerns.

Table 5. Original MPFP Units Forecast at General Plan Buildout

Land Use	North Central	West	Central	Planning Area East	Mace	Core	South	Total
Residential Units								
Single Family	2,112	894	104	165	1,332	0	1,375	5,982
Multi-family	407	901	318	382	477	226	1,063	3,774
Total Residential	2,519	1,795	422	547	1,809	226	2,438	9,756
Non-Residential square footage (x 1,000)								
Retail	0	55	127	72	66	385	101	806
Office	18	123	55	13	210	156	57	632
Industrial	409	0	0	9	129	0	8	555
Business Park	0	22	0	294	1,406	0	947	2,669
Service Commercial	196	0	0	16	120	0	353	685
Total Nonresidential	623	200	182	404	1,931	541	1,466	5,347

Table 6. Revised (April 1997) Units Forecast at General Plan Buildout

Land Use	North Central (1)	West	Central	Planning Area East	Mace	Core	South	Total
Residential Units								
Single Family	2,058	595	39	62	1,271	16	1,323	5,364
Multi-family	499	669	30	226	424	70	865	2,783
Total Residential	2,557	1,264	69	288	1,695	86	2,188	8,147
Non-Residential square footage (x 1,000)								
Retail	0	55	127	72	106	162	101	623
Office	18	123	55	13	292	426	57	984
Industrial	410	0	0	9	129	0	8	556
Business Park	0	117	0	257	1,198	0	947	2,519
Service Commercial	196	0	0	53	108	129	353	839
Total Nonresidential	624	295	182	404	1,833	717	1,466	5,521

NOTE

(1) Assumes current TCE numbers, NOT the proposed Covell Center project. *See* discussion on page 8 [of original document] for more detail.

MPFP Review Committee/Finance and Economics Commission Recommendations

The MPFP Review Committee and FEC recommend two general approaches to deriving development impact fees. First, for the project categories of parks/open space, general government facilities, and public safety, existing facility standards should form the basis for deriving fees. The derivation of such fees include the following general steps:

- Inventory existing facilities in each project category.
- Estimate the current replacement value of the existing facility inventory.
- Determine the appropriate service population for each project category; i.e., residents and/or employees.
- Calculate the dollar value of existing facilities per service population.
- Apply the resulting factor to new increments of service population.

This approach to deriving impact fees satisfies the requirements of state law in the following ways:

- Because fees are based upon existing standards, the purpose of the fee is to maintain existing facility standards as the City grows into the future.

Table 7. Remaining Unbuilt Balance as of June 30, 1997

				Planning Area				
Land Use	North Central (1)	West	Central	East	Mace	Core	South	Total
Residential Units								
Single Family	1,644	198	7	43	648	0	625	3,165
Multi-family	499	519	30	20	337	70	279	1,754
Total Residential	2,143	717	37	63	985	70	904	4,919
Non-Residential square footage (x 1,000)								
Retail	0	32	0	72	106	82	101	393
Office	0	63	37	0	292	421	0	813
Industrial	396	0	0	0	56	0	0	452
Business Park	0	22	0	238	1,198	0	771	2,229
Service Commercial	193	0	0	44	108	129	319	793
Total Nonresidential	589	117	37	354	1,760	632	1,191	4,680

NOTE

(1) Assumes current TCE numbers, NOT the proposed Covell Center project. *See* discussion below for more detail.

- Various facility master planning efforts provide an initial glimpse of the facilities anticipated to be funded in part with the revenue generated by impact fees.
- This study provides the analysis which links the need for facilities to various types of development. By assessing the differential demand created by various types of development, and calculating impact fees accordingly, a reasonable relationship between new facilities funded with impact fee revenue and particular developments is established.
- By showing the facilities intended to be financed with fee revenues, a reasonable relationship between the need for the public facility and the type of development project on which the fee is imposed is established.

Beyond satisfying state legal requirements, basing fees on existing facility standards addresses the following policy issues:

- Reduce divisive arguments about whether new development is providing higher levels of amenities in comparison to those enjoyed by existing development.
- Limit the tendency to add projects or expand existing project scopes unless and until equal-sized cost reductions or project deferrals are identified, or alternative funding sources are found.
- Minimize fluctuations in fee levels over time.

The project categories for which fees are proposed to be calculated using existing standards are those which tend to be incrementally related to population and employment growth. For example, relatively small additions of parks and general government facilities can be constructed to match correspondingly small increases in service population. The use of existing facility standards as the basis for fee calculation does not limit the ability of the City to establish higher standards. It simply limits the extent to which new development is asked to contribute to that increase.

Conversely, roadways, water, sewer, and drainage projects often have "capacity thresholds" at which major improvements may be required as a result of small increases in service demand. Thus, the need for major expansions in these latter categories can be more easily attributed to new developments. For this reason, development impact fees are derived by estimating the cost of projects necessary to adequately serve the general plan and allocating those costs among the service population projected in the General Plan. However, in the event that projects are added to the MPFP over time, or existing project costs increase, only the proportional share of such cost increases should be allocated to remaining new development.

Table 12 illustrates this recommendation relating to project cost increases in the roadways, water, sewer, and drainage categories. Cost increases are broken into two components based on the amount of development elapsed at the time of a cost increase. For example, a hypothetical project in 1998 experiences a cost increase from $2 million to $2.3 million, during which time 2,000 units of development (DUEs) have already been developed. Of that $300,000 increase, only 85.7 percent (12,000 , 14,000) is attributed to the remaining 12,000 DUEs. This amount is shown in the fourth column.

The difference, shown in the far right column, represents the remaining portion (2,000 , 14,000) of the increase that

Table 8. Comparison of Current General Plan and Covell Center Proposal

Land Use	Units	Current General Plan	Covell Ctr Proposal	Difference
Single Family	DU	993	583	(410)
Multi-family	DU	254	105	(149)
Serv. Comm.	sq. ft.	196,000	0	(196,000)
Business Park	acres	0.0	22.0	22.0
Off., LI & SC	acres	0.0	12.0	12.0

Table 9. Average Household Size by Unit Type

Type of Unit	Average persons per unit
Single Family Detached	2.83
Single Family Attached	2.34
Multi-family	2.16
All units	2.46

Source: Sacramento Area Council of Governments Regional Data Center and 1990 Census Summary Tape File 1A.

Table 10 Employment Density

Land Use	Bldg. SF	Employees	Empl. SF
Commercial (non-industrial)	2,800,000	8,640	325
Industrial	1,000,000	800	1,250

should have been paid by development which has already occurred. This amount should not be passed on to future new development in the DUE fee calculation, and would thus have to be funded from some other source. The remaining shaded rows show additional hypothetical cost increases and the resulting proportion of such costs allocated to new development. Based on the remaining development potential (*See* Table 7, in Section II), it is estimated that 70.8 percent of the General Plan DUE capacity remains to be built. Thus, for project categories which have experienced cost increases in excess of inflation, only 70.8 percent of such increases will be included in the impact fee calculation.

This policy may create unfunded liabilities in these four project categories. However, three of the categories (water, sewer and drainage) are operated as enterprise funds and thus have alternative revenue sources potentially available to augment funding needs. For such liabilities in the roadways category, options may include alternative funding sources or reducing project scopes (although projects required as environmental mitigation may not be able to be scaled down without additional analysis). While potentially difficult choices may result, it is fundamentally unfair to place the burden of increasing project costs on ever-decreasing amounts of remaining development.

This approach to deriving impact fees satisfies the requirements of state law in the following ways:

- Because fees are based upon specific analysis of the demand created by the expected development of the adopted General Plan, the purpose of the fee is to provide the means of mitigating public facility demand created by new development.
- The projects listed in Appendices A, B, and C show the facilities anticipated to be funded with the revenue generated by impact fees.
- This study provides the analysis which links the need for facilities to various types of development. By assessing the differential demand created by various types of development, and calculating impact fees accordingly, a reasonable

Table 11. Recommended DUE Conversion Factors

Use Category	Units	Persons per unit	Square Feet per DUE (1)	DUEs per Unit	Service Pop. Land per unit
Single Family Detached	dwelling unit	2.83	NA	1.00	2.83
Single Family Attached	dwelling unit	2.34	NA	0.82	2.34
Multi-family	dwelling unit	2.16	NA	0.76	2.16
Commercial (Non-Industrial)	1,000	325	919.8	1.08	3.08
Industrial	1,000	1,250	3,537.5	0.28	0.80

NOTE
(1) DUE = 2.83 persons

Table 12. Demonstration of Effect of Passing Only Proportional Amount of Project Cost Increases to New Development

Year	Project Cost Estimate	Remaining DUEs	Cost Increase Attributable to Remaining Development	Cost per New DUE	Actual Development (DUEs)	Impact Fee Revenue	Amount to Be Funded from Non-Impact Fee Source
1996	$2,000,000	14,000	$0.00	$142.86	1,000	$142,857	$0
1997	$2,000,000	13,000	$0.00	$142.86	1,000	$142,857	$0
1998	$2,300,000	12,000	$257,142.86	$164.29	1,000	$164,286	$42,857
1999	$2,300,000	11,000	$0.00	$164.29	1,000	$164,286	$0
2000	$2,500,000	10,000	$142,857.14	$178.57	1,000	$178,571	$57,143
2001	$2,500,000	9,000	$0.00	$178.57	1,000	$178,571	$0
2002	$2,700,000	8,000	$114,285.71	$192.86	1,000	$192,857	$85,714
2003	$2,700,000	7,000	$0.00	$192.86	1,000	$192,857	$0
2004	$2,700,000	6,000	$0.00	$192.86	1,000	$192,857	$0
2005	$2,900,000	5,000	$71,428.57	$207.14	1,000	$207,143	$128,571
2006	$2,900,000	4,000	$0.00	$207.14	1,000	$207,143	$0
2007	$2,900,000	3,000	$0.00	$207.14	1,000	$207,143	$0
2008	$3,300,000	2,000	$57,142.86	$235.71	1,000	$235,714	$342,857
2009	$3,300,000	1,000	$0.00	$235.71	1,000	$235,714	$0
2010	$3,300,000	0					
Totals						$2,642,857	$657,143

relationship between new facilities funded with impact fee revenue and particular types of developments is established.

- By analyzing the facility demand created by different types of development and calculating impact fees accordingly, a reasonable relationship between the need for public facilities and the type of development project on which the fee is imposed is established.

Beyond satisfying state legal requirements, limiting fee increases is intended to address the following policy issues:

- Limit the tendency to add projects or expand existing project scopes unless and until equal-sized cost reductions or project deferrals are identified, or alternative funding sources are found.
- Minimize fluctuations in fee levels over time.

The actual fee calculations are shown in the following sections of this study.

Roadways

Roadway Standards

The Transportation and Circulation Element (TCE) of the City's General Plan sets forth policies related to roadways, bicycle, and pedestrian facilities. Guiding policy 4.1A states that the City will provide roadway capacity to maintain peak-hour traffic levels of service (LOS) "D" or better on existing arterial streets and interchanges, and LOS "C" on new streets.[1] Subsequent implementing policies speak to right-of-way reservation, design considerations, and transportation system management techniques. TCE policies also address bicycle and pedestrian transportation facilities including overcrossings of highways, provision of bicycle lanes and/or paths along collector and arterial streets, and adequate bicycle access opportunities. Additional detail about standards for bike paths and lanes can be found in General Plan policy 4.4A.

Roadway Project Summary

Table 13 provides a summary of the transportation and circulation facilities anticipated to be constructed in order to maintain General Plan standards as the City develops. Detailed descriptions of individual projects, including cost estimates and anticipated funding sources can be found in Appendix A of this report [*see* original document].

Table 13 also summarizes the allocation of burden for each project; that is, the share of each project that has been attributed to new development (defined as expansion of facilities) versus that attributed to existing development (defined as enhancement of existing facilities). This summary shows the maximum project burden which could be allocated to new development via impact fees.

However, the policy of the City is that certain types of funding for projects be "taken off the top." Examples of such funding including state and federal contributions, and redevelopment. For projects anticipated to be funded with one of these sources, the amount of such funding is subtracted from the total project cost. The remaining amount is divided according to the burden allocation percentages shown in Table 13, with the proportion allocated to new development included in the impact fee calculation.

Table 14 summarizes these various other funding sources, and shows the amount of remaining costs that have been allocated to new development via the impact fee mechanism. Detailed breakdowns of anticipated funding sources for each project are included in Appendix A [*see* original document].

Roadways Cost Allocation

As shown above, the need for more than $82 million worth of roadways projects have been attributed to new development enabled by the 1987 General Plan. When the MPFP was developed, it was acknowledged that certain projects in the plan would be required early in the General Plan time horizon. Because impact fees are collected over time as development occurs, a mechanism was needed to provide up-front financing for required facilities. In the 1990, the City established a number of Mello-Roos Community Facilities Districts (CFD) to provide this mechanism. In this regard, the Mello-Roos mechanism is simply a way to pay impact fees over time rather than at once.

Therefore, the initial calculation of impact fees includes the value of projects to be funded via Mello-Roos special taxes. Then, a "credit" is calculated for each CFD based upon its share of project costs.

Roadway Costs Not Included in Impact Fee Calculation

As discussed above, the MPFP Review Committee recommended that only a proportionate share of cost increases over time be included in subsequent fee calculations (*see* discussion on page 11). Cost increases, whether from adding new projects or escalation of existing project costs, which exceed the Engineering News

Table 13. Roadway Project Summary

Project Number	Project Description	1996/97 Capital Cost	Burden Distribution New	Existing	Potential Amount of Impact Fee Funding
A01	2nd St Recon. L-Pole Line	$636,835	30%	70%	$191,051
A09	Putah Creek Bike X-ing @ I-80	$3,968,885	33%	67%	$1,309,732
A11	Bicycle Undercrossings	$2,255,848	100%	0%	$2,255,848
A12	Russell Blvd Widening, A to C	$138,530	100%	0%	$138,530
A14	Bike/Ped X-ing East of Monarch	$513,754	100%	0%	$513,754
A16	Pole Line I-80 Overcrossing	$11,783,841	100%	0%	$11,783,841
A17	1st St Widening, B to E Streets	$0	0%	0%	$0
A18	F Street Improvements, 3rd to 7th	$57,600	100%	0%	$57,600
A19	I-80 Bike/Ped Overcrossing	$3,775,680	100%	0%	$3,775,680
A20	Mace Blvd. Interchange Imprvmts	$16,064,205	100%	0%	$16,064,205
A21	Richards Blvd. Corridor Alternatives	$7,503,857	100%	0%	$7,503,857
A22	Richards Blvd. I-80 Overcrossing	$6,578,086	100%	0%	$6,578,086
A23	5th St. Widening, C to L	$696,972	100%	0%	$696,972
A24	Covell Widening, Anderson to F	$1,133,658	33%	67%	$374,107
A25	Covell Widening, Birch to Baywood	$178,048	100%	0%	$178,048
A26	Covell Widening, Baywd to Monarch	$1,407,000	100%	0%	$1,407,000
A27	Covell Widening, Monarch to 32A	$2,200,000	100%	0%	$2,200,000
A29	32A Reconst., Pole Line to Mace	$2,240,518	100%	0%	$2,240,518
A31	Covell Reconst., Lake to Hwy 113	$972,173	100%	0%	$972,173
A32	Pole Line, Covell to C. Limit	$624,720	100%	0%	$624,720
A33	F St., Grande to New Anderson	$115,542	100%	0%	$115,542

Table 13. Roadway Project Summary (continued)

Project Number	Project Description	1996/97 Capital Cost	Burden Distribution New	Existing	Potential Amount of Impact Fee Funding
A34	Drummond Recon, Albany-Montgomery	$234,623	100%	0%	$234,623
A35	Chiles, Resrch Pk to El Cemonte	$1,268,068	100%	0%	$1,268,068
A37	B St. Improvement, 1st to 5th	$103,157	100%	0%	$103,157
A38	F St. Improvement, 7th to Covell	$103,350	100%	0%	$103,350
A40	New Signal, 4th and F	$150,758	100%	0%	$150,758
A41	New Signal, Covell and Birch	$71,808	100%	0%	$71,808
A43	New Signal, Drummond/Chiles/Cowell	$143,295	100%	0%	$143,295
A44	New Signal, Covell and J	$87,117	100%	0%	$87,117
A46	New Signals, South Davis	$596,858	100%	0%	$596,858
A47	New Signal, 1st and B	$158,603	100%	0%	$158,603
A48	New Signal, 5th and D	$144,460	100%	0%	$144,460
A49	New Signal, 2nd and F	$126,480	100%	0%	$126,480
A50	New Signal, 1st and F	$122,884	100%	0%	$122,884
A51	New Signal, 1st and C	$132,398	100%	0%	$132,398
A52	New Signal, 2nd and B	$144,768	100%	0%	$144,768
A53	Transport. System Management Plan	$79,447	100%	0%	$79,447
A54	So. Davis Arterial Extra Features	$635,375	100%	0%	$635,375
A55	New Signal, 8th & Pole Line	$182,088	100%	0%	$182,088
A56	New Signal, Arlington & Shasta	$91,813	100%	0%	$91,813
A57	New Signal, Covell & Denali	$156,544	100%	0%	$156,544
A58	New Signal, Covell & Evergreen	$143,955	100%	0%	$143,955
A59	Bicycle Overcross—Hwy 113/Periph	$1,211,284	100%	0%	$1,211,284
A60	Bicycle Overcross—Covell/L	$1,133,946	100%	0%	$1,133,946
A61	Bicycle Crossing—Pole Line/Donner	$545,671	100%	0%	$545,671
A62	Chiles (Cowell)/Drummond Realign	$245,600	100%	0%	$245,600
A63	Transit Center (SP Depot) Expans	$2,296,550	33%	67%	$757,862
A64	New Signal, SR113 Ramps/Covell Blvd	$212,149	100%	0%	$212,149
A65	New Signal, Covell & Lake	$161,994	100%	0%	$161,994
A66	New Signal, Russell & Arlington	$220,780	100%	0%	$220,780
A67	New Signal, Russell & Lake	$141,056	100%	0%	$141,056
A68	New Signal, 8th & J	$148,480	100%	0%	$148,480
A69	Rd 32A E of Mace—Roadway Reloc	$448,074	100%	0%	$448,074
A70	Drexel/Loyola Connection	$269,694	100%	0%	$269,694
A71	Pole Line Road Corridor Plan	$2,423,202	100%	0%	$2,423,202
AA97	Median Opening on Covell into Marketplace	$78,530	100%	0%	$78,530
AB97	Covell Blvd./SR 113 Interchange Improvements	$4,639,440	100%	0%	$4,639,440
AD95	H Street Bike Lane & Landscaping	$106,646	33%	67%	$35,193
AE01	Additional Core Area Parking Lots	$4,187,610	100%	0%	$4,187,610
AE07	5th & G Streets Parking Structure	$1,750,000	100%	0%	$1,750,000
AE97	Pole Line Road Bus Turnaround	$87,089	100%	0%	$87,089
AG97	Intersection Improvements, Covell/Shasta	$159,300	100%	0%	$159,300
	Roadways Total	$88,190,692			$82,716,062

Record construction cost index are only included within the impact fee calculation in proportion to the amount of remaining development within the General Plan.

Table 15 shows the steps in this calculation.

The City's Transportation and Circulation (TCE) is based upon several levels of analyses. One piece of that analysis is the City's traffic model, which simulates the effect of development as shown in the General Plan on roadway infrastructure. One aspect of that model is the establishment of "trip generation factors," which estimate the amount of traffic that different types of development will impose on the roadway system. Such factors are based on a combination of national and statewide averages, which have been adjusted to account for traffic patterns in Davis. Each trip has two components: its origin and destination. The City's policy is that for purposes of calculating impact fees, the land use responsible for producing the trip—i.e., the trip origin—is charged for the trip. Table 16 shows this set of calculations.

During review of the roadways cost allocation factors, it was noted that certain categories of land use had be aggregated into the originally used categories. It was noted that four categories of residential uses had been aggregated into two. In addition, four categories of retail uses had been combined into a single category. The issue of the appropriate number of residential categories has been addressed by creating an additional type for purposes of DUE conversion factors. After detailed review of assumptions and traffic characteristics, the Finance and Economics Commission (FEC) recommends for the purpose of roadway impact fee calculations that the retail categories be aggregated into two—Core Area retail and auto-related retail in one category, and all other retail in the other. The FEC recommendation is based largely upon the similarity in traffic cost allocation factors (*see* near the bottom of Table 16) between these types of retail uses.

The following table converts the remaining unbuilt General Plan capacity (*see* Table 7 on page 4 [of the original document]) into the land use categories recommended by the FEC, and then converts the resulting land use units into dwelling unit equivalents (DUEs) based on the conversion factors outlined in the discussion on page 8 [of the original document].

Roadway Impact Fee Calculations

Table 18 shows the calculation of roadway impact fees based on the discussion above.

Mello-Roos Credits

When the MPFP was first developed in 1989, certain projects in the roadways categories were anticipated to be needed prior to when money would be available from a pay-as-you-go financing source such as development impact fees. To provide such up-front financing, the City established five Mello-Roos Community Facilities Districts (CFDs), which provide the ability to incur debt secured by special taxes levied on property within the districts. In this regard, Mello-Roos special taxes are simply an alternative method of paying impacts fees over time rather than in a single lump sum. Therefore, development which occurs within one of the City-wide Mello-Roos CFDs should receive a "credit" for that participation in the form of a reduced impact fee.

Costs were allocated among the various CFDs based upon the share of project costs anticipated to be funded via the Mello Roos mechanism. At that time, the City's policy was to allocate costs among various planning areas based on a variety of techni-

Table 14. Anticipated Roadway Funding Sources

Source	Amount	% of Total
State Funds	$15,655,837	17.6%
UC Davis	$2,620,019	2.9%
Redevelopment	$25,685,571	28.8%
Construction Tax	$2,952,273	3.3%
Mello-Roos	$8,489,928	9.5%
Development Impact Fees	$22,716,392	26.5%
Other Revenues	$10,070,673	11.3%
Total	$88,190,692	100.0%

Table 15. Roadway Costs to Be Included in Impact Fee Calculation

1997 Impact Fee Funded Share (including Mello-Roos funding)	$31,206,320
1995 Impact Fee Funded Share (including Mello-Roos funding)	$27,589,685
Increase (Decrease) From Prior Year	$3,616,635
Increase Attributable to Inflation @ 6.85%:	$1,891,080
Increase Above Inflation:	$1,725,555
Share of Increase to Include in Fee (based on proportion of remaining General Plan buildout)	70.8%
Amount of Increase to Include in Fee:	$3,113,442
1997 Adjusted Impact Fee Funded Share:	$30,703,127
(Less: Impact Fees Collected as of 6/97)	($5,665,998)
Roadways Cost to Spread	$25,037,129
Unfunded Roadway Costs	$503,192

Table 16. Traffic Service Standard Cost Allocation Factors

Land Use	Single Family	Duplex/ Condo	Multi-Family	Mobile Home	Light Indus'l	Heavy Indus'l	Bus. Park	Office	Park	Schools	Hospital	UCD Spec. Gen.	UCD Resid'l	Core Area Retail	Retail <100K SF	Retail >100K SF	Car Dealers	Totals
Units	DU	DU	DU	DU	Acres	Acres	Acres	1000 SF	Acres	Students	Each	Trips	Trips	1000 SF	1000 SF	1000 SF	1000 SF	
Quantity	14,195	1,861	11,052	542	105	223	196	1,456	318	11,464	1	56,652	8,193	805	1,377	428	83	
Rate	10.50	9.50	8.50	7.00	60.00	16.00	152.00	17.00	6.00	0.81	4438.00	1.00	1.00	40.00	105.00	70.00	45.00	
Trip Ends	149,048	17,680	93,942	3,794	6,300	3,568	29,792	24,752	1,908	10,428	4,438	50,987	8,193	32,200	144,585	29,960	3,735	615,309
PRODUCTIONS																		
Home based work*	12,162	1,443	7,666	310									669					22,249
Home based other*	82,411	9,775	51,942	2,098									4,530					150,757
Non home based*	9,912	1,176	6,247	252	1,855	1,051	8,774	7,289	91	1,387	1,307	7,750	545	3,977	17,856	3,700	461	73,630
ATTRACTIONS																		
Home based work					666	377	3,151	2,618	0	338	469	6,906		1,181	5,304	1,099	137	22,249
Home based other	11,214	1,330	7,068	285	702	397	3,318	2,757	1,275	5,033	494	13,128	616	15,779	70,850	14,681	1,830	150,757
Non home based	9,912	1,176	6,247	252	1,855	1,051	8,774	7,289	91	1,387	1,307	7,750	545	3,977	17,856	3,700	461	73,630
Internal-External*	13,411	1,591	8,453	341	98	55	462	384	10	73	69	408	737	209	940	195	24	27,459
External-Internal*	1,118	133	705	28	715	405	3,383	2,811	429	1,961	504	7,643	61	6,199	27,833	5,767	719	60,413
TOTAL TRIP ENDS (in Davis)	140,140	16,623	88,328	3,567	5,892	3,337	27,861	23,148	1,895	10,178	4,150	43,586	7,704	31,321	140,639	29,142	3,633	581,14
Peak Hour Percentage	11%	11%	11%	11%	12%	12%	12%	13%	8%	7%	11%	9%	11%	10%	10%	10%	10%	
Allocated Trips *	13,092	1,553	8,251	333	320	181	1,514	1,363	42	239	207	1,422	720	1,038	4,663	966	120	36,026
Adjustments	1,483	176	934	38					(42)	(239)	(207)	(1,422)	(720)					(0)
TOTAL	14,574	1,729	9,186	371	320	181	1,514	1,363	0	0	0	0	0	1,038	4,663	966	120	36,026
Floor Area Ratio					25%	20%	25%											
QTY in 1000 SF					1,143	1,943	2,134											
DUE	14,195	1,861	11,052	542	1,513	857	2,823	1,926						1,065	1,821	566	110	
Charged Trips/DUE	1.03	0.93	0.83	0.68	0.21	0.21	0.54	0.71						0.98	2.56	1.71	1.10	
Cost Allocation Factor	1.01	0.91	0.81	0.67	0.21	0.21	0.53	0.69	0.00	0.00	0.00	0.00	0.00	0.96	2.51	1.67	1.08	

Land Use	Charged Trips	DUE	Trips per DUE	Cost Allocation Factors
Single Family (Detached)	14,574	14,195	1.03	1.00
Duplex/Triplex/Condo (SF Attached)	1,729	1,861	0.93	0.90
Multi Family units (4+ & MH)	9,557	11,594	0.82	0.80
Core Area Retail and Car Dealers	1,159	1,175	0.99	0.96
Retail (all other)	5,629	2,388	2.36	2.30
Industrial	502	2,369	0.21	0.21
Office/Business Park	2,877	4,749	0.61	0.59

cal and policy assumptions. One of recommended changes to the fee methodology discussed in Section II of this study is allocate facility costs on a city-wide rather than area-specific basis. However, because the Mello-Roos special tax rates were predicated upon prior policy, the "credit" calculation must also account for this.

Table 19 shows the steps in deriving the Mello-Roos credit. The Mello-Roos tax rates were based upon escalated project costs in the future. The portion of roadways costs which have been allocated to each CFD are essentially spread across the anticipated amount of development, converted into equally weighted "units" based upon DUE and roadway service cost allocation factors, to derive a credit for each land use.

Table 17. Conversion of Remaining DUEs to Recommended Roadway Land Use Categories

Land Use	No. Central	West	Central	Planning Area East	Mace	Core	South	Total
Residential DUEs								
Single Family Detached (1)	1,480	178	6	39	583	0	563	2,849
Single Family Attached (1)	136	16	1	4	54	0	52	262
Multi-family	381	396	23	15	257	53	213	1,339
Total Residential	1,996	591	30	58	894	53	827	4,449
Non-Residential DUEs								
Core/AC Retail (2)	0	0	0	0	0	89	67	157
Other Retail	210	35	0	126	233	140	389	1,133
Office/Business Park	0	93	40	259	1,620	458	838	3,308
Industrial	112	0	0	0	16	0	0	128
Total Nonresidential	322	128	40	385	1,869	687	1,295	4,725

NOTE

(1) Assumes future detached single family = 90.0% of total single family development

(2) Core Area retail and South Davis Retail in TAZs 53 and 69.

Table 18. Roadway Impact Fee Calculation

Land Use	Remaining DUEs	Cost Allocation Factors	Weighted Units	% of Weighted Units	Share of Costs	Cost per DUE	DUE/ Unit	Cost per Unit or 1,000 SF
Single Family Detached	2,849	1.00	2,848	32.04%	8,022,741	2,816.48	1.00	$2,816
Single Family Attached	262	0.90	235	2.65%	663,364	2,534.83	0.83	$2,096
Multi-family	1,339	0.80	1,070	12.05%	3,016,431	2,253.18	0.76	$1,720
Core/AC Retail	157	0.96	150	1.69%	423,322	2,703.82	1.09	$2,940
Other Retail	1,133	2.30	2,605	29.31%	7,338,922	6,477.90	1.09	$7,043
Office/Business Park	3,308	0.59	1,951	21.95%	5,496,776	1,661.72	1.09	$1,807
Industrial	128	0.21	26	0.30%	75,573	591.46	0.28	$167
Totals	9,174		8,889	100.00%	25,037,129			

Roadway Priorities

The revenues generated by imposition of the above fees will be used, in conjunction with other financing sources, to construct roadway projects identified above. The Finance and Economics Commission worked with the Safety Advisory Commission to establish general priorities for each of the projects within this category.

Funding for the roadways category is the most complicated of any in the MPFP because of the number of different financing sources and the inter-relationship between various projects. For example, the Mace Boulevard interchange project could be funded by either redevelopment or the Citywide Mello-Roos (or some combination of the two). Depending on the extent and timing of projects related to the Richards Boulevard Corridor Alternatives, which are still being defined and scoped, the amount of redevelopment money available for Mace Boulevard is unclear. In turn, the more Mello-Roos funding that is directed toward the Mace Boulevard interchange, the less is available for, say, the I-80 bicycle overcrossing project or relocation of either the police or fire station. Staff is in the process of developing alternative scenarios to test fiscal implications and will be presenting options to the City Council.

Table 19. Mello-Roos Credit Calculation for Roadways Projects

Project	CFD 90-1 (East)	CFD 90-2 (Mace)	CFD 90-3 (N. Central)	CFD 90-4 (South)	CFD 90-5 (West)	Total
Pole Line Road	1,001,633	3,338,775	3,171,836	5,842,856	-	13,355,100
I-80 Overcrossing	-	3,549,673	-	2,789,028	-	6,338,701
Mace Blvd. Interchange	572,824	2,864,119	1,882,135	2,864,119		8,183,197
Covell Widening—Monarch	79,926	72,660	574,011	-	-	726,597
Roadways Totals	1,654,383	9,825,227	5,627,982	11,496,003	-	28,603,595
Percent of Total	5.78%	34.35%	19.68%	40.19%	0.00%	100.00%
Credit to Each CFD Based on 1997 Cost Estimates	491,043	2,916,258	1,670,460	3,412,167	-	8,489,928
Estimated DUEs at Buildout (*see* devel. estimates)						
Land Use						
Single Family Detached	56	1,144	1,852	1,191	536	4,778
Single Family Attached	5	105	170	109	49	439
Multi-family	172	324	381	660	511	2,048
Core/AC Retail	0	0	0	67	0	67
Other Retail	136	233	213	426	60	1,068
Office	294	1,620	20	1,092	261	3,286
Industrial	3	36	116	2	0	157
Totals	665	3,462	2,752	3,548	1,416	11,843
Weighted Units (DUEs X CAFs)						
Land Use						
Single Family Detached	56	1,144	1,852	1,191	536	4,778
Single Family Attached	5	95	153	98	44	395
Multi-family	138	259	305	528	408	1,638
Core/AC Retail	0	0	0	65	0	65
Other Retail	313	535	490	980	138	2,456
Office	173	956	12	644	154	1,939
Industrial	1	8	24	0	0	33
Totals	685	2,996	2,836	3,507	1,280	11,303
Credit per Weighted Unit	717	973	589	973	-	
Credit per DUE (Credit per Weighted Unit X CAFs)						
Single Family Detached	717	973	589	973	0	
Single Family Attached	645	876	530	876	0	
Multi-family	574	779	471	778	0	
Core/AC Retail	688	934	565	934	0	
Other Retail	1,649	2,239	1,355	2,238	0	
Office	423	574	348	574	0	
Industrial	151	204	124	204	0	
Credit per Unit (Credit per DUE X DUE per unit)						
Single Family Detached	717	973	589	973	0	
Single Family Attached	534	724	438	724	0	
Multi-family	438	594	360	594	0	
Core/AC Retail	749	1,016	615	1,016	0	
Other Retail	1,793	2,434	1,473	2,433	0	
Office	460	624	378	624	0	
Industrial	43	58	35	58	0	
Roadways Fees with Mello-Roos Credits						
Single Family Detached	2,099	1,843	2,227	1,843	2,816	
Single Family Attached	1,562	1,372	1,658	1,372	2,096	
Multi-family	1,282	1,125	1,360	1,126	1,720	
Core/AC Retail	2,191	1,924	2,325	1,924	2,940	
Other Retail	5,250	4,609	5,570	4,610	7,043	
Office	1,347	1,182	1,429	1,183	1,807	
Industrial	125	109	132	109	167	

Table 20. Completed MPFP Roadways Projects

Project Number	Project Description
A01	2nd St Recon. L—Pole Line
A16	Pole Line I-80 Overcrossing
A22	Richards Blvd. I-80 Overcrossing
A23	5th St. Widening, C to L
A24	Covell Widening, Anderson to F
A25	Covell Widening, Birch to Baywood
A33	F St., Grande to New Anderson
A38	F St. Improvement, 7th to Covell
A41	New Signal, Covell and Birch
A44	New Signal, Covell and J
A53	Transport. System Management Plan
A55	New Signal, 8th & Pole Line
A56	New Signal, Arlington & Shasta
A58	New Signal, Covell & Evergreen
A70	Drexel/Loyola Connection
AA97	Median Opening on Covell into Marketplace
AG97	Intersection Improvements, Covell/Shasta
1–5 Year Roadway Project Priorities	
A09	Putah Creek Bike X-ing @ I-80
A11	Bicycle Undercrossings
A19	I-80 Bike/Ped Overcrossing
A20	Mace Blvd. Interchange Imprvmts
A26	Covell Widening, Baywd to Monarch
A29	2nd St. Reconst., Pole Line to Mace
A40	New Signal, 4th and F
A47	New Signal, 1st and B
A51	New Signal, 1st and D
A62	Chiles (Cowell)/Drummond Realign
A63	Transit Center (SP Depot) Expans
A69	Rd 32A E of Mace—Roadway Reloc
AD95	H Street Bike Land & Landscaping
AE07	5th & G Streets Parking Structure
6–10 Year Roadway Project Priorities	
A14	Bike/Ped X-ing East of Monarch
A32	Pole Line, Covell to C. Limit*
A60	Bicycle Overcross-Covell/L*
A61	Bicycle Crossing—Pole Line/Donner*
A18	F Street Improvements, 3rd to 7th
A27	Covell Widening, Monarch to 32A
A37	B St. Improvement, 1st to 5th
A50	New Signal, 1st and F
A52	New Signal, 2nd and B
A71	Pole Line Road Corridor Plan
10+ Year Roadway Project Priorities	
A12	Russell Blvd Widening, A to C
A21	Richards Blvd. Corridor Alternatives**
A31	Covell Reconst., Lake to Hwy 113
A34	Drummond Recon, Albany—Montgomery
A35	Chiles, Resrch Pk to El Cemonte
A43	New Signal, Drummond/Chiles/Cowell
A46	New Signals, South Davis
A48	New Signal, 5th and D
A49	New Signal, 2nd and F
A54	So. Davis Arterial Extra Features
A57	New Signal, Covell & Denali
A64	New Signal, SR113 Ramps/Covell Blvd
A65	New Signal, Covell & Lake
A66	New Signal, Russell & Arlington
A67	New Signal, Russell & Lake
A68	New Signal, 8th & J
AB97	Covell Blvd./SR 113 Interchange Improvements
AE01	Additional Core Area Parking Lots
AE97	Pole Line Road Bus Turnaround
A59	Bicycle Overcross—Hwy 113/Periph

* Project staging and priorities may change depending on the timing and extent of development on the proposed Covell Center site

** Project priority depends on cost and extent of alternatives, which are still being defined. Certain components of this project will likely occur earlier than this time frame suggests.

Therefore, the following priorities are based upon the best current information and the assumption that they will be subject to ongoing review and reprioritized accordingly. Thus, they should be viewed as subject to change as future decisions are considered. The priorities within each time frame are not in any particular order.

DEVELOPMENT IMPACT FEE SUMMARY

Effective Feb. 24, 2008

Development Impact Fee Summary - Base Fees Payable Outside of City Wide Mello-Roos Districts

Land Use	Units	Roadways	Water	Storm Sewer	Sewer	Parks	Open Space	Public Safety	General Facilities	Totals (3)
Single Family Detached	dwelling	$7,767	$2,740	$310	$6,150	$5,072	$952	$971	$2,344	$26,305
Single Family Attached	dwelling	$5,780	$2,740	$310	$4,640	$4,194	$787	$803	$1,938	$21,191
Studio/One Bedroom	dwelling	$2,924	$1,472	$87	$3,320	$3,316	$622	$685	$1,226	$13,652
Multi-family	dwelling	$4,742	$1,472	$87	$3,320	$3,871	$727	$741	$1,789	$16,749
Core/AC Retail	1,000 sf	$8,107	Note (1)	$119	Note (2)	$739	$139	$1,055	$910	$11,069
Auto Sales (AC)	1,000 sf	$4,065	Note (1)	$119	Note (2)	$739	$139	$1,055	$910	$7,028
Other Retail[4]	1,000 sf	$19,422	Note (1)	$119	Note (2)	$739	$139	$1,055	$910	$22,384
Office/Business Park	1,000 sf	$4,982	Note (1)	$119	Note (2)	$739	$139	$1,055	$910	$7,944
Institutional	1,000 sf	$3,884	Note (1)	$119	Note (2)	$739	$139	$1,055	$910	$6,847
Industrial	1,000 sf	$461	Note (1)	$119	Note (2)	$192	$36	$274	$237	$1,320

(1) Water connection fees for non-residential uses are flat rate based upon meter size.
(2) Sewer connection fees for non-residential development depend on flow and strength of effluent.
(3) Non-residential fees do not include sewer or water connection fees.
(4) Development that is outside the scope anticipated in the General Plan may trigger a site specific review of impact fee levels.

East Davis Development Impact Fees After Mello-Roos Credits (CFD 1990-1)

Land Use	Units	Roadways	Water	Storm Sewer	Sewer	Parks	Open Space	Public Safety	General Facilities	Totals
Single Family Detached	dwelling	6,988	2,740	310	6,150	5,072	952	494	2,067	24,773
Single Family Attached	dwelling	5,200	2,740	310	4,640	4,194	787	477	1,749	20,097
Studio/One Bedroom	dwelling	2,631	1,472	87	3,320	3,316	622	384	1,065	12,897
Multi-family	dwelling	4,267	1,472	87	3,320	3,871	727	463	1,628	15,835
Core/AC Retail	1,000 sf	7,294	Note (1)	119	Note (2)	739	139	492	793	9,576
Auto Sales (AC)	1,000 sf	3,658	Note (1)	119	Note (2)	739	139	492	793	5,940
Other Retail	1,000 sf	17,476	Note (1)	119	Note (2)	739	139	492	793	19,757
Office/Business Park	1,000 sf	4,483	Note (1)	119	Note (2)	739	139	492	793	6,765
Institutional	1,000 sf	3,495	Note (1)	119	Note (2)	739	139	492	793	5,777
Industrial	1,000 sf	415	Note (1)	119	Note (2)	192	36	236	229	1,227

East Davis/Mace Development Impact Fees After Mello-Roos Credits (CFD 1990-2)

Land Use	Units	Roadways	Water	Storm Sewer	Sewer	Parks	Open Space	Public Safety	General Facilities	Totals
Single Family Detached	dwelling	6,498	2,740	310	6,150	5,072	952	752	2,098	24,572
Single Family Attached	dwelling	4,836	2,740	310	4,640	4,194	787	653	1,770	19,930
Studio/One Bedroom	dwelling	2,447	1,472	87	3,320	3,316	622	547	1,083	12,894
Multi-family	dwelling	3,968	1,472	87	3,320	3,871	727	614	1,646	15,704
Core/AC Retail	1,000 sf	6,783	Note (1)	119	Note (2)	739	139	797	806	9,383
Auto Sales (AC)	1,000 sf	3,401	Note (1)	119	Note (2)	739	139	797	806	6,002
Other Retail	1,000 sf	16,250	Note (1)	119	Note (2)	739	139	797	806	18,850
Office/Business Park	1,000 sf	4,169	Note (1)	119	Note (2)	739	139	797	806	6,769
Institutional	1,000 sf	3,250	Note (1)	119	Note (2)	739	139	797	806	5,850
Industrial	1,000 sf	386	Note (1)	119	Note (2)	192	36	257	230	1,220

North Central Davis Development Impact Fees After Mello-Roos Credits (CFD 1990-3)

Land Use	Units	Roadways	Water	Storm Sewer	Sewer	Parks	Open Space	Public Safety	General Facilities	Totals
Single Family Detached	dwelling	6,071	2,740	310	6,150	5,072	952	155	2,077	23,527
Single Family Attached	dwelling	4,518	2,740	310	4,640	4,194	787	245	1,756	19,189
Studio/One Bedroom	dwelling	2,286	1,472	87	3,320	3,316	622	171	1,070	12,344
Multi-family	dwelling	3,707	1,472	87	3,320	3,871	727	266	1,634	15,083
Core/AC Retail	1,000 sf	6,337	Note (1)	119	Note (2)	739	139	91	797	8,222
Auto Sales (AC)	1,000 sf	3,178	Note (1)	119	Note (2)	739	139	91	797	5,063
Other Retail	1,000 sf	15,181	Note (1)	119	Note (2)	739	139	91	797	17,067
Office/Business Park	1,000 sf	3,894	Note (1)	119	Note (2)	739	139	91	797	5,780
Institutional	1,000 sf	3,036	Note (1)	119	Note (2)	739	139	91	797	4,922
Industrial	1,000 sf	360	Note (1)	119	Note (2)	192	36	209	229	1,146

DEVELOPMENT IMPACT FEE SUMMARY

Effective Feb. 24, 2008

South Davis Development Impact Fees After Mello-Roos Credits (CFD 1990-4)

Land Use	Units	Roadways	Water	Storm Sewer	Sewer	Parks	Open Space	Public Safety	General Facilities	Totals
Single Family Detached	dwelling	6,654	2,740	310	6,150	5,072	952	847	2,183	24,908
Single Family Attached	dwelling	4,952	2,740	310	4,640	4,194	787	718	1,828	20,169
Studio/One Bedroom	dwelling	2,505	1,472	87	3,320	3,316	622	608	1,132	13,062
Multi-family	dwelling	4,063	1,472	87	3,320	3,871	727	669	1,696	15,904
Core/AC Retail	1,000 sf	6,945	Note (1)	119	Note (2)	739	139	910	842	9,694
Auto Sales (AC)	1,000 sf	3,483	Note (1)	119	Note (2)	739	139	910	842	6,231
Other Retail	1,000 sf	16,639	Note (1)	119	Note (2)	739	139	910	842	19,388
Office/Business Park	1,000 sf	4,268	Note (1)	119	Note (2)	739	139	910	842	7,017
Institutional	1,000 sf	3,328	Note (1)	119	Note (2)	739	139	910	842	6,076
Industrial	1,000 sf	395	Note (1)	119	Note (2)	192	36	265	232	1,239

West Davis Development Impact Fees After Mello-Roos Credits (CFD 1990-5)

Land Use	Units	Roadways	Water	Storm Sewer	Sewer	Parks	Open Space	Public Safety	General Facilities	Totals
Single Family Detached	dwelling	7,767	2,740	310	6,150	5,072	952	438	2,170	25,599
Single Family Attached	dwelling	5,780	2,740	310	4,640	4,194	787	439	1,819	20,709
Studio/One Bedroom	dwelling	2,924	1,472	87	3,320	3,316	622	349	1,125	13,215
Multi-family	dwelling	4,742	1,472	87	3,320	3,871	727	431	1,688	16,338
Core/AC Retail	1,000 sf	8,107	Note (1)	119	Note (2)	739	139	426	837	10,366
Auto Sales (AC)	1,000 sf	4,065	Note (1)	119	Note (2)	739	139	426	837	6,325
Other Retail	1,000 sf	19,422	Note (1)	119	Note (2)	739	139	426	837	21,682
Office/Business Park	1,000 sf	4,982	Note (1)	119	Note (2)	739	139	426	837	7,242
Institutional	1,000 sf	3,884	Note (1)	119	Note (2)	739	139	426	837	6,144
Industrial	1,000 sf	461	Note (1)	119	Note (2)	192	36	232	232	1,272

Non-Residential Water Connection Fees

Type of Non-Residential Connection	Connection Fee
Small Comm/Industrial (1)	$6,917
Medium Comm/Industrial (2)	$26,720
Large Comm/Industrial (3)	$66,874

(1) "Small" C/I is defined as any non-residential connection with up to a one-inch meter.

(2) "Medium" C/I is defined as any non-residential connection with a meter greater than one inch, but less than or equal to two inches.

(3) "Large" C/I is defined as any non-residential connection with greater than a two-inch meter.

APPENDIX D

New Housing Trust Fund Nexus Study
Nexus Study Methodology
Executive Summary

Source: City of Sacramento, Environmental and Planning Systems
The following appendix contains the Executive Summary of the City of Sacramento Housing Trust Fund Analysis dated March 2006.

The full Housing Trust Fund Nexus Analysis, which was prepared by Keyser Marston Associates (KMA), may be found in Attachment 3. The nexus study was prepared by KMA with input from a staff technical advisory committee comprised of representatives from SHRA and representatives from City departments, including Development Services, Economic Development and the City Attorney's Office.

Following is a brief overview of the methodology used in the nexus study.

Total New Employees: The nexus analysis begins with six building types: office, retail, hotel, medical, manufacturing/industrial, and warehousing. Assuming a prototypical 100,000-square-foot building, it then estimates the total number of employees working in each building type, based on average employment density. For example, warehouses have a low ratio of employees per square foot of building space while offices, retail, and medical facilities have a much higher density of employees.

Breakdown of Occupations: The study then determines the distribution of occupations for each building type, using data from the Bureau of Labor Statistics. Occupations cut across many different building or industry types. For example, retail establishments include car dealers, apparel and home furnishings stores, grocery stores, restaurants, dry cleaners, etc. Despite the diversity, three main occupation groups dominate retail employment: sales; food preparation and serving; and office and administrative support, accounting for seventy-five percent of all retail employment. Similar occupations characterize the hotel industry, where seventy-seven percent of hotel-related employment is in service-related jobs building and grounds services including maid service, food preparation and serving, and office and administrative support.

Compensation: Sacramento County wage and salary data were linked to these occupations, allowing the study to calculate the number of jobs paying compensation at very low-income and low-income levels in Sacramento County at each building type.

Employees to Employee Households: This step in the analysis recognizes that there is generally more than one worker per household, a calculation that reduces the number of housing units in demand for new workers The Sacramento County average is 1.57 workers per worker household, varying by household size. (The census data used for this factor excludes retired persons, full time student households and unemployed households on public assistance.)

With the number of worker households and wage and salary information, the study can now calculate the number of worker households who fall into each income category for each building type, shown in Table 1 below. ("Worker households" and "employee households" are used interchangeably.)

"Very low-income" is defined as income below fifty percent of the Sacramento area median income, determined annually by the U.S. Department of Housing and Urban Development. "Low-income" is defined as income from fifty to eighty percent of the area median income.

Housing Units: Returning to the building types, the study now determines the number of households by income level that are associated with the building type. Dividing by the prototypical 100,000 square foot space, it can arrive at coefficients of housing units per square foot of building area. That coefficient, multiplied by the affordability gap described below, will ultimately determine the "total nexus cost" or maximum housing trust fund fee justifiable. As shown above in Table 1, retail and hotel have the highest number of low-wage workers compared to other commercial building types.

Because not all worker households will live in Sacramento County, the study adjusts the number of worker house-

Table 1 Worker Households by Income Category						
Income (% AMI)[1]	Office	Hotel	Retail	Ware-house	Manufac-turing	Hospital/Medic al
< 50% Median	3%	39%	36%	11%	6%	5%
50-80% Median	22%	43%	42%	30%	27%	25%
Total	25%	82%	78%	41%	33%	30%

Notes: 1) AMI = Area Median Income. In 2005, the Area Median Income in Sacramento County for a household of four was $64,100.

Table 2 Number of Worker Households by Building Type in 100,000 Square Foot Building						
Households	Office	Hotel	Retail	Ware-house	Manufac-turing	Hospital/Medical
< 50% Median	5.363	37.766	49.954	2.586	6.105	8.948
50-80% Median	42.315	41.734	57.494	7.317	26.243	39.970
Total	47.678	79.500	107.447	9.902	32.347	48.918

Table 3 Number of Housing Units (or Households) per Square Foot of Building Area						
Income	Office	Hotel	Retail	Ware-house	Manufac-turing	Hospital/Medical
< 50% Median	.00005363	.00037766	.00049954	.00002586	.00006105	.00008948
50-80% Median	.00042315	.00041734	.00057494	.00007317	.00026243	.00039970
Total	.00047678	.00079500	.00107447	.00009902	.00032347	.00048918

holds downward by 19.9 percent, using the 2000 census information that 80.1 percent of those who work in Sacramento County also live in Sacramento County. The figures in Table 3 above represent these lower "commute adjustments."

Affordability Gap: Before the last step in the study's methodology, the study determines the affordability gaps for rental and ownership units, using data from recent affordable housing developments in Sacramento. Forty and seventy percent of area median income (AMI) represent the very low-income and low-income categories, respectively, to reflect more closely the actual incomes of tenants residing in housing affordable to those income groups.

The affordability gap for a rental unit is the difference between its development cost and the value (or price) that can be supported by the net operating income of a unit affordable to a very low-income or low-income tenant (rent minus operation cost divided by a capitalization factor).

For an ownership unit, the affordability gap is the difference between the development cost of a condominium unit and the sales price that a low-income household can afford within thirty percent of its income, considering principal, interest, taxes, and insurance payments. Both rental and ownership affordability calculations do not include the potential use of other housing subsidies.

The resulting affordability gaps are as follows:

Total Nexus Costs (Maximum Justifiable Linkage Fee): In the last step, the study multiplies the number of households by income level per square foot of building area by the affordability gap. The result is the maximum justifiable linkage fee (Table 6).

Table 4 Affordability Gap: Rental Units			
Income Category	Development Cost	Affordable Unit Value	Affordability Gap
Very low-income (40% AMI)	$143,000	$35,700	$107,300
Low Income (70% AMI)	$143,000	$110,500	$32,500

Table 5 Affordability Gap: Ownership Units			
Income Category	Development Cost	Affordable Unit Value	Affordability Gap
Low Income (70% AMI)	$183,000	$100,700	$82,300

Table 6 Total Nexus Costs for Six Building Types (in Dollars)			
Building Type	Very Low-Income[1]	Very Low- & Low-Income (All Rental)	Very Low- & Low-Income (Rental & Condo)
Office	$5.75	$19.51	$40.58
Hotel	$40.52	$54.09	$74.87
Retail/Entertainment	$53.60	$72.29	$100.92
Warehousing	$2.77	$5.15	$8.80
Manufacturing/Industrial	$6.55	$15.08	$28.15
Hospital/Medical	$9.60	$22.59	$42.50

Note: 1. The "Very Low-Income" column is shown because the housing trust fund in the county is restricted to housing very low-income persons The city's trust fund benefits both very low-income and low-income persons.

Despite the study's conservative assumptions, described below, the fee is high because of the high cost of housing relative to wages and salaries. Nevertheless, the study recognizes that "the total nexus cost for each building type is far in excess of any reasonable fee amount likely to be considered."

The nexus costs in Table 6 can be calculated by multiplying the housing units per square foot of building area by the affordability gap. For example, the housing unit coefficients for very low- and low-income retail space are .00049954 and .00057494, respectively. Those numbers multiplied by the very low-income and low-income affordability gaps for rental housing ($107,300 + $32,500) equal a total nexus cost per square foot of $53.60 for a very low-income unit and $18.69 for a low-income unit, the total equaling $72.29 per square foot.

Conservative Assumptions: The study contains a number of conservative assumptions. Significant among them is the decision to count only "direct" employees within a workspace. Many indirect employees serve that workspace, such as janitors, landscape maintenance people, building security personnel and others whose services are performed through contracts. Many of these workers receive lower income compensation. Construction workers are also not counted. Nor does the analysis count building multipliers (workers buying food, supplies, gas—using their income to create other jobs in the economy).

Setting the Fee: KMA concluded the nexus analysis with alternatives decision makers could consider in updating a housing trust fund fee. They include setting fees as a percent of the nexus amount or as a percent of a building's total development cost, and setting fees independently for each building type.

While a fee set as a percentage of the nexus cost is straightforward, it can disproportionately burden one building type (usually retail) because of the high density of jobs and high incidence of low-wage workers. Fees set independently for each building type are often employed to arrive at one fee for all commercial buildings, or to reduce a fee for retail buildings because of their contribution to sales tax revenues.

Other local governments have also opted to exempt small projects, areas difficult to develop (such as redevelopment areas), non-profit uses, and certain special uses as child care centers.

KMA recommended considering the different fee-setting approaches and then narrowing the possibilities. However, the housing trust fees are ultimately tailored to the community's conditions; KMA cautions that they should always stand up to the tests of being policy-based and fair.

Tables following the study's final chapter show the development costs for different types of prototypical buildings in Sacramento and provide information on the housing trust fund programs of other jurisdictions. The final chapter also includes a comparison of fee programs, including jobs-housing linkage fees, in other jurisdictions with which Sacramento competes to attract jobs and services.

Table 1-A. Household Distribution

HUD's Income Categories	Professional/ Technical	Clerical	Craft	Operator	Laborer	Service
Less than $11,050	.2%	3%	2%	4%	5%	5%
Less than $12,650	1%	18%	11%	24%	29%	29%
Less than $14,200	2%	37%	23%	50%	60%	60%
Less than $15,800	4%	44%	27%	59%	70%	70%
Less than $17,050	6%	56%	35%	75%	90%	90%

Source: Keyser Marston Associates, Inc., September 1987

Table 1-A. Very Low Income Housing Assistance—Clerical Occupation

Household Size		Less than $11,050	Less than $12,650	Less than $14,200	Less than $15,800	Less than $17,050	Total
		(2.8%)	(18%)	(27.2%)	(43.8%)	(55.8%)	
Size	Distribution						
1	(36%)	1%[1]					1.0%
2	(28%)		5%[2]				5.0%
3	(18%)			6.7%[2]			6.7%
4	(11%)				4.8%[2]		4.8%
5	(7%)					3.9%[2]	3.9%
TOTAL	100%						21.4%[3]

1. This number indicates 1% of all one person clerical households will earn less than $11,050 and thus qualify for very low income assistance. This percentage is calculated by multiplying the percentage of one person households (36%) by the percentage of households earning less than $11,050 (2.8%).
2. Calculated using the same approach as in footnote one.
3. Represents the percentage of clerical households that will meet HUD's very low income criteria.

Source: Keyser Marston Associates, Inc., August 1987

APPENDIX E

Sacramento County Code

The following code section empowers the Board of Supervisors to impose special conditions in conjunction with the rezoning of property.

Title 1, Chapter 15, Article 2
115-18. Action by the Board of Supervisors

The Board of Supervisors may approve, modify or disapprove the recommendation of either Planning Commission, provided that any modification of the proposed ordinance or amendment by the Board of Supervisors which had not been considered by the Planning Commission at its hearing shall first be referred to the Planning Commission which previously heard the matter for a report and recommendation on the proposed modification, but the Planning Commission shall not be required to hold a public hearing thereon.

Failure of the Planning Commission to report within forty (40) days after the reference, or such longer period as may be designated by the Board of Supervisors, shall be deemed to be approval of the proposed modification. The Board of Supervisors may impose conditions to the zoning reclassification of the property where it finds that said conditions must be imposed so as not to create problems inimical to the public health, safety and general welfare of the County of Sacramento. If conditions are imposed on a zoning reclassification, said conditions shall run with the land and shall not automatically be removed by a subsequent reclassification of the property. Said conditions may be removed only by the Board of Supervisors after recommendation by the Planning Commission. Action by the Board of Supervisors shall become effective thirty (30) days from the date of the final hearing or thirty days from the date the Chairperson of the Board of Supervisors signs the approval document, whichever is later, unless a court review thereof is commenced within that thirty-day period.

For purposes of this Section, "approval document" shall mean the ordinance enacting the zoning reclassification unless the Board of Supervisors has imposed conditions on such reclassification. In that event, "approval document" shall mean both the ordinance enacting the reclassification and any agreement or other document setting forth the conditions imposed by the Board of Supervisors. (Amended 1993) property. Said conditions may be removed only by the Board of Supervisors after recommendation by the Planning Commission. Action by the Board of Supervisors shall become effective thirty (30) days from the date of the final hearing or thirty days from the date the Chairperson of the Board of Supervisors signs the approval document, whichever is later, unless a court review thereof is commenced within that thirty-day period.

APPENDIX F

Sacramento County Zoning Agreement

The following agreement is executed and recorded in conjunction with a rezoning action.

Agreement No. _______

THIS AGREEMENT made this ______________ day of ______________________, 20 _____, by and between "First Party," as identified in Item (a) of Exhibit I of this Agreement, and the COUNTY OF SACRAMENTO, a political subdivision of the State of California, herein called "Second Party."

WITNESSETH:

WHEREAS, First Party is the owner of real property, herein called the "Property," situated in the County of Sacramento, which Property is described in Item (e) of Exhibit I of this Agreement; and

WHEREAS, the Property is now zoned as specified in Item (b) of Exhibit I; and

WHEREAS, First Party has applied for a reclassification of zoning of the Property pursuant to which application the Property is being reclassified from its present classification to the classification or classifications specified in Item (c) of Exhibit I; and

WHEREAS, public hearings have been held upon said application before the Board of Supervisors of the County of Sacramento, State of California, and after having considered the matter presented, it has been determined that certain conditions to the zoning reclassification of said real property must be imposed so as not to create any problems inimical to the health, safety and the general welfare of the County of Sacramento;

NOW, THEREFORE, IT IS MUTUALLY UNDERSTOOD AND AGREED that inasmuch as the reclassification specified in Item (c) of Exhibit I is being granted, the said reclassification shall be subject to the conditions specified in the following paragraphs:

1. That Exhibits I and II, as completed and attached hereto, are incorporated into and made a part of this Agreement with the same force and effect as if fully set forth herein.
2. That First Party shall dedicate right-of-way and construct and install, at First Party's own cost and expense, street improvements and necessary drainage facilities in accordance with the Standard Specifications of Second Party in effect at the time of installation.
3. That said Street Improvements shall be of the type and located as specified in Item (a) of Exhibit II.
4. That said Street Improvements and drainage facilities shall be constructed and installed at such time as the Department of Public Works of Second Party determines the necessity therefore.
5. That if First Party or any successor-in-interest of First Party refuses or neglects to construct or install said Street Improvements and drainage facilities after notification by the said Department of Public Works, said Street Improvements and drainage facilities may be installed by the said Department of Public Works and the cost thereof shall become a lien and charge upon the Property.
6. That First Party shall comply with the additional conditions, if any, specified in Item (b) of Exhibit II of this Agreement.
7. In the event First Party, and successor-in-interest of First Party, or any person in possession of the property described in Item (e) of Exhibit I violates or fails to perform any of the conditions of this Agreement within thirty (30) days after notice thereof as provided in Para-

graph 8, the Board of Supervisors of Second Party may instruct the County Counsel of Second Party to institute legal proceedings to enforce the provisions of this Agreement. The Board of Supervisors of Second Party may also initiate public hearings to rezone the property to any suitable classification.

8. Notice of violation of provisions of this Agreement shall be sent to First Party at the address specified in Item (d) of Exhibit I and to the street address of the property described in Item (e) of Exhibit I. Any subsequent title holder, any lien holder, or party in possession of the property shall also receive notice of such violation at an address other than as specified in Item (d) of Exhibit I by filing with the Clerk of the Board of Supervisors of Second Party the address to which the notice is to be sent with reference to this Agreement and the Resolution authorizing its execution.
9. In the event suit is brought by the County Counsel of Second Party to enforce any of the provisions of this Agreement, First Party agrees to pay to Second Party a reasonable sum to be fixed by the Court as attorney's fees.
10. Each and every one of the provisions of this Agreement herein contained shall bind and inure to the benefit of the successor-in-interest of each and every party hereto, in the same manner as if they had herein been expressly named.

IN WITNESS WHEREOF, the parties hereto have executed this Agreement the day and year first above written.

____

[ ]

"First Party"

[SEAL] COUNTY OF SACRAMENTO,
a political subdivision of the
State of California

ATTEST: ___________________________
Clerk of the Board of Supervisors

By:

____

Chairman of the Board of Supervisors
"Second Party"

Exhibit I

Agreement No. ______

(a) "First Party," as used in this Agreement, includes each and all of the following:

(b) The property is now zoned:

(c) The zoning reclassification of the property is from its present zoning to:

(d) Notice to First Party pursuant to Paragraph No. 7 shall be addressed to:

(e) "Property," as used in this Agreement, includes:
all that certain real property situated in the County of Sacramento, State of California, described as follows:

Exhibit II

Agreement No. ______

(a) Street improvements and drainage facilities pursuant to Paragraph Nos. 2 and 3 of this Agreement shall be of the type and shall be constructed and installed as specified below:

1. Grant the County right-of-way for _______________ Avenue, based on a 108-foot standard, and install public street improvements pursuant to the Sacramento County improvement Standards.
2. Grant the County right-of-way for _______________ Road, based on a 108-foot standard, and install public street improvements pursuant to the Sacramento County improvement Standards.
3. Dedicate additional right-of-way on ______________ Road and _____________________ Avenue for intersection widening. These widenings shall be approved by the Transportation Division of the Department of Public Works.
4. Dedicate off-site right-of-way and construct improvements necessary to extend the two-way left turn lane on __________________ Road to the satisfaction of the Transportation Division of the Department of Public Works. Alternatively, provide any substitute traffic safety measures as recommended by the Transportation Division of the Department of Public Works.
5. Dedicate and construct right-of-way for the extension of ________________ Drive to _______________ Road. The total width along the south boundary shall be 50 feet; along the west boundary, the width shall be 45 feet, widening to 51 feet at the driveway into the project site, as shown on Exhibit "X" (revised site plan approved by the Board of Supervisors on ______________________), to the satisfaction of the Transportation Division of the Department of Public Works.
6. Construct and/or modify roadway medians as required by the Department of Public Works.
7. Provide drainage easements pursuant to the Sacramento County Drainage Ordinance and Improvement Standards, including any fee required by Ordinance 1 of the County Water Agency.
8. Off-site drainage easements and improvements shall be provided as necessary pursuant to the Sacramento County Drainage Ordinance and Improvement Standards.

(b) The additional conditions with which First Party shall comply, pursuant to Paragraph No. 6 of this Agreement, are as follows:

1. Zoning on the property shall be in accordance with Exhibit "S," approved by the Board of Supervisors on _________________ .
2. The applicant shall provide funding for the construction and maintenance of a bus shelter adjacent to the area designated as park-and-ride.
3. The applicant shall provide a pro rata development fee for traffic signal improvements of the ____ intersections, as determined by the Director of the Department of Public Works.
4. The location and number of all driveways shall be approved by the Transportation Division of the Department of Public Works.
5. Comply with the submitted Transportation Systems Management Plan, including providing 27 park-and-ride spaces as requested by Regional Transit.
6. Construct an 8-foot high masonry wall adjacent to the RD-5 zoned lots at the southeast end of the project site.

   To ensure convenient pedestrian/disabled access to transit opportunities adjacent to the project site, submit plans for a pedestrian/disabled distribution system connecting the main commercial building area to the streetside sidewalk system. Such a distribution system shall consist of crosswalks and segregated pathways to ensure that pedestrians/disabled do not mingle with vehicular traffic. This system shall be of a hard, paved surface and have a minimum of slope to facilitate wheelchair access.
8. Provide a 30-foot wide landscape buffer adjacent to the RD-5 zoned lots at the southeast end of the project site. The type of landscaping shall be approved by the Sacramento County Sheriff's Department.

9. Outdoor security lighting systems shall be designed so that the luminescence or the light source will be shielded such that unwanted glare will not be visible from adjacent residential properties.

10. All existing Ash trees shall be retained and incorporated into landscaping plans to the greatest extent possible.

11. Comply with the Mitigation Monitoring and Reporting Program (MMRP) for this project as follows:

    a. The project proponent shall comply with the MMRP for this project, including the payment of 100% of the Department of Environmental Review and Assessment staff costs, and the costs of any technical consultant services incurred during implementation of the MMRP. The initial estimate of these costs is $500.00. If the initial estimate of these costs exceeds the actual monitoring costs, the balance shall be refunded to the proponent, and if the actual monitoring costs exceed the initial estimate, the proponent shall be responsible for paying the additional amount.

    b. Until the MMRP has been recorded and the estimated MMRP fee has been paid, no final parcel map or final subdivision map for the subject property shall be approved; and no encroachment, grading, building, sewer connection, water connection or occupancy permit from Sacramento County shall be approved.

Introduction to Appendices G and H

Appendices G and H contain selected provisions from a Disposition and Development Agreement (DDA) and from an Owner Participation Agreement (OPA) entered into by the Sacramento Housing and Redevelopment Agency and various property owners. The DDA is the documentation of the sale of property by a redevelopment agency to a developer and the development agreement between the agency and the developer. The OPA is the documentation of an agreement between a property owner wishing to redevelop his property within a redevelopment project area, and the redevelopment agency. The OPA contains a provision waiving the agency's power of eminent domain so long as the owner redevelops and uses the property in accordance with the OPA (and hence the redevelopment plan).

These provisions are the result of negotiations between the agency and particular developers and owners. The language is appropriate only between these parties and is based on specific circumstances and projects which may or may not be repeated. However, the provisions are typical of types of exactions that a local agency might require through the redevelopment process. The uses, business preferences, architectural and design requirements of the project and non-discrimination clauses in both development and subsequent uses are common. Ten to twelve exhibits are usually attached to these documents. Exhibits may include escrow instructions and the grant deed (in the case of a DDA), preliminary plans, public improvements development agreement, regulatory agreements, and the schedule of performances. DDAs and OPAs are often fifty to sixty pages in length and contain all terms and conditions necessary to ensure the successful development conforming to the redevelopment plan. Standard and usual contract provisions are not included in the attachments.

The first set of documents includes a scope of development and special provisions of the Disposition and Development Agreement providing for art in public places, child care, "best efforts" to obtain a cinema tenant (a key element of the plan), targeted hiring, landscaping and participation in a downtown cultural and entertainment district.

APPENDIX G

Disposition and Development Agreement

Source: Dana W. Phillips, General Counsel, Sacramento, California Housing and Redevelopment Agency

Downtown Expansion Project

I. General

Pursuant to the terms and conditions in the DDA, the Expansion Project shall be designed and developed as an integrated complex in which the new buildings will have architectural excellence, both individually as well as in the context of a total complex and will integrate with existing buildings; but are not intended to match.

The open spaces between buildings, where they exist, shall be designed and developed with the same degree of excellence. The design and development of the improvements within the Site shall sensitively blend the old and the new development of the Site. Particular attention shall be paid to pedestrian activities, massing, scale, color and materials. The total development shall be in acceptable conformity with the Preliminary Plans for the Downtown Plaza Expansion/Remodel, and the Redevelopment and Urban Design Plan for the Downtown Sacramento area. Development shall be in accordance with plans and specifications prepared by the Jerde Partnership dated July 27, 1990, filed with the City of Sacramento Planning and Development Department, Building Division described in the attached as Exhibit 1. Development shall be in accordance with the Schedule of Performance attached as Exhibit 12 to the DDA.

The Agency and Developer will cooperate and direct their respective consultants, architects, and/or engineers to cooperate so as to ensure the continuity and coordination vitally necessary for the proper and timely completion of the Project.

II. Private Development

A. Developer Improvements—The Site

The Developer shall cause to be constructed, a two-level retail expansion of the existing Downtown Plaza regional shopping center. The Project will consist of the addition of approximately 210,000 gross leasable area consisting of the following categories:

1. 150,000 square feet of retail area which may include up to 43,000 square feet of cinema area;
2. 35,000 square feet of restaurant and fast food area; and
3. 25,000 square feet office area.

The Project at completion will contain a total of 600,000 gross leasable area consisting of the following categories:

1. 265,000 square feet of retail area;
2. 35,000 square feet of restaurant and fast food area; and
3. 300,000 square feet of office area.

Without the prior approval of Agency, Developer may vary the above allocations by (i) a figure not to exceed five percent (5%) per category or, (ii) a figure not to exceed ten percent (10%) of the aggregate. The retail center may include such buildings and occupants customarily located in regional shopping centers, such as financial institutions, services and vending carts.

B. Pedestrian Mall

Developer shall construct or cause to be constructed within the K Street Mall area, the Improvements as set forth in Preliminary Plans. The Mall shall be for pedestrian use and related amenities.

C. Architecture and Design

The Improvements shall be consistent with the plans approved by the City Design Review Board on July 3, 1990 and shall be of high architectural quality, shall be landscaped, (as structural capacity within the existing structure may permit) and shall be effectively integrated and aesthetically designed. The shape, scale of volume, exterior design, and exterior finish of each building must be consonant with, visually and physically related to, and enhance each other as well as adjacent buildings within the Project.

D. Landscaping

Landscaping shall embellish the open spaces on the Site to integrate the Developer Improvements with adjacent sites outside the Project. Landscaping includes such materials as paving, trees, shrubs, and other plant materials, landscape containers, top soil preparation, landscape and pedestrian lighting and water elements and is subject to the approval of the Design Review Board as applicable to the extent of their jurisdiction.

E. Signs

All signs on the exteriors of buildings and structures developed as a part of the Developer Improvements shall be subject to approval by the Design Review Board and Agency as applicable to the extent of their jurisdiction and must comply with applicable City ordinances and codes.

F. Art in Public Places

Pursuant to Agency's Aesthetic Improvement Policy, also known as the Art in Public Places Program, Developer shall expend not less than two percent (2%) of the total qualifying Project construction costs on Aesthetic Improvements. Developer shall comply, in all respects, with the APP Guidelines and shall cooperate with the Sacramento Metropolitan Arts Commission in carrying out its obligation under the DDA.

III. Miscellaneous

A. Mitigation Measures

The Negative Declaration for Downtown Plaza prepared in January 1990 and certified on April 3, 1990, provides for the following mitigation measures to be completed by Developer:

1. Hydrology

A qualified structural engineer shall review all proposed construction dewatering operations near existing facilities prior to start of construction. Extraction and disposal methods shall be subject to the review and approval of the Regional Water Quality Control Board. The Developer shall provide written verification from a qualified structural engineer and Regional Water Quality Control Board.

During wet weather, prevent runoff water from entering excavations by collecting water and disposing outside the construction limits. Heavy construction equipment, building materials, excavated soil, and vehicular traffic should not be allowed within 1/3 of the slope height from the top of any sloped excavation. Automobile parking along Fourth Street should be prohibited during construction if necessary. The Developer shall provide written verification from a qualified structural engineer.

2. Cultural Resources

a. During ground disturbance activities, the site shall be monitored by a qualified archeologist. In the event that construction activity reveals evidence of prehistoric remains and/or historic structures, the resources shall be researched, their history identified, and their existence mapped and recorded photographically. The Developer shall provide written verification from an archeological monitor.

b. A survey of adjacent buildings shall be performed prior to driving any test piles. At a minimum, the condition survey should include photographs of the exterior of adjacent structures and the placement and periodic measurement of vertical and horizonal survey monuments affixed to adjacent structures.

c. Prior to pile driving, existing structures should be evaluated by a structural engineer to establish a limiting response spectra. The indicator pile program should include driving indicator piles at the closest point of approach to adjacent structures.

d. During driving, existing structures should be monitored for driving-induced displacements, velocities, and accelerations by an engineering firm qualified in vibration monitoring. If during indicator pile driving the limiting response spectra established by the structural engineer is exceeded, driving should be modified to reduce induced vibrations below acceptable limits. Modifications to pile driving could include predrilling, reducing the energy output of the hammer, and/or mobilizing a pile driver with a lower energy rating.

e. For items b, c, and d above, the Developer shall provide written verification from a qualified structural engineer to Agency.

3. Transportation

Due to the high volume of people who use public regional transit services in the vicinity of the project, the project shall be designed to include and Developer shall provide written verification from Sacramento Regional Transit.

- Signage which emphasizes the location of bus stops and RT Metro Stations;
- Clear and direct access to bus stops and RT Metro Stations;

- Architecturally compatible shelters for passengers at bus stops adjacent to the Downtown Plaza; and
- Transit information signage or kiosks in locations visible to Downtown Plaza employees and patrons.

IV. Special Provisions

A. Art in Public Places

Pursuant to Agency's Aesthetic Improvement Policy, also known as the Art in Public Places Program, Developer shall expend not less than two percent (2%) of the total qualifying Project construction costs on Aesthetic Improvements. Developer shall comply, in all respects, with the APP Guidelines and shall cooperate with the Sacramento Metropolitan Arts Commission in carrying out its obligation under this DDA. As a condition of issuance of a Certificate of Completion, Developer shall designate in writing to Agency the Aesthetic Improvements subject to this DDA. The Project Aesthetic Improvement located immediately west of the northwest corner of the Macy's store in the area identified in the Downtown Plaza Project Site Map and consisting of an eighty-foot metal framework tower designed by R.M. Fischer and electrical and mechanical appurtenances such as lighting and clockworks, an aerial pedestrian bridge connecting the G Garage and the Downtown Plaza Project Site and the base structure which supports such bridge and tower is, collectively referred to herein as the "Tower."

1. Ownership

Except for the Tower, which will be owned by Agency, the Aesthetic Improvements shall be owned by Developer. Developer, however, shall not remove the Aesthetic Improvements from the Downtown Plaza Project Site without the prior written consent of Agency. Developer may, however, move the Aesthetic Improvements within the Downtown Plaza Project, may remove the Aesthetic Improvements and replace them with other Aesthetic Improvements of similar quality as part of a program for sharing, trading or rotating art displays, or any other program which serves the intent of the Art in Public Places Program, without Agency's prior consent.

In the event that an Aesthetic Improvement must be removed from the Downtown Plaza Project Site to permit rehabilitation, remodeling or demolition of the Downtown Plaza Project, Developer shall offer the Aesthetic Improvement for sale to Agency or its allowed designee at fair market value established as reasonably agreed by the parties. Agency shall, in such event be responsible for compliance with California's Art Preservation Act (Civil Code § 987, et seq.) Only a public agency or a public-benefit, nonprofit corporation may be an allowed designee of Agency under this Section 14.1.1. Failure of the Agency to exercise its option to purchase the Aesthetic Improvement within a reasonable period of time (not to exceed forty-five days) after notice has been provided to Agency that a fair market value has been established shall be deemed approval by the Agency of Developer's removal of the Aesthetic Improvement from the Downtown Plaza Project Site.

B. Cinema Assurances

Developer shall use reasonable efforts to locate a cinema in the Project as shown in the Preliminary Plans and described in the Scope of Development. Developer shall, as soon as reasonably possible and with all due diligence, begin negotiation with potential cinema operators for the Project. If Developer is unable to obtain a cinema operator as the initial tenant for space in the Site designated for cinema uses, Developer shall notify Agency and may thereafter proceed to lease the space to any other retail tenant.

C. Child Care

Prior to, or at the time of transfer of the Site to Developer, Developer shall pay to City the sum of Seventy-Six Thousand Dollars ($76,000) to be used by the City to provide child care within the Project Area or as would reasonably benefit the Project Area. In the alternative, Developer may, as a condition of issuance of a Certificate of Completion, provide evidence reasonably acceptable to Agency that such sum has been expended, or security acceptable to Agency assuring that such sum will be expended, to provide a child care facility within or adjacent to the Downtown Plaza Project. Said sum shall constitute Developer's full obligation under this DDA to provide child care services, except for any obligation related to the D1(b) Parcel.

D. Pedestrian Linkage Study Participation

Agency shall enter into a contract with an architect acceptable to Developer and Agency to study and design pedestrian linkages between the Downtown Plaza Project and Old Sacramento Historic District to the west, "Chinatown" and the Southern Pacific site to the north, the proposed Capitol Mall Partners "Lot A Project" to the south and the K Street pedestrian mall to the east of Seventh Street. As a condition of Certificate of Completion, Developer shall contribute one-third of the costs of such study, not to exceed $33,000 which shall be payable within sixty (60) days of execution of this DDA. The study shall be commenced within one (1) year of the date of such payment and diligently prosecuted to completion. This Section shall not be construed as an agreement, commitment or obligation of the Developer to contribute to the costs of such improvements as may be indicated by the study.

E. PIC/SETA

As a condition of issuance of a Certificate of Completion, Developer shall develop an employee recruitment program with the Private Industry Council ("PIC") and the Sacramento Employment Training Agency ("SETA") jobs programs, regarding Downtown Plaza and its tenants, which shall be submitted to the Agency for approval. During construction of the Improvements and for a period of two (2) years after issuance of a Certificate of Completion, Developer shall cause the approved recruitment program to be distributed to all tenants for the Downtown Plaza Project. Developer shall reasonably assist the Agency, no more than two times annually, in obtaining from the tenants sufficient information to review the effectiveness of the recruitment program.

F. Distribution of Information to Future Tenants

During construction of the Improvements and for a period of two years after issuance of a Certificate of Completion, Developer shall, in cooperation with Agency's MBE/WBE coordinator, distribute information regarding MBE/WBE contractors and local contractors and subcontractors with permanent places of business within the County of Sacramento to tenants to aid in their use of such contractors for tenant improvements.

G. Public Vehicular Transportation Plan

As the Public Vehicular Transportation Plan, Developer shall participate in, and contribute not more than Fifteen Thousand Dollars ($15,000), payable within sixty (60) days of execution of this DDA, toward the study of a public vehicular transportation system linking "Old Sacramento Historic District" with "7th" and "K" Street pedestrian mall entrance which system should serve as a transit link with other downtown areas including areas known as "Southern Pacific Railyard Site," "Capitol Mall Lot A Site," Convention Center and peripheral parking areas for downtown. Developer shall reasonably accommodate the operation by the Sacramento Regional Transit District of such a system. This Section shall not be construed as an agreement, commitment or obligation of Developer to contribute to the costs of such system or to adopt the results of such study.

During construction, Developer shall provide two vehicles for use by the Sacramento Regional Transit District to provide public transportation between the Convention Center and the Old Sacramento Historic District.

H. D1(b) Parcel Landscaping

As a condition of issuance of a Certificate of Completion and provided that Agency and Developer reasonably agree that the start of construction on the D1(b) Parcel as described in the DDA shall be more than 120 days following issuance of the Certificate of Completion, Developer shall landscape, in accordance with plans prepared by Developer and reasonably approved by Agency, and maintain, at Developer's cost, the D1(b) Parcel. Developer shall commence such landscaping not later than issuance of the Certificate of Completion for the Site and complete such landscaping in a reasonable period of time. Developer shall make reasonable efforts to use Agency's animal-shaped, children's sculptures currently in front of Macy's as a part of such landscaping. Developer shall return such sculptures to Agency at Agency's corporation yard (currently located at 320 Commerce Circle, Sacramento) upon their removal from the D1(b) Parcel. The termination of any and all of Developer's rights to the D1(b) Parcel or Developer's commencement of construction on the D1(b) Parcel shall terminate its obligations for landscaping and maintenance under this Section.

I. Sacramento Downtown Cultural and Entertainment District

Developer shall participate in the formation of, and join with, the Sacramento Downtown Cultural and Entertainment District ("District") (by whatever name it may be organized), provided that, and so long as, the District shall be organized in accordance with the following provisions: The District shall include the Downtown Business Improvement Area (of which Developer is a member) and the Old Sacramento Business Improvement Area, which improvement areas are currently formed. The District is further defined in the Sacramento Downtown Cultural and Entertainment District Master Plan. Events of the District shall be held to benefit such improvement areas generally and shall be held within the boundaries of such improvement area or within publicly-owned areas and established arts and cultural facilities within a one-half mile radius of such district. Each of the areas comprising such improvement area shall contribute the same proportion of its gross income to the operation of the District as established by the governing body of the District and approved by such improvement area. The governing body of the District shall have at least one representative of each area comprising such improvement area, shall represent equally such areas and shall have no more representatives of arts and cultural organizations than representatives of the areas comprising such improvement area.

If the District is not organized in accordance with this Section, Developer shall participate in formation of the District, shall reasonably cooperate with the District in establishing a fair and equitable formula for any financial contribution and voting and shall participate in the District to a formula deemed fair and equitable by the Developer.

If the District is not formed within five years after issuance of a Certificate of Completion, Developer's obligations under this Section shall terminate.

J. Pedestrian Access During Construction

Developer shall use reasonable efforts to maintain pedestrian access through the K Mall during construction of the Improvements.

* * *

Disposition and Development Agreement

The following provisions have been selectively chosen from the DDA between the Redevelopment Agency of the City of Sacramento and DPA, L.P. (a California limited partnership). Excerpts include purpose.

1. Purpose of the DDA

In furtherance of the objective of the Community Redevelopment Law, the Agency has undertaken a program for the clearance and reconstruction or rehabilitation of blighted areas in the City including a redevelopment project in the Project Area.

The primary purpose of this DDA is to transfer to Developer, for redevelopment, Agency's D1 Parcel and the K Street Mall Parcel which comprise a portion of the Site and to convey or undertake to have the City to convey to Developer certain rights over and in the Fifth Street Bridge and certain air rights over Fifth Street, which rights comprise the balance of the Site. The purpose of this DDA is not for speculation in land holding. To accomplish the transfer and redevelopment, Agency will subdivide the D1 Parcel into D1(a) Parcel, D1(b) Parcel and the Garage Parcel.

By the terms of this DDA, Agency will transfer the Site to Developer solely for redevelopment as two levels of improvements designed for use as retail, cinema, food service, service commercial and ancillary uses, which is the Project. Also as part of the Project, Developer shall remodel Agency's Existing Garages which serve Downtown Plaza (at Agency's cost as provided in this DDA).

In conjunction with the Project and under the Public Improvements Development Agreement, the Developer will develop for Agency, as the Garage Project, a public parking garage (the Garage) within the Garage Parcel (at Agency's cost as provided in this DDA).

Also in conjunction with the Project, Agency and Developer will have the option, exercisable by signing the D1(b) DDA within two years from August 27, 1990, to enter into the D1(b) DDA for the transfer and redevelopment of the D1(b) Parcel. Developer's failure to enter the D1(b) DDA within such time and redevelop the D1(b) Parcel will terminate all rights of Developer in the D1(b) Parcel.

The Site is adjacent to the Downtown Plaza, an existing shopping center owned by Developer. Downtown Plaza is adjacent to major department stores ("Department Stores") owned separately by Macy's and Weinstock's; nevertheless, no party other than Agency and Developer shall have any rights arising out of this DDA. The real property owned by Developer which contains the Downtown Plaza is the Downtown Plaza Site. The Project and the Garage Project are an integral part of the renovation of Downtown Plaza as a first-class, urban retail shopping center. The further purpose of this DDA is such renovation of Downtown Plaza. However, the failure of Developer to carry out such renovation of Downtown Plaza shall not relieve Developer of its obligation to carry out the terms of this DDA and to develop the Project and the Garage Project. Such renovation of Downtown Plaza and the construction of the Project and the Garage Project are collectively referred to as the Downtown Plaza Project.

The Agency represents that the development of the Site, the completion of the Downtown Plaza Project and the fulfillment generally of this DDA are (1) in the vital and best interests of the City and the health, safety, morals and welfare of its residents, (2) for the purpose of community improvement and welfare, (3) for the benefit of the Agency's Redevelopment Project and (3) in accord with the public purposes and provisions of any applicable federal, state and local laws and requirements under which the Downtown Plaza Project is to be undertaken and is being assisted.

* * *

4.1.3. Agency Approval of Plans

Subject to the terms of this DDA, the Agency shall have reasonable rights of architectural review (including landscaping) of the Plans and review of the Plans for conformity to the Preliminary Plans and Scope of Development, and including any proposed changes to the Plans. Agency shall approve or disapprove the Plans, in writing, as soon as practicable, but in any event not later than thirty (30) days of their receipt. Agency shall promptly grant approval of progressively more detailed drawings and specifications which are not in material conflict with the Plans previously approved by Agency.

* * *

4.1.8. Purpose of Approval

Agency's approval of Plans is not an assurance of the adequacy or correctness of the Plans, other than with respect to Agency's Project requirements. Agency's right to approve the Plans is solely (a) to assure that the Plans conform to the Preliminary Plans, further the Redevelopment Plan and are generally suitable to the uses and designs contemplated by this DDA and (b) to assure that Agency funds provided under this DDA are spent for their intended uses.

* * *

5.1.16. Transfer of City-Owned Property

As a condition precedent in favor of Developer and covenant by Agency, and where and if applicable, Agency shall have obtained the transfer of title by City of air rights within the 5th street right-of-way and related support easements which are also within the Site for conveyance by Agency to Developer.

* * *

5.2. Purchase Terms

Subject to all the terms, covenants and conditions of this DDA, including, specifically, the following terms, the Agency shall sell the Site to Developer solely for the purpose of constructing the Improvements consistent with the approved Plans and, thereafter, for the uses set out in this DDA:

[Document specifies prices, square footage and parcels.]

* * *

5.9.4. Agency Access

After the conveyance of the Site by Agency to Developer, Developer shall permit the representatives of Agency, designated by Agency in writing, access to the Downtown Plaza Project at all reasonable times which Agency or its designated representatives deems necessary for the purposes of the DDA, including, but not limited to, inspection of all work being performed in connection with the construction of the Improvements; provided, that Developer may reasonably require Agency representatives to be accompanied by Developer representatives and to take reasonable safety precautions. Agency shall indemnify and hold Developer harmless for any claims or liability arising from Agency's exercise of its rights under this Section.

* * *

5.10. Nondiscrimination

There shall be no discrimination against or segregation of any persons, or group of persons on account on account of sex, marital status, religion, race, color, creed, national origin or ancestry in the sale, lease, sublease, transfer, use or enjoyment of the land, nor shall the transferee himself or any person claiming under or through him, establish or permit any such practice or practices of discrimination or segregation with reference to the selection, location, number, use or occupancy of tenants, lessees, sublessees, subtenants, or vendees of the land.

* * *

6.4. Covenant to Perform

In consideration of Developer's performance in constructing the Improvements and developing the Site, Agency has made significant material concessions for transfer of the Site to Developer. Therefore, the parties agree that such obligations of Developer shall be covenants running with the land and that they shall, in any event, and without regard to technical classification or designation, be to the fullest extent permitted by law and equity, binding for the benefit of the Agency and enforceable by the Agency against the Developer and its successors and assigns. Such covenants shall terminate upon the issuance of a Certificate of Completion as provided in this DDA.

* * *

6.10. Antidiscrimination During Construction

The Developer for itself and its successors and assigns, agrees that the following provisions shall apply to, and be contained in all contracts and sub-contracts for the construction of the improvements on the Site provided for in this DDA.

* * *

6.11. Agency Sign

If Developer places a sign on the Site during construction stating the names of the Downtown Plaza Project principals and lenders, it shall also name "Sacramento Housing and Redevelopment Agency" as a participant in the Downtown Plaza Project. The Agency name on the sign shall be in letters not less than size of letters used to name the lenders for the Downtown Plaza Project.

* * *

6.13. Minority/Women's Business Enterprises Requirements

The provisions of this DDA related to the Site are subject to Agency's minority-owned and women-owned business enterprises ("MBE/WBE") requirements.

6.13.1. In Solicitations

In all services solicitation (whether direct or by bid, Request for Proposal or Request for Qualification), Developer shall cause its contractor to take all reasonable steps necessary to encourage the participation of minority-owned and female-owned businesses. Such steps may include, but are not limited to:

6.13.1.1. Registry

Obtaining and utilizing the Minority and Women's Business Enterprises Registry from the Agency MBE/WBE Coordinator.

(1) Advertising

Advertising the invitation to bid or to submit proposals in the "El Hispano" and the "Sacramento Observer" as well as a newspaper of general circulation.

(2) Direct Contacts

Reviewing the telephone directory or professional organization membership lists, or making direct contact with minority-owned or female-owned businesses for specialized trades and services and inviting such firms to bid.

6.13.2. Documentation

Developer shall maintain or cause to be maintained such documentation of efforts of outreach to minority or female owned businesses as may be reasonably required by Agency.

6.13.3. Goal

The MBE/WBE utilization goal for this Project is 20% of contract dollars for Minority Business Enterprise and 5% of contract dollars for Women's Business Enterprise.

6.13.4. Inclusion in Contracts

The requirements and contract provisions for the Minority and Women's Business Enterprises must be included in all contracts. Contracts for purchases of goods and services over $10,000 must be coordinated with the Agency's MBE/WBE Coordinator.

* * *

6.15. Local Hire

Developer shall require its contractor to use its good faith efforts to hire, or cause to be hired, for no less than fifty percent (50%) of the cost of the work relating to direct labor of the Project local contractors and subcontractors with permanent places of business within the County of Sacramento. To the extent that labor for any portion of the Project is not available within the county, such portion shall not be included in determining the said percentage. Agency shall have the right, within thirty (30) day after the award of such subcontracts, to approve the computations as described in the foregoing sentence. If Agency determines that Developer has failed to comply with the aforesaid, Developer shall give written explanation for such failure including a detailed listing of all efforts made to effect such compliance.

* * *

8. Covenants Regarding Use and Operation of Site

The Developer covenants and agrees for itself, its successors, its assigns and every successor-in-interest to all or any part of the Site, that the Developer, such successors and such assignees shall act as follows:

8.1. Uses

Without the prior written approval of Agency, neither the Project nor any part thereof shall be used, and, subject to the next to last sentence of this Section 8.1 no building or other improvement shall be constructed, maintained or used, except for retail, ancillary office, not more than 30,000 square feet of regular office and service commercial establishments common to a first-class, mall, urban, retail shopping center in California. Service uses may include brokerage and insurance offices, restaurants, movie, travel and other agencies and similar service establishments, provided that service commercial uses other than restaurants and movie theaters will not occupy more than ten percent (10%) of the Floor Area of the Project without the prior written approval of Agency. Notwithstanding the foregoing, no building in the Project shall be used primarily for general office purposes; however, buildings within Downtown Plaza but not part of the Project may be so used.

8.2. Limitation on Detrimental Characteristics

Without the prior written approval of Agency, no use or operation shall be permitted on any part of the Site which use or operation is clearly objectionable to the development or operation of the Project as a first-class urban retail shopping center. Developer shall not lease any portion of the Site for any of the uses or any of the other activities set out in this Section and Developer shall not permit such use or activities on any portion of the Site. Included among the uses or operations which are objectionable are uses or operations which produce or are accompanied by the following characteristics, which list is not intended to be all-inclusive:

8.2.1. Any noise, litter, odor or other activity that may constitute a public or private nuisance.

8.2.12. Any unusual fire, explosive or other damaging or dangerous hazards (including the storage, display or sale of explosives or fireworks).

8.2.3. Any warehouse operation, or any assembling, manufacturing, distilling, refining, smelting, industrial, agricultural, drilling or mining operation.

8.2.4. Any trailer court, mobile home park, lot for sale of new or used motor vehicles, labor camp, junk yard, stock yard or animal raising.

8.2.5. Any dumping, disposal, incineration or reduction of garbage or refuse other than handling or reducing such waste if produced on the premises from authorized uses and if handled in a reasonably clean and sanitary manner.

8.2.6. Any laundry, laundromat or dry cleaning plant.

8.2.7. Any veterinarian's office (not ancillary to a pet shop).

8.2.8. Any car washing establishment or any automobile body and fender repair work.

8.2.9. Any "second hand" or "surplus" stores (but excluding stores primarily selling antiques).

8.2.10. Any flea market, fire sale, bankruptcy sale or auction house operation.

8.2.11. Any skating rink, living quarters (residential or otherwise), or mortuary.

8.2.12. Any operation involving the production, exhibition, rental, distribution or sale of "X-Rated" movies or obscene materials other than a video tape or record retailer who may sell or rent "x-rated" movies or materials as a minor and an incidental part of their business.

8.2.13. Any bar, tavern, dance hall or restaurant where sales from alcoholic beverages exceed sixty percent (60%) of such establishment's annual gross revenue.

8.2.14. Any billiard room or video or other game arcade, except if such use is strictly ancillary to the conduct of an activity otherwise permitted under this Agreement and is consistent with the leasing and operation of a first-class urban, retail shopping center.

8.2.15. Any massage parlor.

8.2.16. Any bowling alley.

8.2.17. Any noise or sound which can be heard in the public pedestrian areas and which is reasonably objectionable due to intermittence, beat, frequency, shrillness or loudness.

8.3. Obligation to Refrain from Discrimination

With regard to the Project and Site, there shall be no discrimination against or segregation of any persons, or group of persons, on account of sex, marital status, race, color, creed, ancestry or national origin of any person. All such deeds, leases or contracts shall contain or be subject to substantially the following nondiscrimination or non-segregation clauses:

[Exact language is found in the Health and Safety Code Section 33436(a) for deeds; 33436(b) for leases; and 33436(c) for contracts.]

* * *

8.5. Effect and Duration of Covenants

The covenants contained in the Grant Deed subject and burden the Site with the covenants regarding use of the Site and regarding nondiscrimination, as covenants running with the land. It is intended and agreed that the agreements and covenants provided in the Grant Deed shall be covenants running with the land and equitable servitudes thereon and that they shall, in any event, and without regard to technical classifications or designation, be binding, to the fullest extent permitted by law and equity, for the benefit and in favor of, and enforceable by, the Agency, the Agency's successors and assigns, any other governmental entity acting within its authority and any successor in interest to all or any part of the Site against the Developer, its successors and assigns and every successor in interest to all or any part of the Site, and any party in possession or occupancy of the Site and any subcontracting party or parties or other transferees under this DDA.

* * *

8.6. Effect of Violation

The Agency is deemed the beneficiary of the terms and provisions of this DDA and the covenants running with the land, both for its own right and for the purposes of protecting the interests of the community and other parties, public or private, in whose benefit this DDA and the covenants running with the land have been provided. The DDA and the covenants shall run in favor of the Agency without regard to whether the Agency has had or does have any interest in the Site. If the covenants against racial discrimination are breached, the Agency shall have the right to exercise all rights and remedies, and to maintain any actions or suits at law or in equity or other proper proceedings to enforce the curing of such breaches to which it or any other beneficiaries of this DDA and covenants are entitled.

* * *

14. Special Provisions

14.1. Art in Public Places

Pursuant to Agency's Aesthetic Improvement Policy, also known as the Art in Public Places Program, Developer shall expend not less than two percent (2%) of the total qualifying Project construction costs on Aesthetic Improvements. Developer shall comply, in all respects, with the APP Guidelines and shall cooperate with the Sacramento Metropolitan Arts Commission in carrying out its obligation under this DDA. As a condition of issuance of a Certificate of Completion, Developer shall designate in writing to Agency the Aesthetic Improvements subject to this DDA. The Project Aesthetic Improvement located immediately west of the northwest corner of the Macy's store in the area identified in the Downtown Plaza Project Site Map and consisting of an eighty-foot metal framework tower designed by R.M. Fischer and electrical and mechanical appurtenances such as lighting and clockworks, an aerial pedestrian bridge connecting the G Garage and the Downtown Plaza Project Site and the base structure which supports such bridge and tower is, collectively referred to herein as the "Tower."

14.1.1. Ownership

Except for the Tower, which will be owned by Agency, the Aesthetic Improvements shall be owned by Developer. Developer, however, shall not remove the Aesthetic Improvements from the Downtown Plaza Project Site without the prior written consent of Agency. Developer may, however, move the Aesthetic Improvements within the Downtown Plaza Project, may remove the Aesthetic Improvements and replace them with other Aesthetic Improvements of similar quality as part of a program for sharing, trading or rotating art displays, or any other program which serves the intent of the Art in Public Places Program, without Agency's prior consent.

In the event that an Aesthetic Improvement must be removed from the Downtown Plaza Project Site to permit rehabilitation, remodeling or demolition of the Downtown Plaza Project, Developer shall offer the Aesthetic Improvement for sale to Agency or its allowed designee at fair market value established as reasonably agreed by the parties. Agency shall, in such event be responsible for compliance with California's Art Preservation Act (Civil Code § 987, et seq.) Only a public agency or a public-benefit, non-profit corporation may be an allowed designee of Agency under this Section 14.1.1. Failure of the Agency to exercise its option to purchase the Aesthetic Improvement within a reasonable period of time (not to exceed forty-five days) after notice has been provided to Agency that a fair market value has been established shall be deemed approval by the Agency of Developer's removal of the Aesthetic Improvement from the Downtown Plaza Project Site.

14.2. Cinema Assurances

Developer shall use reasonable efforts to locate a cinema in the Project as shown in the Preliminary Plans and described in the Scope of Development. Developer shall, as soon as reasonably possible and with all due diligence, begin negotiation with potential cinema operators for the Project. If Developer is unable to obtain a cinema operator as the initial tenant for space in the Site designated for cinema uses, Developer shall notify Agency and may thereafter proceed to lease the space to any other retail tenant.

14.3. Child Care

Prior to, or at the time of transfer of the Site to Developer, Developer shall pay to City the sum of Seventy-Six Thousand Dollars ($76,000) to be used by the City to provide child care within the Project Area or as would reasonably benefit the Project Area. In the alternative, Developer may, as a condition of issuance of a Certificate of Completion, provide evidence reasonably acceptable to Agency that such sum has been expended, or security acceptable to Agency assuring that such sum will be expended, to provide a child care facility within or adjacent to the Downtown Plaza Project. Said sum shall constitute Developer's full obligation under this DDA to provide child care services, except for any obligation related to the D1(b) Parcel.

14.4. Pedestrian Linkage Study Participation

Agency shall enter into a contract with an architect acceptable to Developer and Agency to study and design pedestrian linkages between the Downtown Plaza Project and Old Sacramento Historic District to the west, "Chinatown" and the Southern Pacific site to the north, the proposed Capitol Mall Partners "Lot A Project" to the south and the K Street pedestrian mall to the east of Seventh Street. As a condition of Certificate of Completion, Developer shall contribute one-third of the costs of such study, not to exceed $33,000 which shall be payable within sixty (60) days of execution of this DDA. The study shall be commenced within one (1) year of the date of such payment and diligently prosecuted to completion. This Section shall not be construed as an agreement, commitment or obligation of the Developer to contribute to the costs of such improvements as may be indicated by the study.

14.5. PIC/SETA

As a condition of issuance of a Certificate of Completion, Developer shall develop an employee recruitment program with the Private Industry Council ("PIC") and the Sacramento Employment Training Agency ("SETA") jobs programs, regarding Downtown Plaza and its tenants, which shall be submitted to the Agency for approval. During construction of the Improvements and for a period of two (2) years after issuance of a Certificate of Completion, Developer shall cause the approved recruitment program to be distributed to all tenants for the Downtown Plaza Project. Developer shall reasonably assist the Agency, no more than two times annually, in obtaining from the tenants sufficient information to review the effectiveness of the recruitment program.

14.6. Distribution of Information to Future Tenants

During construction of the Improvements and for a period of two years after issuance of a Certificate of Completion, Developer shall, in cooperation with Agency's MBE/WBE coordinator, distribute information regarding MBE/WBE contractors and local contractors and subcontractors with permanent places of business within the County of Sacramento tenants to aid in their use of such contractors for tenant improvements.

14.7. Public Vehicular Transportation Plan

As the Public Vehicular Transportation Plan, Developer shall participate in, and contribute not more than Fifteen Thousand

Dollars ($15,000), payable within sixty (60) days of execution of this DDA, toward the study of a public vehicular transportation system linking "Old Sacramento Historic District" with "7th" and "K" Street pedestrian mall entrance which system should serve as a transit link with other downtown areas including areas known as "Southern Pacific Railyard Site," "Capitol Mall Lot A Site," Convention Center and peripheral parking areas for downtown. Developer shall reasonably accommodate the operation by the Sacramento Regional Transit District of such a system. This Section shall not be construed as an agreement, commitment or obligation of Developer to contribute to the costs of such system or to adopt the results of such study.

During construction, Developer shall provide two vehicles for use by the Sacramento Regional Transit District to provide public transportation between the Convention Center and the Old Sacramento Historic District.

14.8. D1(b) Parcel Landscaping

As a condition of issuance of a Certificate of Completion and provided that Agency and Developer reasonably agree that the start of construction on the D1(b) Parcel as described in the DDA shall be more than 120 days following issuance of the Certificate of Completion, Developer shall landscape, in accordance with plans prepared by Developer and reasonably approved by Agency, and maintain, at Developer's cost, the D1(b) Parcel. Developer shall commence such landscaping not later than issuance of the Certificate of Completion for the Site and complete such landscaping in a reasonable period of time. Developer shall make reasonable efforts to use Agency's animal-shaped, children's sculptures currently in front of Macy's as a part of such landscaping. Developer shall return such sculptures to Agency at Agency's corporation yard (currently located at 320 Commerce Circle, Sacramento) upon their removal from the D1(b) Parcel. The termination of any and all of Developer's rights to the D1(b) Parcel or Developer's commencement of construction on the D1(b) Parcel shall terminate its obligations for landscaping and maintenance under this Section.

14.9. Sacramento Downtown Cultural and Entertainment District

Developer shall participate in the formation of, and join with, the Sacramento Downtown Cultural and Entertainment District ("District") (by whatever name it may be organized), provided that, and so long as, the District shall be organized in accordance with the following provisions: The District shall include the Downtown Business Improvement Area (of which Developer is a member) and the Old Sacramento Business Improvement Area, which improvement areas are currently formed. The District is further defined in the Sacramento Downtown Cultural and Entertainment District Master Plan. Events of the District shall be held to benefit such improvement areas generally and shall be held within the boundaries such improvement area or within publicly-owned areas and established arts and cultural facilities within a one-half mile radius of such district. Each of the areas comprising such improvement area shall contribute the same proportion of its gross income to the operation of the District as established by the governing body of the District and approved by such improvement area. The governing body of the District shall have at least one representative of each area comprising such improvement area, shall represent equally such areas and shall have no more representatives of arts and cultural organizations than representatives of the areas comprising such improvement area.

If the District is not organized in accordance with this Section, Developer shall participate in formation of the District, shall reasonably cooperate with the District in establishing a fair and equitable formula for any financial contribution and voting and shall participate in the District to a formula deemed fair and equitable by the Developer.

If the District is not formed within five years after issuance of a Certificate of Completion, Developer's obligations under this Section shall terminate.

14.10. Pedestrian Access During Construction

Developer shall use reasonable efforts to maintain pedestrian access through the K Mall during construction of the Improvements.

* * *

21.4. Plans and Data

If this DDA is terminated, for any reason, prior to the completion of the Improvements, Developer shall deliver to Agency any and all data acquired for development of the Site and the portions of the Plans related to the construction of the Garage and other public improvements on the Site. Developer shall thereafter quitclaim all of its rights, title and interest in the Plans to Agency.

* * *

APPENDIX H

Owner Participation Agreement

Source: Dana W. Phillips, General Counsel, Sacramento, California Housing and Redevelopment Agency

The OPA is between the Redevelopment Agency of the City of Sacramento and 8th and J Street Venture (a California Limited Partnership). Excerpted materials include:

1. Purpose of the OPA

In furtherance of the objective of the Community Redevelopment Law, the Agency has undertaken a program for the clearance and reconstruction or rehabilitation of blighted areas in the City of Sacramento including a redevelopment project in the Project Area.

The primary purpose of this OPA is to redevelop the Site at its highest and best use as a mixed use urban development, as more completely described in this OPA.

The Agency has identified the half-block South of J Street and bounded by J, Eighth and Ninth streets and the alley as one which is vital to the redevelopment of the Project Area, and Agency is undertaking the redevelopment of the entire half-block. Developer owns the Site which is at the western end of the half-block, and in response to Agency's redevelopment activities in the half-block, Developer has proposed to develop the Project on the Site.

The Agency represents that the development of the Site and the completion of the Project, under this OPA, and the fulfillment generally of this OPA, are (1) in the vital and best interests of the City and the health, safety, morals and welfare of its residents, (2) for the purpose of community improvement and welfare, (3) for the benefit of Project Area and in accordance with the Agency's Redevelopment Plan and (4) consistent with the Redevelopment Plan.

* * *

2. Waiver of Eminent Domain

In consideration of the performance by Developer of its obligations under this OPA, the Agency waives its authority under Health and Safety Code Section 33391 to acquire the Site by eminent domain for so long as Developer or a transferee permitted under this OPA is the sole and original owner of the Site.

* * *

3.2. Relocation

Developer shall pay all costs of relocation of existing businesses (including goodwill) and residential tenants required by law to be paid by Developer or the Agency as a result of this Project.

* * *

3.4. Agency Approval of Plans

The Agency shall have the right, but not the obligation, to review the Plans to assure their conformity with the Preliminary Plans, the Scope of Development and the provisions of this OPA, and based upon such review the Agency shall have the right to approve or reject the Plans. Agency's right of review shall specifically include the right to review architectural and landscaping designs. If the Agency rejects the Plans, Developer shall obtain no rights to develop the Site under this OPA and take no action on the Site until such time as Developer has modified the Plans and received the Agency's approval of the Plans as modified.

The Plans may be approved by the Agency's Executive Director, without further review by the Agency's governing board, if (a) the Plans conform in all material respects to the Preliminary Plans, (b) no changes which require Agency approval under this OPA have been made to the Preliminary Plans or to Plans previously approved by the Agency, (c) Design Review Board has approved the Plans, and (d) the City is prepared to issue a building permit based upon the Plans.

* * *

5.12. Agency Access to the Site

Developer shall permit Agency representatives access, without charge, to the entire Site at any time and for any purpose which Agency reasonably considers necessary to carry out its obligations and protect its interests under the OPA. Purposes for Agency entry may include, without limitation, inspection of all work being performed in connection with the construction of the Improvements.

* * *

5.13. Agency Sign

If Developer places a sign on the Site during construction stating the names of the Project participants, it shall also name "Sacramento Housing and Redevelopment Agency" as a participant in the Project. The Agency name on the sign shall be in letters not less than size of letters used to name the lenders for the Project.

* * *

5.15. Minority/Women's Business Enterprises Requirements

The provisions of this DDA related to the Site are subject to Agency's minority-owned and women-owned business enterprises ("MBE/WBE") requirements.

5.15.1. In Solicitations

In all services solicitation (whether direct or by bid, Request for Proposal or Request for Qualification), Developer shall cause its contractor to take all reasonable steps necessary to encourage the participation of minority-owned and female-owned businesses. Such steps may include, but are not limited to:

5.15.1.1. Registry

Obtaining and utilizing the Minority and Women's Business Enterprises Registry from the Agency MBE/WBE Coordinator.

1) **Advertising**

Advertising the invitation to bid or to submit proposals in the "El Hispano" and the "Sacramento Observer" as well as a newspaper of general circulation.

2) **Direct Contacts**

Reviewing the telephone directory or professional organization membership lists, or making direct contact with minority-owned or female-owned businesses for specialized trades and services and inviting such firms to bid.

5.15.2. Documentation

Developer shall maintain or cause to be maintained such documentation of efforts of outreach to minority or female owned businesses as may be reasonably required by Agency.

5.15.3. Goal

The MBE/WBE utilization goal for this Project is twenty percent of contract dollars for Minority Business Enterprise and five percent of contract dollars for Women's Business Enterprise.

5.15.4. Inclusion in Contracts

The requirements and contract provisions for the Minority and Women's Business Enterprises must be included in all contracts. Contracts for purchases of goods and services over $10,000 must be coordinated with the Agency's MBE/WBE Coordinator.

* * *

5.16. Local Hire

Developer shall use its best efforts to hire, or cause to be hired, for no less than fifty percent (50%) of the cost of the work relating to direct labor of the Project, local contractors and subcontractors with permanent places of business within the County of Sacramento. To the extent that labor for any portion of the Project is not available within the county, such portion shall not be included in determining the said percentage. Agency shall have the right to approve the computations as described in the foregoing sentence. If Agency determines that Developer has failed to hire, or cause hiring of local contractors and subcontractors as provided in this Section, Developer shall give written justification for such failure including a detailed listing of all efforts made to effect such compliance.

* * *

6.1. Uses

Developer shall develop and operate the Site primarily as office, retail and parking and to other uses necessary and incidental to such uses, all as specified in this OPA, the Agreement containing covenants and the Plans approved by the Agency under this OPA, and shall continue to maintain and use the Site in accordance with said uses.

* * *

6.3. Use Prohibitions

Developer shall not permit any use of the Project for the sale or display of materials containing pornography, nudity, graphic violence or drug paraphernalia. Developer shall not permit any use of the Project as a massage parlor, adult bookstore or second-hand store or to conduct any activity in violation of any law, ordinance, regulation or restriction.

* * *

6.6. Effect and Duration of Covenants

The covenants are contained in the Agreement Containing Covenants, which subjects and burdens the Site with the covenants regarding use of the Site and regarding nondiscrimination, as covenants running with the land. It is intended and agreed that the agreements and covenants provided in this OPA and the Agreement Containing Covenants shall be covenants running with the land and equitable servitudes thereon and that they shall, in any event, and without regard to technical classifications or designation, be binding, to the fullest extent permitted by law and equity, for the benefit and in favor of, and enforceable by, the Agency, the Agency's successors and assigns, any other governmental entity acting within its authority and any successor in interest to all or any part of the Site against the Developer, its successors and assigns and every successor in interest to all or any part of the Site, and any party in possession or occupancy of the Site and any subcontracting party or parties or other transferees under this OPA.

* * *

9. Prohibitions Against Assignment and Transfer

Except as a result of a death of the holder of an interest in Developer, assignment and transfer of Developer's interests under this Agreement without Agency's reasonable, written approval are prohibited, as provided in this Section 9, for the following reasons. The development of the Site is important to the general welfare of the community. Substantial public aids have been made available by law and by the federal and local governments to make development of the Site possible. Prior to issuance of a Certificate of Completion, a transfer of a substantial part of the stock in the Developer, if it is a corporation, or a change in the ownership or identity of its member partners, if it is a partnership, or any other act or transaction involving or resulting in a significant change in the ownership regarding the identity of the parties in control of the Developer or the degree of their control, is for practical purposes a transfer or disposition of the Site which may affect the ability of Developer to carry out its obligations under this OPA.

For the foregoing reasons, the qualifications and identity of the Developer, and its stockholders or member partners, are of particular concern to the community and Agency. Developer understands and acknowledges that it is because of qualifications and identity and in reliance on Developer's promise to perform its obligations under this OPA that Agency is entering into this OPA.

For the foregoing reasons, Developer represents and agrees that its promise to develop the Site, and its other undertakings pursuant to the OPA, are not for speculation in land holding.

* * *

11.3. Child Care

Developer shall pay to the Agency a fee ("Child Care Fee") in the amount of Seventy-Five Thousand Dollars ($75,000) to be used to provide child care within the Project Area or as would reasonably benefit the Project Area. The Child Care Fee shall be due and payable not later than the time of payment of fees for the initial building permits. If, prior to payment of such fee, Agency rescinds its policy requiring negotiations regarding child care (Agency Resolution No. 87-1032), the child care fee shall under this Section 11.3. not be required.

* * *

11.4. City Requirements

The Agency is a legal entity separate and distinct from the City. Developer is not by this OPA relieved of any ordinances or fees of the City of Sacramento, except to the extent superseded by the Agency in exercise of its authority.

In lieu of the City's Housing Trust Fund fee and subject to the approval of the City, the Developer shall pay an amount equal to ninety-seven cents per square foot for the gross square footage of the Improvements direct to the Agency which shall be expended by the Agency for uses in accordance with the purposes of City's Housing Trust Fund Ordinance.

12.5. Agency's Option to Pay Debt or Purchase Site

If, after Developer's default under the OPA relating to construction of the Improvements and after sixty (60) days prior written notice from the Agency to Developer and Lender, either Lender fails to exercise its option to construct the Improvements or Lender undertakes, but does not diligently prosecute, construction of the Improvements to completion after notice from Agency that Lender is not diligently prosecuting construction of the Improvements, Agency shall have the option to take one of the following actions. This option shall be exercisable by Agency upon at least thirty (30) days prior written notice to Lender anytime within nine (9) months from (a) Lender's failure to exercise its option to construct the Improvements or (b) the date of notice from Agency to Lender regarding the Lender's failure to diligently prosecute construction of the Improvements to completion provided Lender has failed to cure such default within thirty (30) days of such notice.

* * *

13.7. Agency Completion of Construction

Notwithstanding any other provision of this OPA and subject to the Lender's security in the Site, if the Developer fails, after commencing construction of the Improvements fails to diligently prosecute the construction of the work in accordance with the Schedule of Performances and substantially complete such construction within ninety (90) days following the date for substantial completion, the Agency may elect, upon ninety (90) days written notice to the Developer and construction lender, and with or without legal process, to take possession of the Site, remove the Developer and all agents, employees and contractors of the Developer from the Site, complete the work of construction and market and sell or lease the Site with the Improvements. Nevertheless, Agency has no obligation to take possession of the Site or to complete the construction of the Improvements. If, prior to expiration of the ninety (90) days following Agency's notice, Lender notifies Agency in writing of its intent to cure Developer default, Lender shall have sixty (60) days following such notice in which to commence cure of Developer's default, and Agency shall have no further rights under this section so long as Lender diligently prosecutes such cure.

* * *

13.7.2. If Agency elects to complete construction and sell the Site under this Section 13.7, Agency shall disburse the proceeds of such sale (a) first, to repay the loans secured by the Site, (b) second, to reimburse Agency for the actual costs to Agency incurred by Agency in conjunction with such sale, including reasonable staff costs and related overhead, and for any other damages to which Agency may be entitled under this OPA, and (c) third, to pay the balance to Developer.

Introduction to Appendices I and J

Appendices I and J are two development agreements. Agreements are consensual in nature. Neither the local government nor the developer can be compelled to enter into an agreement, much less a particular form of agreement. As a result, the agreement has to contain terms acceptable to both sides. Pursuant to the enabling legislation, the parties enjoy few limitations as to the range of issues to be negotiated. Similar to the flexibility of a planned development zoning ordinance, an agreement can be customized to meet the particular needs of the parties. Generally, the thrust of a development agreement is to secure the developer's previously or concurrently obtained land use approvals.

The first agreement was used for the first tier approval of a large scale ski resort project. It operates in conjunction with an earlier initiative which approved a general plan amendment and rezoning, launching the proposed development. The development agreement allows for bank and transfers of development units with the project, special contributions for recreational facility of general public benefit, public access to the golf course amenities, strategies to generate local use and sales tax revenue as part of project development and codifies various mitigation strategies. The development's small lot tentative maps will be filed at a later time.

The second agreement is for a mixed use project. Similar in content when compared to the first agreement, it provides a strong statement of vesting for the developer. The developer remains subject to later enactment of regional traffic impact fees, an issue of particular concern to the County. The County also negotiated for a local-hire provision.

The attached agreement forms are included as illustrations only. No suggestion is made as to the suitability of these agreements in any particular situation.

APPENDIX I

Development Agreement—Public

Source: William W. Abbott,
Abbott & Kindermann LLP

MITIGATION/DEVELOPMENT AGREEMENT
BY AND BETWEEN
THE COUNTY OF ___________ AND
____
RELATIVE TO THE DEVELOPMENT KNOWN AS
____

THIS DEVELOPMENT AGREEMENT is made and entered into this _______ day of _______, 2007, by and between the COUNTY OF __________, a political subdivision of the State of California ("County"), and _________________, a limited liability company ("Developer"), pursuant to the authority of Article 2.5, Chapter 4, Division 1, Title 7 (Government Code section 65864 et seq.) relating to Development Agreements.

RECITALS

1. In order to strengthen the public land use planning process, to encourage private participation in the process, to reduce the economic risk of development and to reduce the waste of resources, the Legislature adopted the Development Agreement Statutes (Government Code section 65864 et seq.).
2. The Development Agreement Law permits cities and counties to contract with private interests for their mutual benefit in a manner not otherwise available to the contracting parties. With respect to the ______________ Project, this Agreement provides an additional vehicle by which the County and ________________________ can assure the public that CEQA mitigation measures identified as part of the programmatic EIR will be incorporated into, and made part of any subsequent development. Such agreements, as authorized by the Development Agreement Law, can also assure property developers they may proceed with projects assured that approvals granted by public agencies will not change during the period of development of their projects. It is the desire of the parties to implement the voter-approved _______________ initiative by creating a legal framework by which the Project proceeds while at the same time, recognizing the County's duty to protect the health, safety and welfare of the ________ County residents. It is also the desire of the parties to create an additional mechanism by which the Board of Supervisors (i) effectively regulate potential environmental impacts associated with the ____________ project, (ii) establish the parameters for the Annual Monitoring and Compliance Reports and (iii) create a framework for the establishment of site specific development standards.
3. The Development Agreement relates to the development known as ____________, a mixed use development located in the western ___________ County. The parties have, in good faith, negotiated the terms hereinafter set forth which carry out the legislative purpose set forth above and will assure the parties to this Agreement of mutually desirable development of the subject property.
4. The completion of the Project will provide a high quality, four-season mountain resort, serving both local residents and tourists, generating property tax, sales tax and transient occupying tax revenue to the County.
5. Developer has a legal interest in that certain real property, more particularly described on **Exhibit "B"** hereto, located in the County of _________, and desires to create thereon a commercial development allowing for mixed uses.
6. The __________ County voters, in 2000, enacted the __________ Initiative, with over 62% of all votes cast in

favor of the measure. The stated purpose of the Initiative was as follows:

A. The People of ________ County find that they can no longer rely primarily on prison facilities and declining timber industry to sustain the County's economy. The people of ________ County find there is limited opportunity for private economic development.

B. The People of ________ County desire to diversify the local economy by attracting major investment for a new four-season mountain resort on ___________. Such a facility would provide recreational opportunities throughout the year, including skiing and golf.

C. The People of ________ County desire to increase the range of recreational opportunities available to County residents, including golf, skiing, fishing, bicycling, hiking, and horseback riding.

D. The People of _________ County find that a four-season mountain resort will provide new full-time and part-time jobs. These job opportunities will generate additional private sector investment and employment throughout the County, enhance existing small businesses and encourage new small businesses.

E. The People of _______ County find that a new four-season mountain resort will help revitalize the County's economy and generate new tax revenues for the County without imposing any new taxes or fees on current _______ County residents.

F. The People of __________ County find with the decline of the timber industry, that there has been limited opportunity for private economic development. In recent years, economic growth has been focused on prison facilities. It is the desire of the people to diversify the local economy by attracting major investment for a four-season mountain resort in the ______________ area. Such a facility would attract tourist activity throughout the year, including skiing, golf, and other recreation uses. A four-season mountain resort will provide direct job benefits in the form of major construction activities as well as ongoing employment to operate the facilities once constructed. These primary employment opportunities will in turn generate additional private sector investment and employment throughout the County.

G. The purpose of this initiative is to make changes to the County General Plan and Zoning Ordinance to allow a four-season mountain resort in the vicinity of _________________. These changes will create the opportunity for golf, skiing, fishing, trails and other resort type recreation facilities, shops, lodges, condominiums, single-family and other residential uses, and commercial facilities such as conference facilities and restaurants, centered around a village and neighborhoods. The four-season mountain resort will serve local day users, overnight visitors and permanent residents.

7. County, in furtherance of the _______________ Initiative, and in response to Developer's applications, after public hearings and extensive environmental analysis, took the following actions:

a. By Resolution No.________, certifying an EIR and approving a Mitigation Monitoring Program,

b. By Resolution No. _______, approving a Large Lot Parcel Map.

8. By Ordinance No._________, the Board of Supervisors authorized the Chairman of the Board to sign this Development Agreement on behalf of the County.

9. Development of the subject property pursuant to the terms and conditions of the various entitlements, the General Plan and the Environmental Impact Report will provide for orderly growth and development consistent with the County's General Plan and other development policies and programs.

10. On ________, 2007, the County Planning Commission, designated by County as the Planning Agency for purposes of Development Agreement review pursuant to Government Code section 65867, considered this Agreement.

11. County and Developer have taken all actions mandated by and fulfilled all requirements set forth in the County Code governing requirements for Development Agreements.

12. Having duly considered this Agreement and having held the noticed public hearings, County finds and declares that the provisions of this Development Agreement are consistent with the maps and text of the County's General Plan.

NOW, THEREFORE, the parties hereto agree as follows:

ARTICLE 1
GENERAL PROVISIONS

Section 1.1. The Project. The Project is a four-season, mountain resort, mixed use development located on the Subject Property, consisting of approximately 7,000± acres, allowing for a maximum of 3259 equivalent dwelling units ("EDUs"), 233,800 square feet of general commercial uses, 51,500 square feet of public uses, 100,000 square feet of mountain resort recreation uses, and 222,600 square feet of common area support uses, as further described in Exhibit "A", incorporated herein by this reference.

Section 1.2. Subject Property. The Project site is more specifically described in Exhibit "B" which is incorporated herein and made part of this Agreement.

Section 1.3. Definitions. As used in the Agreement, the following terms, phrases and words shall have the meanings and be interpreted as set forth in this Section.

(a) **Adopting Ordinance** means Ordinance Number __________ entitled: "Mitigation/Development Agreement By and Between the County of _________ and ______________, relative to the Development Known as _____________" dated , and effective ___________, which approves this Mitigation/Development Agreement as required by Government Code section 65867.5.

(b) **Assumption Agreement** means an agreement substantially conforming to the model assumption agreement described in **Exhibit "C,"** or other agreement in a form approved by the County Counsel, executed by a Landowner with the Developer, expressly assuming various obligations relating to the development of the Project, or portion thereof.

(c) **CEQA** means the California Environmental Quality Act section 21000 et seq., of the Public Resources Code of the State of California.

(d) **Certificate of Occupancy** means either a certificate issued after inspections by the County authorizing a person or persons in possession of property to dwell or otherwise use a specified building or dwelling unit, or the final inspection if a formal certificate is not issued.

(e) **Collective Standards** means this Development Agreement, the Planning Documents and the Existing Land Use Regulations.

(f) **County** means the County of ____________, as administered by the Board of Supervisors, or its designee.

(g) **Developer** means __________________________, a limited liability company, or its successor in interest.

(h) **Director** means the Director of the Community Development Department for the County of ___________.

(i) **Effective Date** means the effective date of the Adopting Ordinance.

(j) **Existing Land Use Regulations** mean the ordinances, resolutions and regulations adopted by the County in effect on the Effective Date including the adopting ordinances that govern the permitted uses of land, the density and intensity of use, the timing of development, the design, improvement, and construction standards and specifications applicable to the development of the Subject Property, including, but not limited to, the General Plan, the zoning ordinance and all other ordinances, codes, rules and regulations of the County establishing subdivision standards, park regulations, building standards and road and infrastructure improvement standards. Development impact fees are excluded from "Existing Land Use Regulations" as used herein.

(k) **Initiative** means the _____________ Initiative, as approved by the voters in November, 2000.

(l) **General Plan** means the General Plan of the County.

(m) **Mitigation Measures** means those mitigation measures approved by the Board of Supervisors attached hereto as Exhibit "D", and the Mitigation Monitoring Program adopted in conjunction therewith; as well as mitigation measures which may be adopted in the future in conjunction with future Project entitlements.

(n) **Landowner** is a party who has acquired any portion of the Subject Property from the Developer who, unless otherwise released as provided in this Agreement, shall be subject to the applicable provisions of this Agreement.

(o) **Planning Documents** mean, and shall be limited to, the Initiative, Project Compliance Reports, Development Manuals, the Mitigation Measures and the Large Lot Parcel Map and conditions of approval referenced in Recital 7.

(p) **Project** means the anticipated development of the Subject Property as specified in Section 1.1 and as provided for in the provisions of this Agreement and all other incorporated exhibits.

(q) **Subject Property** means the property described in Section 1.2, or the remaining portions thereof after releases from the provisions of this Agreement have been executed as authorized by this Agreement.

Section 1.4. Exhibits. Exhibits to this Agreement are as follows:

Exhibit "A" Project Description
Exhibit "B" Subject Property

Exhibit "C"	Assumption Agreement
Exhibit "D"	Mitigation Measures
Exhibit "E"	Building, Road and Snow Storage Standards (E1-E3)
Exhibit "F"	District Assignment and Assumption Agreement
Exhibit "G"	Notice of Termination

Section 1.5. Incorporation of Recitals. Recitals 1 through 12 are incorporated herein, including all exhibits referred to in said Recitals. In the event of inconsistency between the Recitals and the provisions of Articles 1 through 6, the provisions of Articles 1 through 6 shall prevail.

Section 1.6. Parties to Agreement. The parties to this Agreement are:

(a) **The County.** The County of ___________ is a political subdivision of the State of California exercising general governmental functions and power. The principal office of the County is located at ___________.

(b) **Developer.** _________________, is a private enterprise which has a legal interest in the Subject Property. Developer's principal office for the purpose of this Agreement is ___________.

(c) **Landowner.** From time to time, as provided in this Agreement, Developer may sell or otherwise lawfully dispose of a portion of the Subject Property to a Landowner who, unless otherwise released, shall be subject to the applicable provisions of this Agreement related to such portion of the Subject Property.

Section 1.7. Project is a Private Undertaking. It is agreed among the parties that the Project is a private development and that County has no interest therein except as authorized in the exercise of its governmental functions. Nothing in this Agreement shall preclude the Developer from forming any form of private investment entity for the purpose of completing any portion of the Project.

Section 1.8. Term of Agreement. This Agreement shall commence upon the effective date of the Adopting Ordinance approving this Agreement, and shall continue in force for twenty (20) years from the Effective Date unless extended or terminated as provided herein. Following the expiration of the term or extension thereof, or if sooner terminated, this Agreement shall have no force and effect, subject however, to post-termination obligations of Developer or Landowner. The term of the Development Agreement shall be automatically extended in the event of a legal challenge to the Agreement or the Planning Documents until such time as there is a final adjudication of the legal challenge. The Term of any entitlement granted by the County in implementation of the Initiative shall be automatically extended by period of time during which there is a legal challenge to this Agreement or the entitlement, until such time as there is a final adjudication of the legal challenge.

Section 1.9. Extension for Outside Delay. In the event of delay due to litigation, moratorium or other restriction whether direct or indirect and whether implemented by the County or another party, that delays Developer's ability to develop or use the Subject Property, or that interferes with the County's ability to issue building permits or other approvals required for such development, construction or use, the Expiration Date shall be extended by the amount of time of such delay.

Section 1.10. Priority of Enactment. In the event of conflict between various land use documents referenced in this Agreement, the parties agree that the following sequence of approvals establishes the relative priority of the approvals, each approval superior to the approvals listed thereafter: (1) the Initiative; (2) Mitigation Measures; (3) the Development Agreement; (4) the large lot parcel map; and (5) the Existing Land Use Regulations.

Section 1.11. Vested Rights of Developer. During the term of this Agreement, unless sooner terminated in accordance with the terms hereof, in developing the Subject Property consistent with the Project described herein, Developer is assured, and County agrees, that the development rights, obligations, terms and conditions specified in the Collective Standards are fully vested in the Developer and may not be changed or modified by the County except as may be expressly permitted by, and in accordance with, the terms and conditions of this Agreement, or as expressly consented thereto by the Developer to the extent such proposed change or modification is applicable thereto. Subsequent approvals and permits granted by the County shall also be fully vested as provided in this section.

ARTICLE 2
PROJECT DEVELOPMENT

Section 2.1. Vested Right to Develop. Developer shall have the vested right to develop a maximum of 3259 EDUS, 333,800 square feet of commercial uses, mountain resort recreation facilities and supporting facilities in accordance with Section 1.11 of this Agreement, on the Subject Property.

Section 2.2. Permitted Uses, Development Standards and Allocation of Development.

(a)

Permitted Uses:	As specified in the Collective Standards
Maximum Density of Uses:	As specified in the Collective Standards
Maximum Intensity of Use:	As specified in the Collective Standards
Impact Fees:	As required by the Mitigation Measures and as described herein
Land Dedication and Reservation:	As specified by the Existing Land Use Regulations
Building Heights:	Exhibit E1
Building Setbacks:	Exhibit E1
Road Standards:	Exhibit E2
Snow Storage Standards:	Exhibit E3

(b) The parties hereto intend that Collective Standards shall serve as the definitive and controlling document for all subsequent actions, discretionary or ministerial, relating to the development and occupancy of the Project.

(c) Developer shall prepare and submit for County an allocation and accounting of the maximum residential and non-residential uses within the Project for each project phase. This accounting shall consist of such forms, tables and maps as may be approved by the Director. The distribution of the allocation shall be the sole responsibility of the Developer until such time as the Developer submits the final accounting. It is anticipated that the Developer will amend the accounting from time to time as the Project builds out. Total Project development shall not exceed the amount described in Section 1.1 herein.

(d) The allocation and any amendment thereto, shall be filed with the Director, according to a schedule approved by The Director.

(e) The purpose of the accounting is to apprise the County of the overall development pattern and to assure that the maximum development set forth in Section 1.1 herein is not exceeded.

(f) The maximum allowable density and intensity shall be noted on any recorded map creating developable lots for purposes of sale, lease or financing without the intent to further resubdivide. The Developer retains the ability to fully utilize, within the Project boundaries, unallocated development density and intensity. _____________ County Code section 16.08.212 is waived.

Section 2.3. Subsequent Entitlements, Approvals and Permits.

(a) Successful implementation of the Project will require the Developer to obtain additional approvals and permits from the County and from other agencies. The County shall comply with CEQA in the administration of subsequent entitlements, approvals, and permits including compliance with mitigation measures as mandated by CEQA. In acting upon subsequent entitlements, approvals, and permits, the County's exercise of discretion and permit authority shall conform with the Collective Standards.

(b) In the course of implementing the Project, the Developer will file subsequent applications for discretionary approvals such as tentative subdivision maps. The County will process these applications consistent with applicable law, including the California Environmental Quality Act and the Subdivision Map Act. In the course of taking action on these applications, the County will exercise discretion in adopting mitigation measures and condition of approval. The exercise of this discretion is not prohibited by the Agreement, but the exercise of that discretion must be consistent with this Agreement.

(c) In complying with California Environmental Quality Act, the County shall rely on the program environmental impact report (EIR) certified herewith to the extent allowed by CEQA. Nothing in this Agreement shall preclude the evaluation of impacts or consideration of mitigation measures or alternatives as required by the California Environmental Quality Act.

Section 2.4. Recreational Facilities.

(a) For purposes of this section, "Developer" shall include the Foundation referenced in Section 2.30.

(b) Developer shall contribute two hundred thousand dollars ($200,000) (or in kind services) to the County and _________ Community Services District ("_________ CSD") for the purpose of upgrading and rehabilitating parks in the __________ Creek and ___________ communities at the end of Phase I, which phase is defined in Section 2.22 of this Agreement. The County and the __________ CSD shall be responsible for electing and planning all improvements.

Section 2.5. Trail Systems.

(a) Developer shall file with the County, no later then the recording of the first Residential Subdivision Map, a Trail Master Plan.

(b) Developer shall convey a license to use the trail system to a qualified non-profit or public entity, as selected by Developer, on such terms and conditions as may be mutually agreed upon.

Section 2.6. Golf/Ski/Public Access.

(a) Public play will be allowed on at least one golf course.

(b) _________ County residents will be afforded, on the same rates and terms, a local rate for daily golf, daily ski passes, and season ski passes which will be not more than the lowest advertised rate charged for such passes, as offered to the general public by the ski and golf operator. This section shall not apply to (i) ticket and pass offers coupled with other amenities such as lodging promotions or (ii) ticket and passes marketed through independent third party vendors.

(c) Public access to __________ Reservoir at the existing boat launch will be allowed per Mitigation Measures 17.1a and 17.1b.

Section 2.7. Boat Launch. In the event that the County approves a new public boat launch facility at ____________ Reservoir in conformance with the _________ Community Plan, Developer shall contribute two hundred sixty five thousand dollars ($265,000) toward construction costs. At its sole discretion, the County may elect to redirect some or all of the money paid pursuant to this Section if other funds become available for construction of the boat launch.

Section 2.8. Utility/Access Easements. Developer will include, in any final map recorded in furtherance of the Large Lot Parcel Map, easements for ingress, egress and utilities, to the reasonable satisfaction of the County Public Works Director. This requirement shall include the designation of easements for both primary and secondary access to/from the Project. The parties shall cooperate in relocating the easements referenced herein as necessary to implement the Project.

Section 2.9. Property Line Survey. County and Developer agree to cooperate with each other to cause the common boundary of the Project boundary with ______ Lake to be surveyed. Developer to pay cost of survey.

Section 2.10. Secondary Access Requirements

(a) As an Existing Land Use Regulation, Developer shall comply with Chapter 9.16 of the _______ County Code. For purposes of Section 9.16.100, the reference to "publicly maintained road" shall also include a road maintained by Developer in furtherance of the Project, or a road maintained by an owners association, wherein the association has the right to impose a lien for the purpose of collecting assessments, including the right to foreclose upon the lien.

(b) Permanent, year-round secondary access shall be installed prior to development of any residential units south of ___________.

Section 2.11. Use Tax Direct Payment Permit. Developer agrees to obtain a "Use Tax Direct Payment Permit" from the State Board of Equalization ("BOE"). This will allow Developer to defer payment of use taxes at the time of any transaction, and instead self-accrue use taxes and make the payment directly to the BOE, assuring 100 percent allocation of the one percent share of use taxes to the County. (Rev. & Tax. Code, § 7051.3.) Developer agrees to use good faith efforts to receive all subsequent developers and/or general contractors who meet the Five Hundred Thousand and No/100 Dollar ($500,000.00) expenditure criteria of section 7051.3 to obtain separate "Use Tax Direct Payment Permits" for associated activities at the Project.

Section 2.12. Specific and Unique Job-Site. Developer and County agree to work together to have ____________ identified and designated by the BOE as a specific and unique "job-site" in the unincorporated area of the County. All contractors and builders on ____________ shall use the designated job-site code for all sales taxable purchases, transactions, and deliveries.

Section 2.13. Request for Zip Code. Developer and County agree to work together to establish a new zip code for the community of ____________, by submitting a request to the U.S. Postal Service. In the event such a request is denied, Developer and County agree to request realignment of the existing ____________ area zip code to include only __________ County territory, excluding those areas of _______ County that are presently included in the _____ zip code.

Section 2.14. Annual Mitigation Report ("AMR"). No later than thirty days prior to the one year anniversary of the Effective Date, and every anniversary thereafter, Developer shall file with the Community Development Department an Annual Mitigation Report ("AMR"). The AMR may be reviewed in conjunction with the annual review of the Development Agreement as provided for in Section 4.2. The report shall provide a statement of compliance with all applicable mitigation measures, conditions of approval, and provisions of this Agreement. The AMR is a public record, and shall be available to any interested member of the public, in accordance with the Public Records Act. The AMR is not required as to any portion of the Project for which this Agreement is terminated.

Section 2.15. Cost Recovery – Monitoring. No later than the annual review in Section 4.2; the County shall establish its estimated reasonable annual monitoring costs "Annual Costs" for the following twelve month period. The estimate shall include a general breakdown of anticipated costs by staff and consultants. In the event of dispute, the parties shall meet informally to resolve any disagreement over estimated costs. Once approved by the County, the Developer will fund the estimate in four quarterly deposits. At the end of the year, the County will provide the Developer with an accounting of all charges and will credit forward any unexpended funds. In the event of a shortfall, the Developer shall provide additional funds as necessary to eliminate the shortfall. The shortfall payment shall be made within thirty days of delivery of an itemized list of payments from the prior accounting period(s).

Section 2.16. Project Compliance Report ("PCR").

(a) In conjunction with the application for any County permit or approval, the Developer shall file a PCR with the Community Development Department. The PCR may address an individual permit/approval, or a group or series of permits/approvals by type or geographic area. With respect to any permits/ approvals subject of the PCR, the PCR shall state the following:
 1) Applicable Mitigation Measures approved as part of any applicable prior CEQA/NEPA document, including the Program EIR certified herewith.
 2) Applicable Conditions of Approval imposed as part of prior approvals, including this Agreement.
 3) Compliance with any applicable Development Manual.

(b) A PCR shall be required for all discretionary approvals such as tentative subdivision maps, as well as the following approvals: grading plans, improvement plans for utilities or roadways and building permits. A PCR shall not be required for actions taken pursuant to an approval granted by another agency.

(c) No permit/approval for which a PCR has been prepared shall be issued by any County agency unless the Community Development Department determines that the permit/approval is in compliance with the Collective Standards including, without limitation, all applicable mitigation measures and conditions of approval.

(d) A PCR may be combined with a Development Manual (Section 2.17).

(e) The PCR is a public record, and shall be available to any interested member of the public, in accordance with the Public Records Act.

Section 2.17. Development Manual. A Development Manual shall be prepared by the Developer and filed with the Community Development Department for the following project phases and elements:

(a) Required for all commercial, residential, public and maintenance facility phases:

(b) Except as may be waived by the Director, the content shall include the following:
 1) Lot sizes
 2) Allowable lot coverage
 3) Building heights and setbacks or building envelopes
 4) Provision of public services and infrastructure
 5) Road standards
 6) Pedestrian and bicycle paths
 7) Preliminary Grading Plans
 8) Preliminary Drainage Plans
 9) Landscaping
 10) Proposed Uses.
 11) Architectural Standards

(c) Separate Development Manuals may be prepared for individual project areas or types of development. Unless waived by the Director, a preliminary Development Manual shall be submitted with an application for a tentative subdivision map for a development area or Project Phase.

(d) Upon filing of a final Development Manual, staff will review the manual for compliance with the Collective Standards including, without limitation, all applicable mitigation measures and conditions of approval. The County shall have thirty (30) days within which to reject the manual; the basis for rejection to be set forth in writing. The parties shall meet informally to resolve any disputes. The final Development Manual will be submitted concurrently with the final subdivision map (if any) or no later than application for a building permit, if no map is required.

(e) No permit or approval to construct commercial, residential, public facilities or maintenance facilities shall be issued by the County unless it is in compliance with the Development Manual.

(f) A Development Manual may be combined with a PCR (Section 2.16).

(g) The Development Manual is a public record, and shall be available to any interested member of the public, in accordance with the Public Records Act.

(h) The Director shall adopt procedures for amending an approved final Development Manual.

Section 2.18. No Conflicting Enactments. Subject to exceptions contained in Section 2.19 and 2.29, neither the County nor any agency of the County shall enact any ordinance, resolution or other measure that relates to the rate, timing or sequencing of the development or construction of the Subject Property on all or any part of the Subject Property that is in conflict with this Agreement, or any amendments thereto, or that reduces the development rights provided by this Agreement. Without limiting the foregoing general statement, and for all purposes pursuant to this Agreement generally, and this Section specifically, an ordinance, resolution or other measure shall be deemed to conflict with this Agreement if the ordinance, resolution or measure seeks to accomplish any one or more of the following results, either with specific reference to this Subject Property or as part of a general enactment that applies to this Subject Property would or could:

(a) Limit or reduce the density or intensity of the Project development granted by the Collective Standards or otherwise require any reduction in the height, number, size or square footage of lots, structures or buildings;

(b) Limit or control in any manner the timing or phasing of the construction/development of the Project allowed by the Collective Standards;

(c) Limit the location of buildings, structures, grading or other improvements relating to the development of the Project in a manner which is inconsistent with or more restrictive than the Collective Standards;

(d) Limit the processing of applications for or procurement of Subsequent Approvals;

(e) Clauses (a) through (d) above are intended as examples, and not as a comprehensive or exclusive list, of new development requirements that would or could conflict with the Collective Standards, and therefore with this Agreement.

Section 2.19. Changes to Existing Land Use Regulations. The County agrees not to amend the Mountain Resort designation or zoning for the term of this Agreement, except as provided in Section 2.29 herein. Only the following changes to the Existing Land Use Regulations shall apply to the development of the Subject Property:

(a) Land use regulations, ordinances, policies, programs, or resolutions adopted or undertaken by County in order to comply with state or federal laws, plans or regulations, provided that in the event that such state or federal laws, plans or regulations prevent or preclude compliance with one or more provisions of this Agreement, such provision or provisions shall be modified or suspended as may be necessary to comply with such regional, state or federal laws or regulations.

(b) County land use regulations, ordinances, policies, programs, or resolutions adopted after the Effective Date, that are not in conflict with the terms and conditions for development of the Subject Property established by this Agreement or otherwise applicable Existing Land Use Regulations and which do not impose additional burdens on such development.

(c) County land use regulations, ordinances, policies, programs, or resolutions adopted after the Effective Date, which are in conflict with the Existing Land Use Regulations, but the application of which to the development of the Subject Property has been consented to in writing by the Developer and/or the applicable Landowner either through this Agreement or by later separate document.

Section 2.20. Application, Processing and Inspection Fees. Application fees, processing fees and inspection fees that are revised during the term of this Agreement shall apply to the development pursuant to this Agreement, provided that such revised fees apply generally to similar private projects or works within County. Developer shall pay such fees for processing applications, tentative subdivision maps, final maps, building permits, encroachment permits or other ministerial permits, boundary line modifications, mergers, or abandonments as necessary to undertake the Project, and as are applicable to the specific application or permit at the time the application therefore is submitted.

Section 2.21. Development Impact Fees. Developer shall pay those development impact fees and charges of every kind and nature imposed or required by the County, or other authorized entities, applicable to development of the Project as are in effect at the time application therefore is submitted.

Section 2.22. Timing of Development. The parties acknowledge that the most efficient and economic development of the Subject Property depends upon numerous factors, such as market orientation and demand, interest rates, competition and similar factors, and that generally it will be most economically beneficial to the ultimate purchasers to have the rate of development determined by Developer. Accordingly, the timing, sequencing and phasing of the development is solely the responsibility of Developer, and the Board of Supervisors shall not impose, by ordinance, resolution or otherwise, any restrictions on such timing, sequencing or phasing of development within the Subject Property.

Notwithstanding the provisions of this paragraph, the following is a list of proposed project features which have been accepted by the County as integral parts of the Development Concept Plan and project description for the _______________ Resort Project. It is agreed that these features will be incorporated into the development of the project commensurate with the pace and level of overall development of the project – as determined by the County in its deliberation of each development phase. Where it is critical that a given element be developed as a feature of the first development phase it will be grouped under "First Development Phase" below.

A. First Development Phase. As part of the First Development Phase, subject to the timing provisions set forth below, Developer shall construct or install all of the following:

1) First phase of water system
2) First phase of sewage treatment system
3) Development of primary and secondary access to the project in accordance with the Collective Standards
4) First phase fire station/law enforcement facility as described in Mitigation Measures 18.1 and 18.2.
5) Construct fuel break along southern and western boundaries, provide fire evacuation program and refuge areas as specified in the Vegetation Management Plan.
6) Establish volunteer emergency assistance organization (timing: recordation of first small lot subdivision map)
7) Emergency First Aid station (timing: prior to issuance of building permits for residential construction)
8) Establish emergency medical response service (timing: prior to issuance of building permits for residential construction)
9) Not less than forty (40) acres of snow making equipment will be installed.
10) Ski facility including base facilities featuring not fewer than three (3) chairlifts (timing: construction of 400 units (excluding lodging and interval ownership units) or four (4) years after the first final small lot subdivision map for phase I is recorded, whichever is later).
11) An internal trails system to connect the main features of the phase (timing: each final map).
12) Onsite community parks (timing: each final map).
13) Public access to ___________ Reservoir at existing boat launch as specified in Mitigation Measure 17.1a and 17.1b.
14) Guest access to ____________ Reservoir from proposed Village Center (timing: prior to first commercial or residential building permit for Village Center).
15) First phase energy (propane) and communication infrastructure plan
16) Implement National Ski Area Association guidelines to reduce, reuse, and recycle waste (timing: prior to first commercial or residential building permit).
17) Eighteen (18) hole golf course not less than 6,500 yards long (timing: construction of 400 units (excluding lodging and interval ownership units) or four (4) years after the first final small lot subdivision map for phase I is recorded, whichever is later).
18) Permanent, year-round secondary access to be installed prior to development of any residential units south of _____________..

B.Later Development Phases. As part of Later Development Phases, subject to the timing provisions set forth below, Developer shall construct or install all of the following:

1) Remaining phases of water system
2) Remaining phases of sewage treatment system
3) Additional fire station/law enforcement facility capacity per Mitigation Measures 18.1 and 18.2
4) Medical clinic (timing: 75% buildout)
5) Maintain volunteer emergency assistance organization and emergency medical response service
6) A trail system that ties the project site to the _______ Trailhead at the __________Visitors Center (offsite right-of-way to be provided by others).
7) Completion of onsite trail system connecting all project features

8) Additional community parks per Mitigation Measures 17.3a
9) Continued public access to _____________ Reservoir at existing boat launch per Mitigation Measures 17.1a and 17.2a.

Section 2.23. Delivery of Services. Successful implementation and completion of the Project will require the coordination and cooperation of the County and the Developer. Implementation may require that a public entity acquire title to, and operate public infrastructure. This infrastructure will, in nearly all cases, be constructed by the Developer or its designee. The County and Developer shall meet and confer for the purpose of evaluating various alternatives for ownership and operation, but the decision as to the appropriate public entity shall be made by the County, as approved by LAFCo. Developer agrees to file a complete application with LAFCo to form a new district or Community Service District ("CSD") no later than twelve months following the Effective Date. In the event that the County requires and LAFCo approves the formation of a public entity other that a County Service Area, then the County may assign its obligations to cooperate in the financing, construction, and maintenance of public improvements to one or more special districts (independent or dependent), subject to all of the following conditions:

(a) LAFCo specifies, as a condition of organization or reorganization that the district shall succeed to the specified sections of this Agreement.
(b) The district agrees in writing to accept the obligations by execution of the District Assignment and Assumption Agreement, attached hereto as **Exhibit "F,"** and,
(c) A copy of the executed District Assignment and Assumption Agreement is mailed to the Developer, and,
(d) The Developer agrees to the assignment, such assignment not to be unreasonably withheld.
(e) The County enters into a supplemental development agreement or property transfer agreement (or both) with the district(s) which assures the County that the District will provide all assigned duties in a timely manner as may be required to implement the Initiative and this Agreement.

Section 2.24. Operating Memoranda. The provisions of this Agreement require a close degree of cooperation between County and Developer, and refinements and further development of the Project may demonstrate that clarifications with respect to the details of performance of County and Developer or minor revisions to the Project are appropriate. If and when, from time to time, during the term of this Agreement, County and Developer agree that such clarifications or minor modifications are necessary or appropriate, they may effectuate such clarifications through operating memoranda approved by the County and Developer, which, after execution, shall be attached and become part of this Agreement. No such operating memoranda shall constitute an amendment to this Agreement requiring public notice or hearing. The County Counsel shall be authorized to make the determination whether a requested clarification may be effectuated pursuant to this Section or whether the requested clarification is of such a character to require an amendment to this Agreement pursuant to Section 6.7. The Parties acknowledge that modifications which would be categorized as exempt under CEQA, or which, after an initial study made pursuant to CEQA, County determines do not require any further environmental review, or do not increase the density or intensity of use or the maximum height, bulk, size, or architectural style of proposed buildings within the Subject Property, may be effectuated through operating memoranda pursuant to this Section. The County Administrator may execute any operating memoranda hereunder without Board of Supervisors action.

Section 2.25. Public Financing Districts. Nothing in this Agreement precludes the establishment of one or more Community Facilities (Mello-Roos) Districts pursuant to California Government Code section 53311 et seq. and/or assessment districts or other financing mechanisms covering all or a portion of the Subject Property to construct or maintain the Improvements and/or to enable the issuance of tax-exempt bonds to finance the Improvements. County agrees to cooperate with Developer and consider in its reasonable discretion the use of all such financing mechanisms.

Section 2.26. Supplemental Development Agreements. Supplemental development agreements may be entered into between the parties governing all or a part of the Project.

Section 2.27. Covenant of Good Faith and Fair Dealing. Time is of the essence in achieving agreement on the form and substance of all documents, their execution, implementation actions including the grant of approvals and permits, formation of special districts, design, construction and operation of infrastructure, provision of services, and accomplishment of all further undertakings by all parties as contemplated by this Agreement. Implicit in this Agreement are all the covenants of good faith and fair dealing recognized under California law. All parties pledge and agree to use their best efforts to reach accord with respect to all details required to affect the intentions evidenced by this Agreement.

Section 2.28. Cooperation in Project Implementation. The County further agrees to cooperate in the implementation of the Initiative and the Project. This includes the timely review, permitting and inspection of all on-site and off-site buildings, improvements, and finalized construction and maintenance of public facilities.

Section 2.29. County Initiated Rezoning. Upon recordation of a final subdivision map creating developable lots intended for sale, lease or financing without further resubdivision, the County shall have the option to change or modify the zoning with the consent of the Developer, such consent shall not be unreasonably withheld. The purpose of this paragraph is intended to permit the County to apply zoning districts and regulations otherwise applied in the County outside of property designated MR in the County General Plan, which districts shall be similar to, and compatible with, the land use plan and development concept set forth by the Developer for the subdivided area. Unless otherwise agreed to in writing by the Developer the rezoning shall not take effect for 24 months from the date of adoption. The County and developer shall jointly record a notice of termination, as shown on Exhibit "G," which shall take effect upon the rezoning taking effect. For purposes of the Initiative, any rezoning pursuant to this section shall be considered to be modifications to the Initiative agreed to by the Developer.

Section 2.30. Foundation. Within twelve (12) months of the effective date of this Agreement, the Developer will form a 501(c)(3) foundation. The purpose of the foundation will be to fund projects of community benefit in the greater _________ Creek area. This will include, but not be limited to: recreational improvements, areas set aside for scientific production and study, open space, wildlife, and community amenities and services. Funding sources for the foundation will include a property transfer charge imposed at the time of property transfer, on property sales occurring within the Project boundary. The charge will apply to the resale of finished lots or homes but not to initial sales or bulk sales by the Developer.

ARTICLE 3
ENTITLEMENT AND PERMIT PROCESSING, INSPECTIONS

Section 3.1. County Approvals. Subject to Developer's compliance with applicable regulations, the County is bound to permit the uses on the Subject Property that are consistent with the Collective Standards. The County agrees to grant and implement the land use and building approvals, including, but not limited to, planned unit developments, variances, development plans, subdivision improvement plans and agreements, building plans and permits, specifications, landscape plans, grading plans and permits, parcel maps, tentative subdivision maps, final subdivision maps (including phased final subdivision maps), amendments to maps, lot line adjustments, re-subdivisions, use permits and certificates of occupancy (collectively "County Approvals"), reasonably necessary or desirable to accomplish the goals, objectives, policies, standards and plans described in the Collective Standards. County Approvals shall include any applications, permits and approvals required to complete the infrastructure and improvements necessary to develop the Subject Property (collectively, the "Improvements"), in accordance with the Collective Standards, including, without limitation, those related to: (i) clearing the Subject Property; (ii) grading the Subject Property; (iii) construction of roads, storm drainage facilities, sewer facilities and other utility facilities and connections; (iv) construction of water treatment and delivery facilities and storage tanks; and (v) construction of all commercial, industrial and residential structures and all structures and facilities accessory thereto, subject to the limitations set forth in the Collective Standards.

Section 3.2. Duty to Grant and Implement. County's obligation to grant and implement the County Approvals set forth above shall not infringe upon the County's right to withhold such County Approvals for failure to conform to the Collective Standards or if failure to withhold such approvals would place the residents of the subdivision or the immediate community, or both, in a condition dangerous to their health or safety, or both.

Section 3.3. Timely Processing. The aforementioned County Approvals and any environmental review required thereon shall be granted and approved by the County on a timely basis, provided that applications for such approvals are submitted to the County during the term of this Agreement, and provided further that Developer is not in default under the terms and conditions of this Agreement. County agrees to hire and/or retain appropriate personnel and/or consultants to process all County Approvals in an expeditious manner if, and only if, Developer agrees at the time to pay for such consultants or additional staff. Notwithstanding this provision, the County retains its complete discretion over operation and management of its departments, and processing of the County Approvals.

Section 3.4. Cooperation Between County and Developer. Consistent with the terms set forth herein, the County agrees to cooperate with Developer in securing all permits which may be required by the County.

Section 3.5. Consultant Assistance. The County agrees to hire or retain, or both, appropriate personnel and consultants to process all subsequent County Approvals in a timely manner. The County agrees to retain consultants to expedite engineering review of Developer's technical plans if, and only if, Developer agrees at the time to pay for such consultants. The County also agrees to retain consultants to expedite review of building plans and inspection of construction if, and only if, Developer agrees at the time to pay for such consultants. Notwithstanding this provision, the County retains its complete discretion over operation and management of its departments, and processing of the County Approvals.

Section 3.6. Further Consistent Discretionary Actions. Nothing in this Agreement shall be construed to limit the County's right to withhold Subsequent Approvals for failure to conform to the Collective Standards or other requirements imposed by any Law or by County's exercise of its authority as recognized under this Agreement, or to limit the authority or obligation of County to hold legally required public hearings, or to limit the discretion of County or any of its officers or officials in complying with any Law and County's adopted rules, regulations and policies that require County officers and officials to exercise discretion; provided, any such discretionary action exercised after the Adoption Date shall be consistent with the terms of this Agreement and shall not prevent or hinder development or use of the Subject Property as contemplated by the Initiative and this Agreement.

Section 3.7. Term of Tentative Subdivision Maps and Other Approvals. Pursuant to California Government Code sections 65863.9 and 66452.6(a), County and Developer agree that the term and expiration date of any County Approval, including but not limited to any tentative subdivision map or other County permit or approval approved for any development on the Subject Property, shall coincide with the later of (a) the Expiration Date as it may be extended or (b) the term for such approval that otherwise would govern under applicable law, including any extensions permitted under applicable law. The provisions of the Subdivision Map Act regarding the term of tentative maps and procedures for requesting extensions and regarding the timely filing of final maps and subsequent efforts shall apply to subsection (b). The Subdivision Map Act shall govern in the event of any conflict with County subdivision ordinances or any other County regulation.

Section 3.8. Design Review; Design Guidelines. The Developer has prepared or will cause to be prepared, and will adopt Design Guidelines outlining aesthetic and architectural standards and other building criteria. The County will timely review the Design Guidelines solely to determine conformity with applicable Mitigation Measures. A Design Review Board, whose members are appointed by the Developer, will implement the Design Guidelines. Thereafter, the County will not issue a building permit for a residential, public, maintenance or commercial structure unless there is evidence of prior written approval by the Design Review Board. The Developer may amend the Design Guidelines as specified within the document, except that the Developer may not modify and any provision specifically noted as a Mitigation Measure without first obtaining County written approval, such approval shall not be unreasonably withheld. Amendments pursuant to this section shall not require modification to the Development Agreement.

ARTICLE 4
DEFAULT

Section 4.1. General Provisions.

(a) Subject to extensions of time by mutual consent in writing, failure or delay by either party or Landowner not released from this Agreement to perform any term or provision of this Agreement, shall constitute a default. In the event of alleged default or breach of any terms or conditions of this Agreement, the party alleging such default or breach shall give the other party or Landowner not less than sixty (60) days notice in writing specifying the nature of the alleged default and the manner in which said default may be cured. During any such sixty (60) day period, the party or Landowner charged shall not be considered in default for purposes of termination or institution of legal proceedings.

(b) After notice and expiration of the sixty (60) day period, if such default has not been cured or is not being diligently cured in the manner set forth in the notice, the other party or Landowner to this Agreement may, at his option, institute legal proceedings pursuant to this Agreement or give notice of its intent to terminate this Agreement pursuant to California Government Code section 65868 and any regulations of the County implementing said Government Code section.

(c) Following notice of intent to terminate, or prior to instituting legal proceedings, the matter shall be scheduled for consideration and review in the manner set forth in Government Code sections 65865, 65867, and 65868 and County regulations implementing said sections by the County within thirty (30) calendar days.

(d) Following consideration of the evidence presented in said review before the County and an additional thirty (30) day period to cure, either party alleging the default by the other party or Landowner may institute legal proceedings, or may give written notice of termination of this Agreement to the other party; provided, however, a Landowner may only give such notice with respect to such portion of the Subject Property in which Landowner owns an interest.

(e) Evidence of default may also arise in the course of a regularly scheduled periodic review of this Agreement pursuant to Government Code section 65865.1. If either party or Landowner determines that a party or Landowner is in default following the completion of the normally scheduled periodic review, said party or Landowner may give written notice of termination of this Agreement specifying in said notice the alleged nature of the default, and potential actions to cure said default where appropriate. If the alleged default is not cured in sixty (60) days or within such longer period specified in the notice, or the defaulting party or Landowner waives its right to cure such alleged default, this Agreement may be terminated by County as to the Developer or Landowner and the property in which the Developer or Landowner owns an interest.

Section 4.2. Annual Review. County shall, at least every twelve (12) months during the term of this Agreement, review the extent of good faith substantial compliance by Developer and Landowner with the terms of this Agreement. Such periodic review by the Director shall be limited in scope to compliance with the terms of this Agreement pursuant to California Government Code section 65865.1. Failure to complete said review within the prescribed period shall be deemed a finding of good faith substantial compliance. Notice of such annual review shall include the statement that any review may result in amendment or termination of this Agreement. A finding by County of good faith compliance by Developer and Landowner with the terms of the Agreement shall conclusively determine said issue up to and including the date of said review. Any party may appeal a determination by the Director to the Board of Supervisors by filing a written appeal with the Clerk of the Board within ten (10) days of the determination. The County shall deposit in the mail or fax to Developer and/or Landowner a copy of all staff reports and, to the extent practical, related exhibits concerning contract performance at least seven (7) calendar days prior to such periodic review.

Section 4.3. Estoppel Certificates.

(a) County shall at any time upon not less than twenty (20) days prior written notice from Developer, execute, acknowledge and deliver to Developer, lender or investor, an Estoppel Certificate in writing which certifies that this Agreement is in full force, has not been terminated and is enforceable in accordance with its terms.

(b) At Developer's option, the failure to deliver such Estoppel Certificate within the stated time period, or for the County to decline in writing to provide the requested Estoppel Certificate, may/shall be conclusive that the Agreement is in full force and effect, that there are no incurred defaults in Developer's performance of the Agreement or of any County ordinances, regulations and policies regulating the use and development of the Developer's property subject to this Development Agreement.

Section 4.4. Developer Default Limited to Property/Entity; Separate Obligations of Owners. Except as may be specified in Section 4.1, no default hereunder in performance of a covenant or obligation with respect to a particular portion of the Subject Property shall constitute a default applicable to any other portion of the Subject Property, and any remedy arising by reason of such default shall be applicable solely to the portion of property where the default has occurred. Similarly, the obligations of the Developer and Landowners shall be severable and no default hereunder in performance of a covenant or obligation by any one of them shall constitute a default applicable to any other owner who is not affiliated with such defaulting owner, and any remedy arising by reason of such default shall be solely applicable to the defaulting owner and the portion of the Subject Property owned thereby.

Section 4.5. Default by County. In the event County does not accept, review, approve or issue necessary development permits or entitlements for use in a timely fashion as defined by this Agreement, or as otherwise agreed to by the parties, or the County otherwise defaults under the terms of this Agreement, County agrees that Developer or Landowner shall not be obligated to proceed with or complete the Project or any phase thereof, nor shall resulting delays in Developer performance constitute grounds for termination or cancellation of this Agreement.

Section 4.6. Cumulative Remedies of Parties. In addition to any other rights or remedies, County, Developer and any Landowner may institute legal or equitable proceedings to cure, correct or remedy any default, to specifically enforce any covenant or agreement herein, to enjoin any threatened or attempted violation of the provisions of this Agreement.

Section 4.7. Enforced Delay, Extension of Times of Performance. In addition to specific provisions of this Agreement, performance by either party or Landowner hereunder shall not be deemed to be in default where delays or defaults are due to war, insurrection, strikes, walkouts, riots, floods, earthquakes, fires, casualties, acts of God, governmental restrictions imposed or mandated by governmental entities other than the County, enactment of conflicting state or federal laws or regulations, new or supplementary environmental regulation enacted by the state or federal government or litigation. An extension of time for such cause shall be in effect for the period of the enforced delay or longer, as may be mutually agreed upon.

ARTICLE 5
TERMINATION

Section 5.1. Termination Upon Completion of Development. This Agreement shall terminate upon the expiration of the term or when the Subject Property has been fully developed and all of the Developer's obligations in connection therewith are satisfied as determined by the County. Upon termination of this Agreement, the County shall record a notice of such termination in a form satisfactory to the County Counsel that the Agreement has been terminated. This Agreement shall automatically terminate and be of no further force or effect as to any single-family residence, any other residential dwelling unit(s) or any non-residential building, and the lot or parcel upon which such residence or building is located, when it has been approved by the County for occupancy. Upon request of the Developer, the County shall record a Notice of Termination in substantial conformance with Exhibit "G."

Section 5.2. Effect Upon Termination on Developer Obligations. Termination of this Agreement as to the Developer of the Subject Property or any portion thereof shall not affect any of the Developer's obligations to comply with the County General Plan and the terms and conditions of any applicable zoning, or subdivision map or other land use entitlements approved with respect to the Subject Property, any other covenants or any other development requirements specified in this Agreement to continue after the termination of this Agreement, or obligations to pay assessments, liens, fees or taxes.

Section 5.3. Effect Upon Termination on County. Upon any termination of this Agreement as to the Developer of the Subject Property, or any portion thereof, the entitlements, conditions of development, limitations on fees and all other terms and conditions of this Agreement shall no longer be vested hereby with respect to the property affected by such termination (provided vesting of such entitlements, conditions or fees may then be established for such property pursuant to then existing planning and zoning law) and the County shall no longer be limited, by this Agreement, to make any changes or modifications to such entitlements, conditions or fees applicable to such property.

ARTICLE 6
ADDITIONAL GENERAL TERMS

Section 6.1. Assignment and Assumption. Developer shall have the right to sell, assign or transfer this Agreement with all the rights, title and interests therein to any person, firm or corporation at any time during the term of this Agreement. The conditions and covenants set forth in this Agreement and incorporated herein by exhibits shall run with the land and the benefits and burdens shall bind and inure to the benefit of the parties. Developer shall provide County with a copy of the Assumption Agreement as provided for in Section 6.9. Express written assumption by such purchaser, assignee or transferee, to the satisfaction of the County Counsel, of the obligations and other terms and conditions of this Agreement with respect to the Subject Property or such portion thereof sold, assigned or transferred, shall relieve the Developer selling, assigning or transferring such interest of such obligations so expressly assumed. Any such assumption of Developer's obligations under this Agreement shall be deemed to be to the satisfaction of the County Counsel if executed in the form of the Assumption Agreement attached hereto as Exhibit "C" and incorporated herein by this reference, or such other form as shall be approved by the County Counsel.

Section 6.2. Mortgagee and Foreclosure Purchaser as Transferee. No Mortgage (including the execution and delivery thereof to the Mortgagee) or taking of possession by a Mortgagee or acquisition by a Foreclosure Purchaser shall constitute a Transfer. A Mortgagee or a Foreclosure Purchaser shall be a Transferee when such Mortgagee or Foreclosure Purchaser has complied with the provisions of Section 6.1 above.

Section 6.3. Mortgagee Protection. This Agreement shall be superior and senior to the lien of any Mortgage encumbering any interest in the Subject property. Notwithstanding the foregoing, no Event of Default shall defeat, render invalid, diminish, or impair the lien of any Mortgage made for value, but, subject to the provisions of Section 6.4, all of the terms and conditions contained in this Agreement shall be binding upon and effective against any person (including any Mortgagee) who acquires title to the Subject Property, or any portion thereof or interest therein or improvement thereon, by foreclosure, trustee's sale, deed in lieu of foreclosure, or termination of the Mortgage.

Section 6.4. Mortgagee Not Obligated; Mortgagee as Transferee. No Mortgagee shall have any obligation or duty under this Agreement, except that nothing contained in this Agreement shall be deemed to permit or authorize any Mortgagee or Foreclosure Purchaser to undertake any new construction or improvement project, or to otherwise have the benefit of any rights of Developer, or to enforce any obligation of County under this Agreement, unless and until such Mortgagee or Foreclosure Purchaser has become a Transferee in the manner specified in this Article 6.

Section 6.5. Notice of Default to Mortgagee; Right of Mortgagee to Cure. If County receives notice from a Mortgagee requesting a copy of any notice of an Event of Default given to Developer hereunder and specifying the address for service thereof, then County shall deliver to such Mortgagee, concurrently with service thereon to the Developer, any notice given with respect to any claim by County that the Developer has committed an Event of Default. If County makes a determination of noncompliance under this Agreement, County shall likewise serve notice of such noncompliance on such Mortgagee concurrently with service thereof on the Developer. Such Mortgagee shall have the right (but not the obligation) to cure or remedy, or to commence to cure or remedy, the Event of Default claimed or the areas of noncompliance set forth in County's notice within the applicable time periods for cure specified in this Agreement. If, however, the Event of Default or such noncompliance is of a nature which can only be remedied or cured by such Mortgagee upon obtaining possession of the portion of the Subject Property, if such Mortgagee shall elect to cure such Event of Default, such Mortgagee shall seek to obtain possession with diligence and continuity through a receiver or otherwise, and shall thereafter remedy or cure the Event of Default or noncompliance as soon as reasonably possible after obtaining possession. So long as such Mortgagee is pursuing cure of the event of Default or noncompliance in conformance with the requirements of this Section and/or diligently pursuing an action to obtain possession of the Subject Property by receiver or otherwise, County shall not exercise any right or remedy under this Agreement on account of such Event of Default or noncompliance.

Section 6.6. Covenants Running with the Land. Each and every purchaser, assignee or transferee of an interest in the Subject Property, or any portion thereof, shall be obligated and bound by the terms and conditions of this Agreement, and shall be the beneficiary thereof and a party thereto, but only with respect to the Subject Property, or such portion thereof, sold, assigned or transferred to it. Any such purchaser, assignee or transferee shall observe and fully perform all of the duties and obligations of a Developer contained in this Agreement, as such duties and obligations pertain to the portion of the Subject Property sold, assigned or transferred to it. Provided however, notwithstanding anything to the contrary above, if any such sale, assignment or transfer relates to a completed residential or commercial unit or non-residential building or a portion thereof, which has been approved by the County for occupancy, the automatic termination provisions of Section 5.1 herein shall apply thereto and the rights and obligations of Developer hereunder shall not run with respect to such portion of the Subject Property sold, assigned or transferred and shall not be binding upon such purchaser, assignee or transferee. This Agreement shall be binding upon any special district organized, or which by annexation, provides services to the Project and which succeeds to the County's obligations after the Effective Date.

Section 6.7. Amendment to Agreement (Developer and County). This Agreement may be amended by mutual consent of the parties in writing, in accordance with the provisions of Government Code section 65868, provided that: any amendment which relates to the term, permitted uses, density, intensity of use, height and size of proposed buildings, or provisions for reservation and dedication of land shall require a noticed public hearing before the parties may execute an amendment. Unless otherwise provided by law, all other amendments may be approved without a noticed public hearing.

Section 6.8. Releases. Developer, and any subsequent Landowner, may free itself from further obligations relating to the sold, assigned or transferred property, provided that:

(a) The Clerk of the Board of Supervisors receives a copy of the Assumption Agreement provided for in Section 6.1; and

(b) The buyer, assignee or transferee expressly assumes the obligations under this agreement pursuant to Section 6.1 contained herein above.

Section 6.9. Notices. Notices, demands, correspondence and other communication to County and Developer shall be deemed given if dispatched by prepaid first-class mail to the principal offices of the parties as designated in Section 1.6. Notice to the County shall be to the attention of both the County Counsel and the Director. Notices to subsequent Landowners shall be required to be given by the County only for those Landowners who have given the County written notice of their address for such notices. The parties hereto may, from time to time, advise the other of new addresses for such notices, demands or correspondence.

Section 6.10. Recordation of Agreement. Within ten (10) days of the Board of Supervisors entering into this Agreement, the Clerk of the Board shall record this document.

Section 6.11. Applicable Law. This Agreement shall be construed and enforced in accordance with the laws of the State of California.

Section 6.12. Invalidity of Agreement/Severability. If this Agreement in its entirety is determined by a court to be invalid or unenforceable, this Agreement shall automatically terminate as of the date of final entry of judgment. If any provision of this Agreement shall be determined by a court to be invalid and unenforceable, or if any provision of this Agreement is rendered invalid or unenforceable according to the terms of any federal or state statute, which becomes effective after the Effective Date, the remaining provisions shall continue in full force and effect.

Section 6.13. Third Party Legal Challenge. In the event any legal action or special proceeding is commenced by any person or entity challenging this Agreement, any Project approvals, entitlements or components thereof, the environmental impact report for the Project or any approval subsequently granted by the County for the development of ___________, the County and Developer agree to cooperate with each other as set forth herein. County may elect to tender the defense of any lawsuit filed by a third person or entity to Developer and/or Landowner(s) (to the extent the litigation, in part or in whole, seeks to overturn or invalidate this Agreement, any Project approvals, entitlements or components thereof, the environmental impact report for the Project or any subsequent approval granted for the Subject Property held by or granted to Developer and/or Landowner), and, in such event, Developer and/or such Landowner(s) shall indemnify, hold the County harmless from and defend the County from all costs and expenses incurred in the defense of such lawsuit, including, but not limited to, damages, attorneys' fees and expenses of litigation awarded to the prevailing party or parties in such litigation. Developer and/or Landowner shall pay an initial deposit of fifty thousand dollars ($50,000) to the County within thirty (30) days of written notice that a lawsuit has been filed on the Project. Developer shall pay an additional fifty thousand dollar ($50,000) every three (3) months up to a limit of one million dollars ($1,000,000). Said deposit shall be held by the County as security for compliance with this Section and/or the costs of any potential settlement. Developer agrees that the County may draw on the deposit in the event Developer fails to timely pay invoices as required herein or otherwise defaults on its obligations pursuant to this Section. Developer shall replenish deposit funds within thirty (30) days of a written request from County up to a limit of one million dollars ($1,000,000). If at the end of litigation deposit funds remain, the County shall refund same within thirty (30) days of a written request from Developer. For purposes of this section only, "County" shall include all employees, consultants and agents acting on behalf of the County. Neither party shall settle any such lawsuit without the consent of the other party except that if Developer is in default of its obligations as set forth in this Section, the County may settle or otherwise resolve the litigation against it without consent of Developer. Both parties shall act in good faith, and shall not unreasonably withhold consent to settle. The County may elect to participate in the litigation, in which case the Developer and/or Landowner agree to reimburse the County for its litigation costs and fees, including the retention of outside legal counsel and all staff costs as provided herein. Developer and/or Landowner shall pay such fees and costs within thirty (30) days of presentation of a written request or invoice. This provision shall survive the termination of this Agreement. Any violation by Developer or Landowner of the provisions set forth in this section shall be deemed to be a material breach of this Agreement. During such time as the Developer or Landowner is in breach or default of its obligations pursuant to this section, County shall have no obligation to process any applications for County Approvals. This is in addition to any and all other remedies available to the County.

Section 6.14. Resolution of Disputes. In addition to the annual review provisions, all disputes between the Parties may be appealed as provided for in Section 4.2.

Section 6.15. Standard Terms and Conditions.

(a) **Venue.** Venue for all legal proceedings shall be in the Superior Court for the County of ____________.

(b) **Waiver.** A waiver by any party of any breach of any term, covenant or condition herein contained or a waiver of any right or remedy of such party available hereunder at law or in equity shall not be deemed to be a waiver of any subsequent breach of the same or any other term, covenant or condition herein contained or of any continued or subsequent right to the same right or remedy. No party shall be deemed to have made any such waiver unless it is in writing and signed by the party so waiving.

(c) **Completeness of Instrument.** This Agreement, together with its specific references and attachments, constitutes all of the agreements, understandings, representations, conditions, warranties and covenants made by and between the parties hereto. Unless set forth herein, neither party shall be liable for any representations made express or implied.

(d) **Supersedes Prior Agreements.** It is the intention of the parties hereto that this Agreement shall supersede any prior agreements, discussions, commitments, representations or agreements, written or oral, between the parties hereto.

(e) **Captions.** The captions of this Agreement are for convenience in reference only and the words contained therein shall in no way be held to explain, modify, amplify or aid in the interpretation, construction or meaning of the provisions of this Agreement.

(f) **Number and Gender.** In this Agreement, the neuter gender includes the feminine and masculine, and the singular includes the plural, the word "person" includes corporations, partnerships, firms or associations, wherever the context so requires.

(g) **Mandatory and Permissive.** "Shall" and "will" and "agrees" are mandatory. "May" is permissive.

(h) **Term Includes Extensions.** All references to the term of this Agreement or the Agreement Term shall include any extensions of such term.

(i) **Successors and Assigns.** All representations, covenants and warranties specifically set forth in this Agreement, by or on behalf of, or for the benefit of any or all of the parties hereto, shall be binding upon and inure to the benefit of such party, its successors and assigns.

(j) **Modifications.** No modification or waiver of any provisions of this Agreement or its attachments shall be effective unless such waiver or modification is in writing, signed by all parties, and then shall be effective only for the period and on the condition, and for the specific instance for which given.

(k) **Counterparts.** This Agreement may be executed simultaneously and in several counterparts, each of which shall be deemed an original, but which together shall constitute one and the same instrument.

(l) **Other Documents.** The parties agree that they shall cooperate in good faith to accomplish the object of this Agreement and to that end, agree to execute and deliver such other and further instruments and documents as may be necessary and convenient to the fulfillment of these purposes.

(m) **Partial Invalidity.** If any term, covenant, condition or provision of this Agreement is held by a court of competent jurisdiction to be invalid, void or unenforceable, the remainder of the provision and/or provisions shall remain in full force and effect and shall in no way be affected, impaired or invalidated.

(n) **Controlling Law.** The validity, interpretation and performance of this Agreement shall be controlled by and construed under the laws of the State of California.

(o) **Time is of the Essence.** Time is of the essence of this Agreement and each covenant and term a condition herein.

(p) **Authority.** All parties to this Agreement warrant and represent that they have the power and authority to enter into this Agreement in the names, titles and capacities herein stated and on behalf of any entities, persons, estates or firms represented or purported to be represented by such entity(s), person(s), estate(s) or firm(s) and that all formal requirements necessary or required by any state and/or federal law in order to enter into this Agreement have been fully complied with. Further, by entering into this Agreement, neither party hereto shall have breached the terms or conditions of any other contract or agreement to which such party is obligated, which such breach would have a material effect hereon.

(q) **Document Preparation.** This Agreement will not be construed against the party preparing it, but will be construed as if prepared by all parties.

(r) **Advice of Legal Counsel.** Each party acknowledges that it has reviewed this Agreement with its own legal counsel, and based upon the advice of that counsel, freely entered into this Agreement.

(s) **Consent/Subordination.** Unless waived in writing by the County Counsel, Developer shall furnish proof satisfactory to the County, prior to approval of the Agreement, that all persons possessing a legal interest in the property have consented to the recording of this Agreement. Unless waived in writing by the County Counsel, the County shall require subordination by all lenders of record as a condition precedent to the County approval of the Agreement. The County shall have no duty to subordinate its interest in this Agreement.

(t) **Attorneys Fees and Costs.** If any action at law or in equity, including an action for declaratory relief, is brought to enforce or interpret provisions of this Agreement, the prevailing party shall be entitled to reasonable attorneys' fees and costs, which may be set by the Court in the same action or in a separate action brought for that purpose, in addition to any other relief to which such party may be entitled.

(u) **Calculation of Time Periods.** All time periods referenced in this Agreement shall be calendar days, unless the last day falls on a legal holiday, in which case the last day shall be the next business day.

IN WITNESS WHEREOF, this Agreement was executed by the parties thereto on the dates set forth below.

COUNTY OF LASSEN

By: ________________________ Date: _______
Chair

ATTEST:

____
County Clerk

APPROVED AS TO FORM:

____
County Counsel

DEVELOPER

By: ______________________________ Date: _______
Its: ______________________________

APPROVED AS TO FORM:

____

LIST OF EXHIBITS

Exhibit "A" Project Description
Exhibit "B" Subject Property
Exhibit "C" Assumption Agreement
Exhibit "D" Mitigation Measures
Exhibit "E" Road and Snow Storage Standards (E1-E3)
Exhibit "F" District Assignment and Assumption Agreement
Exhibit "G" Notice of Termination

APPENDIX J

Development Agreement—Private

Source: William W. Abbott,
Abbott & Kindermann LLP

DEVELOPMENT AGREEMENT
BY AND BETWEEN
THE COUNTY OF __________ AND
_____________________________________.

RELATIVE TO THE DEVELOPMENT KNOWN AS
____

THIS DEVELOPMENT AGREEMENT is made and entered into this ______ day of ___________, 20__, by and between the **COUNTY OF** ____________, a political subdivision of the State of California ("County"), and _________________ a California corporation ("Developer"), pursuant to the authority of Article 2.5, Chapter 4, Division 1, Title 7 (Government Code section 65864 *et seq.*) relating to Development Agreements.

RECITALS

1. In order to strengthen the public land use planning process, to encourage private participation in the process, to reduce the economic risk of development and to reduce the waste of resources, the Legislature adopted the Development Agreement Statutes (§ 65864 *et seq.* of the Government Code).

2. The Development Agreement Law permits cities and counties to contract with private interests for their mutual benefit in a manner not otherwise available to the contracting parties. Such agreements, as authorized by the Development Agreement Law, can assure property developers they may proceed with projects assured that approvals granted by public agencies will not change during the period of development of their projects. Cities and counties are equally assured that costly infrastructure such as roads, sewers, schools, fire protection facilities, etc., will be available at the time development projects come on line.

3. The Development Agreement relates to the development known as __________, a mixed use development located in the __________ Community Center. The parties have, in good faith, negotiated the terms hereinafter set forth which carry out the legislative purpose set forth above and will assure the parties to this Agreement of mutually desirable development of the subject property.

(a) The completion of the Project will provide a high quality, commercial center, serving both local residents and tourists, reducing trips by local residents going out of the County to shop for necessary goods and services, and in turn generating sales tax revenue to the County. The Project is consistent with the County General Plan as amended, and will, in conjunction with other approved development within the County: maintain an economic and social balance between housing supply and employment opportunities; assure that County revenues meet expenditures necessary to provide an adequate level of municipal services; and establish a balance of land uses that enables the County to provide necessary municipal services.

4. Developer has a legal and/or an equitable interest in that certain real property, more particularly

described on Exhibit "A" hereto, located in the County of _________, and desires to create thereon a commercial development allowing for mixed uses.

5. County, in response to Developer's applications, after public hearings and extensive environmental analysis, has granted the following entitlements:

a. By Resolution No._________, certifying an EIR and approving a Mitigation Monitoring Program,

b. By Resolution No. ________, approving a general plan amendment,

c. By Ordinance No. ________, approving amendments to the zoning code,

d. By separate staff action approving a boundary line adjustment, which upon approval shall be incorporated by reference into this Agreement.

6. By Ordinance No. __________, the Board of Supervisors authorized the Chair of the Board County to sign this Development Agreement on behalf of the County.

7. Development of the subject property pursuant to the terms and conditions of the various entitlements, the General Plan and the Environmental Impact Report will provide for orderly growth and development consistent with the County's General Plan and other development policies and programs.

8. On December 1, 2005, the County Planning Commission, designated by County as the Planning Agency for purposes of Development Agreement review pursuant to Government Code section 65867, considered this Agreement.

9. County and Developer have taken all actions mandated by and fulfilled all requirements set forth in the County Code governing requirements for Development Agreements.

10. Having duly considered this Agreement and having held the noticed public hearings, County finds and declares that the provisions of this Development Agreement are consistent with the maps and text of the County's General Plan.

NOW, THEREFORE, the parties hereto agree as follows:

ARTICLE 1

1 GENERAL PROVISIONS

Section 1.1. <u>The Project</u>. The Project is a mixed use development located on the Subject Property, consisting of approximately twenty seven and 4/10 (27.4) acres +/- in the _________ Community Center area of the County.

Section 1.2. <u>Subject Property</u>. The Project site is more specifically described in **Exhibit "A"** which is incorporated herein and made part of this Agreement.

Section 1.3. <u>Definitions</u>. As used in the Agreement, the following terms, phrases and words shall have the meanings and be interpreted as set forth in this Section.

(a) **Adopting Ordinance** means Ordinance Number __________ entitled: "Development Agreement By and Between the County of ___________ and _________________relative to the Development Known as ___________" dated _________________, and effective ___________________________, which approves this Development Agreement as required by Government Code section 65867.5.

(b) **Assumption Agreement** means an agreement substantially conforming to the model assumption agreement described in Exhibit "B," or other agreement in a form approved by the County Attorney, executed by a Landowner with the Developer, expressly assuming various obligations relating to the development of the Project, or portion thereof.

(c) **CEQA** means the California Environmental Quality Act section 21000, *et seq.*, of the Public Resources Code of the State of California.

(d) **Certificate of Occupancy** means either a certificate issued after inspections by the County authorizing a person or persons in possession of property to dwell or otherwise use a specified building or dwelling unit, or the final inspection if a formal certificate is not issued.

(e) **Collective Standards** means this Development Agreement, the Planning Documents and the Existing Land Use Regulations.

(f) **County** means the County of ____________, as administered by the Board of Supervisors, or its designee.

(g) **Developer** means _______________________, a California corporation, or successor in interest.

(h) **Director** means the Director of Planning for the County of ___________.

(i) **Effective Date** means the effective date of the Adopting Ordinance.

(j) **Existing Land Use Regulations** mean the ordinances, resolutions and regulations adopted by the County in effect on the Effective Date including the adopting ordinances that govern the permitted uses of land, the density and intensity of use, the timing of development, the design, improvement, and construction standards and specifications applicable to the development of the Subject Property, including, but not limited to, the General Plan, the zoning ordinance and all other ordinances, codes, rules and regulations of the County establishing subdivision standards, park regulations, impact or development fees, building standards and road and infrastructure improvement standards.

(k) **General Plan** means the General Plan of the County, including the text and maps, as amended in connection with the Project.

(l) **Landowner** is a party who has acquired any portion of the Subject Property from the Developer who, unless otherwise released as provided in this Agreement, shall be subject to the applicable provisions of this Agreement.

(m) **Planning Documents** mean, and shall be limited to, those approvals set forth in Recital 5.

(n) **Project** means the anticipated development of the Subject Property as specified in Section 1.1 and as provided for in the provisions of this Agreement and all other incorporated exhibits.

(o) **Subject Property** means the property described in Section 1.2, or the remaining portions thereof after releases from the provisions of this Agreement have been executed as authorized by this Agreement.

Section 1.4. Exhibits. Exhibits to this Agreement are as follows:

Exhibit "A"	Subject Property
Exhibit "B"	Assumption Agreement
Exhibit "C"	Zoning Code
Exhibit "D"	________ Town Study (dated November 17, 2005)
Exhibit "E"	_________ Concept Plan showing Project Character and Scale

Section 1.5 Incorporation of Recitals. Recitals 1 through 11 are incorporated herein, including all exhibits referred to in said Recitals. In the event of inconsistency between the Recitals and the provisions of Articles 1 through 5, the provisions of Articles 1 through 5 shall prevail.

Section 1.6 Parties to Agreement. The parties to this Agreement are:

(a) **The County.** The County of _____________ is a political subdivision of the State of California exercising general governmental functions and power. The principal office of the County is located at _________________________.

(b) **Developer.** _____________ is a private enterprise which has an equitable interest in the Subject Property. Developer's principal office for the purpose of this Agreement is __________, California, and whose mailing address is ________________.

(c) **Landowner.** From time to time, as provided in this Agreement, Developer may sell or otherwise lawfully dispose of a portion of the Subject Property to a Landowner who, unless otherwise released, shall be subject to the applicable provisions of this Agreement related to such portion of the Subject Property.

Section 1.7. Project is a Private Undertaking. It is agreed among the parties that the Project is a private development and that County has no interest therein except as authorized in the exercise of its governmental functions. Nothing in this Agreement shall preclude the Developer from forming any form of private investment entity for the purpose of completing any portion of the Project.

Section 1.8. Term of Agreement. This Agreement shall commence upon the effective date of the Adopting

Ordinance approving this Agreement, and shall continue in force for fifteen (15) years from the Effective Date unless extended or terminated as provided herein. Following the expiration of the term or extension thereof, or if sooner terminated, this Agreement shall have no force and effect, subject however, to post-termination obligations of Developer or Landowner.

Section 1.9. Priority of Enactment. In the event of conflict between the Development Agreement, the Planning Documents and the Existing Land Use Regulations, the parties agree that the following sequence of approvals establishes the relative priority of the approvals, each approval superior to the approvals listed thereafter: (1) the Development Agreement; (2) the Planning Documents; and (3) the Existing Land Use Regulations (hereafter referred to as the "Collective Standards").

Section 1.10. Vested Rights of Developer. During the term of this Agreement, unless sooner terminated in accordance with the terms hereof, in developing the Subject Property consistent with the Project described herein, Developer is assured, and County agrees, that the development rights, obligations, terms and conditions specified in the Collective Standards are fully vested in the Developer and may not be changed or modified by the County except as may be expressly permitted by, and in accordance with, the terms and conditions of this Agreement, or as expressly consented thereto by the Developer to the extent such proposed change or modification is applicable thereto.

Section 1.11. Assignment and Assumption. Developer shall have the right to sell, assign or transfer this Agreement with all the rights, title and interests therein to any person, firm or corporation at any time during the term of this Agreement. The conditions and covenants set forth in this Agreement and incorporated herein by exhibits shall run with the land and the benefits and burdens shall bind and inure to the benefit of the parties. Developer shall provide County with a copy of the Assumption Agreement as provided for in Section 1.15. Express written assumption by such purchaser, assignee or transferee, to the satisfaction of the County Counsel, of the obligations and other terms and conditions of this Agreement with respect to the Subject Property or such portion thereof sold, assigned or transferred, shall relieve the Developer selling, assigning or transferring such interest of such obligations so expressly assumed. Any such assumption of Developer's obligations under this Agreement shall be deemed to be to the satisfaction of the County Counsel if executed in the form of the Assumption Agreement attached hereto as **Exhibit "B"** and incorporated herein by this reference, or such other form as shall be approved by the County Counsel

Section 1.12. Covenants Running with the Land. Each and every purchaser, assignee or transferee of an interest in the Subject Property, or any portion thereof, shall be obligated and bound by the terms and conditions of this Agreement, and shall be the beneficiary thereof and a party thereto, but only with respect to the Subject Property, or such portion thereof, sold, assigned or transferred to it. Any such purchaser, assignee or transferee shall observe and fully perform all of the duties and obligations of a Developer contained in this Agreement, as such duties and obligations pertain to the portion of the Subject Property sold, assigned or transferred to it. Provided however, notwithstanding anything to the contrary above, if any such sale, assignment or transfer relates to a completed residential or commercial unit or non-residential building or a portion thereof, which has been approved by the County for occupancy, the automatic termination provisions of Section 5.1 herein shall apply thereto and the rights and obligations of Developer hereunder shall not run with respect to such portion of the Subject Property sold, assigned or transferred and shall not be binding upon such purchaser, assignee or transferee.

Section 1.13. Amendment to Agreement (Developer and County). This Agreement may be amended by mutual consent of the parties in writing, in accordance with the provisions of Government Code section 65868, provided that: any amendment which relates to the term, permitted uses, density, intensity of use, height and size of proposed buildings, or provisions for reservation and dedication of land shall require a noticed public hearing before the parties may execute an amendment. Unless otherwise provided by law, all other amendments may be approved without a noticed public hearing.

Section 1.14. Releases. Developer, and any subsequent Landowner, may free itself from further obligations relating to the sold, assigned or transferred property, provided that:

(a) The Clerk of the Board of Supervisors receives a copy of the Assumption Agreement provided for in Section 1.11; and
(b) The buyer, assignee or transferee expressly assumes the obligations under this agreement pursuant to Section 1.11 contained herein above.

Section 1.15. Notices. Notices, demands, correspondence and other communication to County and Developer shall be deemed given if dispatched by prepaid first-class mail to the principal offices of the parties as designated in Section 1.6. Notice to the County shall be to the attention of both the County Counsel and the Director. Notices to subsequent Landowners shall be required to be given by the County only for those Landowners who have given the County written notice of their address for such notices. The parties hereto may, from time to time, advise the other of new addresses for such notices, demands or correspondence.

Section 1.16. Recordation of Agreement. Within ten (10) days of the Board of Supervisors entering into this Agreement, the Clerk of the Board shall record this document.

Section 1.17. Applicable Law. This Agreement shall be construed and enforced in accordance with the laws of the State of California.

Section 1.18. Invalidity of Agreement/Severability. If this Agreement in its entirety is determined by a court to be invalid or unenforceable, this Agreement shall automatically terminate as of the date of final entry of judgment. If any provision of this Agreement shall be determined by a court to be invalid and unenforceable, or if any provision of this Agreement is rendered invalid or unenforceable according to the terms of any federal or state statute, which becomes effective after the Effective Date, the remaining provisions shall continue in full force and effect.

Section 1.19. Third Party Legal Challenge. In the event any legal action or special proceeding is commenced by any person or entity other than a party or a Landowner, challenging this Agreement or any provision herein.

Developer agrees to defend, indemnify, and hold harmless the County and its agents, officers, and employees from any claim, action, or proceeding against the County or its agents, officers, and employees arising from such approval. The obligation of Developer to defend, indemnify, and hold harmless arises only if the County notifies Developer of any claim, action, or proceeding within a reasonable time after the County knows of the claim, action, or proceeding.

Developer shall, upon written request of the County, prepare a defense for the County at Developer's sole expense. Alternatively, the County, at the County's sole discretion, may prepare its own defense, with Developer paying the reasonable costs of the County's defense. Such costs shall include attorney fees and other related costs of defense, including without limitation, travel, postage, photocopies, and County staff costs.

Developer shall not be required to pay or perform any settlement unless the settlement is approved in advance by the Developer. The County must approve any settlement affecting the rights and obligations of the County.

In all cases, regardless of whether the County or the Developer defends the County, the Developer shall indemnify the County for any judgment, order, or settlement rendered as a result of any claim, action, or proceeding arising from the approval.

At no time shall Developer file any complaint, cross-complaint, or any offensive pleadings in an action arising out of the County's approval without first obtaining the County's written approval.

Developer shall pay to the County, within thirty calendar days upon written demand, any amount owed to the County as a result of the County incurring costs or expenses due to its defense under the terms of this subsection.

Section 1.20. Standard Terms and Conditions.

(a) **Venue.** Venue for all legal proceedings shall be in the Superior Court for the County of ___________.

(b) **Waiver.** A waiver by any party of any breach of any term, covenant or condition herein contained or a waiver of any right or remedy of such party available hereunder at law or in equity shall not be deemed to be a waiver of any subsequent breach of the same or any other term, covenant or condition herein contained or of any continued or subsequent right to the same right or remedy. No party shall be deemed to have made any such waiver unless it is in writing and signed by the party so waiving.

(c) **Completeness of Instrument.** This Agreement, together with its specific references and attachments, constitutes all of the agreements, understandings, representations, conditions, warranties and covenants made by and between the parties hereto. Unless set forth herein, neither party shall be liable for any representations made express or implied.

(d) **Supersedes Prior Agreements.** It is the intention of the parties hereto that this Agreement shall supersede any prior agreements, discussions, commitments, representations or agreements, written or oral, between the parties hereto.

(e) Captions. The captions of this Agreement are for convenience in reference only and the words contained therein shall in no way be held to explain, modify, amplify or aid in the interpretation, construction or meaning of the provisions of this Agreement.

(f) Number and Gender. In this Agreement, the neuter gender includes the feminine and masculine, and the singular includes the plural, the word "person" includes corporations, partnerships, firms or associations, wherever the context so requires.

(g) Mandatory and Permissive. "Shall" and "will" and "agrees" are mandatory. "May" is permissive.

(h) Term Includes Extensions. All references to the term of this Agreement or the Agreement Term shall include any extensions of such term.

(i) Successors and Assigns. All representations, covenants and warranties specifically set forth in this Agreement, by or on behalf of, or for the benefit of any or all of the parties hereto, shall be binding upon and inure to the benefit of such party, its successors and assigns.

(j) Modifications. No modification or waiver of any provisions of this Agreement or its attachments shall be effective unless such waiver or modification is in writing, signed by all parties, and then shall be effective only for the period and on the condition, and for the specific instance for which given.

(k) Counterparts. This Agreement may be executed simultaneously and in several counterparts, each of which shall be deemed an original, but which together shall constitute one and the same instrument.

(l) Other Documents. The parties agree that they shall cooperate in good faith to accomplish the object of this Agreement and to that end, agree to execute and deliver such other and further instruments and documents as may be necessary and convenient to the fulfillment of these purposes.

(m) Partial Invalidity. If any term, covenant, condition or provision of this Agreement is held by a court of competent jurisdiction to be invalid, void or unenforceable, the remainder of the provision and/or provisions shall remain in full force and effect and shall in no way be affected, impaired or invalidated.

(n) Controlling Law. The validity, interpretation and performance of this Agreement shall be controlled by and construed under the laws of the State of California.

(o) Time is of the Essence. Time is of the essence of this Agreement and each covenant and term a condition herein.

(p) Authority. All parties to this Agreement warrant and represent that they have the power and authority to enter into this Agreement in the names, titles and capacities herein stated and on behalf of any entities, persons, estates or firms represented or purported to be represented by such entity(s), person(s), estate(s) or firm(s) and that all formal requirements necessary or required by any state and/or federal law in order to enter into this Agreement have been fully complied with. Further, by entering into this Agreement, neither party hereto shall have breached the terms or conditions of any other contract or agreement to which such party is obligated, which such breach would have a material effect hereon.

(q) Document Preparation. This Agreement will not be construed against the party preparing it, but will be construed as if prepared by all parties.

(r) Advice of Legal Counsel. Each party acknowledges that it has reviewed this Agreement with its own legal counsel, and based upon the advice of that counsel, freely entered into this Agreement.

(s) Consent/Subordination. Unless waived in writing by the County Counsel, Developer shall furnish proof satisfactory to the County, prior to approval of the Agreement, that all persons possessing a legal interest in the property have consented to the recording of this Agreement. Unless waived in writing by the County Counsel, the County shall require subordination by all lenders of record as a condition precedent to the County approval of the Agreement. The County shall have no duty to subordinate its interest in this Agreement.

(t) **Attorneys Fees and Costs.** If any action at law or in equity, including an action for declaratory relief or any arbitration, is brought to enforce or interpret provisions of this Agreement, the prevailing party shall be entitled to reasonable attorneys' fees and costs, which may be set by the Court in the same action or in a separate action brought for that purpose, in addition to any other relief to which such party may be entitled.

ARTICLE 2

2 PROJECT DEVELOPMENT

Section 2.1. Vested Right to Develop. Developer shall have the vested right to develop the Subject Property in accordance with Section 1.10 of this Agreement.

Section 2.2. Permitted Uses and Development Standards. The permitted uses, the density and intensity of use, the maximum height and size of proposed buildings, provisions for reservation and dedication of land or payment of fees in lieu of dedication for public purposes, the construction, installation and extension of public and private improvements, subdivision standards, development guidelines and standards, implementation program for processing of subsequent entitlements and other conditions of development for the Subject Property shall be those set forth in Exhibit "C." The parties hereto intend that Exhibit "C" shall serve as the definitive and controlling document for all subsequent actions, discretionary or ministerial, relating to the development, subdivision, and occupancy of the Project. All development shall be in substantive conformity with Exhibits "C", "D" and "E", and the Mitigation Measures, to the approval of the Planning Director. Except as otherwise stated in this Agreement, subsequent approvals undertaken pursuant to and in conformity with the Project approved concurrently with the adoption of this Agreement, shall not be conditioned upon adherence to other ordinances, rules, regulations or requirements.

Section 2.3. Subsequent Zoning Ordinance Amendment. If the County's zoning ordinance is amended after the effective date of the Adopting Ordinance to authorize greater densities and intensity of use or greater maximum height and size of buildings, the amended provisions shall apply to the development of the Subject Property.

Section 2.4. Amendments. Any amendments to Exhibits "C," "D," or "E" agreed to by the Developer and County do not require an amendment to this Agreement.

Section 2.5. No Conflicting Enactments. Neither the County nor any agency of the County shall enact any ordinance, resolution or other measure that relates to the rate, timing or sequencing of the development or construction of the Subject Property on all or any part of the Subject Property that is in conflict with this Agreement, or any amendments thereto, or that reduces the development rights provided by this Agreement. Without limiting the foregoing general statement, and for all purposes pursuant to this Agreement generally, and this Section specifically, an ordinance, resolution or other measure shall be deemed to conflict with this Agreement if the ordinance, resolution or measure seeks to accomplish any one or more of the following results, either with specific reference to this Subject Property or as part of a general enactment that applies to this Subject Property would or could:

(a) Limit or reduce the density or intensity of the Project development granted by the Collective Standards or otherwise require any reduction in the height, number, size or square footage of lots, structures or buildings;

(b) Expand or increase Developer's obligations under the Collective Standards with respect to the provision of parking spaces, streets, roadways and/or any other public or private improvements or structures;

(c) Directly limit public services or facilities otherwise available (e.g., water, drainage, sewer or sewage treatment capacity) to, within or available for use by the Project;

(d) Limit or control in any manner the timing or phasing of the construction/development of the Project allowed by the Collective Standards;

(e) Limit the location of buildings, structures, grading or other improvements relating to the development of the Project in a manner which is inconsistent with or more restrictive than the Collective Standards;

(f) Limit the processing of applications for or procurement of Subsequent Approvals;

(g) Establish, enact or increase in any manner applicable to the Project, or impose against the Project, any fees, taxes (including, without limitation, general, special, and excise taxes), assessments, liens or other financial obligations other than: (i) those specifically permitted by this Agreement; or

(h) Initiate, support or establish any assessment district or other public financing mechanism that would include or otherwise burden or effect the Project or the Subject Property that has not been established prior to the Effective Date.

Clauses (a) through (h) above are intended as examples, and not as a comprehensive or exclusive list, of new development requirements that would or could conflict with the Collective Standards, and therefore with this Agreement.

Section 2.6. **Changes to Existing Land Use Regulations.** Only the following changes to the Existing Land Use Regulations shall apply to the development of the Subject Property:

(a) Land use regulations, ordinances, policies, programs, resolutions or fees adopted or undertaken by County in order to comply with regional, state or federal laws, plans or regulations, provided that in the event that such regional, state or federal laws, plans or regulations prevent or preclude compliance with one or more provisions of this Agreement, such provision or provisions shall be modified or suspended as may be necessary to comply with such regional, state or federal laws or regulations.

(b) County land use regulations, ordinances, policies, programs, resolutions or fees adopted after the Effective Date, that are not in conflict with the terms and conditions for development of the Subject Property established by this Agreement or otherwise applicable Existing Land Use Regulations and which do not impose additional burdens on such development.

(c) County land use regulations, ordinances, policies, programs, resolutions or fees adopted after the Effective Date, which are in conflict with the Existing Land Use Regulations, but the application of which to the development of the Subject Property has been consented to in writing by the Developer and/or the applicable Landowner either through this Agreement or by later separate document.

(d) RIM and _________ Basin transportation fees, as long as the fees apply generally to similar types of development, said fees to apply prospectively only.

Section 2.7. **Application, Processing and Inspection Fees.** Application fees, processing fees and inspection fees that are revised during the term of this Agreement shall apply to the development pursuant to this Agreement, provided that such revised fees apply generally to similar private projects or works within County.

Section 2.8. **Timing of Development.** The parties acknowledge that the most efficient and economic development of the Subject Property depends upon numerous factors, such as market orientation and demand, interest rates, competition and similar factors, and that generally it will be most economically beneficial to the ultimate purchasers to have the rate of development determined by Developer. Accordingly, the timing, sequencing and phasing of the development is solely the responsibility of Developer, and the Board of Supervisors shall not impose, by ordinance, resolution or otherwise, any restrictions on such timing, sequencing or phasing of development within the Subject Property.

Section 2.9. **Obligation and Rights of Mortgage Lenders.** The holder of any mortgage, deed of trust or other security arrangement with respect to the Subject Property, or any portion thereof, shall not be obligated under this Agreement to construct or complete improvements or to guarantee such construction or completion, but shall otherwise be bound by all of the terms and conditions of this Agreement which pertain to the Subject Property or such portion thereof in which it holds an interest. Any such holder who comes into possession of the Subject Property, or any portion thereof, pursuant to a foreclosure of a mortgage or a deed of trust, or deed in lieu of such foreclosure, shall take the Subject Property, or such portion thereof, subject to any pro rata claims for payments or charges against the Subject Property, or such portion thereof, which accrue prior and subsequent to the time such holder comes into possession. Nothing in this Agreement shall be deemed or construed to permit or authorize any such holder to devote the Subject Property, or any portion thereof, to any uses, or to construct any improvements thereon, other than those uses and improvements provided for or authorized by this Agreement, subject to all of the terms and conditions of this Agreement.

Section 2.10. Priority for Hiring of County Residents for Building Construction. To the full extent permitted by state and federal law, the Developer and its contractors and subcontractors, shall give priority in the employment of individuals who reside in __________ County for performance of work in the building construction phase of development, so long as those individuals are as equally qualified, competent and competitive in wage rates as individuals applying for work who reside outside the County. This provision shall not be construed so as to do any of the following:

(a) Interfere with or create a violation of the terms of valid collective bargaining agreements;

(b) Require the Developer or contractor to hire an unqualified individual;

(c) Interfere with, or create a violation of, any federal affirmative action obligation of the Developer or contractor for hiring; or,

(d) Interfere with, or create a violation of, the requirements of Section 12990 of the Government Code.

ARTICLE 3

2 ENTITLEMENT AND PERMIT PROCESSING, INSPECTIONS

Section 3.1. County Approvals. Subject to Developer's compliance with applicable regulations, the County is bound to permit the uses on the Subject Property that are consistent with the Collective Standards. The County agrees to grant and implement the land use and building approvals, including, but not limited to, planned unit developments, variances, development plans, subdivision improvement plans and agreements, building plans and permits, specifications, landscape plans, grading plans and permits, parcel maps, tentative subdivision maps, final subdivision maps (including phased final subdivision maps), amendments to maps, lot line adjustments, re-subdivisions, use permits and certificates of occupancy (collectively "County Approvals"), reasonably necessary or desirable to accomplish the goals, objectives, policies, standards and plans described in the Collective Standards. County Approvals shall include any applications, permits and approvals required to complete the infrastructure and improvements necessary to develop the Subject Property (collectively, the "Improvements"), in accordance with the Collective Standards, including, without limitation, those related to: (i) clearing the Subject Property; (ii) grading the Subject Property; (iii) construction of roads, storm drainage facilities, sewer facilities and other utility facilities and connections; (iv) construction of water treatment and delivery facilities and storage tanks; and (v) construction of all commercial, industrial and residential structures and all structures and facilities accessory thereto, subject to the limitations set forth in the Collective Standards.

Section 3.2. Duty to Grant and Implement. County's obligation to grant and implement the County Approvals set forth above shall not infringe upon the County's right to withhold such County Approvals for failure to conform to the Collective Standards.

Section 3.3. Timely Processing. The aforementioned County Approvals and any environmental review required thereon shall be granted and approved by the County on a timely basis, provided that applications for such approvals are submitted to the County during the term of this Agreement, and provided further that Developer is not in default under the terms and conditions of this Agreement.

Section 3.4. Cooperation Between County and Developer. The County agrees to cooperate with Developer in securing all permits which may be required by the County.

ARTICLE 4

3 DEFAULT

Section 4.1 General Provisions. Subject to extensions of time by mutual consent in writing, failure or delay by either party or Landowner not released from this Agreement to perform any term or provision of this Agreement, shall constitute a default. In the event of alleged default or breach of any terms or conditions of this Agreement, the party alleging such default or breach shall give the other party or Landowner not less than sixty (60) days notice in writing specifying the nature of the alleged default and the manner in which said default may be cured. During any such sixty

(60) day period, the party or Landowner charged shall not be considered in default for purposes of termination or institution of legal proceedings.

After notice and expiration of the sixty (60) day period, if such default has not been cured or is not being diligently cured in the manner set forth in the notice, the other party or Landowner to this Agreement may, at his option, institute legal proceedings pursuant to this Agreement or give notice of its intent to terminate this Agreement pursuant to California Government Code section 65868 and any regulations of the County implementing said Government Code section. Following notice of intent to terminate, or prior to instituting legal proceedings, the matter shall be scheduled for consideration and review in the manner set forth in Government Code sections 65865, 65867, and 65868 and County regulations implementing said sections by the County within thirty (30) calendar days.

Following consideration of the evidence presented in said review before the County and an additional thirty-day period to cure, either party alleging the default by the other party or Landowner may institute legal proceedings, including compulsory arbitration, or may give written notice of termination of this Agreement to the other party; provided, however, a Landowner may only give such notice with respect to such portion of the Subject Property in which Landowner owns an interest.

Evidence of default may also arise in the course of a regularly scheduled periodic review of this Agreement pursuant to Government Code section 65865.1. If either party or Landowner determines that a party or Landowner is in default following the completion of the normally scheduled periodic review, said party or Landowner may give written notice of termination of this Agreement specifying in said notice the alleged nature of the default, and potential actions to cure said default where appropriate. If the alleged default is not cured in sixty (60) days or within such longer period specified in the notice, or the defaulting party or Landowner waives its right to cure such alleged default, this Agreement may be terminated by County as to the Developer or Landowner and the property in which the Developer or Landowner owns an interest.

Section 4.2. **Annual Review.** County shall, at least every twelve (12) months during the term of this Agreement, review the extent of good faith substantial compliance by Developer and Landowner with the terms of this Agreement. Such periodic review by the Planning Director shall be limited in scope to compliance with the terms of this Agreement pursuant to California Government Code section 65865.1. Failure to complete said review within the prescribed period shall be deemed a finding of good faith substantial compliance. Notice of such annual review shall include the statement that any review may result in amendment or termination of this Agreement. A finding by County of good faith compliance by Developer and Landowner with the terms of the Agreement shall conclusively determine said issue up to and including the date of said review. Any party may appeal a determination by the Planning Director to the Board of Supervisors by filing a written appeal with the Clerk of the Board within ten (10) days of the determination.

The County shall deposit in the mail or fax to Developer and/or Landowner a copy of all staff reports and, to the extent practical, related exhibits concerning contract performance at least seven (7) calendar days prior to such periodic review.

Section 4.3. **Estoppel Certificates.**

(a) County shall at any time upon not less than twenty (20) days prior written notice from Developer, execute, acknowledge and deliver to Developer, lender or investor, an Estoppel Certificate in writing which certifies that this Agreement is in full force, has not been terminated and is enforceable in accordance with its terms.

(b) At Developer's option, the failure to deliver such Estoppel Certificate within the stated time period may/shall be conclusive that the Agreement is in full force and effect, that there are no incurred defaults in Developer's performance of the Agreement or of any County ordinances, regulations and policies regulating the use and development of the Developer's property subject to this Development Agreement.

Section 4.4. **Developer Default Limited to Property/Entity; Separate Obligations of Owners.** Except as may be specified in Section 4.1, no default hereunder in performance of a covenant or obligation with respect to a particular portion of the Subject Property shall constitute a default applicable to any other portion of the Subject Property, and any remedy arising by reason of such default shall be applicable solely to the portion of property where the default has occurred. Similarly, the obligations of the Developer and Landowners shall be severable and no default hereunder in performance of a covenant or obligation by any one of them shall constitute a default applicable to any other owner who is not affiliated with such defaulting owner, and any remedy arising by reason of such default shall be solely applicable to the defaulting owner and the portion of the Subject Property owned thereby.

Section 4.5. Default by County. In the event County does not accept, review, approve or issue necessary development permits or entitlements for use in a timely fashion as defined by this Agreement, or as otherwise agreed to by the parties, or the County otherwise defaults under the terms of this Agreement, County agrees that Developer or Landowner shall not be obligated to proceed with or complete the Project or any phase thereof, nor shall resulting delays in Developer performance constitute grounds for termination or cancellation of this Agreement.

Section 4.6. Cumulative Remedies of Parties. In addition to any other rights or remedies, County, Developer and any Landowner may institute legal or equitable proceedings to cure, correct or remedy any default, to specifically enforce any covenant or agreement herein, to enjoin any threatened or attempted violation of the provisions of this Agreement.

Section 4.7. Enforced Delay, Extension of Times of Performance. In addition to specific provisions of this Agreement, performance by either party or Landowner hereunder shall not be deemed to be in default where delays or defaults are due to war, insurrection, strikes, walkouts, riots, floods, earthquakes, fires, casualties, acts of God, governmental restrictions imposed or mandated by governmental entities other than the County, enactment of conflicting state or federal laws or regulations, new or supplementary environmental regulation enacted by the state or federal government or litigation. Notwithstanding the foregoing sentence, delays incurred in conjunction with the delivery of water or sewer service shall not result in any extensions. An extension of time for such cause shall be granted in writing by County for the period of the enforced delay or longer, as may be mutually agreed upon, but in no case shall the cumulative extensions add more than five (5) years to the effective period of this Agreement.

Section 4.8. Arbitration. As an alternative to the remedies specified in Section 4.6, either party may elect to resolve such disputes through compulsory arbitration. The scope of arbitration shall include all claims, defenses and offsets that the party would be allowed to raise or assert in a court of law. The party seeking arbitration must give ten (10) days written notice of intent to proceed with arbitration under this section. The arbitration shall be conducted in the County, (or such other location that may be agreed to by the parties), in accordance with California Code of Civil Procedure sections 1280-1294.2. Such arbitration shall be conducted by a single arbitrator, unless the parties agree to a greater number. All notices relating to such arbitration, including any notices under Code of Civil Procedure section 1290.4, shall be provided to the addresses specified in Section 1.6 above.

NOTICE: BY INITIALING IN THE SPACE BELOW YOU ARE AGREEING TO HAVE ANY AND ALL DISPUTES DECIDED BY NEUTRAL ARBITRATION AS PROVIDED BY CALIFORNIA LAW AND YOU ARE GIVING UP ANY RIGHTS YOU MIGHT POSSESS TO HAVE THE DISPUTE LITIGATED IN A COURT OR JURY TRIAL. BY INITIALING IN THE SPACE BELOW YOU ARE GIVING UP YOUR JUDICIAL RIGHTS TO DISCOVERY AND APPEAL. IF YOU REFUSE TO SUBMIT TO ARBITRATION AFTER AGREEING TO THIS PROVISION, YOU MAY BE COMPELLED TO ARBITRATE UNDER THE AUTHORITY OF THE CALIFORNIA CODE OF CIVIL PROCEDURE. YOUR AGREEMENT TO THIS ARBITRATION PROVISION IS VOLUNTARY.

WE HAVE READ AND UNDERSTAND THE FOREGOING AND AGREE TO SUBMIT DISPUTES REFERENCED IN PARAGRAPH 4.3 TO NEUTRAL ARBITRATION.

On behalf of
COUNTY, initials _______ Developer's initials ___
By: Chairman

ARTICLE 5

4 TERMINATION

Section 5.1. Termination Upon Completion of Development. This Agreement shall terminate upon the expiration of the term or when the Subject Property has been fully developed and all of the Developer's obligations in connection therewith are satisfied as determined by the County. Upon termination of this Agreement, the County shall record a notice of such termination in a form satisfactory to the County Attorney that the Agreement has been terminated. This Agreement shall automatically terminate and be of no further force or effect as to any single-family residence, any other residential dwelling unit(s) or any non-residential building, and the lot or parcel upon which such residence or building is located, when it has been approved by the County for occupancy.

Section 5.2. **Effect Upon Termination on Developer Obligations.** Termination of this Agreement as to the Developer of the Subject Property or any portion thereof shall not affect any of the Developer's obligations to comply with the County General Plan and the terms and conditions of any applicable zoning, or subdivision map or other land use entitlements approved with respect to the Subject Property, any other covenants or any other development requirements specified in this Agreement to continue after the termination of this Agreement, or obligations to pay assessments, liens, fees or taxes.

Section 5.3. **Effect Upon Termination on County.** Upon any termination of this Agreement as to the Developer of the Subject Property, or any portion thereof, the entitlements, conditions of development, limitations on fees and all other terms and conditions of this Agreement shall no longer be vested hereby with respect to the property affected by such termination (provided vesting of such entitlements, conditions or fees may then be established for such property pursuant to then existing planning and zoning law) and the County shall no longer be limited, by this Agreement, to make any changes or modifications to such entitlements, conditions or fees applicable to such property.

IN WITNESS WHEREOF, this Agreement was executed by the parties thereto on the dates set forth below.

COUNTY OF ______________

By: ________________________ Date ____________
By: Chairman

ATTEST:

____
County Clerk

APPROVED AS TO FORM:

____
County Counsel

DEVELOPER

By: ________________________ Date ____________

Its: ______________________________

APPROVED AS TO FORM :

____

LIST OF EXHIBITS

Exhibit "A"	Subject Property
Exhibit "B"	Assumption Agreement
Exhibit "C"	Zoning Code
Exhibit "D"	_________________ Town Study, dated __________, 200__
Exhibit "E"	____________ Concept Plan showing Project Character and Scale

APPENDIX K

Sample Impact Fee Ordinance

CHAPTER 9. DEVELOPMENT IMPACT FEES

TABLE INSET:

ARTICLE 1. GENERAL PROVISIONS AND DEFINITIONS

TABLE INSET:

Sec. 8-9100. Authority and reference to chapter.
This chapter 9 of title VIII of the Fremont Municipal Code may be referred to as the "Impact Fee Ordinance," and is adopted pursuant to the authority of Article XI, Section 7 of the California Constitution, Government Code sections 66000 et seq., (hereinafter "Mitigation Fee Act"), Government Code sections 65000, et seq. (the Planning and Zoning Law of the State of California), Government Code section 66477 (the Quimby Act), and in accordance with the findings set forth in the ordinance codified herein (andall amendments thereto) .
(Ord. No. 2463, § 1, 6-4-02.)

Sec. 8-9101. Purpose of fees.
Pursuant to this chapter, the city has established fees which will be imposed upon development projects for the purpose of mitigating the impacts that the development projects have upon the city's ability to provide public facilities.
(Ord. No. 2463, § 1, 6-4-02.)

Sec. 8-9102. Use of fees.
(a) The fees imposed by the city pursuant to this chapter shall be used to pay, in whole or in part, the estimated reasonable cost of providing specified public facilities, as described in implementing resolutions.
(b) As described in each implementing resolution, the specified public facilities will be categorized into separate and distinct sets of public facilities based upon the type of public facility to be provided, or other identifying features. Each separate set of specified public facilities described in an implementing resolution shall be referred to in this chapter as a "public facility category." Public facility categories include, but are not limited to: traffic, park land dedication, park facilities, capitalfacilities, and fire facilities.
(c) For each separate public facility category, a separate fee shall be calculated and imposed, and each separately imposed fee shall be collected by the city and deposited in a separate and distinct "fee fund," subject to the accounting requirements of the Mitigation Fee Act.
(d) In order to more effectively mitigate the impact of new development, and maximize the use of fee revenues, fee revenues may be used as temporary loans from one fee fund to another fee fund only if the director makes findings, subject to the review and approval of the city council, of the following:

(1) Based upon planned phasing of the public facilities, and anticipated timing of fee revenues to be collected, it is in the city's best interests to allow the temporary loan.
(2) The development projects which are required to pay fees to the fee fund from which the loan is made will receive a benefit from the use of the loan by the separate fee fund to which the loan is made.
(3) All requirements of the Mitigation Fee Act have been satisfied, including a specification of the amount loaned, the date of repayment, and the interest rate to be paid.
(Ord. No. 2463, § 1, 6-4-02.)

Sec. 8-9103. Calculation of fees by implementing resolutions.
(a) Pursuant to the Mitigation Fee Act, in any action establishing, increasing, or imposing a fee as a condition of approval of a development project, a technical report shall be prepared for each public facility category, subject to city council approval by implementing resolution. In addition to the findings supporting the adoption of impact fees identified in the impact fee ordinance, each implementing resolution shall include the following:
(1) Identify the purpose of the fee by identifying the estimated types and quantities of development projects subject to the fee, and the public facility category to be funded by the fees.
(2) Identify the use of the fee by identifying the specified public facilities to be funded by the fees.
(3) Determine how there is a reasonable relationship between the city's use of the fee and the types of development projects on which the fee is to be imposed, by demonstrating how the development projects will benefit from the specified public facilities to be funded by the fees.
(4) Determine how there is a reasonable relationship between the need for the specified public facilities and the types of development projects on which the fee is to be imposed, by demonstrating how the development projects create a demand for the construction of the specified public facilities to be funded by the fees.
(5) Determine how there is a reasonable relationship between the amount of the fee and the cost of the specified public facility attributable to the development projects on which the fee is to be imposed. This shall include two elements: (i) a quantification of the estimated reasonable cost of providing the specified public facility, which may include the estimated costs of land acquisition, design, construction, construction administration, general administration (including establishment and enforcement) of the fee program, and contingencies; and (ii) an identification of the method by which the city quantifies the proportionate responsibility of each development project for the cost of the specified public facilities, which may be satisfied by establishing a formula which reasonably quantifies the proportionate responsibility of various types of development projects using standardized units of measurement.
(Ord. No. 2463, § 1, 6-4-02.)

Sec. 8-9104. Definitions.
As used in this chapter, all words, phrases, and terms shall be interpreted in accordance with the definitions set forth in the Mitigation Fee Act, unless otherwise defined herein.
"Applicant" means any person, or other legal entity, which applies to the city for approval of a development project.
"Change of use" means any proposed use of an existing structure (or a previously existing structure) on a parcel which: (a) requires a building permit or other permit or city approval (such as a conditional use permit or a zoning administrator permit), and (b) the proposed use is included in a different property use category (as defined in implementing resolutions) than the last legal use of the existing structure, and (c) the proposed use results in impacts greater than the last legal use of the existing structure.
"Development project" means any project undertaken for the purpose of development, as defined in the Mitigation Fee Act, and shall specifically include any building permit, or any other permit or city approval required for a change of use. Development project shall specifically include any change of use or remodel.
"Director" means the Director of the Department of Development and Environmental Services of the City of Fremont, or any person designated by the city manager or director to perform the functions of the "director" specified in this chapter.
"Fee" means, for the purpose of this chapter, a development impact fee imposed by the city in accordance with this chapter.
"Fee fund" means each of the separate and distinct funds into which fees for each public facility category are deposited.
"Impact fee ordinance" means this chapter 9 of title VIII of the Fremont Municipal Code.
"Implementing resolution" means a resolution of the City Council of the City of Fremont, including any technical

report incorporated by reference, in which the findings specified in section 8-9103 are made for each public facility category.

"Inflation index" means a recognized standard index (such as the Consumer Price Index), as determined by the director to be a reasonable method of calculating the impact of inflation upon cost estimates set forth in implementing resolutions.

"Mitigation Fee Act" means California Government Code sections 66000 et seq.

"Public facility" means any public improvements, public services, or community amenities, as defined by the Mitigation Fee Act and the Quimby Act, including, but not limited to: traffic improvements, park land dedication, park facility improvements, capital facilities (such as public buildings), fire facilities, and any similar public improvement for which the city has adopted an implementing resolution pursuant to this chapter.

"Public facility category" means a separate and distinct set of public facilities as described in section 8-9102(b).

"Quimby Act" means Government Code section 66477.

"Remodel" means any proposed improvement or reconstruction of an existing structure (or a previously existing structure) on a parcel which: (a) requires a building permit or other permit or city approval (such as a conditional use permit or a zoning administrator permit), and (b) results in impacts greater than the last legal use of the existing structure.

"Specified public facility" means those public facilities described in each implementing resolution, the total program costs of which are used as the basis for the calculation of a fee, as described in section 8-9102.

"Vested development rights" means an applicant's right to proceed with development of a development project in substantial compliance with the local ordinances, policies, and standards in effect at the time that the rights vest, as the term is defined in the vesting tentative map statutes (Government Code sections 66498.1--66498.9), development agreement statutes (Government Code sections 65864--65869.5), and state law.

(Ord. No. 2463, § 1, 6-4-02.)

ARTICLE 2. PAYMENT OF FEES

TABLE INSET:

Sec. 8-9200. Obligation to pay fees.

(a) Each applicant for city approval of a development project (including applications for a change of use and remodels) shall pay impact fees to the city, in accordance with the amounts set forth in implementing resolutions, unless the applicant establishes, to the satisfaction of the Director, entitlement to a fee credit pursuant to Article 3, a fee adjustment pursuant to Article 4, or a fee exemption or exception pursuant to this Article 2.

(b) The obligation to pay impact fees pursuant to this chapter shall not replace an applicant's obligation to mitigate development project impacts in accordance with other requirements of state or local law.

(Ord. No. 2463, § 1, 6-4-02.)

Sec. 8-9201. Timing of payment.

The fee for each unit of development within a development project shall be paid in-full prior to the issuance of the city permit required for that unit of development, unless otherwise authorized by the Mitigation Fee Act. If an applicant receives a permit from the city for a unit of development, and the fee has not been paid, the applicant shall pay the fee in-full within 30 days of written notice from the city.

(Ord. No. 2463, § 1, 6-4-02.)

Sec. 8-9202. Amount of payment.

(a) The fee to be paid for each unit of development within a development project shall be the amount of the fee in effect, pursuant to implementing resolution, at the time that full payment is made to the city.

(b) The fee to be paid for a change of use shall be: (1) the amount of the fee required pursuant to subsection 8-9202(a) for the proposed use, (2) minus the amount of the fee for the last legal use of the existing structure.

(c) The fee to be paid for a remodel shall be the amount of the fee required pursuant to subsection 8-9202(a) for that portion of the remodel which generates impacts greater than the last legal use of the existing structure.

(d) In the event that a previous partial fee payment is made for any unit of development, the full fee to be paid for that unit shall be the amount of the fee in effect, pursuant to implementing resolution, at the time that full payment is made to the city, less the amount of the previous partial payment.

(e) The applicant shall have the burden of proving the amount of any fee previously paid, the date on which payment was made, and the unit of development for which payment was made.

(Ord. No. 2463, § 1, 6-4-02.)

Sec. 8-9203. Park land dedication fees.

The city's approval of each residential development project shall be conditioned upon the dedication of park land, or the payment of a park land dedication fee in lieu thereof, or a combination of both, in an amount proportionate to the number of residents estimated to reside within the development project, and sufficient to maintain the city's park fee standard of five acres of park land per 1,000 persons. The city's implementing resolution for park land dedication fees shall identify the method for establishing the estimated number of residents per development project. If park land dedication is required, the applicant shall receive a credit against park land dedication fees, in accordance with Article 3 of this chapter. In implementing the park land dedication requirements of this section, the city shall comply with all requirements of the Quimby Act.

(Ord. No. 2463, § 1, 6-4-02.)

Sec. 8-9204. Fee adjustments by the city.

The city reserves the right to update and adjust each fee from time to time, in accordance with the Mitigation Fee Act. The fee in effect at the time any applicant has obtained a vested development right shall be subject to adjustment by the city, as incorporated in updated implementing resolutions in effect at the time that full payment of the fee is made, based upon any or all of the following criteria:

(a) Adjustments in the amount of the estimated construction costs of providing the specified public facilities based upon adjustments in accordance with the inflation index.

(b) Adjustments to replace estimated costs with actual costs (including carrying costs) of providing the specified public facilities.

(c) Adjustments to reflect more accurate cost estimates of providing the specified public facilities based upon more detailed analysis or design of the previously identified specified public facilities.

(Ord. No. 2463, § 1, 6-4-02.)

Sec. 8-9205. Exemptions and exceptions.

(a) Non-residential development projects are exempt from impact fees for park land dedication fees and park facility fees.

(b) Residential development projects are exempt from impact fees for any remodel, as long as it does not result in a change of use.

(c) A reconstruction of a razed structure shall receive a fee credit only if the applicant submits documentation to the satisfaction of the director establishing that the razed structure was in existence in accordance with the timing requirements of this subsection 8-9205(c). If a development project receives a credit pursuant to this subsection 8-9205(c), the amount of the fee to be paid shall be: (i) the amount of the fee required pursuant to subsection 8-9202(a) for the entire new structure, (ii) minus the amount of the fee which would have been required pursuant to subsection 8-9202(a) for the last legal use of the razed structure.

(1) In order to be entitled to a credit for a fire impact fee, the razed structure is required to have been in existence on or after May 16, 1989.

(2) In order to be entitled to a credit for a traffic impact fee, or a capital facility fee, or a parks facility fee, the razed structure is required to have been in existence on or after June 11, 1991.

(3) In order to be entitled to a credit for a park dedication in lieu fee, the razed structure is required to have been in existence on or after April 18, 1972.

(d) An applicant may request a refund of a fee previously paid in accordance with this chapter only if the applicant provides written documentation to the satisfaction of the director that: (1) the building permit (including any permit or city approval on which the fee was imposed) is cancelled or voided, and (2) work has not progressed on the building permit which would allow commencement of a new use or change of use, and (3) the city has not already committed the fees to the construction of public facilities. Any refund made pursuant to this subsection may, in the discretion of the director, include a deduction to cover the city's administrative costs of processing the refund.

(e) A development project shall be exempt from the requirements of this impact fee ordinance if the applicant provides documentation, to the satisfaction of the director, of federal, state, or local law (including a duly adopted resolution of the city council) which establishes entitlement to the exemption.

(Ord. No. 2463, § 1, 6-4-02.)

ARTICLE 3. CREDITS AND REIMBURSEMENTS

TABLE INSET:

Sec. 8-9300. Application for potential credit.

An applicant may be eligible for a credit against impact fees otherwise owed, in return for providing a public facility to the city, only if the applicant submits a written application to the director which establishes compliance with all of the following requirements to the satisfaction of the director:

(a) Describe the specified public facilities (or portion thereof) proposed to be provided by the applicant, with a cross-reference to the description of the specified public facilities in the relevant implementing resolution.

(b) Identify the estimated cost of providing the specified public facilities (including construction, design, and/or land acquisition, as set forth in section 8-9103) for which the applicant is requesting credit.

(c) Describe the development project or projects to which the fee credit is requested to apply. The description shall be limited to all or a portion of the development project for which specified public facilities are a condition of approval.

(d) Document that either: (1) the applicant is required, as a condition of approval for the development project, to construct the specified public facilities; or (2) the applicant requests to build one or more specified public facilities which benefit the development project, and the director determines in writing prior to the commencement of construction that it is in the city's best interests for the specified public facilities to be built by the applicant.

(e) To the extent that credit for land acquisition costs are requested, document that: (1) the location of the land is advantageous to the public facility needs of the city; and (2) the amount of credit for the land acquisition is equal to a reasonable estimate of the fair market value of the land based upon either: (i) documentation provided by the applicant to the city, or (ii) in the event that the director determines that the documentation provided by the applicant does not provide a reasonable basis for determining the fair market value of the land, the applicant shall pay for the costs of a property appraisal by an expert selected by the director which is qualified to express an opinion as to the value of the property (pursuant to Code of Civil Procedure section 1255.010).

(Ord. No. 2463, § 1, 6-4-02.)

Sec. 8-9301. Timing of application.

The application for credit shall be submitted by the applicant to the director in accordance with the following timing requirements: (a) to the extent that the applicant requests credit for design or construction, the application shall be submitted concurrently with the submittal of improvement plans; (b) to the extent that the applicant requests credit for land dedication, the application shall be submitted prior to the recordation of the final map or parcel map for the development project. The applicant may submit a late application only if the applicant establishes, to the satisfaction of the director, that, in light of new or changed circumstances, it is in the city's best interests to allow the late application.

(Ord. No. 2463, § 1, 6-4-02.)

Sec. 8-9302. Amount of potential credit.

In the event that the director determines that the applicant has submitted a timely application in compliance with section 8-9301, and it is in the city's best interest to allow the applicant to provide the proposed specified public facility, the applicant shall be entitled to credit against fees otherwise owed in accordance with this chapter, provided that the applicant enters into an agreement with the city which includes the following essential terms:

(a) The design of the specified public facility is approved by the city.

(b) The applicant agrees to provide the specified public facilities in return for the credit to be allocated in accordance with the terms of the agreement and this chapter.

(c) The amount of credit available to the applicant shall not exceed the lesser of: (i) the applicant's actual cost of providing the specified public facility, to be evidenced by the submittal of written documentation to the satisfaction of the director, and (ii) the estimated cost of providing the specified public facility, as identified in the implementing resolution.

(d) The amount of credit available to the applicant for land dedication shall be equal to the amount identified in section 8-9300(e).

(e) The applicant provides improvement security in a form and amount acceptable to the city.

(f) The applicant identifies the development projects to which the credit will be applied.

(g) The credit may only be applied to fees which would otherwise be owed for the public facility category relevant to the specified public facility.

(Ord. No. 2463, § 1, 6-4-02.)

Sec. 8-9303. Request for reimbursement.

To the extent that the applicant has a balance of credit available, the applicant may submit a written request for reimbursement to the director. The applicant shall be entitled to potential reimbursement from the city only if the applicant submits a written request to the director which establishes the following:

(a) The request shall be made no later than 180 days after the later to occur of: (i) issuance of the last permit within the development project for which the application for credit was made, or (ii) the date of the city's acceptance of the specified public facilities as complete.

(b) The request shall identify the specific dollar amount of the credit balance for which the applicant requests reimbursement, along with documentation in support thereof. This documentation shall include a calculation of the total credit available (pursuant to section 8-9302(c)) less amount of credit previously allocated to offset fees pursuant to section 8-9302(f).

(c) The request must include a designation of the name and address of the legal entity to which reimbursement payments are to be made.

(Ord. No. 2463, § 1, 6-4-02.)

Sec. 8-9304. Allocation of reimbursements.

(a) In the event the director determines that the applicant has properly submitted a request for reimbursement pursuant to section 8-9303, the director shall prepare a written determination which will identify the dollar amount of the potential reimbursement. The dollar amount of the reimbursement shall equal the amount specified in the applicant's request (not to exceed the actual credit available to the applicant, less the total of all credit allocations to offset fees pursuant to section 8-9302, as determined by the director).

(b) The city shall make reimbursement payments to the applicant (or the entity identified by the applicant pursuant to section 8-9303). The right to receive reimbursement payments, if any, shall not run with the land.

(c) The city shall make reimbursement payments pursuant to a schedule to be established by the director, and consistent with the approved capital improvement program. The city shall make no reimbursements to any applicant in excess of the amount of fees deposited in the relevant reimbursement account.

(d) No reimbursement payment shall be made to an applicant until after the completion of construction by the applicant, and acceptance of improvements by the city.

(Ord. No. 2463, § 1, 6-4-02.)

ARTICLE 4. FEE PROTESTS, APPEALS, AND ADJUSTMENTS

TABLE INSET:

Sec. 8-9400. Notice of protest rights.

(a) Each applicant is hereby notified that, in order to protest the imposition of any impact fee required by this chapter, the protest must be filed in accordance with the requirements of this chapter and the Mitigation Fee Act. Failure of any person to comply with the protest requirements of this chapter or the Mitigation Fee Act shall bar that person from any action or proceeding or any defense of invalidity or unreasonableness of the imposition.

(b) On or before the date on which payment of the fee is due, the applicant shall pay the full amount required by the city and serve a written notice to the director with all of the following information: (1) a statement that the required payment is tendered, or will be tendered when due, under protest; and (2) a statement informing the city of the factual elements of the dispute and the legal theory forming the basis for the protest.

(c) After receipt of the notice from the applicant, and prior to the informal hearing to be scheduled in accordance with section 8-9401, the director shall investigate the factual and legal adequacy of the applicant's protest. At the request of the director, the applicant shall provide additional information or documentation in substantiation of the protest.

(d) The applicant shall bear the burden of proving, to the satisfaction of the director, entitlement to a fee adjustment. The evidence (information and documentation) to be submitted by the applicant in support of the protest shall include, but not be limited to, an identification of the amount of the fee which the applicant alleges should be imposed upon the development project, and all factual and legal bases for the allegation. The applicant shall identify each portion of this impact fee ordinance and any implementing resolution which the applicant claims supports the allegation. The applicant

shall identify each portion of this impact fee ordinance (in particular the elements summarized in section 8-9103) and each portion of any implementing resolution (in particular the technical reports incorporated therein) which the applicant claims fails to support the city's imposition of the fee upon the development project.
(Ord. No. 2463, § 1, 6-4-02.)

Sec. 8-9401. Informal hearing.
(a) The director shall schedule an informal hearing regarding the protest, to be held no later than 60 days after the imposition of the impact fees upon the development project, and with at least ten days prior notice to the applicant (unless either dates are otherwise agreed by the director and the applicant).
(b) During the informal hearing, the director shall consider the applicant's protest, relevant evidence assembled as a result of the protest, and any additional relevant evidence provided during the informal hearing by the applicant and the city. The director shall provide an opportunity for the applicant to present additional evidence at the hearing in support of the protest. However, in weighing relevant evidence, the director may consider the extent to which the applicant provided requested substantiating evidence prior to the hearing.
(Ord. No. 2463, § 1, 6-4-02.)

Sec. 8-9402. Director's determination.
When the director determines that sufficient evidence has been submitted to decide the protest, the director shall close the informal hearing, and issue a written determination regarding the protest. The director may continue the informal hearing in order to assemble additional relevant evidence. The director's determination shall support the fee imposed upon the development project unless the applicant establishes, to the satisfaction of the director, entitlement to an adjustment to the fee.
(Ord. No. 2463, § 1, 6-4-02.)

Sec. 8-9403. Appeal of director's determination.
Any applicant who desires to appeal a determination issued by the director pursuant to section 8-9402 shall submit a written appeal to the director and the city manager. A complete written appeal shall include a complete description of the factual elements of the dispute and the legal theory forming the basis for the appeal of the director's determination. An appeal received by the city manager more than ten calendar days after the director's determination may be rejected as late. Upon receipt of a completeand timely appeal, the city manager shall appoint an independent hearing officer to consider and rule on the appeal.
(Ord. No. 2463, § 1, 6-4-02.)

Sec. 8-9404. Appeal hearing.
The independent hearing officer shall, in coordination with the applicant and the director, set the time and place for the appeal hearing, and provide written notice thereof. The independent hearing officer may issue directives related to the conduct of the hearing in an effort to facilitate resolution of the dispute or narrow the issues in dispute, including pre-hearing or post-hearing briefs pursuant to a briefing schedule, and scheduling presentation of evidence during the hearing. The independent hearing officer shall consider relevant evidence, provide an opportunity for the applicant and the city to present additional non-cumulative evidence at the hearing, and preserve the complete administrative record of the proceeding.
(Ord. No. 2463, § 1, 6-4-02.)

Sec. 8-9405. Decision of independent hearing officer.
Within thirty days after the independent hearing officer closes the hearing and receives post-hearing briefs (if any), the independent hearing officer shall issue a written decision on the appeal hearing which shall include a statement of findings of fact in support of the decision. The independent hearing officer's discretion shall be limited to a determination that either supports the director's determination, or orders the city to refund all or a portion of the impact fees to the applicant. The applicantshall bear the burden of proving entitlement to a fee adjustment. The decision of the hearing officer is final and conclusive, and is subject to judicial review only in accordance with Chapter 6 of Title 1 of the Fremont Municipal Code.
(Ord. No. 2463, § 1, 6-4-02.)

Sec. 8-9406. Costs of protest.
The applicant shall pay all city costs related to any protest or appeal pursuant to this chapter, in accordance with the fee schedule adopted by the city. At the time of the applicant's protest, and at the time of the applicant's appeal, the applicant shall pay a deposit in an amount established by the city to cover the estimated reasonable cost of processing the protest and appeal. If the deposit is not adequate to cover all city costs, the applicant shall pay the difference within 20 days after receipt ofwritten notice from the director.
(Ord. No. 2463, § 1, 6-4-02.)

Sec. 8-9407. Applicant's acknowledgment of adjustment or waiver.

As a condition of any adjustment or waiver made for a fee imposed upon a particular development project, the applicant may be required by the director or the independent hearing officer to provide an acknowledgment and waiver, in a form acceptable to the director, of any further right to protest or appeal the city's imposition of fees for that development project.

(Ord. No. 2463, § 1, 6-4-02.)

APPENDIX L

Sample Timeline for AB 1600 Fee Ordinance

Source:Abbott & Kinderman, LLP

The following timeline is a representative schedule for completing and implementing a new fee or increase in a fee. This time line assumes the use of an enabling ordinance as well as an implementing resolution. The law permits the use of ordinances only to adopt fees. The latter action actually sets the fee. The actual timeline can vary depending upon the frequency of regularly scheduled meetings of the Board of Supervisors or City Council. Other factors that will affect the timeline will include CEQA as well as whether or not the local agency elects to act on the basis of an urgency ordinance.

Number of Days Before or After Public Hearing	Required Action
-28	At least 14 days before the regularly scheduled meeting, mail out notice to any interested party who requests notice of the adoption of new or increased impact fees. (Gov. Code, §§ 66016(a), 54986(a))
-24	At least 10 days before the "open and public meeting," a local agency is to make available to the public, data indicating the cost of the service, and the revenue sources anticipated to provide the service. (Gov. Code, §§ 66016(a), 54986(a))
-14	A local agency shall conduct at least "one open and public meeting" as part of a regularly scheduled meeting. (Gov. Code, §§ 66016(a), 54986(a)) Recommendation: that this occur at the regularly scheduled meeting at which the fee ordinance is introduced (see next step).
0	Conduct public hearing; introduction and first reading of ordinance.
+14	Adopt ordinance at next regularly scheduled meeting; adopt fee resolution contingent upon effective date of ordinance.
+15	File CEQA notice of exemption or determination.
+45	Ordinance takes effect.
+74	Resolution takes effect 60 days after adoption. (Gov. Code, § 66017(a).)

APPENDIX M

Sample Petition for Writ of Mandate

SUPERIOR COURT OF THE STATE OF CALIFORNIA
COUNTY OF PLACER

RICHLAND COMMUNITIES, INC., a California corporation, RICHLAND ROSEVILLE, L.P., a Florida limited partnership, HIGHLAND RESERVE NORTH, L.P., a Delaware limited partnership, OAKVILLE RESERVE, L.P., a Florida corporation, RICHLAND IRVINE, INC., a Florida corporation, and PARKLAND RESERVE, INC., a California corporation,
Petitioners and Plaintiffs,

No.
PETITION FOR WRIT OF MANDATE AND COMPLAINT FOR DECLARATORY RELIEF

v.

CITY OF ROSEVILLE; CITY COUNCIL OF THE CITY OF ROSEVILLE, and DOES 1-20,
Respondents and Defendants.

COUNTY OF PLACER,

Real Party In Interest

Petitioners and Plaintiffs ("Petitioners"), by this verified petition and complaint ("petition"), allege as follows:

PARTIES

1. Petitioners are the owners and developers of property covered by the Highland Reserve North Specific Plan, the Northeast Roseville Specific Plan and the North Central Roseville Specific Plan in the City of Roseville. Petitioners' development projects in the City of Roseville include multi-family (with significant affordable housing components), single-family, office, industrial, commercial and warehouse development.

2. Petitioner Richland Roseville, L.P., a Florida limited partnership, is the owner and developer of property within the Northeast Roseville Specific Plan in the City of Roseville. Petitioners Highland Reserve North, L.P., a Delaware limited partnership, and Oakville Reserve, L.P., a Florida corporation, are the owners and developers of property within the Highland Reserve North Specific Plan in the City of Roseville. Petitioners Richland Irvine, Inc., a Florida corporation, and Parkland Reserve, Inc., a California corporation, are the owners and

developers of property within the North Central Roseville Specific Plan in the City of Roseville.

3. Respondent and Defendant City of Roseville ("City") is a municipal corporation organized and existing under the laws of the State of California. Respondent and Defendant City Council of the City of Roseville is the governing body of the City.

4. Real party in interest County of Placer ("County") is a political subdivision of the State of California.

5. The true names and capacities of Defendants and Respondents Does 1 through 20 are unknown to Petitioners, who will amend this petition to insert their true names and capacities when Petitioner has ascertained them. Petitioners are informed and believe and on that basis allege that, at all relevant times, each of the Respondents and Defendants, including Does 1 through 20, was the agent or employee of each of the remaining Respondents and Defendants, and, while acting within the scope and course of that agency or employment, took part in the acts and omissions alleged in this petition. Petitioners are informed and believe and on that basis allege that Does 1 through 20 are responsible or liable in some manner for the occurrences alleged in this petition. Each charging allegation in this petition, and each reference to "Respondents," "City," or "City Council" refers to both the named Respondents and Defendants, and to Respondents and Defendants Does 1 through 20.

GENERAL ALLEGATIONS

6. On or about October 15, 1996, the Placer County Board of Supervisors adopted Ordinance No. 4768-B, which added Chapter 38 to the Placer County Code establishing and levying a capital facilities impact fee (the "Fee") on new development in the unincorporated areas of Placer County to pay for anticipated impacts of development on County facilities.

7. The Fee was adopted by the County with the stated purpose of mitigating the impact of new development on a wide variety of County public facilities, including court and criminal justice facilities, general administrative and office facilities, warehouses and archive facilities, outdoor animal control pens/storage, domestic and predatory animal control offices and storage facilities, agricultural department office and lab storage facilities, and morgue/coroner facilities.

8. At various times between 1997 and 2000, the County requested that the Roseville City Council adopt and impose the Fee on new development within the City. The City Council reviewed and considered this request at three Council meetings (on April 2, 1997, June 3, 1998, and July 15, 1998), but did not adopt the Fee on any of those occasions, citing concerns about uniformity of application in other Placer County cities, location of County facilities to be funded, adoption of a reciprocal fee by the County to mitigate traffic impacts, waivers for affordable housing and economic development, and other issues.

9. On February 16 and March 1, 2000, the Roseville City Council again considered adoption of the Placer County Fee. Petitioners appeared at these Council meetings, and, prior to and at these meetings, submitted written and oral comments regarding the proposed Fee, and urged the City Council not to adopt the Fee in light of various legal issues described in the written and oral submittals.

10. On or about February 15, 2000, pursuant to Government Code section 66024, Petitioners requested copies of all documents relied upon by Respondents to establish that the Fee does not or will not exceed the cost of the facilities, services or regulatory activities for which it is or will be imposed.

11. On or about February 15, 2000, pursuant to Government Code section 66006(b), Petitioners requested copies of all information required to be made available to the public regarding the Fee.

12. On or about March 1, 2000, City Council adopted "Resolution No. 00-84 Implementing Placer County Capital Facilities Impact Fees." Pursuant to the terms of Resolution 00-84, the Fee was to become effective upon the later of (i) May 1, 2000; (ii) adoption of a comparable fee by the City of Rocklin; or (iii) adoption of an agreement between the City and the County defining the process for collection of the Fee and requiring the County to indemnify, defend and hold harmless the City from any claim or suit arising out of adoption or imposition of the Fee (the "Implementation Agreement").

13. On or about June 7, 2000, the Roseville City Council approved the Implementation Agreement and thereby caused the Fee to become effective in the City of Roseville pursuant to the terms of Resolution No. 00-84.

14. Petitioners are informed and believe and thereon allege that Respondents intend to apply, levy and collect the Fee from all of Petitioners' development projects within the City pursuant to Resolution 00-84. This petition pertains to any Fee imposed to date or that may be imposed in the future by Respondents on any project owned or developed by Petitioners.

15. Petitioners have exhausted all administrative remedies available to them. Petitioners lack an adequate legal remedy, as no legal remedy is available that would direct Respondents to vacate and set aside the decisions they have made regarding the Fee.

FIRST CAUSE OF ACTION
(Petition for Writ of Mandate)
Against All Respondents

16. Petitioners incorporate by reference the allegations of all preceding paragraphs as though set forth here in full.

17. The California and United States Constitutions require a nexus or rough proportionality between the burden a development project will impose on the community and the exactions imposed as a condition of approval of that development project. Any exaction that lacks this nexus or rough proportionality violates the constitutional prohibition against taking private property for public use without just compensation.

18. The California Mitigation Fee Act (Government Code sections 66000-66025) requires local agencies that take any action to establish, increase or impose fees on development projects to make certain determinations and findings regarding the reasonable relationship between the fees and the impacts of development. Government Code sections 66001(a)(3) and 66001(b) require local agencies to demonstrate the reasonable relationship between the need for the public facility and the type of development project on which the fee is imposed, and the reasonable relationship between the amount of the fee and the cost of the public facility attributable to the development upon which the fee is imposed.

19. Respondents did not independently make the findings required under the Mitigation Fee Act and the evidence before the City Council did not demonstrate the reasonable relationships mandated by the Mitigation Fee Act. Respondents made no independent attempt to determine the reasonable relationship, nexus, or rough proportionality between the Fee imposed and the burden of new development—either residential or non-residential—on County facilities. Respondents did not consider the most recent data available regarding facilities needs and costs, recent and projected growth, and alternative (non-development) funding sources, and their decision to adopt the Fee was not based upon substantial evidence.

20. Resolution No. 00-84 was adopted verbatim as submitted by the County. Respondents relied entirely upon the County's 1996 findings, which in turn were based on a study ("Study") prepared on behalf of the County by Recht Hausrath & Associates in 1994. The Study was based on population and employment projections obtained from the California Department of Finance and the 1993 Placer County General Plan EIR. The Study did not discuss the amount, location or timing of new development, and did not contain an analysis of the impact of new development. The Study assumed that all population and employment increases were attributable exclusively to new residential and non-residential development. It did not analyze the influence of other demographic factors on population growth and employment, such as birth rates and changes in household density. The Study did not contain an analysis of the impact of non-residential development on County facilities and did not analyze the connection between specific services and either residential or non-residential land uses.

21. The authors of the Study recommended that the County review the demographic assumptions, existing facilities standards, alternative funding sources, and assumptions regarding cost allocation relied upon in the Study approximately every five years. Petitioners are informed and believe and thereon allege that neither the County nor Respondents have reviewed these factors since the Study was completed in 1994.

22. The Fee will have a disproportionately detrimental impact on affordable housing, conflicting with the policies of the City's general and specific plans. The Implementation Agreement restricts the ability of the City to grant waivers or deferrals of the Fee and may hamper or preclude attainment of affordable housing goals and policies reflected in the City's general and specific plans and infringe on the City's discretionary land use authority.

23. There is no reasonable relationship, nexus, or rough proportionality between the amount of Fee imposed and the burden new development, either residential or non-residential, will place on County facilities. As a result of the substantive and procedural deficiencies described above, the Fee is invalid and void ab initio. Petitioners are entitled to issuance of a writ of mandate directing the City Council to vacate and set aside any decision it has made to adopt or impose the Fee. Petitioners also are entitled to a writ directing the City to refund any portion of the Fee paid by Petitioners as of the date of judgment, with interest, pursuant to Government Code section 66020 and other applicable law.

SECOND CAUSE OF ACTION
(Declaratory Relief)
Against All Respondents

24. Petitioners incorporate by reference the allegations of all preceding paragraphs as though set forth in full at this place.

25. Petitioners make the contentions set forth above. Petitioners are informed and believe and on that basis allege that Respondents dispute these contentions. Petitioners accordingly desire a judicial declaration as to the validity of their contentions. A judicial declaration is necessary and appropriate at this time so that the parties may ascertain their rights and duties in connection with the matters alleged in this petition, and to avoid a multiplicity of actions.

WHEREFORE, Petitioners pray relief as set forth below:

1. For a peremptory writ of mandate declaring the Fee to be invalid and void ab initio and directing the Roseville City Council to vacate and set aside any decision it has made to adopt or impose the Fee and to refund any Fee paid by Petitioners as of the date of judgment, with interest;
2. For an alternative writ of mandate directing the Roseville City Council to take the actions set forth in the immediately preceding paragraph or show cause before this Court why it has not done so;
3. For a judicial declaration of the rights and remedies of the parties with respect to the Fee;
4. For Petitioners' costs of suit herein; and
5. For such other legal and/or equitable relief as the Court or jury may deem proper.

DATED: October __, 2000

McCUTCHEN, DOYLE, BROWN & ENERSEN, LLP

By:____

Geoffrey L. Robinson
Attorneys for Petitioners and PlaintiffsRichland Communities, Inc., Richland Roseville, L.P., Highland Reserve North, L.P., Oakville Reserve, L.P., Richland Irvine, Inc., and Parkland Reserve, Inc.

APPENDIX N

California Codes
Government Code
Section 66000-66008

66000. As used in this chapter, the following terms have the following meanings:

(a) "Development project" means any project undertaken for the purpose of development. "Development project" includes a project involving the issuance of a permit for construction or reconstruction, but not a permit to operate.

(b) "Fee" means a monetary exaction other than a tax or special assessment, whether established for a broad class of projects by legislation of general applicability or imposed on a specific project on an ad hoc basis, that is charged by a local agency to the applicant in connection with approval of a development project for the purpose of defraying all or a portion of the cost of public facilities related to the development project, but does not include fees specified in Section 66477, fees for processing applications for governmental regulatory actions or approvals, fees collected under development agreements adopted pursuant to Article 2.5 (commencing with Section 65864) of Chapter 4, or fees collected pursuant to agreements with redevelopment agencies that provide for the redevelopment of property in furtherance or for the benefit of a redevelopment project for which a redevelopment plan has been adopted pursuant to the Community Redevelopment Law (Part 1 (commencing with Section 33000) of Division 24 of the Health and Safety Code).

(c) "Local agency" means a county, city, whether general law or chartered, city and county, school district, special district, authority, agency, any other municipal public corporation or district, or other political subdivision of the state.

(d) "Public facilities" includes public improvements, public services, and community amenities.

66000.5. This chapter, Chapter 6 (commencing with Section 66010), Chapter 7 (commencing with Section 66012), Chapter 8 (commencing with Section 66016), and Chapter 9 (commencing with Section 66020) shall be known and may be cited as the Mitigation Fee Act.

66001. (a) In any action establishing, increasing, or imposing a fee as a condition of approval of a development project by a local agency, the local agency shall do all of the following:

(1) Identify the purpose of the fee.

(2) Identify the use to which the fee is to be put. If the use is financing public facilities, the facilities shall be identified. That identification may, but need not, be made by reference to a capital improvement plan as specified in Section 65403 or 66002, may be made in applicable general or specific plan requirements, or may be made in other public documents that identify the public facilities for which the fee is charged.

(3) Determine how there is a reasonable relationship between the fee's use and the type of development project on which the fee is imposed.

(4) Determine how there is a reasonable relationship between the need for the public facility and the type of development project on which the fee is imposed.

(b) In any action imposing a fee as a condition of approval of a development project by a local agency, the local agency shall determine how there is a reasonable relationship between the amount of the fee and the cost of the public facility or portion of the public facility attributable to the development on which the fee is imposed.

(c) Upon receipt of a fee subject to this section, the local agency shall deposit, invest, account for, and expend the fees pursuant to Section 66006.

(d) (1) For the fifth fiscal year following the first deposit into the account or fund, and every five years thereafter, the local agency shall make all of the following findings with respect to that portion of the account or fund remaining unexpended, whether committed or uncommitted:

(A) Identify the purpose to which the fee is to be put.

(B) Demonstrate a reasonable relationship between the fee and the purpose for which it is charged.

(C) Identify all sources and amounts of funding anticipated to complete financing in incomplete improvements identified in paragraph (2) of subdivision (a).

(D) Designate the approximate dates on which the funding referred to in subparagraph (C) is expected to be deposited into the appropriate account or fund.

(2) When findings are required by this subdivision, they shall be made in connection with the public information required by subdivision (b) of Section 66006. The findings required by this subdivision need only be made for moneys in possession of the local agency, and need not be made with respect to letters of credit, bonds, or other instruments taken to secure payment of the fee at a future date. If the findings are not made as required by this subdivision, the local agency shall refund the moneys in the account or fund as provided in subdivision (e).

(e) Except as provided in subdivision (f), when sufficient funds have been collected, as determined pursuant to subparagraph (F) of paragraph (1) of subdivision (b) of Section 66006, to complete financing on incomplete public improvements identified in paragraph (2) of subdivision (a), and the public improvements remain incomplete, the local agency shall identify, within 180 days of the determination that sufficient funds have been collected, an approximate date by which the construction of the public improvement will be commenced, or shall refund to the then current record owner or owners of the lots or units, as identified on the last equalized assessment roll, of the development project or projects on a prorated basis, the unexpended portion of the fee, and any interest accrued thereon. By means consistent with the intent of this section, a local agency may refund the unexpended revenues by direct payment, by providing a temporary suspension of fees, or by any other reasonable means. The determination by the governing body of the local agency of the means by which those revenues are to be refunded is a legislative act.

(f) If the administrative costs of refunding unexpended revenues pursuant to subdivision (e) exceed the amount to be refunded, the local agency, after a public hearing, notice of which has been published pursuant to Section 6061 and posted in three prominent places within the area of the development project, may determine that the revenues shall be allocated for some other purpose for which fees are collected subject to this chapter and which serves the project on which the fee was originally imposed.

(g) A fee shall not include the costs attributable to existing deficiencies in public facilities, but may include the costs attributable to the increased demand for public facilities reasonably related to the development project in order to (1) refurbish existing facilities to maintain the existing level of service or (2) achieve an adopted level of service that is consistent with the general plan.

66002. (a) Any local agency which levies a fee subject to Section 66001 may adopt a capital improvement plan, which shall indicate the approximate location, size, time of availability, and estimates of cost for all facilities or improvements to be financed with the fees.

(b) The capital improvement plan shall be adopted by, and shall be annually updated by, a resolution of the governing body of the local agency adopted at a noticed public hearing. Notice of the hearing shall be given pursuant to Section 65090. In addition, mailed notice shall be given to any city or county which may be significantly affected by the capital improvement plan. This notice shall be given no later than the date the local agency notices the public hearing pursuant to Section 65090. The information in the notice shall be not less than the information contained in the notice of public hearing and shall be given by first-class mail or personal delivery.

(c) "Facility" or "improvement," as used in this section, means any of the following:

(1) Public buildings, including schools and related facilities; provided that school facilities shall not be included if Senate Bill 97 of the 1987-88 Regular Session is enacted and becomes effective on or before January 1, 1988.

(2) Facilities for the storage, treatment, and distribution of nonagricultural water.

(3) Facilities for the collection, treatment, reclamation, and disposal of sewage.

(4) Facilities for the collection and disposal of storm waters and for flood control purposes.

(5) Facilities for the generation of electricity and the distribution of gas and electricity.

(6) Transportation and transit facilities, including but not limited to streets and supporting improvements,

roads, overpasses, bridges, harbors, ports, airports, and related facilities.

(7) Parks and recreation facilities.

(8) Any other capital project identified in the capital facilities plan adopted pursuant to Section 66002.

66003. Sections 66001 and 66002 do not apply to a fee imposed pursuant to a reimbursement agreement by and between a local agency and a property owner or developer for that portion of the cost of a public facility paid by the property owner or developer which exceeds the need for the public facility attributable to and reasonably related to the development. This chapter shall become operative on January 1, 1989.

66004. The establishment or increase of any fee pursuant to this chapter shall be subject to the requirements of Section 66018.

66005. (a) When a local agency imposes any fee or exaction as a condition of approval of a proposed development, as defined by Section 65927, or development project, those fees or exactions shall not exceed the estimated reasonable cost of providing the service or facility for which the fee or exaction is imposed.

(b) This section does not apply to fees or monetary exactions expressly authorized to be imposed under Sections 66475.1 and 66477.

(c) It is the intent of the Legislature in adding this section to codify existing constitutional and decisional law with respect to the imposition of development fees and monetary exactions on developments by local agencies. This section is declaratory of existing law and shall not be construed or interpreted as creating new law or as modifying or changing existing law.

66006. (a) If a local agency requires the payment of a fee specified in subdivision (c) in connection with the approval of a development project, the local agency receiving the fee shall deposit it with the other fees for the improvement in a separate capital facilities account or fund in a manner to avoid any commingling of the fees with other revenues and funds of the local agency, except for temporary investments, and expend those fees solely for the purpose for which the fee was collected. Any interest income earned by moneys in the capital facilities account or fund shall also be deposited in that account or fund and shall be expended only for the purpose for which the fee was originally collected.

(b) (1) For each separate account or fund established pursuant to subdivision (a), the local agency shall, within 180 days after the last day of each fiscal year, make available to the public the following information for the fiscal year:

(A) A brief description of the type of fee in the account or fund.

(B) The amount of the fee.

(C) The beginning and ending balance of the account or fund.

(D) The amount of the fees collected and the interest earned.

(E) An identification of each public improvement on which fees were expended and the amount of the expenditures on each improvement, including the total percentage of the cost of the public improvement that was funded with fees.

(F) An identification of an approximate date by which the construction of the public improvement will commence if the local agency determines that sufficient funds have been collected to complete financing on an incomplete public improvement, as identified in paragraph (2) of subdivision (a) of Section 66001, and the public improvement remains incomplete.

(G) A description of each interfund transfer or loan made from the account or fund, including the public improvement on which the transferred or loaned fees will be expended, and, in the case of an interfund loan, the date on which the loan will be repaid, and the rate of interest that the account or fund will receive on the loan.

(H) The amount of refunds made pursuant to subdivision (e) of Section 66001 and any allocations pursuant to subdivision (f) of Section 66001.

(2) The local agency shall review the information made available to the public pursuant to paragraph (1) at the next regularly scheduled public meeting not less than 15 days after this information is made available to the public, as required by this subdivision. Notice of the time and place of the meeting, including the address where this information may be reviewed, shall be mailed, at least 15 days prior to the meeting, to any interested party who files a written request with the local agency for mailed notice of the meeting. Any written request for mailed notices shall be valid for one year from the date on which it is filed unless a renewal request is filed. Renewal requests for mailed notices shall be filed on or before April 1 of each year. The legislative body may establish a reasonable annual charge for sending notices based on the estimated cost of providing the service.

(c) For purposes of this section, "fee" means any fee imposed to provide for an improvement to be constructed to serve a development project, or which is a fee for public improvements within the meaning of subdivision (b) of Section 66000, and that is imposed by the local agency as a condition of approving the development project.

(d) Any person may request an audit of any local agency fee or charge that is subject to Section 66023, including fees or charges of school districts, in accordance with that section.

(e) The Legislature finds and declares that untimely or improper allocation of development fees hinders economic growth and is, therefore, a matter of statewide interest and concern. It is, therefore, the intent of the Legislature that this section shall supersede all conflicting local laws and shall apply in charter cities.

(f) At the time the local agency imposes a fee for public improvements on a specific development project, it shall identify the public improvement that the fee will be used to finance.

66006.5. (a) A city or county which imposes an assessment, fee, or charge, other than a tax, for transportation purposes may, by ordinance, prescribe conditions and procedures allowing real property which is needed by the city or county for local transportation purposes, or by the state for transportation projects which will not receive any federal funds, to be donated by the obligor in satisfaction or partial satisfaction of the assessment, fee, or charge.

(b) To facilitate the implementation of subdivision (a), the Department of Transportation shall do all of the following:

(1) Give priority to the refinement, modification, and enhancement of procedures and policies dealing with right-of-way donations in order to encourage and facilitate those donations.

(2) Reduce or simplify paperwork requirements involving right-of-way procurement.

(3) Increase communication and education efforts as a means to solicit and encourage voluntary right-of-way donations.

(4) Enhance communication and coordination with local public entities through agreements of understanding that address state acceptance of right-of-way donations.

66007. (a) Except as otherwise provided in subdivision (b), any local agency that imposes any fees or charges on a residential development for the construction of public improvements or facilities shall not require the payment of those fees or charges, notwithstanding any other provision of law, until the date of the final inspection, or the date the certificate of occupancy is issued, whichever occurs first. However, utility service fees may be collected at the time an application for utility service is received.

If the residential development contains more than one dwelling, the local agency may determine whether the fees or charges shall be paid on a pro rata basis for each dwelling when it receives its final inspection or certificate of occupancy, whichever occurs first; on a pro rata basis when a certain percentage of the dwellings have received their final inspection or certificate of occupancy, whichever occurs first; or on a lump-sum basis when the first dwelling in the development receives its final inspection or certificate of occupancy, whichever occurs first.

(b) (1) Notwithstanding subdivision (a), the local agency may require the payment of those fees or charges at an earlier time if (A) the local agency determines that the fees or charges will be collected for public improvements or facilities for which an account has been established and funds appropriated and for which the local agency has adopted a proposed construction schedule or plan prior to final inspection or issuance of the certificate of occupancy or (B) the fees or charges are to reimburse the local agency for expenditures previously made. "Appropriated," as used in this subdivision, means authorization by the governing body of the local agency for which the fee is collected to make expenditures and incur obligations for specific purposes.

(2) (A) Paragraph (1) does not apply to units reserved for occupancy by lower income households included in a residential development proposed by a nonprofit housing developer in which at least 49 percent of the total units are reserved for occupancy by lower income households, as defined in Section 50079.5 of the Health and Safety Code, at an affordable rent, as defined in Section 50053 of the Health and Safety Code. In addition to the contract that may be required under subdivision (c), a city, county, or city and county may require the posting of a performance bond or a letter of credit from a federally insured, recognized depository institution to guarantee payment of any fees or charges that are subject to this paragraph. Fees and charges exempted from paragraph (1) under this paragraph shall become immediately due and payable when the residential development no longer meets the requirements of this paragraph.

(B) The exception provided in subparagraph (A) does not apply to fees and charges levied pursuant to Chapter 6 (commencing with Section 17620) of Part 10.5 of Division 1 of Title 1 of the Education Code.

(c) (1) If any fee or charge specified in subdivision (a) is not fully paid prior to issuance of a building permit for construction of any portion of the residential development encumbered thereby, the local agency issuing the building permit may require the property owner, or lessee if the lessee's interest appears of record, as a condition of issuance of the building permit, to execute a contract to pay the fee or charge, or applicable portion thereof, within the time specified in subdivision (a). If the fee or charge is prorated pursuant to subdivision (a), the obligation under the contract shall be similarly prorated.

(2) The obligation to pay the fee or charge shall inure to the benefit of, and be enforceable by, the local agency that imposed the fee or charge, regardless of whether it is a party to the contract.

The contract shall contain a legal description of the property affected, shall be recorded in the office of the county recorder of the county and, from the date of recordation, shall constitute a lien for the payment of the fee or charge, which shall be enforceable against successors in interest to the property owner or lessee at the time of issuance of the building permit. The contract shall be recorded in the grantor-grantee index in the name of the public agency issuing the building permit as grantee and in the name of the property owner or lessee as grantor. The local agency shall record a release of the obligation, containing a legal description of the property, in the event the obligation is paid in full, or a partial release in the event the fee or charge is prorated pursuant to subdivision (a).

(3) The contract may require the property owner or lessee to provide appropriate notification of the opening of any escrow for the sale of the property for which the building permit was issued and to provide in the escrow instructions that the fee or charge be paid to the local agency imposing the same from the sale proceeds in escrow prior to disbursing proceeds to the seller.

(d) This section applies only to fees collected by a local agency to fund the construction of public improvements or facilities. It does not apply to fees collected to cover the cost of code enforcement or inspection services, or to other fees collected to pay for the cost of enforcement of local ordinances or state law.

(e) "Final inspection" or "certificate of occupancy," as used in this section, have the same meaning as described in Sections 305 and 307 of the Uniform Building Code, International Conference of Building Officials, 1985 edition.

(f) Methods of complying with the requirement in subdivision (b) that a proposed construction schedule or plan be adopted, include, but are not limited to, (1) the adoption of the capital improvement plan described in Section 66002, or (2) the submittal of a five-year plan for construction and rehabilitation of school facilities pursuant to subdivision (c) of Section 17017.5 of the Education Code.

66008. A local agency shall expend a fee for public improvements, as accounted for pursuant to Section 66006, solely and exclusively for the purpose or purposes, as identified in subdivision (f) of Section 66006, for which the fee was collected. The fee shall not be levied, collected, or imposed for general revenue purposes.

66010. As used in this chapter:

(a) "Development project" means a development project as defined in Section 66000.

(b) "Fee" means a monetary exaction or a dedication, other than a tax or special assessment, which is required by a local agency of the applicant in connection with approval of a development project for the purpose of defraying all or a portion of the cost of public facilities related to the development project, but does not include fees for processing applications for governmental regulatory actions or approvals.

(c) "Local agency" means a local agency, as defined in Section 66000.

(d) "Public facilities" means public facilities, as defined in Section 66000.

(e) "Reconstruction" means the reconstruction of the real property, or portion thereof, where the property after reconstruction is substantially equivalent to the property prior to damage or destruction.

66011. No fee may be applied by a local agency to the reconstruction of any residential, commercial, or industrial development project that is damaged or destroyed as a result of a natural disaster, as declared by the Governor. Any reconstruction of real property, or portion thereof, which is not substantially equivalent to the damaged or destroyed property, shall be deemed to be new construction and only that portion which exceeds substantially equivalent construction may be assessed a fee. The term substantially equivalent, as used in this section, shall have the same meaning as the term in subdivision (c) of Section 70 of the Revenue and Taxation Code.

66012. (a) Notwithstanding any other provision of law which prescribes an amount or otherwise limits the amount of a fee or charge which may be levied by a city, county, or city and county, a city, county, or city and county shall have the authority to levy any fee or charge in connection with the operation of an aerial tramway within its jurisdiction.

(b) If any person disputes whether a fee or charge levied pursuant to subdivision (a) is reasonable, the auditor, or if there is no auditor, the fiscal officer, of the city, county, or city and county shall, upon request of the legislative body of the city, county, or city and county, conduct a study and determine whether the fee or charge is reasonable.

66013. (a) Notwithstanding any other provision of law, when a local agency imposes fees for water connections or sewer connections, or imposes capacity charges, those fees or charges shall not exceed the estimated reasonable cost of providing the service for which the fee or charge is imposed, unless a question regarding the amount of the fee or charge imposed in excess of the estimated reasonable cost of providing the services or materials is submitted to, and approved by, a popular vote of two-thirds of those electors voting on the issue.

(b) As used in this section:

(1) "Sewer connection" means the connection of a structure or project to a public sewer system.

(2) "Water connection" means the connection of a structure or project to a public water system, as defined in subdivision (f) of Section 116275 of the Health and Safety Code.

(3) "Capacity charge" means a charge for public facilities in existence at the time a charge is imposed or charges for new public facilities to be acquired or constructed in the future that are of proportional benefit to the person or property being charged, including supply or capacity contracts for rights or entitlements, real property interests, and entitlements and other rights of the local agency involving capital expense relating to its use of existing or new public facilities. A "capacity charge" does not include a commodity charge.

(4) "Local agency" means a local agency as defined in Section 66000.

(5) "Fee" means a fee for the physical facilities necessary to make a water connection or sewer connection, including, but not limited to, meters, meter boxes, and pipelines from the structure or project to a water distribution line or sewer main, and that does not exceed the estimated reasonable cost of labor and materials for installation of those facilities.

(6) "Public facilities" means public facilities as defined in Section 66000.

(c) A local agency receiving payment of a charge as specified in paragraph (3) of subdivision (b) shall deposit it in a separate capital facilities fund with other charges received, and account for the charges in a manner to avoid any commingling with other moneys of the local agency, except for investments, and shall expend those charges solely for the purposes for which the charges were collected. Any interest income earned from the investment of moneys in the capital facilities fund shall be deposited in that fund.

(d) For a fund established pursuant to subdivision (c), a local agency shall make available to the public, within 180 days after the last day of each fiscal year, the following information for that fiscal year:

(1) A description of the charges deposited in the fund.

(2) The beginning and ending balance of the fund and the interest earned from investment of moneys in the fund.

(3) The amount of charges collected in that fiscal year.

(4) An identification of all of the following:

(A) Each public improvement on which charges were expended and the amount of the expenditure for each improvement, including the percentage of the total cost of the public improvement that was funded with those charges if more than one source of funding was used.

(B) Each public improvement on which charges were expended that was completed during that fiscal year.

(C) Each public improvement that is anticipated to be undertaken in the following fiscal year.

(5) A description of each interfund transfer or loan made from the capital facilities fund. The information provided, in the case of an interfund transfer, shall identify the public improvements on which the transferred moneys are, or will be, expended. The information, in the case of an interfund loan, shall include the date on which the loan will be repaid, and the rate of interest that the fund will receive on the loan.

(e) The information required pursuant to subdivision (d) may be included in the local agency's annual financial report.

(f) The provisions of subdivisions (c) and (d) shall not apply to any of the following:

(1) Moneys received to construct public facilities pursuant to a contract between a local agency and a person or entity, including, but not limited to, a reimbursement agreement pursuant to Section 66003.

(2) Charges that are used to pay existing debt service or which are subject to a contract with a trustee for bondholders that requires a different accounting of the charges, or charges that are used to reimburse the local agency or to reimburse a person or entity who advanced funds under a reimbursement agreement or contract for facilities in existence at the time the charges are collected.

(3) Charges collected on or before December 31, 1998.

(g) Any judicial action or proceeding to attack, review, set aside, void, or annul the ordinance, resolution, or motion imposing a fee or capacity charge subject to this section shall be brought pursuant to Section 66022.

(h) Fees and charges subject to this section are not subject to the provisions of Chapter 5 (commencing with Section 66000), but are subject to the provisions of Sections 66016, 66022, and 66023.

(i) The provisions of subdivisions (c) and (d) shall only apply to capacity charges levied pursuant to this section.

66014. (a) Notwithstanding any other provision of law, when a local agency charges fees for zoning variances; zoning changes; use permits; building inspections; building permits; filing and processing applications and petitions filed with the local agency formation commission or conducting preliminary proceedings or proceedings under the Cortese-Knox-Hertzberg Local Government Reorganization Act of 2000, Division 3 (commencing with Section 56000) of Title 5; the processing of maps under the provisions of the Subdivision Map Act, Division 2 (commencing with Section 66410) of Title 7; or planning services under the authority of Chapter 3 (commencing with Section 65100) of Division 1 of Title 7 or under any other authority; those fees may not exceed the estimated reasonable cost of providing the service for which the fee is charged, unless a question regarding the amount of the fee charged in excess of the estimated reasonable cost of providing the services or materials is submitted to, and approved by, a popular vote of two-thirds of those electors voting on the issue.

(b) The fees charged pursuant to subdivision (a) may include the costs reasonably necessary to prepare and revise the plans and policies that a local agency is required to adopt before it can make any necessary findings and determinations.

(c) Any judicial action or proceeding to attack, review, set aside, void, or annul the ordinance, resolution, or motion authorizing the charge of a fee subject to this section shall be brought pursuant to Section 66022.

66020. (a) Any party may protest the imposition of any fees, dedications, reservations, or other exactions imposed on a development project, as defined in Section 66000, by a local agency by meeting both of the following requirements:

(1) Tendering any required payment in full or providing satisfactory evidence of arrangements to pay the fee when due or ensure performance of the conditions necessary to meet the requirements of the imposition.

(2) Serving written notice on the governing body of the entity, which notice shall contain all of the following information:

(A) A statement that the required payment is tendered or will be tendered when due, or that any conditions which have been imposed are provided for or satisfied, under protest.

(B) A statement informing the governing body of the factual elements of the dispute and the legal theory forming the basis for the protest.

(b) Compliance by any party with subdivision (a) shall not be the basis for a local agency to withhold approval of any map, plan, permit, zone change, license, or other form of permission, or concurrence, whether discretionary, ministerial, or otherwise, incident to, or necessary for, the development project. This section does not limit the ability of a local agency to ensure compliance with all applicable provisions of law in determining whether or not to approve or disapprove a development project.

(c) Where a reviewing local agency makes proper and valid findings that the construction of certain public improvements or facilities, the need for which is directly attributable to the proposed development, is required for reasons related to the public health, safety, and welfare, and elects to impose a requirement for construction of those improvements or facilities as a condition of approval of the proposed development, then in the event a protest is lodged pursuant to this section, that approval shall be suspended pending withdrawal of the protest, the expiration of the limitation period of subdivision (d) without the filing of an action, or resolution of any action filed. This subdivision confers no new or independent authority for imposing fees, dedications, reservations, or other exactions not presently governed by other law.

(d) (1) A protest filed pursuant to subdivision (a) shall be filed at the time of approval or conditional approval of the development or within 90 days after the date of the imposition of the fees, dedications, reservations, or other exactions to be imposed on a development project. Each local agency shall provide to the project applicant a notice in writing at the time of the approval of the project or at the time of the imposition of the fees, dedications, reservations, or other exactions, a statement of the amount of the fees or a description of the dedications, reservations, or other exactions, and notification that the 90-day approval period in which the applicant may protest has begun.

(2) Any party who files a protest pursuant to subdivision (a) may file an action to attack, review, set aside, void, or annul the imposition of the fees, dedications, reservations, or other exactions imposed on a development project by a local agency within 180 days after the delivery of the notice. Thereafter, notwithstanding any other law to the contrary, all persons are barred from any action or proceeding or any defense of invalidity or unreasonableness of the imposition. Any proceeding brought pursuant to this subdivision shall take precedence over all matters of the calendar of the court except criminal, probate, eminent domain, forcible entry, and unlawful detainer proceedings.

(e) If the court finds in favor of the plaintiff in any action or proceeding brought pursuant to subdivision (d), the court shall direct the local agency to refund the unlawful portion of the payment, with interest at the rate of eight percent per annum, or return the unlawful portion of the exaction imposed.

(f) (1) If the court grants a judgment to a plaintiff invalidating, as enacted, all or a portion of an ordinance or resolution enacting a fee, dedication, reservation, or other exaction, the court shall direct the local agency to refund the unlawful portion of the payment, plus interest at an annual rate equal to the average rate accrued by the Pooled Money Investment Account during the time elapsed since the payment occurred, or to return the unlawful portion of the exaction imposed.

(2) If an action is filed within 120 days of the date at which an ordinance or resolution to establish or modify a fee, dedication, reservation, or other exactions to be imposed on a development project takes effect, the portion of the payment or exaction invalidated shall also be returned to any other person who, under protest pursuant to this section and under that invalid portion of that same ordinance or resolution as enacted, tendered the payment or provided for or satisfied the exaction during the period from 90 days prior to the date of the filing of the action which invalidates the payment or exaction to the date of the entry of the judgment referenced in paragraph (1).

(g) Approval or conditional approval of a development occurs, for the purposes of this section, when the tentative map, tentative parcel map, or parcel map is approved or conditionally approved or when the parcel map is recorded if a tentative map or tentative parcel map is not required.

(h) The imposition of fees, dedications, reservations, or other exactions occurs, for the purposes of this section, when they are imposed or levied on a specific development.

66021. (a) Any party on whom a fee, tax, assessment, dedication, reservation, or other exaction has been imposed, the payment or performance of which is required to obtain governmental approval of a development, as defined by Section 65927, or development project, may protest the establishment or imposition of the fee, tax, assessment, dedication, reservation, or other exaction as provided in Section 66020.

(b) The protest procedures of subdivision (a) do not apply to the protest of any tax or assessment (1) levied pursuant to a principal act that contains protest procedures, or (2) that is pledged to secure payment of the principal of, or interest on, bonds or other public indebtedness.

66022. (a) Any judicial action or proceeding to attack, review, set aside, void, or annul an ordinance, resolution, or motion adopting a new fee or service charge, or modifying or amending an existing fee or service charge, adopted by a local agency, as defined in Section 66000, shall be commenced within 120 days of the effective date of the ordinance, resolution, or motion.

If an ordinance, resolution, or motion provides for an automatic adjustment in a fee or service charge, and the automatic adjustment results in an increase in the amount of a fee or service charge, any action or proceeding to attack, review, set aside, void, or annul the increase shall be commenced within 120 days of the effective date of the increase.

(b) Any action by a local agency or interested person under this section shall be brought pursuant to Chapter 9 (commencing with Section 860) of Title 10 of Part 2 of the Code of Civil Procedure.

(c) This section shall apply only to fees, capacity charges, and service charges described in and subject to Sections 66013, 66014, and 66016.

66023. (a) Any person may request an audit in order to determine whether any fee or charge levied by a local agency exceeds the amount reasonably necessary to cover the cost of any product or service provided by the local agency. If a person makes that request, the legislative body of the local agency may retain an independent auditor to conduct an audit to determine whether the fee or charge is reasonable.

(b) Any costs incurred by a local agency in having an audit conducted by an independent auditor pursuant to subdivision (a) may be recovered from the person who requests the audit.

(c) Any audit conducted by an independent auditor to determine whether a fee or charge levied by a local agency exceeds the amount reasonably necessary to cover the cost of providing the product or service shall conform to generally accepted auditing standards.

(d) The procedures specified in this section shall be alternative and in addition to those specified in Section 54985.

(e) The Legislature finds and declares that oversight of local agency fees is a matter of statewide interest and concern. It is, therefore, the intent of the Legislature that this chapter shall supersede all conflicting local laws and shall apply in charter cities.

(f) This section shall not be construed as granting any additional authority to any local agency to levy any fee or charge which is not otherwise authorized by another provision of law, nor shall its provisions be construed as granting authority to any local agency to levy a new fee or charge when other provisions of law specifically prohibit the levy of a fee or charge.

66024. (a) In any judicial action or proceeding to validate, attack, review, set aside, void, or annul any ordinance or resolution providing for the imposition of a development fee by any city, county, or district in which there is at issue whether the development fee is a special tax within the meaning of Section 50076, the city, county, or district has the burden of producing evidence to establish that the development fee does not exceed the cost of the service, facility, or regulatory activity for which it is imposed.

(b) No party may initiate any action or proceeding pursuant to subdivision (a) unless both of the following requirements are met:

(1) The development fee was directly imposed on the party as a condition of project approval.

(2) At least 30 days prior to initiating the action or proceeding, the party requests the city, county, or district to provide a copy of the documents which establish that the development fee does not exceed the cost of the service, facility, or regulatory activity for which it is imposed. In accordance with Section 6257, the city, county, or district may charge a fee for copying the documents requested pursuant to this paragraph.

(c) For purposes of this section, costs shall be determined in accordance with fundamental fairness and consistency of method as to the allocation of costs, expenses, revenues, and other items included in the calculation.

66025. "Local agency," as used in this chapter, means a local agency as defined in Section 66000.

APPENDIX O

Stirling Fee Conversion Chart

Former Government Code section	53080	53080.1	53080.15	53080.2	53080.3	53080.4	53080.6
Recodified as Education Code section	17620	17621	17622	17623	17624	17625	17626

Notes

Chapter 1

1. Dean Misczynski injected "fiscalization" into the public lexicon in 1986. Dean J. Misczynski, "The Fiscalization of Land Use," Chapter 3 in Kirlin and Winkler, eds., *California Policy Choices*, volume 3, published by the University of Southern California School of Public Administration, Sacramento, California (1986).
2. The State Treasurer cited these projections by the American Society of Civil Engineers and the California Transportation Commission in *Looking Beyond the Horizon: Investment Planning for the 21st Century*, State Treasurer's Office, Sacramento, California (October 2007), pp. 14–15.
3. The cake similes by Macmahon, Grodzin, and Wildavsky appear in Richard P. Nathan, et al., *Reagan and the States*, published by Princeton University Press (1987), pp. 358–359.
4. *Friends of "B" Street v, City of Hayward* (1980) 106 Cal.App.3d 988.
5. *Policy entrepreneurs* invest their own political resources to achieve the results that they favor. This process links problems, policies, and politics. *See* John W. Kingdon, *Agendas, Alternatives, and Public Policies*, Harper Collins (1995, second edition).
6. John J. Kirlin, et al., "Reframing State Dialogue on Infrastructure," chapter 8, in Kirlin and Winkler, eds., *California Policy Choices*, volume 5, University of Southern California, School of Public Administration, Sacramento (1989).
7. Misczynski, op. cit., pp. 74–75.
8. Data from Table 21C, "Revenues Distributed to Special Districts From Transactions and Use Tax, 2005-06," California State Board of Equalization, *2005–2006 Annual Report*.
9. California Constitution, article XIII A.
10. Arthur O'Sullivan, et al., *the Future of Proposition 13 in California*, University of California's California Policy Seminar, Berkeley, California (1993). *See also*, "Property Taxes: Why Some Local Governments Get More Than Others," Legislative Analyst's Office, Sacramento, California (1997).
11. California Constitution, article XIII B, § 6.
12. California Constitution, article XIII C.
13. Gov't Code §53750 – §53754. *See also, Assessing The Benefits of Benefit Assessments: A Citizen's Guide to Benefit Assessments in California, 2nd Edition*, Senate Local Government Committee, Sacramento, California (2004).
14. California Constitution, article XIII D.
15. "Situs" is from the Latin word meaning "place" or "site."
16. California Constitution, article XIII, § 29, and Gov't Code § 55700 *et seq.*
17. Community redevelopment agencies use property tax increment financing to pay for their activities, including funding for their tax allocation bonds. The concept is simple. A redevelopment agency's activities stimulates private investment in a redevelopment project area, resulting in assessed valuations higher than would have otherwise occurred. The property tax revenue that results from this increased in assessment valuation is called property tax increment revenue. The property tax increment revenue pays for the principal and interest on redevelopment agencies' indebtedness, including property tax allocation bonds. For more on redevelopment agencies and property tax increment funding, *see Redevelopment in California (Fourth Edition)*, Gerald Ramiza, et al., Solano Press Books, Point Arena, California (2009).
18. *County of Riverside v. City of Murietta* (4th Dist. 1998) 65 Cal. App. 4th 616.
19. *Shifting Gears, Rethinking Property Tax Shift Relief*, published by the Legislative Analyst's Office, Sacramento, California, 1999. *See also, Tension and Ambiguity: A Legislative Guide to Recent Efforts to Reform California's State-Local Fiscal Relationship*, Candace Carpenter, Senate Local Government Committee, Sacramento, California, March 2001.
20. *Population Projections for California and Its Counties 2000–2050*, State Department of Finance, Sacramento, California (July 2007.)
21. An excellent review appears in a series of articles, "Infrastructure Finance: What Works? What Might Work?" Dean Misczynski, ed., *Land Use Forum*, volume 1, number 3, (Spring 1992), published by the Continuing Education of the Bar (1992).
22. California Constitution, article XVI, § 18, requires counties and cities to win two-thirds voter approval before incurring debts that exceed their annual revenues. School districts need 55 percent voter approval.
23. California Constitution, article XIII A, §§ 1(b)(2) and 1(b)(3).
24. Gov't Code §54300 *et seq. See also California Debt Issuance Primer*, published by the California Debt and Investment Advisory Commission, Sacramento California (March 2006).
25. *Assessing The Benefits of Benefit Assessments A Citizen's Guide to Benefit Assessments in California (Second Edition)*, published by the Senate Local Government Committee, Sacramento, California (December 2004). *See also California Debt Issuance Primer*, published by the California Debt and Investment Advisory Commission, Sacramento California (March 2006).
26. The Improvement Bond Act of 1915, Streets & Highways Code § 8500 *et seq.*, and the Improvement Bond Act of 1915, Streets & Highways Code § 5000 *et seq.*
27. California Constitution article XIII D and Gov't Code § 53750 *et seq.*
28. For an overview of redevelopment, *see* "Redevelopment" (chapter 15), *Guide to California Planning (Third Edition)*, by William Fulton & Paul Shigley, published by Solano Press Books, Point Arena, California (2005). A more detailed treatment is in *Redevelopment in Cali-*

fornia (Fourth Edition), Gerald Ramiza, et al., Solano Press Books, Point Arena, California (2009).

29. Community Redevelopment Law, Health & Safety Code § 33000 *et seq.*
30. *Subsidizing Redevelopment*, Michael Dardia, published by the Public Policy Institute of California, San Francisco, California (1998).
31. California Constitution article XVI, § 16, and Health & Safety Code § 33670.
32. Health & Safety Code § 33030.
33. Proposition 13 (1978) eliminated the ability of voters to pass local general obligation bonds. The voters rejected Proposition 4, which would have restored local governments' ability to issue general obligation bonds, in 1980. It wasn't until 1986, that the voters passed Proposition 46 to amend the California Constitution to permit local general obligation bonds with two-thirds voter approval.
34. Gov't Code § 53311 *et seq.*
35. Special taxes levied under the Mello-Roos Act can pay for a limited number of services. *See* chapter 9.
36. For a detailed discussion, *see* "Exactions" (chapter 13), *Curtin's California Land Use and Planning Law (Twenty-Ninth Edition)*, by Cecily TalbertLarcky, published by Solano Press Books, Point Arena, California (2009).
37. *See* chapter 4.
38. *See* chapter 6.
39. Antonia Dolar, "'Exotic' Techniques," *Land Use Forum*, volume 1, number 3 (Spring 1992), published by the Continuing Education of the Bar, Berkeley, California (1992).
40. *Rider v. City of San Diego* (1998) 18 Cal. 4th 1035.
41. Gov't Code § 6584 *et seq.*
42. For an explanation of joint powers authorities, see *Governments Working Together: A Citizen's Guide to Joint Powers Agreements*, published by the Senate Local Government Committee, Sacramento, California (2007).
43. *A Review of the Marks-Roos Local Bond Pooling Act of 1985*, published by the California Debt and Investment Advisory Commission, Sacramento, California (1998).
44. *Ibid.*
45. Gov't Code §50665.1 *et seq. See also City of Redondo Beach v. Taxpayers* (1960) 54 Cal. 2d 126.
46. Gov't Code § 53175 *et seq.*
47. Dolar, op. cit.
48. Gov't Code § 53395 *et seq.*
49. 81 Ops. Cal. Atty. Gen. 45 (1998).
50. For the City and County of San Francisco, see Gov't Code § 53395.8; for the cities that are members of the Orangeline Development Authority, see Gov't Code § 53395.85; for the Salton Sea Authority, see Gov't Code § 53395.9; for the Border Area Development Zone, see Gov't Code § 53398 *et seq.*
51. Gov't Code § 53835 *et seq.*
52. Woodrow Wilson, "The Study of Administration," *Political Science Quarterly*, volume 2 (1887), reprinted in Shafritz & Hyde, eds., *Classics of Public Administration, Fourth Edition*, published by Harcourt Brace College Publishers, Fort Worth, Texas (1997).

Chapter 2

1. The term exaction as used in the Mitigation Fee Act does not include conditions of approval related to use. *Fogarty v. City of Chico*, (2007) 148 Cal. App. 4th 537.
2. Robert H. Freilich and Stephen P. Chinn, "Fine Tuning the Taking Equation: Applying It to Development Exactions, Part I," *Land Use Law* (February 1988), pp. 3–9, presentation at the League of California Cities Conference, June 1989.
3. Duncan Associates National Impact Fee Survey: 2007, August 2007. *See* http://www.impactfees.com/publications%20pdf/2007survey.pdf. Only 38 California Cities were included in the Survey.
4. City of Glendale, Draft 2006–2014 Housing Element, pp. 120–122.
5. Joel Bell, "California Opens the Door for Municipalities to Obtain Greater Revenue from Subdivision Exactions," 22 *Real Property, Probate and Trust Journal* (Summer 1987), pp. 345, 346.
6. All code sections refer to the California Government Code unless stated otherwise. The text of these sections may be found in Appendix N.
7. Bell, *supra*, p. 349.
8. Section 4, article XIII A, of the California Constitution requires a special tax to be approved by two-thirds of the voters.
9. It is important to remember that many of the fees discussed in this section cannot be used for operation and maintenance. Section 65913.8 prohibits the use of such fees for operation and maintenance, although the statute provides some limited exceptions.
10. James Longtin, *California Land Use Regulations*, Local Government Publications (1987, second edition, and 1998 Supplement), pp. 771–772.
11. Brian W. Blaesner and Christine M. Kentopp, "Impact Fees: The Second Generation," 38 *Washington University Journal of Urban and Contemporary Law* (Fall 1990), pp. 55, 64.
12. Blaesner and Kentopp, *supra*, p. 69.
13. Blaesner and Kentopp, *supra*, p. 71.
14. Benjamin Kaufman, "Planning After *Ehrlich*," presentation to the 1997 American Planning Association National Conference in San Diego, California (Supreme Court holds that city may impose fee to mitigate impacts of loss of land use designation and upholds general legislative fee).
15. Connors et al., "The Expanding Circle of Exactions: From Dedication to Linkage," 50 *Law & Contemporary Problems* (1987), p. 70.
16. California Office of Planning and Research, *Land Use Bulletin* (September–October 1988), p. 9.
17. Longtin, *supra*, p. 789.
18. The "incidence" of an exaction encompasses who and/or what it affects and in what manner.
19. The authority to impose payroll taxes is limited to charter cities.
20. Daniel J. Curtin, Jr., "Legal Aspects of Impact Fees and Dedications, a Developer's Perspective," presentation to the League of California Cities–Annual Conference, Small Cities Session (October 15, 1991), pp. 28–29.
21. California Association of Realtors, *California Ballot Monitor: A Guide to Local Land Use and Taxation Measures* (May 1992), p. 2.
22. *Ibid.*
23. Daniel J. Curtin, Jr., "Legal Aspects of Takings, Dedications, and Development Fees–An Update," presentation to the Real Property Roundtable–Fresno County Bar Association (June 18, 1991), p. 39.
24. Misczynski, *supra*, p. 76.
25. *Rider v. County of San Diego* (1991) 1 Cal. 4th 1, 12.
26. *Santa Clara County Local Transportation Authority v. Guardino* (1995) 11 Cal. 4th 220, 239.
27. Joseph T. Henke and Miles Woodlief, "The Effect of Proposition 13 Court Decisions on California Local Government Revenue Sources," 22 *University of San Francisco Law Review* (1988), pp. 251, 268.
28. Blaesser and Kentopp, *supra*, p. 67
29. The court relied on cases such as *Solvang Municipal Improvement District v. Board of Supervisors* (2d Dist. 1980) 112 Cal. App. 3d 545; *City of San Diego v. Holodnak* (4th Dist. 1984) 157 Cal. App. 3d 759, 763; *City Council of Fresno v. Malmstrom* (5th Dist. 1979) 94 Cal. App.3d 974; and *City Council of the City of San Jose v. Kent South* (1st Dist. 1983) 146 Cal. App. 3d 320.

Chapter 3

1. "The powers not delegated to the United States by the Constitution, nor prohibited by it to the States, are reserved to the States respectively, or to the people." U.S. Constitution, Tenth Amendment.
2. Charles Rhyne, *The Law of Local Government Operations*, § 19.1, 1980, Washington, D.C.: Law of Local Government Operations Project.
3. A jurisdiction-wide enactment need not apply to all property within that jurisdiction but may be limited to a particular type of use (*see, e.g., San Remo Hotel v. City and County of San Francisco* (2002) 27 Cal. 4th 643, where a requirement applied to all hotels converting from residential to tourist-serving use) or, presumably, a geographic portion of the jurisdiction.

4. All code sections refer to the California Government Code unless stated otherwise. The text of these sections may be found in Appendix N.

5. The Fifth Amendment, made applicable to the states through the Fourteenth Amendment, provides in full:

   > No person shall be held to answer for a capital, or otherwise infamous crime, unless on a presentment or indictment of a grand jury, except in cases arising in the land or naval forces, or in the militia, when in actual service in time of war or public danger; nor shall any person be subject for the same offense to be twice put in jeopardy of life or limb; nor shall be compelled in any criminal case to be a witness against himself, nor be deprived of life, liberty or property, without due process of law; *nor shall be private property be taken for public use, without just compensation*." [Emphasis added.]

6. Note that some cases and commentators do not apply the term "regulatory taking" to exactions that require conveying an interest in land (*e.g.*, an easement for public access). *See, e.g., Blue Jeans Equities West v. City and County of San Francisco* (1st Dist. 1992) 3 Cal. App. 4th 164, 169. Others include under the umbrella of regulatory taking both "restrictions on use" (*e.g.*, development standards and "downzoning") and exactions (*see, e.g., Nollan v. California Coastal Commission* (1987) 483 U.S. 835). This book takes the latter approach.

7. In *Monks v. City of Rancho Palos Verdes* (2008) 167 Cal. App. 4th 2, the court addressed the identified "exception" to the categorical rule that a land use regulation that denies a property owner all economically beneficial use is a regulatory taking. In *Lucas v. South Carolina Coastal Council,* 112 S. Ct. 2886 (1992), the U.S. Supreme Court held that such a regulation is a taking, even if established in order to prevent serious harm to the public welfare. However, the Court said, such a regulation does not result in a taking to the degree it restricts a use that is prohibited by "background principles of [state] law of property and nuisance." *Lucas* at 2900. In *Monks,* the court considered whether a moratorium on the construction of new homes in the vicinity of recent landslides had met the requirements for the exception. Noting that the City had the burden of justifying the moratorium under the exception, the court found that the City had failed to do so.

8. "Adjudicative" decisions are also variously known as "quasi-judicial," "administrative," and "adjudicatory," each being "non-legislative." Although the conceptual basis for distinguishing these decisions from legislative approvals is well-settled (legislative acts establish rules of general applicability while adjudicative acts implement those rules on a case-by-case basis), different states draw the line between the two broad categories somewhat differently. (Compare, *e.g.*, California's rule, expressed in *Arnel Development Company v. City of Costa Mesa* (1980) 28 Cal. 3d 511, with the Oregon rule, laid out in *Fasano v. Board of County Commissioners of Washington County* (1973) 264 Ore. 574.Chapter 4

Chapter 4

1. Comprehensive discussions of these laws may be found in Daniel J. Curtin, Jr., *Curtin's California Land Use and Planning Law* (2000, twentieth edition); Beatty, Coomes et al., *Redevelopment in California* (1995, second edition, and 1999 Supplement); and Daniel J. Curtin, Jr. and Robert Merritt, *Subdivision Map Manual* (1998); all published by Solano Press Books.
2. All code sections refer to the California Government Code unless stated otherwise.
3. For a list of common optional general plan elements, see *The Planners Book of Lists,* produced by the Governor's Office of Planning and Research and available on the Land Use Planning and Information Network (LUPIN), www.ceres.ca.gov/planning.
4. "Administrative" approvals, also known as "adjudicative," adjudicatory," or "quasi- judicial" acts, are discussed more fully in chapter 3, endnote 7.
5. Distinct provisions apply to "granny units"—second units intended solely for one or two adults aged 62 or over. § 65852.1. No limitations on exactions are provided with regard to these units.

Chapter 5

1. All code sections refer to the California Government Code unless stated otherwise.
2. The reference to "financing" in section 66001(a)(2) would appear to limit the circumstances in which specific improvements must be listed. However, "financing" is not defined, but as a result of the use of the phrase, "[i]f the use is for financing public facilities, the facilities shall be identified[,]" the Legislature apparently intended that a specific listing of improvements was the exception and not the rule. As a result of this language, the local agency adopting the fee should leave itself maximum flexibility in order to adjust the timing and nature of the specific improvements to be constructed.
3. Both the *Shapell* and *Garrick* cases upheld the school districts' generalized cost estimates as well within their legislative discretion without the need for a concrete construction plan. The courts are also reluctant to "micro plan" a jurisdiction's capital facilities. For example, the school district's choice between constructing permanent and moveable classrooms was one which the court in *Garrick* declined to second guess. *Garrick, supra,* at 333.
4. Section 65090 requires publication once in a newspaper of general circulation at least ten days prior to the hearing.
5. Daniel J. Curtin, Jr., *Curtin's California Land Use and Planning Law,* published by Solano Press Books (2000, twentieth edition), p. 251.

Chapter 6

1. SB 50 or Proposition 1A when used in this chapter refers to both SB 50 and Prop. 1A.
2. The Stirling fee law, Government Code section 53080 et seq., has been recodified in Education Code section 17620 et seq. A conversion table can be found in Appendix ??.
3. All code sections refer to the California Government Code unless stated otherwise.
4. The text of these enactments may be found in Appendix ??.
5. This is subject to periodic adjustment. § 65995(b)(3).
6. Nominally, the Stirling fee requirements were preempted as to school fees and facility financing, even as to local legislative powers. § 65995(e). This preemption was recognized by the appellate court in *Murrieta* in circumstances involving non-legislative acts. *Murrieta Valley Unified School District v. County of Riverside* (4th Dist. 1991) 228 Cal. App. 3d at 1234. The scope of preemption is limited to fees, however, leaving room for other land use control measures.

   > Neither section 65995(e) nor section 65996, preempted a county's authority or prohibits it from considering and providing feasible mitigating measures for land use and development in an EIR, and in the general plan amendment to which it relates, because the general plan amendment allegedly contributes to student overcrowding which adversely affects the existing inadequate school facilities in a school district. As mentioned by the district, those measures could include reduction of residential densities or imposing a controlled phasing of single- and multiple-family residential development within those attendance areas of the district which have inadequate school facilities. *Murrieta, supra,* p. 1234.

   For all practical purposes, since a city or county could exercise one of the other forms of allowable land use controls, local government should be able to offer a "developer buyout" option. For example, if a developer voluntarily elects to pay fees in lieu of compliance with a phasing restriction, the question of preemption becomes academic.
7. CEQA is not a regulatory catchall that may be relied upon to solve the need for school facilities. In reviewing a school district challenge to an EIR prepared by the Regents of the University of California, that took place prior to SB 50 and Proposition 1A, the appellate court determined that:

   > Classroom overcrowding by itself did not automatically constitute a significant effect on the environment pursuant to CEQA.
   >
   > CEQA requires the lead agency to address the physical impacts resulting from project approval and how to mitigate those impacts. The EIR is not required to address how the district should expand its facilities.

CEQA did not mandate that the Regents provide monetary mitigation of impacts. *Goleta Union School District v. Regents of the University of California* (2d Dist. 1995) 37 Cal. App. 4th 1025.

8. The Stirling fee law, Government Code section 53080 et seq., has been recodified in Education Code section 17620 et seq. A conversion table can be found in Appendix ??.
9. As defined in Civil Code section 51.3, Health and Safety Code section 1569.2(j), and Government Code section 15432(d)(9); and for adult mobile home parks, with both rental and resident ownership. § 65599.2.
10. The only exception applies to the Lodi Unified School District. § 65980.1.

Chapter 7

1. All code sections refer to the California Government Code unless stated otherwise. The text of these sections may be found at Appendix ??.
2. The term "exactions" is not defined in the Mitigation Fee Act and has not yet been subject to interpretation through case law. However, usage of the term "exactions" in section 66020 is broad and encompasses fees, dedications, and reservations. Section 66021 further incorporates taxes and assessments under the protest procedures found in section 66022. See (chapter 2, former section A) page ?? for additional guidance on defining these terms.
3. In the unique setting of airport land use plans and local legislative acts, the 5th District Court of Appeal recently concluded that, because approval of a 401+ acre specific plan was adjudicatory in nature, the stricter findings requirements were necessary for ordinance review pursuant to Code of Civil Procedure section 1094.5. *California Aviation Council v. City of Ceres* (5th Dist. 1992) 9 Cal. App. 4th 1384.
4. Even though the term "quasi-legislative" can be used interchangeably with "legislative," throughout this chapter these actions are referred to as "legislative."
5. Title 14, California Code of Regulations.
6. In 1990, the California legislature made extensive technical revisions to sections of the Government Code relating to local government fees, effective January 1, 1991. Consolidating certain provisions of existing law without substantive change, they made technical, clarifying, and corrective changes. Discussions in this section refer to the current code sections unless indicated otherwise.
7. Only those familiar with the frailties of California's legislative process can understand why two statutes exist instead of one—in other words, no rationale exists. Section 66020 is the successor statute to the former section 66008, formerly section 65913.5, whereas section 66021 was preceded by section 65009 and former section 65958.
8. Section 66021 explicitly allows challenges to taxes and assessments as long as a specific protest statute under the enabling act does not apply, or where the monies are not otherwise pledged. § 66021(b).
9. Effective January 1, 1996, former section 66475.4, which set forth special procedures to challenge excessive dedications under the Subdivision Map Act, was repealed by its own terms.
10. Section 66020 is clearly tied to subdivision map approvals. In contrast, section 66021 is linked to the broader definition of development found at section 65927, bringing within its purview a greater range of entitlements. Section 65927 defines development as follows:

    "Development" means, on land, in or under water, the placement or erection of any solid material or structure; discharge or disposal or any dredged material or of any gaseous, liquid, solid, or thermal waste; grading, removing, dredging, mining, or extraction of any materials; change in the density or intensity of use of land, including, but not limited to, subdivision pursuant to the Subdivision Map Act (commencing with § 66410), and any other division of land except where the land division is brought about in connection with the purchase of such land by a public agency for public recreational use; change in the intensity of use of water, or of access thereto; construction, reconstruction, demolition, or alteration of the size of any structure, including any facility of any private, public, or municipal utility; and the removal or harvesting of major vegetation other than for agricultural purposes, kelp harvesting, and timber operations which are in accordance with a timber harvesting plan submitted pursuant to the provisions of the Z'berg-Nejedly Forest Practice of 1973 (commencing with § 4511 of the Public Resources Code).

    As used in this section, "structure" includes, but is not limited to, any building, road, pipe, flume, conduit, siphon, aqueduct, telephone line, and electrical power transmission and distribution line.

    Nothing in this section shall be construed to subject the approval of disapproval of final subdivision maps to the provisions of this chapter.

    "Development" does not mean a "change of organization," as defined in section 56021, or a "reorganization," as defined in section 56073.
11. Title 14, California Code of Regulations. These requirements are discussed at length in Michael H. Remy et al., *Guide to the California Environmental Quality Act*, published by Solano Press Books (1996, second edition).
12. Section 66499.37 provides in part: "Any action or proceeding to attack, review, set aside, void or annul the decision of an advisory agency, appeal board or legislative body concerning a subdivision, or of any of the proceedings, acts or determinations taken, done or made prior to such decision, or to determine the reasonableness, legality or validity of any condition thereto shall not be maintained by any person unless such action or proceeding is commenced and service of summons effected within 90 days after the date of such decision."

Chapter 8

1. Sections 5506.3 to 5506.10.

Chapter 9

1. Proposition 1A and Proposition 22 were intended to limit this practice.
2. Property-based exactions are the focus of this chapter, however several user-based exactions can also be utilized, such as user fees and charges for particular services.
3. All code sections referenced are to the California Government Code unless otherwise stated.
4. Section 53970 defines "local agency" as any city, county, city and county, or a district, public authority, or any other political subdivision in the state.
5. Charter cities may enact their own procedural ordinances under their charter power for assessment district formation and financing. *J.W. Jones Companies v. City of San Diego* (4th Dist. 1984) 157 Cal. App. 3d 745. Generally these proceedings must comply with article XVI, section 19 of the California Constitution, which provides charter entities with a method of avoiding compliance with the provisions of the Special Assessment Investigation, Limitation and Majority Protest Act of 1931. Streets and Highways Code § 2800 et seq.
6. Proposition 218 provides exemptions for certain types of assessments existing at the time the Proposition was enacted. California Constitution, article XIIID, section 5. The exemptions include assessments where bonds were issued, assessments approved by the voters, assessments imposed pursuant to a petition of all landowners subject to the assessment, and assessments imposed solely to finance capital cost or maintenance of certain listed types of improvements. Any assessment existing on November 6, 1996 can be reviewed to determine whether it falls within one of the exemptions.
7. This is particularly confounding in the context of Lighting and Landscape Assessment Districts that require the local agency to be liable for payments of all amounts assessed on public property. Streets and Highways Code § 22663.
8. The Legislature did enact section 5854 in 1997 to ensure that section 3 of article XIIIC of the California Constitution is not construed against owners of municipal securities that were purchased on or before the passage of Proposition 218 on November 5, 1996, such that they "assume the risk of, in any way consent to, any action by initiative measure that constitutes an impairment of contractual rights protected by [section] 10 of article I of the United States Constitution."

9. For an excellent discussion of the bonding methods available, see *The California Debt Financing Primer*, produced by the California Debt Issuance Advisory Commission (CDIAC) and Orrick, Herrington & Sutcliffe. This publication was revised in April 1998 and is available through CDIAC at (916) 653-3269 or www.treasurer.ca.gov/ stoca.htm.
10. Traditional mechanisms include assessments, special taxes (e.g., police or fire special tax or Mello-Roos community facilities districts), and special districts.
11. A Community Service District is not a mechanism to be used by an existing governmental entity in the same manner as other mechanisms discussed in this chapter; rather a CSD is an autonomous special district requiring separate formation.
12. For more on this subject, see the Urban Land Institute's *Ten Principles for Successful Public/Private Partnerships* (2005).
13. Many utilities operate in a "reactive" maintenance mode with the "if it ain't broke, don't fix it" approach. Alternatively, the "planned" maintenance approach focuses on preventive and predictive maintenance activities to reduce long-term maintenance costs.

Glossary

AB 1600

A statutory scheme that governs the type of "nexus" or connection that must be shown between the amount of the fee, its purpose, and the project on which it is imposed. AB 1600 requires local governments to make certain findings before a fee is established and imposed, and contains provisions for refunds, reimbursements, and accounting. Commonly referred to as the "nexus" legislation. (Government Code § 66000 et seq.)

Accounting

With some statutory schemes such as AB 1600, the local agency is required to deposit the fee collected for an identified improvement in a separate capital facilities fund or account in a manner that avoids commingling the fees with other revenues and funds. The local agency may only expend those fees for the purpose for which they were collected. The accounting takes place when the local agency makes available to the public the beginning and ending balance for the fiscal year, including the fee, interest, and other income, the amount of expenditure by public facility, and the amount of refunds made during the fiscal year.

Ad Valorem Property Taxes

A tax based on some percentage of the value of the property.

Adjudicatory Act

Involves the application of an existing rule to a specific set of facts. An adjudicatory act determines rights or obligations of any kind concerning matters or transactions which already exist and have transpired. It implements a plan, policy, or rule already adopted by the legislative body. The terms "quasi-adjudicatory," "administrative," and "adjudicatory act" are often used interchangeably. Review of adjudicatory decisions is by administrative mandamus pursuant to California Code of Civil Procedure § 1094.5.

Aesthetic Regulation

The regulation of building design and site developments in the interest of appearance. The courts have consistently upheld a local government's power to protect and enhance the visual character of the community.

Annexation

The addition of land to an existing district or municipality, with a resulting change in the legal boundaries of the annexing jurisdiction.

Appropriation

Appropriation occurs when a local agency makes expenditures and incurs obligations for the specific purposes for which the fee was collected.

Assembly Constitutional Amendment (ACA)

A constitutional measures the state assembly submits to the electorate for a vote.

Assessable Space

A factor used to determine the maximum school fee allowable for residential buildings defined as all the square footage within the perimeter of a residential structure, but not including a carport, walkway, garage, overhang, patio, enclosed patio, detached accessory structure, or similar area.

Assessment

A charge imposed on real property for local public improvements of direct benefit to that property. Also called "fees," "charges," "special taxes," or "special property taxes."

Assessment Districts

An area within a public agency's boundaries that receives a special benefit from the construction of one or more public facilities. An Assessment District, which is strictly a financing mechanism for providing public infrastructure as allowed under the Streets and Highways Code, has no legal life of its own and cannot act by itself. Bonds may be issued to finance the improvements, subject to repayment by assessments charged against the benefitting properties. Creation of an Assessment District enables property owners in a specific area to cause the construction of public facilities or to maintain them—for example, a downtown, or the grounds and landscaping of a specific area—by contributing their fair share of the construction and/or installation and operating costs.

Bond

An interest-bearing certificate issued by a government entity promising to pay the holder a specified sum on a specified date. Bonds are a common means of raising capital funds.

Brown Act

Also known as the Open Meeting Act or the Secret Meeting Law, the Brown Act requires that certain meetings be public and that deliberations and actions of public commissions, boards and councils, and other public agencies in the state be conducted and taken openly. Meetings conducted on the subject of fees or charges are also subject to the notice requirements provided in the Brown Act. (Government Code § 54950 et seq.)

California Environmental Quality Act (CEQA)

A state law requiring state and local agencies to regulate activities with consideration for environmental protection. If a proposed activity has the potential for a significant adverse environmental impact, an Environmental Impact Report (EIR) must be prepared and certified as to its adequacy before taking action on the proposed project. Otherwise, the local agency must rely upon a Negative Declaration or exemption. (Public Resources Code § 21000, et seq.)

Capacity Charges

Charges for facilities in existence at the time the charge is imposed, or charges for new facilities to be constructed in the future, which benefit the person or property being charged.

Capital Improvement Plan or Program (CIP)

A plan or program, administered by a city or county government and reviewed by its planning commission, that provides a schedule for permanent improvements, usually for a minimum of five years in the future, to fit the projected fiscal capability of the local jurisdiction. The program generally is reviewed annually for conformance to and consistency with the general plan.

Certificate of Participation (COP)

A Certificate of Participation, which like a bond evidences a promise to pay money at a specified time, is typically issued in connection with lease financing. A COP is used as a convenient alternative when certain statutory requirements place restrictions–such as interest rate limitations and election restrictions–preclude use of traditional forms. COPs can be used to finance any real or personal property that the public entity is statutorily authorized to lease, including land, buildings, relocatable school structures, vehicles, computers, and other equipment. Lease financing, however, is inappropriate for expendable supplies and for operation and maintenance expenses because items such as these are not properly the subject of a lease.

Chargeable Covered and Enclosed Space

For commercial and industrial projects, the building department of a local agency calculates the amount of a school fee based on chargeable covered and enclosed space. Garages, parking structures, unenclosed walkways, and areas for storage, utilities, and disposal incidental to the principle use are excluded from this calculation.

Charter City

A charter city is a city organized under a charter as opposed to the general law. A city organized under general law has only those powers the legislature expressly confers and those powers which are incident to those expressly granted. The parameters of a charter city's authority are decided on a case-by-case basis. The charter is not a grant of power, and the powers the charter enumerates do not constitute an exclusion or limitation on the city's authority.

Clean Water Act

The Federal Water Pollution Control Act, generally referred to as the Clean Water Act, is the major body of federal legislation dealing with water quality. Enacted in 33 U.S.C. §§ 1251–1376, its objective is to restore and maintain the chemical, physical, and biological integrity of the nation's waters. To this end, the Act establishes various programs including programs for distributing grants for water pollution control, technology research, and for constructing publicly operated treatment works. The Clean Water Act requires the states to adopt water quality standards to protect the public health or welfare, enhance the quality of water, and serve the purposes of the Act.

Committed

Many statutes require that fees be "committed" as opposed to "spent." The authors suggest that the terms were not intended to be used interchangeably. It is likely that a court would be satisfied by a commitment of funds similar to the definition of "appropriated" under AB 1600.

Community Development Block Grants (CDBG) Program

A program to distribute money to communities around the country as opposed to distribution to large cities, permitting local governments to pay for a wide variety of infrastructure investments.

Community Redevelopment Act

Enabling legislation found in California Health & Safety Code § 33000 et seq. granting cities and counties power to acquire property within redevelopment areas by eminent domain, even if private development projects were planned for the site. The Act also permits cities and counties to create "tax-increment financing" districts called "project areas" enabling them to issue bonds against the future property tax increases inside the project area.

Conditional or Contract Zoning

An infrequently used, uncodified, alternative technique for imposing conditions.

Cortese-Knox Act

The Cortese-Knox Local Government Reorganization Act of 1985 governs annexations and incorporations. This Act is the most recent recodification of the power and duties of the Local Agency Formation Commission. The Act replaces the Municipal Organization Act of 1977, the District Reorganization Act of 1965, and the Knox-Nisbet Act. (Government Code §§ 56000–57550) AB 1600 applies to fees imposed by conducting authorities pursuant to the Cortese-Knox Act in Government Code § 57004. It provides that the conducting authority may establish a schedule of processing fees for the estimated expenses to comply with procedures required or authorized by the Act or a local ordinance under the Act.

Community Service District (CSD)

An independent special district with its own elected board of directors formed in response to the need for higher service levels in developing areas. These special districts, or CSDs, allow counties to isolate the costs of providing a higher level of service than otherwise provided throughout the county.

Dedication

The voluntary act of a private owner setting aside a portion of land or an interest in land for the use of the public. Dedications for roads, parks, school sites, or other public uses are often made conditions for approval of development by a city or a county.

Dedication, In Lieu of

Fees that may be required of an owner or developer of private land as a substitute for a dedication of land, usually calculated in dollars per lot or per square foot of land area.

Development Agreement

A legal and enforceable instrument binding the city and a developer equally, that may specify conditions, terms, restrictions and regulations pertaining to all aspects of a development. Development agreements are subject to public hearings, the making of findings as to consistency with the city's general plan, and recordation with the county recorder. They are authorized by California planning law as a means for "locking in" the specific terms of a city-developer arrangement and for formalizing vested rights in a development plan.

Disposition and Development Agreement (DDA)

The agreement between a city and the developer who will be building a project called for in a redevelopment plan.

Final Map

A map of an approved subdivision filed in the county recorder's office. It shows surveyed lot lines, street rights-of-way, easements, monuments, and distances, angles, and bearings, pertaining to the exact dimensions of all parcels, street lines, and so forth.

Entitlement

In the land use context, an entitlement is a permit or authorization from a governmental entity conferring a right to undertake specific activities as outlined in the permit or authorization on the land for which the entitlement is sought.

Equivalent Dwelling Unit (EDU)

Used in fee studies undertaken pursuant to AB 1600 to calculate the equivalent demand for the facility or service per square foot of commercial or residential uses. The EDU represents the proportionate demand for the facility.

Exaction

An exaction is a development requirement imposed by a city or county for the purpose of offsetting or mitigating the impact of the development on public services, facilities, and the taxpayers who use them. Most often an exaction takes the form of dedication of land for public use, construction of public facilities, payment of fees, or some combination thereof.

Excise Taxes

Excise taxes, or "privilege" taxes, are collected for the exercise of the right or privilege to develop or use property or municipal services. The tax is imposed on the occupants of property rather than on the actual property owners. An excise or privilege tax is not a property tax within the meaning of Proposition 13. The primary purpose of an excise tax must be to raise revenue, and not to regulate.

Fees

A form of monetary exaction other than a tax or assessment a local agency charges an applicant for the purpose of defraying all or a portion of the cost of public facilities or services related to the development project. There are three major types of fees: (1) fees for benefits and services, commonly referred to as "service fees," "user fees," or "connection fees;" (2) fees for regulatory activities; and (3) development fees. The three types of development fees are: (a) in-lieu fees; (b) impact fees, including a variation called "linkage" fees; and (c) mitigation fees.

Finding(s)

The result(s) of an investigation and the basis upon which decisions are made. Findings are used by government agencies to justify action taken by the entity. In general, findings are required for land use decisions that are adjudicatory in nature. In an adjudicatory decision, a reviewing body holds a hearing, takes evidence, and uses discretion to determine the facts and bases its decision on the facts. The decision involves applying a fixed rule, standard, or law to a specific set of existing facts. By comparison, findings are not necessary for legislative or quasi-legislative acts, unless specifically required by statute. Legislative acts may also entail holding a hearing, taking evidence, and using discretion to determine the facts and making a decision based on those facts. However, legislative acts generally formulate a rule to apply to all future cases as compared to applying an existing rule and existing facts as in an adjudicatory action.

Gann Initiative

Proposition 4, which in 1979 added Article XIII B to the California Constitution, placed new fiscal limits on state and local governments by establishing 1978–79 as the base year for tax-financed government expenditures. Proposition 4 also limited the growth of those expenditures in succeeding years to adjustments for population growth plus the lesser of either the Consumer Price Index (CPI) or per capita income growth. This cap on expenditures, called the "Gann Limit," excludes (a) user fees, (b) proceeds from the sale of bonds, (c) revenues to pay debt service, and (d) block grants.

General Plan

A compendium of city or county policies regarding long-term development, in the form of maps and accompanying text. The General Plan is a legal document required of each local agency by Government Code § 65301 and adopted by the city council or board of supervisors. In California, the General Plan has seven mandatory elements (Circulation, Conservation, Housing, Land Use, Noise, Open Space, Safety and Seismic Safety) and may include any number of optional elements (such as Air Quality, Economic Development, Hazardous Waste, and Parks and Recreation). The General Plan may also be called a "City Plan," "Comprehensive Plan," or "Master Plan."

General Obligation Bond (G.O. Bond)

Monies used by the state to pay for infrastructure. Includes both state G.O. bonds which must be repaid out of the general tax revenue and local G.O. bonds which are typically repaid by an increase in the local property tax rate. If a local G.O. bond is issued, each property owner's taxes must be increased to pay off the bond.

General Tax

A tax, the proceeds of which are deposited or dedicated in the agency's general fund for general governmental purposes.

Habitat Conservation Plan

A plan by which some private development or activity that involves an incidental take of an endangered species or alteration of habitat is allowed in exchange for an agreement by the landowners to preserve, donate, or sell critical pieces of land for wildlife conservation purposes.

Impact Fees

Fees levied on the developer of a project by the city as compensation for unmitigated impacts the project with produce.

Improvement

The addition of one or more structures or utilities on a parcel of land.

Infrastructure

Public facilities such as sewage disposal systems, water supply systems, other utility systems, and roads.

Infrastructure Financing District

Legally constituted government entities authorized by Government Code §§ 53395- 53397.11 solely to provide regional public capital facilities.

Integrated Financing District Act

Government Code §§ 53175–53199 sets forth a financing method to construct an expensive public project such as a wastewater treatment plant that might not otherwise be built if a single developer were required to bear the cost merely because other property owners in the surrounding area were not yet ready to develop their property.

Interim Ordinance

A provisional law or regulation adopted by a governmental authority for a limited duration to address a specific situation. The ordinance usually contains specific language identifying the duration of the ordinance.

Inverse Condemnation

In the land use context, inverse condemnation occurs where a land use ordinance, regulation, or decision is so restrictive as to deprive the owner of an economically viable use of the property.

Joint Powers Authority (JPA)

A legal arrangement that enables two or more units of government to share authority in order to plan and carry out a specific program or set of programs serving both units.

Local Agency Formation Commission (LADFCO)

A county commission that reviews and evaluates all proposals for formation of special districts, incorporation of cities, annexation to special districts or cities, consolidation of districts, and merger of districts with cities. Each county's LAFCO is empowered to approve, disapprove, or conditionally approve these proposals.

Lease Financing

Enables public entities to finance capital assets over a multi-year period. In Certificate of Participation (COP) structured lease financing, the public agency leases property from a nonprofit corporation, a Joint Powers Authority (JPA), or another third party. If necessary, the public agency may even lease property to a third party in order to lease it back from the third party. Sold to investors much as bonds are, the COPs are evidence of the undivided proportionate interest of the owners and the lease payments to be made by the public agency under the lease. The lease must be structured so that it does not violate California Constitution Article XVI, §§ 1 and 18, which prevent the state and local governments from incurring any indebtedness that cannot be repaid in the year incurred without the approval of two-thirds of the voters. A lease must be for a proper public purpose and must abide by all the various statutory provisions which govern leasing practices of cities, counties, and special districts.

Legislative Act

A legislative or quasi-legislative act generally predetermines what the rules will be for future cases falling under its provisions. In the land use context, the most commonly recognized form of legislative acts are adoption of or amendments to zoning ordinances, general and specific plans, and development agreements.

Linkage Fees

Linkage fees are exactions in the form of fees imposed on commercial projects that can be used to finance larger public facilities such as mass transit and affordable housing, even though the facilities eventually built with the funds are not physically adjacent to the site or directly related to the physical design of the specific project.

Local Agency

A county, city (whether formed by general law or charter), school district, special district, authority, agency, and any other municipal corporation, district, or other political subdivision of the state.

Marks-Roos Local Bond Pooling Act

Enacted in 1985 pursuant to Government Code §§ 6584–6599, the Act allows governmental entities in concert with, or as part of a Joint Powers Authority, to use a "pool" financing technique for a broad array of public capital improvements.

Mello-Roos Community Facilities Act of 1982

Permits the creation of a Community Facilities District (CFD) to impose a special tax on property located within the district to fund public improvements in the district's area. (Government Code section 55311 et seq.)

Mello-Roos Community Facilities District (CFD)

Districts that raise funds from property owners within a given area in order to provide public improvements in that area. Similar to assessment districts, their enabling legislation is the Mello-Roos Community Facilities Act of 1982, Government Code § 55311 et seq.

Mello-Roos Taxes

Funds collected from property owners within a given area to fund a Mello-Roos Community Facilities District. Mello-Roos Districts are authorized to float tax-exempt bonds, and the Mello-Roos taxes received from property owners in the CFD are used to pay back the bonds.

Mitigate

To ameliorate, alleviate, or avoid to the extent reasonably feasible.

Nexus

A direct connection between an exaction required and the proposed development to which the exaction is attached. The legal interpretation of nexus has expanded to permit local governments to impose exactions that are not as clearly and directly related to development.

Notice of Determination (NOD)

A brief notice filed by a pubic agency after it approves or determines to carry out a project.

Notice of Exemption (NOE)

A brief notice that may be filed by a public agency after it has decided to carry out or approve a project for which an exemption to CEQA applies.

Ordinance

A law or regulation set forth and adopted by a governmental authority, usually a city or county, pursuant to specified procedures.

Parcel Map

A map depicting the establishment of up to four new lots by splitting a recorded lot. Parcel maps are subject to the California Subdivision Map Act and a city's subdivision regulations.

Parcel Taxes

Taxes levied as a flat rate upon each parcel or classification of parcel regardless of the value of the property. Considered to be "special" taxes under Proposition 13, parcel taxes require approval by two-thirds of the voters for passage.

Permit Streamlining Act

The Act, which applies to certain local land use decisions, requires the local government to follow a standardized process and to finish its review and make its decisions on development projects within the specific time limit set forth in the Act. If the local government fails either to approve or disapprove the project within the time strictures, the project is automatically deemed approved by operation of law. (Government Code §§ 65920–65963.1)

Police Power

Article XI, § 7 of the California Constitution permits cities and counties to exercise their police power to protect public health, safety, and welfare which includes regulation of development within their respective boundaries. According to article XI, § 7, "a county or city may make and enforce within its limits, all local police, sanitary, and other ordinances and regulations not in conflict with the general laws." Under this broad grant of authority, local governments enact a wide range of regulatory controls, particularly in the realm of land use and zoning.

Preemption

A local ordinance is preempted when it conflicts with or interferes with a state law on the same subject matter. Where a state law preempts the local regulation, the local enactment is invalid. Preemption may occur either expressly or by legislative implication when a local regulation duplicates, contradicts, or enters into an area fully occupied by general law. Likewise, state law may be preempted by federal law.

Property Taxes

A tax based on some percentage of value of the property. (See also, Ad Valorem Property Tax.)

Proposition 13

Article XIII A of the California Constitution (Proposition 13), adopted by the voters in 1978, dramatically reduced the size of property tax revenues in the state. Accomplishing five major objectives, article XIII A (1) capped the nominal property tax rate at 1% of assessed valuation; (2) rolled back assessed values to their 1975–76 level; (3) limited annual increases and assessed valuation to no more than 2% except when property is exchanged or transferred; (4) prohibited override of the 1% property tax limitation; and (5) required two-thirds voter approval of increases and "special non-property tax liability."

Quimby Act (Parkland Dedication)

The Quimby Act gives the legislative body of a city or county the authority to require by ordinance the dedication of land, the payment of fees, or a combination of both for park or recreational purposes. (Government Code § 66477)

Redevelopment

The legally-authorized process of rehabilitating or rebuilding a deteriorated section of a city using municipal powers and finances to assemble properties, replace infrastructure, or otherwise assist in creating new facilities and stimulating private development.

Regulatory Taking

An ordinance, regulation, or decision promulgated by a local agency that is so restrictive as to deprive the owner of economically viable use of the property. A regulatory taking results in inverse condemnation.

Reimbursement Agreement

An agreement between a local agency and private property owner or developer for that portion of the cost of a public facility paid by the property owner or developer which exceeds the need for the public facility attributable to, and reasonably related to, the development.

Reservation

A compulsory requirement for a subdivider to offer to sell a portion of his or her property at a predetermined rate for public purposes. (Government Code §§ 66479–66482)

SB 90

Passed in 1972, SB 90 establishes a comprehensive system of local government property tax rate limitations, implements a state-mandated reimbursement program for local government, and reinforces school finance to make it less dependent on local property tax revenues.

SB 1287

Legislation enacted in 1992 (Government Code §§ 65995–65996) which added language to the Stirling legislation offering school districts an additional $1.00 per foot in potential fees. Contains a sunset provision, at the time of the statewide vote on ACA 6 (November 1993). If the voters approve ACA 6, SB 1287 continues in effect. If the voters disapprove ACA 6, the limitation of SB 1287 expires, and the prior statutory language kicks in.

School Facilities Act

Authorizes a city or county to require dedication of land, payment of fees, or both, for interim or temporary classroom and related interim or temporary facilities as a condition of approval for a residential development. (Government Code § 65970 et seq.)

Sewer Connection

The connection of a building to a public sewer system.

Special Assessment

A charge imposed on a particular real property parcel for local public improvement of direct benefit to that property. The assessed property receives a special benefit over and above that received by the general public.

Special Tax

A tax, the proceeds of which are deposited or dedicated to a specific fund or purpose and not to funds deposited in the agency's general fund for general governmental purposes.

Specific Plan

A special set of development standards that apply to a particular geographical area.

Statute of Limitations

The period of time, defined by statute, within which a specific cause of action may be filed in court. Once the statute of limitations has "run," meaning the deadline within which to bring a cause of action has passed, that cause of action may not be pursued.

Stirling Legislation

In 1986, the legislature adopted the Stirling legislation which enabled school districts to directly adopt and impose exactions on developers for school construction and reconstruction. This enactment authorizes the governing body of any school district to impose fees, charges, dedications, or other requirements on new construction within the limitations contained therein (Government Code § 53080)

Stirling Fees

The permitted range of school facilities for which Stirling fees can be collected is quite broad. The legislation caps fees that can be imposed on new construction at $1.50 per square foot for residential development and $0.25 per square foot for commercial/ industrial development, subject to biannual adjustments for inflation.

Subdivision

The division of a tract of land into defined interests for purposes of sale, lease, or financing.

Subdivision Map Act

Division 2 of Title 7 (§§ 66410 et seq.) of the California Government Code. This Act vests in local legislative bodies the regulation and control of the design and improvement of subdivisions, including the requirement for tentative and final maps. (See "Subdivision.")

Taking

The broad and flexible authority of the police power is limited by the "takings" clause of the Fifth Amendment to the United States Constitution, made applicable to the states by the Fourteenth Amendment. A taking may occur either physically where the government entity physically takes private property without compensation, or via regulation which may be unduly restrictive so as to cause a taking of the landowner's property without just compensation. In the context of exactions, when conditioning development on payment of a fee or some other exaction, a local agency cannot restrict the use of the property which is the subject of the exaction in such a manner that will constitute a taking of private property without compensation. (See "Police Power.")

Tax

A compulsory exaction imposed by legislative power on persons or property for the purpose of raising revenue to fund a governmental endeavor. A tax may be levied to raise revenue for a general or specific purpose, and can cover a wide or narrow range of persons, property, or activity. The four major types of taxes related to land development are property taxes, parcel taxes, excise taxes, and special taxes.

Tentative Map

The initial map setting forth in detail a proposed land subdivision that must comply with the city's or county's subdivision and zoning regulations and the state Subdivision Map Act. The subdivision of land depicted on the tentative map does not take effect until approval and recordation of the final map.

Tolling

A statute of limitation is postponed or suspended until an issue or dispute is resolved. Tolling stops the running of the statute of limitation.

Transit Impact Development Fee (TIDF)

An exaction imposed on new development which requires participation in a funding mechanism to assure adequate transit services to the area of the local government in which the project is located.

Uniform Protest Act

Provisions in Government Code §§ 66020-66025 that govern protests, legal challenges, and audits for dedications or requirement for fees.

Urban Development Action Grant (UDAG Program)

A federal grant program established to assist local governments. This program provided financing for commercial revitalization projects, often in downtown areas.

Use Permit

The discretionary and conditional review of a use within a particular zoning ordinance. Often referred to as a special use, special permit, or conditional use permit.

Variance

A departure from any provision of the zoning requirements for a specific parcel, except use, without changing the zoning ordinance or the underlying zoning of the parcel. A variance is usually granted only when the peculiarity of the property in relation to other properties in the same zone district demonstrates hardship.

Vesting (Vested Right)

Vesting operates as a shield from the application of later development requirements. In common law vesting, a property owner, who has performed substantial work and incurred substantial liabilities in good faith reliance on a permit issued by the government, acquires a vested right to complete construction in accordance with the terms of the permit. Consequently, construction cannot be prohibited by virtue of a change in the zoning laws.

Vesting Tentative Map

A tentative map refers to a map made in order to show the design of, improvements to, and conditions for a proposed subdivision. Approval of a Vesting Tentative Map grants a vested right to proceed with development in substantial compliance with the ordinances, policies, and standards in effect at the time the map is approved or conditionally approved. (See "Vesting.")

Water Connection

The connection of a building to a public water system as defined in Health and Safety Code § 4010.1e.

Zoning

The division of a city or county by legislative regulations into areas, or zones, that specify allowable uses for real property and size restrictions for buildings within these areas; a program that implements policies of the General Plan.

Zoning Law

Codified in Government Code §§ 65800-65912, the state law sets forth procedural controls for the local enactment of ordinances which specify allowable uses for real property and size restrictions for buildings within these areas. Zoning implements policies of a jurisdiction's General Plan.

Suggested Reading

If this book falls short in fully explaining the planning process from the planning agency's perspective and from the builder-developer perspective, the following documents and books should be consulted:

California Land Use Practice
CEB 300 Frank H. Ogawa Plaze, Suite 410
Oakland, CA 94612-2001

CEQA Deskbook
1999–2000 (second) edition
Includes 2001 Supplement
By Ronald E. Bass, Albert I. Herson, and Kenneth M. Bogdan
A practical user's guide that explains, in a step-by-step fashion, how to proceed from the beginning to the end of the environmental review process. It summarizes the California Environmental Quality Act and the CEQA Guidelines, and focuses on the procedural and substantive requirements of CEQA. Formerly called Successful CEQA Compliance.

Solano Press Books, P.O. Box 773,
Point Arena, CA 95468, (800) 931-9373

General Plan Guidelines
November 1998

Governor's Office of Planning and Research, Sacramento, California

A complete guide to the planning process and to the preparation of general plans.

Governor's Office of Planning and Research, 1400 Tenth Street, Sacramento, CA 95814

Guide to the California Environmental Quality Act (CEQA)
1999–2000 (tenth) edition

By Michael H. Remy et al.

An overview of existing requirements for adequate environmental review. Included are an examination of the statutes, the implementing guidelines, current case law, and a rigorous analysis and commentary on the means of avoiding redundancy when preparing EIRs. Current case summaries are provided in the appendix; also included are the entire Act, updated through January 1999, and the entire text of the existing CEQA Guidelines, updated through February 1999.

Solano Press Books, P.O. Box 773,
Point Arena, CA 95468, (800) 931-9373

Guide to California Planning 1999 (second) edition

By William Fulton

An extensive account of what land use planning is supposed to be and what it is in California, including the processes and laws that must be observed, and how these processes and laws are used for better or for worse. Prepared for those members of the general public and for students who wish to understand the fundamentals of the current practice of land use planning in California.

Solano Press Books, P.O. Box 773,
Point Arena, CA 95468, (800) 931-9373

Land Use Initiatives and Referenda in California
2000 (second) edition

By Michael P. Durkee et al.

A summary of the constitutionally established power of initiatives and referenda and the limits on the use of both at the local government level to effect land use policies and projects and to enact slow-growth or no-growth measures in California.

Solano Press Books, P.O. Box 773,
Point Arena, CA 95468, (800) 931-9373

Longtin's California Land Use 1987 (second) edition
(two volumes/annual supplement)

By James Longtin

This publication should be consulted by those interested in a detailed legal analysis of California land use law.

Local Government Publications, P.O. Box 10087, Berkeley, CA 94709, (800) 345-0899

Redevelopment in California
1995 edition with 2001 supplement

By David F. Beatty, Joseph E. Coomes, Jr., et al.

A guide to detailed provisions of the Community Redevelopment Law and to the authority given cities and counties to establish and manage redevelopment agencies and to prepare, adopt, implement and finance redevelopment projects.

Solano Press Books, P.O. Box 773,
Point Arena, CA 95468, (800) 931-9373

Subdivision Map Act Manual
2000 edition

By Daniel J. Curtin, Jr.
and Robert E. Merritt

A summary and discussion of the substantive and procedural features of the statute and current case law. Includes any statutory or case law changes that occurred through June 2000. The full text of the Act is provided, updated through December 1999.

Solano Press Books, P.O. Box 773,
Point Arena, CA 95468, (800) 931-9373

Blogs:

ww.aklandlaw.com

Table of Authorities

CASES

Health and Safety Code

Labor Code

Public Contract Code

Public Resources Code

Public Utilities Code

Revenue and Taxation Code

Streets and Highways Code

Uniform Building Code

Index

Index entries having page numbers with suffix (sb) indicates that information will be found the gray-shaded sidebars on that page.

B

C

D

E

F

G

H

I

P

Q

R

S

T

U

V

W

Y

Z